LET US KNOW WHAT YOU THINK

In order to produce a guidebook that will serve you best, we ask that you take a few moments to fill out this short feedback form. Feel free to photocopy this form and/or attach additional sheets. You can also provide feedback via email at guidebook@envirofront.org.

Overall, are you pleased with the format and/or contents of *The Guidebook*?
Yes:___   No:___

If no, what suggestions do you have for future editions of *The Guidebook*?

_____

_____

_____

What specific organizations/entities and/or resources would you like to see added to *The Guidebook*?

_____

What would you like to see removed from *The Guidebook*?

_____

Which Section(s) is MOST useful/of interest to you?

___Section 1: Environmental NGOs   _____Section 5: Business Groups and Labor Unions
___Section 2: Governmental Organizations _____Section 6: "Opposing View" Groups
___Section 3: Multilaterals   _____Section 7: Other Entities and Websites of Note
___Section 4: Political Organizations

Which Section(s) is LEAST useful/of interest to you?

___Section 1: Environmental NGOs   _____Section 5: Business Groups and Labor Unions
___Section 2: Governmental Organizations _____Section 6: "Opposing View" Groups
___Section 3: Multilaterals   _____Section 7: Other Entities and Websites of Note
___Section 4: Political Organizations

Would you be interested in purchasing *The Guidebook* on CD-ROM?
Yes:___   No:___

Additional comments can be made on the back of this sheet (or attached additional sheets).

MAIL TO: **Environmental Frontlines**
                      P.O. Box 43
                      Menlo Park, CA 94026

OR FAX AT: 650-323-8452

OR EMAIL AT: guidebook@envirofront.org

THANKS FOR YOUR FEEDBACK!

— First Edition —

THE ENVIRONMENTAL GUIDEBOOK:

A Selective Reference Guide to Environmental Organizations and Related Entities

Jeff Staudinger

Published By

P.O. Box 43
Menlo Park, CA 94026
650/323-8452
info@envirofront.org
www.envirofront.org

Environmental Frontlines is a non-profit organization established to generate and disseminate educational materials to the public regarding environmentally-related issues.

Purchasers of this Guide can also obtain a bookmark/favorite file which includes website links to the organizations and entities profiled in this book. Contact *Environmental Frontlines* for further details.

Printed on recycled paper (85% recovered fiber and 30% post-consumer waste) in the U.S.A.

The following trade/service marks appear in this book:

Environmental Law Institute; The Great American Cleanup (a program of Keep America Beautiful); National Wildlife Federation (and NWF publications: Ranger Rick; Your Big Backyard; and Wild Animal Baby; along with NWF programs: Schoolyard Habitats; Backyard Wildlife Habitat; Earthsavers; NatureLink; Keep the Wild Alive; and Campus Ecology); Hypercars and The Hypercar Center (both associated with the Rocky Mountain Institute); Sierra Club (along with its slogan "Explore, enjoy and protect the planet"); LEED (the green building rating system offered by the U.S. Green Building Council); Canon Envirothon; The EnviroMentors Project (offered by the National Environmental Education and Training Foundation); Growing Smart (an initiative of the American Planning Association); Energy Star (a joint program of the U.S. Dept. of Energy and the U.S. Environmental Protection Agency); Responsible Care (a program of the American Chemistry Council); Sustainable Forestry Initiative (a program of the American Forest and Paper Association); Project Learning Tree (a program of the American Forest Foundation); REALTORS (as used by the National Association of Realtors); The Human Internet (the slogan of About.com); The Online Environmental Community (the slogan of the EnviroLink Network); Environmental Yellow Pages; FirstGov (a U.S. government website); ENN (the abbreviation for the Environmental News Network); and Yahoo!.

Cover Photo: El Capitan, Yosemite National Park, California.

Cataloguing-in-Publication Data
    Staudinger, Jeff.
        The environmental guidebook: a selective reference guide to environmental organizations and related
            entities / by Jeff Staudinger and Environmental Frontlines.--1st ed.
        p. cm.
        Includes index.
        ISBN 0-9720685-0-3 (paperback)
        1. Environmental Protection -- U.S. -- Directories. 2. Conservation of Natural Resources -- U.S. --
        Directories. 3. Environmental Policy -- U.S. -- Directories.
        I. Environmental Frontlines. II. Title.

The Environmental Guidebook may be purchased by contacting *Environmental Frontlines* as follows (an order form is also included as the last page of this book):

Environmental Frontlines	650/323-8452
P.O. Box 43	info@envirofront.org
Menlo Park, CA 94026	www.envirofront.org

If you have any questions or comments regarding **The Environmental Guidebook** or *Environmental Frontlines*, please contact us using the information provided above.

Printed and bound in the United States of America using recycled paper (30% post-consumer waste).

TABLE OF CONTENTS

TD
171
.S76
2002

Acknowledgements

While many people and associated entities contributed to the final product that is this Guidebook, several deserve special acknowledgment with respect to actually getting the finished book to print, namely: the West Valley Design Group of Saratoga, CA (www.wvdg.westvalley.edu), which provided technical design services for the cover "at cost" (thank you!); Malloy Lithographing of Ann Arbor, MI (www.malloy.com), which printed the book while carefully explaining and guiding the author through the maze of steps involved; Maria Yip, who provided much-needed technical expertise in dealing with the daunting computer/software-related issues encountered along the way; and Dan Poynter (ParaPublishing.com), whose book, *The Self-Publishing Manual*, was found to be exactly the resource it is billed to be, namely a "must-have" for anyone seeking to publish a book. Overall, if there was one lesson learned from this exercise, it was that publishing a book is not anything like "publishing" a report – the real challenge with a book begins <u>after</u> the last word is written. Without the aforementioned help, that challenge would not have been met by this novice author acting alone.

In addition, the author wishes to acknowledge Professor Steve Yaffee of the University of Michigan, School of Natural Resources and Environment, for planting the seeds that ultimately led to this book. On behalf of the multitude of students who have taken his well-known and respected "Resource Policy and Administration" class over the years, thanks for helping us truly understand the policy process and for teaching us the practical skills required for effective policy-making and implementation.

Finally, through this book, the author acknowledges the "frontline" efforts being made every day by the organizations and entities profiled within in addressing the important environmental issues of the day. Through such efforts, it is hoped that we can collectively leave the world a better place for our children and grandchildren.

About the Author and the Organization

About the Author

Jeff Staudinger is the Founding Director of ***Environmental Frontlines***. A registered Professional Engineer with 15 years of professional experience in the environmental protection field, he holds graduate degrees in both Environmental Engineering and Environmental/Resource Policy from Stanford University and the University of Michigan, respectively. He is a past recipient of the U.S. Environmental Protection Agency's Science to Achieve Results (STAR) fellowship award and also served as a Doris Duke Foundation Conservation Fellow for 1999-2001.

About Environmental Frontlines

Environmental Frontlines (EF) is a non-profit organization established to generate and disseminate educational materials to the public regarding environmentally-related issues. It is an independent entity which focuses on monitoring – and reporting on – what is occurring on the frontlines of "environmentalism," broadly defined to include a wide range of specific issues and activities. Such monitoring/reporting efforts are perhaps best reflected in the publication of this Guidebook, which is designed to serve as an essential reference guide profiling key organizations and other entities actively engaged in environmental issues or other significant environmentally-related activities.

From this monitoring effort, EF seeks to advance environmentalism via three distinct avenues, namely by:

- Acting as a "one-stop," independent source for information on current issues and/or the work of others.
- Disseminating the "best of the best" in terms of information, ideas, tools and other resources culled from the organizations/entities and other sources EF monitors.
- Becoming actively involved ourselves in select instances where we feel we can make a significant difference.

Overall, ***Environmental Frontlines*** seeks to serve as a reliable guidepost to all parties interested and/or involved in environmentally-related issues/activities.

Please contact us as follows for further information on our specific activities, as well as to order additional copies of this publication (an order form is also included on the last page of this book):

Environmental Frontlines   (650) 323-8452
P.O. Box 43   info@envirofront.org
Menlo Park, CA 94026   www.envirofront.org

Finally, if you like what you see with ***Environmental Frontlines***, please consider making a donation – a Supporter Donation Form is enclosed on the last page of this book. Thanks in advance for your generous contribution to EF!

Introduction

This is the first edition of ***The Environmental Guidebook: A Selective Reference Guide to Environmental Organizations and Related Entities*** (the Guide). The Guide is designed – as its title suggests – to be an essential reference book profiling key environmental organizations and other entities actively engaged in environmental issues or other environmentally-related activities. Key guiding principles used in development of the Guide include:

- **Selective in terms of listings**. The Guide focuses in on identified "key players" (as opposed to attempting to be an "all-inclusive," directory-type publication).

- **Extensively researched to provide relevant/essential information.** Rather than relying on organization-supplied information (such as generic mission statements), the Guide is based on active, in-depth research aimed at identifying and detailing relevant/essential activities, contributions and viewpoints of listed organization/entities, as well as specifying what each organization/entity has to offer to interested parties in terms of active participation opportunities, tools/resources, and publications and other information sources (particularly as provided through the organization's/entity's Internet website(s)).

- **Profiles much more than just environmentally-focused public interest groups.** While the Guide does profile such groups (see Section 1), it also profiles a full range of interested parties, including governmental organizations (see Section 2), multilaterals such as the United Nations (see Section 3), political organizations including political parties (see Section 4), business groups and labor unions (see Section 5), and media-related entities and job/career organizations (see Section 7). In addition, the Guide's "opposing views" section (see Section 6) profiles non-business groups that are typically labeled as "anti-environmental" by critics/observers. Finally, profiles are included for associated "websites of note" (namely Internet directories and information/data resource websites/gateways) within Section 7.

- **Adopts a relatively wide definition of "environmental" work**, considering not only the traditional areas of conservation (i.e., protecting nature/wildlife and other natural resources) and environmental protection (i.e., addressing pollution issues), but also key associated issue areas such as agriculture, energy, public health, trade/commerce, and transportation, as well as more underlying factors such as consumerism, land use, and population growth.

- **Identifies key reports and other key publications.** In compiling relevant profile information, reports and other publications were identified that are judged to represent "essential reading" for interested parties. These key reports/publications are noted within the individual profiles, as well as compiled in a summary list contained in Appendix B.

- **Provides key contact information for readers to obtain further information,** including through the Internet.

In developing the Guide, the major challenge encountered was in attempting to provide relevant listings and specific/detailed information without it resulting in "information overload" for readers. To that end, a few key ground rules were utilized in the Guide's development, namely:

- **A U.S. focus.** While groups such as Conservation International (which, while U.S.-based, works exclusively abroad) are included in the Guide, in general the distinct focus is on the U.S. The main exception to this rule occurs with the listing of multilateral organizations (such as the United Nations). These organizations were included in the Guide owing to: 1) their global scope (thereby affecting U.S. interests) and 2) the U.S. presence within the profiled organizations as an active (and typically influential) member.

- **A national focus.** While many worthy regional- and state-specific groups exist (such as the Chesapeake Bay Foundation), opening up the Guide to such groups would require extensive additional research efforts, as well as result in significant expansion of the Guide's overall size. Thus, such profiling was not undertaken with the Guide's focus being restricted to profiling national organizations. However, where applicable, appropriate note of sub-national groups within national organizations (e.g., regional, state or local chapters) is made.

- **Limited scientific research-related listings.** A multitude of scientific research organizations/entities (particularly within universities) perform environmentally-related research. However, identifying and compiling those activities represents a very large task, while such information is likely to be of relatively limited interest to most readers. Thus, such profiling was not specifically undertaken. However, it should be noted that some of the organizations/entities listed in the Guide do oversee and/or perform pertinent scientific research as part of their activities (for instance, the U.S. Department of Energy oversees and/or conducts extensive energy-related research with significant environmental implications), and such activities are noted as warranted within those organizations'/entities' profiles.

- **Limited higher education-related listings.** Profiling environmentally-related degree programs at colleges and universities – while a noble task – was not undertaken due to both the effort involved as well as the fact that other readily-available publications already provide such information (e.g., Peterson's Guides). Instead, profiling of higher education-related organizations/entities within the Guide was focused on campus-based groups (such as the Sierra Club's Campus Ecology Program) and broad-based higher education efforts (such as University Leaders for a Sustainable Future).

To help fill in some of above-identified missing elements, the interested reader is referred to the National Wildlife Federation's annual *Conservation Directory*, which is billed as "a guide to worldwide environmental organizations" and is viewed as a complementary reference resource to this Guide (to find out more about the *Conservation Directory*, contact the National Wildlife Federation at 703-790-4000; to purchase the Directory, contact The Lyons Press at 800-836-0510).

Finally, while extensive efforts were made to ensure both the accuracy and sufficiency of the information provided in this Guide, errors, omissions, and/or inconsistencies may be encountered, especially with respect to Internet-related information (due to re-designed websites, changing web addresses, etc.). Thus, we apologize in advance to readers encountering such errors, omissions, and/or inconsistencies and respectfully ask that readers forward information concerning such problems to our attention for investigation/correction. Further, we welcome all comments and/or feedback on this Guide to help enhance its effectiveness/usefulness (including suggestions for additional organizations/entities that you feel should be included in the Guide). Please forward such information to us using the following contact information (a formal feedback form is also included as the first page of this book):

Environmental Frontlines   650/323-8452
P.O. Box 43   info@envirofront.org
Menlo Park, CA 94026   www.envirofront.org

Additional copies of the Guide can be obtained by contacting us as noted above or by using the order form contained on the last page of this book. (A Supporter Donation Form is also included on the last page if you wish to make a charitable contribution to Environmental Frontlines.)

Thank you.

User's Guide

Nearly 500 profile entries (493 to be exact) are listed in this Guide, arranged based on seven fundamental categories, with each category presented within a separate section as follows:

Section 1: Environmental Non-Governmental Organizations (NGOs)	(182 entries)
Section 2: Governmental Organizations	(103 entries)
Section 3: Multilaterals (Multinational Organizations)	(26 entries)
Section 4: Political Organizations	(6 entries)
Section 5: Other Interested Parties (Business Groups and Labor Unions)	(89 entries)
Section 6: "Opposing View" Groups	(35 entries)
Section 7: Other Entities and Websites of Note	(52 entries)

Each of the overall categories noted above have been further broken down into appropriate sub-categories, with each sub-category presented within separate subsections (see the Table of Contents or the beginning of each section for a detailed breakdown). Because not every organization/entity profiled clearly falls into one of the established categories/sub-categories, in such cases individual entries have been cross-referenced for convenience under a second appropriate category/sub-category listing.

Each profile entry is assigned a unique Profile Number (listed at the beginning of each entry), starting with "1" for the first entry appearing and proceeding numerically in the order that the entries appear within the Guide up through 493 (the number of the final profile provided). This unique number is used for cross-referencing and indexing purposes.

Specific information contained within each profile entry varies depending upon the specific category/sub-category considered – thus, more detailed information on the exact format used is contained at the beginning of each section/sub-section. In general, however, the entries typically are listed alphabetically and for organizations, provide a description of the group (typically covering current activities, programs, services, viewpoints, publications and other information resources, relevant financial information, etc.), along with basic contact information (at a minimum, the main telephone number for the organization) and the group's Internet website address (nearly every organization profiled maintains a website). For the "Websites of Note" entries listed in Section 7 (profiling selected Internet directories and information/data resource websites/gateways), the descriptions provided focus on the information/data offered by/through the listed websites/gateways.

Finally, two appendices are included within this Guide: Appendix A, providing a summary listing of all organizations and other entities profiled, and Appendix B, providing a summary listing of identified "key reports/publications" (reports and other publications judged to represent "essential reading" for interested parties).

SECTION 1: ENVIRONMENTAL NON-GOVERNMENTAL ORGANIZATIONS (NGOs)

INTRODUCTION/USER'S GUIDE:

In this section, 182 separate profiles of environmentally-focused/relevant non-governmental organizations (NGOs) and associated entities are provided, divided into the following five subsections:

1.1 – Policy Research Institutions ("Think Tanks")	(7 entries)
1.2 – Public Interest Groups and Coalitions	(127 entries)
1.3 – Progressive Business Groups and Coalitions	(3 entries)
1.4 – Student- and Education-Oriented Groups	(12 entries)
1.5 – Professional Societies	(33 entries)

The "Public Interest" sub-category is the largest and most wide-ranging sub-category listed; it essentially represents environmental NGOs judged not to best-fit into one of the other listed sub-categories (in questionable cases, organizations have been cross-referenced for convenience under a second appropriate sub-category listing).

In terms of individual entry contents, a descriptive outline of standardized profile information provided for each organization listed within this section is presented on the following two pages (please note that the exact contents provided varies by organization, being dependant upon applicability and/or availability).

The standard structure employed for the informational entries contained within this section is designed to give a relatively brief – but detailed – profile and current snapshot of the organization, with the information provided organized as follows:

- **Basic Characterization of the Organization:** The upper block of the entry from the "General Focus Areas" through the "Unique" sub-entries, designed to provide insight into what the organization does (including its current activities and programs/focus areas), as well as what it has to offer to interested parties (including its publications and tools/resources).

- **Website Characterization:** The short block in the middle of the entry consisting of the "Associated Websites," "Website Notes," and "Check Out on the Web" sub-entries, designed to provide relevant information regarding the organization's website(s), particularly in terms of key contents "worth a look."

- **Basic Facts:** The lower block of the entry beginning with the "(Year) Founded" sub-entry and continuing to the end, designed to provide a host of supplemental material, including (when available) information characterizing the relative size of the organization (i.e., staffing level and approximate budget). Likely of particular interest is the breakdown of the organization's expenses – where a detailed breakdown of program service expenses is provided (based on IRS records or other information sources), it can offer additional insight as to the operating structure and activities/priorities of the organization (based on where/how the organization chooses to spends its money).

Outline of Standardized Profile Information Provided

[Profile #] Organization Name (Website Address) – An "Earth Share" Charity*

*– Included if the organization is a member charity for "Earth Share" (which acts as the equivalent of the United Way, collecting workplace donations for qualifying non-profit environmental organizations – See Profile #44).

General Focus Area(s): See the next page for details regarding the designations used for this sub-entry.

A Top Federal Lobbying Group Per Fortune Magazine's Annual Survey: Noted as applicable with the organization's ranking for 2001 specified.

Slogan: As adopted/used by the organization.

Description/Mission: A short summary of the organization, particularly in regards to its basic mission/focus.

Basic Activities: Potential entries include: public awareness/education; policy research/analysis; advocacy; communication/information dissemination; training/technical assistance; outreach/organizing; field operations/activities; scientific/technical research; youth education; litigation.

Lobbying/Political Activities: Included if the organization is registered as a federal lobbyist under the Lobbying Disclosure Act (LDA) and/or maintains a Political Action Committee (PAC), with the name of the PAC specified.

Programs/Issues (and activities/focus areas): Providing specifics on the organization's activities/concerns.

Campaigns/Key Initiatives: Highlighting the organization's "high priority" issues/activities.

Periodicals: Listing magazines, newsletters and bulletins offered by the organization, providing: title, publication frequency and noting if they are available online at the organization's website.

Other Publications: Listing the relative quantity ("a couple"; "various"; "a multitude") and type (reports, fact sheets, etc.) and noting if they are available online at the organization's website.

Key Reports/Publications: Listing specific reports and other publications judged to represent "essential reading" for interested parties, and noting if they are available online at the organization's website. (A summary listing of all such reports/publications is also provided in Appendix B.)

Annual Report: Only included if the report is available online at the org's website; if so, the latest year available is specified. (Represents a key additional source of information on the organization's activities/accomplishments.)

Online Activist Tools: Noting what is specifically provided on the organization's website (typically includes an "action alert" system allowing participants to send comments to key officials on specific issues of concern).

Unique: Listing programs/activities and/or website features not seen elsewhere and of particular note.

Associated Websites: Listing distinct websites separate from the organization's main website, along with a short description and corresponding web address (URL).

Website Notes: Significant notes regarding the organization's main website – navigating hints, content notes, etc.

Check Out on the Web: Listing website-related content/features that particularly stand out ("worth a look").

Founded: Beginning year specified **Membership:** Noted if applicable and figures made available **Coverage:** Geographical coverage; possible entries: U.S.; Int'l; Global **Staff:** Overall staffing level **Regional/State/Local Offices:** Noted as applicable **NP Status:** Formal IRS non-profit status (typically 501(c)(3) – exempt) **Budget:** Approximate ("ballpark") figure based on IRS submittals (IRS Form 990) or other sources (annual report, etc.).

Revenue: Providing a percentage breakdown based on IRS submittals (IRS Form 990). Categories considered: Contributions (non-governmental public support from individuals, foundations, businesses, etc.); Government Grants; Program Service Revenues; Other (a variety of miscellaneous sources including: membership dues; investment income; special events; inventory sales [typically publications]).

Expenses: Providing a percentage breakdown based on IRS submittals (IRS Form 990). Categories considered: Program Services (broken down by specific program/service when available); Management and General (administration and overhead expenses); Fundraising.

Public Support Sources: Noting the types of public support received (from individuals, foundations, businesses, government, etc.) and – when available – the relative amount received (e.g., "40% individuals; 60% foundations")

Affiliated Orgs: Noted as applicable; based on IRS submittals and other sources (annual report, website, etc.).

Contact Info: Providing: Street/mailing address; general telephone number; general email address (if available).

Key Personnel: Typically citing the name and title of key executives (President, Executive Director, etc.).

In terms of cited "General Focus Areas," the two main designations used are:

  Conservation (i.e., protecting nature/wildlife and/or other natural resources)

  Pollution (i.e., addressing pollution issues)

In addition, a host of other designations were generated for use (reflecting the wide range of activities conducted by the listed organizations), consisting of the following:

Academic Competition	Implications of Science and Technology
Action Alert Center (devoted online center)	Information Disclosure/Right-to-Know
Activism Support/Training	Internet Hosting
Activist Network	Media-Related
Agriculture	Politics
Arbor Day/Tree Planting	Population
Business Practices	Product Standards
Community Service	PR Watch (public relations industry watchdog)
Consumerism	Public Health
Corporations/Globalization	Religious-Based
Earth Day	Scenic Conservation
Economics	Scientific Research
Ecotourism	Senior Citizen Involvement
Energy	Sprawl/Smart Growth
Environmental Education	Sustainable Development
Global Issues	Trail Building
Global Warming (climate change)	Transportation
Government Watchdog	Whistleblower Support
Green Building Construction	Workplace Giving

For organizations with multiple (more than three) general focus areas, a "Multiple Focus Areas" tag was assigned as an alternative identifier, indicating organizations with relatively broad agendas (typical of larger advocacy groups such as Greenpeace or the Sierra Club).

Subsection 1.1: Policy Research Institutions ("Think Tanks")

Introduction/User's Guide:

Within this subsection, 7 policy research institutions ("think tanks") focused on environmentally-related issues are profiled. A "think tank" is a somewhat loosely defined term typically applied to independent organizations whose main activity consists of research/analysis of public policy issues and whose main output typically is in the form of written reports and/or briefs primarily aimed at policy-/decision-makers. At traditional think tanks – such as the Brookings Institution – an academic environment is maintained, with research staff being formally referred to as "scholars."

For purposes of this Guide, a relatively loose definition of a "think tank" was used; of the organizations so-listed herein, only Resources for the Future likely meets the definition of a traditional think tank.

Organizational profiles for this subsection are listed beginning on the next page, presented in alphabetical order. In terms of individual entry contents, the reader is referred back to the beginning of Section 1 where a descriptive outline of standardized profile information provided is presented.

Subsection 1.1: Policy Research Institutions ("Think Tanks")

1. **Center for Clean Air Policy (CCAP)** (www.ccap.org)

General Focus Areas: Pollution; Global Warming

Description/Mission: Policy research center focused on examining market-based approaches to major air quality-related issues. Founded by a bipartisan group of state governors.

Basic Activities: Policy research/analysis; information dissemination.

Programs (and focus areas): Air Quality (reducing electric power plant emissions); Domestic and Int'l Climate Change (emissions banking; joint implementation in developing countries; other market-based options); Transportation/Land Use (emissions reduction via market-based measures): Education and Exchange (international exchange program for professionals).

Periodicals: In the Air (monthly newsletter; online)

Other Publications: Various publications in each program area (most online)

Check Out on the Web: Highlights of State Initiatives on Global Climate Change (11/00 report; online)

Founded: 1985 **Coverage:** U.S./Int'l **Staff:** 20 **NP Status:** 501(c)(3) **Budget:** $2 million

Revenue (FY00): Contributions (51%); Government Grants (47%); Program Service Revenues (0%); Other (2%).

Expenses (FY00): Program Services (95%; for: air quality program –16%; domestic climate change program – 25%; international climate change program –42%; transportation/land use program –7%; education and exchange program –5%); Management and General (4%); Fundraising (1%).

Contact Info: 750 1ˢᵗ St. NE, Suite 940, Washington, DC 20002; (202) 408-9260; general@ccap.org

Key Personnel: Ned Helme (Executive Director)

2. **Environmental and Energy Study Institute (EESI)** (www.eesi.org) – **An "Earth Share" Charity**

General Focus Areas: Multiple Focus Areas

Description/Mission: Policy research institute promoting environmental sustainability through work on environmental and energy issues. Target audience is policymakers, particularly Congress (originally founded by bipartisan group of Congressional members). Primarily works behind the scenes to bring stakeholders together.

Basic Activities: Policy research/analysis; briefings and roundtables; information dissemination.

Programs (and focus areas): Energy and Climate (energy efficiency; renewable energy technologies); Water and Sustainable Communities (sprawl-water resource connections); Transportation ("clean vehicles"; alternative transportation); Economic and Fiscal Policy (market-based policies: tax measures; tradable emissions permits; elimination of harmful subsidies)

Periodicals: ECO (**E**thanol, **C**limate Protection and **O**il Reduction; monthly newsletter; online)

Other Publications: Briefing Summaries (reports on EESI congressional briefings; online); Facts Sheets (online)

Annual Report: 1999 report online.

Check Out on the Web: Briefing Summaries (summary reports on cutting-edge environmental and energy issues).

Founded: 1984 **Coverage:** U.S. **Staff:** 10 **NP Status:** 501(c)(3) **Budget:** $0.7 million

Revenue (2000): Contributions (72%); Government Grants (21%); Program Service Revenues (0%); Other (7%).

Expenses (2000): Program Services (84%; for: energy and climate program –40%; sustainable communities program –20%; transportation program –21%; special projects –3%); Management and General (10%); Fundraising (6%).

Contact Info: 122 C St. NW, Suite 700, Washington, DC 20001; (202) 628-1400; eesi@eesi.org

Key Personnel: Carol Werner (Executive Director)

3. H. John Heinz Center for Science, Economics and the Environment (www.heinzctr.org)

General Focus Areas: Conservation; Global Warming

Description/Mission: Policy research center dedicated to improving the scientific and economic foundation for environmental policy, with a focus on emerging issues. Specific studies are chosen that mostly likely benefit from multi-sector (business, environmental groups, government and academia) collaborations. Founded in memory of the late Senator John Heinz.

Basic Activities: Policy research/analysis; information dissemination.

Programs (and focus areas): Environmental Reporting (focused on creating a "report card" on the health of the nation's ecosystems); Global Climate Change (domestic greenhouse gas control); Sustainable Oceans, Coasts and Waterways (coastal hazard impacts; impacts of dam removal; marine fisheries management; integrated governance approaches).

Publications: Various reports (most online)

Founded: 1995 **Coverage:** U.S. **Staff:** 16 **NP Status:** 501(c)(3) **Budget:** $3 million

Revenue (FY00): Contributions (50%); Government Grants (49%); Program Service Revenues (0%); Other (<1%).

Expenses (FY00): Program Services (93%; for: sustainable oceans, coasts and waterways program –61%; environmental reporting program –23%; global climate change program –9%); Management and General (5%); Fundraising (2%).

Contact Info: 1001 Pennsylvania Ave. NW, Suite 735 South, Washington, DC 20004; (202) 737-6307; info@heinzcenter.org

Key Personnel: William Merrell (President)

4. Inform, Inc. (www.informinc.org) – An "Earth Share" Charity

General Focus Areas: Pollution; Business Practices; Transportation

Slogan: "Strategies for a better environment."

Description/Mission: Policy research center focused on identifying practical solutions to problems related to business practices and transportation issues, with an emphasis on pollution prevention and waste reduction. Seeks to translate ideas into action.

Basic Activities: Applied policy research/analysis; education; information dissemination.

Programs (and focus areas): Chemical Hazards Prevention (materials accounting/right-to-know; business practices); Resource Protection (sustainable products and practices; extended producer responsibility; solid waste prevention); Sustainable Transportation (cleaner vehicles/fuels).

Periodicals: Inform Reports (quarterly newsletter; online)

Other Publications: Various books, reports, fact sheets (many online).

Key Publications (all online): Expanding the Public's Right-to-Know: Materials Accounting Data as a Tool for Promoting Environmental Justice and Pollution Prevention; Extended Producer Responsibility: A Materials Policy for the 21st Century; Waste at Work: Prevention Strategies for the Bottom Line (practical strategies and case studies for businesses).

Check Out on the Web: Community Waste Prevention Toolkit (tools to help design/implement local solid waste prevention programs); Purchasing for Pollution Prevention Project (aimed at helping government purchase alternatives to PBT chemical-containing products); Extended Producer Responsibility (a hub of information on EPR/product stewardship)

Founded: 1974 **Membership:** 1,000 **Coverage:** U.S. **Staff:** 17 **NP Status:** 501(c)(3) **Budget:** $1 million

Revenue (FY00): Contributions (71%); Government Grants (3%); Program Service Revenues (3%); Other (23%; from a 25th anniversary special event).

Expenses (FY00): Program Services (73%); Management and General (21%); Fundraising (6%).

FY01 Financials online

Contact Info: 120 Wall St., 16th Floor, New York, NY 10005; (212) 361-2400

Key Personnel: Joanna Underwood (President)

5. Resources For the Future (RFF) (www.rff.org)

General Focus Areas: Multiple Focus Areas

Description/Mission: Policy research institute devoted exclusively to natural resource and environmental protection issues, conducting policy research/analysis rooted primarily in economics and other social sciences. Champions two fundamental principles: 1) must balance – if only in a qualitative way – costs/benefits of proposed policy alternatives and 2) seek to accomplish environmental goals in most inexpensive way possible, often via economic incentives (such as tradable permits or pollution charges) in lieu of command-and-control regulation. Operates the Center for Risk Management which conducts research on cost/benefits and management of environmental risk. RFF neither lobbies nor takes positions on specific legislative or regulatory proposals.

Basic Activities: Policy research/analysis; information dissemination.

Programs (and focus areas): Environment (air; water; climate; solid waste; hazardous waste and Superfund; regulatory policy); Natural Resources (forests; minerals; energy; biodiversity; land use; open space; resource policy; fisheries); Intersections (electricity restructuring; urban transportation; sustainable development; technological innovation; nuclear weapons cleanup; public health; food); Methods, Tools and Techniques (non-market valuation; cost-benefit analysis; risk analysis; modeling; regulatory design).

Periodicals: Resources (quarterly newsletter; online); CRM [Center for Risk Management] Newsletter (semi-annual newsletter; online).

Other Publications: Comprehensive publications library (for each program area, provides online access to: Project Summaries; Discussion Papers; Issue Briefs; Lectures and Conference Proceedings; Reports; *Resources* Magazine Articles; Congressional Testimony).

Key Publications (books): The RFF Reader in Environmental and Resource Management (primer on environmental policy); Climate Change Economics and Policy: An RFF Anthology (a collection of relevant Issues Briefs); A Vision for the U.S. Forest Service – Goals for the Next Century.

Key Publications (non-books) (all online): Experience with Market-Based Environmental Policy Instruments (summary of policies implemented worldwide); National Environmental Policy During the Clinton Years; The Role of Renewable Resources in U.S. Electricity Generation – Experience and Prospects; Cleaning Up the Nuclear Weapons Complex: Does Anyone Care?.

Check Out on the Web: Weathervane (online forum providing analysis/commentary on U.S./global climate change policy initiatives).

Founded: 1952 **Coverage:** U.S./Int'l **Staff:** 100 **Researchers:** 40 **NP Status:** 501(c)(3) **Budget:** $10 million

Revenue (FY00): Contributions (40%); Government Grants (15%); Program Service Revenues (1%); Other (44%; from: investment income –30%; rental income –13%; misc. –1%).

Expenses (FY00): Program Services (80%; for: "quality of the environment" research –22%; energy and natural resources research –20%; Center for Risk Management –11%; education and publications –10%; building operations –10%; "academic relations" grants and fellowships –3%; other misc. –4%); Management and General (15%); Fundraising (5%).

Contact Info: 1616 P St. NW, Washington, DC 20036; (202) 328-5000

Key Personnel: Paul R. Portney (President)

6. Tellus Institute (www.tellus.org)

General Focus Areas: Energy; Business Practices; Sustainable Development

Description/Mission: Policy research institute and consulting organization focused on environmental stewardship and equitable development. Tellus' work centers around research projects contracted for by both governmental and non-governmental organizations.

Basic Activities: Policy research/analysis; consulting; communication/information dissemination.

Programs (and focus areas): Energy (markets and regulation; energy efficiency; energy, environment and economy); Business and Sustainability (environmental accounting; governance and accountability; public policy; supply chain management); Sustainable Communities (sustainable futures; community initiatives and strengthening local participation; solid waste management); Stockholm Environment Institute-Boston (international research focusing on sustainable development with programs in: sustainable development strategies; energy, environment and climate; water and development).

Periodicals: Environmental Perspectives (risk analysis and solid waste groups newsletter; semi-annual; online), Energy Perspectives (energy group newsletter; semi-annual; online)

Other Publications: A multitude of reports, articles, etc. (many online).

Key Publications (all online): The American Way to the Kyoto Protocol: An Economic Analysis to Reduce Carbon Pollution; Coal: America's Past, America's Future? (a critical look at coal as an energy source).

Unique: Each research group has developed computer software models to assist planning professionals in their analyses.

Check Out on the Web: Chemical Strategies Partnership (seeking to reduce chemical use, waste, risks and costs by redefining the way chemicals are used and sold; located under "Business and Sustainability").

Founded: 1976 **Coverage:** U.S./Int'l **Staff:** 50 **NP Status:** 501(c)(3) **Budget:** $4 million

Revenue (2000): Contributions (0%); Government Grants (0%); Program Service Revenues (84%; from: non-governmental research contracts/fees –59%; government research contracts/fees –25%); Other (15%).

Expenses (2000): Program Services (90%); Management and General (10%); Fundraising (0%).

Contact Info: 11 Arlington St., Boston, MA 02116; (617) 266-5400; info@tellus.org

Key Personnel: Paul Raskin (President)

World Resources Institute (WRI) (www.wri.org)

See Profile #133 (located within Subsection 1.2 – "Public Interest Groups and Coalitions").

7. **Worldwatch Institute (www.worldwatch.org)**

General Focus Areas: Multiple Focus Areas

Description/Mission: Policy research institute focused on emerging global environmental issues and trends, including links with other key issues (including: food and agriculture; energy; economic development; transportation; health and social issues; military). Focuses on information dissemination.

Basic Activities: Policy research/analysis; publications/information dissemination.

Programs (and focus areas): Energy (climate change; transportation; materials; energy); Economy (globalization and governance; sustainable economics; information technology; security; consumption); People (population; urbanization; food; water); Nature (freshwater ecosystems; natural disasters; bio-invasion; pollution; forests; oceans; disease; species).

Periodicals: World Watch (bi-monthly magazine; highlights online)

Other Publications: Various books and papers (papers available online at a nominal cost).

Key Reports: State of the World (annual report on current global environmental issues); Vital Signs (annual report on global trends in environmental and related areas).

Founded: 1974 **Coverage:** Global **Staff:** 40 **NP Status:** 501(c)(3) **Budget:** $4 million

Revenue (2000): Contributions (85%); Government Grants (0%); Program Service Revenues (0%); Other (15%).

Expenses (2000): Program Services (59%; for research and publications); Management and General (36%); Fundraising (5%).

Contact Info: 1776 Massachusetts Ave. NW, Washington, D.C. 20036; (202) 452-1999; worldwatch@worldwatch.org

Key Personnel: Lester Brown (Chairman of the Board); Christopher Flavin (President)

Subsection 1.2: Public Interest Groups and Coalitions

Introduction/User's Guide:

Within this subsection, 127 profiles are provided of public interest groups and coalitions (and related entities) working on environmentally-related issues. As previously noted at the beginning of this overall section, the "Public Interest" sub-category is the largest and most wide-ranging sub-category of environmental NGOs; it essentially represents organizations judged not to best-fit into one of the other listed environmental NGO sub-categories (in questionable cases, organizations have been cross-referenced for convenience under a second appropriate sub-category listing).

As a result, the compiled listing presented in this subsection runs the full range from very large, widely-recognized organizations with broad agendas (e.g., Greenpeace, the Sierra Club) to very small, narrowly-focused, independent projects (e.g., the Appliance Standards Awareness Project). And in keeping with a key guiding principle adopted for the Guide – utilizing a relatively wide definition of "environmental" work/organizations – the compiled listing contains organizations with general focus areas extending beyond the traditional areas of conservation (i.e., protecting nature/wildlife and other natural resources) and environmental protection (i.e., addressing pollution-related issues) to include closely-associated issue areas such as agriculture, energy, public health, trade/commerce, and transportation, as well as more underlying factors such as consumerism, land use, and population growth.

Organizational profiles for this subsection are listed beginning on the next page, presented in alphabetical order. In terms of individual entry contents, the reader is referred back to the beginning of Section 1 where a descriptive outline of standardized profile information provided is presented.

A Closer Look – Federal Lobbying Efforts:

One note can be made regarding the relative perceived ability of environmental public interest groups to influence federal policy-making via lobbying efforts. Based on Fortune magazine's annual survey for 2001, only one such group – the Sierra Club – was included as a "top federal lobbying group" (ranked #52 of 87 listed groups). In contrast, as detailed in Section 5, 21 business trade associations – as well as 8 labor unions – profiled in this Guide were included in the Fortune survey ranking for 2001.

Subsection 1.2: Public Interest Groups and Coalitions

8.   20/20 Vision (www.2020vision.org**)**

General Focus Areas: Action Alert Center

Slogan: "Busy people taking action for peace and the environment."

Description/Mission: Works to increase citizen participation in public policy decisions on "progressive" issues – the environment, military spending, handguns, and campaign financing. Concentrates on public education and promoting grassroots activism through its Education Fund; also engages in lobbying through its affiliated National Project organization.

Basic Activities: Public education; grassroots activism.

Periodicals: Viewpoint (quarterly newsletter; online)

Online Activist Tools: Action Center (provides action alerts, posted online and sent via email); Tools For Citizens (contents: writing letters; phone calls; meeting with local Congressional members; generating local media attention; "magnifying the impact"); Sample Letters.

Founded: 1986 **Membership:** 20,000 **Coverage:** U.S. **Staff:** 6 **NP Status:** 501(c)(3) [Ed Fund]; 501(c)(4) [National Project]; **Budget (Ed Fund):** $0.4 million

Revenue (Ed Fund; 2000): Contributions (99%); Government Grants (0%); Program Service Revenues (0%); Other (1%).

Expenses (Ed Fund; 2000): Program Services (81%); Management and General (10%); Fundraising (9%).

Contact Info: 1828 Jefferson Place NW, Washington, DC, 20036; (202) 833-2020 / (800) 669-1782; vision@2020vision.org

Key Personnel: Jim Wyerman (Executive Director)

9.   African Wildlife Foundation (AWF) (www.awf.org**) – An "Earth Share" Charity**

General Focus Areas: Conservation

Slogan: "Conserving wildlife. Respecting all life."

Description/Mission: Works on species and habitat conservation in Africa. 80% of staff members are Africans working in the field throughout Africa.

Basic Activities: In-field species and habitat conservation; conservation policy and strategy; training; institutional development; education.

Programs (and activities/focus areas): Heartlands (manage large African landscapes – Heartlands, extending across state, private, and community lands – to be both environmentally viable for wildlife and economically successful for people); Conservation Service Centers (help African communities build viable and environmentally-friendly business ventures, typically eco-tourism); Critical Species Projects (research on endangered species); Training, Institutional Development and Education (variety of activities).

Periodicals: African Wildlife News (quarterly newsletter)

Other Publications: Lists of recommended books provided online.

Annual Report: 2000 report online.

Check Out on the Web: Individual African animal summaries taken from the AWF's "Wild Lives Guidebook" (online).

Founded: 1961 **Coverage:** Africa **Staff:** 80+ **NP Status:** 501(c)(3) **Budget:** $8 million

Revenue (FY00): Contributions (61%); Government Grants (25%); Program Service Revenues (1%); Other (13%).

Expenses (FY00): Program Services (75%; for: Heartlands program –35%; policy and conservation strategy – 15%; conservation service centers –13%; training, institutional development and education program –12%); Management and General (10%); Fundraising (15%).

Contact Info: 1400 16th Street NW, Suite 120, Washington, DC 20036; (202) 939-3333; africanwildlife@awf.org

Key Personnel: R Michael Wright (President/CEO)

10. Alliance to Save Energy (ASE) (www.ase.org)

General Focus Areas: Energy

Description/Mission: Coalition of business, government, environmental and consumer groups promoting the efficient and clean use of energy worldwide. Primary focus is on demonstration programs. Founded by former Senators Charles Percy and Hubert Humphrey. Officers on ASE's Board of Directors includes 4 current Congressmen.

Basic Activities: Research/Pilot Projects; Education; Communications; Policy Research/Analysis; Advocacy.

Lobbying/Political Activities: Registered lobbyist under the LDA.

Programs (and focus areas): Energy Efficiency (residential; federal; school; industrial; commercial); Consumer Energy Education; Energy Policy Reform; Appliance Standards; International Development.

Periodicals: Alliance Update (quarterly newsletter; online), E-Efficiency News (newsletter; online)

Other Publications: Various reports/guides/booklets (online).

Annual Report: 1999 report online.

Online Activist Tools: Alliance Activist program (action alerts sent via email)

Website Notes: Separate webpages provided devoted to: Consumers; Educators; Media; Energy Industry Professionals.

Founded: 1977 **Coverage:** U.S./Int'l **Staff:** 60+ **NP Status:** 501(c)(3) **Budget:** $4 million

Revenue (1999): Contributions (38%); Government Grants (60%); Program Service Revenues (0%); Other (2%).

Expenses (1999): Program Services (92%; for: demonstration programs –79%; policy programs –9%; communications program –4%); Management and General (1%); Fundraising (7%).

Public Support Sources: Federal government; industry/utilities; foundations.

Contact Info: 1200 18th St. NW, Suite 900, Washington, DC 20036; (202) 857-0666; info@ase.org

Key Personnel: David M. Nemtzow (President); Senator Byron Dorgan [D-ND] (Chairman, Board of Directors)

11. American Council for an Energy-Efficient Economy (ACEEE) (www.aceee.org)

General Focus Areas: Energy

Slogan: "Economic prosperity and a cleaner environment through energy efficiency."

Description/Mission: Promotes energy efficiency through collaborative projects and initiatives with government, utilities, research institutions, businesses and public interest groups. Co-founded the Clean Car Campaign (see Profile #25, located within this subsection).

Basic Activities: Technical/policy assessments; advising governments and utilities; information dissemination; technical conferences; advocacy/lobbying.

Lobbying/Political Activities: Registered lobbyist under the LDA.

Programs: National, Regional and State Energy Policy; Buildings, Appliances and Equipment; Utilities; Industry; Transportation; International.

Publications: Extensive, including: Books; Conference Proceedings; Consumer Guides; Research Reports.

Key Publications: Green Book: The Environmental Guide to Cars and Trucks (annual; highlights online); Most Energy Efficient Appliances (annual; online); Consumer Guide to Home Energy Savings (periodically revised).

Annual Report: 2000 report online.

Online Activist Tools: "Efficiency Net" (action alerts sent via email).

Founded: 1980 **Coverage:** U.S. **Staff:** 28 **NP Status:** 501(c)(3) **Budget:** $3 million

Revenue (2000): Contributions (36%); Government Grants (17%); Program Service Revenues (46%; from: conference revenue –25%; government fees/contracts –21%); Other (1%).

Expenses (2000): Program Services (99%; for programs [see above] –74%; conferences –24%; publications –1%; lobbying –<1%); Management and General (1%); Fundraising (0%).

Public Support Sources: Government, industry/utilities, foundations, national labs/research institutions.

Contact Info: 1001 Connecticut Ave. NW, Suite 801, Washington, DC 20036; (202) 429-8873; info@aceee.org

Key Personnel: Steven Nadel (Executive Director)

12. American Farmland Trust (AFT) (www.farmland.org) – **An "Earth Share" Charity**

General Focus Areas: Conservation

Description/Mission: Focused on farmland conservation and promotion of environmentally-friendly farming practices. Nearly 60,000 acres of farmland in 22 states are currently under agricultural conservation easements held or created by AFT.

Basic Activities: Public education; technical assistance; research; policy development; direct farmland protection projects; advocacy.

Lobbying/Political Activities: Registered lobbyist under the LDA.

Programs (and focus areas): Center for Agriculture and the Environment (research on: farmland protection; conservation practices; integrated pest management); Farmland Information Library (www.farmlandinfo.org; offers a variety of resources); Competition for Land Project (research on value/use of private lands and policy reforms to protect farmlands and other natural resources); Farming on the Edge (mapping project of lost/threatened farmlands); grassfarmer.com (information on grass-based farming systems; www.grassfarmer.com); Agricultural Conservation Innovation Center (develop/make available economically practical solutions to agricultural-environmental problems; www.agconserv.com); Public Policy; Around the Country (AFT regional activities).

Periodicals: American Farmland (quarterly magazine; select articles online)

Other Publications: Various articles, reports, papers, and fact sheets (from AFT and others; most fully online)

Key Publication: Top 20 Most Threatened Farming Areas (part of the 3/97 "Farming on the Edge" report).

Annual Report: 1999 report online.

Online Activist Tools: GR@SSROOTS (action alerts sent via e-mail)

Associated Websites: See above under "Programs"

Check Out on the Web: The Farmland Information Library (extensive list of online resources and publications)

Website Notes: Offers a personalized start page option.

Founded: 1980 **Membership:** 50,000 **Coverage:** U.S. **Staff:** 90 **Regional Offices:** 7 **NP Status:** 501(c)(3) **Budget:** $12 million

Revenue (FY00): Contributions (47%); Government Grants (10%); Program Services (3%); Other (40%; from investment income –39%; misc. –1%).

Expenses (FY00): Program Services (80%); Management and General (5%); Fundraising (15%);

Contact Info: 1200 18th St. NW, Suite 800, Washington, DC 20036; (202) 331-7300; info@farmland.org

Key Personnel: Ralph Grossi (President)

13. American Forests (www.americanforests.org) – **An "Earth Share" Charity**

General Focus Areas: Conservation

Slogan: "People caring for tress and forests since 1875."

Description/Mission: Stated mission of "helping people improve the environment with trees and forests." Known for its tree-planting activities, as well as publication of *The National Register of Big Trees*. Through its Global ReLeaf Center, has planted 15+ million trees through 500+ projects in the U.S. and 21 countries worldwide.

Basic Activities: Forest restoration/maintenance; forest policy research/analysis; public education; communications.

Programs (and activities/focus areas): Global ReLeaf Center (work with local partners to develop/implement forest ecosystem restoration projects and urban/community forest projects); Forest Policy Center (ecosystem restoration and maintenance; community-based forestry/ecosystem management; urban-rural initiative); Urban Forests Center (national sprawl initiative; regional ecosystem analysis); Famous and Historic Trees Program (seeks to bring history alive through famous trees – e.g., Johnny Appleseed apple trees).

Key Campaigns/Initiatives: No Trees, No Tigers (reforest Siberian tiger habitat); Trees for Sarajevo (reforest war-torn Sarajevo); Wildfire ReLeaf (plant native trees in forest ecosystems damaged by the wildfires of 2000); A Tree for Every Child (environmental education and action program).

Periodicals: American Forests (magazine; online), ForestBytes (monthly email newsletter; online); The National Register of Big Trees (biennial).

Other Publications: A few books and reports.

Annual Report: 1999 report online.

Founded: 1875 **Coverage:** U.S. **Staff:** 44 **NP Status:** 501(c)(3) **Budget:** $5 million

Revenue (2000): Contributions (54%); Government Grants (0%); Program Service Revenues (40%; from: grants –38%; publications sales –2%); Other (6%).

Expenses (2000): Program Services (81%; for: Global ReLeaf program –37%; urban forests program –14%; communications –9%; rural forests program –7%; famous and historic trees program 7%; membership –7%); Management and General (16%); Fundraising (3%).

Public Support Sources: Corporations; Foundations; Individuals; Agencies and Associations.

Contact Info: PO Box 2000, 910 17th St. NW, Suite 600, Washington, DC 20013; (202) 955-4500; info@amfor.org

Key Personnel: Deborah Gangloff (Executive Director)

14. American Oceans Campaign (AOC) (www.americanoceans.org)

General Focus Areas: Conservation; Pollution

Description/Mission: Ocean and coastal water protection. Co-founded by Actor Ted Danson.

Basic Activities: Public Awareness and Education; Communications; Outreach and Partnerships; Legislation and Advocacy/Lobbying; Litigation.

Key Programs: Healthy Oceans Business Alliance (alliance with local coastal businesses to adopt/promote environmentally-sound practices and raise public awareness of beach issues); Fish Habitat Protection (seek to protect critical fish habitats and minimize destructive fishing practices); Healthy Beaches Campaign (national public awareness campaign regarding contaminated beach water).

Issue Areas (and specific issues/activities): Water (beach water quality; stormwater and polluted runoff; estuaries); Fish (fisheries; fish habitat; Marine Fish Conservation Network [coalition of 100+ groups seeking to make conservation a top priority of marine fisheries management]; Great American Fish Count); Special Places (Alaska; California).

Periodicals: Splash (newsletter; 2-3 times/yr; online); DC Splash (newsletter distributed to members of Congress; 3-4 times/yr; online)

Other Publications: Fish Briefs (plain language summary of scientific papers; online).

Online Activist Tools: Action Network (action alerts sent via email)

Founded: 1987 **Membership:** 22,000 **Coverage:** U.S. **Staff:** 14 **Offices:** 2 **NP Status:** 501(c)(3) **Budget:** $2 million

Revenue (FY00): Contributions (98%); Government Grants (0%); Program Service Revenues (0%); Other (2%).

Expenses (FY00): Program Services (92%; for: marine fish conservation network –25%; fish habitat program –23%; water quality public awareness program –17%; public education –15%; healthy oceans business alliance –9%; lobbying –3%); Management and General (6%); Fundraising (2%).

Contact Info: 600 Pennsylvania Ave SE, Suite 210, Washington DC 20003; (202) 544-3526; info@americanoceans.org

Key Personnel: Barbara Jeanne Polo (Executive Director)

15. American Rivers (www.amrivers.org) – An "Earth Share" Charity

General Focus Areas: Conservation

Slogan: "Restore. Protect. Enjoy."

Description/Mission: River conservation group focused on protecting wild rivers, restoring hometown rivers and repairing large rivers. Cited preservation results: 22,000 river-miles, 5.5 million acres of riverside (riparian) lands.

Basic Activities: River conservation efforts; policy reform efforts/advocacy; public awareness and education.

Lobbying/Political Activities: Registered lobbyist under the LDA.

Key Issues: Army Corps Reform; Community Riverfronts; Dam Removal; Hydropower Dam Reform; Fish and Wildlife; Floodplains and Wetlands; Land Use and Urban Sprawl; Water Quality; Water Quantity/ Instream Flow; Wild and Scenic Rivers.

Campaigns: Columbia River; Missouri River; Mississippi River; Ohio River; Snake River; Yellowstone; Rivers of Lewis and Clark; River Budget (federal money for river protection and restoration).

Periodicals: American Rivers (quarterly newsletter); RiverCurrents (weekly e-newsletter); The River Monitor (focused on the Missouri and Mississippi Rivers; monthly; online).

Key Publications: Most Endangered Rivers (annual report; online); River Budget (annual report advocating for increased federal funding for river protection/restoration; online)

Annual Report: 2000 report online.

Online Activist Tools: Take Action Center (contents: action alerts; online activist [action alerts sent via email]; find elected officials; Congress watch; look up Congressional bills; helping local rivers).

Website Notes: A large web site containing a plethora of information/resources, including an online "Community Center" for "river activists and friends."

Founded: 1973 **Members:** 31,000 **Coverage:** U.S. **Staff:** 40 **Regional Offices:** 8 **NP Status:** 501(c)(3) **Budget:** $6 million

Revenue (FY00): Contributions (79%); Government Grants (1%); Program Service Revenues (4%); Other (16%; from: membership dues –14%; misc. –2%).

Expenses (FY00): Program Services (75%; for: protection of nationally significant rivers via policy reform – 21%; hydropower policy reforms –21%; endangered species, western water program, clean water and urban rivers program –23%; public awareness and education –10%); Management and General (5%); Fundraising (20%).

Contact Info: 1025 Vermont Ave. NW, Suite 720, Washington, DC 20005; (202) 347-7550; amrivers@amrivers.org

Key Personnel: Rebecca Wodder (Executive Director)

16. Appliance Standards Awareness Project (ASAP) (www.standardsasap.org)

General Focus Areas: Energy

Description/Mission: Campaign targeting the U.S. Dept. of Energy to modernize energy efficiency standards for water heaters, clothes washers, central air conditioners and fluorescent lamp ballasts. Founded by the Alliance to Save Energy, the American Council for an Energy-Efficient Economy, and the Natural Resources Defense Council (see separate profiles for each within this subsection).

Basic Activities: Advocacy; research; public education.

Publications: A couple of reports (online).

Key Report: Opportunity Knocks: Capturing Pollution Reductions and Consumer Savings from Updated Appliance Efficiency Standards (online).

Online Activist Tools: Take Action Now (action alerts posted online)

Coverage: U.S.

Contact Info: 20 Belgrade Ave., Suite 1, Boston, MA 02131; (617) 363-9101

Key Personnel: Andrew deLaski (Executive Director)

Audubon Society (www.audubon.org)

See Profile #77 for "National Audubon Society" (located within this subsection).

17. Beyond Pesticides/ National Coalition Against the Misuse of Pesticides (www.beyondpesticides.org) – An "Earth Share" Charity

General Focus Areas: Public Health

Slogan: "Because freedom from pesticides is everybody's right."

Description/Mission: National network committed to pesticide safety and adoption of alternative pest management strategies. Primary goal is to affect change through local action. Acts as an information clearinghouse. Also organizes an annual National Pesticide Forum designed to bring together scientists and activists.

Basic Activities: Information dissemination and public education; community assistance; advocacy; annual conference.

Programs (and activities/focus areas): Children and Schools (pesticides and alternative pest management in schools); Wood Preservatives (seeking a complete ban on use of inorganic arsenicals, pentachlorophenol and creosote); Genetic Engineering (focused on food crops – seeking labeling and regulatory review); Organic Foods (implementation of the Organic Foods Production Act); West Nile Virus and Mosquito Management (contends that spray programs are of limited efficacy); National Pesticide Forum (annual forum to bring together scientists and activists); Pesticide Watchdog (government watchdog activities); Golf and the Environment (work with golf course industry to effect changes in pesticide use); Center for Community Pesticides and Alternatives Information (information on pesticide hazards and alternatives to their use); Pesticides Incident Reports (database of reports of illnesses due to pesticide exposure).

Periodicals: Pesticides and You (quarterly newsletter; online); Technical Report (monthly)

Other Publications: Various reports, compilations, brochures (available at minimal cost); various fact sheets (online); website also provides a list of recommended books.

Check Out on the Web: Safety Source for Pest Management (directory of pest management firms offering "least toxic" control methods)

Online Activist Tools: Action alerts with sample letters

Founded: 1981 **Coverage:** U.S. **Staff:** 7 **NP Status:** 501(c)(3) **Budget:** $0.6 million

Revenue (2000): Contributions (92%); Government Grants (0%); Program Service Revenues (4%); Other (4%)

Expenses (2000): Program Services (95%; for: community information and assistance –45%; "children and schools" program –24%; "stop the poisoning" program regarding West Nile virus spraying –16%; annual National Pesticide Forum –7%; other –4%); Management and General (3%); Fundraising (2%).

Contact Info: 701 E St. SE , Suite 200, Washington DC 20003; (202) 543-5450; info@beyondpesticides.org

Key Personnel: Jay Feldman (Executive Director)

18. Breakthrough Technologies Institute (BTI) / Fuel Cells 2000 (www.fuelcells.org)

General Focus Areas: Energy

Description/Mission: Promotes the development and commercialization of advanced environmental and energy technologies. Currently focused on promoting fuel cell technology via its "Fuel Cells 2000" project.

Basic Activities: Public education; information dissemination; briefings and seminars.

Periodicals: Fuel Cell Quarterly (quarterly newsletter).

Other Publications: Variety of books, reports, articles, market studies, etc. (some online).

Key Publication: Fuel Cell Directory (listing of fuel cell related businesses, research institutes and various orgs; updated semi-annually).

Website Notes: Billed as "the online fuel cell information center," the website provides information on both transportation and stationary (building, residences, etc.) fuel cell applications, as well as on "fuel cell basics." Also has a fuel cell-related career center.

Check Out on the Web: Online Card Catalog (gateway to collected fuel cell information; content areas: Fuel Cell and Energy Basics; Stationary Applications; Automotive Applications; Portable/Small Fuel Cells; Technology-Specific; Fuels for Fuel Cells; Fuel Cell Components; Markets Studies; Periodicals; Searchable Online Energy and Science Libraries).

Founded: 1993 **Coverage:** U.S./Int'l **Budget:** $0.7 million

Revenue (1999): Contributions (84%); Government Grants (6%); Program Service Revenues (9%; from reports and seminars); Other (1%).

Expenses (1999): Program Services (74%; all for the Fuel Cells 2000 Education Project); Management and General (18%); Fundraising (8%).

Contact Info: 1625 K St. NW, Suite 725, Washington DC, 20006; (202) 785-4222

Key Personnel: Robert Rose (Executive Director)

19. Campaign for Safe and Affordable Drinking Water (CSADW) (www.safe-drinking-water.org)

General Focus Areas: Public Health

Description/Mission: Alliance of 300+ organizations working to protect drinking water in the U.S. A primary campaign of the Clean Water Fund (see Profile #27, located within this subsection).

Basic Activities: Public education; advocacy.

Issues: Right-to-Know [Consumer Confidence] Reports; EPA Rulemaking (focused on arsenic regulation); Water Infrastructure Funding; Protecting Vulnerable People (children, elderly, etc.).

Publications: A couple of fact sheets and reports (all online).

Key Report: Measuring Up: Grading the First Round of Right To Know Reports.

Founded: 1994 **Coverage:** U.S.

Contact Info: 4455 Connecticut Avenue NW, Suite A-300, Washington, DC 20008; (202) 895-0420, ext. 109; csadw@cleanwater.org

20. Center for Health, Environment and Justice (CHEJ) (www.chej.org) – An "Earth Share" Charity

General Focus Areas: Pollution; Public Health; Activism Support and Training

Description/Mission: Environmental justice-oriented organization, focused on grassroots community organizing and empowerment, providing technical and organizing assistance. Also runs its own national campaigns. Has worked with 8000+ community-based groups nationwide. Founded by Lois Gibbs of Love Canal fame. Formerly known as the Citizens Clearinghouse for Hazardous Waste.

Basic Activities: Scientific and Technical Assistance; Organizing and Leadership Training; Information Services; Research; Advocacy.

Campaigns: Stop Dioxin Exposure (seeking to modify/shut down dioxin-emitting facilities – waste incinerators, paper mills, certain manufacturing plants); Health Care Without Harm (international coalition to eliminate dioxin and mercury emissions from the health care industry; see Profile #62, located within this subsection); Child Proofing Our Communities (addressing environmental threats to children's health).

Periodicals: Everyone's Backyard (quarterly magazine), Environmental Health Monthly (monthly magazine).

Other Publications: 140+ guidebooks and "fact packs" on various organizing, scientific, corporate and legal issues (available at a nominal cost).

Online Activist Tools: Action alerts sent via email.

Founded: 1981 **Coverage:** U.S. **Staff:** 9 **NP Status:** 501(c)(3) **Budget:** $2 million

Revenue (2000): Contributions (96%); Government Grants (0%); Program Service Revenues (1%); Other (3%).

Expenses (2000): Program Services (93%; for: environmental education outreach –71%; Health Care Without Harm campaign –22%); Management and General (3%); Fundraising (5%).

Contact Info: PO Box 6806, 150 S Washington St., Suite 300, Falls Church, VA 22040; (703) 237-2249; chej@chej.org

Key Personnel: Lois Gibbs (Executive Director)

Center for Marine Conservation (CMC) (www.cmc-ocean.org)

See Profile #87 for "Ocean Conservancy" (located within this subsection).

Center for Media and Democracy (CMD) (www.prwatch.org)

See Profile #98 for "PR Watch" (located within this subsection).

21. Center for a New American Dream (CNAD) (www.newdream.org)

General Focus Areas: Consumerism

Description/Mission: Promotes sustainable policies and practices by helping individuals and institutions reduce and shift patterns of consumption.

Basic Activities: Public education; organizing and outreach; web and network services.

Campaigns/Programs: Junk Mail; Kids and Commercialism (tips for parents); Simplify the Holidays; Faith Based Programs; Government Procurement Strategies; Action Network (two programs: Turn-the-Tide, promoting 9 consumer-related actions to help improve the environment; Step-by-Step, providing monthly actions for individuals designed to impact the decisions/actions of communities, governments, businesses).

Periodicals: Enough! (quarterly newsletter; selected articles online); In Balance (monthly email bulletin; online).

Other Publications: A couple of guides (available at a nominal cost).

Key Publication: More Fun, Less Stuff Starter Kit (practical tips on how to simplify your life, free up time, money, personal energy, and protect the environment).

Check Out on the Web: "New Dream Puzzle" – a 16 piece "consumption puzzle" showing how various issues fit together to form a "new American dream," along with action tips, articles, research, links, and recommended reading.

Founded: 1996 **Coverage:** U.S./Canada **Staff:** 20 **NP Status:** 501(c)(3) **Budget:** $1 million

Revenue (2000): Contributions (93%); Government Grants (0%); Program Service Revenues (<1%); Other (7%).

Expenses (2000): Program Services (63%; for: public education –28%; web and network services –15%; organizing and outreach –14%; government procurement strategies program –5%; children and commercialism program –1%); Management and General (20%); Fundraising (17%).

Contact Info: 6930 Carroll Ave., Suite 900, Takoma Park, MD 20912; (301) 891-3683; newdream@newdream.org

Key Personnel: Betsy Taylor (Executive Director)

22. Center for Renewable Energy and Sustainable Technology (CREST) / Renewable Energy Policy Project (REPP) (www.crest.org)

General Focus Areas: Energy

Description/Mission: Information center for renewable energy and energy efficiency technologies. Formerly known as Solstice. Also includes the Renewable Energy Policy Project (REPP), which focuses on renewable energy policy research (publishing 30+ research reports and issue briefs and 15+ interactive CD-ROMs and web-based tools).

Basic Activities: Policy research/analysis; information dissemination.

Publications: Various research reports and issue briefs (online).

Website Notes: Runs differently from most websites – most of the information is held in a database; thus it is not visible until one searches for it. Searching done using the "Global Energy Marketplace" (GEM) gateway.

Founded: 1993 **Coverage:** U.S./Int'l **Staff:** 6 **NP Status:** 501(c)(3) **Budget:** $0.8 million

Revenue (1998): Contributions (5%); Government Grants (54%); Program Service Revenues (41%; from: contract income –18%; internet services –16%; product sales 6%).

Expenses (1998): Program Services (48%; for: U.S. DOE-funded development of an energy efficiency CD-ROM –14%; U.S. EPA-funded effort providing public information on market-based energy efficiency opportunities – 7%; U.S. EPA-funded effort providing information on potential greenhouse gas reduction actions –4%; U.S. AID-funded program to produce an energy website for India –3%; non-government contracts –21%); Management and General (52%); Fundraising (0%).

Contact Info: 1612 K Street NW, Suite 202, Washington, DC 20006; (202) 293-2898; info@crest.org

Key Personnel: George Sterzinger (Executive Director)

23. Children's Environmental Health Network (CEHN) (www.cehn.org)

General Focus Areas: Public Health

Description/Mission: National project dedicated to protecting the fetus and children from environmental hazards. The Network itself is composed of experts in the fields of medicine, nursing, research and policy. CEHN maintains 3 Advisory Committees (in Education, Policy, and Science/Research) corresponding to each of

CEHN's program areas. Sponsored by the Public Health Institute, a large ($50+ million budget) public health non-profit organization.

Basic Activities/Programs: Education (works with medical, nursing and public health professionals); Policy; Scientific Research (focus areas: asthma and respiratory diseases; childhood cancer; neurodevelopmental effects; endocrine and sexual disorders; cross-cutting issues).

Key Publication: *Training Manual on Pediatric Environmental Health: Putting It Into Practice* (training manual for health care faculty; online)

Check Out on the Web: *Resource Guide on Children's Environmental Health* (Internet gateway providing information and links to relevant groups, projects, and data/information sources).

Founded: 1992 **Coverage:** U.S. **Staff:** 8

Contact Info: 110 Maryland Ave. NE, Suite 511, Washington, DC 20002; (202) 543-4033; cehn@cehn.org

Key Personnel: Daniel J. Swartz (Executive Director)

24. Clean Air Trust (CAT) (www.cleanairtrust.org)

General Focus Areas: Pollution

Slogan: "Working to achieve a strong and effective Clean Air Act."

Description/Mission: Promotes and defends the Clean Air Act. Founded by former Senators Edmund Muskie and Robert Stafford.

Basic Activities: Public education; advocacy.

Check Out on the Web: "Clean Air Villain" awards (issued monthly).

Website Notes: A small website, mainly providing press releases along with issuance of monthly "Clean Air Villain" awards.

Founded: 1995 **Coverage:** U.S. **NP Status:** 501(c)(4)

Contact Info: 1625 K St. NW, Suite 790, Washington, DC 20006; (202) 785-9625; frank@cleanairtrust.org

Key Personnel: Frank O'Donnell (Executive Director)

25. Clean Car Campaign (www.cleancarcampaign.org)

General Focus Areas: Pollution

Description/Mission: Campaign promoting development and sale of vehicles meeting the "Clean Car Standard" – increased fuel efficiency, reduced emissions and clean production practices. Also spearheading a related campaign to remove mercury from vehicles. Coordinated by a coalition of 6 environmental/energy groups (see below).

Key Coalition Members (see separate profiles for each within this subsection): American Council for an Energy Efficient Economy; Environmental Defense; Union of Concerned Scientists.

Basic Activities: Public education; advocacy.

Publications: A couple of guides and reports (online).

Key Report: *Toxics in Vehicles: Mercury* (examines the implications for recycling and disposal; online).

Check Out on the Web: "Clean Car Pledges" – consumers showing their interest in purchasing vehicles meeting the Clean Car Standard (nearly 100,000 have signed the Pledge).

Coverage: U.S.

Contact Info: 1875 Connecticut Ave. NW, Suite 1016, Washington, DC 20009; (202) 387-3500; info@cleancarcampaign.org

26. Clean Water Action (CWA) (www.cleanwateraction.org)

General Focus Areas: Activism Support; Politics

Description/Mission: Focuses on organizing grassroots groups, coalitions and campaigns on water-related and other environmental issues. Also campaigns to elect environmental candidates at all government levels. CWA is affiliated with the Clean Water Fund (see Profile #27, located within this subsection), sharing facilities, equipment and employees.

Basic Activities: Grassroots organizing; public education; advocacy.

Lobbying/Political Activities: Registered lobbyist under the LDA; maintains a PAC (Clean Water Action Vote Environment – a.k.a. Clean WAVE).

National Priorities: Arsenic in Drinking Water; Clean Air Act; Water Infrastructure Funding; Safe Drinking Water Act Right To Know (Consumer Confidence) Reports.

Periodicals: Clean Water Action News (newsletter).

Founded: 1971 **Coverage:** U.S. **Members:** 750,000 **State Chapters:** 17 **NP Status:** 501(c)(4)

Contact Info: 4455 Connecticut Ave. NW, Suite A300, Washington, DC 20008; (202) 895-0420; cwa@cleanwater.org

Key Personnel: Kathy Aterno (Executive Director); Paul Schwartz (Policy Coordinator)

27. Clean Water Fund (CWF) (www.cleanwaterfund.org) – An "Earth Share" Charity

General Focus Areas: Pollution; Public Health

Description/Mission: Develops local grassroots campaigns for cleaner water and air and protection from toxic pollution. CWF is affiliated with Clean Water Action (see Profile #26, located within this subsection), sharing facilities, equipment and employees. CWF's programs build on and complement those of CWA.

Basic Activities: Grassroots organizing; research; public education; advocacy.

Programs (and focus areas): Clean and Safe Water (water supply resource protection; drinking water safety); Environment-Economy Initiative (material reuse and recycled market development; infrastructure [sewage and drinking water facilities]; fees, charges and funding strategies to support environmental investments and reward pollution prevention; trade-related environmental concerns; smart growth); Sustainable Energy (electric power plant emissions; consumer education; electric utility deregulation); Environmental Health (programs focused on preventing pollution from persistent poisons); Research, Training, Outreach and Education (field office-based programs/activities to assist citizens/local communities facing environmental hazards).

Campaigns/Initiatives: Campaign for Safe and Affordable Drinking Water (see Profile #19, located within this subsection); Safe Foods (genetically engineered foods); Preventing Harm (a resource and action center on children and the environment; initiatives focus on arsenic, dioxin, dursban and mercury).

Publications: A couple of reports (online).

Key Report: In Harm's Way (examines toxic threats to child development; online).

Founded: 1978 **Coverage:** U.S. **NP Status:** 501(c)(3) **Budget:** $2.5 million

Revenue (FY00): Contributions (95%); Government Grants (5%); Program Service Revenues (0%); Other (<1%).

Expenses (FY00): Program Services (82%; for: clean and safe water programs –32%; environment-economy initiative and sustainable energy programs –25%; environmental health programs –18%; research, training, outreach and education –7%); Management and General (12%); Fundraising (6%).

Contact Info: 4455 Connecticut Ave. NW, Suite A300-16, Washington, DC 20008; (202) 895-0432; cwf@cleanwater.org

Key Personnel: David Zwick (Executive VP); Kathy Aterno (Executive Director)

28. Clean Water Network (CWN) (www.cwn.org)

General Focus Areas: Pollution

Description/Mission: Alliance of 1000 organizations (representing environmentalists, farmers, fishermen, boaters, etc.) endorsing a platform paper – the National Agenda for Clean Water (key elements: Prevent Pollution and Achieve Zero Discharge; Protect Critical Ecosystems; Enforce the Law – Close Loopholes).

Basic Activities: Public education; advocacy.

Issues: Coastal Issues; Clean Water Act Enforcement; Factory Farms; Mixing Zones; Polluted Runoff; Raw Sewage (Wet Weather) Pollution; Impaired Waters; Water Quality Standards; Wetlands.

Publications: Some reports and fact sheets (online).

Online Activist Tools: Legislative Action Center (contents: elected officials; issues and legislation; guide to the media).

Check Out on the Web: "State Information," providing for each state: 1) Clean Water State Fact Sheet, 2) EPA Report on State Water Quality and 3) Local Advocacy Information.

Coverage: U.S. **Staff:** 5

Contact Info: 1200 New York Avenue NW, Suite 400, Washington, DC 20005; (202) 289-2395; cleanwaternt@igc.org

Key Personnel: Eddie Scher (Director)

29. Clear the Air Campaign (www.cleartheair.org)

General Focus Areas: Pollution; Public Health

Slogan: "The national campaign against dirty power."

Description/Mission: National campaign to improve air quality by reducing emissions from coal-burning power plants. A joint project of the Clean Air Task Force, National Environmental Trust (see Profile #78, located within this subsection) and the U.S. PIRG Education Fund (see Profile #101, located within this subsection). Initiated by the Pew Charitable Trusts.

Basic Activities: Research; public education; advocacy.

Publications: Some reports and fact sheets (all online).

Key Publications (both online): Power to Kill (projects death and disease from 51 power plants charged with violating the Clean Air Act's New Source Review regulations); Death, Disease and Dirty Power (quantifies the health impacts of fine-particle air pollution – soot – from power plants, as well as expected health benefits from reduction of such emissions).

Online Activist Tools: Take Action section (action alerts sent via email).

Coverage: U.S.

Contact Info: 1200 18th Street NW, 5th Floor, Washington, DC 20036; (202) 887-1715; info@cleartheair.org

Key Personnel: Angela Ledford (Director)

30. Climate Action Network (CAN) (www.climatenetwork.org)

General Focus Areas: Global Warming

Description/Mission: Global network of nearly 300 NGOs (including the World Wildlife Fund, Greenpeace and Friends of the Earth), working on climate change issues. Organized around 8 regional offices worldwide, including a U.S. office.

Basic Activities: Public education; advocacy.

Periodicals: Hotline (newsletter; online).

Website Note: Main website principally serves as a gateway to the websites of the 8 regional offices of CAN, including the U.S. office.

Founded: 1989 **Coverage:** Global **Regional Offices:** 8

Contact Info (U.S.): 1367 Connecticut Ave NW, Suite 300, Washington, DC 20036; (202) 785-8702; info@climatenetwork.org

Key Personnel: Nathalie Eddy (U.S. Coordinator)

31. Coalition for Environmentally Responsible Economies (CERES) (www.ceres.org)

General Focus Areas: Business Practices

Description/Mission: Coalition of 70+ environmental, investor, and advocacy groups working in partnership with companies to promote/improve corporate environmental responsibility worldwide. Known for development/promotion of standardized corporate environmental reporting practices. 50+ corporate partners have formally endorsed the "CERES Principles," a 10-point code of environmental conduct that includes commitment to annual public issuance of a CERES-style environmental report.

Basic Activities: Research/guideline development; conferences; communications; outreach.

Initiatives: Global Reporting Initiative (develop guidelines for reporting on economic, environmental and social performance; initially for corporations, eventually for any business, governmental or non-governmental organization; coordinated by CERES in partnership with the United Nation Environment Programme); Green Hotel Initiative (catalyze the demand and supply of environmentally-responsible hotel services).

Periodicals: CERES News (monthly newsletter via email; online).

Other Publications: A couple of reports (free, but must order from CERES).

Founded: 1989 **Coverage:** U.S./Int'l **Staff:** 12 **NP Status:** 501(c)(3) **Budget:** $2 million

Revenue (2000): Contributions (57%); Government Grants (0%); Program Service Revenues (17%; from conference fees); Other (26%; from: membership dues –20%; misc. –6%).

Expenses (2000): Program Services (80%); Management and General (14%); Fundraising (6%).

Contact Info: 11 Arlington Street, 6th Floor, Boston, MA 02116; (617) 247-0700; info@ceres.org

Key Personnel: Robert Massie (Executive Director)

32. Coastal Conservation Association (CCA) (www.joincca.org)

General Focus Areas: Conservation

Description/Mission: Organization of recreational fishermen seeking to protect recreational fish in coastal waters through education, lobbying/legislation and restoration. An active litigant, with 100+ lawsuits pending against the National Marine Fisheries Service. Active in conservation and restoration of fisheries, but at the same time opposes "no fish" zones.

Basic Activities: Fisheries conservation/restoration; education; policy/legislation; advocacy/lobbying; litigation.

Periodicals: Tide (bi-monthly magazine); Rising Tide (quarterly magazine for youth); Capital Ideas (monthly newsletter; online).

Founded: 1977 **Membership:** 75,000 **Coverage:** U.S. **Staff:** 60 **State/Local Chapters:** 15/164 **NP Status:** 501(c)(3) **Budget:** $7 million

Revenue (2000): Contributions (40%); Government Grants (0%); Program Service Revenues (0%); Other (60%; from: special events [includes: dinners; auctions; angling tournaments] –47%; membership dues –7%; misc. –6%)

Expenses (2000): Program Services (84%; for: information dissemination –62%; *Tide* magazine –10%; projects – 9%; state chapter newsletters – 2%; college scholarships – <1%); Administration (15%); Other (<1%).

Contact Info: 6919 Portwest, Suite 100, Houston, TX 77024; (713) 626-4234 / 800-201-FISH; ccantl@joincca.org

Key Personnel: Alex Jernigan (President)

33. Concern, Inc. (no web address)

General Focus Areas: Sustainable Development

Description/Mission: Environmental education organization focused on sustainability issues. In partnership with 16 other orgs, directs the Sustainable Communities Network (see Profile #121, located within this subsection), an online information network promoting sustainable communities. Also involved in local and regional sustainability projects and conducts various outreach activities.

Basic Activities: Public education; information dissemination; outreach; local and regional sustainability projects.

Coverage: U.S./Int'l **NP Status:** 501(c)(3) **Budget:** $0.2 million

Revenue (FY00): Contributions (56%); Government Grants (0%); Program Service Revenues (41%; from government fees/contracts); Other (3%).

Expenses (FY00): Program Services (95%; for: Sustainable Communities Network –67%; national and international outreach –13%; local and regional sustainability projects –11%; community outreach –4%); Management and General (3%); Fundraising (2%).

Contact Info: 1794 Columbia Road NW, Suite 6, Washington, DC 20009; concern@concern.org

34. (The) Conservation Fund (www.conservationfund.org) – An "Earth Share" Charity

General Focus Areas: Conservation

Description/Mission: Focuses on land and water resource conservation through land acquisition, community initiatives and leadership training. Since inception, has conserved 3+ million acres of forest, wetlands, recreation areas, historical sites and working landscapes. Works in partnership with the private sector, NGOs, and public agencies. Also operates the Freshwater Institute (which develops aquaculture technologies) and manages the Conservation Leadership Network (a government/NGO alliance for building the capacity of natural resource conservation professionals and organizations – housed at National Conservation Training Center in Shepherdstown, WV).

Basic Activities: Land acquisition; community initiatives; leadership training; technical research.

Projects: New England's Forests; Forestland Habitat; Sensitive Wetlands; Meadowlands; Desert Habitat; Rangeland; America's Greenways; Civil War Battlefield Preservation.

Periodicals: Common Ground (bimonthly newsletter; online).

Other Publications: A few books and guides.

Founded: 1985 **Coverage:** U.S. **NP Status:** 501(c)(3) **Budget:** $50 million

Revenues (2000): Contributions (87%; includes: cash contributions –78%; gifts of land –9%); Government Grants (5%); Program Service Revenues (4%); Other (4%).

Expenses (2000): Program Services (95%); Management and General (4%); Fundraising (1%).

Contact Info: 1800 North Kent St., Suite 1120, Arlington, VA 22209; (703) 525-6300.

Key Personnel: Lawrence Selzer (President)

35. Conservation International (CI) (www.conservation.org) – An "Earth Share" Charity

General Focus Areas: Conservation; Business Practices

Description/Mission: Focuses on preservation of tropical and temperate ecosystems, working in 30+ countries on 4 continents (Africa, Asia-Pacific, Mexico/Central America, South America). Works in partnership with governments, local communities, and businesses. Practical and community-centered, 75% of CI staff work on the frontlines and 90% are citizens of the countries they work in.

Basic Activities: Field programs/support; scientific research; communication and education; conservation funding/grants; conservation enterprises.

Geographical Focus Areas: Biodiversity Hotspots (25 threatened ecoregions); Major Tropical Wilderness Areas (namely: Amazonia; Africa's Congo Basin; the island of New Guinea); Key Marine Ecosystems (15 specific ecosystems); Select Major Wetlands (namely Brazil's Pantanal wetland and the Okavango Delta of Botswana).

Programs (and activities/focus areas): Research and Science (conservation biology; conservation economics; strategic planning; regional analysis; Geographic Information Systems); Business and Environment (agriculture and fisheries; energy and mining; travel and leisure; carbon offsets; water); Protected Areas (research; conservation funding); Conservation Grants (Critical Ecosystem Partnership Fund for creating working alliances with key multilaterals – see Profile #304, located within Subsection 3.1.5 – "UN-Associated Partnership Programs"); Conservation Enterprise Fund (funds directed to businesses engaged in: agro-forestry, ecotourism or wild-harvest products); Conservation Enterprises (conservation coffee; conservation cocoa; ecotourism; wild-harvest products; marine seaweed); Resource Economics (focused on China, Ecuador, and Mexico); Ecotourism; Biodiversity Reporting Award (to promote news coverage); Environmental Education; Tropical Wilderness Protection Fund (cash fund to respond to "conservation emergencies").

Key Centers (and activities/focus areas): Center for Applied Biodiversity Science (collect/interpret biodiversity data; develop strategic plans for conservation; establish conservation partnerships; promote public awareness/involvement); Center for Environmental Leadership in Business (partnership to advance conservation solutions and educate consumers/employees on biodiversity protection).

Periodicals: News from the Front (quarterly newsletter; online).

Other Publications: Some fact sheets, policy papers, books (some online).

Key Report: The Top 10 Coral Reef Hotspots (study conducted by CI's Center for Applied Biodiversity Science).

Annual Report: 2000 report online.

Check Out on the Web: Investigate Biodiversity (educational tool for science students developed by CI in partnership with Intel Corporation).

Founded: 1987 **Coverage:** International **Staff:** 600 **NP Status:** 501(c)(3) **Budget:** $50 million

Revenue (FY00): Contributions (92%; includes: cash –83%; non-cash –9%); Government Grants (5%); Program Service Revenues (1%); Other (2%)

Expenses (FY00): Program Services (84%; for: field programs/support –64%; Center for Applied Biodiversity Science –12%; communication and education –6%; Center for Environmental Leadership in Business –2%; Critical Ecosystem Partnership Fund –<1%); Management and General (10%); Fundraising (6%).

Funding Sources (FY00): Individuals (40%); Governments, NGOs and Multilaterals (25%); Foundations (18%); Corporations (14%); Other (3%).

Contact Info: 1919 M St. NW, Suite 600, Washington, DC 20036; (202) 912-1000 / (800) 406-2306.

Key Personnel: Russell Mittermeier (Executive Director)

36. Consortium for Energy Efficiency (CEE) (www.cee1.org)

General Focus Areas: Energy

Description/Mission: Coalition promoting the manufacture and purchase of energy-efficient products and services. CEE develops specifications that define "high efficiency" for certain products/equipment. CEE members include utilities, research orgs, state/regional energy offices/programs, while CEE partners include manufacturers, retailers and government agencies (both the DOE and EPA provide major funding support).

Basic Activities: Technical research and information; specification development.

Programs (and focus areas): Residential (clothes washers; home appliances; lighting; central air conditioning and heat pumps; gas heating); Commercial (air conditioning and heat pumps; clothes washers; gas boilers; buildings); Industrial (motor systems; premium motors; compressed air; transformers); Government (state and local government purchasing; apartment-sized refrigerators; traffic signals).

Periodicals: Market Transformer News (tri-annual newsletter; online).

Other Publications: Various program-related documents (facts sheets; initiative descriptions; program summaries; efficiency specs; qualifying product lists; all online).

Check Out on the Web: Fact Sheets (individual "snapshots" of CEE program areas; located within the "Resource Library"); M-T Primer (a short primer on "market transformation" – what CEE is attempting to accomplish overall; located under "About CEE").

Founded: 1991 **Coverage:** U.S. **Staff:** 13 **NP Status:** 501(c)(3) **Budget:** $1.5 million

Revenue (2000): Contributions (57%); Government Grants (38%); Program Service Revenues (0%); Other (5%).

Expenses (2000): Program Services (69%; for various energy efficiency initiatives); Management and General (31%); Fundraising (0%).

Contact Info: 1 State St., Suite 1400, Boston MA 02109; (617) 589-3949.

Key Personnel: Marc Hoffman (Executive Director)

37. Corporate Watch / CorpWatch.org (www.corpwatch.org)

General Focus Areas: Corporations; Globalization

Slogan: "Holding corporations accountable."

Description: Organization dedicated to "countering corporate-led globalization through education and activism." Focuses on human rights, labor rights and environmental justice. Formerly known as the Transnational Resource and Action Center (TRAC). A Project of the Tides Center (see Profile #123, located within this subsection).

Basic Activities: Research and monitoring; public education and information dissemination; advocacy.

Issues: Beyond 9-11; Biotechnology; Globalization 101 (an introduction); Grassroots Globalization; Internet Politics; Money and Politics; Oil, Gas and Coal; Sweatshops; Tobacco; Trade Agreements; World Bank/IMF; WTO.

Key Campaigns (and specific activities): Alliance for a Corporate-Free UN (international coalition of orgs examining human rights and environmental records of companies forming partnerships with the UN; calls on the UN to forgo such collaborations); Climate Justice (works with communities affected by the oil industry worldwide); Greenwash (bimonthly awards to corporations judged to focus more on PR campaigns than on actually protecting the environment).

Publications: A couple of reports and books (reports provided online).

Key Publications (both online): Greenhouse Gangsters vs. Climate Justice (examines oil companies records and tactics and calls for "climate justice"); Tangled Up in Blue (explores corporate partnerships at the United Nations and calls for a "corporate-free UN").

Online Activist Tools: Cyber-Action Team (action alerts sent via email).

Check Out on the Web: "Research" (provides the CorpWatch Research Guide – an interactive guide to researching corporations via the Internet).

Founded: 1996 **Coverage:** U.S./Int'l **Staff:** 7

Contact Info: PO Box 29344, San Francisco, CA 94129; (415) 561-6568; corpwatch@corpwatch.org

Key Personnel: Joshua Karliner (Executive Director)

38. Cousteau Society (www.cousteausociety.org)

General Focus Areas: Conservation

Description/Mission: Focuses on protection and improvement of oceans and associated marine ecosystems. Founded by Jacques Cousteau, world-renown ocean explorer whose scientific expeditions aboard the ship *Calypso* were documented in 120 television films.

Basic Activities: Scientific research; public education; publication and films; environmental education.

Issues: Coral Reefs; Marine Protected Areas; Whales; Fisheries (focused on: toothfish; sharks; seahorses; sturgeon).

Programs (and specific activities): Dolphin Log in the Classroom (provide copies of the Society's children's magazine to classrooms); Waters of Peace (exploring the natural resources of the Caspian Sea); Cousteau Label (provided to communities that protect ocean or lake shores in accord with the "Cousteau Charter"); Coastal Workers (promoting employment for such workers); Ecotechnie (promoting an integrated environmental education program that combines ecology, economics, social sciences and technology).

Periodicals: Calypso Log (bimonthly; online); Dolphin Log (for kids ages 8-12; bimonthly; online).

Other Publications: Various books, along with films and videos.

Check Out on the Web: Lists of books, films and videos put out by Jacques Cousteau / the Cousteau Society.

Founded: 1973 **Membership:** 150,000 **Coverage:** Global **NP Status:** 501(c)(3) **Budget:** $5 million

Revenue (2000): Contributions (90%); Government Grants (0%); Program Service Revenues (7%; includes publications and films); Other (3%).

Expenses (2000): Program Services (64%; for: research and films –32%; membership support –18%; public education –14%); Management and General (19%); Fundraising (17%).

Contact Info: 870 Greenbrier Circle, Suite 402, Chesapeake, VA 23320; (800) 441-4395; cousteau@cousteausociety.org

Key Personnel: Francine Cousteau (President)

39. Defenders of Wildlife (www.defenders.org) – An "Earth Share" Charity

General Focus Areas: Conservation

Description/Mission: Focuses on wildlife and habitat protection. Known for its work on endangered species issues, particularly predators such as brown bears and gray wolves. Also advocates for wildlife conservation to protect species before they become endangered.

Basic Activities: Wildlife restoration; education and communication; research; legislation; advocacy; litigation.

Lobbying/Political Activities: Registered lobbyist under the LDA.

Programs/Issues (and focus areas): Species Conservation (bears; big cats; wolves; wild birds; prairie species; marine mammals; meso-carnivores); Habitat Conservation (Habitat Conservation Plans; national wildlife refuges;

state biodiversity clearinghouse; ecosystems and lands legacy; anti-environmental riders; global warming; habitats and highways); Policy (endangered species and biodiversity); Canadian Programs (Boreal forest; endangered species; Great Canadians; carnivore conservation).

Periodicals: Defenders (semi-annual magazine; online); DENlines (bi-weekly e-newsletter; online); WILDLines (weekly e-newsletter on state wildlife issues; online); WolfLines (bi-weekly e-newsletter on wolf issues; online).

Other Publications: Some reports (all online).

Key Report: Amber Waves of Gain (an exposé of the American Farm Bureau trade association).

Annual Report: 2000 report online.

Online Activist Tools: Defenders Electronic Network (consists of: Action Center; biweekly email updates).

Unique: "Adopt a Polar Bear" program.

Associated Website: Kid's Planet (for kids; www.kidsplanet.org).

Founded: 1947 **Members/Supporters:** 320,000 **Coverage:** U.S./Canada **Regional Offices:** 11 **NP Status:** 501(c)(3) **Budget:** $18 million

Revenue (1999): Contributions (92%); Government Grants (0%); Program Service Revenues (0%); Other (8%).

Expenses (1999): Program Services (80%; for: wildlife action program –40%; information, education and communication –32%; membership development –7%); Management and General (7%); Fundraising (13%).

Contact Info: 1101 14th St. NW, Suite 1400, Washington, DC 20005; (202) 682-9400; info@defenders.org

Key Personnel: Rodger Schlickeisen (President/CEO)

40. Ducks Unlimited (DU) (www.ducks.org)

General Focus Areas: Conservation

Slogan: "World leader in wetlands conservation."

Description/Mission: Focuses on wetland and waterfowl conservation. Cites conservation of nearly 10 million acres of wetland habitat across North America. Conducts 5000+ grassroots events annually.

Basic Activities: Waterfowl conservation; restoration of grasslands, watersheds and forests; establishing conservation easements and management agreements; scientific research; public education; policy/advocacy.

Lobbying/Political Activities: Registered lobbyist under the LDA.

Key Programs (and activities/focus areas): Conservation Easements; Institute for Wetland and Waterfowl Research (science arm of DU); Matching Aid to Restore States Habitat (MARSH – provides matching funds/grants to public and private agencies and organizations to acquire and enhance waterfowl habitat within each state); International Programs (covering: Canada; Mexico; Latin American and the Caribbean; Australia; New Zealand); Governmental Affairs (focused on 3 areas: North American Wetlands Conservation Act; conservation reserve program; wetlands reserve program); Taking Wing (working with the U.S. Forest Service to improve wetland habitat for waterfowl on National Forests and National Grasslands).

Periodicals: Unlimited (bimonthly magazine; archives partially online); DU Newsletter (quarterly newsletter); Puddler (quarterly magazine for kids).

Key Publication: DU's Conservation Plan (identifies important habitat priority areas and other waterfowl conservation issues).

Annual Report: 2001 report online.

Unique: TV series, "The World of Ducks Unlimited" (features waterfowl hunting action; weekly; shown on TNN).

Check Out on the Web: State Fact Sheets (summary information on state-level activities); Wood Duck Nesting Box Plan (information on how to construct and locate such boxes); "Greenwings" (for kids; focus on waterfowl and wetlands).

Founded: 1937 **Membership:** 700,000 **Coverage:** U.S./Int'l **Regional Offices:** 5 **NP Status:** 501(c)(3) **Budget:** $125 million

Revenue Sources (FY01): Conservation Easements (27%); Federal/State Habitat Reimbursements (24%); DU Events (15%); Membership (11%); Major Gifts and Endowments (9%); Sponsors (8%); Other (6%).

Revenue (FY01): Contributions (58%; includes contributions from independent DU chapters); Government

Grants (33%); Program Service Revenues (0%); Other (9%).

Expenses (FY01): Program Services (81%; for: North American waterfowl habitat conservation projects –68%; public education program –11%; membership services –2%; federal public policy/lobbying program –<1%); Management and General (4%); Fundraising (15%).

Associated Org: Wetlands America Trust (DU trust fund set up to acquire, monitor and maintain conservation easements to protect wetland ecosystems in the U.S.; for FY01, $48 million worth of such easements were acquired by DU through the Trust).

Contact Info: 1 Waterfowl Way, Memphis, TN 38120; (800) 45-DUCKS.

Key Personnel: L.J. Mayeux (President); Don Young (Executive VP)

41. Earth Day Network (www.earthday.net)

General Focus Areas: Earth Day; Energy

Description/Mission: Coordinating body of/clearinghouse for worldwide Earth Day activities. The Network includes 5,000+ organizations in 184 countries. Also coordinates worldwide campaigns focused on "clean energy."

Basic Activities: Earth Day coordination; public education; advocacy.

Worldwide Campaigns (unifying theme – clean energy): Human Rights and the Environment (focus on oil extraction by multinationals in Burma, Nigeria, Chad and Cameroon, Ecuador); Adopt Clean Energy; Fund Clean Energy (shift international funding from fossil fuel towards renewable energy); No Nuclear Energy; Energy Efficiency; Car Free Day (Earth Day); Clean Energy in the U.S.

Periodicals: Grist (online magazine).

Annual Report: 2000-01 report online.

Online Activist Tools: "Do Good" section (contents: posted action alerts, arranged into 15 "action categories").

Website Notes: The website itself is focused on energy-related issues, along with providing Earth Day-related news and resources.

Check Out on the Web: Grist magazine, a "must-read" online environmental magazine (see Profile #478, located within Subsection 7.3 – "Media-Related Entities").

Founded: 1989 **NP Status:** 501(c)(3) **Budget:** $3 million

Revenue (2000): Contributions (92%); Government Grants (0%); Program Service Revenues (0%); Other (8%).

Expenses (2000): Program Services (97%); Management and General (3%); Fundraising (0%).

Contact Info: 811 1st Ave., Suite 454, Seattle, WA 98104; (206) 876-2000; earthday@earthday.net

Key Personnel: Denis Hayes (Chairman); Kelly Evans (Executive Director)

42. Earth Island Institute (EII) (www.earthisland.org)

General Focus Areas: Activism Support and Training

Slogan: "Innovative action for the environment."

Description/Mission: Operates as a "campaign incubator," sponsoring, supporting and promoting environmental projects worldwide focused on education and activist campaigns. Has resulted in a consortium of 30+ grassroots campaigns, each functioning independently while sharing resources and administrative/organizational support. Also known for its *Earth Island Journal* publication. Founded by veteran environmentalist, the late David Brower.

Basic Activities: Funding/support of independent grassroots campaigns; communications; public education; advocacy.

Periodicals: Earth Island Journal (quarterly magazine; online); Island Wire (email newsletter).

Annual Report: 2000-01 report online.

Online Activist Tools: Activist Toolbox (contents: "activate-the-web"; progressive connections; federal officials feedback sites); Action Alerts.

Check Out on the Web: Web pages of EII-sponsored projects.

Founded: 1982 **Membership:** 20,000 **Coverage:** U.S./Int'l **NP Status:** 501(c)(3) **Budget:** $5 million

Revenue (2000): Contributions (85%); Government Grants (4%); Program Service Revenues (7%); Other (4%).

Expenses (2000): Program Services (87%); Management and General (7%); Fundraising (6%).

Contact Info: 300 Broadway, Suite 28, San Francisco, CA 94133; (415) 788-3666.

Key Personnel: John Knox and David Phillips (Executive Directors)

43. Earthjustice Legal Defense Fund (www.earthjustice.org) – An "Earth Share" Charity

General Focus Areas: Conservation; Pollution; Public Health

Slogan: "Because the earth needs a good lawyer."

Description/Mission: Environmental law firm (50 lawyers on staff) serving 500+ environmental organizations free-of-charge. Also runs Environmental Law Clinics at Stanford University and the University of Denver. Formerly the Sierra Club Legal Defense Fund.

Basic Activities: Litigation; public education and information; advocacy.

Lobbying/Political Activities: Registered lobbyist under the LDA.

Program Areas: Air; Forests; Health and Communities; Oceans; Public Lands; Water; Wildlife; International.

Campaigns: Fish-Trees-Water (safeguarding and restoring the Great Northwest); National Wild Forests (public lands protection).

Periodicals: E-Brief (monthly e-mail newsletter).

Annual Report: 2000 report online.

Online Activist Tools: Take Action section (action alerts sent via email).

Unique: "Earthjustice Channel" – an online (RealPlayer-based) video covering five key Earthjustice activity areas (Endangered Species; Health and Communities; Fish, Trees, Water Campaign; Marine Protection; Water).

Check Out on the Web: "Urgent Cases" (key current legal cases).

Founded: 1971 **Coverage:** U.S./Int'l **Staff:** 130 **Regional Offices:** 10 **NP Status:** 501(c)(3) **Budget:** $20 million

Revenue (FY00): Contributions (84%; from: individuals –53%; foundations –31%); Government Grants (0%); Program Service Revenues (0%); Other (16%; from court awards –9%; investment income –7%).

Expenses (FY00): Program Services (73%; for: litigation –57%; public information –16%); Management and General (8%); Fundraising (19%).

Contact Info: 180 Montgomery St., Suite 1400, San Francisco, CA 94104; (415) 627-6700; eajus@earthjustice.org

Key Personnel: Vawter "Buck" Parker (Executive Director)

44. Earth Share (www.earthshare.org)

General Focus Areas: Workplace Giving

Slogan: "One environment. One simple way to care for it."

Description/Mission: Manages workplace-giving (payroll deduction) campaigns for national environmental and conservation charities just as the United Way does for health and human services charities. Raises $8+ million in pledges per year, along with another $40+ million in in-kind contributions. Its 40+ member charities represent a wide array of environmental groups; each must meet a 17-point list of criteria for membership. Has 16 state-specific partner organizations (for example, Earth Share of California), 14 of which have their own separate websites.

Basic Activities: Operates workplace giving program; public education.

Periodicals: Sharing News (annual newsletter from member charities; online).

Associated Websites: State-specific partner organization websites.

Check Out on the Web: Environmental Resource Guides (listing of publications, videos, etc. from member organizations; organized in two ways: 1) for citizens and 2) for teachers/students; online under "News and Resources").

Founded: 1988 **Coverage:** U.S./Int'l **Staff:** 19 **NP Status:** 501(c)(3) **Budget:** $9 million

Revenue (FY01): Contributions (99%); Government Grants (0%); Program Service Revenues (<1%).

Expenses (FY01): Program Services (90%; for: allocation of campaign contributions to member orgs –71%; conduct campaigns on behalf of member orgs –19%; USEPA grant to promote "EPA Green" –1%); Management and General (6%); Fundraising (4%).

Contact Info: 3400 International Dr. NW, Suite 2K, Washington, DC 20008; (202) 537-7100 / (800) 875-3863.

Key Personnel: Kalman Stein (President)

45. Earthwatch Institute / Earthwatch Expeditions (www.earthwatch.org**)**

General Focus Areas: Scientific Research

Description/Mission: Sponsors scientific field research worldwide by recruiting volunteers from the general public to help field scientists with their research. Volunteers collect data and work as full-fledged expedition members. Each year, 4000 member volunteers work in some 700 research teams led by 200 research scientists on projects in 50+ countries worldwide. Also offers expedition fellowships to K-12 teachers and high school students. The formal legal name of the Institute is Earthwatch Expeditions, Inc.

Basic Activities: Scientific field research; public education.

Research Areas: Endangered Ecosystems; Oceans; Biodiversity; Cultural Diversity; Global Change; World Health; Archaeology.

Founded: 1971 **Coverage:** U.S./Int'l **Staff:** 84 **NP Status:** 501(c)(3) **Budget:** $7 million

Revenue (FY00): Contributions (90%); Government Grants (0%); Program Service Revenues (0%); Other (10%; from: membership dues –8%; misc. –2%).

Expenses (FY00): Program Services (71%; for research expeditions and public education); Management and General (22%); Fundraising (7%).

Affiliated Org: Center for Field Research (develops the research program for Earthwatch by evaluating research grant applications solicited from scientists; the grant program works based on "participant funding" – most funds granted to projects come from payments made by participating volunteers).

Contact Info: Box 75, 3 Clock Tower Place, Suite 100, Maynard, MA 01754; (800) 776-0188; info@earthwatch.org

Key Personnel: Roger Bergen (President/CEO)

Ecotourism Society (www.ecotourism.org**)**

See Profile #369 for "(The) International Ecotourism Society" (TIES), located within Subsection 5.1 – "Business Trade Associations, Coalitions/Councils and Related Entities."

46. Endangered Species Coalition (ESC) (www.stopextinction.org**)**

General Focus Areas: Conservation

Description/Mission: Coalition of 430 environmental, scientific and religious organizations seeking to broaden and mobilize public support for protecting endangered species and supporting the Endangered Species Act.

Basic Activities: Public education; advocacy.

Issues/Campaigns: Endangered Species Act Funding; Stop the Anti-Environmental Riders Campaign; Endangered Species Act Reauthorization; Regional Issues.

Periodicals: ESA Today (quarterly news magazine; online); On Top of The Hill (weekly legislative and policy report; online).

Online Activist Tools: Action Alerts; Activist Toolbox (contents: fact sheets; skill sheets; sample materials).

Check Out on the Web: "About ESA" – a practical introduction to the Endangered Species Act program.

Founded: 1982 **Coverage:** U.S. **Staff:** 10

Contact Info: 1101 14th Street NW, Suite 1001, Washington, DC 20005; (202) 682-9400; esc@stopextinction.org

Key Personnel: Brock Evans (Executive Director)

47. Environmental Alliance for Senior Involvement (EASI) (www.easi.org) – An "Earth Share" Charity

General Focus Areas: Senior Citizen Involvement

Description/Mission: Provides opportunities for older adults to help protect and improve the environment in their local communities. Over 300 partnering organizations, with a national network of 12,000 local organizations (spanning all 50 states) serving as program hosts. EASI also has chartered local "Senior Environment Corps" programs in all 50 states, which has resulted in 100,000+ seniors taking part in a variety of environmental projects. Founded by USEPA and AARP. Nearly all work funded via state/federal grants.

Basic Activities: Environmental projects for senior citizens.

Project Areas: Energy Conservation; Environmental Education; Environmental Health; Environmental Monitoring; Environmental Restoration; Pollution Prevention.

Periodicals: EASI Does It (quarterly newsletter; online).

Annual Report: 1999-2000 report online.

Check Out on the Web: Briefing Paper on EASI (succinct summary of the organization, including future initiatives; online under "Publications").

Founded: 1991 **Coverage:** U.S. **Staff:** 13 **NP Status:** 501(c)(3) **Budget:** $0.9 million

Income (ordinary income; FY00): Contributions (19%); Government Grants (81%); Program Service Revenues (0%).

Expenses (FY00): Program Services (83%; for: state grant work –49%; federal grant work –32%; non-grant work –3%); Management and General (12%); Fundraising (5%).

Contact Info: PO Box 250, Catlett, VA 20119; (540) 788-3274; easi@easi.org

48. Environmental Defense (ED) (www.environmentaldefense.org) – An "Earth Share" Charity

General Focus Areas: Multiple Focus Areas

Slogan: "Finding the ways that work."

Description/Mission: Multi-faceted environmental advocacy organization emphasizing scientific evaluation of environmental problems and use of economic incentives to address such issues. Formerly known as the Environmental Defense Fund (EDF).

Basic Activities: Scientific, economic and policy research/analysis; public education; advocacy; business partnerships.

Lobbying/Political Activities: Registered lobbyist under the LDA.

Strategic Initiatives: Biodiversity; Climate; Health; Oceans.

Programs: Ecosystem Restoration; Energy; Environmental Alliances (with businesses); Environmental Health; Environmental Justice; Global and Regional Air; Oceans; Transportation; International Program.

Periodicals: EDF Letter (4-6 times/yr; online); e-mail newsletter (monthly).

Publications: Extensive amount of reports, brochures, fact sheets (many online).

Annual Report: 2000 report online.

Online Activist Tools: Action Alerts (posted online and sent via email).

Key Associated Websites: Scorecard (www.scorecard.org; provides data/information on various pollution-related issues – see Profile #465, located within Subsection 7.2 – "Information and Data Resource Websites and Gateways"); Action Network (online activist tool; actionnetwork.org); Act Global (www.actglobal.org; information and activist network on international environmental, economic and social issues); ForMyWorld (www.formyworld.com; provides detailed, zip-code-specific environmental information).

Check Out on the Web: "Publications" section – in addition to ED-produced documents, provides feature stories from E – The Environmental Magazine.

Founded: 1967 **Members:** 300,000 **Coverage:** U.S./Int'l **Staff:** 216 **Regional Offices:** 5 **NP Budget:** $35 million

Revenue (FY00): Contributions (87%; from: individuals –57%; foundations –30%); Government Grants (1%); Program Service Revenues (3%); Other (9%).

Expenses (FY00): Program Services (80%; for: biodiversity initiative –21%; climate initiative –24%; health initiative –16%; oceans initiative –7%; education activities –10%; membership activities –2%); Management and General (5%); Fundraising (15%).

Contact Info: 257 Park Ave. South, New York, NY 10010; (212) 505-2100; Contact@environmentaldefense.org

Key Personnel: Fred Krupp (Executive Director)

49. Environmental Law Institute (ELI) ® (www.eli.org) – An "Earth Share" Charity

General Focus Areas: Multiple Focus Areas

Description/Mission: Environmental law-focused institute most well known for its training courses and associated educational publications. Also conducts a significant amount of policy research and development (see below).

Basic Activities: Information dissemination; training/seminars; policy research/analysis; law and policy development.

Programs (and focus areas) – Research and Policy Division: Sustainability and Resource Protection (sustainable land use; state biodiversity; water pollution prevention; wetlands; mining; brownfields; green building); Center for Public Health and Law (indoor environments; radiation; risk assessment; community environmental health; stewardship of contaminated sites); Environmental Management and Capacity Building; International.

Periodicals: Environmental Law Reporter (multi-component subscription service covering environmental law and litigation; full subscription – $1000/yr); The Environmental Forum (bi-monthly policy journal); National Wetlands Newsletter (bi-monthly newsletter on wetland regulation, policy, science, and management).

Other Publications: Various research reports and briefs (online); various books.

Key Report: Cleaner Power: The Benefits and Costs of Moving from Coal Generation to Modern Power Technologies (online).

Annual Report: 2000 report online.

Check Out on the Web: National Database on Environmental Management Systems (a joint project with USEPA and the Univ. of North Carolina to determine how implementing Environmental Management Systems – ISO 14000, etc. – affects businesses).

Founded: 1969 **Coverage:** U.S. **Staff:** 68 **NP Status:** 501(c)(3) **Budget:** $5 million

Revenue (2000): Contributions (39%); Government Grants (29%); Program Service Revenues (20%; from: reference material subscriptions –14%; misc. –6%); Other (12%; from: membership dues –8%; misc. –4%).

Expenses (2000): Program Services (77%; for: research, policy and training –45%; publications –20%; membership and outreach –13%); Management and General (17%); Fundraising (6%).

Contact Info: 1616 P St. NW, Suite 200, Washington, DC 20036; (202) 939-3800; law@eli.org

Key Personnel: J. William Futrell (President)

50. Environmental Media Association (EMA) (www.ema-online.org)

General Focus Areas: Media

Description/Mission: Seeks to mobilize the Hollywood entertainment community to educate people worldwide about environmental problems and inspire them to act. EMA's Board of Directors includes Michael Eisner, Norman Lear, Warren Littlefield, John Travolta, and Ted Turner.

Basic Activities: Briefing seminars; consultation on story ideas; fact-checking and research services; clipping service; providing environmental props; EMA Awards Festival (annually honoring film and TV productions).

Periodicals: Green Light (tri-annual newsletter; online).

Key Publication: Environmental Production Guide (information to produce films and TV programs in an environmentally-friendly manner; online).

Founded: 1989 **Coverage:** U.S. **NP Status:** 501(c)(3) **Budget:** $0.6 million

Revenue (2000): Contributions (39%); Government Grants (0%); Program Service Revenues (60%; from: EMA awards festival –55%; "Pets 911" –6%); Other (1%).

Expenses (2000): Program Services (84%; for: EMA awards festival –32%; other programs –52%); Management and General (5%); Fundraising (11%).

Contact Info: 10780 Santa Monica Blvd., Suite 210, Los Angeles, CA 90025; (310) 446-6244; ema@ema-online.org

Key Personnel: Debbie Levin (Executive Director)

Environmental Research Foundation (www.rachel.org**)**
See Profile #483 for "Rachel's Environment and Health Weekly," located within Subsection 7.3 – "Media-Related Entities."

51. Environmental Working Group (EWG) (www.ewg.org)

General Focus Areas: Pollution; Public Health

Slogan: "Cutting-edge research on health and the environment."

Description/Mission: "Content provider" (information and policy analysis) to public interest groups and individuals, providing reports, articles, technical assistance and development of computer database and Internet resources. Many generated reports are state-level studies released in collaboration with other public interest groups. Also operates several associated websites (see below).

Basic Activities: Information Dissemination; Policy Analysis; Technical Assistance.

Specific Focus Areas: Air Pollution; Drinking Water; Environmental Enforcement; Federal Farm Subsidies; Pesticides.

Publications: Reports and memos (online)

Key Publications (both online): Above the Law: How the Government Lets Major Air Polluters Off the Hook. (analysis of Clean Air Act violations by industry and associated government enforcement activities); Prime Suspects: The Law Breaking Polluters America Fails to Inspect (analysis of state environmental enforcement programs).

Associated Websites: Chemical Industry Archives (internal documents from the chemical industry and its national trade associations concerning health risks of toxic chemicals; www.chemicalindustryarchives.org); FoodNews.org (promoting healthier food choices, pesticide-free foods and organic farming; www.foodnews.org); BanDursban.org (focused on the banned pesticide Dursban; www.bandursban.org); Dirty Money Tracker (tracking donations by industries and coalitions to members of Congress); California (focused on: methyl bromide; pesticides; children's health).

Founded: 1993 **Staff:** 18 **NP Status:** 501(c)(3)

Contact Info: 1718 Connecticut Ave. NW, Suite 600, Washington, DC 20009; (202) 667-6982; info@ewg.org

Key Personnel: Kenneth Cook (President)

52. Essential Information (www.essential.org)

General Focus Areas: Activism Support and Training

Slogan: "Encouraging activism."

Description/Mission: Provides information on issues/topics neglected by the mass media and policy makers, including those related to the environment. Disseminates information in various ways (books, reports, magazines, the Internet, seminars and conferences). Efforts are designed to encourage activism by citizens. Founded by Ralph Nader.

Basic Activities: Research and analysis; publications and information dissemination.

Programs (and activities/focus areas): Essential Action (alerts activists to current international campaigns); Multinationals Resource Center (provides information to Southern country activists, groups, and journalists); Geographic Information Systems Project; Good Works (careers in social change); Essential Books.

Periodicals: Multinational Monitor (monthly newsletter tracking corporate activity, particularly in the Third World; online).

Other Publications: A few books.

Online Activist Tools: Essential Action (posted action alerts).

Founded: 1982 **Coverage:** International **NP Status:** 501(c)(3) **Budget:** $2 million

Revenue (2000): Contributions (91%); Government Grants (0%); Program Service Revenues (8%;); Other (<1%).

Expenses (2000): Program Services (98%; for: Internet program –53%; democracy, corporate accountability and human rights program –28%; health and environment program –17%); Management and General (2%); Fundraising (0%).

Contact Info: PO Box 19405, Washington, DC 20036; (202) 387-8034.

Key Personnel: Russell Mokhiher (President)

Focus Project (www.ombwatch.org**)**

See Profile **#88** for "Office of Management and Budget (OMB) Watch," located within this subsection.

53. Forest Service Employees for Environmental Ethics (FSEEE) (www.afseee.org)

General Focus Areas: Conservation

Description/Mission: Membership-based organization of U.S. Forest Service employees, other resource professionals and concerned citizens working to change from within the USFS's basic management philosophy to a land ethic yielding ecologically and economically sustainable management.

Basic Activities: Guidance and legal support to USFS employees; monitoring and organizing; technical assistance; public education; youth education.

Programs (and activities/focus areas): Public Education (publications and speaking tours); Monitoring and Organizing (watchdog over the USFS); Protecting Integrity and Ethics (helping USFS whistleblowers); The Secret Forest (field-based forest ecology curriculum for middle school students).

Periodicals: Forest (bi-monthly magazine; online).

Online Activist Tools: E-Activist (electronic activist journal sent via e-mail).

Check Out on the Web: "Forest Service in the News" (news about the USFS and natural resource management in the U.S. and internationally; updated daily).

Founded: 1989 **Membership:** 13,000 **Coverage:** U.S. **Staff:** 7 **NP Status:** 501(c)(3) **Budget:** $0.8 million

Revenue (2000): Contributions (96%); Government Grants (0%); Program Service Revenues (2%); Other (2%).

Expenses (2000): Program Services (87%; for: public education –36%; membership development –23%; assistance in writing forest management plans –14%; guidance and legal support to USFS employees –11%; misc. other programs –3%); Management and General (6%); Fundraising (7%).

Contact Info: PO Box 11615, Eugene, OR 97440; (541) 484-2692; fseee@fseee.org

Key Personnel: Andy Stahl (Executive Director)

54. Forest Stewardship Council U.S. (FSC-US) / U.S. Working Group (www.fscus.org)

General Focus Areas: Conservation

Description/Mission: Promotes forest stewardship by establishing management standards and policies and certifying forest management programs and associated wood products obtained from such forests (via issuance of an "FSC label"). As of 11/01, 78 forests (covering 7.5 million acres) were FSC-certified in the U.S. Council partners include environmental and conservation groups, the timber industry, the forestry profession, indigenous peoples' organizations, community forestry groups and forest product certification organizations from 25 countries. FSC-US is part of the Forest Stewardship Council International, a membership organization with nearly 300 members from over 40 countries. The formal legal name of FSC-US is the U.S. Working Group.

Basic Activities: Public information and education; management standards development; product and management certification programs.

Periodicals: FSC News and Views (e-newsletter; online).

Associated Website: Certified Forest Products Council (database of FSC-certified products and forests; also provides a comparison of different forest certification systems; www.certifiedwood.org).

Check Out on the Web: "Current Issues" (discussion of unresolved issues and ongoing debates in FSC certification; located under "Standards and Policies").

Founded: 1993 **Coverage:** U.S. **NP Status:** 501(c)(3) **Budget:** $3 million

Revenue (2000): Contributions (99%); Government Grants (0%); Program Service Revenues (0%); Other (<1%).

Expenses (2000): Program Services (72%; for: public education; standards development; grants to FSC-Canada and FSC-Mexico); Management and General (18%); Fundraising (10%).

Contact Info: 1134 29th St. NW, Washington, DC 20007; (877) 372-5646; info@foreststewardship.org

Key Personnel: Jamison Ervin (Executive Director)

55. Friends of the Earth (USA) (FoE) (www.foe.org) – An "Earth Share" Charity

General Focus Areas: Multiple Focus Areas

Description/Mission: Multi-faceted environmental advocacy organization dedicated to preserving the health and diversity of the planet. Particular emphasis is placed on economic issues. Works on both national and local grassroots levels.

Basic Activities: Research; public education; outreach; advocacy.

Lobbying/Political Activities: Registered lobbyist under the LDA; maintains a PAC (Friends of the Earth Political Action Committee).

Programs (and focus areas): Economics ("Green Scissors" program to cut targeted government subsidies; environmental tax reform; earth budget; transportation); International (trade and investment; international finance; corporate accountability); Community Health and Environment (community activists support; safer foods/safer farms; "Healing the Atmosphere" [ozone depletion]; DC environmental network); Justice (enforcement of, and compliance, with environmental laws); Northwest Programs (focus on: river restoration; salmon).

Periodicals: Atmosphere (tri-annual magazine focused on ozone/global warming; online).

Other Publications: Various reports (most online).

Key Reports (all online): Green Scissors (annual report identifying environmentally harmful and wasteful government programs); Paying for Pollution (identifies existing tax subsidies for polluting energy sources); Clean Water Report Card (grades each state on its Clean Water Act program).

Online Activist Tools: Action Alerts (posted online); Legislative Resources; Environmental Laws (full text and summaries).

Founded: 1969 **Members:** 20,000 **Coverage:** U.S./Int'l **NP Status:** 501(c)(3) **Budget:** $4 million

Revenue (FY00): Contributions (96%); Government Grants (0%); Program Service Revenues (<1%); Other (4%).

Expenses (FY00): Program Services (83%; for: international program –24%; outreach –23%; "economics for the earth" tax and budget program –18%; "protect the planet" activist support program –15%; membership services – 3%); Management and General (9%); Fundraising (8%).

Affiliated Org: FOE Action, Inc. (a 501(c)(4) non-profit).

Contact Info: 1025 Vermont Ave. NW, Suite 300, Washington, DC 20005; (202) 783-7400; foe@foe.org

Key Personnel: Brent Blackwelder (President)

56. Friends of the Earth International (FoEI) (www.foei.org)

General Focus Areas: Multiple Focus Areas

Description/Mission: Federation of 66 autonomous national environmental organizations (including FoE-USA) located in 68 countries around the world. Approximately one-half of member groups use "Friends of the Earth" in their name. Member orgs: 1) work on both national and grassroots levels, 2) work on the main environmental issues confronting their countries (i.e., no single-issue groups), 3) participate in international campaigns, and 4) educate and do research.

Basic Activities: Research; public education; outreach and organizing; advocacy.

Campaigns/Programs: Antarctic; Climate Change; Desertification; Ecological Debt; Forests; Gender; Genetically Modified Organisms; Human Rights; International Financial Institutions; Maritime; Mining; Rio Plus Ten (the UN-sponsored 2002 World Summit for Sustainable Development); Sustainable Societies; Trade,

Environment and Sustainability; Transnational Corporations; Wetlands.

Periodicals: Link (quarterly magazine; online); Interlinkages (monthly bulletin; online); BIFI (monthly bulletin focused on FoEI's International Financial Institutions program; online).

Other Publications: Various reports in all program areas (some online).

Annual Report: 1999 report online.

Founded: 1971 **Members/Supporters:** 1 million **Coverage:** International **Staff (combined):** 700 **Budget (1998; combined):** $200 million

Public Support Sources: Membership Dues (from member groups); Governments; Foundations.

Contact Info: P.O. Box 19199, 1000 GD Amsterdam, The Netherlands; foei@foei.org

Key Personnel: Marijke Torfs (International Coordinator)

Fuel Cells 2000 (www.fuelcells.org**)**

See Profile #18 for "Breakthrough Technologies Institute," located within this subsection.

Global Cities Project Online (www.globalcities.org**)**

See Profile #456 located within Subsection 7.2 – "Information and Data Resource Websites and Gateways.".

57. Grassroots Recycling Network (GRRN) (www.grrn.org**)**

General Focus Areas: Pollution

Slogan: "Some day, there will be no such thing as trash."

Description/Mission: Network of recycling and community-based activists who advocate policies and practices to: 1) achieve zero waste, 2) end government subsidies for waste, and 3) create sustainable jobs from discards. Known for its campaigns targeting specific large corporations (see below).

Basic Activities: Public education; advocacy; research.

Campaigns (and activities/focus areas): Coke and Pepsi (pushing for 25% recycled content in their plastic soda containers and an 80% recycling rate for all their beverage containers by 2005); Dow (pushing for removal of Dow's persistent herbicide, Confront, and other persistent, clopyralid-containing herbicides from the marketplace, due to their potential to undermine the marketability of compost products); Staples (pushing for Staples to: 1) eliminate products made from old growth forests and/or from U.S. national forests and 2) phase out sale of all products that are made using 100% virgin wood fiber); Electronic Scrap (promoting computer recycling and reuse, particularly via manufacturer "take-it-back" programs); Recycle Congress (pushing for establishment of an effective recycling program on Capital Hill).

Publications: Variety of articles, reports, plans, fact sheets (most online under "Learn More").

Key Publications (both online under "Learn More"): Wasting and Recycling in the U.S. (details the state of both "wasting" and recycling, along with a proposed "agenda for action"); Welfare for Waste (details how federal taxpayer subsides discourage recycling).

Online Activist Tools: Take Action section ("e-letter" campaigns).

Founded: 1995 **Coverage:** U.S. **Staff:** 5 **NP Status:** 501(c)(3) **Budget:** $0.2 million

Revenue (2000): Contributions (95%); Government Grants (0%); Program Service Revenues (1%); Other (4%).

Expenses (2000): Program Services (29%); Management and General (71%); Fundraising (0%).

Contact Info: PO Box 49283, 205 Three Oaks Dr., Athens, GA 30604; (706) 613-7121; zerowaste@grrn.org

Key Personnel: Bill Sheehan (Executive Director)

Green Business Network (www.greenbiz.com**)**

See Profile #457 for "GreenBiz.com," located within Subsection 7.2 – "Information and Data Resource Websites and Gateways."

58. Green Corps (www.greencorps.org)

General Focus Areas: Activism Support and Training

Description/Mission: Billed as "the field school for environmental organizing" with a stated mission of "training the next generation of environmental leaders while making a difference on important environmental campaigns." Primary focus is on training recent college graduates for environmental organizing and advocacy careers. Also has helped lead 50+ wilderness and public health campaigns in partnership with 25 national, state and local environmental and related groups.

Basic Activities: Activist leadership training; organizing/advocacy support to NGOs.

Programs (and activities): Environmental Leadership Training Program (offering one-year, full-time, paid positions for 20-30 recent college grads that include: classroom training, hands-on experience as an organizer, and job placement for program graduates); Partner With Us Program (provides short-term field organizing and advocacy support to environmental and related non-profits).

Key Environmental Campaigns (2000-01): Fighting Global Warming (with World Wildlife Fund); Defending Public Health (with the Toxics Action Center); Protecting National Forests (with Rain Forest Action Network); Artic National Wildlife Refuge (with Alaska Wilderness League).

Founded: 1992 **Coverage:** U.S. **NP Status:** 501(c)(3) **Budget:** $1 million

Revenue (FY00): Contributions (80%); Government Grants (0%); Program Service Revenues (19%; from technical services to other exempt orgs); Other (1%).

Expenses (FY00): Program Services (90%); Management and General (3%); Fundraising (7%).

Contact Info: 29 Temple Place, Boston, MA 02111; (617) 426-8506

Key Personnel: Leslie Samuelrich (Executive Director)

59. Greenpeace (International) (www.greenpeace.org)

General Focus Areas: Multiple Focus Areas

Description/Mission: Multi-faceted environmental advocacy organization known for its highly visible public protests (including hanging large protest signs) and use of monitoring ships (particularly the *Rainbow Warrior*). Maintains national/regional offices in 41 countries.

Basic Activities: Non-violent direct action; advocacy; public education; communications and outreach; research.

Specific Focus Areas: Climate; Forests; Genetic Engineering; Nuclear; Oceans/Ocean Dumping; Toxics.

Annual Report: 2001 report online.

Online Activist Tools: Cyberactivist Community (features: receive monthly activist news e-zine and emergency campaign alerts, both via email; participate in "Cybercentre" discussion board).

Unique: Photo and Video Library (can purchase photos and videos).

Check Out on the Web: Streaming Videos (RealPlayer-based videos on various Greenpeace campaigns/actions).

Founded: 1971 **Coverage:** Int'l **Membership:** 2,500,000 **Budget (combined worldwide ops):** $125 million

Revenue (combined worldwide ops; FY00): Individuals (82%); Legacies and Bequests (9%); Foundations (3%); Major Donors (3%); Other (3%).

Expenses (combined worldwide ops; FY00): Program Services (57%; for: campaigns addressing: climate; forests; genetic engineering; oceans; nuclear and disarmament; toxics –34%; marine operations and action support –10%; media and communications –9%; public information and outreach –4%); Management and Support (14%); Fundraising (29%);

Contact Info: Keizersgracht 176, 1016 DW Amsterdam, The Netherlands; supporter.services@ams.greenpeace.org

Key Personnel: Gerd Leipold (Executive Director)

60. Greenpeace (USA) (www.greenpeaceusa.org)

General Focus Areas: Multiple Focus Areas

Description/Mission: Multi-faceted environmental advocacy organization known for its highly visible public protests (including hanging large protest signs). Part of Greenpeace International (see Profile #59, located within this subsection).

Basic Activities: Non-violent direct action; advocacy; public education; communications and outreach; research.

Specific Focus Areas: Forests; Genetic Engineering; Global Warming/Energy; Nuclear Disarmament; Oceans; Toxics.

Periodicals: Greenpeace Newsletter (e-newsletter).

Other Publications: Multitude of fact sheets/brochures/briefings/reports (all online).

Annual Report: 1999 report online.

Online Activist Tools: Take Action section (action alerts – posted online and sent via email).

Unique: Send a free email postcard online (see "Green Room").

Website Notes: Well-constructed website, especially the web pages dedicated to each focus area (forests, genetic engineering, etc.)

Check Out on the Web: "Current Features" (summary of recent Greenpeace actions); "Videos" (RealPlayer-based videos on various Greenpeace campaigns/actions; located under "Media Center").

Founded: 1971 **Coverage:** U.S. **Membership:** 250,000 **NP Status:** 501(c)(3) (Greenpeace Fund); 501(c)(4) (Greenpeace, Inc.) **Budget ("GP Fund"):** $9 million **Budget ("GP Inc."):** $14 million

Revenue ("Fund"; 1999): Contributions (96%); Government Grants (0%); Program Service Revenues (0%); Other (4%).

Revenue ("Inc."; 1999): Contributions (67%); Government Grants (0%); Program Service Revenues (0%); Other (33%; from: Greenpeace Fund –30%; misc. –3%).

Expenses ("Fund"; 1999): Program Services (82%; for: grants to Greenpeace Int'l –39%; grants to Greenpeace Inc. for campaigns on: climate; forests oceans; toxics –24%; grants to Greenpeace Inc. for public information and education –14%; grant to Greenpeace Inc. for "action resources" –5%); Management and General (4%); Fundraising (14%).

Expenses ("Inc."; 1999): Program Services (57%; for: campaigns on: climate; forests; oceans; toxics; misc. other –34%; public information and education –18%; "action resources" –5%); Management and General (2%); Fundraising (41%).

Contact Info: 702 H St. NW, Suite 300, Washington, DC 20001; (202) 462-1177 / (800) 326-0959; greenpeace.usa@wdc.greenpeace.org

Key Personnel: John Passacantando (Executive Director)

61. Green Seal (www.greenseal.org)

General Focus Areas: Product Standards

Description/Mission: Identifies and promotes "environmentally preferable" products and practices. Most well known for its Green Seal product certification program (see below).

Basic Activities: Develop product standards; evaluate products/services/companies; technical assistance; public education.

Programs/Projects (and activities/focus areas): Green Seal Certification Program (sets product standards and awards – based on those standards – a "Green Seal of Approval" to "environmentally-preferable consumer products"; 30+ standards established thus far); Environmental Partners (green buying assistance to businesses and other orgs; 450 members currently); Greening Your Government (assist all levels of government with green purchasing, operations and plant improvement); Global Eco-Labeling Network (association of national environmental labeling programs from around the world; www.gen.gr.jp); Environmental Production Guide (interactive web site providing film/TV producers with information for using environmentally responsible products/services; www.epg.org); Hotel Projects (green purchasing and ecotourism); USEPA's Energy Star ® Homes Program (work with builders and developers to increase energy efficiency and improve indoor air quality).

Periodicals: Choose Green Report (monthly report; identifies specific products/services as "environmentally responsible").

Other Publications: Developed "green standards" (all online); various reports (online).

Key Publication: Office Green Buying Guide (100+ page guide).

Coverage: U.S./Int'l **Staff:** 4 **NP Status:** 501(c)(3) **Budget:** $0.6 million

Revenue (FY00): Contributions (58%); Government Grants (0%); Program Service Revenues (41%; from: fees for evaluating companies/products –40%; informational materials –1%); Other (1%).

Expenses (FY00): Program Services (79%); Management and General (15%); Fundraising (6%).

Contact Info: 1001 Connecticut Ave. NW, Suite 827, Washington, DC 20036; (202) 872-6400; greenseal@greenseal.org

Key Personnel: Arthur Weissman (President)

62. **Health Care Without Harm (HCWH)** (www.noharm.org)

General Focus Areas: Pollution; Public Health

Slogan: "The campaign for environmentally responsible health care."

Description/Mission: Collaborative campaign of 300+ organizations in 27 countries promoting environmentally responsible health care, focused on pollution prevention and the use of environmentally safe materials, technology and products. Coordinated through the Center for Health, Environment and Justice (see Profile #20, located within this subsection); also associated with the Institute for Agriculture and Trade Policy (see Profile #64, located within this subsection).

Basic Activities: Advocacy; public education; communications and outreach; research.

Issues (and focus areas): Mercury (phase-out of household mercury thermometers and mercury-containing medical products/devices); Incineration (eliminate non-essential incineration of medical waste); PVC (phase out of PVC-based medical products); Pesticides (reduce exposure to pesticides and other toxins found in health care settings); Pollution Prevention (address the environmental impacts of health care).

Publications: Various HCWH and non-HCWH reports and fact sheets (provided online under "Resources").

Key Publication: Going Green (a resource kit for pollution prevention in health care; online).

Founded: 1996 **Coverage:** U.S./Int'l

Public Support Sources: Foundations; Center for Health, Environment and Justice (see Profile #20, located within this subsection).

Contact Info: 1755 S Street NW, Suite 6B, Washington DC 20009; (703) 237-2249; hcwh@chej.org

Key Personnel: Jolie Patterson (Key Contact)

63. **Health Track** (www.health-track.org)

General Focus Areas: Pollution; Public Health

Slogan: "Your health. Your community. Your right to know."

Description/Mission: Promotes a nationwide health-tracking network to identify and track the links between environmental hazards and illnesses. Also seeks to provide researchers and public health officials with tools to prevent disease. Supported by The Pew Charitable Trusts; has 19 partner groups consisting of various national public/environmental health groups and associations of public health officials.

Basic Activities: Research; public education.

Publications: Various case studies and reports (all online).

Check Out on the Web: "Your Community" (provides state-level information on the environment and chronic disease); Health Track Mapping (maps cancer deaths and toxic releases).

Coverage: U.S. **Staff:** 4

Contact Info: 2233 Wisconsin Ave. NW, Suite 525, Washington, DC 20007; (202) 687-0736; info@health-track.org

Key Personnel: Jim O'Hara (Executive Director)

64. **Institute for Agriculture and Trade Policy (IATP)** (www.iatp.org)

General Focus Areas: Agriculture

Description/Mission: Policy-oriented research and education organization focused on agriculture and trade issues.

Basic Activities: Policy Research; Education/Outreach; Training/Technical Assistance; Coalition Building/Int'l Networking; Advocacy.

Programs (and focus areas): Environment and Agriculture (watershed organizing and protection; marketing sustainable agriculture; certified forestry; nutrient and pesticide management; toxins and industrial pollutants); Food and Agriculture (global food policy; sustainable food systems; inter-American integration projects); Forestry (Forest Stewardship Council certification; market development; carbon credits; ecological landscape assessments); Globalism and Global Governance (international policymaking institutions; cross-border organizing and collaboration); Trade and Agriculture (international trade policies, practices and treaties; Uruguay Round Agreements on Agriculture; trade-related aspects of intellectual property rights; genetic engineering).

Periodicals: IATP News (online); Agriculture and Biodiversity News (monthly news bulletin; online).

Other Publications: A couple of reports (online) and a few books.

Online Activist Tools: Action Alerts (posted online).

Check Out on the Web: Eat Well, Eat Antibiotic-Free (a consumer guide for finding meat raised without antibiotics; online); Genetically Engineered Food: A Self-Defense Guide for Consumers.

Founded: 1986 **Coverage:** Global **Staff:** 35 **NP Status:** 501(c)(3) **Budget:** $3 million

Revenue (2000): Contributions (87%); Government Grants (2%); Program Service Revenues (11%; from: contract service fees –10%; misc. other sources –1%); Other (<1%).

Expenses (2000): Program Services (81%; for: environment, agriculture and forestry –38%; trade and agriculture –15%; food and agriculture –10%; globalism and global governance –9%; information technology –9%); Management and General (9%); Fundraising (10%).

Contact Info: 2105 1st Ave. South, Minneapolis, MN 55404; (612) 870-0453; iatp@iatp.org

Key Personnel: Mark Ritchie (President)

65. Institute for Global Communications (IGC) (www.igc.org)

General Focus Areas: Internet Hosting

Slogan: "Connecting people who are changing the world."

Description/Mission: Seeks to bring Internet tools and online services to progressive public interest groups. Known for being an Internet host for smaller groups. Operates four member networks including EcoNet, which lists about 220 organizations/websites. IGC is a project of the Tides Center.

Basic Activities: Internet hosting/service provider; Internet support services.

Periodicals: IGC Newsletter (weekly email newsletter).

Online Activist Tools: Advocacy Tips.

Founded: 1986 **Coverage:** Global

Contact Info: P.O. Box 29904, Presidio Building 1012, 1st Floor, Torney Ave., San Francisco, CA 94129; (415) 561-6100; support@igc.apc.org

66. Institute for Local Self-Reliance (ILSR) (www.ilsr.org)

General Focus Areas: Sustainable Development

Description/Mission: Promotes the sustainable economic development of local communities. Also operates Self-Reliance, Inc., a consulting affiliate providing technical assistance and professional services regarding sustainable, green industrial development.

Basic Activities: Research; Public Education; Information Dissemination; Consulting/Technical Assistance; Policy/Advocacy.

Programs (and focus areas): New Rules Project (identify innovative public policies that strengthen local communities; covers 10 sectors, including: environment; agriculture; energy); Carbohydrate Economy Clearinghouse (information on moving from a petrochemical- to a plant matter-based economy); Waste to Wealth (information on community development through reuse and recycling; focused on: scrap-based manufacturing; zero-waste campaign; building re-hab/deconstruction; extended product responsibility for manufacturers);

Healthy Building Network (seeking phase out of 4 targeted building materials: PVC plastic [vinyl]; plywood and chipboard; formaldehyde; arsenic-treated wood); Energy Policy (focused on Minnesota).

Periodicals: The New Rules (tri-annual newsletter; back issues online); The Carbohydrate Economy (quarterly newsletter).

Other Publications: Various fact sheets, monographs, case studies (some online).

Key Publications: The Poisonwood Rivals ("a report on the dangers of touching arsenic-treated wood"; online); The Home Town Advantage ("how to defend your Main Street against chain store and why it matters").

Founded: 1974 **Coverage:** U.S. **Staff:** 15 **NP Status:** 501(c)(3) **Budget:** $1 million

Revenue (FY00): Contributions (64%); Government Grants (13%); Program Service Revenues (22%; from: consulting –18%; publications –4%); Other (1%).

Expenses (FY00): Program Services (79%; for "new rules" project –20%; carbohydrate economy program –16%; DC initiative –12%; building deconstruction program –10%; "waste-to-wealth" program –7%; "macredo" regional program –5%: energy policy –5%; healthy building network –4%); Management and General (16%); Fundraising (5%).

Affiliated Org: Self-Reliance, Inc. (professional consulting arm of ILSR).

Contact Info: 2425 18th St. NW, Washington, DC 20009; (202) 232-4108; info@ilsr.org

Key Personnel: Neil Seldman (President)

67. Interfaith Center on Corporate Responsibility (ICCR) (www.iccr.org)

General Focus Areas: Business Practices

Slogan: "Inspired by faith, committed to action."

Description/Mission: International coalition of 275 Protestant, Roman Catholic and Jewish institutional investors seeking to merge social values with investment decisions. Unlike the typical passive approach offered for socially-conscious investing – simply buying/selling stock based on company policies/practices – ICCR members actively press corporations to change their behavior/activities through a variety of means (shareholder resolutions; public hearings and investigations; publishing special reports; sponsoring special actions such as prayer vigils, letter writing campaigns and consumer boycotts). ICCR members also make investments (surpassing $900 million) to promote economic development in low income and minority communities. The combined portfolio value of ICCR's member organizations is estimated to be $110 billion. ICCR members work through 6 Issue Groups, including "Energy and Environment."

Basic Activities: Research; communications; public education/info dissemination; special actions (shareholder resolutions; public hearings and investigations; prayer vigils; letter writing campaigns; consumer boycotts).

Energy and Environment Issues (and focus areas): Genetic Engineering (genetically engineered food); Energy and Climate Change (global warming; renewable energy); Accountability and Disclosure (standardized public environmental reporting; endorsement of the CERES Principles for public environmental accountability; disclosure of environmental liabilities); Chlorine Compounds (paper bleaching; contamination of the Hudson River with PCBs); Particular Member Issues.

Periodicals: Corporate Examiner (monthly newsletter; reports on policies/practices of major U.S. corporations).

Other Publications: A few reports/briefs (available at nominal cost).

Coverage: U.S. **Staff:** 13 **Budget:** $1 million

Revenue (FY00): Contributions (16%; from an endowment fund); Government Grants (0%); Program Service Revenues (17%); Other (67%); from: membership dues –41%; special events –17%; misc. –9%).

Expenses (FY00): Program Services (66%); Management and General (25%); Fundraising (9%).

Contact Info: 475 Riverside Drive, Room 550, New York, NY 10115; (212) 870-2295; info@iccr.org

Key Personnel: Patricia Wolf (Executive Director); Ariane van Buren (Director, Energy & Environment Group)

International Union for Conservation of Nature and Natural Resources (IUCN) (www.iucn.org)

See Profile #307, located within Subsection 3.2 – "Other Multilaterals and Associated Entities."

68. International Right to Know Campaign (IRTK) (www.irtk.org)

General Focus Areas: Information Disclosure; Right-to-Know

Description/Mission: Alliance of 200+ public interest organizations campaigning to enact an international right-to-know law requiring U.S.-based corporations to disclose information on their environmental impacts, labor practices, and human rights practices wherever they operate. Coordinated by Friend of the Earth USA (see Profile #55, located within this subsection).

Basic Activities: Public education; advocacy.

Online Activist Tools: Action Center (contents: email list; elected officials; issues and legislation; media guide)

Coverage: U.S.-based corporations

Contact Info: 1025 Vermont Ave. NW, Washington, DC 20005; (202) 783-7400; info@irtk.org

Key Personnel: Lisa Archer (Field Organizer)

69. Izaak Walton League of America (IWLA) (www.iwla.org) – An "Earth Share" Charity

General Focus Areas: Conservation

Description/Mission: Grassroots natural resource conservation group, founded by hunters, anglers and other recreationalists.

Basic Activities: Community-based conservation; technical assistance; public education; policy and legislative tracking; advocacy.

Key Issues/Campaigns (and activities/focus areas): American Wetlands (promoting local wetland stewardship); Fish Kills Advisory Network (for the Upper Mississippi River); Midwest Power Plants (seek to clean up old coal-fired power plants); Outdoor Ethics (for all outdoor recreationalists); Save Our Steams (education and technical assistance for grassroots watershed conservation); Sustainability Education (public education focused on local/regional sustainability concerns).

Periodicals: Outdoor America (quarterly magazine; partially online).

Other Publications: Some "special reports" (all online).

Annual Report: 2000 report online.

Online Activist Tools: Action Alerts (posted online and sent via email).

Founded: 1922 **Members/Supporters:** 50,000 **Coverage:** U.S. **State-Specific Offices:** 21 **Local Chapters:** 300+ **NP Status:** 501(c)(3) **Budget:** $4 million

Revenue (2000): Contributions (82%); Government Grants (3%); Program Service Revenues (1%); Other (14%).

Expenses (2000): Program Services (85%; for: Midwest clean air campaign –17%; general conservation activities –10%; "save our streams" program –9%; *Outdoor America* magazine –9%; membership –8%; energy efficiency program –6%; forestry monitoring –3%; membership marketing –3%; sustainability education –3%; outdoor ethics program –3%; Midwest office –3%; misc. other programs/services –11%); Management and General (3%); Fundraising (12%).

Contact Info: 707 Conservation Lane, Gaithersburg, MD 20878; (301) 548-0150; general@iwla.org

Key Personnel: Paul Hansen (Executive Director)

70. Jane Goodall Institute (JGI) (www.janegoodall.org)

General Focus Areas: Conservation

Description/Mission: Focuses on conservation and understanding of wildlife, particularly chimpanzees and other primates. (Jane Goodall is considered the world's foremost authority on chimpanzees, having closely observed their behavior for the past quarter century in the jungles of the Gombe Game Reserve in Africa.)

Basic Activities: Scientific Research; Education; Wildlife Habitat Conservation; Animal Welfare Activities.

Key Programs/Centers (and activities/focus areas): Sanctuaries (care for orphaned chimpanzees in Uganda, Congo, Kenya and Tanzania); Gombe Stream Research Center (observation of chimps and baboons in Tanzania); ChimpanZoo (study of chimpanzees in zoos and other captive settings); TACARE (Lake Tanganyika Catchment Reforestation and Education project in Tanzania); Roots and Shoots (youth education; see below under "Unique"); Congo Basin Project (addressing the commercial bushmeat trade in Central Africa); Jane Goodall

Center for Primate Studies (research center).

Periodicals: World Report (yearly newsletter with quarterly project updates); Roots and Shoots Network (semi-annual newsletter; online).

Other Publications: Website provides a list of Jane Goodall-related books and videos.

Unique: "Roots and Shoots" – school-based program (pre-school through college) aimed at hands-on local projects helping the environment, animals, and human communities. Over 1,000 registered groups in 50 countries worldwide participate.

Founded: 1977 **Membership:** 17,000 **Coverage:** Global **NP Status:** 501(c)(3) **Budget:** $4 million

Revenue (2000): Contributions (80%); Government Grants (0%); Program Service Revenues (15%; from: honoraria and lecture tour –14%; misc. –1%); Other (5%).

Expenses (2000): Program Services (77%; for: wildlife research –20%; education and communication programs – 32%; animal welfare and conservation –24%); Management and General (5%); Fundraising (18%).

Contact Info: PO Box 14890, 8700 Georgia Ave., Suite 500, Silver Springs, MD 20911; (301) 565-0086; jgiinformation@janegoodall.org

Key Personnel: Fred Thompson (President)

71. Keep America Beautiful (KAB) (www.kab.org)

General Focus Areas: Pollution; Public Health

Description/Mission: Promotes beautification, litter prevention and improved waste handling practices at the local level. Has 22 state / 500 community affiliates. Known for its "Crying Indian" public service TV campaign in 1971, which is credited with helping awaken environmental consciousness in the U.S.

Basic Activities: Community partnerships; field training services and technical assistance; communications and public education; youth education.

Programs (and activities/focus areas): Affiliate Program (team up with local communities to implement the Keep America Beautiful System); Great American Cleanup™ (spring neighborhood cleanups; 10,000 communities participated in 2000); Graffiti Hurts (education and community-based efforts for graffiti abatement/ prevention); Waste in Place (elementary school curriculum for litter prevention); Close the Loop (consumer education for purchasing recycled/ recyclable products); Charge Up to Recycle (promote recycling of nickel cadmium (Ni–Cd) rechargeable batteries); Vision for America Awards (annual award to a selected corporate leader).

Periodicals: Network News (quarterly newsletter; online).

Other Publications: A couple of brochures and some educational materials for teachers.

Unique: Litter Index (quantifying – through visual assessments – the relative amount of litter present in a community).

Founded: 1953 **Coverage:** U.S. **NP Status:** 501(c)(3) **Budget:** $3 million

Revenue (2000): Contributions (73%); Government Grants (0%); Program Service Revenues (12%; from: national convention/regional meeting –5%; affiliate fees –3%; certification fees –2%; publications –2%); Other (15%; from: "Vision for America" awards dinner –11%; misc. –4%).

Expenses (2000): Program Services (77%; for: program and field training services –68%; communication and public education –9%); Management and General (8%); Fundraising (15%).

Public Support Sources: Corporations; Affiliate Fees; Individuals.

Contact Info: 1010 Washington Blvd., Stamford, CT 06901; (203) 323-8987.

Key Personnel: G. Ray Empson (President)

72. Land Trust Alliance (LTA) (www.lta.org) – An "Earth Share" Charity

General Focus Areas: Conservation

Description/Mission: Promotes voluntary land conservation and provides information, skills and resources for individual land trusts. Membership includes approximately 850 land trusts across the U.S.

Basic Activities: Field Services and Technical Assistance; Training and Education; Information Dissemination;

Funding (grants and training scholarships); Advocacy.

Programs/Services Offered (and activities/focus areas): Technical Assistance; Public Policy (focused on federal policy); Training (National Land Trust Rally – annual conference for land conservationists); Land Conservation Leadership Program (regional conferences; local training sessions); Funding ($400,000+ awarded annually in grants and training scholarships); Regional Programs (technical services and assistance); Publications; Standards and Practices.

Periodicals: Exchange (magazine); Landscape (tri-annual newsletter).

Other Publications: Library of land trust information.

Key Publication: "Standards and Practices Guidebook" – step-by-step information for land trusts.

Annual Report: 2000 report online.

Check Out on the Web: Land Trust Census (snapshot of the land conservation movement).

Founded: 1982 **Membership:** 2100 **Coverage:** U.S. **Staff:** 40 **Regional Offices:** 5 **NP Status:** 501(c)(3) **Budget:** $4 million

Revenue (2000): Contributions (75%); Government Grants (2%); Program Service Revenues (21%; from: annual conference and workshops –17% publication sales –4%); Other (2%).

Expenses (2000): Program Services (83%; for: field services –35%; training and education –19%; land trust information –18%; general program and membership –6%; public policy –5%); Management and General (3%); Fundraising (14%).

Contact Info: 1331 H St. NW, Suite 400, Washington DC 20005; (202) 638-4725; lta@lta.org

Key Personnel: Rand Wentworth (President)

73. League of Conservation Voters (LCV) (www.lcv.org)

General Focus Areas: Politics

Slogan: "The political voice of the environment."

Description/Mission: Watchdog group focused on holding elected officials (particularly Congressional members) accountable on the environment. Also has an associated research and education organization – the LCV Education Fund (see Profile #74, located within this subsection).

Basic Activities: Information Dissemination; Public Education.

Lobbying/Political Activities: Maintains a PAC (League of Conservation Voters Political Action Committee).

Programs (and activities/focus areas): National Environmental Scorecard (tracking and making available – online and in-print – the voting records of all Congressional members); Eye on the Administration ("watchdog" monitoring of the current Presidential Administration); State LCVs (seeks to hold state and local elected officials accountable on the environment).

Publications: National Environmental Scorecard (annual report on congressional voting records).

Online Activist Tools: Take Action (contents: action center [2000 scorecard; issues and legislation; media guide; congress today]; capital hill basics).

Check Out on the Web: Links to 27 state-specific LCV web sites seeking to hold state and local elected officials accountable on the environment.

Founded: 1970 **Membership:** 25,000 **Coverage:** U.S. **NP Status:** 501(c)(4)

Associated Org: League of Conservation Voters Education Fund (see Profile #74, located within this subsection).

Contact Info: 1920 L St. NW, Suite 800, Washington, DC 20036; (202) 785-8683; lcv@lcv.org

Key Personnel: Deb Callahan (President)

74. League of Conservation Voters Education Fund / Vote Environment (www.voteenvironment.org) – An "Earth Share" Charity

General Focus Areas: Politics

Description/Mission: Provides the public and other environmental organizations with information and educational services regarding elections and current environmental policy issues. The Ed Fund is separate from the main LCV organization (see Profile #73, located within this subsection), although it does use regular LCV staff and has common management.

Basic Activities: Information Dissemination; Public Education; Training and Technical Support; Research; Advocacy.

Key Programs (and activities/focus areas): Capacity-Building (enhance capacity/effectiveness of state/local environmental orgs via: strategic planning and organizing; communication tools; new/latest technology); Leadership Development/Training (workshops and seminars for activists via LCV's Environmental Leadership Institute); Public Engagement (public opinion research; public education campaigns; "ask the candidate" campaigns).

Check Out on the Web: "Ask Your Elected Official" (lists key questions to ask officials; covers 10 general issue areas, plus state-specific issues); "About the Issues" (background briefs on key issue areas with links to further information); "State Resources" (provides state-specific: contacts; public interest groups; "ask the candidate" questions; public poll results; news).

Founded: 1985 **Coverage:** U.S. **Regional Offices:** 7 **NP Status:** 501(c)(3) **Budget:** $12 million

Revenue (2000): Contributions (99%); Government Grants (0%); Program Service Revenues (0%); Other (1%).

Expenses (2000): Program Services (94%; for: public education –62%; civic participation/voter drive –10%; assist with development of state/local environmental groups –9%; community leadership development training – 7%; state lobbying –6%); Management and General (4%); Fundraising (2%).

Associated Orgs: League of Conservation Voters (see Profile #73, located within this subsection)

Contact Info: 1920 L St. NW, Suite 800, Washington, DC 20036; (202) 785-0730; ed_fund@lcv.org

Key Personnel: Deb Callahan (President); Elizabeth Sullivan (Executive Director)

75. Mineral Policy Center (MPC) (www.mineralpolicy.org)

General Focus Areas: Pollution; Public Health

Slogan: "Protecting communities and the environment."

Description/Mission: Dedicated to cleaning up and preventing pollution from mining. Seeks to serve as an information clearinghouse regarding the impact of mineral policies and development on other natural resources and the environment.

Basic Activities: Research; public education; advocacy/legislative reform efforts; activist support and technical assistance.

Programs/Campaigns (and activities/focus areas): Mining Law and Regulatory Reform (1872 mining law; claim location rule; "3809" surface mining rule; Toxics Release Inventory); Protecting Communities and Ecosystems (provide support to local activists); Corporate Responsibility; Abandoned Mine Cleanup; Mining/Media/Message; International.

Periodicals: MPC News (bi-annual newsletter; online); MineWire (newsletter for activists; online).

Other Publications: Various books and reports, issue papers, fact sheets, position papers (most online).

Online Activist Tools: Take Action section (contents: sign petition; contact your senator/rep/president).

Check Out on the Web: The Photo Gallery (documenting mining impacts); Mining Conservation Directory (list of conservation groups with a mining focus, includes links to their websites).

Founded: 1988 **Membership:** 2500 **Coverage:** U.S./Int'l **Staff:** 8 **Field Offices:** 2 **NP Status:** 501(c)(3) **Budget:** $1 million

Revenue (2000): Contributions (98%); Government Grants (0%); Program Service Revenues (0%); Other (2%).

Expenses (2000): Program Services (79%; for: 1872 mining law reform programs –32%; media and communications –15%; "circuit rider" community programs –12%; corporate accountability –8%; publications – 7%; general program development –5%); Management and General (12%); Fundraising (9%).

Contact Info: 1612 K St. NW, Suite 808, Washington, DC 20006; (202) 887-1872; mpc@mineralpolicy.org

Key Personnel: Steve D'Esposito (President)

76. National Arbor Day Foundation (www.arborday.org)

General Focus Areas: Arbor Day/Tree Planting

Description/Mission: Promotes Arbor Day, general tree planting and associated environmental stewardship. Provides 8+ million trees for planting each year. Also operates the Arbor Day Farm in Nebraska City, NE.

Basic Activities: Tree plantings; public education; youth education; conferences/seminars/workshops; recognition programs.

Programs (and activities/focus areas): Celebrate Arbor Day; Trees for America (year-round plantings; 8+ million trees distributed for planting annually); Tree City USA (recognizing 2500+ communities meeting certain standards); Tree Line USA (recognizing utilities meeting certain standards); Building with Trees (recognizing builders/developers); Conservation Trees (aimed at farmers and ranchers); Rainforest Rescue (campaign to save threatened rainforest areas); Youth Education (focus on environmental stewardship); Arbor Day Farm (education facility dedicated to tree planting and conservation).

Periodicals: Arbor Day (bimonthly newsletter).

Unique: Can order 10 free tree seedlings for planting.

Check Out on the Web: "Trees" section (everything you want to know about trees, including an online tree identification guide).

Founded: 1971 **Membership:** 1,000,000 **Coverage:** U.S. **NP Status:** 501(c)(3) **Budget:** $22 million

Revenue (FY01): Contributions (25%); Government Grants (2%); Program Service Revenues (15%; from: tree sales –9%; misc. –6%); Other (58%; from: membership dues –47%; sales of inventory –6%; misc. –5%).

Expenses (FY01): Program Services (86%; for: "trees for America" program –43%; Arbor Day farm –14%; youth education program –10%; "conservation trees" program –5%; other programs –15%); Management and General (2%); Fundraising (12%).

Contact Info: 100 Arbor Ave., Nebraska City, NE 68410; (402) 474-5655; info@arborday.org

Key Personnel: John Rosenow (President)

77. National Audubon Society (NAS) (www.audubon.org) – An "Earth Share" Charity

General Focus Areas: Conservation

Description/Mission: Seeks to conserve and restore ecosystems, focusing on birds and other wildlife. Operates 12 education centers and 100+ sanctuaries. Well-known for its *Field Guides* on birds and wildlife.

Basic Activities: Field operations; science and field research; policy research and advocacy; public education; youth education.

Lobbying/Political Activities: Registered lobbyist under the LDA.

Campaigns: Agriculture Policy; Bird Conservation; Endangered Species; Everglades Restoration; Forest Habitat; Marine Wildlife/Oceans; National Wildlife Refuges; Population and Habitat; San Francisco Bay Restoration; Protecting the Upper Mississippi River; Wetlands.

Key Education Programs: Audubon Adventures (for grades 4 to 6); Camps (for youth, teachers, adults, families); Audubon Expedition Institute (for college students).

Periodicals: Audubon (bi-monthly magazine; online); Audubon Advisory (bi-weekly legislative update sent via e-mail); Population and Habitat (bi-monthly newsletter).

Other Publications: A couple of reports (online); various books/guides.

Key Report: Refuges in Crisis (identifies 10 key National Wildlife Refuges in crisis; online).

Annual Report: 2000 report online.

Online Activist Tools: Take Action section (contents: "Armchair Activist"; "letter-of-the-month" club).

Unique: "Adopt a Puffin" program.

Check Out on the Web: Watch List (identifies North American bird species needing help); Christmas Bird Count (annual national survey conducted by volunteers for over 100 years); Refuge Guide (location and description of National Wildlife Refuges).

Founded: 1905 **Members:** 550,000 **Coverage:** U.S. **Staff:** 300 **Field Offices:** 19 **Chapters:** 500+ **NP Status:** 501(c)(3) **Budget:** $70 million

Revenue (FY00): Contributions (60%); Government Grants (2%); Program Service Revenues (10%; from: subscriptions –6%; misc. –4%); Other (28%; from: membership dues –12%; investment income –13%; misc. –

3%).

Expenses (FY00): Program Services (82%; for: field operations –39%; marketing and communication –26%; public policy and government affairs –9%; science and field research –5%; centers and education –3%); Management and General (9%); Fundraising (9%).

Contact Info: 700 Broadway, New York, NY 10003; (212) 979-3000.

Key Personnel: John Flicker (President/CEO)

National Coalition Against the Misuse of Pesticides (www.beyondpesticides.org)

See Profile #17 for "Beyond Pesticides / National Coalition Against the Misuse of Pesticides," located within this subsection.

National Council for Science and the Environment (NCSE) (cnie.org)

See Profile #461 for "National Library for the Environment," located within Subsection 7.2 – "Information and Data Resource Websites and Gateways."

National Environmental Education and Training Foundation (NEETF) (www.neetf.org)

See Profile #142, located within Subsection 1.4 – "Student- and Education-Oriented Groups."

78. National Environmental Trust (NET) (environet.policy.net)

General Focus Areas: Multiple Focus Areas

Slogan: "The environmental action network for the 21st Century."

Description/Mission: Conducts public education campaigns on selected environmental issues.

Basic Activities: Public education; advocacy; research.

Lobbying/Political Activities: Registered lobbyist under the LDA.

Campaigns (and focus areas): Air Pollution (coal-fired electric utilities); Children's Environmental Health (exposure to toxics); Genetic Engineering; Global Warming; Heritage Forests (National Forests); Marine Conservation (overfishing; bycatch; habitat degradation; fisheries privatization schemes).

Publications: Several reports (all online).

Key Report: Polluting Our Future (documents toxic chemical releases of concern for child development, learning and behavior; online).

Online Activist Tools: Take Action section (action alerts sent via e-mail).

Website Notes: For each designated campaign, the website provides: The Issue (basic facts); Solutions; Take Action; Newsroom; More Info.

Founded: 1994 **Coverage:** U.S. **NP Status:** 501(c)(3) **Budget:** $18 million

Revenue (FY00): Contributions (99%); Government Grants (0%); Program Service Revenues (0%); Other (1%).

Expenses (FY00): Program Services (89%; for: global warming policy campaign –74%; clean air/coal-fired electric utilities campaign –8%; children's environmental health campaign –3%; forests campaign –2%; general environment campaign –1%; biotechnology campaign –1%; marine conservation campaign –<1%); Management and General (9%); Fundraising (2%).

Associated Org: NET Action Fund (a 501(c)(4) non-profit).

Contact Info: 1200 18th St. NW, Suite 500, Washington, DC 20036; (202) 887-8800; netinfo@environet.org

Key Personnel: Philip Clapp (President)

79. National Fish and Wildlife Foundation (NFWF) (www.nfwf.org)

General Focus Areas: Conservation

Slogans: "We make conservation your best business decision." "Partnerships that work; solutions that last."

Description/Mission: Established by Congress to foster public and private partnerships aimed at conservation of fish, wildlife and plants and associated habitats via issuance of challenge grants. In FY99, $17 million in federal funds (matched with $50 million in non-federal funds) were awarded to support nearly 600 on-the-ground conservation projects. Partners with government, corporations, private foundation and non-profit orgs.

Basic Activities: Challenge grant-making.

Basic Funding Areas: Conservation Education; Habitat Protection and Restoration; Natural Resource Management.

Check Out on the Web: "Funded Program" section (provides short, state-based descriptions of funded projects).

Founded: 1984 **Coverage:** U.S. **Regional Offices:** 8 **NP Status:** 501(c)(3) **Budget:** $50 million

Revenue (FY00): Contributions (51%); Government Grants (39%); Program Service Revenues (3%); Other (7%).

Expenses (FY00): Program Services (96%); Management & General (2%); Fundraising (2%).

Contact Info: 1120 Connecticut Ave. NW, Suite 900, Washington, DC 20036; (202) 857-0166.

Key Personnel: John Berry (Executive Director)

80. National Geographic Society (www.nationalgeographic.com)

General Focus Areas: Conservation; Scientific Research

Description/Mission: Billed as "the world's largest nonprofit scientific and educational organization," seeking to "increase and diffuse geographic knowledge in its broadest sense." Well-known for its self-titled magazine. Also produces "Explorer" (TV specials shown on MSNBC), operates its own cable TV channel (the National Geographic channel) and runs the free-admission "Explorers Hall" museum in Washington, DC.

Basic Activities: Scientific research and exploration; public education; youth education; publications and TV.

Key Programs (and activities/focus areas): Committee for Research and Exploration (awards $4 million annually in grants for scientific research and exploration; has awarded 6500+ such grants totaling $80+ million since 1890); EarthPulse Conservation Partnership (partnership with Ford Motor Company to promote conservation); Education Foundation (grants to K-12 teachers and educational institutions for geography education).

Periodicals: National Geographic (monthly magazine; current issue features online); National Geographic for Kids (bi-monthly classroom magazine for grades 3-6; website provides supplemental information, tied into the print copy); National Geographic World (monthly magazine for kids 8-14 years old; archives online); National Geographic Traveler (educational travel magazine; 8 times/yr.).

Other Publications: Various books, videos, and CD-ROMs.

Check Out on the Web: EarthPulse page (promoting the EarthPulse Conservation Partnership; provides news, interactive maps, virtual worlds, event listings, and monthly features; check out the Wild World Conservation Atlas in particular, which provides interactive maps of the Earth's eco-regions).

Founded: 1888 **Coverage:** U.S./Int'l **Staff:** >1000 **NP Status:** 501(c)(3) **Budget:** $500 million

Revenue (1999): Contributions (1%); Government Grants (0%); Program Service Revenues (45%; from: books and other merchandise –18%; periodical advertising –13%; *Traveler*, *World*, and *Adventure* magazines –5%; *National Geographic* magazine –4%; misc. –5%); Other (54%; from: membership dues –38%; investment income –14%; misc. –2%).

Expenses (1999): Program Services (95%; for: *National Geographic* magazine –53%; books and other merchandise –23%; *Traveler*, *World*, and *Adventure* magazines –11%; school publishing –3%; geography education –2%; research grants and allocations –1%; expeditions council –1%; various other programs –1%); Management and General (5%); Fundraising (<1%).

Contact Info: 1145 17th St. NW, Washington, DC 20036; (202) 857-7000.

Key Personnel: John Fahey (President/CEO)

81. National Parks Conservation Association (NPCA) (www.npca.org) – An "Earth Share" Charity

General Focus Areas: Conservation

Description/Mission: Citizen "watchdog" group for the U.S. National Park System. Originally established under the guidance of the first Director of the National Park Service, Stephen Mather.

Basic Activities: Public education; outreach; advocacy; litigation.

Lobbying/Political Activities: Registered lobbyist under the LDA.

Programs (and focus areas): Wildlife Protection; Marine and Coastal Protection (beaches; coral reefs; marine wildlife; wetlands); Wild Alaska; Cultural Diversity; Across the Nation ("state of the parks"; park funding and management; park visitor experience).

Periodicals: National Parks (bi-monthly magazine; partially online).

Other Publications: A few reports and fact sheets (all online).

Key Report: 10 Most Endangered Parks (annual list; online).

Annual Report: 2000 report online.

Online Activist Tools: Take Action section (contents: action alerts [posted online and sent via email]; park planning participation; chat room).

Check Out on the Web: Explore the Parks (virtual visits).

Founded: 1919 **Membership:** 500,000 **Coverage:** U.S. **Regional Offices:** 7 **NP Status:** 501(c)(3) **Budget:** $20 million

Revenue (FY00): Contributions (85%); Government Grants (0%); Program Service Revenues (1%); Other (14%; from: membership dues –7%; misc. –7%).

Expenses (FY00): Program Services (62%; for: park visitor experience program –28%; park resource protection program –20%; public support and advocacy program –9%; park funding and management program –6%); Management and General (24%); Fundraising (14%).

Contact Info: 1300 19th St. NW, Suite 300, Washington, DC 20036; (800) 628-7275; npca@npca.org

Key Personnel: Thomas Kiernan (President)

82. National Recycling Coalition (NRC) (www.nrc-recycle.org)

General Focus Areas: Pollution

Description/Mission: Broad-based coalition promoting recycling, source reduction, composting, and reuse. Coalition members include recycling and environmental non-profit groups, businesses, federal, state and local government entities, and individuals. NRC supports America Recycles Day (Nov. 15).

Basic Activities: Technical information and assistance; training and education; outreach; advocacy; annual Congress/conference.

Programs/Initiatives (and activities/focus areas): Buy Recycled Business Alliance (promoting procurement of recycled content products); Climate Change and Waste Reduction (integrate waste reduction into state/local Climate Change Action Plans); Electronics Recycling Initiative; National Recycling Financing Initiative (focuses on small and start-up recycling businesses); National Recycling Economic Information Project (collecting economic data on recycling); Recycling Works (recycling industry networking); Source Reduction Forum (generating tools and resources).

Periodicals: Connection (NRC newsletter); Newswire (monthly email newsletter); Recycling Policy Reporter (monthly email newsletter).

Other Publications: Various reports, case studies and fact sheets (a couple online).

Key Reports (both online): Level the Playing Field for Recycling (identifies virgin material and waste disposal subsides that negatively impact recycling; online); U.S. Recycling Economic Information Study (study of the U.S. recycling and reuse industry).

Check Out on the Web: Defending Recycling: How to Respond to Attacks on Recycling (fact sheet; online).

Founded: 1978 **Coverage:** U.S. **Members:** 4500 **Staff:** 12 **NP Status:** 501(c)(3) **Budget:** $2 million

Revenue (FY00): Contributions (39%); Government Grants (20%); Program Service Revenues (33%; from: annual Congress/conference –30%; misc. –3%); Other (8%; from membership dues).

Expenses (FY00): Program Services (97%; for: various recycling initiatives –30%; annual Congress/conference – 28%; Buy Recycled Business Alliance –16%; membership –9%; board and committees – 7%; other services – 7%); Management and General (1%); Fundraising (3%).

Contact Info: 1727 King St., Suite 105, Alexandria, VA 22314; (703) 683-9025; info@nrc-recycle.org

Key Personnel: Kate Krebs (Acting Executive Director)

83. National Religious Partnership for the Environment (NRPE) (www.nrpe.org)

General Focus Areas: Religious-Based Focus

Description/Mission: Partnership of 4 religious-based environmental education programs (see below for specific participants).

Basic Activities: Public education; partnerships/outreach.

Participants (and focus areas): Coalition on the Environment and Jewish Life (interested in a wide range of issues); Evangelical Environmental Network (focused on: air pollution; endangered species; energy; global warming); National Council of the Churches of Christ in the USA (focused on: climate change; energy; environmental justice); U.S. Catholic Conference (focused on environmental justice).

Founded: 1993 **Coverage:** U.S. **NP Status:** 501(c)(3) **Budget:** $1.5 million

Revenue (FY00): Contributions (96%); Government Grants (0%); Program Service Revenues (0%); Other (4%).

Expenses (FY00): Program Services (83%; for: affiliates program –47%; general program –36%); Management and General (15%); Fundraising (2%).

Contact Info: 1047 Amsterdam Ave., New York, NY 10025; (212) 316-7441; nrpe@nrpe.org

Key Personnel: Paul Gorman (Executive Director)

84. National Wildlife Federation (NWF) ® (www.nwf.org) – An "Earth Share" Charity

General Focus Areas: Conservation

Slogan: "Education and action to keep the wild in our world."

Description/Mission: Focuses on wildlife and other natural resource conservation, with a particular emphasis on public education efforts. Also conducts a significant advocacy program (see listing of "programs" below). Founded as a nationwide federation of grassroots conservation activists; prides itself as being the most "local" national conservation group. Particularly known for its "Ranger Rick®" kids magazine. Runs National Wildlife Productions, which produces film, TV and multimedia projects on nature/conservation. Also operates the Campus Ecology ® program which provides ideals/assistance for greening college campuses (see Profile #138, located within Subsection 1.4 – "Student- and Education-Oriented Groups").

Basic Activities: Wildlife and ecosystem conservation; public and community education; youth education; outreach; publications and film; advocacy.

Lobbying/Political Activities: Registered lobbyist under the LDA.

Programs (DC Office): Artic Refuge Protection; Conservation Funding; Climate Change and Wildlife; Keep the Wild Alive ® (protecting endangered species); Smart Growth and Wildlife; Population and the Environment; Finance and the Environment (int'l financial institutions); International Trade and Environment; Everglades Restoration; Floodplains Management.

Periodicals (all magazines): National Wildlife ® (bimonthly; online); International Wildlife ® (bimonthly; online); Wild Animal Baby ® (for ages 1-3); Your Big Backyard ® (for ages 3-6); Ranger Rick ® (for ages 7-12).

Other Publications: Various books and reports (many online).

Key Publications: Conservation Directory (annual; listing of 3000+ conservation-oriented public interest groups, government agencies, educational institutions and information resources); Pollution Paralysis II: Code Red for Watersheds (examines and grades state-level watershed protection programs; online); Troubled Waters: Congress, the Corps of Engineers, and Wasteful Water Projects (identifies the 25 most wasteful and damaging water projects in the U.S.; online).

Annual Report: 2000 report online.

Unique: Backyard Wildlife Habitat ™ program (shows how to create a mini-wildlife habitat in one's backyard; 25,000+ sites officially certified).

Online Activist Tools: Take Action section (contents: action alerts [posted online and sent via email]; action toolkit [personal advocacy; organizing your community; using the news]; action updates; Enviro-Action [monthly newsletter; online]; Conservation Directory online).

Website Notes: The website is as advertised: "a treasure trove of conservation information."

Check Out on the Web: Kid's Zone (contents: games; tours; outdoor stuff; reader's corner); Get Outdoors (contents: backyard wildlife habitats' nature link; expeditions; family summits).

Founded: 1936 **Members:** 4 million **Coverage:** U.S. **Regional Offices:** 11 **State Affiliates:** 46 **NP Status:** 501(c)(3) **Budget:** $100 million

Revenue (FY00): Contributions (39%); Government Grants (<1%); Program Service Revenues (<1%); Other (60%; from: sales of inventory [nature education materials] –35%; membership dues –19%; misc. –6%).

Expenses (FY00): Program Services (85%; for: education, outreach, publications and films –21%; other nature education materials –36%; conservation advocacy –14%; membership education –14%); Management and General (6%); Fundraising (9%).

Associated Orgs: National Wildlife Federation Endowment (serves to invest and preserve NWF funds; a 501(c)(3) non-profit); National Wildlife Action (a 501(c)(4) non-profit); National Wildlife Productions (film, TV, and multimedia arm; a 501(c)(3) non-profit with a $2 million budget for FY00; President – Christopher Palmer).

Contact Info: 11100 Wildlife Center Dr., Reston, VA 20190; (703) 438-6000.

Key Personnel: Mark Van Putten (President/CEO)

85. Natural Resources Defense Council (NRDC) (www.nrdc.org) – An "Earth Share" Charity

General Focus Areas: Multiple Focus Areas

Slogan: "The Earth's best defense."

Description/Mission: Multi-faceted environmental advocacy organization dedicated to protecting America's natural resources. Well-known for its litigation activities.

Basic Activities: Advocacy; litigation; communications; public education; research.

Lobbying/Political Activities: Registered lobbyist under the LDA.

Issues (and focus areas): Clean Air and Energy (air pollution; energy; transportation); Global Warming; Clean Water and Oceans (drinking water; water pollution; oceans; water conservation and restoration; the Everglades); Wildlife and Fish (animals and birds; fish; whales and marine mammals; habitat preservation); Parks/Forests/Wildlands (parks; forests; wilderness preservation; land use); Toxic Chemicals and Health (health threats and effects; kids' health; pesticides; farming and organic food); Nuclear Weapons and Waste; Cities and Green Living (smart growth/sprawl; green building; recycling; green living; cleaner manufacturing).

Key Initiative: BioGems (saving endangered wildlands of exceptional natural value).

Periodicals: On Earth (quarterly magazine; online); Legislative Watch (tracks legislation in Congress; biweekly via email; latest online).

Other Publications: Numerous program-related reports (many online).

Key Publication: A Responsible Energy Policy for the 21st Century (online).

Online Activist Tools: Earth Action Center (bi-weekly emailed action alerts; current alerts posted online)

Check Out on the Web: Reference/Links section – well thought out and put together, especially the references.

Founded: 1970 **Membership:** 500,000 **Coverage:** U.S./Int'l **Staff:** 150 **Regional Offices:** 3 **NP Status:** 501(c)(3) **Budget:** $35 million

Revenue (FY00): Contributions (87%); Government Grants (2%); Program Service Revenues (6%); Other (5%).

Expenses (FY00): Program Services (80%; for: environmental programs –49%; communications and public education –24%; membership services –6%; legislative activities –1%); Management and General (8%); Fundraising (12%).

Associated Orgs: NRDC Action Fund (a 501(c)(4) non-profit).

Contact Info: 40 West 20th St., New York, NY 10011; (212) 727-2700; nrdcinfo@nrdc.org

Key Personnel: John H. Adams (President)

86. (The) Nature Conservancy (TNC) (www.nature.org) – An "Earth Share" Charity

General Focus Areas: Conservation

Slogan: "Saving the last great places."

Description/Mission: Focused on land conservation through purchasing/managing threatened lands and waters. Manages 1400 private preserves worldwide; 90% of the preserves remain open to the public. Protects 12 million acres in the U.S., 80 million outside the U.S. (in Canada, Latin America, the Caribbean, Asia and the Pacific). Partners with landowners, corporations, and government. For FY00, received gifts of land valued at $91 million, while selling $82 million worth of land to government and other conservation agencies.

Basic Activities: Land acquisition and management; scientific research; training and technical support; general conservation activities; communications and outreach.

Lobbying/Political Activities: Registered lobbyist under the LDA.

Global Initiatives (and activities/focus areas): Land Acquisition (focused on lands of high ecological value); Coastal and Marine Conservation (focused on Asia and the Western Pacific); Forest Protection (focused on rainforests); Community-Based Conservation (improving relationships between communities and nearby natural areas); Cross-Border Partnerships (focused on N. American grassland birds); Conservation Blueprint (strategic vision for conservation work worldwide).

Special Initiatives (and activities/focus areas): Adopt-an-Acre (critical rainforest protection); Berkshire Taconic Landscape Program; Center for Compatible Economic Development (programs: community-based conservation; business and product development); Climate Change (large-scale conservation to reduce greenhouse emissions); EcoEnterprises Fund (venture capital and technical assistance for environmentally-compatible businesses in the Caribbean and Latin America); Ecotourism (work with local groups to develop ecotourism in 15 countries); Freshwater Initiative (freshwater conservation in the U.S., Latin America, and the Caribbean); Great Lakes Program (protect biodiversity of the region); Rescue the Reef (protect warm water reefs); Wings of the Americas (protect critical bird habitats in the Americas).

Key Campaign: Campaign for Conservation – Saving The Last Great Places (ambitious plan to invest $1 billion in saving 200 key threatened landscapes in the U.S., Latin America and the Pacific).

Key Divisions: Conservation Science (provides methods, training and tech support to field staff and partners, focusing on: conservation planning; ecological management and restoration; freshwater conservation).

Periodicals: Nature Conservancy (bimonthly magazine; online); Nature News (1-2 times/mo. email update; online); Global Currents (tri-annual international program newsletter; online).

Key Report: Precious Heritage: The Status of Biodiversity in the U.S. (book published by Oxford Univ. Press).

Annual Report: 2000 report online.

Check Out on the Web: Conservation Beef ("beef with a mission" – buy free-range, hormone-free beef); ConserveOnline (collection of practical information for the conservation practitioner); Conservation Journeys (trips to TNC project areas worldwide).

Founded: 1951 **Members:** 1 million **Coverage:** U.S./Int'l. **Staff:** 2800 **Local Chapters:** In each state and in 27 countries **NP Status:** 501(c)(3) **Budget:** $600 million

Revenue (FY00): Contributions (57%; includes: cash –45%; gifts of land –12%); Government Grants (0%); Program Service Revenues (21%; from: land sales to government/other conservation agencies –10%; government agency fees/contracts –8%; activity and contract fees –3%); Other (22%; from investment income).

Expenses (FY00): Program Services (78%; for: conservation programs –73%; communication and outreach – 5%); Management and General (10%); Fundraising (12%).

Private Funding Sources (FY00): Individuals (61%); Foundations (29%); Corporations (8%); Other (2%).

Key Associated Org: Nature Conservancy Action Fund (a 501(c)(4) non-profit).

Contact Info: 4245 North Fairfax Dr., Suite 100, Arlington, VA 22203; (703) 841-5300 / (800) 628-6860; comment@tnc.org

Key Personnel: Steven McCormick (President/CEO)

87. Ocean Conservancy (www.oceanconservancy.org) – **An "Earth Share" Charity**

General Focus Areas: Conservation

Slogan: "Advocates for wild, healthy oceans."

Description/Mission: Focuses on marine conservation (both species and habitats). Formerly known as the Center for Marine Conservation.

Basic Activities: Research; policy analysis/advocacy; public education.

Strategic Goals: Conserve/recover vulnerable marine wildlife; conserve/restore marine fish populations; protect ocean ecosystems and establish ocean wilderness areas; clean/restore coastal and ocean waters.

Programs (and focus areas): Marine Ecosystem Protection (marine reserves; marine sanctuaries; clean oceans campaign; Caribbean Reef campaign); Marine Wildlife and Fisheries Conservation (Alaskan Seas campaign; threatened and endangered marine wildlife); Marine Conservation of Biological Diversity.

Key Specific Program: International Coastal Cleanup (annual one-day event to remove debris from shorelines, waterways, and beaches – in 2000, collected 4+ million pounds in the U.S., 14 million pounds worldwide).

Key Campaign: Ocean Wilderness Challenge (protect at least 5% of U.S. oceans as ocean wilderness).

Periodicals: Marine Conservation News (quarterly newsletter).

Key Report: Conserving America's Oceans: A Blueprint (policy blueprint for the Bush Administration).

Online Activist Tools: Ocean Action Network (action alerts – posted online and sent via email).

Founded: 1971 **Membership:** 120,000 **Coverage:** U.S./Int'l **Regional Offices:** 4 **Field Offices:** 4 **NP Status:** 501(c)(3) **Budget:** $15 million

Revenue (FY00): Contributions (63%); Government Grants (4%); Program Service Revenues (<1%); Other (33%; from investment income).

Expenses (FY00): Program Services (72%; for: wildlife conservation –18%; public education and member services –17%; international initiatives –12%; ecosystem protection –12%; citizens outreach and monitoring – 10%; regional impact –3%); Management and General (14%); Fundraising (14%).

Contact Info: 1725 DeSales St. NW, Suite 600, Washington, DC 20036; (202) 429-5609; cmc@dccmc.org

Key Personnel: Roger McManus (President)

88. Office of Management and Budget (OMB) Watch / Focus Project (www.ombwatch.org)

General Focus Areas: Government Watchdog

Slogan: "Promoting government accountability."

Description/Mission: Government watchdog organization that focuses on federal budget issues and other key areas (see "focus areas" below). Legally known as the Focus Project. Started the Right-to-Know Network in 1989, now an online service providing environmental and housing/bank loan data (see Profile #464, located within Subsection 7.2 – "Information and Data Resource Websites and Gateways"). OMB Watch is listed here as environmentally-related federal programs can be (and have been) significantly impacted by the budgetary decisions that OMB Watch monitors.

Basic Activities: Research/monitoring; information dissemination; public education; advocacy.

Specific Focus Areas: Federal Budget; Government Performance/Accountability; Government Information Policy; Nonprofit Issues (advocacy protection; use of technology); Federal Regulatory Matters (monitoring regulations).

Periodicals: OMB Watcher (bimonthly online newsletter).

Other Publications: Several reports (a few online).

Key Publication: A Guide to Environmental Statutes and Regulations That Promote Public Access Activities (Appendix C of "A Citizen's Platform for Our Environmental Right-to-Know"; provides summaries of major statutes and associated key Internet and other resources; online).

Check Out on the Web: Right-To-Know Network (see Profile #464, located within Subsection 7.2 – "Information and Data Resource Websites and Gateways").

Founded: 1983 **Staff:** 12 **NP Status:** 501(c)(3) **Budget:** $1 million

Revenue (FY00): Contributions (87%); Government Grants (0%); Program Service Revenues (13%; from: computer network expense reimbursements –7%; technical assistance –5%; publications –<1%); Other (<1%).

Expenses (FY00): Program Services (81%); Management and General (9%); Fundraising (9%).

Contact Info: 1742 Connecticut Ave. NW, Washington, D.C. 20009; (202) 234-8494; ombwatch@ombwatch.org

Key Personnel: Gary Bass (Executive Director)

89. <u>Peregrine Fund</u> (<u>www.peregrinefund.org</u>) **– An "Earth Share" Charity**

General Focus Areas: Conservation

Slogan: "Working to conserve wild populations of birds of prey."

Description/Mission: Focuses on conservation/restoration of birds of prey and their habitats, both nationally and internationally. Best known for Peregrine falcon recovery work in the U.S. A "hands-on" organization. Currently working at/on 28 separate sites/projects around the world. Operates the World Center for Birds of Prey in Boise, Idaho.

Basic Activities: Species Restoration; Conservation; Education/Training; Research.

Periodicals: Fund Newsletter (semi-annual); E-Newsletter (via email).

Annual Report: 2000 report online.

Founded: 1970 **Coverage:** U.S./Int'l **Staff:** 70 **NP Status:** 501(c)(3) **Budget:** $6 million

Revenue (FY00): Contributions (64%); Government Grants (21%); Program Service Revenues (0%); Other (15%; from: investment income –10%; misc. –5%).

Expenses (FY00): Program Services (94%; for: species restoration –60%; conservation programs –27%; education/information –7%); Management and General (4%); Fundraising (2%).

Contact Info: 566 West Flying Hawk Lane, Boise, ID 83709; (208) 362-3716; <u>tpf@peregrinefund.org</u>

Key Personnel: William Burnham (President/CEO)

90. <u>Pesticide Action Network (International) (PAN)</u> (<u>www.pan-international.org</u>)

General Focus Areas: Pollution; Public Health

Description/Mission: Network of 600+ NGOs, institutions, and individuals in 60+ countries worldwide seeking to replace pesticides with ecologically sound alternatives. PAN projects and campaigns are coordinated by 5 autonomous Regional Centers (North America, Latin America, Europe, Africa, Asian and the Pacific – see Profile #91 for PAN-North America, located within this subsection).

Basic Activities: Research and community monitoring; policy development; education; communications; demos of alternatives; advocacy.

International Campaigns (and activities): Day of No Pesticide Use (December 3rd – the anniversary of the Bhopal, India disaster); Pesticide Use (community monitoring and other studies); Corporate Activities (research and advocacy); Food Security Without Pesticides (research and advocacy).

Website Notes: The website itself basically serves as a gateway to websites of the 5 PAN Regional Centers, including PAN-North America.

Coverage: Global

91. <u>Pesticide Action Network North America (PANNA)</u> (<u>www.panna.org</u>) **– An "Earth Share" Charity**

General Focus Areas: Pollution; Public Health

Slogan: "Advancing alternatives to pesticides worldwide."

Description/Mission: Network of 100+ mixed interest groups in North America seeking to replace pesticides with ecologically sound alternatives. Part of PAN International (see Profile #90, located within this subsection).

Basic Activities: Research and community monitoring; policy development; education; communications; demos of alternatives; advocacy.

Campaigns/Issues (and activities/focus areas): Californians for Pesticide Reform (coalition of 135 orgs); Farmworkers Rights (focus on: pesticide poisoning incidents; pesticide use and reduction); Genetic Engineering (seek labeling of GE foods and a moratorium on approval of GE crops); Kids and Pesticides (reduce pesticide use in schools and parks); Methyl Bromide Phase-Out; Organic Cotton (offers the International Organic Cotton Directory); Persistent Organic Pollutants Elimination; Sustainable California; World Bank Monitoring/Reform (focus on alternative pest management).

Periodicals: Pesticide Action Network Updates Service – PANUPS (international news service; online); Partners Update (semi-annual newsletter; online); Global Pesticide Campaigner (tri-annual pesticide and sustainable agriculture news magazine).

Other Publications: Various reports, backgrounders/briefs, fact sheets (some online).

Key Report: Nowhere to Hide: Persistent Toxic Chemicals in the U.S. Food Supply (online).

Annual Report: 2000 report online.

Online Activist Tools: PAN Alert (action alerts sent via email).

Check Out on the Web: The Pesticide Advisor (offering help with specific pest/pesticide problems); PAN Pesticide Database (human toxicity, ecotoxicity and regulatory data/information on 5400 pesticide ingredients and 100,000+ formulated pesticide products; at www.pesticideinfo.org).

Founded: 1982 **Coverage:** N. America **Staff:** 14 **NP Status:** 501(c)(3) **Budget:** $2 million

Revenue (2000): Contributions (91%); Government Grants (6%); Program Service Revenues (2%); Other (<1%).

Expenses (2000): Program Services (86%; for: campaigns and joint projects –30%; coalitions –30%; regional/int'l networking –16%; research and communications –9%); Management and General (5%); Fundraising (9%).

Contact Info: 49 Powell St., Suite 500, San Francisco, CA 94102; (415) 981-1771; panna@panna.org

Key Personnel: Monica Moore (Programs Director); Stephen Scholl-Buckwald (Managing Director)

92. Pew Center on Global Climate Change (www.pewclimate.org)

General Focus Areas: Global Warming

Slogan: "Working together because climate change is serious business."

Description/Mission: Provides information and proposes solutions to address global climate change. Established and funded by the Pew Charitable Trust. Part of Strategies for the Global Environment (see Profile #118, located within this subsection), a non-profit that also serves as an umbrella organization for the Pew Oceans Commission (see Profile #93, located within this subsection).

Basic Activities: Research; education; information dissemination.

Affiliated Org: Business Environmental Leadership Council (30 major companies agreeing to a joint Statement of Principles recognizing global warming risks and a need to take action; serves in an advisory capacity to the Pew Center).

Publications: Numerous research reports (on environmental impacts, economics and policy of global climate change) and a couple of briefs (all online); one book (see below).

Key Publication: Climate Change: Science, Strategies and Solutions (book; partially online).

Check Out on the Web: The "Reports" section (research reports divided into 4 series: Solutions; Economics; Environmental Impacts; Policy).

Founded: 1998 **Coverage:** Global **Staff:** 12 **NP Status:** 501(c)(3) **Financial Information:** See Profile #118 for "Strategies for the Global Environment," located within this subsection.

Contact Info: 2101 Wilson Blvd., Suite 550, Arlington, VA 22201; (703) 516-4146.

Key Personnel: Eileen Claussen (President)

93. Pew Oceans Commission (www.pewoceans.org)

General Focus Areas: Conservation

Slogan: "Connecting people and science to sustain marine life."

Description/Mission: A 17-person commission (headed by former White House Chief of Staff Leon Panetta) established to "examine threats to living resources in U.S. waters and the measures needed to restore and sustain the health of the marine environment." Principal output will be a report to Congress scheduled for publication in Fall of 2002. Also seeks to educate the public on the principal threats to marine biodiversity as well as the importance of coastal resources to the U.S. economy. Part of Strategies for the Global Environment (see Profile #118, located within this subsection), a non-profit that also serves as an umbrella organization for the Pew Center on Global Climate Change (see Profile #92, located within this subsection).

Basic Activities: Research; public education.

Issues (and focus areas): Status of Marine Life; Fishing and Agriculture (overfishing; bycatch; habitat degradation and loss; altered marine ecosystems); Coastal Development (residential building; recreation; facilities for hydroelectric power and oil and gas); Marine Pollution; Law and Programs.

Periodicals: e-newsletter (via email).

Coverage: U.S. **NP Status:** 501(c)(3) **Financial Information:** See Profile #118 for "Strategies for the Global Environment," located within this subsection.

Contact Info: 2101 Wilson Blvd., Suite 550, Arlington, VA 22201; (703) 516-0624.

Key Personnel: Leon Panetta (Commission Chairman)

94. Physicians for Social Responsibility (PSR) (www.psr.org**)**

General Focus Areas: Pollution; Public Health

Description/Mission: Addresses 3 perceived threats to global survival: nuclear weapons and waste, global environmental pollution and gun violence. Originally formed to eliminate nuclear weapons.

Basic Activities: Education (public and professional); research; link activists with issue experts; national/int'l policy; advocacy.

Programs (and focus areas): Environment and Health (persistent organic pollutants; medical waste incineration and dioxin; climate change and human health; children's environmental health; drinking water and health); Nuclear/Security (nuclear weapons abolition; health and environmental effects of nuclear weapons; nuclear weapons testing and development; nuclear waste and cleanup); Violence Prevention.

Periodicals: PSR Reports (quarterly newsletter; online).

Other Publications: A few reports/primers (all online).

Online Activist Tools: EnviroHealthAction (contents: legislative action center [action alerts; elected officials; issues and legislation; media guide]; quick-links).

Founded: 1961 **Membership:** 20,000 **Coverage:** U.S./Int'l **Chapters:** In 21 states **NP Status:** 501(c)(3) **Budget:** $3 million

Revenue (2000): Contributions (79%); Government Grants (1%); Program Service Revenues (1%); Other (19%; from: membership dues –16%; misc. –3%).

Expenses (2000): Program Services (77%; for: public and medical information –62%; media and public affairs –8%; chapter development –8%); Management and General (9%); Fundraising (14%).

Contact Info: 1875 Connecticut Ave. NW, Suite 1012, Washington, DC 20009; (202) 667-4260; psrnatl@psr.org

Key Personnel: Robert Musil (Executive Director and CEO)

95. Pinchot Institute (www.pinchot.org**)**

General Focus Areas: Conservation

Slogan: "Leadership in forest conservation."

Description/Mission: Continues conservation leader Gifford Pinchot's legacy in supporting sustainable forest management. Also jointly manages Grey Towers, Pinchot's home in Milford, PA, which is a national historical landmark. (Pinchot served as the first head of the U.S. Forest Service.)

Basic Activities: Policy research and analysis; convening and facilitation; technical assistance and training; leadership development.

Programs (and activities/ focus areas): Community-Based Forest Stewardship (providing technical assistance and training); Conservation Policy and Organizational Change (focused in policy implementation); Conservation Leadership Training (leadership workshops; professional development seminars).

Periodicals: The Pinchot Letter (semi-annual newsletter; online).

Other Publications: Some books, reports, papers (a few online).

Biennial Report: 1998-99 online.

Founded: 1963 **Coverage:** U.S. **Staff:** 16 **NP Status:** 501(c)(3) **Budget:** $1 million

Revenue (2000): Contributions (64%); Government Grants (33%); Program Service Revenues (1%); Other (2%).

Expenses (2000): Program Services (78%; for: general natural resource management issues –18%; sustainable rural development program –17%; public forest land green certification –8%; leadership training program –8%; other program services –27%); Management and General (22%); Fundraising (0%).

Contact Info: 1616 P St. NW, Suite 100, Washington, DC 20036; (202) 797-6580; pinchot@pinchot.org

Key Personnel: V. Alaric Sample (President)

96. Population Action International (PAI) (www.populationaction.org)

General Focus Areas: Population

Description/Mission: Works to strengthen public awareness and political/financial support worldwide for population and family planning programs grounded in individual rights. Seeks to make clear the linkages between population, reproductive health, the environment and development. Seeks to serve as a bridge between the academic and policymaking communities. Covers 6 issue areas, including "Environment."

Basic Activities: Research; Advocacy; Communications.

Lobbying/Political Activities: Registered lobbyist under the LDA.

Environment Issues (and focus areas): Community-Based Population and Environment (integrating resource conservation and reproductive health); Populations Linkages to Natural Resources (biodiversity loss; forest use; freshwater availability).

Publications: Various reports and fact sheets (most online).

Key Reports (all online): People in the Balance – Population and Natural Resources at the Turn of the Millennium (concise summary exploring population linkages with: water; land; forests; fisheries; carbon dioxide emissions; biodiversity); Forest Futures – Population, Consumption and Wood Resources (explores the link between population and forests); Nature's Place – Human Population and the Future of Biodiversity (explores the link between population and biodiversity).

Online Activist Tools: Take Action section (contents: action network [action alerts – posted online and sent via email]; key issues and legislation; guide to congress; capitol hill basics).

Check Out on the Web: Publications (reports containing a multitude of figures and graphs).

Founded: 1965 **Coverage:** Global **Staff:** 30 **NP Status:** 501(c)(3) **Budget:** $5 million

Revenue (FY00): Contributions (91%); Government Grants (0%); Program Service Revenues (<1%); Other (8%).

Expenses (FY00): Program Services (81%; for: U.S./Int'l population activities –53%; capacity-building for colleague NGOs –17%; communications –11%); Management and General (13%); Fundraising (6%).

Contact Info: 1300 19th St. NW, Suite 200, Washington, DC 20036; (202) 557-3400; pai@popact.org

Key Personnel: Amy Coen (President)

97. Population Reference Bureau (PRB) (www.prb.org)

General Focus Areas: Population

Slogan: "Providing timely and objective population information."

Description/Mission: Provides data/information on U.S. and international population trends and their implications. Has 4 focus areas, including "Environment." Maintains a large library (open to the general public) containing 13,000+ books/monographs and 350 periodicals.

Basic Activities/Programs (and focus areas): Publications/Communications; Technical Assistance (developing/implementing policy communication strategies); Training (on policy communications); Technical Research (aimed at journalists); Education (materials/training for middle and high school education); Reference Service (library and reference staff); Policy Studies.

Periodicals: Population Today (newsletter; 8 times/yr; online); Population Bulletin (in-depth focus on a specific topic; quarterly; online).

Other Publications: Various articles, datasheets, and reports (many online).

Key Associated Website: PopPlanet (PopPlanet.org; provides information about population, health, and environment connections in different regions; information provided through in-depth Country Briefing Books – currently covers 15 countries in Africa, central America and Southeast Asia).

Check Out on the Web: U.S. in the World (compares U.S. and developing country trends; key products are "U.S. State-Developing Country Profiles," which comparatively match 41 individual U.S. states with specific developing countries facing similar demographic, environmental and socioeconomic challenges – for example, California/South Africa; all profiles available online).

Founded: 1938 **Coverage:** Global **NP Status:** 501(c)(3) **Budget:** $7 million

Revenue (FY00): Contributions (1%); Government Grants (0%); Program Service Revenues (89%; from: international programs –63%; publications/communications –11%; policy studies –11%; information and education –4%); Other (9%).

Expenses (FY00): Program Services (79%; for: international programs –55%; publications/communications – 11%; policy studies –7%; information and education –6%); Management and General (20%); Fundraising (1%).

Contact Info: 1875 Connecticut Ave. NW, Suite 520, Washington, DC 20009; (202) 483-1100; popref@prb.org

Key Personnel: Peter J. Donaldson (President)

98. PR Watch / Center for Media and Democracy (CMD) (www.prwatch.org)

General Focus Areas: Public Relations Industry

Description/Mission: Investigative reporting on the public relations industry, focused on health, consumer safety, environmental, democracy and world peace issues. Best known for their books (see below). A project of the Center for Media and Democracy.

Basic Activities: Research; publications/reporting; information dissemination.

Periodicals: PR Watch (quarterly newsletter; online).

Other Publications: Three books: Toxic Sludge is Good for You: Lies, Damn Lies and the Public Relations Industry; Mad Cow USA: Could the Nightmare Happen Here?; Trust Us – We're Experts: How Industry Manipulates Science and Gambles with Your Future.

Check Out on the Web: Spin of the Day (examines current PR-related activities/campaigns).

Founded: 1993 **Coverage:** U.S. **Staff:** 3 **NP Status:** 501(c)(3) **Budget (CMD):** $0.1 million

Revenue (CMD; 2000): Contributions (67%); Government Grants (0%); Program Service Revenues (26%; from publications); Other (7%).

Expenses (CMD; 2000): Program Services (88%); Management and General and Fundraising (12%).

Contact Info: 520 University Ave., Suite 310, Madison, WI 53703; (608) 260-9713; editor@prwatch.org

Key Personnel: John Stauber (Executive Director)

99. Public Citizen (www.citizen.org)

General Focus Areas: Pollution; Public Health

Slogan: "Protecting health, safety and democracy."

Description/Mission: Consumer protection group with 6 divisions (see below) including the Critical Mass Energy and Environment Program (CMEP). Consists of two affiliated non-profit organizations: Public Citizen, Inc. (a 501(c)(4) non-exempt group) and Public Citizen Foundation (a 501(c)(3) exempt group). Originally formed by Ralph Nader.

Basic Activities: Research; public education; communications; government watchdog activities; advocacy; litigation.

Lobbying/Political Activities: Registered lobbyist under the LDA.

Divisions: Critical Mass Energy and Environment Program (CMEP); Auto Safety; Congress Watch; Global Trade Watch; Health Research Group; Litigation Group.

CMEP Programs (and focus areas): Energy (electricity deregulation; energy efficiency and renewable energy; oil and gas; Price-Anderson Act); Food Safety/Food Irradiation; Global Safe Food Alliance (focused on meat production); Nuclear Power Plants (decommissioning; nuclear revival; reactor safety); Nuclear Waste (high-level waste; low level waste); Water for All (water and wastewater system privatization).

Publications: A multitude of reports (all the latest online).

Online Activist Tools: Take Action section (contents: action alerts [posted online and sent via email]; finding federal/state representatives; key votes; today in the House; today in the Senate).

Check Out on the Web: Atomic Atlas Project (high-level nuclear waste transport routes associated with the proposed central nuclear waste repository at Yucca Mountain).

Founded: 1971 **Coverage:** U.S. **Supporters:** 150,000 **Staff (CMEP only):** 14 **NP Status:** 501(c)(3) (PC Foundation); 501(c)(4) (PC Inc.) **Budget (PC Foundation):** $8 million **Budget (PC Inc.):** $5 million

Revenue (FY00; PC Foundation): Contributions (87%); Government Grants (0%); Program Service Revenues (3%; from courts awards); Other (10%).

Revenue (FY00; PC Inc.): Contributions (89%); Government Grants (0%); Program Service Revenues (2%); Other (9%).

Expenses (FY00; PC Foundation): Program Services (87%; for: publications –22%; health research group – 15%; litigation group –13%; global trade watch division –10%; public information and education –9%; critical mass energy project –8%; congress watch division –5%; PC Texas –5%); Management and General (5%); Fundraising (8%).

Expenses (FY00; PC Inc.): Program Services (64%; for: public information and education –30%; congress watch division –16%; global trade watch division –5%; critical mass energy project –5%; publications –5%; PC Texas –2%; "Buyers Up" program –1%); Management and General (14%); Fundraising (22%).

IRS Form 990: FY00 online for both PC Inc. and PC Foundation.

Contact Info: 1600 20th St. NW, Washington, DC 20009; (202) 588-1000; cmep@citizen.org

Key Personnel: Joan Claybrook (President); Wenonah Hauter (CEMP Director)

100.   Public Employees for Environmental Responsibility (PEER) (www.peer.org)

General Focus Areas: Whistleblower Support

Slogan: "Protecting employees who protect the environment."

Description/Mission: Works with, and on behalf of, government environmental/natural resource professionals seeking to: 1) defend/strengthen the legal rights of public employees who speak out about environmental/natural resource issues (including providing free legal assistance), 2) monitor government environmental/natural resource agencies, 3) inform government officials, the media and the public about substantive environmental/natural resource issues.

Basic Activities: Legal assistance; "watchdog" activities; research; public education; advocacy.

Periodicals: PEEReview (quarterly newsletter; tables of contents online).

Other Publications: White Papers (anonymous reports written and reviewed by public employees explaining environmental/resource issues or exposing alleged agency malfeasance; Executive Summaries available online); Employee Surveys (specific government agency surveys; summary results online).

Check Out on the Web: White Papers and Employee Surveys (see above).

Founded: 1992 **Coverage:** U.S. **Staff:** 7 **State/Regional Chapters:** 11 **NP Status:** 501(c)(3) **Budget:** $0.8 million

Revenue (FY00): Contributions (99%); Government Grants (0%); Program Service Revenues (0%); Other (1%).

Expenses (FY00): Program Services (77%; for: field offices –41%; membership –18%; "wise use" program –7%; employee defense –6%; fish and wildlife program –3%; coal project –1%; timber theft program –1%); Management and General (20%); Fundraising (3%).

Contact Info: 2001 S St. NW, Suite 570, Washington DC 20009; (202) 265-7337; info@peer.org

Key Personnel: Jeff Ruch (Executive Director)

101.   Public Interest Research Group (PIRG) (www.uspirg.org) – An "Earth Share" Charity

General Focus Areas: Multiple Focus Areas

Description/Mission: Research and advocacy organization focused on environmental preservation, consumer protection and government accountability issues. Originally started at the state-level in 1971, USPIRG was formed in 1983 to work on issues at the federal level. Also operates an Education Fund with a common Board of Directors.

Basic Activities: Investigative research; media exposes; grassroots organizing; advocacy; litigation.

Lobbying/Political Activities: Registered lobbyist under the LDA.

Programs (and focus areas): Environmental (Arctic wilderness protection; arsenic in drinking water; clean air; clean water; endangered species; energy; environmental protection; forests protection; global warming; "polluter pork"; Superfund; toxics and environmental health); Consumer Protection (various issues including genetically modified foods); Democracy/Open Government (voter participation; campaign finance reform); Higher Education.

Publications: A multitude of reports (all online).

Key Reports: Congressional Scorecard (annual report on Congressional members public interest voting records; online); Lethal Legacy (identifies nearly 600 "dirty" power plants; online); Polluters' Playground (examines facilities in "significant non-compliance" with their Clean Water Act permits; online); Green Scissors (annual report identifying environmentally harmful and wasteful government programs; online); A New Energy Future (energy policy blueprint; online).

Online Activist Tools: e-Activist (e-mailed Action Alerts).

Key Associated Website: State PIRGs (www.pirg.org; gateway to 26 separate state-level PIRGs; each state PIRG is independent and locally based, while working together and with USPIRG to share ideas and resources).

Check Out on the Web: Reports section (plenty of reports; all available online); the 26 state-level PIRG websites.

Founded: 1971 **Members:** 1 million **Coverage:** U.S. **NP Status:** USPIRG – 501(c)(4); USPIRG Ed Fund – 501(c)(3) **Budget (Ed Fund):** $2.5 million

Revenue (Ed Fund; FY00): Contributions (97%); Government Grants (0%); Program Service Revenues (0%); Other (3%).

Expenses (Ed Fund; FY00): Program Services (97%; for: environmental programs –74%; toxics right-to-know program –13%; regional programs –6%; open government program –2%; consumer education –2%); Management and General (2%); Fundraising (1%).

Contact Info: 218 D St. SE, Washington DC 20003; (202) 546-9707; uspirg@pirg.org

Key Personnel: Gene Karpinski (Executive Director)

---

102. **Rails-to-Trails Conservancy (RTC)** (www.railtrails.org) – **An "Earth Share" Charity**

General Focus Areas: Trail-Building

Description/Mission: Promotes conversion of abandoned rail corridors and connecting open spaces into a nationwide network of public trails (more than 1100 such "rail-trails" – spanning 11,000+ miles – already exist nationwide, with an additional 2400 rail-trail projects – spanning another 30,000 miles – currently in progress). Works with state/local agencies and groups in establishing the trails; RTC itself does not look to become a long-term owner or manger of the trails.

Basic Activities: Technical Assistance/Research; Outreach; Public Education; Policy/Advocacy; Litigation.

Lobbying/Political Activities: Registered lobbyist under the LDA.

Periodicals: Rails-to-Trails (quarterly magazine).

Other Publications: Guide books and directories.

Annual Report: 2000 report online.

Related Websites (all accessible from the RTC homepage): National Transportation Enhancements Clearinghouse (identifying federal funding sources); TrailLink.com (for finding recreational trails); Trails and Greenways Clearinghouse (offering technical assistance and resources for trail builders); Millennium Trails (pubic/private national trails initiative).

Founded: 1986 **Coverage:** U.S. **Members/Donors:** 100,000+ **Staff:** 50+ **State Field Offices:** 6 **NP Status:** 501(c)(3) **Budget:** $6 million

Revenue (FY00): Contributions (37%); Program Service Revenues (21%; from: consulting –14%; annual bike trip –4%; misc. –3%); Other (42%; from: membership dues –35%; misc. –7%).

Expenses (FY00): Program Services (81%; for: membership development –20%; direct project assistance/research –19%; field office outreach –19%; public information and education –14%; trail conservancy –5%; national policy program –4%); Management and General (7%); Fundraising (12%).

Contact Info: 1100 17th St. NW, 10th Floor, Washington DC 20036; (202) 331-9696; railtrails@transact.org

Key Personnel: David Burwell (President)

103.   Rainforest Action Network (RAN) (www.ran.org) – An "Earth Share" Charity

General Focus Areas: Conservation

Description/Mission: Focused on protecting rainforests and defending the rights of indigenous people. Known for its direct action efforts and corporation-focused campaigns.

Basic Activities: Education; grassroots organizing; non-violent direct action; grant making.

Programs (and activities/focus areas): Grassroots (informs and mobilizes a worldwide activist network of 150 local Rainforest Action Groups – RAGs); Protect-an-Acre (providing grants to organizations and communities in rainforest regions); Education (providing student and teacher information).

Campaigns: Old Growth (focus on logging by Boise Cascade); Citigroup (addressing the company's financial investments); U'wa (Occidental Petroleum drilling on the ancestral territory of the U'wa people in Columbia).

Periodicals: World Rainforest Report (bi-annual newsletter; online).

Other Publications: Various fact sheets and a couple of reports (all online).

Key Report: Drilling To The Ends Of The Earth: The Case Against New Fossil Fuel Exploration (online).

Annual Report: 2000 report online.

Activist Tools Online: Action Center (contents: action alerts [posted online and sent via email]; activist toolbox [media skills; fundraising skills; direct action tools]).

Associated Website: rainforestweb.org (world rainforest information portal with 1500+ links).

Founded: 1985 **Membership:** 15,000 **Coverage:** U.S./Int'l **Staff:** 28 **NP Status:** 501(c)(3) **Budget:** $3 million

Revenue (2000): Contributions (87%; includes: cash –73%; non-cash –14%); Government Grants (0%); Program Service Revenues (0%); Other (13%; from membership dues).

Expenses (2000): Program Services (77%; for: public education and membership –57%; grassroots campaigning and community organizing –20%); Management and General (12%); Fundraising (11%).

Contact Info: 221 Pine St., Suite 500, San Francisco, CA 94104; (415) 398-4404; rainforest@ran.org

Key Personnel: Randall Hayes (President); Christopher Hatch (Executive Director)

104.   Rainforest Alliance (www.rainforest-alliance.org) – An "Earth Share" Charity

General Focus Areas: Conservation

Description/Mission: Seeks to conserve tropic forests via development/promotion of economically viable and socially desirable alternatives to destruction.

Basic Activities: Education; communications; research; product certification; partnerships with businesses, governments, and local peoples; grant-making.

Programs (and activities/focus areas): Allies in the Rainforest (local fundraising for specific rainforest projects); Catalyst Grants (grants to local rainforest-based conservation groups); Conservation Agriculture Network (certification of "environmentally-sound" agricultural products); Conservation Media Center (tropical conservation news hub for Latin America, based in Costa Rica); SmartWood Certification (timber certified as coming from sustainably-managed forests), SmartVoyager (certifies "responsibly-managed" tour boats in the Galapagos Islands); Research Projects and Fellowships.

Periodicals: The Canopy (bi-monthly newsletter; feature article online), Eco-Exchange (bi-monthly newsletter on neotropical conservation; online); Rainforest Matters (bi-monthly email newsletter; online).

Annual Report: 2000 report online.

Associated Website: Eco-Index (www.eco-index.org, searchable almanac of current and past conservation projects in Mesoamerica).

Check Out on the Web: Both the "Resources/Facts" and "For Kids and Teachers" sections.

Founded: 1986 **Members/Supporters:** 14,000 **Coverage:** U.S./Int'l **Staff:** 40 **NP Status:** 501(c)(3) **Budget:** $4 million

Revenue (FY00): Contributions (58%); Government Grants (1%); Program Service Revenues (32%; from: wood certification review fees –31%; misc. –1%); Other (9%).

Expenses (FY00): Program Services (80%; for: smart wood certification project –45%; conservation agriculture network/ "eco-OK" project –13%; communications –12%; special projects –4%; conservation media center –3%; catalysts grants program –2%; natural resources and rights program –1%); Management and General (3%); Fundraising (17%).

Contact Info: 65 Bleecker St., New York, NY 10012; (212) 677-1900; canopy@ra.org

Key Personnel: Tensie Whelan (Executive Director)

105. Redefining Progress (www.rprogress.org)

General Focus Areas: Economics

Description/Mission: Economics-focused organization that: 1) offers alternative means of measuring "progress" (particularly via its "Genuine Progress Indicator," offered as an alternative to use of Gross Domestic Product–GDP), 2) identifies and promotes market-based environmental policies to promote sustainability and social equity.

Basic Activities: Research; public education; policy/advocacy; outreach and technical assistance.

Programs (and focus areas): Accurate Prices (environmental tax reform); Climate Change Justice (equitable and low-cost climate protection; climate change and environmental justice); Common Assets (revitalizing common assets like schools, housing, transportation and parks); Sustainability (examining "ecological deficit spending").

Projects (and activities/focus areas): Community Indicators Project (working with 200 community-based groups to develop local indicators/benchmarks of "progress"); Ecological Footprint (measures what nations and households consume of nature); Genuine Progress Indicator (alternative means of measuring "progress" that incorporates environmental sustainability and social equity along with economic growth; offered as an alternative to use of Gross Domestic Product–GDP).

Publications: Various reports and backgrounders (most online).

Key Reports: Tax Waste, Not Work (proposes a revenue-neutral tax shift to resource taxes or emission permits; summary online); Genuine Progress Report (annual report based on RP's Genuine Progress Indicator; online).

Check Out on the Web: Ecological Footprint section (calculate your own; view national footprints).

Founded: 1994 **Coverage:** U.S. **Staff:** 15 **NP Status:** 501(c)(3) **Budget:** $1 million

Revenue (FY00): Contributions (91%); Government Grants (0%); Program Service Revenues (7%); Other (3%).

Expenses (FY00): Program Services (77%; for: accurate prices program –38%; indicators program –37%; climate change justice project –2%); Management and General (15%); Fundraising (8%).

Contact Info: 1904 Franklin St., 6th Floor, Oakland, CA 94612; (510) 444-3041; info@rprogress.org

Key Personnel: Michel Gelobter (Executive Director)

Renewable Energy Policy Project (REPP)

See Profile #22 for the "Center for Renewable Energy and Sustainable Technology (CREST)," located within this subsection.

REP America/ Republicans for Environmental Protection (www.repamerica.org)

See Profile #317, located within Subsection 4.2 – "Other Political Groups.".

106. Resource Renewal Institute (RRI) (www.rri.org)

General Focus Areas: Sustainable Development

Description/Mission: Advocates development and use of state and national "Green Plans" (comprehensive, integrated, long-term environmental management strategies designed to achieve sustainability) modeled on those of the Netherlands and New Zealand. Acts as a clearinghouse for information on Green Plans.

Basic Activities: Education/Outreach; Advocacy; Analysis.

Key Programs (and activities/focus areas): States Campaign (promote development/implementation of state-level Green Plans); Green Plan Leadership Program / "Seeing is Believing" Tours (educate/inspire key leaders); Green Plan Center (information clearinghouse).

Periodicals: The International Green Planner (semi-annual newsletter; online).

Other Publications: A couple of books and reports/papers (some online).

Key Publication: Green Plans: A Primer (online).

Annual Report: 1999 report online.

Check Out on the Web: "Best Practices" section (comprised of: Environmental Atlas, providing comprehensive summaries of environmental policies/agencies/organizations in the U.S., E.U. and other selected nations; Case Studies, covering 3 U.S. states and 11 foreign countries; "State of the Environment" Reports, a database of U.S. state-level "State of the Environment" Reports).

Founded: 1985 **Coverage:** U.S./Int'l **Staff:** 15 **NP Status:** 501(c)(3) **Budget:** $0.9 million

Revenue (2000): Contributions (93%); Government Grants (0%); Program Service Revenues (6%); Other (1%).

Expenses (2000): Program Services (73%; for: states campaign program –22%; green plan leadership program – 12%; green plan center –7%; other green plan projects –23%; subsidiary projects –9%); Management and General (14%); Fundraising (12%).

Contact Info: Pier 1, Fort Mason Center, San Francisco, CA 94123; (415) 928-3774; info@rri.org

Key Personnel: Huey Johnson (President)

107.   River Network (www.rivernetwork.org)

General Focus Areas: Conservation

Slogan: "Helping people understand, protect and restore rivers and their watersheds."

Description/Mission: Two-pronged effort: 1) support 500+ grassroots river conservation groups and link them into a national movement ("Watershed Program" – see below for details) and 2) acquire/protect key riverlands – 40,000 acres so far – from private landholders including corporations, utilities and families ("River Conservancy" program). Merged with the River Watch Network in 10/99.

Basic Activities: Acquire key riverlands; technical assistance/consultation; training; information dissemination; financial assistance.

Assistance Offered: Workshops/Training; Publications; Consultation; 1-800 Resource Line; River Rally (annual activist event); Partnership Program; Resource Library; Grants; Directory of River Groups; Case Studies; Ask Our Staff.

Watershed Programs (and activities/focus areas): River Source Center (information clearinghouse); River Watch (watershed monitoring); Organizational Development (help establish and build watershed conservation groups/programs); River Protection and Restoration Tools (education/assistance on techniques, programs and laws); Networking.

Periodicals: Streamlines (general newsletter); River Voices (quarterly newsletter for partner groups); Volunteer Monitor (bi-annual newsletter for volunteer monitoring groups).

Other Publications: Various books/directories (geared towards helping other river groups).

Key Publications: River and Watershed Conservation Directory (annual; lists 3700+ grassroots river and watershed conservation groups, local agencies, and governments; searchable database available online); Directory of Funding Sources for Grassroots River and Watershed Conservation Groups (annual; lists 300+ private, corporate and federal funding sources; searchable database available online).

Annual Report: 1999 report online.

Activist Tools Online: Resource Library (hundreds of resources for river and watershed activists); Directory of River Groups; Funding Sources.

Check Out on the Web: 'Resource Library" – that's where it's all at!

Founded: 1988 **Coverage:** U.S. **Staff:** 34 **Offices:** 4 **NP Status:** 501(c)(3) **Budget:** $5 million

Revenue (FY00): Contributions (90%; includes: cash –67%; gifts of land –23%); Government Grants (6%); Program Service Revenues (1%); Other (3%).

Expenses (FY00): Program Services (88%; for: river conservancy program –49%; watershed program –39%); Management and General (6%); Fundraising (6%).

Contact Info: 520 SW 6th Ave., Suite 1130, Portland, OR 97204; (503) 241-3506; info@rivernetwork.org

Key Personnel: Ken Margolis (President)

108. Rocky Mountain Elk Foundation (RMEF) (www.rmef.org)

General Focus Areas: Conservation

Description/Mission: Wildlife habitat conservation group focused on North American elk. Has enhanced and/or protected 3+ million acres of wildlife habitat throughout the U.S. and Canada, including via land acquisition (with 40,000 acres acquired in 2000) and nearly 3000 conservation projects. While focused on conservation, the Foundation also "strongly supports hunting practiced in a legal, responsible and ethical manner."

Basic Activities: Conservation projects; land acquisition; public education.

Programs/Projects (and focus areas): Land Program (land acquisitions; conservation easements; real estate donations; contributions/cooperative participation/land exchanges); Conservation Projects (habitat enhancements; wildlife management; hunter education; conservation education).

Key Initiative: Pass It On Campaign (5-year effort to raise $250 million for conservation and enhancement of another 2 million acres of "elk country").

Periodicals: Bugle (bi-monthly; partially online); Wild Outdoor World (bi-monthly kid's magazine).

Annual Report: 2000 report online.

Founded: 1984 **Members:** 120,000 **Coverage:** N. America **Local Chapters:** 500+ **NP Status:** 501(c)(3) **Budget:** $30 million

Revenue (2000): Cash Donations (44%); Conservation Easements (29%); Special Events and Subscription Revenue (15%; includes local "Big Game Banquets"); Land Sales (9%); Merchandise Sales (3%).

Expenses (2000): Program Services (86%; for: landscapes program –56%; learning about wildlife program – 11%; elk futures program –9%; membership services –10%); Management and General (9%); Fundraising (5%).

Contact Info: PO Box 8249, 2291 W. Broadway, Missoula, MT 59807; (406) 523-4500; info@elkfoundation.org

Key Personnel: Rich Lane (President/CEO)

109. Rocky Mountain Institute (RMI) (www.rmi.org) – An "Earth Share" Charity

General Focus Areas: Multiple Focus Areas

Slogan: "Vision across boundaries."

Description: A market-oriented, applied research and consulting organization which brings a business and science/technology-based perspective in dealing with relevant resource issues. A common focus is in improving efficiency and eliminating waste. Activities increasingly based on the book "Nature Capitalism" – co-written by RMI co-founders Hunter and Amory Lovins – which promotes an environmentally-friendly business model. Also known for promoting "Hypercars" ® (super-clean/efficient cars); has spun off Hypercar, Inc. to produce such cars. Also manages the Windstar Land Conservancy as a demo lab for restorative land-management techniques.

Basic Activities: Research; Consulting; Education and Outreach.

Key Programs (and focus areas): Energy (energy efficiency; hydrogen/fuel cell technology); Water (efficient use); Climate (promoting market-based measures to reduce greenhouse-gas emissions); Buildings and Land Development (green development; home resource efficiency); Transportation ("Hypercars" – super-clean/efficient cars); Business Practices ("natural capitalism" – an environmentally-friendly business model); Communities ("economic renewal" – growing sustainably).

Periodicals: RMI Solutions (tri-annual newsletter; online).

Other Publications: Various books, reports, articles, etc. (most online).

Key Publications (books): Natural Capitalism (promoting an environmentally-friendly business model; online); The Economic Renewal Guide (toolkit for communities to achieve sustainable economic development; partially online); Brittle Power: Energy Strategy for National Security (examines vulnerability of U.S. energy systems to attack/disaster; online).

Key Publications (non-books): A Strategy for Hydrogen Transition (using fuel cells for energy generation; online); Climate: Making Sense and Making Money (argues that the global climate can be protected not at a cost but at a profit; online).

Annual Report: 2000-01 report online.

Associated Websites: Hypercar, Inc. (focuses on commercial production of super-clean/efficient cars; www.hypercar.com); Natural Capitalism (focuses on the book, which is made available online; www.natcap.org)

Check Out on the Web: Home Resource Efficiency (compendium of information on how to increase a home's efficiency; located under "Buildings and Land"); Home Energy Briefs (practical household energy tips; located in the "Library" under "Energy").

Founded: 1982 **Coverage:** U.S./Int'l **Staff:** 55 **NP Status:** 501(c)(3) **Budget:** $5 million

Revenue (2000): Contributions (41%); Government Grants (0%); Program Service Revenues (42%; from: consulting fees –39%; misc. –2%); Other (17%; from investment income).

Expenses (2000): Program Services (79%); Management and General (14%); Fundraising (7%).

Contact Info: 1739 Snowmass Creek Road, Snowmass, CO 81654; (970) 927-3851; outreach@rmi.org

Key Personnel: Amory B. Lovins (Research CEO); L. Hunter Lovins (Strategy CEO)

110. **Safe Energy Communication Council (SECC) (www.safeenergy.org) – An "Earth Share" Charity**

General Focus Areas: Energy

Description/Mission: Coalition of 10 national energy, environmental and media public interest groups promoting energy efficiency and renewable energy policies while simultaneously identifying the liabilities of nuclear power. Focuses on empowering grassroots activists through media training, technical assistance, and information dissemination.

Key Coalition Members (see separate profiles for each within this subsection): Friends of the Earth; Greenpeace; Sierra Club; Public Interest Research Group.

Basic Activities: Communications; outreach; education/organizing; workshops and technical assistance.

Programs (and activities/focus areas): Media Training (workshops and training sessions); Wildlife Project (examining nuclear power related effects on marine wildlife and ocean habitat); Power Boosters (publicizing energy efficiency success stories); Nuclear Waste Reprocessing (seeking to discourage plutonium disposition via reprocessing and use of mixed-oxide fuel); Responding to Nuclear Advertising (countering the nuclear industry's public relations and advertising claims); Electric Utility Restructuring Program (seeking to insure full accountability of the economic and environmental liabilities of nuclear power in a restructured electric market).

Publications: A few reports (available at a nominal cost).

Founded: 1980 **Coverage:** U.S. **Staff:** 7 **NP Status:** 501(c)(3) **Budget:** $0.6 million

Revenue (2000): Contributions (89%); Government Grants (8%); Program Service Revenues (1%); Other (2%).

Expenses (2000): Program Services (84%; for: education/organizing –32%; communications –21%; outreach –18%; workshops and technical assistance –12%); Management and General (12%); Fundraising (4%).

Contact Info: 1717 Massachusetts Ave. NW, Suite 106, Washington, DC 20036; (202) 483-8491; safeenergy@erols.com

Key Personnel: Scott Denman (Executive Director)

111. **Save Our Environment Action Center (www.saveourenvironment.org)**

General Focus Areas: Action Alert Center

Slogan: "A national partnership for the environment."

Description/Mission: An internet-based action center run collaboratively by 19 of the nation's largest environmental/conservation advocacy groups. Seeks to increase public awareness and activism on key environmental/conservation issues.

Basic Activities: Public awareness and education; advocacy/activism.

Campaigns (and focus areas): National Energy Policy; Wild Forests (roadless area conservation rule); Bush Administration's Environmental Rollbacks; Global Warming (regulate greenhouse gas emissions).

Online Activist Tools: Action Center (posted action alerts for the campaigns cited above).

Coverage: U.S.

Contact Info: info@saveourenvironment.org

112. **Save The Redwoods League** (www.savetheredwoods.org)

General Focus Areas: Conservation

Description/Mission: Seeks to preserve the redwood forests of California by purchasing such lands and turning them over to public parks or reserves. Since 1918, the League's members have donated $150+ million for the purchase and protection of 130,000+ acres of redwood forest. The League has assisted in acquisition of 60% of the total acreage in California's 37 Redwood Parks. Also conducts redwoods-associated research and education activities. For FY00, purchased nearly 4800 acres of redwood forests.

Basic Activities: Land acquisition and preservation; research and education; grant-making.

Programs: Redwood Land Purchase; Tree Planting; Memorial and Honor Groves; Education and Research Activities (including grant-making).

Periodicals: Redwoods Bulletin (bi-annual bulletin; online).

Other Publications: A couple of booklets about redwoods (available at a nominal cost).

Biennial Report: 1999-2000 online.

Founded: 1918 **Coverage:** U.S. **Staff:** 12 **NP Status:** 501(c)(3) **Budget:** $15 million

Revenue (FY00): Contributions (73%; includes: cash –40%; gifts of land –33%); Government Grants (18%); Program Service Revenues (<1%); Other (9%).

Expenses (FY00): Program Services (84%; for land purchase and other land preservation activities); Management and General (8%); Fundraising (8%).

Contact Info: 114 Sansome St., Suite 1200, San Francisco, CA 94104; (415) 362-2352; info@savetheredwoods.org

Key Personnel: Katherine Anderton (Executive Director)

113. **Scenic America** (www.scenic.org) – **An "Earth Share" Charity**

General Focus Areas: Scenic Conservation

Slogan: "Change is inevitable; ugliness is not."

Description/Mission: Promotes "scenic conservation" (preserving/enhancing the scenic character of America's communities and countryside) with a primary goal of building a citizens movement for such conservation. Seeks to reduce "visual pollution" (such as billboards and signs) and works on related issues such as land use and community and highway design. Principal focus is on helping citizens on state and local issues through its two general programs (see below).

Basic Activities: Public education and communication; technical assistance; policy/advocacy.

Lobbying/Political Activities: Registered lobbyist under the LDA.

General Programs: Resource Center (provides free assistance to 700 communities annually); Affiliate Development Program (seeks to create a network of state/local scenic conservation groups).

Projects/Issues: Billboard and Sign Control; Community Design; Context-Sensitive Highway Design; Scenic Byways (designation and protection of scenic roads); Smart Growth; Tree Conservation; Wireless Telecommunications Tower Siting; Scenic View Protection.

Periodicals: Viewpoints (tri-annual newsletter; online); Grassroots Advocate (summary of state/local efforts; 9 times/yr; online).

Other Publications: Various reports, technical bulletins, action guides, and "Facts for Action" (some online, especially the "Facts for Action").

Key Reports: Last Chance Landscapes (annual list of key national landscapes with both a pending threat and a potential solution; online); Federal Laws Scenic Report Card (evaluates federal laws relating to scenic conservation).

Online Activist Tools: Action Center (posted action alerts concerning the projects/issues cited above).

Check Out on the Web: "Photo Gallery" (photos designed to expose "the hypocrisy of the billboard industry").

Founded: 1978 **Coverage:** U.S. **Staff:** 10 **Affiliated State-Level Programs:** 9 **NP Status:** 501(c)(3) **Budget:** $1 million

Revenue (FY01): Contributions (91%); Government Grants (0%); Program Service Revenues (4%); Other (5%).

Expenses (FY01): Program Services (78%; for: Resource Center –22%; general program and technical assistance –20%; special projects –16%; public policy –12%; press and public information –8%; lobbying –<1%); Management and General (11%); Fundraising (11%).

Contact Info: 801 Pennsylvania Ave. SE, Suite 300, Washington, DC 20003; (202) 543-6200; webmaster@scenic.org

Key Personnel: Meg Maguire (President)

114.　SeaWeb (www.seaweb.org)

General Focus Areas: Conservation

Description/Mission: Seeks to advance ocean conservation via public education efforts.

Basic Activities: Information dissemination; public education; scientific and policy research; advocacy.

Key Programs: Aquaculture Clearinghouse (information clearinghouse on salmon-related aquaculture issues; see below for online contents); Compass (seeks to stimulate/enhance ties between marine science and conservation policy).

Key Issues: Overfishing; Marine Reserves; Sustainable Seafood Consumption; Aquaculture.

Campaigns: Sturgeon Protection; Swordfish Overfishing.

Periodicals: Ocean Update (monthly newsletter; online).

Aquaculture Clearinghouse Online Contents: Issue Papers; Background Reports; Policy and Regulation; Bibliography; News and Info.

Check Out on the Web: Ocean Briefing Book (overview and synthesis of specific issues); Ocean Citations (selected scientific research citations on ocean issues).

Founded: 1995 **Coverage:** U.S./Int'l **Staff:** 12 **NP Status:** 501(c)(3) **Budget:** $2.5 million

Revenue (FY00): Contributions (99%); Government Grants (0%); Program Service Revenues (0%); Other (<1%).

Expenses (FY00): Program Services (82%; for: North Atlantic swordfish campaign –23%; Compass marine science program –14%; communications –12%; aquaculture clearinghouse –9%; marine sanctuaries program –7%; Latin America program –5%; consumer marketing program –5%; aquarium network –4%; coral reefs program –4%); Management and General (18%); Fundraising (0%).

Contact Info: 1731 Connecticut Ave. NW, 4th Floor, Washington, DC 20009; (202) 483-9570; seaweb@seaweb.org

Key Personnel: Vikki Spruill (Executive Director)

115.　Sierra Club ® (www.sierraclub.org) – An "Earth Share" Charity

General Focus Areas: Multiple Focus Areas

A Top Federal Lobbying Group Per Fortune Magazine's Annual Survey: Ranking for 2001: #52

Slogan: "Explore, enjoy and protect the planet."®

Description/Mission: Multi-faceted environmental advocacy organization founded by John Muir. Known for its club outings (which includes wilderness trips, both national/international, and local chapter/group outings). Also operates the Sierra Student Coalition, a national, student-run grassroots activist network (see Profile #145, located within Subsection 1.4 – "Student- and Education-Oriented Groups"). Financially supported through the Sierra Club Foundation, an environmental grant-making foundation.

Basic Activities: Policy/legislation; advocacy; litigation; public education; wilderness outings.

Lobbying/Political Activities: Registered lobbyist under the LDA; maintains a PAC (Sierra Club Political Committee).

Priority Issues/Campaigns: Energy; Free Trade; Global Warming; Human Rights and the Environment (including international right-to-know); Global Population and the Environment; Logging (seeks an end to commercial logging in National Forests); Sprawl; Water (focus on: factory farms; wetlands; water quality); Wildlands (a campaign to protect 100 million acres of "wild America").

Periodicals: Sierra (bi-monthly magazine; online); Sierra Club Currents (bi-weekly activist news bulletin; online); The Plane (monthly activist newsletter; online).

Other Publications: Various issue-specific reports, articles and fact sheets (all online).

Key Publications (all online): Sprawl Reports (a continuing series of reports – 5 thus far – on sprawl impacts and solutions); Seeing the Forests for Their Green (details the economic benefits of forest protection, recreation and restoration); SPARE America's Wildlands (a blueprint for the Club's wildlands protection campaign).

Annual Report: 2000 report online for the Sierra Club Foundation.

Online Activist Tools: Take Action section (contents: action alerts [posted online and sent via email]; letter writing tips; congress contact information).

Check Out on the Web: Inner City Outings (provides low-income, inner city youth with trips to the wilderness); Environmental 911 Program (for obtaining information to address local environmental issues – call 415-977-5520 or e-mail at environmental911@sierraclub.org); John Muir Exhibit (an extensive tribute to the Club's founder).

Website Notes: Site provides individual state-level pages for all 50 states plus DC and Canada.

Founded: 1892 **Members:** 700,000 **Coverage:** U.S./Int'l **State Chapters:** 50 **Field Offices:** 26 **NP Status:** SC – 501(c)(4); SC Foundation – 501(c)(3) **Budget (SC Foundation):** $45 million

Revenue (SC Foundation; 2000): Contributions (96%; includes: cash –28%; non-cash –68%); Government Grants (0%); Program Service Revenues (0%); Other (4%).

Expenses (SC Foundation; 2000): Program Services (91%; for: direct grants to the SC –59%; other grants – 32%); Management and General (3%); Fundraising (6%).

Contact Info (Sierra Club): 85 2nd St., 2nd Floor, San Francisco, CA 94105; (415) 977-5500; information@sierraclub.org

Contact Info (Sierra Club Foundation): 85 2nd St., Suite 750; San Francisco, CA 94105; (415) 995-1780; sierraclub.foundation@sierraclub.org

Key Personnel: Carl Pope (Executive Director – SC); John DeCock (Executive Director – SC Foundation)

116.   Smart Growth Network (SGN) (www.smartgrowth.org)

General Focus Areas: Sprawl/Smart Growth

Slogan: "Development that serves economy, community and environment."

Description/Mission: Creating/aiding national, regional, and local coalitions to encourage metropolitan development that is environmentally, fiscally, economically, and socially "smart." Focused on acting as an information clearinghouse and building partnerships; not an advocacy organization. Partners with 24 governmental and public interest groups.

Organizational Structure: Organizational home – International City/County Management Association (see Profile #255, located within Subsection 2.3 – "Governmental Associations and Councils"); coordinated by the USEPA's Division of Development, Community and Environment; website maintained by the Sustainable Communities Network (see Profile #121, located within this subsection).

Basic Activities: Education/outreach; technical assistance; research.

Key Resources Provided: Tool Catalogue (covers: general tools; brownfields and infill redevelopment; financing and fiscal analysis; green building and industrial ecology); Bibliographies; Presentations; Library (contents: document index; case studies; PDF index; bibliographies/bibliography database); Bookstore (SGN member publications).

Issues (and focus areas): Buildings (green construction; demolition and waste management); Community; Economics (quality of life and of place); Environment (air quality; water quality; open space); Financing ("smart" real estate financing); Fiscal Impacts (residential land use; non-residential land use; location and density); Implementation (smart growth policy database); Infrastructure (water supply, waste and conservation; solid waste reduction and recycling; roads, highways and public transit; using existing infrastructure); Land Use (development patterns; leveraging growth; alternatives); Redevelopment (reducing public costs and increasing private returns; saving natural resources; creating better access; preserving a sense of place); Regionalism (metropolitan expansion; regional cooperation); Transportation.

Periodicals: Getting Smart! (bimonthly newsletter).

Other Publications: Articles, case studies, fact sheets, guidebooks and reports (obtained from various sources; all online).

Check Out on the Web: Issue Area Overviews (concise summaries of key issue areas, along with relevant online resources); Smart Growth State by State (state-level issue tracking).

Coverage: U.S.

Contact Info: (202) 328-8160; info@smartgrowth.org

117. Sprawl Watch Clearinghouse (www.sprawlwatch.org)

General Focus Areas: Sprawl/Smart Growth

Description/Mission: Collect and disseminate information on land use practices designed to manage growth.

Basic Activities: Information dissemination; public education; research.

Key Resources Provided: Resources (books, reports, articles, and organizations, listed by category, namely: cities; demographic trends; economy; environment; equity; farmlands; historic preservation; housing; public policies; suburbia; superstore sprawl and small town decline; public health; religious community; transportation; who's involved with smart growth); In the States (state-specific resources); Best Practices (to revitalize cities and arrest sprawl); Policy (federal and state); Communications.

Periodicals: Sprawl Watch (bi-monthly newsletter; online).

Other Publications: Various books, reports and articles obtained from various sources.

Online Activist Tools: What You Can Do section (general strategies to stem sprawl and promote smart growth).

Check Out on the Web: "Communications" section, providing: "Backgrounder on Pro-Sprawl Players and Messages," "Myth and Fact Soundbites," and "Research on Pro-Sprawl Players and Messages."

Founded: 1998 **Coverage:** U.S. **Staff:** 3

Public Support Sources: Foundations.

Contact Info: 1400 16th St. NW, Suite 225, Washington, DC 20036; (202) 332-7000; allison@sprawlwatch.org

Key Personnel: Allison Smiley (Executive Director)

118. Strategies for the Global Environment (no web site)

General Focus Areas: Global Issues

Description/Mission: Umbrella organization for both the Pew Center on Global Climate Change and the Pew Oceans Commission (see Profiles #92 and 93, respectively, both located within this subsection).

Coverage: Global **NP Status:** 501(c)(3) **Budget:** $6 million

Revenue (2000): Contributions (97%); Government Grants (0%); Program Service Revenues (<1%); Other (2%).

Expenses (2000): Program Services (94%; for: domestic and international policy on global climate change –44%; education/outreach on global climate change –25%; Pew Oceans Commission –23%; innovative business solutions addressing global climate change –2%); Management and General (5%); Fundraising (1%).

Contact Info: 2101 Wilson Blvd., Suite 550, Arlington, VA 22201; (703) 516-4146.

Key Personnel: Eileen Claussen (President)

119. Surface Transportation Policy Project (STPP) (www.transact.org)

General Focus Areas: Transportation

Description/Mission: Nationwide network of 250+ organizations seeking to improve the nation's transportation system, emphasizing the needs of people rather than vehicles. Also operates a California-specific program.

Basic Activities: Public education; policy research/analysis; advocacy.

Key National Programs: Policy Project (leading the National Smart Growth Coalition to develop federal policy on smart growth and transportation related issues); Quality of Life Campaign (promoting transportation policy reform via public education and work with local activists); New Directions Initiative (seeking to shift control of transportation funding to local communities)

Periodicals: Progress (bimonthly newsletter; online); Transfer (biweekly electronic news bulletin; online).

Other Publications: Various reports (many online).

Online Activist Tools: Advocate's Toolbox (contents: using data and information; effective programs; generating media for your issue; other useful tools).

Check Out on the Web: "Quality of Life" publications addressing practical, real-world issues including: Road Rage; Road Construction Trade-Offs; Pedestrian Safety; "High Mileage Moms;" Sprawl-Congestion Connection.

Coverage: U.S. **NP Status:** 501(c)(3) **Budget:** $2 million

Revenue (FY00): Contributions (77%); Government Grants (0%); Program Service Revenues (17%; from: government fees/contracts –9%; contracts with other NGOs –8%); Other (6%).

Expenses (FY00): Program Services (99%; for: California campaign –33%; policy project –22%; network/MIS – 11%; quality of life campaign –10%; smart growth –9%; access program –4%; DC campaign –2%; other misc. programs –9%); Management and General (<1%); Fundraising (0%).

Contact Info: 1100 17th St. NW, 10th Floor, Washington, DC 20036; (202) 466-2636; stpp@transact.org

Key Personnel: David Burwell (President/CEO)

120.   **Surfrider Foundation (**www.surfrider.org**) – An "Earth Share" Charity**

General Focus Areas: Conservation; Pollution

Description/Mission: Focused on coastal protection, working primarily on a grassroots, local community level. Operates in Japan, Brazil, France and Australia as well as the U.S. Originally founded by surfers and maintains a strong connection with surfing and popular culture.

Basic Activities: Conservation; Advocacy/Activism; Research; Education.

Key Programs (and focus areas): Respect the Beach (K-12 environmental education modules); Blue Water Task Force (coastal water testing and monitoring); Beachscape (document/map coastal resources); Clean Water (address non-point source pollution); Surf Site Stewardship (preserve surf bioregions); Snowrider Project (environmental education for "snow-riders").

Periodicals: Making Waves (bi-monthly magazine; online); Surfrider Chapter News (bi-monthly newsletter; online).

Key Report: State of the Beach (annual report summarizing the health of U.S. beaches; online).

Unique: Music for Our Mother Ocean (MOM) (music CDs made to benefit Surfrider).

Online Activist Tools: Legislative Updates and Action Alerts (posted online).

Founded: 1984 **Members:** 27,000 **Coverage:** U.S./Int'l **Staff:** 17 **Chapters:** 50+ **NP Status:** 501(c)(3) **Budget:** $2 million

Revenue (2000): Contributions (61%); Government Grants (0%); Program Service Revenues (1%); Other (38%; from: membership dues –31%; sales of inventory –6%; misc. –1%).

Expenses (2000): Program Services (89%; for: environmental activism; educational programs); Management and General (7%); Fundraising (4%).

IRS Form 990: 1999 online.

Contact Info: 122 S. El Camino Real, PMB #67, San Clemente, CA 92672; (949) 492-8170; info@surfrider.org

Key Personnel: Christopher Evans (Executive Director)

121.   **Sustainable Communities Network (SCN) (**www.sustainable.org**)**

General Focus Areas: Sustainable Development

Slogan: "Linking citizens to resources and to one another to create healthy, vital, sustainable communities."

Description/Mission: Online information network promoting sustainable communities. Directed by Concern Inc. (see Profile #33, located within this subsection) in partnership with 16 other organizations.

Basic Activities: Information dissemination.

Resources Provided: Links, readings, and case studies divided into the following gateways: Creating Community; Smart Growth; Growing a Sustainable Economy; Protecting Natural Resources; Governing Sustainably; Living Sustainably.

Publications: Various documents obtained from various sources (many online).

Founded: 1993 **Coverage:** U.S./Int'l **Staff:** 2 **NP Status:** 501(c)(3) **Financial Information:** See Profile #33 for "Concern, Inc.," located within this subsection.

Contact Info (c/o Concern, Inc.): 1794 Columbia Road NW, Suite 6, Washington, DC 20009; concern@concern.org

Key Personnel: Susan Boyd (Director)

122.   Teaming With Wildlife (TWW) (www.teaming.com)

General Focus Areas: Conservation

Slogan: "A natural investment."

Description/Mission: National campaign to secure funding for state-level non-game wildlife conservation and related education and recreation programs. 3,000+ organizations and businesses have endorsed TWW, including all 50 state and wildlife agencies. TWW is run by a 10-member Steering Committee consisting of various wildlife conservation groups, along with the International Association of Fish and Wildlife Agencies (see Profile #271, located within Subsection 2.3 – "Governmental Associations and Councils"), which also owns and operates TWW's website.

A Closer Look: TWW's originally proposed funding mechanism involves extending the existing user fee on hunting and fishing gear to additional outdoor gear. However, TWW also supports the proposed Conservation and Reinvestment Act (CARA), which would dedicate a portion of federal income from offshore oil and natural gas leases for a variety of purposes, including the goals of TWW.

Basic Activities: Public education; legislation/advocacy.

Key Report: State Wildlife Diversity Program Funding: A 1998 Survey (online).

Online Activist Tools: Action Alert (contents: sample faxes; contact Senate/House/President; action kit).

Check Out on the Web: Fast Facts (a summary of why CARA is needed; online under "Press Kit").

Coverage: U.S.

Contact Info: c/o International Association of Fish and Wildlife Agencies, 444 N. Capitol St. NW, Suite 544, Washington DC, 20001; (202) 624-7890; teaming@sso.org

123.   Tides Center (www.tides.org)

General Focus Areas: Activism Support and Training

Slogan: "Strengthening resources for change."

Description/Mission: Provides a fiscal home and infrastructure support to new/emerging charitable organizations not incorporated as a nonprofit. As a 501(c)(3) exempt nonprofit itself, the Tides Center serves as the incorporated structure for accepted organizations, referred to as "Tide Projects." In 1999, the Center served as the home for 350 projects working in 40 states and 12 countries. The Center itself is part of the "Tides family" – a group of nonprofit orgs committed to positive social change, innovation, and environmental sustainability.

Basic Activities: NGO support (fiscal and infrastructure support).

Key Tides-Sponsored Orgs (see Profiles #37 and #65, respectively, both located within this subsection): CorpWatch.org; Institute for Global Communications (IGC Internet).

Founded: 1996 **Coverage:** U.S./Int'l **NP Status:** 501(c)(3) **Budget:** $45 million

Revenue (1999): Contributions (80%); Government Grants (3%); Program Service Revenues (14%; from fees to administer public education programs for Center projects); Other (3%).

Expenses (1999): Program Services (91%); Management and General (9%); Fundraising (0%).

Contact Info: PO Box 29907, Presidio Building 1014, San Francisco, CA 94129; (415) 561-6300.

Key Personnel: Drummond Pike (President); David Salniker (Executive Director)

124.   Trout Unlimited (TU) (www.tu.org)

General Focus Areas: Conservation

Description/Mission: Focused on conservation, protection and restoration of North American trout and salmon coldwater fisheries and their watersheds.

Basic Activities: Conservation and restoration; scientific research; policy/advocacy; public education and communications.

Lobbying/Political Activities: Registered lobbyist under the LDA.

2001 National Conservation Agenda (and focus areas): Water Quality (polluted runoff/Clean Water Act; acid mine drainage; home rivers initiative; acid rain; habitat loss from hard-rock mining; federal lands; local land use/development; land exchange impacts); In-Stream Flows (FERC re-licensing; non-FERC hydropower management; water programs; small dam removal); Pacific and Atlantic Salmon Recovery; Wild Salmonid Conservation.

Key Operating Programs (and activities): Coldwater Conservation Fund (funding projects linking scientific and economic research/analysis to practical applications in watershed management; $1+ million budget); Embrace-A-Stream (matching grants program awarding $270,000 of funds to TU chapters/councils for fisheries conservation projects).

Priority Campaigns: Snake River Salmon; Acid Rain; Atlantic Salmon; Small Dam Removal; Western Water Project (water for trout and salmon).

Periodicals: Trout (quarterly magazine; partially online); Lines to Leaders (monthly newsletter; online).

Other Publications: Various reports (all online under "Conservation Library").

Annual Report: 2000 report online.

Online Activist Tools: Trout Action (contents: action alerts [sent via email]; legislative action center [action alerts; elected officials; issues and legislation; media guide; congress today]; advice on effective advocacy).

Unique: Operates Trout Unlimited TV – a TV series providing "adventures in angling and conservation," shown on ESPN/ESPN2.

Founded: 1959 **Membership:** 125,000 **Coverage:** N. America **Staff:** 45 **State/Local Chapters:** 500 **NP Status:** 501(c)(3) **Budget:** $8 million

Revenue (FY00): Contributions (53%); Government Grants (<1%); Program Service Revenues (2%); Other (45%; from: membership dues –39%; misc. –6%).

Expenses (FY00): Program Services (75%; for: resources department –23%; regional support –21%; member/chapter support –16%; communications department –14%; merchandise –1%); Management and General (2%); Fundraising (22%).

Contact Info: 1500 Wilson Blvd., Suite 310, Arlington, VA 22209; (703) 522-0200; trout@tu.org

Key Personnel: Charles Gauvin (President/CEO)

125.   Trust for Public Land (TPL) (www.tpl.org) – An "Earth Share" Charity

General Focus Areas: Conservation

Slogan: "Conserving land for people."

Description/Mission: Focused on land conservation for public use (for both recreation and "spiritual nourishment"). Has completed 2100 open space and park projects protecting 1.3 million acres in 45 states and Canada. Works with public land-protection agencies or communities to purchase land for preservation; TPL-purchased land is usually transferred to those public agencies or community land trusts. For FY01, TPL acquired $405 million worth of land/easements for $320 million, while selling $365 million worth of land/easements for $270 million. At the end of FY01 (3/31/01), the fair market value of TPL land holdings was $145 million.

Basic Activities: Land acquisition and conveyance to others; technical and financial assistance; information and public education; policy/advocacy.

Lobbying/Political Activities: Registered lobbyist under the LDA.

National Programs (and activities/focus areas): Greenprint for Growth (land conservation as a smart growth strategy); Conservation Finance Program (promote state/local conservation funding measures); Green Cities

Initiative (create parks and protect greenspace in urban areas); Tribal Lands Initiative (bring traditional Native American lands under tribal ownership); Big Picture Project (explore the larger meaning of TPL's work).

Regional/Local Programs: California; Mid-Atlantic; Mid-West; Minnesota; New York City; Southeast.

Periodicals: Land and People (semi-annual magazine; online); State-Specific Newsletters/Bulletins (online).

Other Publications: Several reports (some online).

Check Out on the Web: "Research Room" (information resources on: federal funding; state and local funding; watershed conservation; urban conservation; economic benefits; open space programs).

Founded: 1971 **Members:** 10,000 **Coverage:** U.S./Canada **Regional/Field/Project Offices:** 45 **NP Status:** 501(c)(3) **Budget** (includes net land/easement acquisitions and sales): $150 million

Revenue (FY01): Net Value of Land Acquired (53%); Contributions and Grants (38%); Other (9%).

Expenses (FY01): Program Services (94%; for: land conveyed to public agencies and other NGOs –62% [based on fair market value less consideration received]; open space conservation programs –32%); Management and General (5%); Fundraising (1%).

Affiliated Org: The Conservation Campaign (a 501(c)(4) non-profit organization).

Contact Info: 116 New Montgomery St., 4th Floor, San Francisco, CA 94105; (415) 495-4014; info@tpl.org

Key Personnel: Will Rogers (President)

126. Turning Point Project (www.turnpoint.org)

General Focus Areas: Global Issues

Description/Mission: A general public education project involving a series of educational ads (appearing in The New York Times in 1999) concerning perceived major issues of the new millennium. A coalition of nearly 100 public interest groups signed the ads.

Basic Activities: Public education; information dissemination.

Ad Series: Extinction Crisis (4 ads); Genetic Engineering (5 ads); Industrial Agriculture (6 ads); Economic Globalization (5 ads); Technomania (5 ads).

Publications: See above-mentioned ads.

Website Notes: In addition to the actual ads, the website provides a resource guide listing coalition organizations, related organizations and a bibliography.

Coverage: Global

Contact Info: 666 Pennsylvania Ave. SE, Suite 302, Washington, DC 20003; (800) 249-8712; info@turnpoint.org

Key Personnel: John Perry (Project Contact Person)

127. Union of Concerned Scientists (UCS) (www.ucsusa.org) – An "Earth Share" Charity

General Focus Areas: Multiple Focus Areas

Slogan: "Citizens and scientists for environmental solutions."

Description/Mission: A multi-faceted organization conducting scientific analysis and advocacy to protect the environment and curtail nuclear arms proliferation.

Basic Activities: Scientific and policy research/analysis; public education; advocacy.

Lobbying/Political Activities: Registered lobbyist under the LDA.

Advocacy Programs (and focus areas): Food and Environment (antibiotic resistance; biotechnology; sustainable agriculture); Clean Vehicles (health and environment; advanced vehicles; cars and SUVs; trucks and buses); Global Environment (biodiversity; global warming; environmental connections); Clean Energy (renewable energy; health and environment; nuclear safety); Global Security/Nuclear Arms Control.

Service Programs (and activities/focus areas): Sound Science Initiative (2000 scientists providing information to government and the media, particularly regarding biodiversity and global warming); Communicating Ecosystem Services (tools for scientists to engage the public on key ecosystem services – pollination; water purification; forest carbon storage; flood damage control).

Periodicals: Nucleus (quarterly magazine; highlights online); Earthwise (quarterly newsletter).

Other Publications: Variety of reports (many online).

Key Publications: The Consumer's Guide to Effective Environmental Choices (book); Clean Energy Blueprint (proposed national energy policy; online).

Annual Report: 1999 report online.

Online Activist Tools: Action Center (posted action alerts); Action Network (action alerts sent via email).

Check Out on the Web: Great Green Web Game (experience the consequences of common consumer choices).

Founded: 1969 **Members:** 50,000 **Coverage:** U.S./Int'l **Staff:** 57 **NP Status:** 501(c)(3) **Budget:** $7 million

Revenue (FY00): Contributions (97%); Government Grants (0%); Program Service Revenues (0%); Other (3%).

Expenses (FY00): Program Services (77% for: global environment program –20%; clean vehicle/transportation program –15%; global security/nuclear arms control program –15%; energy program –13%; food and environment program –12%; legislative program –1%); Management and General (6%); Fundraising (17%).

Contact Info: PO Box 9105, 2 Brattle Square, Cambridge, MA 02238; (617) 547-5552; ucs@ucsusa.org

Key Personnel: Howard Ris (President)

128.   United States Green Building Council (USGBC) (www.usgbc.org)

General Focus Areas: Green Building Construction

Description/Mission: Promotes adoption of green building practices, technologies, policies and standards. The Council itself represents a coalition of 800+ international organizations including business (e.g., Carrier, Herman Miller, Armstrong), environmental orgs (e.g., Audubon Society, Natural Resources Defense Council, Rocky Mountain Institute), retailers (e.g., Gap, Target), financial (e.g., Bank of America) and building and design professionals.

Basic Activities: Technical research; standards setting; technical training and certification.

Key Program: LEED Green Building Rating System™ (a voluntary, consensus-based, market-driven building rating system based on existing proven technology; for new and existing commercial, institutional, and high-rise residential buildings; projects can be officially certified and registered as "LEED"; a LEED accreditation exam is also offered to building professionals).

Key Publication: Sustainable Building Technical Manual (green building practices for design, construction, and operations).

Website Notes: Website does not provide much information aimed at the general public.

Founded: 1993 **Coverage:** U.S./Int'l

Contact Info: 1015 18th St. NW, Suite 805, Washington, DC 20036; (202) 828-7422; info@usgbc.org

U.S. Public Interest Research Group (PIRG) (www.uspirg.org)

See Profile #101 for "Public Interest Research Group," located within this subsection.

129.   Water Keeper Alliance (www.keeper.org)

General Focus Areas: Pollution

Slogan: "Clean water. Strong communities."

Description/Mission: Umbrella organization for 70 "Water Keeper" programs located throughout the U.S. and in North and Central America. (A "Water Keeper" is a non-governmental ombudsperson serving as a public advocate for a particular water body, including acting as a "neighborhood watch" / citizen's patrol to monitor and protect that water body. All "Keepers" have a boat that they use to help monitor their water body. Water Keepers are self-described as "part investigator, scientist, lawyer, lobbyist and PR agent.")

Basic Water Keeper Activities: Water quality monitoring; participating in planning and regulatory meetings; public education; litigation.

Basic Water Keeper Alliance Activities: Review/approve new Water Keeper programs; legal initiatives; annual conferences.

Campaigns: Hog Campaign (a broad legal initiative targeting the corporate hog industry).

Check Out on the Web: Keeper Programs (lists individual Keeper programs, about half of which have their own websites).

Founded: 1992 **Coverage:** U.S./Int'l **Members:** 70 "Keepers" **NP Status:** 501(c)(3) **Budget:** $0.4 million

Revenue (FY00): Contributions (91%); Government Grants (0%); Program Service Revenues (0%); Other (9%).

Expenses (FY00): Program Services (78%); Management and General (16%); Fundraising (6%).

Contact Info: 78 North Broadway, E Building, White Plains, NY 10603; (914) 422-4410.

Key Personnel: Robert F. Kennedy, Jr. (President); Kevin Madonna (Executive Director)

130.   (The) Wilderness Society (TWS) (www.wilderness.org) – An "Earth Share" Charity

General Focus Areas: Conservation

Description/Mission: Seeks to preserve America's wilderness/wildlife and develop a nationwide network of wild lands. Operates the Wilderness Support Center which aids grassroots wilderness groups with an ultimate goal of adding public lands to the National Wilderness Preservation System.

Basic Activities: Public education; scientific/economic analysis; advocacy; assist grassroots groups.

Lobbying/Political Activities: Registered lobbyist under the LDA.

Campaigns (and focus areas): Artic National Wildlife Refuge Protection (seeks to designate ANWR as a National Monument); BLM Lands (management and protection); Conservation Coast-to-Coast (regional office-specific campaigns/ programs); Energy and National Lands; Land and Water Conservation Fund/CARA; National Forests (roadless area policy; road management policy; forest planning regulations); National Monument Protection; Off-Road Vehicle Damage Control; Roadless Area Protection; Wilderness Campaigns (seeks to establish a nationwide "network of wild lands," plus various state-level initiatives); Wildfires.

Publications: Various reports, articles, and fact sheets (most online).

Key Reports: Most Endangered Wildlands (annual report; online); The Economic Value of Forest Ecosystem Services (a review of economic value estimates).

Annual Report: 1999 report online.

Online Activist Tools: Take Action section (contents: posted action alerts; legislative directory; legislative tracker); WildAlert Action Center (e-mailed weekly newsletter with action alerts)

Check Out on the Web: Fact Sheets (2-3 page issue overviews; see "Library" webpage); What You Own (interactive map providing public land statistics).

Founded: 1935 **Membership:** 200,000 **Coverage:** U.S. **Staff:** 110+ **Regional Offices:** 8 **NP Status:** 501(c)(3) **Budget:** $17 million

Revenue (FY00): Contributions (95%); Government Grants (0%); Program Service Revenues (<1%); Other (4%).

Expenses (FY00): Program Services (70%; for: conservation projects –44%; public education –26%); Management and General (9%); Fundraising (21%).

Public Support Sources (FY99): Individuals (84%); Foundations (14%); Corporations (2%).

Contact Info: 1615 M St. NW, 2nd Floor, Washington, DC 20036; (202) 833-2300.

Key Personnel: William H. Meadows (President)

131.   Wildlife Conservation Society (WCS) (www.wcs.org) – An "Earth Share" Charity

General Focus Areas: Conservation

Slogan: "Saving wildlife and wild lands."

Description/Mission: Focused on wildlife and wildlands conservation, working in 53 nations across Africa, Asia, Latin America and North America. Also operates a network of wildlife parks in New York City – the Bronx Zoo (site of WCS's headquarters), the New York Aquarium and the Central Park, Queens and Prospect Park wildlife centers – which altogether attract 4+ million visitors annually.

Basic Activities: Conservation; scientific research; training; education; zoo/wildlife center and aquarium operation.

Conservation Programs (and focus areas): Regional Initiatives (in: Africa; Asia; Latin America; North America); Marine Conservation (focus areas: fisheries conservation; coral research; coastal zone conservation; coastal sharks and pelagic fishes; bycatch); Wildlife in Sustainable Forests (wildlife conservation in forests managed for timber production); Landscape Ecology (examines how ecosystems are arranged); Field Herpetological Conservation (seeks to save endangered reptiles and amphibians); Global Carnivore (advance the knowledge of carnivore biology and apply it to their conservation).

Science Programs (and focus areas): Wildlife Health Sciences; Conservation Genetics (apply molecular biology techniques to conserve wildlife); Geographic Information Systems (apply to landscape ecology); Species Survival Programs (coordinate breeding management in zoos and aquariums).

Periodicals: Wildlife Conservation (bi-monthly magazine; online).

Other Publications: Various books; bibliography of scientific research journal articles (online).

Unique: WCS on the Radio (two radio spots on wildlife – Nature Watch and Ocean Report – 4 times/wk.; archived on the website – can access over the Internet using RealAudio).

Founded: 1895 **Membership:** 100,000 **Coverage:** U.S./Int'l **NP Status:** 501(c)(3) **Budget:** $110 million

Revenue (FY00): Contributions (25%); Government Grants (23%); Program Service Revenues (16%; from: admission fees –15%; misc. –1%); Other (36%; from: investment income –12%; membership dues –6%; misc. – 18%).

Expenses (FY00): Program Services (85%; for: Bronx Zoo –44%; New York Aquarium –12%; New York wildlife centers –12%; international programs –15%; other programs/services –2%); Management and General (10%); Fundraising (5%).

Contact Info: 2300 Southern Blvd., Bronx, New York 10460; (718) 220-5100.

Key Personnel: William Conway (President)

132. Working for Change / Working Assets (www.workingforchange.com)

General Focus Areas: Action Alert Center / Activist Support and Training

Description/Mission: Website devoted to various progressive issues (see below), including the environment. Established by Working Assets (the telecommunications company that donates a portion of its revenues to various non-profits).

Basic Activities: Public education and information.

Activism Categories Covered: Environment; U.S. Politics; Rights and Society; Health and Science; Global Affairs; Work and Economy; Family and Education.

Programs/Main Website Divisions: Act for Change (allows individuals to speak out on urgent issues of the day by providing a direct link to decision makers); Give for Change (online donations to hundreds of non-profits); Volunteer for Change (lists of nationwide volunteer opportunities from two other sites – Volunteer Match [from Impact Online] and Idealist [from Action Without Borders]); Radio for Change (news and talk radio); Shop for Change (100+ stores; 5% of purchase price donated to progressive organizations).

Online Activist Tools: Activism section (contents: action alerts [posted online and sent via email]; activism tips [congressional directory; legislative resource center; tips for activism; media resource center]).

Coverage: U.S.

Contact Info: (877) 255-9253

World Conservation Union (www.iucn.org)

See Profile #307 for "International Union for Conservation of Nature and Natural Resources," located within Subsection 3.2 – "Other Multilaterals and Associated Entities."

133. World Resources Institute (WRI) (www.wri.org)

General Focus Areas: Multiple Focus Areas

Slogan: "Human – Nature: Make the connection."

Description/Mission: Policy- and science-oriented research center focused on global environmental issues within four broad areas: climate change; ecosystems; material use and waste generation; environmental information and decision-making. Particularly known for its biennial *World Resources* report that examines global environmental trends. Maintains a number of associated websites ("project sites" for specific projects – see below).

Basic Activities: Policy and scientific research/analysis; publications/information dissemination.

Programs (and focus areas): Biological Resources (agriculture; biodiversity; ecosystems; forests; oceans and coasts; water resources); Climate, Energy and Pollution (partnering with businesses to identify policies and business strategies to achieve climate protection goals); Economics and Population; Global Forest Watch (an international forest data and mapping network); Information (global and country-level data on sustainable development); Institutions and Governance (ecosystem management); Management Institute for Environment and Business (business education; capital markets; climate change and business; economics; UN Global Compact); *World Resources* Report.

Global Research Topics (and focus areas): Agriculture and Food (agricultural practices and policy); Biodiversity and Protected Areas; Business and Economics (partnering with businesses); Climate and Atmosphere (global climate change); Coastal and Marine Ecosystems (management and conservation of resources); Energy and Material Resources; Environmental Governance and Institutions (developing and transitional nations); Forests and Grasslands; Population, Health, and Human Well-Being; Water Resources and Freshwater Ecosystems.

Key Projects (and associated websites): Millennium Ecosystem Assessment (www.millenniumassessment.org; a $21-million, 4-year effort to assess the world's ecosystems); Access Initiative (www.accessinitiative.org; promotes information access, participation and equity/justice in environmental decision-making); Global Warming – Early Warning Signs (www.climatehotmap.org; offering a global map illustrating the local consequences of global warming); Safe Climate (www.safeclimate.net; calculates the carbon dioxide "footprint" of individuals or businesses); GHG Protocol Initiative (www.ghgprotocol.org; seeks to establish international accounting and reporting standards for greenhouse gas emissions); Global Forest Watch (www.globalforestwatch.org; international data and mapping network for the world's forests).

Publications: Various books, reports, etc. (many online).

Key Publications (all online): World Resources report (biennial report of global environmental trends); Pilot Analysis of Global Ecosystems Reports (a "big picture" view of the world's ecosystems; five separate reports, covering: agro-ecosystems; forests; grasslands; coastal and marine ecosystems; freshwater ecosystems); The Weight of Nations (material outflows from industrial economies); Critical Consumption Trends and Implications (evaluates the global food, fiber, and fisheries sectors, arguing that production and consumption patterns are integrally linked); Watersheds of the World (assesses the ecological value and vulnerability of the world's watersheds); Reefs at Risk (a map-based indicator of threats to the world's coral reefs); A Climate and Environmental Strategy for U.S. Agriculture; Fertile Ground – Nutrient Trading's Potential to Cost Efficiently Improve Water Quality (focused on U.S. watersheds).

Check Out on the Web: "Earth Trends" section (information portal providing – for each Global Research Topic [see above] – the following: searchable database; data tables; country profiles; maps of relevant data; feature articles); Beyond Grey Pinstripes Program (preparing MBA students for social and environmental stewardship).

Founded: 1982 **Coverage:** Global **Staff:** 130 **NP Status:** 501(c)(3) **Budget:** $20 million

Revenue (FY00): Contributions (37%); Government Grants (12%); Program Service Revenues (0%); Other (51%; from investment income).

Expenses (FY00): Program Services (81%; for: institutions and governance program –17%; biological resources program –11%; Management Institute for Environment and Business –10%; communications –8%; global forest watch data and mapping network –7%; information program –7%; special studies and fellows –6%; *World Resources* report –6%; climate, energy and pollution program –5%; economics and population program –4%); Management and General (14%); Fundraising (5%).

Contact Info: 10 G St. NE, Suite 800, Washington, DC 20002; (202) 729-7600; front@wri.org

Key Personnel: Jonathan Lash (President)

134.   **World Wildlife Fund (WWF) (www.worldwildlife.org) – An "Earth Share" Charity**

General Focus Areas: Conservation

Slogan: "Working together, we can leave our children a living planet."

Description/Mission: Focuses on wildlife and wildlands conservation, especially in the tropical forests of Latin America, Asia, and Africa. Since inception, WWF has been involved in 13,000+ projects in 157 countries. Has national organizations or representatives in 50+ countries worldwide with conservation projects in Africa, Asia, Latin America, and North America. Known for its Panda bear logo.

Basic Activities: Conservation field projects; scientific and policy research; training; education; outreach; advocacy.

Lobbying/Political Activities: Registered lobbyist under the LDA.

Overall Goals (Living Planet Campaign): Protect endangered spaces; save endangered species; address global threats.

Key Issues/Programs (and focus areas): Endangered Spaces (focus on preserving the "Global 200": key terrestrial, freshwater, and marine habitats); Endangered Species (wildlife trade; pandas; rhinos; elephants; tigers; whales; other species); Forests (establishing protected areas; certifying to Forest Stewardship Council standards; alliance with the World Bank; climate change and forest conservation); Climate Change ("climate savers" program, helping businesses develop/implement climate and energy solutions; Florida campaign); Oceans (endangered species; global threats; protected areas; marine stewardship; Great Barrier Reef); Toxic Chemicals (endocrine disrupters; persistent organic pollutants; agricultural pesticides).

Periodicals: Living Planet (quarterly magazine); Focus (bi-monthly newsletter).

Other Publications: Various reports (most online).

Key Publication: The Global 200: A Representative Approach to Conserving the Earth's Distinctive Ecoregions (guiding strategy for conserving global biodiversity; online).

Annual Report: 2000 report online.

Online Activist Tools: Wildlife Activist section (Conservation Activist Network – action alerts posted online and sent via email).

Check Out on the Web: Pennies for the Planet (annual kids campaign linking environmental education and action); Travel with WWF (trips to areas rich in wildlife).

Website Notes: Site provides navigation options based on visitor type: WWF Member; Wildlife Lover; Activist; Kids; Educator.

Founded: 1961 **Members** (U.S.): 1.2 million **Coverage:** Global **NP Status:** 501(c)(3) **Budget:** $110 million

Revenue (FY00): Contributions (67%); Government Grants (20%); Program Service Revenues (1%); Other (13%).

Expenses (FY00): Program Services (82%; for: conservation field and policy program –66%; public education – 16%); Management and General (5%); Fundraising (13%).

Contact Info: 1250 24th St. NW, Washington, DC 20037; (202) 293-4800.

Key Personnel: Kathryn Fuller (President)

Subsection 1.3: Progressive Business Groups and Coalitions

Introduction/User's Guide:

Within this subsection, 3 groups and coalitions comprised exclusively of businesses/corporations that work in a relatively progressive fashion on environmental issues are profiled (traditional business trade associations and other business groups of interest are separately profiled within Section 5 – "Other Interested Parties").

Organizational profiles for this subsection are listed beginning on the next page, presented in alphabetical order. In terms of individual entry contents, the reader is referred back to the beginning of Section 1 where a descriptive outline of standardized profile information provided is presented.

A Closer Look – Related Efforts:

In addition to the business-only groups listed here, a key related group that also focuses on business practices is the Coalition for Environmentally Responsible Economies (CERES, listed as Profile #31 within Subsection 1.2 – "Public Interest Groups and Coalitions"). CERES is a coalition of environmental, investor and advocacy groups that works in partnership with businesses regarding corporate environmental responsibility, work very similar to that conducted by the business-only groups listed within this subsection.

Finally, it should be noted that: 1) some environmental public interest groups have formed significant partnerships with businesses in recent years (e.g., Environmental Defense's "Alliance for Environmental Innovation" program) and 2) as large power consumers, businesses tend to be quite interested – for obvious financial reasons – in energy issues (especially energy efficiency issues) and hence are often active participants in energy-related public interest groups (e.g., the Alliance to Save Energy and the American Council for an Energy-Efficient Economy – both listed within Subsection 1.2 – "Public Interest Groups and Coalitions").

Subsection 1.3: Progressive Business Groups and Coalitions

135. **Business for Social Responsibility (BSR)** (www.bsr.org)

General Focus Areas: Business Practices

Description/Mission: A non-profit business association promoting corporate social responsibility (CSR) globally by helping firms implement and improve CSR policies and practices; covers 8 core CSR issues, including "Environment." Comprised of 1400+ member and affiliated companies; member companies are diverse in both size and business sector. Has an affiliated non-profit organization – the BSR Education Fund – managed by same Board of Directors. The BSR Ed Fund runs several CSR-related programs, including "Business and the Environment" through which BSR works with companies to develop/implement more sustainable business strategies and practices both within their own operations and throughout their supply chains.

Key Corporate Members: Chevron-Texaco; Shell; Ford; General Motors; Dow; DuPont.

Basic Activities: Education; training; technical assistance; research.

Key Issues: Climate Change; Energy Efficiency; Extended Product Responsibility; Green Power; Sustainable Business Practices (the focus of the BSR Ed Fund).

Key Working Groups (and activities/focus areas): Clean Cargo and Green Freight Groups (movement of goods from source to market with minimal environmental impact); Green Power Market Development Group (develop corporate markets for green power); Sourcing Environmentally Responsible Forest Products (sustainable forestry sourcing policies); Supply Chain Environmental Network (implementing environmental programs with suppliers, including collaboration on green product design techniques and reusable shipping packaging).

Check Out on the Web: Topic Overviews (online under "Library"; for each identified CSR issue, examines: business benefits; recent developments; external standards; implementation steps; leadership examples; sample policies; awards and recognition programs; and links to additional resources).

Founded: 1992 **Coverage:** U.S./Int'l **NP Status:** BSR – 501(c)(6); BSR Ed Fund – 501(c)(3) **Budget (BSR Ed Fund):** $5 million

Revenue (BSR Ed Fund; FY00): Contributions (50%); Government Grants (0%); Program Service Revenues (47%; from: fees for service –26%; government awards –9%; BSR affiliate revenue –6%; training workshops and seminars –6%); Other (3%).

Expenses (BSR Ed Fund; FY00): Program Services (82%; for: education, training and technical assistance); Management and General (16%); Fundraising (2%).

Contact Info: 609 Mission St., 2nd Floor, San Francisco, CA 94105; (415) 537-0888.

Key Personnel: Robert Dunn (President/CEO)

136. **Global Environmental Management Initiative (GEMI)** (www.gemi.org)

General Focus Areas: Business Practices

Description/Mission: Alliance of 40+ major companies promoting a worldwide business ethic for environmental, health and safety management through example and leadership.

Basic Activities: Management tools development; benchmarking; communications and information exchange.

Main Working Groups (and activities/focus areas): Tools (create specific "tools" to improve businesses' environmental, health and safety activities); Benchmarking (identifies and benchmarks key environmental, health and safety management practices).

Publications: Various reports aimed at businesses (online).

Associated Websites: Business and Climate (www.businessandclimate.org; focuses on business opportunities and risks related to global climate change; main website divisions: business and climate change [background information]; formulate a strategy [tips for business planning]; practical steps [ways to reduce emissions]; measurement and metrics [how to measure and report emissions]); HSE Web Depot (www.hsewebdepot.org; Internet-based information resource for development/improvement of health, safety and environment management information systems).

Founded: 1993 **Coverage:** Global **NP Status:** 501(c)(3)-PF **Budget:** $0.7 million

Revenue (2000): Contributions (91%); Government Grants (0%); Program Service Revenues (0%); Other (9%).

Expenses (2000): Direct Charitable Activities (55%; for: "management tools" project –37%; communications and marketing committee –12%; membership program –5%); Other (45%).

Contact Info: 1 Thomas Circle NW, 10th Floor, Washington, DC 20005; (202) 296-7449; gemi@worldweb.net

Key Personnel: Steve Hellem (Executive Director)

GreenBiz.com / Green Business Network (www.greenbiz.com)
See Profile #457, located within Subsection 7.2 – "Information and Data Resource Websites and Gateways."

137.   World Business Council for Sustainable Development (WBCSD) (www.wbcsd.ch)

General Focus Areas: Business Practices; Sustainable Development

Description/Mission: Coalition of 150 international companies with a mission to "provide business leadership as a catalyst for change toward sustainable development, and to promote the role of eco-efficiency, innovation and corporate social responsibility." Members are drawn from 30+ countries and 20 major industrial sectors and includes many leading multinational corporations. Also maintains a network of 30 national and regional Business Councils for Sustainable Development and has partner organizations in Africa, Asia, Europe, the Americas and Oceania.

Basic Activities: Business Leadership; Policy Development; Best Practice Identification; Global Outreach.

Key Projects (and focus areas): Sustainability through the Market (make a business case for sustainable development); Corporate Social Responsibility; Climate and Energy (policy; future energy systems; business as a "solutions provider"); Innovation and Technology; Sustainable Development Reporting; Natural Resources (biodiversity; access to water – management and use of fresh water); Eco-Efficiency; Sectorial Projects (cement; electric utilities; forestry; mining; mobility).

Periodicals: Sustain (quarterly newsletter; online).

Other Publications: Various reports, project briefs and books (all online except for the books).

Key Publications (both online): Sustainability Through the Market – Seven Keys to Success (how sustainability can be achieved using market forces; 30 case studies included); Eco-Efficiency – Creating More Value With Less Impact (reference source for eco-efficiency).

Annual Report: 2000 report online.

Founded: 1990 **Coverage:** Global **HQ:** Geneva, Switzerland

Contact Info: Geneva, Switzerland; (41 22) 839 3100; info@wbcsd.org

Key Personnel: Philip Watts (Chairman of the Executive Committee; also serves as the Chairman of the Royal Dutch/Shell Group)

Subsection 1.4: Student- and Education-Oriented Groups

Introduction/User's Guide:

Within this subsection, 12 student- and education-oriented groups conducting environmentally-relevant work are profiled, ranging from youth community service-learning programs (e.g., the Student Conservation Association and the YMCA's Earth Services Corps) through college-based activist programs (e.g., the Sierra Student Coalition). Also included are groups seeking high-level change in higher education (e.g., Second Nature and the Higher Education Network for Sustainability and the Environment), as well as the leading professional organization for environmental education at all levels (i.e., the North American Association for Environmental Education).

Organizational profiles for this subsection are listed beginning on the next page, presented in alphabetical order. In terms of individual entry contents, the reader is referred back to the beginning of Section 1 where a descriptive outline of standardized profile information provided is presented.

Subsection 1.4: Student- and Education-Oriented Groups

Association of Environmental Engineering and Science Professors (AEESP) (www.aeesp.org)
See Profile #163, located within Subsection 1.5 – "Professional Societies."

138.   **Campus Ecology ® Program (National Wildlife Federation)** (www.nwf.org/campusecology)
General Focus Areas: Conservation

Description/Mission: Higher education program with a stated mission to "assist students, faculty, staff and administrators in transforming colleges and universities into learning and teaching models of environmental sustainability." Focused on assisting with the design and implementation of practical conservation projects on campuses and in the surrounding communities, with 2000+ projects completed thus far. Both entire campuses and individuals can formally enroll in the program (about 100 campuses are currently enrolled). A project of the National Wildlife Federation (see Profile #84, located within Subsection 1.2 – "Public Interest Groups and Coalitions").

Basic Activities: Technical assistance and training; communications and networking; project documentation and lesson sharing.

Periodicals: The Connection Newsletter (annual program newsletter; online).

Other Publications: Various books and reports (mainly case studies and/or "how-to-do" documents; some online).

Key Reports: Ecodemia (documenting environmental management innovations at college campuses); State of the Campus Environment (a national report card on environmental performance and sustainability in higher education; online).

Check Out on the Web: Campus Environmental Yearbooks (annual report on campus greening projects; online); Campus Ecology Fellowship Program (assists college students in advancing their environmental initiatives; recipients receive a modest grant, project support, and recognition of accomplishments).

Founded: 1989 **Coverage:** U.S. **Staff:** 3

Contact Info: 8925 Leesburg Pike, Vienna, VA 22184; (703) 438-6262; campus@nwf.org

Key Personnel: Julian Keniry (Program Manager)

139.   **Center for Environmental Citizenship (CEC)** (www.envirocitizen.org)
General Focus Areas: Activism Support and Training

Slogan: "Networking young leaders to protect the environment."

Description/Mission: Founded by young activists to encourage college students to become "environmental citizens." In particular, CEC seeks to "educate, train, and organize a diverse, national network of young leaders to protect the environment."

Basic Activities: Voting drives; leadership training; organizing and networking; conferences.

Programs (and activities/focus areas): Campus Green Vote (electoral training program; "vote environment" campaigns; training for student leaders and groups); National Environmental Wire for Students (provides articles and news releases to campus media outlets; hosts annual Environmental Journalism Academy); EarthNet (online program operating a campus listserv and the CEC's website).

Online Activist Tools: Take Action Online section (action alerts posted online).

Check Out on the Web: EarthNet (contents: news; jobs; events – conferences and training; EnviroNation – state-based listing of student environmental organizations).

Founded: 1992 **Coverage:** U.S. **Staff:** 17 **Field Offices:** 3 **NP Status:** 501(c)(3) **Budget:** $1 million

Revenue (2000): Contributions (99%); Government Grants (0%); Program Service Revenues (0%); Other (1%).

Expenses (2000): Program Services (88%; for: Campus Green Vote program –61%; National Environmental Wire for Students –18%; EarthNet –9%); Management and General (11%); Fundraising (1%).

Contact Info: 200 G St. NE, Suite 300, Washington, DC 20002; (202) 547-8435; cec@envirocitizen.org

Key Personnel: Susan Comfort (Executive Director)

Environmental Education Link (EE-Link) (www.eelink.net)
See Profile #451, located within Subsection 7.2 – "Information and Data Resource Websites and Gateways."

140.   **Envirothon ® (www.envirothon.org)**
General Focus Areas: Academic Competition

Description/Mission: Billed as "North America's largest high school environmental competition." Five-member teams compete based on knowledge in four natural resource areas (aquatics, forestry, soils, wildlife) along with a varying "current environmental issue." Winners of individual state-/province-level competitions meet in a North American finals competition. Finals winners are awarded college scholarships. All teams must be affiliated with their local conservation district or an equivalent conservation agency. Envirothon is formally sponsored by Canon Corporation (the official name of the competition is the "Canon Envirothon" ®) and local conservation districts, in partnership with the Monsanto Corporation, the U.S. Forest Service, the U.S. Environmental Protection Agency, and the National Association of Conservation Districts.

Basic Activities: Academic Competition; Environmental Education; Youth Education.

Founded: 1979 **Coverage:** N. America **NP Status:** 501(c)(3) **Budget:** $0.3 million

Revenue (2000): Contributions (69%); Government Grants (6%); Program Service Revenues (0%); Other (25%; from: membership dues –22%; misc. –3%).

Expenses (2000): Program Services (78%); Management and General (17%); Fundraising (5%).

Contact Info (program info): Kay Asher, Program Coordinator: PO Box 855, League City, TX 77574; (800) 825-5547 (x16); kay-asher@nacdnet.org

Contact Info (org HQ): 315 East 5th North, Saint Anthony, ID 83445; (208) 624-3341.

Key Personnel: Clay Burns (Executive Director); Kay Asher (Program Coordinator)

Green Corps (www.greencorps.org)
See Profile #58, located within Subsection 1.2 – "Public Interest Groups and Coalitions."

141.   **National Association of University Fisheries and Wildlife Programs (NAUFWP)**
        (www.ag.iastate.edu/departments/aecl/naufwp)
General Focus Areas: Environmental Education

Description/Mission: Member-based association representing college and university fisheries and wildlife programs. Offers information exchange between member university programs as well as with related federal agencies, employers of student graduates, and other organizations/groups. Also seeks to promote public education and understanding of fisheries and wildlife management and conservation issues. Currently based out of Iowa State University.

Basic Activities: Information exchange; public education.

Founded: 1991 **Membership:** 55 universities **NP Status:** 501(c)(3) **Budget:** $0.02 million

Contact Info: Dept of Animal Ecology, 124 Science II, Iowa State University, Ames, IA 50011.

Key Personnel: Dr. Bruce Menzel (President)

142.   **National Environmental Education and Training Foundation (NEETF) (www.neetf.org)**
General Focus Areas: Environmental Education

Slogan: "Building a stronger economic, societal and ecological future through environmental learning."

Description/Mission: An organization created by the U.S. Congress in 1990 to develop and support environmental learning programs to meet social goals, such as improved health, better education, and "greener," more profitable business. Initiates programs and public/private partnerships targeting several different audiences – K-12 students, adults, health care professionals and business professionals.

A Closer Look: The organization receives all its funding via government grants.

Basic Activities: Education targeting different audiences (youth; adults; professionals); training; research; challenge grant-making; public/private partnerships.

Major Programs (and key activities/projects): K-12 Education (key program – EnvironMentors™, matching urban teenagers with professionals to work on research or community service projects); Adult Learning (focused on drinking water quality and watershed protection); Health and Environment (education for doctors, nurses, and public health care providers); Green Business Network (joint partnership with GreenBiz.com to provide resources and training to businesses – see Profile #457, located within Subsection 7.2 – "Information and Data Resource Websites and Gateways"); Grants (challenge grants to leverage non-federal investment in environmental education and training); National Public Lands Day (volunteers gather the last Saturday every September to help improve public lands; in 2001, nearly 60,000 volunteers worked on 375 sites, providing $8 million worth of improvements); National Report Card (annual survey of adult Americans on environmental attitudes, knowledge and behavior); Partners in Resource Education (partnership with 5 federal agencies – BLM, NPS, NRCS, FWS, and USFS – to link students, teachers and parents to their lands, promoting resource conservation and understanding of ecosystems).

Publications: Various program-related reports (most online).

Key Report: National Report Card on Environmental Attitudes, Knowledge and Behaviors (annual report; Executive Summary online).

Associated Websites: Water Quality Reports (provides supplementary information on Consumer Confidence Reports issued by public water systems; www.waterqualityreports.org); EnviroMentors Project (matching urban teenagers with professionals to work on research or community service projects; www.enviromentors.org); National Public Lands Day (promoting a day dedicated to volunteers improving public lands; occurs the last Saturday of September; www.npld.com).

Founded: 1990 **Coverage:** U.S. **Staff:** 30 **NP Status:** 501(c)(3) **Budget:** $1 million

Revenue (1999): Contributions (0%); Government Grants (99%); Program Service Revenues (0%); Other (1%).

Expenses (1999): Program Services (89%; for education, training and research); Management & General (11%); Fundraising (0%).

Contact Info: 1707 H St. NW, Suite 900, Washington, DC 20006; (202) 833-2933.

Key Personnel: Kevin J. Coyle (President); Raymond Lovett (Executive Director)

143.   **North American Association for Environmental Education (NAAEE)** (www.naaee.org)

General Focus Areas: Environmental Education

Description/Mission: Professional association of environmental educators that seeks to take a cooperative, non-confrontational, scientifically-balanced approach in promoting environmental education. Members include professionals along with students and volunteers working in both student and adult education programs throughout North America. NAAEE provides continuing education/training and publications/information services, while also conducting education policy/guideline development through its EE Policy Institute (see below). Also operates Environmental Education Link (EE-Link; see Profile #451, located within Subsection 7.2 – "Information and Data Resource Websites and Gateways").

Basic Activities: Information dissemination; training; networking; annual conference and workshops; policy/guideline development.

Programs (and activities/focus areas): Affiliate Partnership (network of professional environmental education associations throughout North America); EE Policy Institute (develops "summit papers" – discussion papers on important topics in the field; National Project for Excellence in Environmental Education – establishes guidelines for the development of balanced, scientifically-accurate, and comprehensive environmental education programs); Environmental Education Training and Partnership (EETAP; a consortium of leading education organizations working to advance environmental education and literacy); International Program.

Publications: Various profession-oriented publications.

Key Publication: Environmental Educational Materials: Guidelines for Excellence Workbook (online).

Founded: 1971 **Coverage:** N. America **Staff:** 7 **NP Status:** 501(c)(3) **Budget:** $2.5 million

Revenue (1999): Contributions (1%); Government Grants (79%); Program Service Revenues (0%); Other (20%;

from: annual conference –14%; misc. –6%).

Expenses (1999): Program Services (84%; for: fulfilling contract and grant agreements –58%; annual conference, workshops and publications –26%); Management and General (13%); Fundraising (3%).

Contact Info: 410 Tarvin Road, Rock Spring, GA 30739; (706) 764-2926; email@naaee.org

Key Personnel: Elaine Andrews (President)

144.   Second Nature (www.secondnature.org)

General Focus Areas: Sustainable Development

Slogan: "Education for sustainability."

Description/Mission: Works to incorporate sustainability concepts into all aspects of college life, promoting "Education for Sustainability" to make sustainability "second nature." Co-founded by Sen. John Kerry (D-MA).

Basic Activities: Information dissemination; training and workshops; outreach and college/university partnerships.

Programs/Services (and activities/focus areas): Workshops (for administrators, faculty, staff and students); Outreach (presentation and consultation services); On-Line Resources (Resource Center – repository of materials submitted by individuals from across higher education; Resource Guides – guides to "Education to Sustainability"); Partnerships (with college consortia nationwide); Sustainable Design (integrate sustainable principles into the education and practice of architects); Consortium for Environmental Education in Medicine (seek to make the link between human health and the environment an integral part of medical education).

Check Out on the Web: On-line "Resource Guides" for faculty, students and administrators.

Founded: 1993 **Coverage:** U.S. **Staff:** 12 **NP Status:** 501(c)(3) **Budget:** $1 million

Revenue (FY01): Contributions (93%); Government Grants (0%); Program Service Revenues (5%; from faculty training); Other (2%).

Expenses (FY01): Program Services (75%; for faculty training); Management and General (11%); Fundraising (14%).

Affiliated Org: Consortium for Environmental Education in Medicine (a 501(c)(3) non-profit organization).

Contact Info: 99 Chauncy St., 6th Floor, Boston, MA 02111; (617) 292-7771; info@secondnature.org

Key Personnel: Anthony Cortese (President)

145.   Sierra Student Coalition (SSC) (www.ssc.org)

General Focus Areas: Multiple Focus Areas

Description/Mission: Student-run arm of the Sierra Club (see Profile #115 under "Public Interest Groups and Coalitions"). Cites 100+ groups on college campuses and in high schools.

Basic Activities: Activist training and organizing; public education; advocacy; wilderness trips.

Programs (and activities/focus areas): Conservation (runs national campaigns – see listing below); Networks (develops local networks of activists); Trainings (conducts workshops year-round; runs the Student Environmental Training Academy – weekend-long student activist training sessions); Outings (organizes trips into the wilderness).

National Campaigns (and focus areas): Forest Protection ("watchdog" monitoring of the U.S. Forest Service; seek to modify the behavior of companies selling forest products); Global Warming; Artic Wilderness (seek to block opening the Arctic National Wildlife Refuge to oil exploration/drilling); Utah Wilderness (seek passage of America's Redrock Wilderness Act); Student Action on the Global Economy (seek World Bank reform).

Periodicals: Generation-E (quarterly newsletter; latest online).

Online Activist Tools: Get Connected section (activist networking); Take Action (action alerts posted online).

Founded: 1991 **Coverage:** U.S. **Members:** 24,000 **Staff (HQ):** 4 **Local (Campus) Chapters:** 100+

Contact Info: PO Box 2402, Providence, RI 02906; (888) JOIN-SSC.

Key Personnel: Myke Bybee (Director)

146. **Student Conservation Association (SCA)** (www.sca-inc.org) – **An "Earth Share" Charity**

General Focus Areas: Conservation

Slogan: "Changing lives through service to nature."

Description/Mission: Provides hands-on conservation service opportunities, outdoor education, and career training for both high school and college-age youth. SCA volunteers and interns annually perform 1+ million hours of conservation service in national parks, forests, refuges and urban areas in all 50 states. Annually places 2500+ students in hands-on conservation service positions. Length of service varies from one month to one year; voluntary, internship and paid positions are available. SCA's primary partners include key government agencies – NPS, BLM, USFS, FWS, USGS – and The Nature Conservatory.

Basic Activities: Hands-on conservation projects; outdoor education; career/leadership training.

Key Programs (and activities/focus areas): High School Conservation Work Crew Program (volunteers work under SGA crew leaders to perform trail and restoration work on public lands, often in remote settings; place 100 crews of 6-10 nationwide annually); Conservation Internships (full-time internships with partnering organizations for 3-12 months; aimed at college students, but need not be a student to qualify); Diversity Initiatives (Internship Program for college students; Urban Youth Corps for high school students); Leadership Programs; Alternative School Break Program (college students working in National Parks and other areas).

Periodicals: e-Volunteer (monthly electronic newsletter).

Founded: 1957 **Membership:** 24,000 **Coverage:** U.S. **Regional Offices:** 6 **NP Status:** 501(c)(3) **Budget:** $11 million

Revenue (FY00): Contributions (10%); Government Grants (0%); Program Service Revenues (72%; from: student placement fees –71%; publication income –1%); Other (18%; from: membership dues –14%; misc. –4%).

Expenses (FY00): Program Services (83%); Management and General (10%); Fundraising (7%).

Contact Info: PO Box 550, 689 River Road, Charlestown, NH 03603; (603) 543-1700; ask-us@sca-inc.org

Key Personnel: Dale Penny (President/CEO)

147. **Student Pugwash USA** (www.spusa.org)

General Focus Areas: Application of Science and Technology

Description/Mission: The U.S. student affiliate of the Pugwash Conferences on Science and World Affairs which seeks to bring together influential scholars and public figures concerned with reducing the danger of armed conflict and seeking cooperative solutions for global problems (see www.pugwash.org for details). Student Pugwash seeks to promote socially responsible application of science and technology, encouraging students to examine the ethical, social, and global implications of science and technology. Chooses themes (see below) around which it organizes its publications and outreach efforts.

Basic Activities: Information dissemination; public education; research; meetings and conferences.

Programs (and activities/focus areas): Global Issues (sponsors meetings to explore solutions to identified global problems); Chapter Development (establishes/develops chapters on college campuses); New Careers (career resources for students).

National Themes (2001-03; upcoming): Nuclear Weapons; Human Genetics; Information Technology; Feeding the World (genetically modified foods and biotechnology in general); Indigenous Knowledge and Modern Science; Environment, Energy, and Security.

National Themes (1999-2000; still active): Access, Education, and the Future of Science; Communicating in the 21st Century; Genetics, Biotechnology, and Social Responsibility; Global Climate Change and Technological Imperatives; Science, Technology, and Human Rights; Terrorism and Weapons of Mass Destruction.

Periodicals: Pugwash (monthly newsletter; online).

Other Publications: Various other documents and career resources (all online).

Key Publications (both online): Mind-Full (issue briefs; "brain snacks for future leaders with ethical appetites"); 200 Employers You Can Live With (organizations that work at the crossroads of science, technology, and society).

Check Out on the Web: "The Pledge" (a program encouraging student scientists and engineers to sign a Hippocratic-type oath; over 5000 pledges collected).

Founded: 1979 **Coverage:** U.S./Int'l **Staff:** 4 **NP Status:** 501(c)(3) **Budget:** $0.3 million

Revenue (2000): Contributions (99%); Government Grants (0%); Program Service Revenues (<1%); Other (<1%).

Expenses (2000): Program Services (94%; for: campus chapter development –69%; students' "new careers" program –24%; global issues meetings 1%); Management and General (6%); Fundraising (0%).

Contact Info: 815 15th St. NW, Suite 814, Washington, DC 20005; (202) 393-6555; spusa@spusa.org

Key Personnel: Susan Veres (Executive Director)

148. University Leaders for a Sustainable Future (ULSF) (www.ulsf.org)

General Focus Areas: Sustainable Development

Description/Mission: Seeks to make sustainability a major focus of teaching, research, operations and outreach at colleges and universities worldwide. Also serves as the Secretariat for signatories of the Talloires Declaration, a 10-point action plan committing institutions to sustainability and environmental literacy in teaching and practice (275 institutions in over 40 countries – 67 in the U.S. – have signed the Declaration). While promoting the signing and implementation of the Declaration, ULSF members include institutions that have yet to sign the Declaration. ULSF is the higher education program of the Center for Respect of Life and Environment (a $1.2 million non-profit focused on animal and environmental protection and related to the Humane Society).

Basic Activities/Programs: Public Education; Site Visits and Evaluations; Conferences and Workshops; Case Study Project.

Periodicals: The Declaration (semi-annual report; online); International Journal of Sustainability in Higher Education (tri-annual academic journal).

Key Publications (both online under "Programs and Services"): Talloires Declaration (10-point action plan committing institutions to sustainability and environmental literacy in teaching and practice); Sustainability Assessment Questionnaire (offers a qualitative assessment of the extent to which a college or university is "sustainable").

Founded: 1990 **Coverage:** U.S./Int'l **Staff:** 7 **NP Status:** 501(c)(3)

Contact Info: 2100 L St. NW, Washington, DC 20037; (202) 778-6133; info@ulsf.org

Key Personnel: Richard M. Clugston (Director)

149. YMCA Earth Services Corps (YESC) (www.yesc.org)

General Focus Areas: Community Service

Slogan: "We build strong kids, strong families, strong communities."

Description/Mission: Service-learning program providing teens with opportunities to initiate environmental community service projects, such as tree plantings, water quality monitoring, and recycling. Operates in 111 YMCAs in 30 states; over its 10 year history, has involved nearly 20,000 teens, resulting in over 1 million hours of service.

Basic Activities: Community service-learning projects.

Program Components: Leadership Development; Environmental Education; Action Projects ("learning by doing"); Cross-Cultural Awareness ("thinking globally, acting locally").

Periodicals: Youth Voice (online newsletter).

Key Publication: Program Handbook (online under "Tools and Training").

Founded: 1989 **Coverage:** U.S.

Contact Info: 909 4th Ave., Seattle, WA 98104; (800) 733-YESC; info@yesc.org

Subsection 1.5: Professional Societies

Introduction/User's Guide:

Within this subsection, 33 environmentally-oriented "professional societies" – membership groups primarily open to, comprised of, and focused on servicing a particular group of professionals (e.g., the American Society of Landscape Architects) – are profiled.

Organizational profiles for this subsection are listed beginning on the next page, presented in alphabetical order.

In terms of individual entry contents, the following is a descriptive outline of standardized profile information provided for each organization listed within this subsection (please note that the exact contents provided varies by organization, being dependant upon applicability and/or availability).

[Profile #] Organization Name (Website Address)

Description: A short summary of the organization, focusing on its target membership, basic activities, and organizational structure.

A Closer Look: Providing additional relevant information judged to be of particular interest.

Lobbying/Political Activities: Included if the organization is registered as a federal lobbyist under the Lobbying Disclosure Act (LDA) and/or maintains a Political Action Committee (PAC), with the name of the PAC specified.

Key Internal Groups: Noting relevant committees, working groups, advisory groups, task forces, etc.

Programs/Issues (and activities/focus areas): Providing specifics on the organization's activities/concerns.

Key Initiatives/Policy Priorities: Highlighting the organization's "high priority" activities/issues.

Key Periodicals: Listing title, description, publication frequency and noting if they are available online at the organization's website.

Other Key Publications: Listing title and noting if they are available online at the organization's website.

Website Notes: Significant notes concerning the organization's website – navigating hints, content notes, etc.

Check Out on the Web: Listing website-related content/features that particularly stand out ("worth a look").

Founded: Beginning year specified **Membership:** Noted if applicable and figures made available **HQ:** Noting city and state **Staff:** Overall staffing level **NP Status:** Formal IRS non-profit status (typically 501(c)(3) – exempt)

Budget: Approximate ("ballpark") figure based on IRS submittals or other sources of information.

Contact Info: Providing: General telephone number; general email address (if available).

Key Personnel: Typically citing the name and title of key executives (President, Executive Director, etc.).

A Closer Look – Reason for Inclusion:

Inclusion of this category of organizations was done based on the potential for professional societies to significantly influence environmental policy and/or outcomes – both overtly through advocacy work (the current level of which varies from organization to organization), as well as more indirectly through their professional education/training activities.

Subsection 1.5: Professional Societies

150. **Air and Waste Management Association (AWMA)** (www.awma.org)

Description: Professional membership association of environmental professionals – scientists, engineers, policymakers, attorneys and consultants – in 65 countries. Provides continuing education/training and publications/information services. Divided into 33 regional sections, 67 local chapters, and 40 student chapters worldwide.

Key Periodicals: Journal of the AWMA (monthly research-oriented journal); EM (monthly journal for environmental managers).

Founded: 1907 **Membership:** 16,000 **HQ:** Pittsburgh, PA **Staff:** 45 **NP Status:** 501(c)(3) **Budget:** $5 million

Contact Info: (412) 232-3444; info@awma.org

Key Personnel: Dennis Mitchell (Executive Director)

151. **American Chemical Society (ACS)** (www.acs.org)

Description: Professional society covering all fields of chemistry. Provides continuing education/training and publications/information services. Divided into 33 technical divisions, including "Environmental Chemistry." A large operation budget-wise ($300+ million), mainly due to its Chemical Abstract Service (CAS) division which provides technical information services on chemicals and chemical research.

A Closer Look: A little-known facet of ACS is its involvement with the Petroleum Research Fund. The Fund was established in 1944 by seven major oil companies to advance scientific education and research in the petroleum field, specifically through ACS. In 1999, this nearly $500 million trust fund provided the ASC with $18 million which was used to award 440 petroleum-related academic research grants.

Lobbying/Political Activities: Registered lobbyist under the LDA.

Key Initiative: Green Chemistry Institute (an affiliated non-profit promoting "green chemistry" [a science-based approach to pollution prevention]; focuses on research and education through government–industry collaboration with universities and national laboratories).

Key Periodicals: Environmental, Science and Technology (bi-weekly research-oriented journal; online).

Founded: 1876 **Membership:** 163,000 members (60% from industry) **HQ:** Washington, DC **Staff:** 1750 **NP Status:** 501(c)(3) **Budget:** $320 million (mostly due to ACS's Chemical Abstract Service and other information services provided)

Contact Info: (800) 227-5558 / (202) 872-4600; help@acs.org

Key Personnel: John Crum (Executive Director)

152. **American Fisheries Society (AFS)** (www.fisheries.org)

Description: Professional society representing fisheries scientists and other professionals. Provides continuing education/training and publications/information services. Also seeks to promote "the conservation, development and wise use of fisheries." Has 100+ chapters, divisions and sections, including student subunits.

Key Periodicals: Fisheries (monthly membership magazine; feature articles online); Transactions of the American Fisheries Society (bi-monthly research-oriented journal; current issue online); North American Journal of Fisheries Management (quarterly management-oriented journal; current issue online).

Founded: 1870 **Membership:** 9200 **HQ:** Bethesda, MD **Staff:** 23 **NP Status:** 501(c)(3) **Budget:** $3 million

Contact Info: (301) 897-8616; main@fisheries.org

Key Personnel: Paul Brouha (Executive Director)

153. **American Institute of Hydrology (AIH)** (www.aihydro.org)

Description: Professional society of professionally-certified hydrologists and hydrogeologists. Focused on providing professional certification and registration of hydrologists/hydrogeologists. Also provides continuing education/training and publications/information services.

Founded: 1981 **Membership:** 1000 (900 professionals; 100 students) **HQ:** St. Paul, MN **Staff:** 2 **Budget:** $0.1

million
Contact Info: (651) 484-8169
Key Personnel: Helen Klose (Executive Director)

154. <u>**American Planning Association (APA)**</u> (www.planning.org)

Description: Professional membership association of planning professionals; two-thirds of members are employed by state and local government agencies. Provides continuing education/training and publications/information services. Also conducts research in city and regional planning and is an active policy advocate (see below). Runs the American Institute of Certified Planners, which sets professional and ethical standards and offers professional certification. Has 46 regional chapters and 17 divisions of specialized planning interests.

Key Initiatives: Growing Smart ^{SM} (project to draft the next generation of model planning and zoning legislation for the U.S.; includes development of a legislative guidebook to help decision-makers update state land use laws to fit modern uses); City Parks Forum (explore and promote the benefits of urban parks).

National Legislative Priorities (and APA's positions): Federal Assistance to Promote Smart Growth; Takings (opposes expansion of "takings" doctrines); Federal Preemption (opposes preemption of local land-use decision-making).

State Legislative Priorities (and APA's positions): Takings (opposes expansion of "takings" doctrines); Implementation of Growing Smart; Licensing/Credentialing.

Key Periodicals: Planning (monthly magazine); Journal of the APA (quarterly journal); Zoning News (monthly newsletter on local land-use controls); Land Use Law and Zoning Digest (monthly law journal).

Key Publications (both online under "Growing Smart" on the "Planning Research" webpage): Growing Smart Legislative Handbook (model statutes for planning and change management); Planning Communities for the 21st Century (report card on the status of state planning/enabling statutes and statutory reform efforts in the U.S.).

Check Out on the Web: "State Summaries" (individual summaries of the planning statutes for all 50 states; online under "Growing Smart" on the "Planning Research" webpage).

Founded: 1909 **Membership:** 30,000 **HQ:** Chicago, IL **Staff:** 70 **NP Status:** 501(c)(3) **Budget:** $12 million
Contact Info: (312) 431-9100; APA@planning.org
Key Personnel: Frank So (Executive Director)

155. <u>**American Public Health Association (APHA)**</u> (www.apha.org)

Description: Billed as the oldest and largest association of public health professionals in the world, representing members from 50+ public health occupations. Provides continuing education/training and publications/information services. Also an active policy advocate. Organized into 25 discipline-based Sections, including one on "Environment."

Lobbying/Political Activities: Registered lobbyist under the LDA.

Key Periodicals: American Journal of Public Health (monthly).

Founded: 1872 **Membership:** 32,000 **HQ:** Washington, DC **Staff:** 65 **NP Status:** 501(c)(3) **Budget:** $13 million
Contact Info: (202) 777-2500; comments@apha.org
Key Personnel: Mohammad Akhter, MD (Executive Director)

156. <u>**American Public Works Association (APWA)**</u> (www.pubworks.org)

Description: Professional association of public agencies, private sector companies, and individuals involved with "public works" projects/services (that is, "community infrastructure" such as water/wastewater systems, roads and public transit, and solid waste management). Provides continuing education/training and publications/information services. Offers professional management accreditation for public works agencies. Also an active policy advocate on both a federal and state level. Maintains 67 chapters (organized into 9 regions) covering the U.S. and Canada.

A Closer Look: In 9/99, APWA adopted a new strategic plan identifying public policy advocacy as one of its 3 long-range goals (and lists it first on their website). Following that plan, they have adopted an aggressive advocacy approach more akin to a business trade association than a professional association.

Key Committees: Solid Waste Management; Water Resources Management; Government Affairs (public policy advocacy).

General Advocacy Principles: 1) Support for adequate investment in public infrastructure; 2) Respect for local authority; 3) Reasonable regulations and protection from unfunded mandates.

Advocacy Priorities for 2002-2003 (and APWA's positions): Transportation (increase federal funding in infrastructure and programs; protect the integrity of transportation trust funds and the framework of TEA-21); TEA-21 (support full/timely implementation); Clean Water (increase federal funding in clean water infrastructure); Stormwater Management (support funding for development of best management practices); Air Quality Standards (support solutions that "promote the efficient and cost-effective delivery of public works services"); Local Control of Public Rights-of-Way (oppose preemption of local control).

Check Out on the Web: APWA Policy and Positions (provides a multitude of written statements on relevant, public works-related issues).

Founded: 1937 **Membership:** 26,000 **HQ:** Kansas City, MO **Staff:** 44 **NP Status:** 501(c)(3) **Budget:** $8 million

Contact Info: (816) 472-6100; apwa@apwa.org

Key Personnel: Peter King (Executive Director)

157. American Society of Landscape Architects (ASLA) (www.asla.org)

Description: Professional society representing the "landscape architecture profession" (includes the areas of site planning, garden design, environmental restoration, town and urban planning, park and recreation planning, regional planning, and historic preservation; in all but 5 states, Landscape Architects are subject to professional licensing requirements). Provides continuing education/training and publications/information services. Also advocates on selected policy issues affecting members. Serves as the accreditation body for landscape architecture programs at universities/colleges. Maintains 47 chapters across the U.S.

Key Periodicals: Landscape Architecture (monthly magazine; online); Landscape Architecture News Digest (online newsletter; 10 times/yr).

Founded: 1899 **Membership:** 13,000 **HQ:** Washington, DC **Staff:** 45 **Budget:** $5 million

Contact Info: (202) 898-2444

Key Personnel: Peter Kirsch (Executive VP)

158. American Water Resources Association (AWRA) (www.awra.org)

Description: Scientific/technical society exclusively devoted to water resources and related issues. Provides continuing education/training and publications/information services. Maintains individual State Sections and various Student Chapters. Has 15 Technical Committees, including one on "Policy."

Key Periodicals: Journal of the American Water Resources Association.

Founded: 1964 **Membership:** 3400 **HQ:** Middleburg, VA **Staff:** 6 **NP Status:** 501(c)(3) **Budget:** $1 million

Contact Info: (540) 687-8390; info@awra.org

Key Personnel: Kenneth Reid (Executive Director)

159. American Water Works Association (AWWA) (www.awwa.org)

Description: Professional association of drinking water supply professionals. Membership includes 4000 public utilities supplying water to 180 million people in North America. Provides continuing education/training and publications/information services. Also advocates on selected policy issues affecting members. Conducts/supports technical/scientific research through its affiliated AWWA Research Foundation and supports water-related projects in developing countries through its affiliated Water for People program.

Lobbying/Political Activities: Registered lobbyist under the LDA.

Key Affiliated Programs/Organizations: AWWA Research Foundation (separate non-profit overseeing drinking water-related research funded through government grants; www.awwarf.org); Water for People (separate non-profit supporting sustainable drinking water, sanitation and hygiene projects in developing countries;

www.waterforpeople.org); Water Wiser (water efficiency clearinghouse operated in conjunction with the U.S. Bureau of Reclamation; www.waterwiser.org).

Key Periodicals: Journal AWWA (monthly research- and management-oriented journal; executive summaries online).

Founded: 1881 **Membership:** 50,000 individuals; 4800 orgs **HQ:** Denver, CO **Staff:** 130 **NP Status:** 501(c)(3)

Budget: $30 million (AWWA); $20 million (AWWA Research Foundation); $1 million (Water for People).

Contact Info: (303) 794-7711

Key Personnel: Jack Hoffbuhr (Executive Director)

160.   Association for Environmental Health and Sciences (AEHS) (www.aehs.com)

Description: Professional membership association of environmental professionals involved in soil protection and cleanup. Provides continuing education/training and publications/information services.

Key Periodicals: Soil and Sediment Contamination (bi-monthly technical, regulatory, and legal journal); Human and Ecological Risk Assessment (quarterly technical journal); Environmental Forensics (quarterly scientific journal).

Key Publication: Survey of States' Soil and Groundwater Cleanup Standards (annual survey; online).

Founded: 1989 **Membership:** 600 **HQ:** Amherst, MA **Staff:** 6 **NP Budget:** $0.25 to 0.5 million

Contact Info: (413) 549-5170; info@aehs.com

Key Personnel: Paul Kostecki (Executive Director)

161.   Association of Energy Engineers (AEE) (www.aeecenter.org)

Description: Professional membership association of energy engineers. Provides continuing education/training and publications/information services. Also offers 9 different technical certifications. Organized into 5 Divisions, including the Environmental Engineers and Managers Institute. Maintains 67 local/regional chapters.

Founded: 1977 **Membership:** 8500 **HQ:** Atlanta, GA **Staff:** 12 **NP Budget:** $1 to 2 million

Contact Info: (770) 447-5083; info@AEEcenter.org

Key Personnel: Albert Thurmann (Executive Director)

162.   Association of Environmental and Resource Economists (AERE) (www.aere.org)

Description: Professional membership association of economists working in the areas of environmental and resource economics. Established "as a means of exchanging ideas, stimulating research, and promoting graduate training." Members come from academic institutions, the public sector, and private industry. AERE draws from traditional economics, agricultural economics, forestry, and natural resource schools.

A Closer Look: AERE's business office is located within Resources for the Future, an environmental think tank (see Profile #5, located within Subsection 1.1 – "Policy Research Institutions").

Key Periodicals: Journal of Environmental Economics and Management (bi-monthly research journal).

Founded: 1979 **Membership:** 1000 **HQ:** Washington, DC **NP Status:** 501(c)(3) **Budget:** $0.04 million

Contact Info: (202) 328-5077

Key Personnel: Marilyn Voigt (Business Office Manager)

163.   Association of Environmental Engineering and Science Professors (AEESP) (www.aeesp.org)

Description: Professional membership association of professors (and students) in college environmental engineering and science programs worldwide. Affiliate membership is open to individuals associated with academic programs but not meeting the professor/student criteria. Provides continuing education/training and publications/information services. Also promotes graduate training.

Founded: 1963 **Membership:** 700 **Staff:** 1 **HQ:** Champaign IL **Budget:** $0.025 to 0.05 million

Contact Info: (217) 398-6969

Key Personnel: Joanne Fetzner (Business Office Manager)

164. **Ecological Society of America (ESA)** (esa.sdsc.edu)

Description: Professional society of scientists working on ecological issues. Provides continuing education/training and publications/information services. Also offers a professional certification program for ecologists.

A Closer Look: A key part of ESA is its Sustainable Biosphere Initiative (SBI), established in 1992, which now operates as the science program office for ESA. Through a variety of activities, SBI seeks to "ensure that sound ecological information is incorporated into natural resource decision-making."

Key Periodicals: Bulletin of the Ecological Society of America (quarterly); Ecology (research journal; 8 times/yr.; current issue online); Ecological Applications (quarterly research and discussion papers relevant to environmental management and policy; current issue online).

Key Other Publications: Issues in Ecology (a continuing series presenting major ecological issues in a format targeting non-scientists; 9 reports thus far; online); Ecological Fact Sheets (short summaries of key issues, along with a list of contacts for further information; online).

Founded: 1915 **Membership:** 7600 **HQ:** Washington, DC **Staff:** 26 **NP Status:** 501(c)(3) **Budget:** $4 million
Contact Info: (202) 833-8773; esahq@esa.org
Key Personnel: Katherine McCarter (Executive Director)

165. **Forest History Society (FHS)** (www.lib.duke.edu/forest)

Description: Member-based society focused on forest history in the U.S. and Canada. Affiliated with Duke University; incorporated as a nonprofit educational institution. Maintains an extensive library (the Carl Weyerhaeuser Library, holding 7,500 books, 200+ periodicals and various archival collections), conducts research, sponsors conferences, and issues publications.

Key Program: USDA Forest Service History Program (supports publications, oral history projects, and historical scholarship).

Key Periodicals: Environmental History (quarterly interdisciplinary journal; table of contents online); Forest History Today (semi-annual magazine; online); Issues Series (booklets providing a historical context to current issues in forestry/natural resource management).

Founded: 1946 **Membership:** 2000 **HQ:** Durham, NC **Staff:** 8 **NP Status:** 501(c)(3) **Budget:** $0.6 million
Contact Info: (919) 682-9319; recluce2@duke.edu
Key Personnel: Steve Anderson (President)

166. **Golf Course Superintendents Association of America (GCSAA)** (www.gcsaa.org)

Description: Professional association of golf course superintendents. Provides technical education and training (including professional certification), communications tools and programs, and representation (including policy advocacy efforts).

Affiliated Orgs: GCSAA Foundation (devoted to education, research and historical preservation initiatives); GCSAA Communications (for-profit arm offering various programs/services).

Key Programs/Initiatives: Environmental Management Program (technical management training in 5 environmentally-related areas); Environmental Stewardship (works with allied golf associations and environmental groups on relevant issues); Environmental Leaders in Golf Awards (annual awards to superintendents for environmental stewardship efforts).

Key Periodicals: Golf Course Management (monthly); Greens and Grassroots (legislative and regulatory tracking newsletter).

Key Publications: Environmental Principles for Golf Courses (a set of voluntary principles for environmental excellence in golf course planning and siting, design, construction, maintenance and facility operations; developed and endorsed in cooperation with several golf and environmental organizations, along with the U.S. Environmental Protection Agency; online).

Founded: 1926 **Membership:** 21,000 **HQ:** Lawrence, KS **Staff:** 115 **Chapters:** 102 **NP Status:** 501(c)(6) (GCSAA); 501(c)(3) (GCSAA Foundation) **Budget (combined operations):** $20 million

Contact Info: (800) 472-7878 / (785) 841-2240; infobox@gcsaa.org
Key Personnel: Stephen Mona (CEO)

167.   National Association for Environmental Management (NAEM) (www.naem.org)

Description: Professional association of private and public sector environmental / environmental, health and safety (EHS) managers. Provides continuing education/training and publications/information services. Has 9 regional chapters.
Founded: 1990 **Membership:** 1,000 **HQ:** Washington, DC **Staff:** 3 **Budget:** $0.25 to 0.5 million
Contact Info: (202) 986-6616 / (800) 391-NAEM; naem@msn.com
Key Personnel: Carol Neurelt (Executive Director)

168.   National Association of Environmental Professionals (NAEP) (www.naep.org)

Description: Professional association of environmental professionals. Promotes ethical practices, technical competency and professional standards. Has 19 State and Regional chapters covering much of the U.S.
Key Periodicals: Environmental Practice (quarterly interdisciplinary journal linking environmental science and policy; abstracts online); NAEP National News (e-newsletter; online).
Founded: 1975 **Membership:** 2,000 **HQ:** Bowie, MD **Staff:** 3 **NP Status:** 501(c)(3) **Budget:** $0.3 million
Contact Info: (888) 251-9902 / (301) 860-1140; office@naep.org
Key Personnel: Bruce Hasbrouck (President)

169.   National Environmental Health Association (NEHA) (www.neha.org)

Description: Professional association for environmental health practitioners. A majority of members work in the public sector (many in county health departments). Provides continuing education/training and publications/information services. Also offers 8 professional credentials. Has 25 state-level affiliate programs. Membership committees are divides into 9 technical sections (see below).
Technical Sections: Air/Land/Water; Environmental Health Management; Food Protection; General Environmental Health; Injury Prevention/Occupational Health; Institutional Environmental Health; Hazardous and Toxic Substances; On-Site Wastewater Management; International Environmental Health.
Key Periodicals: Journal of Environmental Health (professional journal; 10 times/yr.); Environmental News Digest (quarterly newsletter).
Founded: 1937 **Membership:** 5,700 **HQ:** Denver, CO **Staff:** 21 **NP Status:** 501(c)(3) **Budget:** $2.5 million
Contact Info: (303) 756-9090; staff@neha.org
Key Personnel: Nelson Fabian (Executive Director)

170.   National Environmental Training Association (NETA) (www.ehs-training.org)

Description: Professional association "dedicated to promoting competency and excellence in environmental and safety and health training." Members include academic, government, industrial, utility and consulting trainers and training managers. Provides continuing education/training and publications/information services. Also offers two professional training certifications and issues training standards. Founded with support and encouragement from the U.S. EPA.
Founded: 1977 **Membership:** 1600 **HQ:** Phoenix, AZ **Staff:** 6 **NP Status:** 501(c)(3) **Budget:** $0.5 million
Contact Info: (602)956-6099; neta@ehs-training.org
Key Personnel: Charles Richardson (Executive Director)

171.   National Ground Water Association (NGWA) (www.ngwa.org)

Description: Professional membership association for ground water professionals (mainly contractors, scientists and engineers, manufacturers, and suppliers). Provides continuing education/training and publications/information services. Particularly known for its professional education program. Also an active policy advocate and maintains a Political Action Committee. Has state-level affiliate programs in all 50 states.

Lobbying/Political Activities: Registered lobbyist under the LDA; maintains a PAC (National Ground Water Association PAC).

Affiliated Orgs: National Ground Water Educational Foundation (focuses on achieving a broader public understanding of ground water); National Ground Water Information Center (a fee-based groundwater information retrieval service).

Key Periodicals: Journal of Ground Water (bimonthly academic journal); Ground Water Monitoring and Remediation (quarterly technical journal).

Founded: 1948 **Members:** 16,500 **HQ:** Westerville, OH **Staff:** 41 **Budget:** $6 million

Contact Info: (800) 551-7379 / (614) 898-7791; ngwa@ngwa.org

Key Personnel: Kerin McCray (Executive Director)

172.   <u>**National Wildlife Rehabilitators Association (NWRA)**</u> (www.nwrawildlife.org)

Description: Membership organization seeking to support the science and profession of wildlife rehabilitation and its practitioners (wildlife rehabilitation being the treatment and temporary care of injured, diseased and displaced indigenous wildlife with subsequent return to appropriate wild habitats). Provides continuing education/training and publications/information services. Members range from experienced wildlife rehabilitation professionals to interested beginners. About one-quarter of members are veterinarians or veterinary technicians, while others are affiliated with humane societies or zoos.

Founded: 1982 **Members:** 2000 **HQ:** St. Cloud, MN **Staff:** 2 **NP Status:** 501(c)(3) **Budget:** $0.15 million

Contact Info: (320) 259-4086; nwra@nwrawildlife.org

Key Personnel: Elaine Thrune (President)

173.   <u>**Outdoor Writers Association of America (OWAA)**</u> (www.owaa.org)

Description: Membership organization of "professional communicators dedicated to sharing the outdoor experience." Members include writers, editors, book authors, broadcasters, film and video producers, photographers, artists and lecturers. Provides educational services (workshops and seminars) and publications/information services. Also sets professional standards, including a code of ethics.

Founded: 1927 **Members:** 2000 **HQ:** Missoula, MT **Staff:** 3 **NP Status:** 501(c)(3) **Budget:** $0.1 million

Contact Info: (406) 728-7434

Key Personnel: Steve Wagner (Executive Director)

174.   <u>**Renewable Natural Resources Foundation (RNRF)**</u> (www.rnrf.org)

Description: Consortium of 15 professional societies (see below) that seeks to "advance sciences and public education in renewable natural resources." Conducts workshops/meetings and issues publications. Also holds legislative briefings and public-policy round tables, and conducts international outreach activities.

Key Members (see separate profiles within this subsection): American Fisheries Society; American Society of Landscape Architects; American Water Resources Association; Society of Environmental Toxicology and Chemistry; Soil and Water Conservation Society; (The) Wildlife Society.

General Interest Areas: Sustainability; Ecosystems; Biological Diversity; Cultural Diversity; Human Populations; Resources Management; Water Quality and Management; Air Quality; Science; Education; Information Services.

Key Periodicals: Renewable Resources Journal (quarterly public policy-focused journal).

Founded: 1972 **Members:** 15 societies **HQ:** Bethesda, MD **Staff:** 5 **NP Status:** 501(c)(3) **Budget:** $0.5 million

Contact Info: (301) 493-9101; info@rnrf.org

Key Personnel: Robert D. Day (Executive Director)

175.   <u>**Society for Ecological Restoration (SER)**</u> (www.ser.org)

Description: International membership society of individuals and organizations engaged in ecologically-sensitive repair and management of ecosystems worldwide. Provides continuing education/training and publications/information services. Also promotes awareness of and public support for restoration and restorative management and engages in public policy discussions. Has 13 chapters serving regions of North America, England, Australia and India.

Key Periodicals: Restoration Ecology (quarterly scientific/technical journal); Ecological Restoration (quarterly practitioner's guide, summarizing current projects and techniques).

Founded: 1988 **Members:** 2800 **HQ:** Tucson, AZ **Staff:** 3 **NP Status:** 501(c)(3) **Budget:** $0.7 million

Contact Info: (520) 622.5485; info@ser.org

Key Personnel: Steve Gatewood (Executive Director)

176.   Society of American Foresters (SAF) (www.safnet.org)

Description: Professional society for foresters (billed as the largest such society), originally founded by Gifford Pinchot (who served as the first Chief of the U.S. Forest Service). Provides continuing education/training and publications/information services. Also acts as the accreditation authority for professional forestry education in the U.S. and offers a "Certified Forester" program. Undertakes forest policy work. Has 28 technical working groups (see below), 33 state/multi-state chapters and 264 local chapters.

Technical Working Groups: Resources Measurements; Forestry Systems; Ecology and Biology; Management and Utilization; Decision Sciences; Social and Related Sciences.

Key Periodicals: Journal of Forestry (monthly scholarly journal; abstracts online); Forest Science (quarterly research journal; abstracts online); The Forestry Source (monthly SAF newsletter; highlights online).

Key Reports: Task Force Report on Forest Management Certification Programs (compares 6 specific programs; online); Forest of Discord: Options for Governing Our National Forests and Federal Public Lands (task force report analyzing critical policy issues; executive summary online).

Check Out on the Web: Top Ten Forestry Advances (cites key advances in the U.S. over the past century; located under "About Forestry").

Founded: 1900 **Membership:** 19,000 **HQ:** Bethesda, MD **Staff:** 30 **NP Status:** 501(c)(3) **Budget:** $4 million

Contact Info: (301) 897-8720; safweb@safnet.org

Key Personnel: William Banzhaf (Executive VP)

177.   Society of Environmental Journalists (SEJ) (www.sej.org)

Description: Professional society of environmental journalists. Provides continuing education/training and publications/information services. Also performs specialized outreach aimed at editors and general assignment staff.

A Closer Look: SEJ membership is restricted to journalists, educators and students. However, non-members can attend conferences, subscribe to SEJ's journal or contact members via SEJ's mailing list or email services.

Key Periodicals: SEJournal (quarterly; back issues online); TipSheet (weekly news tips; online).

Website Notes: Website itself has good news/journalism content open to non-members.

Founded: 1990 **Members:** 1,000 **HQ:** Philadelphia, PA **Staff:** 7 **NP Status:** 501(c)(3) **Budget:** $0.8 million

Contact Info: (215) 836-9970; sejoffice@aol.com

Key Personnel: Beth Parke (Executive Director)

178.   Society of Environmental Toxicology and Chemistry (SETAC) (www.setac.org)

Description: Professional society with membership consisting primarily of environmental scientists (biologists, chemists, toxicologists, ecologists) and environmental engineers. Promotes the use of multidisciplinary approaches to solve problems regarding the impact of chemicals and technology on the environment. Provides continuing education/training and publications/information services. Has 16 Regional Chapters in North America. Technical work carried out by 7 Advisory Groups (see below).

A Closer Look: Unique in that SETAC by-laws mandate equal representation from academia, business, and government for its officers, Board of Directors, and Committees.

Affiliated Orgs: SETAC Foundation for Environmental Education (public outreach, training and education arm); Sister Groups (in Europe, Asia/Pacific and Latin American).

Advisory Groups: Life-Cycle Assessment; Ecological Risk Assessment; Environmental Assessment of Soils; Fate and Exposure Modeling; Pesticides Microbiological; Metals; Whole Effluent Toxicity.

Key Periodicals: Environmental Toxicology and Chemistry (monthly scientific journal).

Check Out on the Web: "SETAC Graduate Programs" (online directory providing essential information on graduate programs in environmental chemical, engineering and toxicology in the U.S., Canada and Europe).

Founded: 1979 **Members:** 5000 **HQ:** Pensacola, FL **Staff:** 13 **Budget:** $1 to 2 million

Contact Info: (850) 469-1500; setac@setac.org

Key Personnel: Rodney Parrish (Executive Director)

179.   Soil and Water Conservation Society (SWCS) (www.swcs.org)

Description: Scientific and educational association serving as an advocate for the soil and water conservation profession and for science-based conservation policy. Promotes sustainable soil, water, and related natural resource management, particularly on privately owned agricultural and forest lands ("working lands"). Provides continuing education/training and publications/information services. Also conducts policy development and research regarding land and water use. Maintains 80+ chapters.

Key Periodicals: Journal of Soil and Water Conservation (quarterly applied research journal; archives online).

Founded: 1945 **Membership:** 11,000 **HQ:** Ankeny, IA **Staff:** 17 **NP Status:** 501(c)(3) **Budget:** $2 million

Contact Info: (515) 289-2331; swcs@swcs.org

Key Personnel: Craig Cox (Executive VP)

180.   Solid Waste Association of North America (SWANA) (www.swana.org)

Description: Professional association of public and private sector individuals involved in solid waste management in the U.S. and Canada (small businesses can also apply for direct membership). Provides continuing education/training and publications/information services. Also an active policy advocate on both the federal and state levels. Offers professional certification in 6 disciplines. Maintains 8 Technical Divisions (see below). Has 46 chapters (mostly state-level).

Key Technical Divisions: Landfill Management; Landfill Gas Management; Special Waste Management; Waste Reduction, Recycling and Composting; Waste-to-Energy.

Key Legislative and Regulatory Issues: Consumer Labeling Initiative (focus on pesticide disposal instructions); Environmental Justice; Landfill Gas Issues (focus on tax credits); Landfill Sitings Near Public Airports; Bioreactor Landfill Technology Issues; Waste Flow Control and Transboundary Transport.

Founded: 1961 **Membership:** 6000 individuals; 1500 companies **HQ:** Silver Spring, MD **Staff:** 25 **NP Status:** 501(c)(3) **Budget:** $4 million

Contact Info: (800) 467-9262; info@swana.org.

Key Personnel: John Skinner (Executive Director)

181.   Water Environment Federation (WEF) (www.wef.org)

Description: Professional association of water quality professionals, including public utilities. Primary focus areas are wastewater treatment and water quality protection. Provides continuing education/training and publications/information services. Also conducts/supports technical/scientific research through its affiliated WEF Research Foundation. Composed of 79 Member Associations and 6 Corresponding Associations located throughout the world. Maintains 20 Technical Committees (see below).

Affiliated Org: Water Environment Research Foundation (scientific research arm).

Key Technical Committees: Air Quality; Collection Systems; Disinfection; Ecology; Environmental Management Systems; Groundwater; Hazardous Wastes; Industrial Wastes; Non-Point Pollution Sources; Plant Operations and Maintenance; Residuals and Biosolids; Toxics Substances; Water Reuse; Watershed Management.

Key Periodicals: Water Environment Research (bi-monthly research journal); Water Environment and

Technology (monthly covers wastewater treatment and watershed management issues).

Founded: 1928 **Membership:** 41,000 individuals **HQ:** Alexandria, VA **Staff:** 115 **NP Status:** 501(c)(3) **Budget:** $20 million (WEF); $8 million (WEF Research Foundation)

Contact Info: (800) 666-0206 / (703) 684-2400; csc@wef.org

Key Personnel: Quincalee Brown (Executive Director)

182.   (The) Wildlife Society (TWS) (www.wildlife.org)

Description: Scientific and educational organization of professionals and students engaged in wildlife research, management, education and administration. Provides continuing education/training and publications/information services. Also offers professional certifications for wildlife biologists. An active policy advocate (see below), operating a Wildlife Policy Program that issues policy statements and white papers. Has 15 Working Groups.

Policy Priorities: Arctic National Wildlife Refuge; Budgets for Federal Land Management and Research Agencies; Farm Bill Implementation/2002 Farm Bill; Non-Game Wildlife Funding/Conservation and Reinvestment Act (CARA).

Key Periodicals: The Journal of Wildlife Management (quarterly wildlife research and management); Wildlifer (bimonthly newsletter; highlights online); Wildlife Policy News (bi-monthly newsletter on relevant policy issues; online); Wildlife Society Bulletin (scientific quarterly).

Check Out on the Web: Celebrating Our Wildlife Conservation Heritage (COWCH) Project (interviewing the first generation of wildlife professionals for historical purposes).

Founded: 1937 **Membership:** 9700 **HQ:** Bethesda, MD **Staff:** 11 **NP Status:** 501(c)(3) **Budget:** $2 million

Contact Info: (301) 897-9770; tws@wildlife.org

Key Personnel: Harry Hodgdon (Executive Director)

SECTION 2: GOVERNMENTAL ORGANIZATIONS

INTRODUCTION/USER'S GUIDE:

In this section, 103 profiles of environmentally-relevant governmental organizations – and related entities – are provided, divided into the following three subsections:

2.1 – Congressional Committees	(8 entries)
2.2 – Federal Governmental Agencies/Entities	(61 entries)
2.3 – Governmental Associations and Councils	(34 entries)

In terms of individual entry contents, a descriptive outline of standardized profile information provided for each organization listed is given at the beginning of each subsection.

Subsection 2.1: Congressional Committees

Introduction/User's Guide:

Within this subsection, 8 key congressional committees (4 House and 4 Senate committees) working on environmentally-related issues are profiled. The committees profiled cover not only the traditional issue areas of conservation and environmental protection, but also key associated issue areas, namely agriculture, energy, transportation, and trade/commerce.

For each committee, the following profile information is provided (as based on the current 107th Congress which will finish its term at the end of 2002):

[Profile #] Committee Name (Website Address)
Description: Noting the key issue areas covered by the committee and its associated subcommittees (something not always conveyed by just the committee's/sub-committee's name).
Members: Noting the total number of committee members and providing an associated breakdown by party affiliation (D-Democrat; R-Republican; I-Independent).
Subcommittees (and corresponding chairman): For Chairmen, providing specific names and state affiliations (for the 107th Congress, all House Chairman are Republicans; all Senate Chairman are Democrats).
Key Federal Agencies Under the Committee's Jurisdiction: Focusing on the agencies/entities profiled under Subsection 2.2 – "Federal Governmental Agencies/Entities." A key to the abbreviations used for the listed agencies/entities is provided below.
Contact Info: Providing: Street/mailing address; general telephone number; general email address (if established/available).
Chairman / Ranking Minority Member: Providing specific names and state/party affiliations (for the 107th Congress, all House Chairman are Republicans; all Senate Chairman are Democrats, except for the Senate Committee on Environment and Public Works, where James Jeffords – an Independent – is Chairman).

The abbreviations used for identifying federal agencies/entities within this subsection are as follows, with associated Cabinet-level Department names noted in parentheses:

ACE:	Army Corps of Engineers (Dept. of Defense)
ATSDR:	Agency for Toxic Substances and Disease Registry (Dept. of Health and Human Services)
BIA:	Bureau of Indian Affairs (Dept. of the Interior)
BLM:	Bureau of Land Management (Dept. of the Interior)
CDC:	Centers for Disease Control (Dept. of Health and Human Services)
DOE:	Dept. of Energy
DOI:	Dept. of the Interior
DOT:	Dept. of Transportation
EPA:	Environmental Protection Agency
FAA:	Federal Aviation Administration (Dept. of Transportation)
FDA:	Food and Drug Administration (Dept. of Health and Human Services)
FTA:	Federal Transit Administration (Dept. of Transportation)
FWHA:	Federal Highway Administration (Dept. of Transportation)
FWS:	Fish and Wildlife Service (Dept. of the Interior)
HHS:	Dept. of Health and Human Services
MMS:	Minerals Management Service (Dept. of the Interior)

NIH:	National Institutes of Health (Dept. of Health and Human Services)
NMFS:	National Marine Fisheries Service (part of NOAA)
NOAA:	National Oceanic and Atmospheric Administration (Dept. of Commerce)
NOS:	National Ocean Service (part of NOAA)
NPS:	National Park Service (Dept. of the Interior)
NRC:	Nuclear Regulatory Commission
NRCS:	Natural Resources Conservation Service (Dept. of Agriculture)
OAR:	Office of Oceanic and Atmospheric Research (part of NOAA)
OSM:	Office of Surface Mining Reclamation and Enforcement (Dept. of the Interior)
RSPA:	Research and Special Programs Administration (Dept. of Transportation)
USBR:	Bureau of Reclamation (Dept. of the Interior)
USCG:	Coast Guard (Dept. of Transportation)
USDA:	Dept. of Agriculture
USFS:	Forest Service (Dept. of Agriculture)
USGS:	Geological Service (Dept. of the Interior)

Specific committee profiles are provided beginning on the next page, listed alphabetically and grouped by Congressional division – House committees presented first in Subsection 2.1.1, followed by Senate committees in Subsection 2.1.2.

2.1.1 House Committees

183.   **House Committee on Agriculture** (agriculture.house.gov)

Description: House committee focused on agricultural and related issues, including biotechnology.

Members: 51 (27-R; 24-D)

Subcommittees (and corresponding chairman): 1) Ag Department Operations, Oversight, Nutrition and Forestry (Bob Goodlatte, R-VA); 2) Livestock and Horticulture (Richard Pombo, R-CA); 3) Specialty Crops and Foreign Agriculture Programs (Terry Everett, R-AL); 4) Conservation, Credit, Rural Development and Research (Frank Lucas, R-OK); 5) General Farm Commodities and Risk Management (Saxby Chambliss, R-GA).

Key Federal Agencies Under the Committee's Jurisdiction: All USDA agencies (including USFS and NRCS); EPA (focusing on water quality and pesticide issues); FDA (focus on biotechnology issues).

Contact Info: 1301 Longworth House Office Bldg., Washington, DC 20515; (202) 225-2171; agriculture@mail.house.gov

Chairman: Larry Combest (R-TX); **Ranking Minority Member:** Charles Stenholm (D-TX)

184.   **House Committee on Energy and Commerce** (energycommerce.house.gov)

Description: House committee focused on energy and commerce issues, including international trade issues. Also oversees environmental protection issues through its Environment and Hazardous Materials subcommittee and health issues – including public health – through its Health subcommittee.

Members: 57 (31-R; 26-D)

Subcommittees (and corresponding chairman): 1) Commerce, Trade and Consumer Protection (Cliff Stearns, R-FL); 2) Energy and Air Quality (Joe Barton, R-TX); 3) Environment and Hazardous Materials (Paul Gillmor, R-OH); 4) Health (Michael Bilirakis, R-FL); 5) Oversight and Investigations (James C. Greenwood, R-PA); 6) Telecommunications and the Internet (Fred Upton, R-MI).

Key Federal Agencies Under the Committee's Jurisdiction: DOE, EPA; NRC; all HHS agencies (including ATSDR, CDC, FDA, and NIH).

Contact Info: 2125 Rayburn House Office Bldg., Washington, DC 20515; (202) 225-2927.

Chairman: W. J. "Billy" Tauzin (R-LA); **Ranking Minority Member:** John Dingell (D-MI)

185.   **House Committee on Resources** (resourcescommittee.house.gov)

Description: House committee focused on natural resource and related issues. Also oversees the National Fish and Wildlife Foundation (see Profile #79, within Subsection 1.2 – "Public Interest Groups and Coalitions").

Members: 52 (28-R; 24-D)

Subcommittees (and corresponding chairman): 1) Fisheries Conservation, Wildlife and Oceans (Wayne Gilchrest, R-MD); 2) National Parks, Recreation, and Public Lands (George Radanovich, R-CA); 3) Energy and Mineral Resources (Barbara Cubin, R-WY); 4) Water and Power (Ken Calvert, R-CA); 5) Forests and Forest Health (Scott McInnis, R-CO).

Key Federal Agencies Under the Committee's Jurisdiction: USFS and NRCS; NOAA (including NOS, NMFS and OAR); ACE; all DOI agencies – FWS, NPS, USBR, USGS, BLM, MMS, OSM, BIA); EPA (limited to: marine and estuary issues; fish and wildlife issues; NEPA assessments).

Contact Info: 1324 Longworth House Office Bldg., Washington, DC 20515; (202) 225-2761; resources.committee@mail.house.gov

Chairman: James Hansen (R-UT); **Ranking Minority Member:** Nick Rahall, II (D-WV)

186.   **House Committee on Transportation and Infrastructure** (www.house.gov/transportation)

Description: House committee focused on transportation and infrastructure issues. Also oversees water resource-related issues (focus areas: water resources policy; water-related infrastructure; groundwater and watershed protection; coastal pollution and coastal zone management; hazardous waste cleanup) through its Water Resources and Environment subcommittee.

Members: 75 (41-R; 34-D)

Subcommittees (and corresponding chairman): 1) Aviation (John Mica, R-FL); 2) Coast Guard and Maritime Transportation (Frank LoBiondo, R-NJ); 3) Economic Development, Public Buildings and Emergency Management (Steven LaTourette, R-OH); 4) Highways and Transit (Thomas Petri, R-WI); 5) Railroads (Jack Quinn, R-NY); 6) Water Resources and Environment (John Duncan, R-TN).

Key Federal Agencies Under the Committee's Jurisdiction: All DOT agencies (including FAA, FHWA, FTA, and RSPA); USCG; ACE; EPA.

Contact Info: 2165 Rayburn House Office Bldg., Washington, DC 20515; (202) 225-9446.

Chairman: Don Young (R-AK); **Ranking Minority Member:** James Oberstar (D-MN)

2.1.2 Senate Committees

187. Senate Committee on Agriculture, Nutrition, and Forestry (www.senate.gov/~agriculture)

Description: Senate committee focused on agriculture, nutrition and forestry issues.

Members: 21 (11-D; 10-R)

Subcommittees (and corresponding chairman): 1) Production and Price Competitiveness (Kent Conrad, D-ND); 2) Marketing, Inspection, and Product Promotion (Max Baucus, D-MT); 3) Forestry, Conservation, and Rural Revitalization (Blanche Lincoln, D-AR); 4) Research, Nutrition, and General Legislation (Patrick Leahy, D-VT).

Key Federal Agencies Under the Committee's Jurisdiction: All USDA agencies (including USFS and NRCS); EPA (focus on water quality and pesticide issues); FDA (focus on food safety issues, including biotechnology).

Contact Info: SR-328A Russell Senate Office Bldg., Washington, DC 20510; (202) 224-2035.

Chairman: Tom Harkin (D-IA); **Ranking Minority Member:** Richard Lugar (R-IN)

188. Senate Committee on Commerce, Science, and Transportation (www.senate.gov/~commerce)

Description: Senate committee focused on commerce, science and transportation/public transit issues. Also deals with ocean/coastal and fisheries issues through its Oceans, Atmosphere and Fisheries subcommittee.

Members: 23 (12-D; 11-R)

Subcommittees (and corresponding chairman): 1) Aviation (John D. Rockefeller IV, D-WV); 2) Communications (Daniel Inouye, D-HI); 3) Consumer Affairs, Foreign Commerce, and Tourism (Byron Dorgan, D-ND); 4) Oceans, Atmosphere and Fisheries (John F. Kerry, D-MA); 5) Science, Technology and Space (Ron Wyden, D-OR); 6) Surface Transportation and Merchant Marine (John Breaux, D-LA).

Key Federal Agencies Under the Committee's Jurisdiction: FAA, FTA, and RSPA; USCG; NOAA.

Contact Info: 508 Dirksen Senate Office Bldg., Washington, DC 20510; (202) 224-5115.

Chairman: Ernest Hollings (D-SC); **Ranking Minority Member:** John McCain (R-AZ)

189. Senate Committee on Energy and Natural Resources (energy.senate.gov)

Description: Senate committee focused on energy and natural resource issues.

Members: 23 (12-D; 11-R)

Subcommittees (and corresponding chairman): 1) Energy (Bob Graham, D-FL); 2) Public Lands and Forests (Ron Wyden, D-OR); 3) National Parks (Daniel Akaka, D-HI); 4) Water and Power (Byron Dorgan, D-ND).

Key Federal Agencies Under the Committee's Jurisdiction: DOE; NRC; all DOI agencies – FWS, NPS, USBR, USGS, BLM, MMS, OSM, BIA.

Contact Info: 364 Dirksen Senate Office Bldg., Washington, DC 20510; (202) 224-4971; committee@energy.senate.gov

Chairman: Jeff Bingaman (D-NM); **Ranking Minority Member:** Frank Murkowski (R-AK)

190. <u>**Senate Committee on Environment and Public Works**</u> (www.senate.gov/~epw)

Description: Senate committee focused on environmental and public works/infrastructure issues, including global climate change. Also delves into certain natural resource issues through its Fisheries, Wildlife and Water subcommittee.

Members: 19 (10-D; 9-R)

Subcommittees (and corresponding chairman): 1) Clean Air, Wetlands and Climate Change (Joseph Lieberman, D-CT); 2) Transportation, Infrastructure and Nuclear Safety (Harry Reid, D-NV); 3) Fisheries, Wildlife and Water (Bob Graham, D-FL); 4) Superfund, Toxics, Risk and Waste Management. (Barbara Boxer, D-CA).

Key Federal Agencies Under the Committee's Jurisdiction: EPA; FHWA; ACE; FWS; USCG; NOAA; NRCS.

Contact Info: 410 Dirksen Senate Office Bldg., Washington, DC 20510; (202) 224-8832; guest@epw.senate.gov

Chairman: James Jeffords (I-VT); **Ranking Minority Member:** Bob Smith (R-NH)

Subsection 2.2: Federal Governmental Agencies/Entities

Introduction/User's Guide:

Within this subsection, 61 federal governmental agencies (and similar/related entities) working on environmentally-relevant issues are profiled. A relatively wide net was cast in identifying relevant organizations; as a result, 52 agencies/entities are profiled, including 49 which span eight Cabinet-level Departments (namely: Agriculture; Commerce; Defense; Energy; Health and Human Services; Interior; Justice; Transportation), along with 3 independent agencies/entities (namely: the Chemical Safety and Hazard Investigation Board; the Environmental Protection Agency; and the Nuclear Regulatory Commission). Also profiled are 4 multi-agency programs of note (namely: the Clean Water Initiative; the Energy Star® Program; the U.S. Global Change Research Program; and the Wildfire Initiative). Finally, the General Accounting Office is profiled since – as Congress's investigative arm – it can (and does) evaluate the federal agencies/entities and associated programs listed herein.

Organizational profiles for this subsection are presented following this introductory material, grouped into three categories and listed in the following order:

      2.2.1 – Cabinet Department-Associated Agencies/Entities (arranged by Department)   (49 entries)
      2.2.2 – Independent Agencies/Entities (arranged alphabetically)   (8 entries)
      2.2.3 – Multi-Agency Programs (arranged alphabetically)   (4 entries)

In presenting the profiles of the agencies/entities located within federal Cabinet-level Departments, separate entries are provided starting at the overall Department level and working one's way down to the agency/entity of interest (for example, separate entries are provided first for the Commerce Department overall, then for the National Oceanic and Atmospheric Administration [NOAA] located within the Commerce Department, and finally for the National Marine Fisheries Service located within NOAA). This profile entry ordering method was used in an attempt to provide the reader with an overall picture of the general operating environment in which the specific agencies/entities work.

In terms of individual entry contents, the following is a descriptive outline of standardized profile information provided for each agency/entity listed within this subsection (please note that the exact contents provided varies by organization, being dependant upon applicability and/or availability):

[Profile #] Agency/Entity Name (Website Address)
Description/Mission: Providing a background summary of the agency's/entity's mission and activities.
A Closer Look: Providing additional relevant information judged to be of particular interest.
Facts and Figures: Providing background facts/data that helps put the agency's/entity's mission in perspective (for example, noting that the Forest Service oversees 155 National Forests and 20 National Grasslands).
Operating/Organizational Structure: Focusing on key sub-entities (for example, listing key offices).
Programs/Key Programs (and activities/focus areas): Indicating specific activities/areas of concern and/or current priorities for the agency/entity.
Key Multi-Agency Programs: Noting as applicable the multi-agency programs identified in Subsection 2.2.3.
Key Activities/Initiatives/Issues: Highlighting the agency's/entity's "high priority" activities/issues.
Key Reports/Publications: Listing specific reports and other publications judged to represent "essential reading" for interested parties, and noting if they are available online at the agency's/entity's website. (A summary listing of all such reports/publications is also provided in Appendix B.)
Main Website Divisions: As obtained from the agency's/entity's homepage. Listed to provide insight as to what their website has to offer overall. (As one might expect, these websites tend to be very large in size.)

Website Notes: Significant notes concerning the agency's/entity's website – navigating hints, content notes, etc.

Check Out on the Web: Listing website related content/features that particularly stand out ("worth a look").

Established: Year specified **Employees:** Overall staffing level **Regional Offices**: Noted as applicable **Budget**: As obtained from government budget documents (typically the request for FY02).

Budget Breakdown: As obtained from government budget documents (typically the request for FY02).

Budget Info Online: Specifying where budget-related information is located on the agency's/entity's website.

GPRA Reports Online: Specifying what is available online and where it is located on the agency's/entity's website (see text below for further details on the GPRA reports themselves).

OIG Reports Online: Specifying what is available online and where it is located on the agency's/entity's website (see text below for further details on the OIG – Office of the Inspector General – and its associated reports).

Major Management Challenges/Program Risks (per the GAO): Noted as applicable, as obtained from the General Accounting Office's "Performance and Accountability and High Risk Series" report for the agency/entity – see text below for further details on these reports.

Contact Info: Providing: Street/mailing address; general telephone number; general email address (if established/available).

Agency/Entity Head: Citing the person's name and title.

The above reporting structure is designed to give a relatively brief – but detailed – profile and current snapshot of the agency/entity, with the information provided organized as follows:

- **Agency/Entity Characterization:** The upper block of the entry from the "Description/Mission" through the "Key Reports/Publications" sub-entries, designed to provide insight into what the agency/entity does (in terms of current activities and programs/focus areas), as well as what it has to offer to interested parties (principally in terms of reports/publications).

- **Website Characterization:** The short block in the middle of the entry consisting of "Main Website Divisions," "Website Notes," and "Check Out on the Web" sub-entries, designed to provide relevant information regarding the agency's/entity's website, particularly in terms of key contents "worth a look." (As one might expect, these websites tend to be very large in size.)

- **Basic Facts and Government Accountability Information:** The lower block of the entry beginning with the "(Year) Established" sub-entry and continuing to the end, designed to provide a host of supplemental material, including relevant financial (i.e., budget) information (when available) and government accountability information (see below for details). Likely of particular interest is the budget breakdown – where a detailed breakdown is provided, it can offer additional insight as to the operating structure and activities/priorities of the agency/entity (based on where/how the agency/entity desires to spend money).

A few words regarding government accountability information are warranted here. First, through the Government Performance and Results Act (GPRA) program, all "major" Departments and Agencies are required to prepare three basic documents: an Annual Performance Report (documenting accomplishments from the previous fiscal year); an Annual Performance Plan (outlining planned activities/goals for the next fiscal year); and a Strategic Plan (a long-term planning document, typically covering five years in outlook). In addition, the General Accounting Office (GAO) is tasked with investigating and reporting on the "major management challenges and program risks" facing "major" Departments and Agencies. The resulting reports – termed the GAO's "Performance and Accountability and High Risk Series" – are made publicly available by the GAO, including online at its website (www.gao.gov).

Second, all "major" Departments and Agencies have independent Inspector General (IG) offices within their organizations which serve as internal "watchdogs," particularly in terms of reviewing financial matters. While some IGs appear to focus strictly on technical accounting-related matters, others appear to delve into more substantive matters. Standard IG office outputs include: individual audit and inspection reports; semiannual reports to Congress; and an annual "Management Challenges" report.

Thus, both the GPRA-related and the IG-generated reports represent key additional sources of information on Departments' and Agencies' performance; hence they are listed within the corresponding profiles provided within this subsection. In addition, as applicable, a short summary of the "Major Management Challenges/Program Risks" found by the GAO is included in the individual profiles.

A Closer Look – An Overall Perspective:

To provide an overall perspective on current federal governmental agency operations and challenges, the following two key summary tables were prepared by extracting relevant information from the individual profiles presented within this subsection:

- **Summary of FY02 Budget Requests Made by Profiled Federal Governmental Agencies/Entities:** Providing the FY02 requests made by environmentally-relevant agencies/entities, along with the requests made by the corresponding Cabinet-level Departments (the latter included to lend perspective on the budgeting allocations employed by the various Departments involved).

- **Summary of Major Environmentally-Related Management Challenges/Program Risks Identified by the GAO at Profiled Federal Governmental Agencies/Entities:** Summarizing key findings and/or recommendations made by the GAO based on their investigation of "major" Departments and Agencies.

The tables themselves are presented separately on the following pages.

Summary of FY02 Budget Requests Made By Profiled Federal Governmental Agencies/Entities

Department / Agency Name	Profile No.	FY02 Budget Request [billions]
Agricultural Department	191	$95
Forest Service	192	$4.6
Natural Resources Conservation Service	193	$1.1
Chemical Safety and Hazard Investigation Board	240	$0.01
Commerce Department	194	$4.8
National Oceanic and Atmospheric Administration (NOAA)	195	$3.3
National Marine Fisheries Service (under NOAA)	196	$0.7
National Ocean Service (under NOAA)	197	$0.4
Office of Oceanic and Atmospheric Research (under NOAA)	198	$0.3
Defense Department	199	$310
Army Corps of Engineers	200	$3.9
Energy Department	201	$19
Energy Information Administration	203	$0.08
National Energy Technology Laboratory	204	$0.44
National Renewable Energy Laboratory	205	$0.13
Office of Civilian Radioactive Waste Management	206	$0.45
Office of Energy Efficiency and Renewable Energy	207	$1.03
Office of Environmental Management	208	$5.91
Office of Fossil Energy	209	$0.45
Office of Nuclear Energy, Science and Technology	210	$0.22
Environmental Protection Agency	241	$7.3
Water Programs	245	$3.2
Waste Management Programs	244	$1.5
Air Programs	242	$0.6
Pollution Prevention Programs	243	$0.3
Regulatory Compliance and Enforcement Programs	---	$0.4
Health and Human Services Department	211	$473
Centers for Disease Control (CDC)	212	$4.1
Agency for Toxic Substances and Disease Registry (under the CDC)	213	$0.08
National Center for Environmental Health (under the CDC)	214	$0.14
Food and Drug Administration	215	$1.4
Center for Food Safety and Applied Nutrition	216	$0.14
National Institutes of Health (NIH)	217	$23
National Institute of Environmental Health Sciences (under the NIH)	218	$0.56
Interior Department	219	$13
Bureau of Land Management	220	$2.0
Bureau of Reclamation	221	$0.9
Fish and Wildlife Service	222	$1.8
Geological Service	223	$0.8
Minerals Management Service	224	$1.2
National Park Service	225	$2.8
Office of Surface Mining Reclamation and Enforcement	226	$0.4
Justice Department	227	$25
Environment and Natural Resources Division	228	$0.07
Nuclear Regulatory Commission	247	$0.5

Summary of FY02 Budget Requests Made By Profiled Federal Governmental Agencies/Entities (concluded)

Department / Agency Name	Profile No.	FY02 Budget Request [billions]
Transportation Department	231	$60 / $6.6*
Coast Guard	232	$5.2 / $1.1*
Federal Aviation Administration	233	$13 / $0.5*
Federal Highway Administration	235	$33 / $2.7*
Federal Transit Administration	236	$6.7 / $2.3*
Research and Special Programs Administration	237	$0.11 / $0.02*
Multi-Agency Programs		
Clean Water Initiative	248	$2.8
U.S. Global Change Research Program	250	$1.6
Wildfire Management Initiative	251	$2.0

* – Cited figures are: Overall Total Budget / Budgetary Allocation for "Environment."

<u>Summary of Major Environmentally-Related Management Challenges/Program Risks</u>

<u>Identified by the GAO at Profiled Federal Governmental Agencies/Entities</u>

<u>Dept. of Agriculture – U.S. Forest Service</u>

- **Financial Accountability**: Serious concerns raised over basic financial accountability, leading to the Forest Service making the GAO's 2001 "High-Risk" list – the only environmental agency so listed.

- **Performance Accountability**: GAO recommends providing a clearer understanding of what is accomplished with appropriated funds; as a result, the Forest Service is moving towards: 1) activity-based management (tracking costs of 80 core business activities) and 2) performance-based budgeting (linking dollars to work outputs).

<u>Dept. of Defense</u>

- **Uncertain Environmental Liability**: No comprehensive inventory is available detailing all potential DoD environmental cleanup and disposal liabilities.

<u>Dept. of Energy</u>

- **Environmental Cleanup**: GAO recommends integrating work both among and within sites requiring active cleanup; in response, DOE has established an Office of Integration and Disposition.

- **Contract Management** (including environmental cleanup contracts): Identified problems include: cost and schedule overruns; inadequate oversight of contractors' activities; inability to hold contractors accountable.

<u>Department of the Interior</u>

- **National Park Service Management**: GAO recommendations: 1) prioritize the scientific assessment of the condition of NPS resources for planning/budgeting purposes; 2) gather more accurate data on the maintenance backlog to better set project/budget priorities; 3) improve Park Managers' accountability for achieving results; 4) address identified management problems in the concessions program, namely: inadequate staff qualifications/training, use of out-of-date practices, and general lack of accountability; 5) better manage the structural fire safety program for NPS's 30,000 building structures by fully specifying minimum expected standards and placing a higher priority on structural fire safety in general.

- **Land Exchanges (focusing on the Bureau of Land Management):** GAO recommendations: 1) better demonstrate that an exchange is necessary and that exchanged lands are of approximately equal value; 2) guarantee that funds used are properly managed/controlled; 3) highlight the need for increased funding for operating/maintaining newly acquired lands in Congressional budget requests.

- **Ecosystem Restoration Management**: GAO recommendations: 1) work with outside entities to develop plans and strategies to achieve restoration and management goals; 2) improve coordination with multiple entities in such efforts; 3) develop a succession plan to replace retiring fire management personnel.

<u>Dept. of Transportation</u>

- **Federal Transit Administration - Transit Grants**: GAO recommendations: 1) increased federal funding to FTA for project oversight; 2) additional prioritization of eligible projects to ensure that the most promising are funded.

- **Office of Pipeline Safety - Pipeline Safety**: Concerns raised over: 1) implementing a risk-based management approach before fully evaluating the results of a demonstration program; 2) relying less on states to inspect interstate pipelines; 3) pursuing an approach of working constructively with pipeline companies and reducing OPS's reliance on fines in enforcing regulations without first evaluating the effect of such actions on regulatory compliance rates.

- **Surplus Maritime Administration**: Concerns raised over surplus ships (112 as of FY99), which pose environmental threats both in storage and when scrapped/disposed of.

Environmental Protection Agency

- **Environmental and Performance Information Management**: GAO recommendations: 1) fill critical information gaps on environmental conditions and corresponding effects on human health; 2) achieve compatibility among federal/state databases to permit data aggregation; 3) establish more results-oriented – as opposed to output-oriented – performance measures; 4) strengthen security over computer information systems; 5) develop a comprehensive information management strategy addressing the aforementioned concerns.

- **EPA-State Working Relationships**: Urges the EPA to address long-standing problems/disagreements – particularly in the area of regulatory enforcement – and to develop a more effective partnership system; EPA is attempting to address this through its National Environmental Performance Partnership System.

- **Superfund Program**: While much-improved according to the GAO, EPA has still not agreed with the GAO's recommendation to use a performance measure(s) to track cleanup cost recovery outcomes.

- **EPA's Human Capital**: Recommends that the EPA to formally assess human capital needs and align those needs with strategic goals.

Nuclear Regulatory Commission

- **Nuclear Power Plants**: Identifies the need for the NRC to overcome obstacles to implementing a risk-informed regulatory approach; GAO recommendations: 1) develop a comprehensive implementation strategy; 2) obtain staff "buy-in" and ensure that the general public is confident about the new approach; 3) reconsider making compliance with the new approach voluntary, effectively resulting in a dual regulatory system.

- **Nuclear Material Licensees**: Identifies the need for the NRC to: 1) overcome difficulties in implementing a risk-informed regulatory approach, mainly due to the sheer number of licensees involved – over 20,000 – and the diversity of activities they conduct and 2) adjust as more states assume responsibility for regulating nuclear material users.

- **Management Issues**: GAO recommendations: 1) Develop a succession plan to address gaps due to retiring personnel, particularly in terms of maintaining technical competency; 2) improve the NRC's new information system – ADAMS – which was developed to provide timely document access to both NRC staff and the general public, but is experiencing significant start-up problems.

2.2.1 Cabinet Department-Associated Agencies/Entities (arranged by Department)

191.   **Dept. of Agriculture (USDA) (www.usda.gov)**

Description/Mission: Federal Cabinet-level department responsible for supporting the production of agriculture. Also charged with management of the National Forest System (consisting of National Forests and National Grasslands) on a multi-use, sustained yield basis (carried out through the USDA's Forest Service – see Profile #192).

Operating/Organizational Structure: Organized into 7 mission areas, including Natural Resources and Environment, which, in turn, is carried out through two agencies – the Forest Service and the Natural Resources Conservation Service (see Profiles #192 and 193, respectively).

Key Dept. Agencies: Forest Service (USFS; see Profile #192); Natural Resources Conservation Service (NRCS; see Profile #193).

Key Program: Conservation Reserve Program (pays agricultural producers to voluntarily retire environmentally sensitive cropland for 10 to 15 years; $1.8 billion budget requested for FY02; payments made though the Commodity Credit Corporation; 34 million acres currently enrolled, with a maximum program cap of 36 million acres; administered through USDA's Farm Service Agency).

Key Multi-Agency Program: Clean Water Initiative / Clean Water Action Plan (see Profile # 248).

Key Publication: Agriculture Fact Book 2000 (information on U.S. agriculture and all USDA programs; covers: food safety, nutrition, rural issues, research, education, and natural resources; online).

Main Website Divisions: Welcome to USDA; Newsroom; Services and Programs; Agencies; Search/Help.

Check Out on the Web: Biotechnology website (www.usda.gov/agencies/biotech); provides an overview of regulatory oversight of biotechnology by federal agencies, namely: USDA, EPA, and FDA).

Established: 1862 **Employees:** 98,000 **Budget (FY02 Request):** $95 billion

Budget Info Online: FY02 Budget (on the Office of Budget and Program Analysis webpage)

GPRA Reports Online (all on the Office of the Chief Financial Officer's webpage): Annual Performance Plan (FY02); Annual Performance Report (FY00); Strategic Plan (FY00-05).

OIG Reports Online: Audit and inspection reports; semiannual reports to Congress.

Contact Info: 14th and Independence Ave. SW, Washington, DC 20250; (202) 720-2791.

Agency/Entity Head: Ann M. Veneman (Secretary)

192.   **Dept. of Agriculture – Forest Service (FS or USFS) (www.fs.fed.us)**

Description/Mission: Federal agency (under the USDA) overseeing National Forests and National Grasslands, including management of their resources for multiple-use on a sustained-yield basis. Provides technical and financial assistance to state and private forestry agencies/organizations. Also serves as the largest forestry research organization in the world.

Facts and Figures: Known collectively as the "National Forest System," there are 155 National Forests and 20 National Grasslands in the U.S., encompassing nearly 200 million acres in total or about 9% of the total land area in the U.S. Expected timber sales from FS lands in FY02 were 1 to 2 million board-feet including salvage sales. Total revenues (FS receipts plus other income) generated from FS lands average about $1 billion per year.

Operating/Organizational Structure: Organized on four levels: national, regional (9 regions), national forest (155 National Forests and 20 National Grasslands); ranger district (600+, each with a staff size of 10 to 100).

Key Program: Forest Inventory and Analysis (conducting a national "forest census," inventorying and analyzing trends, considering all forests, both public and private; conducted by the Research and Development Division of the USFS's National Headquarters).

Key Multi-Agency Programs: Clean Water Initiative / Clean Water Action Plan (see Profile #248); Wildfire Management / National Fire Plan (see Profile #251).

Key Publication: FS Manual and Handbook (codifies the agency's policies, practices and procedures; "the Bible" to FS employees; online)

Key Report: Resources Planning Act (RPA) Assessment of Forest and Range Lands (focused on the criteria for, and indicators of, sustainable forest and range management; online).

Main Website Divisions: National Forests Web Sites; National Headquarters; Enjoying Your National Forests; Fire Information; News; Library; Contacts; Search; Site Index.

Associated Website: Roadless Area Conservation (www.roadless.fs.fed.us; provides current information on roadless area policy as it affects the FS).

Check Out on the Web: National Forests Web Sites (gateway to individual websites for both national forests and national grasslands); Urban Tree House Program (environmental education structures built outdoors in urban parks or other green spaces; located within the "Research and Development" webpage under "National Headquarters"); Passport in Time (volunteer-based archaeology and historic preservation program at FS sites; located under "Enjoying Your National Parks").

Established: 1905 **Employees:** 35,000 **Budget** (FY02 Request): $4.6 billion

Budget Breakdown (FY02 Request; $ in billions): National Forest System ($1.31); Forest and Rangeland Research ($0.24); State and Private Forestry ($0.24 million; for grants and technical assistance); Wildland Fire Management ($1.28; mainly for: preparedness –$0.62; suppression –$0.33; hazardous fuel reduction –$0.21); Capital Improvement and Maintenance ($0.52); Land Acquisition ($0.13); Mandatory Accounts ($0.86; for: permanent working funds –$0.23; payments to states –$0.39; trust funds –$0.24).

FS Receipts (FY99): $628 million (from: timber harvest –65%; mineral and energy extraction –19%; recreation use –10%; other misc. –6%).

Budget Info Online (use the Site Index to obtain): FY02 Budget (select "Budget Justification").

GPRA Reports Online (use the Site Index to obtain): Annual Performance Plan (FY02) (select "Budget Justification" – attached to the FY02 Budget Justification document); Strategic Plan (2000).

Major Management Challenges/Program Risks (per the GAO): Financial Accountability (serious concerns raised over basic financial accountability, leading to the FS making the GAO's 2001 "High-Risk" list – the only environmental agency so listed); Performance Accountability (providing a clearer understanding of what is accomplished with appropriated funds; as a result, the FS is moving towards activity-based management [tracking costs of 80 core business activities] and performance-based budgeting [linking dollars to work outputs]).

Contact Info: PO Box 96090, 201 14th St. SW, Washington, DC 20090-6090; (202) 205-8333; wo_fs-contact@fs.fed.us

Agency/Entity Head: Mark Rey (Chief)

193.   Dept. of Agriculture – Natural Resources Conservation Service (NRCS) (www.nrcs.usda.gov)

Description/Mission: Federal agency (under the USDA) responsible for conserving natural resources (soil, water and related resources) on private lands. Formerly known as the Soil Conservation Service. Works with conservation districts nationwide to help farmers and ranchers develop "conservation systems" (various approaches and techniques designed primarily to reduce erosion and improve soil and water quality). Agency focus is on providing technical, educational and financial assistance through local, county-based field offices. NRCS also leads the National Cooperative Soil Survey Program (NCSS), a multi-party partnership providing soil survey information to interested parties.

Facts and Figures: Conservation districts are local units of government established under state law to work with cooperating landowners and operators in managing and protecting land and water resources on private lands. There are some 3000 conservation districts nationwide.

Operating/Organizational Structure: Most of NRCS's employees serve in USDA's national network of local, county-based offices.

Programs (and focus areas): Conservation Operations; Resource Conservation and Community Development; Watersheds and Wetlands; Animal Husbandry and Clean Water Programs; International Programs; Soil Survey and Resource Inventory/Assessment; Science and Technology (economics/social science; engineering; ecological science).

Key Multi-Agency Program: Clean Water Initiative / Clean Water Action Plan (see Profile #248).

Key Report: National Resources Inventory (statistically assesses conditions and trends of soil, water, and related resources on non-Federal lands; provides data on: land cover and use, soil erosion, prime farmland soils, wetlands, habitat diversity and selected conservation practices; issued every 5 years; online).

Main Website Divisions: What's New; About NRCS; Partners and Customers; Volunteers; General Information; Science and Technology; Teachers and Students; Media Information; Programs.

Check Out on the Web: Plants Database (source of extensive, standardized information about plants); Backyard Conservation (10 conservation practices scaled down for use by homeowners and city residents); State of the Land (provides data and analysis on: land use, soil erosion and soil quality, water quality, wetlands).

Established: 1935 **Employees:** 11,000 **Budget** (FY02 Request): $1.1 billion

Budget Breakdown (FY02 Request; $ in millions): Conservation Operations ($773; mainly for: technical assistance –$678; soil surveys –$80); Environmental Quality Incentive Program ($174; for helping producers make changes that conserve/improve soil, water and related natural resources); Watershed and Flood Prevention Operations ($100; for technical assistance and project implementation); Resource Conservation and Development ($43; for aid to state/local government and nonprofits in rural areas to plan, develop and carry out programs for resource conservation and development); Watershed Surveys and Planning ($11).

Budget Info Online: See Profile #191 for the Dept. of Agriculture as a whole.

GPRA Reports Online: Strategic Plan (FY00-05; located under "About NRCS"); Accomplishments Report (FY00; on the NRCS home page); also see "PRMS" (web-based database that lists agency accomplishments and progress towards strategic and performance goals).

Contact Info: PO Box 2890, 14th St. and Independence Ave. SW, Washington, DC 20013; (202) 720-3210.

Agency/Entity Head: Pearlie S. Reed (Chief)

194.   Dept. of Commerce (DOC) (home.doc.gov)

Description/Mission: Federal Cabinet-level department charged with promoting job creation and economic growth.

Operating/Organizational Structure: Comprised of 10 main organizations, including the National Oceanic and Atmospheric Administration (NOAA; see Profile #195).

Key Dept. Agencies: National Oceanic and Atmospheric Administration (NOAA; see Profile #195).

A Closer Look: Budget-wise, NOAA is by far the largest organization within the DOC, accounting for nearly two-thirds of the overall requested budget for the DOC as a whole.

Established: 1903 **Employees:** 37,000 **Budget** (FY02 Request): $4.8 billion

Budget Info Online: FY02 Budget Request (located under "About DOC").

GPRA Reports Online (both located under "About DOC"): Strategic Plan (FY00-05); Annual Performance Plan (FY02) and Annual Performance Report (FY00).

OIG Reports Online: Audit and inspection reports; semiannual reports to Congress; "top 10" management challenges list.

Major Environmentally-Related Management Challenges/Program Risks (per the GAO): None identified.

Contact Info: 15th St. and Constitution Ave. NW, Washington, DC 20230; (202) 219-3605.

Agency/Entity Head: Donald Evans (Secretary)

195.   Dept. of Commerce – National Oceanic and Atmospheric Administration (NOAA) (www.noaa.gov)

Description/Mission: Federal agency (under the DOC) charged with a variety of tasks involving the oceans and atmosphere, including coastal zone and marine fisheries management, ocean- and atmospheric-related research (including climate change research) and weather prediction services.

Operating/Organizational Structure: Comprised of 6 major organizations: National Marine Fisheries Service (NMFS; also known as "NOAA Fisheries"); National Ocean Service (NOS); Office of Oceanic and Atmospheric Research (OAR; also known as "NOAA Research"); National Environmental Satellite, Data and Information Service (NESDIS); National Weather Service (NWS); Office of Marine and Aviation Operations (OMAO).

Key NOAA Orgs (and key activities/focus areas) (see Profiles #196-198, respectively): National Marine Fisheries Service (marine fisheries management); National Ocean Service (oversee coastal zone management via federal-state partnerships; manage the National Marine Sanctuaries system and the National Estuarian Reserves system; provide navigation services); Office of Oceanic and Atmospheric Research (science-based research of marine, atmospheric and climate systems).

Key NOAA Center: Climate Diagnostics Center (seeks to identify nature and causes of climate variations on time scales ranging from a month to centuries).

Key Multi-Agency Program: Clean Water Initiative / Clean Water Action Plan (see Profile #248).

Key Research Initiatives: Climate observations/services; ocean exploration; coral reef watch.

Key Report: Turning to the Sea: America's Ocean Future (proposed ocean policy "blueprint" recommending nearly 150 actions in 25 key areas to protect, restore, and explore America's ocean resources; online).

Main Website Divisions: NOAA News; Check This Out; Cool NOAA Websites; Media Advisories; About NOAA; Organizations; Opportunities; Education. (The site also provides gateway access based on 8 topic areas: Weather; Climate; Oceans; Coasts; Fisheries; Charting and Navigation; Satellite Imagery; Research.)

Check Out on the Web: One-Stop Shopping for Information on the Earth's Ozone Layer; NOAA's Climate Data At-A-Glance (106 years of U.S. weather data); 3-D Weather Images (graphics of severe weather events); NOAA's Ark (photos library of 16,000+ images sorted either by type or by NOAA program).

Established: 1969 **Employees:** 14,000 **Budget** (FY02 Request): $3.3 billion

Budget Breakdown (FY02 Request; $ in million): National Marine Fisheries Service ($734); National Ocean Service ($398); Office of Oceanic and Atmospheric Research ($341); National Weather Service ($728); National Environmental Satellite, Data and Information Service ($738); Office of Marine and Aviation Operations ($124); Program Support ($237); Facilities ($18).

Budget Info Online: FY02 Budget Request (located under "Public Affairs").

GPRA Reports Online: Strategic Plan (1995-2005; located on the NOAA home page); Annual Performance Plan (FY02) and Annual Performance Report (FY00) (included as part of the Dept. of Commerce's overall Plan and Report, available on the DOC website under "About DOC").

Contact Info: 14th St. and Constitution Ave. NW, Washington, DC 20230; (202) 482-6090; answers@noaa.gov

Agency/Entity Head: Conrad Lautenbacher (Administrator)

196.   **Dept. of Commerce – NOAA – National Marine Fisheries Service (NMFS or "NOAA Fisheries")**
             (www.nmfs.noaa.gov)

Description/Mission: Federal agency (under NOAA) responsible for the living marine resources within the U.S.'s Exclusive Economic Zone (EEZ; the area extending 200 miles off the nation's coastlines). The basic goals of the NMFS are to: 1) rebuild and/or maintain sustainable fisheries, 2) facilitate recovery of protected species, and 3) protect/maintain coastal marine habitats. The NMFS works in partnership with 8 Regional Fishery Management Councils to manage marine fish stocks in the EEZ (the Councils themselves prepare regional fishery management plans; Council membership includes fishermen, marine scientists, and federal/state fisheries managers). In addition, the NMFS enforces fisheries regulations and is responsible for implementing the Endangered Species Act as it applies to marine and anadromous species.

Organizational Structure – Key Program Offices (and office divisions): Sustainable Fisheries (highly migratory species; domestic fisheries; international fisheries; financial services – financial assistance to the fishing industry and fisheries stakeholders); Protected Resources (marine mammal conservation; endangered species; marine biodiversity; permits and authorization; international activities); Habitat Conservation (habitat protection; habitat conservation; watersheds; Chesapeake Bay); Science and Technology (fisheries statistics and economics; scientific research and analysis; international science and technology).

Key Initiative: Modernization Initiative (seeking to modernize research, management and enforcement programs).

Key Reports: Status of Fisheries of the U.S. (annual report to Congress; online); Our Living Oceans: Report on the Status of U.S. Living Marine Resources (triennial report; online).

Main Website Divisions: HQ Offices; Regional Offices and Science Centers; Legislation and Budget; Publications; Seafood Inspection Program; Search; Kids Corner.

Website Information Topic Areas: Aquaculture; Commercial Fisheries; Endangered Species; Essential Fish Habitat; Fisheries Economics; Fisheries Trade; International Interests; Marine Mammals; Partnerships;

Recreational Fisheries; Strandings (beached marine animals).

Established: 1970 **Employees:** 2800 **Regional Offices:** 5 **Budget** (FY02 Request): $734 million

Budget Breakdown (FY02 Request; $ in millions): Conservation and Management Operations ($303; for: fisheries management –$140; protected species management –$105; enforcement and surveillance –$47); Information Collection and Analysis ($274; for: resource information –$201; fisheries industry information –$47; information analysis and dissemination –$26); Pacific Coastal Salmon Recovery Fund ($90; for grants to states and Indian tribes for salmon recovery planning and implementation); State and Industry Assistance ($21; for product quality and safety research); Pacific Salmon Treaty ($20; for two restoration funds established by treaty); Procurement, Acquisition and Construction ($15; for two specific facility building projects); Environmental Improvement and Restoration Fund ($5; for grants for marine research in the North Pacific).

Budget Info Online: See Profile #195 for NOAA as a whole.

GPRA Reports Online: See Profile #195 for NOAA as a whole.

GAO Report Recommendations to NMFS on Fisheries Management (4/00): 1) Strengthen fisheries data collection efforts, 2) improve communications with the fishing industry, 3) improve economic analysis, focusing on developing alternatives that minimize adverse impacts to fishing communities, and 4) identify the costs of achieving compliance with the Magnuson-Stevens Act's fish habitat provisions.

Contact Info: 1315 East-West Highway, Silver Spring, MD 20910; (301) 713-2239; cyber.fish@noaa.gov

Agency/Entity Head: William T. Hogarth (Assistant Administrator)

197.   Dept. of Commerce – NOAA – National Ocean Service (NOS) (www.nos.noaa.gov)

Description/Mission: Federal agency (under NOAA) responsible for observation, measurement, assessment, and management of the nation's coastal and ocean areas (particularly within the Exclusive Economic Zone, the area extending 200 miles off the nation's coastlines), as well as conducting response and restoration activities in those areas. Also manages the National Marine Sanctuary system (currently at 13 sanctuaries) and the National Estuarine Research Reserve system (currently at 25 reserves) and – in partnership with 33 states with approved coastal management programs – manages the nation's coastal zone. Generally most well known for its navigation services, particularly its nautical maps and charts which are sold to the general public.

Operating/Organizational Structure: Five "Program Offices": Coast Survey; National Geodetic Survey; Ocean and Coastal Resource Management; Response and Restoration; National Centers for Coastal Ocean Science.

Main Website Divisions: About NOS; News and Events; Publications and Products; Programs; Education and Outreach; For NOS Employees.

Check Out on the Web: "Marine Protected Areas" and "National Marine Sanctuaries" web pages (providing information on the 25 reserves and 13 sanctuaries overseen by NOS).

Employees: 1200 **Budget** (FY02 Request): $398 million

Budget Breakdown (FY02 Request; $ in million): Navigation Services ($107; mainly for: mapping and charting –$45; geodesy –$24; tide and current data –$17); Ocean Resources Conservation Assessment ($117; mainly for: ocean assessment –$72; response and restoration activities –$17); Ocean and Coastal Management ($141; mainly for: coastal zone management grants to states –$69; National Estuarine Research Reserves –$16; National Marine Sanctuary program –$36; marine protected areas program –$3); Procurement, Acquisition and Construction ($28; mainly for: National Estuarine Research Reserves –$16; National Marine Sanctuary program –$10); Environmental Improvement and Restoration Fund ($5; for grants for marine research in the North Pacific).

Budget Info Online: FY02 Budget Request (under "About NOS") (Note: a "lightweight" document – see Profile #195 for NOAA as a whole for better budget information on NOS).

GPRA Reports Online: Annual Report (2000); Strategic Plan (99-04) (both under "About NOS") (Note: "lightweight" documents – see Profile #195 for NOAA as a whole for better GPRA reports on NOS).

Contact Info: 1305 East-West Highway, Silver Spring, MD 20910; (301) 713-3074; nos.info@hermes.nos.noaa.gov

Agency/Entity Head: Margaret A. Davidson (Director)

198.   Dept. of Commerce – NOAA – Office of Oceanic and Atmospheric Research (OAR or "NOAA Research") (www.oar.noaa.gov)

Description/Mission: Federal agency (under NOAA) responsible for research into the earth's atmospheric, climate, and marine (ocean and coastal) systems.

Operating/Organizational Structure: A national network of NOAA labs and universities/independent research institutions carry out NOAA's research agenda, coordinated/overseen by OAR (see below for specific research components).

Organizational Structure – Components of NOAA Research: 1) 12 NOAA labs and 11 "Joint Institute" research partners (research-oriented universities/institutions); 2) National Sea Grant College Program (network of 30 different programs; engaging 200+ universities/research institutions in conducting scientific research, education, and outreach projects on ocean, coastal and Great Lakes issues); 3) Office of Global Programs (manages NOAA's Climate and Global Change Research Program); 4) National Undersea Research Program (network of 6 regional centers providing scientific tools and expertise for undersea research).

Key Initiative: Ocean Exploration ("discovery and exploration of the last major frontier on earth"; a cross agency, multi-institution partnership; focus areas: new ocean resources; exploring ocean acoustics; America's maritime heritage [historic shipwrecks and archeological sites]; exploring ocean frontiers; census of marine life).

Main Website Divisions: Welcome; Atmosphere; Climate; Oceans; Organization; Education; Newsroom; Search.

Check Out on the Web: NOAA Research Backgrounders (short descriptions of OAR, its themes and research units); "Education" webpage (provides science-oriented materials/resources for students, teachers and the general public).

Employees: 930 (plus 900 contractors at the 11 Joint Institutes) **Budget** (FY02 Request): $341 million

Budget Breakdown (FY02 Request; $ in millions): Climate and Air Quality Research ($159; focused on research to increase climate/air quality modeling accuracy); Atmospheric Programs ($52; for: weather research –$46; solar-terrestrial services and research –$6); Oceans and Great Lakes Programs ($120; for: National Sea Grant Programs –$62; marine environmental research –$30; ocean exploration –$14; undersea research –$14); Procurement, Acquisition and Construction ($11; for two specific projects).

Budget Info Online: See Profile #195 for NOAA as a whole.

GPRA Reports Online: See Profile #195 for NOAA as a whole.

Contact Info: 1315 East-West Highway, Silver Spring, MD 20910; (301) 713-2458.

Agency/Entity Head: David L. Evans (Assistant Administrator)

199.   Dept. of Defense (DoD) (www.defenselink.mil)

Description/Mission: Federal Cabinet-level department responsible for the common defense of the nation, its citizens and its allies. Protects/advances U.S. interests around the world. Also involved in large water resources-related civil/public works projects and facilities through the Army Corps of Engineers (see Profile #200).

Operating/Organizational Structure: Main military organizations are the Army, Navy, Air Force, and Marine Corps. Also manages 14 defense agencies such as the Defense Logistics Agency. In times of war (or as directed by the President), oversees the U.S. Coast Guard through the Secretary of the Navy (otherwise, the Coast Guard is overseen by the Dept. of Transportation).

Key Dept. Agency (see Profile #200): Army Corps of Engineers (environmental focus areas: water resources-related civil/public works projects and facilities; cleanup of contaminated military and Dept. of Energy sites and facilities; permitting agency for "Section 404" dredge and fill permits for waterways and associated wetlands).

Key Issue: Contaminated Site Cleanup/Installation Restoration (performed through the Defense Environmental Restoration Program [DERP]; consists of three basic programs – see below for details; DERP information is available on the DoD "Environmental Cleanup" home page [www.dtic.mil/envirodod]; each military organization [Army, Navy, etc.] executes the actual cleanup work, overseen by the DoD's Office of Environmental Cleanup [part of the Office of the Secretary of Defense for Environmental Security]).

DERP Programs: Base Realignment and Closure (BRAC; consists of closure and environmental restoration of targeted Army, Navy, Air Force, and Defense Logistics Agency bases, with restored bases ultimately transferred to local communities and/or federal/state agencies for potential reuse; nearly 5000 "sites" in the program; as of 9/99, necessary actions completed at 55% of the sites; $490 million budgeted for cleanup in FY02); Formerly Used Defense Sites (FUDS; formerly owned, operated, or leased Dept. of Defense properties; 9200 "sites" in the program; as of 9/99, necessary actions completed at 25% of the sites); Installation Restoration Program (IRP; active defense installations; 18,500 "sites" in the program; as of 9/99, necessary actions completed at 70% of the sites). NOTE: "Sites" are discrete locations containing contamination on installations/bases; they do not represent the entire installation/base (thus, one installation/base can be home to multiple "sites" requiring cleanup).

Key Report: Defense Environmental Restoration Program [DERP] Annual Report to Congress (outlines the status of DoD's DERP programs [see above for details]; online).

Employees: 3.4 million (1.4 active duty; 1.3 military guard and reserves; 0.7 civilian) **Budget:** $310 billion

Major Environmentally-Related Management Challenges/Program Risks (per the GAO): Uncertain Environmental Liability (no comprehensive inventory of all potential DoD environmental cleanup and disposal liabilities).

Contact Info: The Pentagon, Washington, DC 20301; (703) 697-5737 (Public Affairs).

Agency/Entity Head: Donald H. Rumsfeld (Secretary)

200.   Dept. of Defense – Army Corps of Engineers (ACE or "the Corps") (www.usace.army.mil)

Description/Mission: Federal agency (under the DoD) responsible for planning, designing, building and operating water resources-related and other civil/public works projects and facilities (for navigation, flood control, environmental protection, disaster response, etc.). Also designs and manages the construction of military facilities for the Army and Air Force. Other key duties include management/oversight of environmental cleanup activities at contaminated military and Dept. of Energy sites/facilities and serving as the permitting agency for so-called "Section 404" dredge and fill permits for waterways and associated wetlands.

Facts and Figures: Operates and maintains nearly 300 deep-draft harbors, 275 locks, 12,000 miles of navigable waterways, 383 major lakes and 8,500 miles of levees. Also manages 4,340 recreation sites at 456 lakes and reservoirs. Produces one-fourth of the nation's hydropower, operating 75 hydropower plants.

Operating/Organizational Structure: Organized geographically into 8 divisions and 41 subordinate districts.

Key Activities: Waterways/Wetlands Oversight (permitting agency for so-called "Section 404" permits – dredge and fill permits for waterways and associated wetlands); Contaminated Site Cleanup Management/Oversight (of both military and Dept. of Energy sites through several programs – BRAC [Army and Air Force base closures]; FUDS [9000+ formerly owned or leased Dept. of Defense sites]; FUSRAP [46 formerly utilized Dept. of Energy sites]; IRP [10,000+ active Army sites and 25 active Air Force bases]; EPA's Superfund and Brownfields cleanup programs).

Key Multi-Agency Program: Clean Water Initiative / Clean Water Action Plan (see Profile #248).

Main Website Divisions: Hot Topics and Issues; Who We Are; Where We Are; Services for the Military; Services for the Public: Doing Business with Us; Working for Us; News and Information; Search and Reference; Sitemap.

Check Out on the Web (but see note below): Civil Works Digital Project Notebook (interactive GIS/map-based system of all ACE civil works projects; located under "Services to the Public"); National Inventory of Dams (information on 76,000 U.S. dams; located under "Services to the Public"); Digital Library (graphic/photo/historic library of nearly 6000 images; located under "Search and Reference"); Corps Facts (key program statistics; listed on the "Public Affairs Office" page). (**NOTE:** Post-Sept. 11, public access to both the Civil Works Digital Project Notebook and the National Inventory of Dams has been suspended indefinitely).

Employees: 35,000 (nearly all civilians – less than 1000 are military) **Budget** (FY02 Request): $3.9 billion

Budget Breakdown (FY02 Request; $ in millions): Operations and Maintenance ($1745; for existing facilities); General Construction ($1324; for new and major rehabilitation); Mississippi River-Related Flood Control ($280); Formerly Utilized Sites Remedial Action Program [FUSRAP] ($140; for remediation of contaminated Dept. of Energy sites); "Dredge and Fill Material" Regulatory Permit Program [Section 404 Program] ($128); General Investigations ($130); General Expenses ($153).

Budget Info Online: FY02 Budget Request (obtained from a 4/9/01 press release posted on the ACE website).

Contact Info: 20 Massachusetts Ave. NW, Washington, DC 20314; (202) 761-0660.

Agency/Entity Head: Lt. General Robert B. Flowers (Commander)

201.   Dept. of Energy (DOE) (www.energy.gov)

Description/Mission: Federal Cabinet-level department primarily responsible for: 1) maintaining a "secure and reliable" national energy system and 2) managing the U.S. nuclear arsenal. DOE also: conducts/sponsors basic science research (being the third largest government sponsor behind the National Science Foundation and the National Institutes of Health); oversees cleanup of nuclear weapons research and production facilities; is responsible for disposing of spent nuclear fuel from commercial nuclear reactors and high-level radioactive waste resulting from defense activities.

A Closer Look: DOE contracts out for operation and management of most of its major facilities. As such, it is the largest civilian contracting agency in the federal government, using 100,000+ prime contractor employees at its facilities. For FY99, about 90% of all budgetary obligations ($15.5 billion in total) went to contractors.

Facts and Figures: DOE maintains a network of 26 laboratories (including 16 national labs) conducting scientific research. It is also the landlord for 2.4 million acres of land and nearly 20,000 facilities across the U.S., with 50+ major installations present in 35 states.

Operating/Organizational Structure: Organized into two basic operating Divisions: Nuclear Security (focused on nuclear weapons) and Energy, Science, and Environment (including nuclear power and cleanup of nuclear weapons and power facilities). In addition, there are 17 independent entities within DOE, consisting of various Offices, Administrations, Boards, and Commissions. Thrown into this mix are DOE's research lab network (26 labs in total) which maintains various affiliations with DOE's other entities. Finally, the Federal Energy Regulatory Commission is an independent regulatory agency falling within DOE but having only "dotted line" reporting responsibility to the Energy Secretary (FERC members being appointed by the President and confirmed by the Senate). See below for identified key entities within DOE.

Key Independent Entities Within DOE: Energy Information Administration (provides official energy statistics – data, analyses and forecasts; see Profile #203 for details); Power Marketing Administrations (sells and distributes $3+ billion worth of electric power generated at Federal hydropower plants; consists of 4 separate Administrations); Federal Energy Regulatory Commission (regulates key interstate aspects of electric power, natural gas, oil pipelines, and hydroelectric industries).

Key National Laboratories (see Profiles #204 and #205, respectively, for details): National Renewable Energy Laboratory (conducts research on alternative renewable energy resources); National Energy Technology Laboratory (focus on development of advanced technologies related to fossil fuels – coal, natural gas, and oil).

Key Offices – Energy, Science, and Environment Division (and activities/focus areas) (see Profiles #206-210, respectively, for details): Civilian Radioactive Waste Management (CRWM; responsible for disposing of: 1) commercial spent nuclear fuel and 2) high-level radioactive waste resulting from defense activities); Energy Efficiency and Renewable Energy (EERE; organized into 5 sub-offices dealing with separate energy sectors, namely: industry; transportation; buildings; power; federal agencies); Environmental Management (manages cleanup of: 1) nuclear weapons research and production facilities and 2) nuclear energy research facilities); Fossil Energy (FE; conducts research and development of fossil energy technologies and manages the Strategic Petroleum Reserve – emergency storage of up to 700 million barrels of crude oil); Nuclear Energy, Science, and Technology (NE; focus areas: nuclear power research and development; space and defense power systems; isotope production and distribution; nuclear facilities management; science education).

Key Energy Initiative: Proposed Clean Coal Power Initiative (a 10-year, $2 billion plan for research in coal-based power technologies; builds upon the existing Clean Coal Technology program begun in 1985).

Key Multi-Agency Program: Energy Star® program (see Profile #249).

Key Publications (all online): International Energy Outlook 2001 (international energy projections through 2020); Annual Energy Review (historical U.S. and international energy statistics from 1949 on; annual report); Annual Energy Outlook (midterm [20 year] forecasts of energy supply, demand and prices for the U.S.); Emissions of Greenhouse Gases in the U.S. (annual report); Voluntary Reporting of Greenhouse Gases (annual report on voluntarily-reported emissions reductions and carbon sequestration projects).

Main Website Divisions: Information is presented within two contexts: 1) "Energy and your ___" (health; house; transportation; school; business; community; world; future) and 2) "Energy and ___" (data and prices; efficiency;

environmental quality; national security; science and technology; sources and production).

Website Notes: If you have a specific topic or interest in mind, use the "A-Z Index" to find relevant information.

Check Out on the Web: Free Subscriptions (access to a multitude of email alerts, magazines, and online newsletters); In Your State (state-level perspectives on energy information and resources; located under "Energy and Your Community"); National Library (gateway to accessing DOE publications); Center of Excellence for Sustainable Development (www.sustainable.doe.gov; information and services on sustainable development aimed at local communities).

Established: 1977 **Employees:** 16,000 (federal); 100,000+ (contractors) **Regional Offices:** 6 **Field/Operations Offices:** 11 **Special Purpose Offices:** 7 **Other Facilities (excluding labs):** 14 **National Labs:** 16 **Other Labs**: 10 **Budget** (FY02 Request): $19 billion

Budget Breakdown (by organization; FY02 Request; $ in billions): National Nuclear Security Programs ($7.2); Environmental Quality ($6.5; for: Office of Environmental Management –$5.9; Office of Civilian Radioactive Waste Management –$0.44; Office of Environment, Safety and Health –$0.14); Science and Technology ($3.2); Energy Resources ($2.3; for: Energy Efficiency and Renewable Energy Office [$1.03 – $0.76 for energy efficiency, $0.28 for renewable energy]; Fossil Energy Office –$0.75; Nuclear Energy, Science, and Technology Office –$0.22; Power Marketing Administrations –$0.21; Energy Information Administration –$0.08); Corporate Management ($0.15); Federal Energy Regulatory Commission ($0 – self-financed through collected fees/charges).

Budget Info Online: FY02 Budget Justification (on the "Office of the Chief Financial Officer" web page).

GPRA Reports Online (all on the "Office of the Chief Financial Officer" web page): Performance and Accountability Report (FY00); Performance Plan (FY02); Strategic Plan (FY01-05).

OIG Reports Online: Audit and inspection reports; semiannual reports to Congress; special report on management challenges (issued 11/00).

Major Environmentally-Related Management Challenges/Program Risks (per the GAO): Environmental Cleanup (GAO recommends integrating work both among and within sites requiring active cleanup; in response, DOE has established an Office of Integration and Disposition); Contract Management (including environmental cleanup contracts; identified problems include: cost and schedule overruns; inadequate oversight of contractors' activities; inability to hold contractors accountable).

Contact Info: Forrestal Bldg., 1000 Independence Ave. SW, Washington, DC 20585; (202) 586-5000 / (800) DIAL-DOE.

Agency/Entity Head: Spencer Abraham (Secretary)

202.   Dept. of Energy – Energy Efficiency and Renewable Energy Network (EREN) (www.eren.doe.gov)
Description/Mission: An Internet gateway for accessing information and resources on energy efficiency and renewable energy. Provides access to 600+ relevant web-links and 80,000 relevant documents as well as serves as the gateway to DOE's Office of Energy Efficiency and Renewable Energy (EERE – see Profile #207).

Main Website Divisions (and sub-divisions): Technologies (energy efficiency technologies; renewable energy technologies); Specialized Resources (news; ask an energy expert; kids; solicitations; newsletter subscription; consumers; education; financing; states); Featured Sites.

Check Out on the Web: News section (links to 30+ relevant online newsletters and magazines).

203.   Dept. of Energy – Energy Information Administration (EIA) (www.eia.doe.gov)
Description/Mission: Independent entity within the DOE, providing policy-independent data, analyses, and forecasts regarding energy and its interaction with the economy and the environment. Many of EIA's activities are required by statute, while other activities are in response to requests from policymakers, the energy industry and the general public.

Key Publications (all online): International Energy Outlook 2001 (international energy projections through 2020); Annual Energy Review (historical U.S./international energy statistics from 1949 on; annual report); Annual Energy Outlook (midterm [20 year] forecasts of energy supply, demand and prices for the U.S.); Emissions of Greenhouse Gases in the U.S. (annual report); Voluntary Reporting of Greenhouse Gases (annual report on voluntarily-reported emissions reductions and carbon sequestration projects).

Main Website Divisions (and sub-divisions): Can access information by: Geography (international; states; U.S. regions; country briefs); Fuel; Sector (residential; commercial; industrial; transportation); Price; Specific Subject Area (process; environment; forecasts; analyses). The "Environment" subject area is broken down into: Transportation; Utilities/Electricity; Greenhouse Gas Emissions/Climate Change; Voluntary Reporting of Greenhouse Gases; Legislation/ International Agreement; Publications/Reports/Analyses; Fuels; Geography; Forecasts/Analyses.

Established: 1977 **Employees:** 375 (plus 250 contractors) **Budget** (FY02 Request): $75.5 million

Budget Info Online: See Profile #201 for DOE as a whole.

GPRA Reports Online: EIA Strategic Plan (FY00-05; located under "About Us"); also see Profile #201 for DOE as a whole.

Contact Info: Forrestal Bldg., 1000 Independence Ave. SW, Washington, DC 20585; (202) 586-8800; infoctr@eia.doe.gov

Agency/Entity Head: Mary Jean Hutzler (Acting Administrator)

204.   Dept. of Energy – National Energy Technology Laboratory (NETL) (www.netl.doe.gov)

Description/Mission: DOE national lab with a primary mission of developing fossil-energy based technologies (i.e., using coal, natural gas and oil) for DOE's Office of Fossil Energy (see Profile #209). Also involved in developing and deploying environmental remediation technologies supporting cleanup of DOE's weapons complex through DOE's Office of Environmental Management (see Profile #208). Research and development activities are conducted both in-house and through partnerships and other agreements with industry, universities/private research institutions and other national/federal labs. Nearly 1100 research, development and demonstration projects are in NETL's portfolio. NETL was formerly known as the Federal Energy Technology Center.

Organizational Structure – Key Offices: Strategic Center for Natural Gas; National Petroleum Technology Office; Office of Coal and Environmental Systems; Office of Fuels and Energy Efficiency; Office of Science and Technology (focused on: gas energy system dynamics; carbon sequestration science; computational energy science; ultra clean fuels); Office of Environmental Management and Defense Programs.

Main Website Divisions: What's New; Business; Career Ops; Events; Publications; Technologies; On-Site R&D; People; Maps; Cool Science; NETL TV; Newsroom.

Established: 1996 (predecessor orgs date back to 1910) **Employees:** 550 (plus 700+ contractors) **Budget** (FY02 Request): $440 million

Budget Info Online: See Profile #201 for DOE as a whole.

GPRA Reports Online: Institutional (Strategic) Plan (FY99-03; available under "Publications"); also see Profile #201 for DOE as a whole.

Contact Info: P.O. Box 10940, 626 Cochrans Mill Road, Pittsburgh, PA 15236-0940; (412) 386-6000 .

Agency/Entity Head: Rita Bajura (Director)

205.   Dept. of Energy – National Renewable Energy Laboratory (NREL) (www.nrel.gov)

Description/Mission: DOE national lab seeking to develop and transfer to the private sector renewable energy and energy efficiency technologies. Runs 13 research and development programs through 5 Centers (see below for details). Operated for DOE by Midwest Research Institute, with Battelle Memorial Laboratory and Bechtel Corporation as major subcontractors.

A Closer Look: Nearly completely funded (90+%) by DOE's Office of Energy Efficiency and Renewable Energy (see Profile #207). About 50% of NREL's budget is used to fund research by industry and universities in a cost-share arrangement (NREL has research partnership agreements with about 125 industry partners, 60 universities and 45 non-profit organizations).

Organizational Structure – NREL Centers: Biotechnology Center for Fuels and Chemicals; National Center for Photovoltaics; National Wind Technology Center; Center for Buildings and Thermal Systems; Center for Transportation Technologies and Systems.

Organizational Structure – Research & Development Programs: Biofuels; Biomass Power; Biomass-Derived Chemicals; Geothermal; Hydrogen; Photovoltaics; Solar Power and Thermal Systems; Wind Energy; Waste-to-Energy; Advanced Vehicles (hybrids, electrical, fuel cells); Energy-Efficient Buildings; Industrial Processes; Superconductivity.

Key Issue: Deep budget cuts proposed for FY02 ($130 million for FY02 compared to $187 million in FY00)

Main Website Divisions: Research and Technology; National and International Applications; Technology Transfer; News and Events; Data and Documents; Clean Energy Basics; Education Partnerships.

Check Out on the Web: Photographic Information eXchange (PIX) (collection of renewable energy and energy efficiency technology photographs with extensive documentation provided; located on "Data and Documents" page).

Established: 1977 **Employees:** 850 **Budget** (FY02 Request): $130 million

Budget Info Online: See Profile #201 for DOE as a whole.

GPRA Reports Online: NREL Institutional (Strategic) Plan (FY01-05; located on the home page); also see Profile #201 for DOE as a whole.

Contact Info: 1617 Cole Blvd., Golden, CO 80401-3393; (303) 275-3000.

Agency/Entity Head: Richard H. Truly (Director)

206.   Dept. of Energy – Office of Civilian Radioactive Waste Management (OCRWM) (www.rw.doe.gov)

Description/Mission: Office (within DOE's Energy, Science, and Environment Division) responsible for developing and managing a federal system for disposing of: 1) spent nuclear fuel from commercial nuclear reactors and 2) high-level radioactive waste resulting from defense activities. (Note: Licensing and regulatory oversight of radioactive waste management activities/facilities is the responsibility of the Nuclear Regulatory Commission – see Profile #247, located within Subsection 2.2.2 – "Independent Agencies/Entities"). OCRWM is also responsible for the transportation of civilian waste for ultimate disposal.

A Closer Look: Two notes: 1) per the Nuclear Waste Policy Amendments Act of 1987, OCRWM was directed to evaluate only Yucca Mountain, Nevada as a national, permanent waste disposal site (OCRWM issued a positive recommendation in 1/02); 2) funding for civilian nuclear waste disposal comes from two fees levied on owners and generators of civilian spent nuclear fuel, deposited into the Nuclear Waste Fund (as of 9/1/00, $15.1 billion in fees had been collected, with $5.5 billion spent, leaving $9.6 billion in the Fund).

Main Website Divisions: Program Overview; Yucca Mountain Project; Quality Assurance; Waste Acceptance and Transportation; Program Management; Program Docs; Technical Reports; Announcements; Related Links; Search.

Established: 1982 **Employees:** 200 (plus 2300 contractors) **Budget** (FY02 Request): $445 million

Budget Breakdown By Funding (FY02 request: $ in millions): Defense Waste Disposal ($310); Civilian Waste Disposal ($135).

Budget Breakdown By Activities (FY02 request: $ in millions): Site Characterization ($355); Program Direction and Integration ($84); Waste Acceptance, Storage and Transportation ($6).

Budget Info Online: See Profile #201 for DOE as a whole.

GPRA Reports Online: OCRWM Program (Strategic) Plan (issued 2/00; located under "Program Documents"); also see Profile #201 for DOE as a whole.

Contact Info: Forrestal Bldg., 1000 Independence Ave. SW, Washington, DC 20585; (202) 586-5000.

Agency/Entity Head: Ronald Milner (Acting Director)

207.   Dept. of Energy – Office of Energy Efficiency and Renewable Energy (EERE or OEERE)
    (www.eren.doe.gov/ee.html)

Description/Mission: Office (within DOE's Energy, Science, and Environment Division) responsible for DOE's energy efficiency and renewable energy programs.

A Closer Look: Provides nearly all the funding (90+%) for the National Renewable Energy Laboratory (see Profile #205).

Operating/Organizational Structure: Organized around 5 energy sectors, namely: industry (Office of Industrial Technologies), transportation (Office of Transportation Technologies), buildings (Office of Building Technology, State and Community Programs), power generation and delivery (Office of Power Technologies), and federal government facilities (Federal Energy Management Program).

Key Issue: Deep budget cuts proposed in most programs for FY02 (except for the weatherization grant program).

Main Website Divisions: About EERE; Working With Us; News.

Employees: 500 **Budget** (FY02 Request): $1.03 billion

Budget Breakdown (FY02 Request; $ in millions): Energy Efficiency ($795; for: weatherization grants –$273; transportation sector –$239; building technology, excluding weatherization grants –$94; industry sector –$88; power technology –$47; federal energy management program –$13; policy and management –$40); Renewable Energy ($237; for: biomass/biofuels –$81; solar –$43; wind –$21; geothermal –$14; hydrogen –$14; hydropower –$3; electric energy systems and storage –$34; National Renewable Energy Lab infrastructure needs –$5; support and implementation –$5; program direction –$19).

Budget Info Online: See Profile #201 for DOE as a whole.

GPRA Reports Online: EERE Strategic Plan (10-year plan issued 3/00; on home page); also see Profile #201 for DOE as a whole.

Contact Info: Forrestal Bldg., 1000 Independence Ave. SW, Washington, DC 20585; (202) 586-9220; eeremailbox@ee.doe.gov

Agency/Entity Head: David K. Garman (Assistant Secretary)

208.   Dept. of Energy – Office of Environmental Management (EM or OEM) (www.em.doe.gov)

Description/Mission: Office (within DOE's Energy, Science, and Environment Division) responsible for managing the cleanup (and long-term stewardship, as required) of both: 1) defense-related nuclear weapons research and production facilities and 2) non-defense-related research facilities that conducted federally-sponsored nuclear energy and basic science research. Also responsible for the Waste Isolation Pilot Plant (WIPP – located in Carlsbad, New Mexico), the designated permanent disposal site for defense-related radioactive waste from the research and production of nuclear weapons.

A Closer Look: EM is responsible for environmental cleanup at 113 geographic sites; at the end of FY00, active cleanup had been completed at 71 of those sites, with a goal of completing active cleanup at another 20 sites by the end of FY06. (In addition to the 113 sites overseen by EM, another 46 DOE sites are being cleaned up through the Army Corps of Engineers' Formerly Utilized Sites Remedial Action Program [FUSRAP] program).

Main Website Divisions: Hot Topics; Featured Items; Press Releases; Learn About EM; EM HQ Programs; Budget; Planning and Execution; Laws and Regulations; Cost Engineering; Resources; Interested Audiences; Publications; Calendar of Events.

Established: 1989 **Budget** (FY02 Request): $5.9 billion

Budget Breakdown (FY02 Request; $ in billions): Defense Environmental Restoration and Waste Management ($4.55; for defense-related DOE sites to be cleaned up by the end of FY06 with DOE using the sites after cleanup); Defense Facilities Closure Projects ($1.05; for defense-related DOE sites to be cleaned up by the end of FY06 with DOE not using the sites after cleanup); Uranium Facilities Maintenance and Remediation ($0.36; focused on cleanup at the nation's 3 gaseous diffusion plants); Non-Defense Environmental Management ($0.23; for cleanup at non-defense-related DOE sites that conducted nuclear energy and basic science research); Defense Environmental Management Privatization ($0.14; for selected DOE waste storage, treatment, or disposal projects undertaken by private contractors assuming most of the up-front risk for a project). (Note: EM was budgeted to receive $0.42 billion in discretionary payments from the Uranium Enrichment D&D Fund in FY02).

Budget Info Online: FY02 Budget (available under "Budget"); also see Profile #201 for DOE as a whole.

GPRA Reports Online: See Profile #201 for DOE as a whole.

Contact Info: Forrestal Bldg., 1000 Independence Ave. SW, Washington, DC 20585; (202) 586-5000.

Agency/Entity Head: Jessie Roberson (Assistant Secretary)

209.   Dept. of Energy – Office of Fossil Energy (FE or OFE) (www.fe.doe.gov)

Description/Mission: Office (within DOE's Energy, Science, and Environment Division) conducting research and development of fossil energy technologies (in joint partnership with industry, universities/private research institutions, and national labs). Oversees 500+ active research and development projects. Also manages the Strategic Petroleum Reserve (consisting of emergency storage of up to 700 million barrels of crude oil).

Key Initiative: Proposed Clean Coal Power Initiative (a 10-year, $2 billion plan for research in coal-based power technology; builds upon the existing Clean Coal Technology program begun in 1985).

Main Website Divisions: Electric Power R&D; Oil/Gas R&D; Fuels R&D; Oil Reserves; Electricity Regulation; Gas Regulation.

Employees: 1000 **Budget** (FY02 Request): $449 million

Budget Breakdown (FY02 Request: $ in millions): Fuels and Power Systems ($160); Clean Coal Initiative ($150); Program Direction/Support ($70); Petroleum ($31); Natural Gas ($21); Environmental Restoration ($10); Other ($8).

Budget Info Online: FY02 Budget (available under "Budget"); also see Profile #201 for DOE as a whole.

GPRA Reports Online: See Profile #201 for DOE as a whole.

Contact Info: Forrestal Bldg., 1000 Independence Ave. SW, Washington, DC 20585; (202) 586-6503.

Agency/Entity Head: Michael Smith (Assistant Secretary)

210.   Dept. of Energy – Office of Nuclear Energy, Science, and Technology (NE or ONEST) (www.ne.doe.gov)

Description/Mission: Office (within DOE's Energy, Science, and Environment Division) promoting nuclear technologies for energy production and others uses (namely: medical, industrial, and general research uses).

Key Initiative: Scoping study of potential sites for new nuclear power plants in the U.S. (being conducted under NE's Early Site Permit demonstration program).

Main Website Divisions: From the Director; Organization Chart; Program Offices; Press Releases; Public Information; Advisory Committee; Web Connections; Diversity Activities; Job Opportunities; Contact Us.

Budget (FY02 Request): $223 million

Budget Breakdown (FY02 Request; $ in millions): Infrastructure ($81; for: Argonne National Lab-West –$34; Fast Flux Test Facility –$38; Test Reactor Area –$8); Nuclear Facilities Management ($30; focused on shutdown and deactivation of the Experimental Breeder Reactor-II); Advanced Radioisotope Power Systems ($29; for developing power systems for NASA space missions); Nuclear Energy Research and Development ($27); Program Direction ($25); Isotope Support and Production ($18; for providing a reliable supply of radioactive isotopes for use in medicine, industry and research); University Reactor Fuel Assistance and Support ($12; for: operation and upgrade of university research reactors; student fellowships and scholarships; nuclear engineering research grants).

Budget Info Online: See Profile #201 for DOE as a whole.

GPRA Reports Online: NE Strategic Plan 2000 (available on the NE home page); also see Profile #201 for DOE as a whole.

Contact Info: 19901 Germantown Road, Germantown, MD 20874.

Agency/Entity Head: William Magwood IV (Director)

211.   Dept. of Health and Human Services (HHS) (www.hhs.gov)

Description/Mission: Federal Cabinet-level department responsible for protecting public health and providing essential human services.

Operating/Organizational Structure: Organized into 10 Operating Divisions, including (see Profiles #212, 215 and 217, respectively): the Centers for Disease Control and Prevention (CDC, comprised of 11 national centers/institutes/programs); the Food and Drug Administration (FDA); the National Institutes of Health (NIH, comprised of 18 separate institutes of health).

Key Agencies/Programs (see Profiles #213, 214, 216 and 218, respectively): Agency for Toxic Substances and

Disease Registry (ATSDR; administered by the CDC); Center for Food Safety and Applied Nutrition (CFSAN; part of the FDA); National Center for Environmental Health (NCEH; part of the CDC); National Institute of Environmental Health Sciences (NIEHS; part of the NIH).

Main Website Divisions: Search; News; Agencies; Opportunities; About Us; Related Sites.

Established: 1953 **Employees:** 65,000 **Budget** (FY02 Request): $473 billion

Budget Info Online: FY02 Budget Justification (under "About HHS")

GPRA Reports Online (both under "About HHS"): Performance Plan (FY02) and Performance Report (FY00); Strategic Plan (FY01-06).

OIG Reports Online: Audit and inspection reports; semiannual reports to Congress; annual "Red Book" (list of cost-saving recommendations not implemented).

Major Environmentally-Related Management Challenges/Program Risks (per the GAO): None identified.

Contact Info: 200 Independence Ave. SW, Washington, DC 20201; (202) 619-0257; hhsmail@os.dhhs.gov

Agency/Entity Head: Tommy Thompson (Secretary)

212.   **Dept. of Health and Human Services – Centers for Disease Control (CDC)** (www.cdc.gov)

Description/Mission: Federal agency (under HHS) responsible for developing and applying disease prevention and control nationwide. Also performs many of the administrative functions for the Agency for Toxic Substances and Disease Registry (ATSDR – see Profile #213), a sister agency of the CDC.

Operating/Organizational Structure: Comprised of 11 national centers/institutes/programs, including the National Center for Environmental Health (NCEH – see Profile #214).

Established: 1946 **Employees:** 8500 **Budget** (FY02 Request): $4.1 billion

Budget Info Online: FY02 Budget Request (under "About CDC"); also see Profile #211 for HHS as a whole.

GPRA Reports Online: See Profile #211 for HHS as a whole.

Contact Info: 1600 Clifton Rd., Atlanta, GA 30333; (404) 639-3311.

Agency/Entity Head: Dr. Jeffrey P. Koplan (Director)

213.   **Dept. of Health and Human Services – CDC – Agency for Toxic Substances and Disease Registry (ATSDR)** (www.atsdr.cdc.gov)

Description/Mission: Federal agency (under HHS and managed as part of the CDC) that evaluates the effects of hazardous chemicals/substances in the environment on public health with its primary focus being on the federal Superfund (hazardous waste site cleanup) program. A health-science-based agency; not a regulatory agency.

A Closer Look: Prior to FY01, was funded by the Environmental Protection Agency; now funded through a VA/HUD appropriation.

Basic Activities: Public health assessments; health surveillance and registries; applied research; education; training.

Key Report: Top 20 Hazardous Substances (priority listing by ATSDR and EPA; online).

Web Site Divisions (by topic): Hazardous Substances; Hazardous Waste Sites; Emergency Response; Measuring Health Effects; Environmental Health Education; Special Initiatives; Spotlight (news); Information Sources; Publications.

Web Site Divisions (by audience group): Children and Parents; Communities; Healthcare Professionals; Tribal Affairs.

Check Out on the Web: ToxFAQs (fact sheets on 100+ individual hazardous chemicals/substances); Maps of Hazardous Waste Sites ("GATHER system"; maps out federal Superfund sites and provides health evaluation data from ATSDR's database).

Established: 1980 **Staff:** 400 **Regional Offices:** 10 **Budget** (FY02 Request): $78 million

Budget Info Online: See Profile #211 for HHS as a whole.

GPRA Reports Online: See Profile #211 for HHS as a whole.

Contact Info: 1600 Clifton Rd., Atlanta, GA 30333; (888) 42-ATSDR / (404) 498-0110; ATSDRIC@cdc.gov

Agency/Entity Head: Dr. Jeffrey Koplan (Director)

214.   Dept. of Health and Human Services – CDC – National Center for Environmental Health (NCEH) (www.cdc.gov/nceh)

Description/Mission: Federal agency (under HHS as part of the CDC) focused on public health issues related to the environment (with the "environment" broadly defined to include natural events such as hurricanes, earthquakes, etc.).

A Closer Look: About one-half of NCEH's total budget is directed towards addressing two specific issues: childhood lead poisoning and asthma.

Key Programs (and focus areas): Emergency and Environmental Health Sciences (demilitarization of chemical weapons; disaster epidemiology; emergency preparedness and response; environmental health services; international emergency and refugee health; national pharmaceutical stockpile program; vessel sanitation); Environmental Hazards and Health Effects (air pollution and respiratory health; asthma; health studies branch; childhood lead poisoning prevention; radiation studies; Gulf War chemical exposures); Division of Laboratory Sciences (a.k.a. Environmental Health Laboratory; conducts lab research on: bio-monitoring; cardiovascular disease; chemical terrorism; diabetes; genetics; lead; newborn screening; nutrition; tobacco/smoking).

Key Report: National Report on Human Exposure to Environmental Chemicals (assessment of the U.S. population's exposure to 27 environmental chemicals using bio-monitoring).

Employees: 500 **Budget** (FY02 Request): $137 million

Budget Breakdown (FY02; $ in millions): Childhood Lead Poisoning ($42); Environmental Health Laboratory ($34); Environmental Health Activities ($33); Asthma ($28).

Budget Info Online: See Profile #211 for HHS as a whole.

GPRA Reports Online: NCEH Strategic Plan (FY99-03; under "About NCEH"); also see Profile #211 for HHS as a whole.

Contact Info: Atlanta GA; (770) 488-7000; ncehinfo@cdc.gov

Agency/Entity Head: Richard Jackson, MD (Director)

215.   Dept. of Health and Human Services – Food and Drug Administration (FDA) (www.fda.gov)

Description/Mission: Federal regulatory agency (under HHS) responsible for protecting public health by ensuring that: 1) foods are safe, wholesome, sanitary, and properly labeled; 2) human and veterinary drugs are safe and effective; 3) cosmetics are safe and properly labeled; and 4) the public's health and safety is protected from electronic product radiation.

Operating/Organizational Structure: Divided into 9 Centers/Offices, including the Center for Food Safety and Applied Nutrition (see Profile #216).

Established: 1930 **Employees:** 9500 **Budget** (FY02 Request): $1.4 billion

Budget Info Online: FY02 Budget (under "About FDA"); also see Profile #211 for HHS as a whole.

GPRA Reports Online: Program Priorities (on home page); also see Profile #211 for HHS as a whole.

Contact Info: 5600 Fishers Lane, Rockville, MD 20857; (888) 463-6332.

Agency/Entity Head: Bernard Schwetz (Acting Commissioner)

216.   Dept. of Health and Human Services – FDA – Center for Food Safety and Applied Nutrition (CFSAN) (www.cfsan.fda.gov)

Description/Mission: Federal regulatory agency (under HHS as part of the FDA) responsible for ensuring that the nation's food supply is "safe, sanitary, wholesome, and honestly labeled" and that cosmetic products are safe and properly labeled. Sets standards and develops regulations for the food industry. (Note: The FDA does not regulate meat, poultry, and eggs [which are instead regulated by the USDA's Food Safety and Inspection Service] and drinking water [which is instead regulated by the EPA]. In addition, the EPA also establishes acceptable limits for pesticide residues in foods.)

A Closer Look: FDA regulations cover 30,000+ U.S. food processors and manufacturers, 20,000+ food warehouses, and 3,500 cosmetic firms (restaurants and grocery stores are separately regulated by state and local authorities with technical assistance provided by FDA). The FDA does not regulate food growers, only food processors and manufacturers.

Operating/Organizational Structure: Operates in 12 program areas, including: Biotechnology; Pesticides and Chemical Contaminants.

Overall Program Priorities/Focus Areas: Food Safety; Food Additives; Dietary Supplements; Food Biotechnology.

Key Issue: Bioengineered (Genetically Modified) Food (specific issues include: manufacturers notifying the FDA prior to marketing such foods; labeling issues; assessment for allergy potential).

Employees: 900 **Budget** (FY02 Request): $135 million (NOTE: Budget numbers are for Center activities only; an additional 1600 employees and $184 million is budgeted for field-based activities – primarily inspections – within FDA's overall "Foods" program).

Budget Info Online: FY02 Budget Request (under "About FDA" on the FDA home page); also see Profile #211 for HHS as a whole.

GPRA Reports Online: CFSAN FY01 Program Priorities (on home page); also see Profile #211 for HHS as a whole.

Contact Info: 200 C St. SW, Washington, DC 20204; (888) 723-3366.

Agency/Entity Head: Joseph A. Levitt (Director)

217.   Dept. of Health and Human Services – National Institutes of Health (NIH) (www.nih.gov)

Description/Mission: Federal agency (under HHS) serving as the federal focal point for medical research in the U.S. The vast majority of research is conducted by outside research institutions through NIH grants and research contracts. NIH also supports medical training programs nationwide.

Operating/Organizational Structure: Comprised of 18 separate institutes of health, including the National Institute of Environmental Health Sciences (see Profile #218).

Budget (FY02 Request): $23 billion

Budget Info Online: FY02 Budget Request (on the "News" page); also see Profile #211 for HHS as a whole.

GPRA Reports Online (both on the "News" page): Performance Plan (FY02) and Performance Report (FY00); NIH Investments, Progress and Plans (FY99-03); also see Profile #211 for HHS as a whole.

Contact Info: 1 Center Drive, Bethesda, Maryland 20892; (301) 496-4000; NIHInfo@od.nih.gov

Agency/Entity Head: Dr. Ruth Kirschstein (Acting Director)

218.   Dept. of Health and Human Services – NIH – National Institute of Environmental Health Sciences (NIEHS) (www.niehs.nih.gov)

Description/Mission: Federal research institute (under HHS as part of the NIH) conducting basic research on environmental health and environment-related diseases. Primary focus is on preventing disease rather than treating illnesses. NIEHS also supports 22 university-based environmental research centers (known as Centers for Environmental Health Studies). These Centers each have a specific research focus and each maintains a Community Outreach and Education Program. The NIEHS is also responsible for leadership of the National Toxicology Program (NTP), a multi-agency organization that conducts toxicological research on a broad array of public-nominated chemical compounds and substances.

Organizational Structure – Research Areas: Women's Health; Children's Health; Health Disparities (how poverty, environmental pollution and health interrelate); Birth and Development Defects, Sterility, Breast and Testicular Cancers (focus on chemical-induced root causes); Alzheimer's and Other Neurological Disorders (focus on chemical toxins as potential root causes); Lead Poisoning Treatments; Agricultural Pollution (both from natural materials and from chemicals used in agricultural); Animal Alternatives (seek to reduce the number of animals used in research); Biomarkers (indicators to measure the body's exposure to, and up-take of, toxins).

Check Out on the Web: "Environmental Health Info" (provides a multitude of fact-sheets and pamphlets geared for the general public); NIEHS Online Library (provides more technical information).

Established: 1966 **Budget** (FY02 Request): $562 million

Budget Info Online: See Profile #211 for HHS as a whole.

GPRA Reports Online: NIEHS Strategic Plan (FY01-05; under "Welcome to NIEHS"); also see Profile #211 for HHS as a whole.

Contact Info: 111 Alexander Drive, Research Triangle Park, NC 27709; (919) 541-3345.

Agency/Entity Head: Kenneth Olden (Director)

219.   Department of the Interior (DOI) (www.doi.gov)

Description/Mission: Federal Cabinet-level department serving as the nation's principal conservation agency, overseeing 451 million acres of federally-owned land, representing 70% of all federally-owned land and about 1/5 of the total U.S. land surface. Also manages mineral leasing and operations on more than 700 million acres of onshore mineral estate underlying both federal and non-federal surface lands, and nearly 1.8 billion acres comprising the Outer Continental Shelf (generally the zone between 3 and 200 miles offshore).

Facts and Figures: Of the 451 million acres overseen by DOI as a whole: 264 million are "public lands" overseen by the Bureau of Land Management; 94 million comprise the National Wildlife Refuge system overseen by the Fish and Wildlife Service; 84 million comprise the National Park System overseen by the National Park Service.

A Closer Look: DOI collected $9 billion in gross receipts in FY00, about two-thirds of which was derived from mineral leasing revenues (mainly for oil, gas and coal). DOI also paid out $1.8 billion to the states in FY00 through 13 separate programs.

Operating/Organizational Structure: Organized into eight major bureaus, reporting to four Assistant Secretaries as follows: Fish and Wildlife and Parks (National Park Service –NPS; Fish and Wildlife Service – FWS); Land and Minerals Management (Bureau of Land Management –BLM; Minerals Management Service – MMS; Office of Surface Mining, Reclamation and Enforcement –OSM); Water and Science (U.S. Geological Survey –USGS; Bureau of Reclamation –USBR); Indian Affairs (Bureau of Indian Affairs –BIA). See Profiles #220-227 detailing each bureau (except for Indian Affairs). Historically, DOI has been a highly decentralized Department, allowing each bureau relatively wide latitude to develop their own systems and processes for managing programs.

Key Multi-Agency Programs (see Profiles #248 and 251)**:** Clean Water Initiative / Clean Water Action Plan; Wildfire Management Initiative / National Fire Plan.

Main Website Divisions: News; About DOI; Bureaus; Offices; Index.

Check Out on the Web: Budget Background Information (on the "Office of the Budget" page under "About DOI"): Provides current and historic budget-related information (revenues, payments to states, staffing levels, etc.).

Established: 1849 **Employees:** 69,400 **Budget** (FY02 Request): $12.8 billion

Budget and Employee Breakdown (FY02 Request; $ in billions): National Park Service ($2.8; 20,400); Bureau of Indian Affairs ($2.2; 9,900); Bureau of Land Management ($2.0; 10,800); Fish and Wildlife Service ($1.8; 8,700); Mineral Management Service ($1.1; 1,800); Bureau of Reclamation ($0.9; 5,600); U.S. Geological Survey ($0.8; 9,000); Departmental Offices ($0.7; 2,600); Office of Surface Mining ($0.4; 640).

Budget Info Online: FY 02 Budget (located under "About DOI").

GPRA Reports Online (both located under "About DOI"): Annual Performance Plan (FY02) / Annual Performance Report (FY00); Strategic Plan (FY00-05).

OIG Reports Online: Audit and inspection reports; semiannual reports to Congress.

Major Management Challenges/Program Risks (per the GAO): National Park Service Management (see the National Park Service Profile – #225 – for details); Ecosystem Restoration Management (recommendations: 1) work with outside entities to develop plans and strategies to achieve restoration and management goals; 2) improve coordination with multiple entities in such efforts; 3) develop a succession plan to replace retiring fire management personnel); Land Exchanges (focus on the BLM; recommendations: 1) better demonstrate that an exchange is necessary and exchanged lands are of approximately equal value; 2) guarantee that funds used are properly managed/controlled; 3) highlight the need for increased funding for operating/maintaining newly acquired lands in Congressional budget requests).

Contact Info: 1849 C St. NW, Washington, DC 20240; (202) 208-3100.

Agency/Entity Head: Gale Norton (Secretary)

220.   Dept. of Interior – Bureau of Land Management (BLM) (www.blm.gov)

Description/Mission: Federal agency (under the DOI) responsible for federally-owned "public" lands (which are primarily located in 11 western states and Alaska), including management of their resources both for commercial activities (including for energy and mineral commodities, forest products, livestock grazing forage, and special uses such as right-of-ways for pipelines and transmission lines) and for outdoor recreational activities (such as hunting, fishing, boating, off-road vehicle driving, biking, etc.). Overall, BLM manages 264 million acres (representing about 1/8 of the nation's land) and about 700 million additional acres of subsurface mineral resources. BLM lands host over 50 million visitors annually.

Facts and Figures: BLM-managed lands are mostly extensive grasslands, forests, high mountains, arctic tundra, and deserts. 88 of the 264 million acres are designated "special management areas" (collectively known as the National Landscape Conservation System) which includes: 9 National Conservation Areas; 35 National Wild and Scenic Rivers; 138 Wilderness Areas and 618 Wilderness Study Areas; 10 Historic/Scenic National Trails; 7 National Monuments; 200 Herd Management Areas (for wild, free-roaming horses and burros); and 740 "Areas of Critical Environmental Concern."

A Closer Look: The estimated market value of "production" (from energy and minerals, grazing and timber resources) occurring on BLM public lands in FY00 was $14 billion, with total (direct and indirect) economic impact estimated at $29 billion for FY00. Government-received revenues from energy-related production on public lands (including rents, royalties and bonuses) amounted to $1.5 billion in FY00 ($928 million from oil and gas and $308 from coal, with 50% of each returned to the states). Grazing, timber and land sales netted the federal government an additional $100 million in FY00.

Primary Agency Program Activities: Recreation; Commercial Use; Natural and Cultural Heritage Preservation; Public Health, Safety and Property Protection; Economic and Technical Assistance; Land, Resource and Title Information; Land Health Assessments; Land Health Restoration and Maintenance.

Key Multi-Agency Program: Clean Water Initiative / Clean Water Action Plan (see Profile #248).

Key Initiative: National Assessment Prototype (representing the first step towards developing a systematic assessment of land health and resource use on public lands).

Key Issue: Revision of existing Land Use Plans (the plans guide decisions on land management and resource use; 122 of the 162 plans were completed prior to 1989 and are scheduled for update).

Key Reports: Public Lands Statistics (annual; online); Public Rewards from Public Lands (quantifies the worth of the BLM-managed public lands in economic, social and environmental terms; online).

Main Website Divisions: News; Information (various topics); What We Do; BLM Facts; Directory (phone; email; organization chart; other BLM web pages); FOIA.

Established: 1946 **Employees:** 10,800 **State Offices:** 12 **Budget** (FY02 Request): $2.0 billion

Budget Breakdown (FY02 Request; $ in millions): Management of Lands and Resources ($760); Wildland Fire Management ($658; for fighting wildfires); Payment in Lieu of Taxes ($150; for payments to counties containing certain federal lands); Oregon and California Grant Lands ($105; mainly for managing Western Oregon lands for sustainable-yield timber production); Land and Water Acquisition Fund ($48; for funding 28 specific projects in 11 states); Permanent Operating Funds and Appropriations ($228).

Budget Info Online: FY02 Budget Justification (located under "Budget Information" on the "Information" web page).

GPRA Reports Online: Strategic Plan (FY00-05; located under "BLM Facts"); Annual Performance Plan (FY02) / Annual Performance Report (FY00) (located under "Budget Information" on the "Information" web page).

Contact Info: 1849 C St. NW, Washington, DC 20240; (202) 452-5125 (Public Affairs).

Agency/Entity Head: Kathleen Clarke (Director)

221.   Dept. of Interior – Bureau of Reclamation (USBR or BoR) (www.usbr.gov)

Description/Mission: Federal agency (under the DOI) focused mainly on providing and managing water in 17 western states. Best known for construction of dams, power plants and canals in these western states. Now the largest water wholesaler in the U.S. (delivering 10 trillion gallons of water for irrigation, municipal, rural and industrial use; servicing 31 million people) and the second largest producer of hydroelectric power in the nation (generating 40+ billion kilowatt-hours of energy each year). USBR facilities include 348 reservoirs (with a combined storage capacity of 245 million acre-feet), 58 hydroelectric power plants, and 300+ recreation sites (providing recreation activities for 90 million visitor-days a year).

Key Agency Activities: Water and Energy Management and Development (focused on dam and power plant operations); Land Management and Development (focused on recreation area operations); Fish and Wildlife Management and Development (focused on wetlands and watershed issues); Facility Operations, Maintenance and Rehabilitation (focused on dam and power plant operations).

Main Website Divisions: What We Do; Newsroom; Programs; DataWeb (data on USBR's facilities/projects); Feature (featured webpages); Search; Water Supply (current water supply information); Publications; Employment; Comments.

Check Out on the Web: Data Web (electronic presentation of the Bureau´s Project Data Book, providing data on its dams and reservoirs, power plants, and individual projects [**NOTE:** Post-Sept. 11, public access to the Project Data Book has been reduced]); Written in Water Video (describes the USBR; available online using Real Player; located under "What We Do"); Resource Stewardship Report 2000 (examines stewardship issues facing the USBR; listed under "Newsroom").

Established: 1902 **Employees:** 5600 **Regional Offices:** 5 **Budget** (FY02 Request): $860 million

Budget Breakdown (FY02 Request; $ in millions): Water and Related Resources ($648; for 24 specific major projects/programs plus a host of smaller projects/programs); Central Valley Project Restoration Fund ($55; for fish and wildlife habitat and population restoration in California's Central Valley); Policy and Management ($53; for overhead charges); California Bay-Delta Restoration ($20); Colorado River Dam Fund ($80; a mandatory appropriation for operations and maintenance).

Budget Info Online: See Profile #219 for the DOI as a whole.

GPRA Reports Online (both listed under "Newsroom"): Strategic Plan (FY00-05); Annual Performance Plan (FY02) / Annual Performance Report (FY00).

Contact Info: 1849 C St. NW, Washington, DC 20240; (202) 513-0575 (Public Affairs).

Agency/Entity Head: John Keys (Commissioner)

222.   Dept. of Interior – Fish and Wildlife Service (FWS) (www.fws.gov)

Description/Mission: Federal agency (under the DOI) responsible for conservation of migratory birds, threatened and endangered species, certain marine mammals and freshwater and anadromous fish. Manages the National Wildlife Refuge System (consisting of 535 refuges and 38 wetland management districts spanning 94 million acres) and implements the Endangered Species Act as it applies to terrestrial and freshwater species. Also operates 70 national fish hatcheries (producing 200+ million fish annually), 64 fisheries resource offices, and 78 ecological services field stations. Functions in an advisory capacity to the Army Corps of Engineers for so-called "Section 404" permits (dredge and fill permits for waterways and associated wetlands). Hosts 38 million visitors to its refuges and fish hatcheries annually.

Key Multi-Agency Program: Clean Water Initiative / Clean Water Action Plan (see Profile #248).

Key Publications: Threatened and Endangered Species Recovery Plans (various; online); Threatened and Endangered Species Habitat Conservation Plans (various); Comprehensive Conservation Plans (various; online); Status and Trends of Wetlands – 1986 to 1997 (online).

Main Website Divisions: Conserving Wildlife and Habitats; Working with Others; Educating for Conservation; Learning About Us.

Website Notes: This is a deceptively large web site with 630 different sub-sites (representing 20,000 web pages). Try using the Index/Site Map to find information and/or navigate the site.

Check Out on the Web: Conservation Issues (lists current key conservations issues; located under "Conserving

Wildlife and Habitats").

Established: 1940 **Employees:** 8700 **Budget** (FY02 Request): $1.78 billion

Budget Breakdown – Overall (FY02 Request; $ in millions): Resource Management ($807; see below for a breakdown); Sport Fish Restoration Account ($352; for a grant program to states providing up to 75% of costs for sport fish management, boating access and aquatic education projects; funded by an excise tax on sport fishing equipment); Federal Aid in Wildlife Restoration ($240; for a grant program to states providing up to 75% of costs for restoration of wild birds and mammals [including acquiring, developing and managing their habitats], for the education of hunters, and for development and management of shooting ranges; funded by an excise tax on sporting arms, ammunition, archery equipment, and handguns); Land Acquisition ($164; for acquiring federal refuge lands and for private landowner incentive programs); Cooperative Endangered Species Fund ($90; for grants to states and for acquiring Habitat Conservation Plan lands); Migratory Bird Conservation Account ($44; for acquiring migratory bird areas; principally funded by sales of duck stamps [special U.S. postage stamps] and import duties on arms and ammunition); Construction ($36; for specific projects on wildlife refuges and hatcheries); National Wildlife Refuge Fund ($18); North American Wetlands Conservation Fund ($16; for wetlands conservation grants); Misc. Other ($15).

Budget Breakdown – Resource Management Programs/Activities (FY02 Request; $ in millions): National Wildlife Refuge System ($341; for: refuge operations and maintenance –$315; migratory bird management –$25); Ecological Services ($198; for: endangered species –$112; habitat conservation –$76; environmental contaminants –$10); Fisheries ($93; for: fish hatcheries operations and maintenance –$49; fish and wildlife management assistance –$44); Law Enforcement ($50); General Administration ($124).

Budget Info Online: FY02 Budget Proposal (located under "Learning About Us").

GPRA Reports Online (both located under "Learning About Us"): Annual Performance Plan (FY02) / Annual Performance Report (FY00); Strategic Plan (FY00-05).

Contact Info: 1849 C St. NW, Washington, DC 20240; (202) 208-5634; Contact@fws.gov

Agency/Entity Head: Steven Williams (Director)

223.   **Dept. of Interior – Geological Service (USGS)** (www.usgs.gov)

Description/Mission: Federal agency (under the DOI) providing geologic, topographic and hydrologic information to resource managers, planners and other interested parties. A physical-science based agency; not a regulatory agency. Most well known for its earthquake research and production of topographic maps. Also a primary source of data on the quality and quantity of the nation's water resources.

Agency Focus Areas: Natural Hazards (earthquakes, volcanic eruptions, landslides, etc.); Resources (assessing the quantity, quality, and availability of natural resources); The Environment (understanding natural systems and human impacts on those systems).

Key Multi-Agency Program: Clean Water Initiative / Clean Water Action Plan (see Profile #248).

Key Reports (both online): Our Living Resources: A Report to the Nation on the Distribution, Abundance, and Health of U.S. Plants, Animals, and Ecosystems; Status and Trends of the Nation's Biological Resources (a comprehensive description of U.S. biological resources and the factors affecting them).

Main Website Divisions: Can navigate the site either by: 1) focus area (namely: biology; geology; mapping; water; products); 2) topic (15 main headings listed); 3) audience (namely: Congress; other government; news agencies; scientists; teachers and students); 4) products and data.

Check Out on the Web: Earthquake Information/National Earthquake Information Center (provides near real-time, world-wide earthquake information); Center for Integration of Natural Disaster Information (provides access to information concerning natural disasters – droughts, earthquakes, floods, geomagnetism, hurricanes, landslides, volcanoes wildfires, and wildlife diseases); Picturing Science (online science tours); Mineral Publications and Data Products (provides a multitude of data on U.S. mineral resources, including an interactive mapping feature – Mineral Resources Online); NWIS Data (access to over 100 years of water resources data collected at 1.5 million sites throughout the U.S.); Water Use (provides extensive data on U.S. water use, including comprehensive reports issued every five years).

Established: 1879 **Employees:** 9,000 **Budget** (FY02 Request): $813 million (also conducts $270 million of reimbursable work annually)

Budget Breakdown (FY02 Request; $ in millions): Geologic Assessments ($214); Water Resource Investigations ($159); Biological Research ($149); National Mapping Program ($124).

Budget Info Online: FY02 Budget (located under "About USGS").

GPRA Reports Online (both located under "About USGS"): Annual Performance Plan (FY02) / Annual Performance Report (FY00); Strategic Plan (FY00-05).

Contact Info: 12201 Sunrise Valley Dr., Reston, VA 20192; (703) 648-4000; ask@usgs.gov

Agency/Entity Head: Charles Groat (Director)

224.   Dept. of Interior – Minerals Management Service (MMS) (www.mms.gov)

Description/Mission: Federal agency (under the DOI) responsible for managing the nation's natural gas, oil and mineral resources on the outer continental shelf (OCS, generally the zone between 3 and 200 miles offshore, covering nearly 1.8 billion acres in total). MMS also collects, accounts for, and disburses money obtained from mining/drilling leases (mainly for extracting natural gas, oil, and coal) involving federal offshore and onshore lands, as well as for such leases involving Indian lands (for FY00, the total revenue so collected was $6.3 billion).

A Closer Look: Historically, collected revenues are distributes as follows: U.S. Treasury (62%); Special Purpose Funds (24%; comprised of: Land and Water Conservation Fund – $900 million annually; Historic Preservation Fund – $150 million annually; Reclamation Fund – variable amount); States (11%); Native Americans (3%).

Organizational Structure – MMS Environmental Program: Organized into two branches: Environmental Assessment (focused on environmental compliance with applicable laws and regulations, including NEPA) and Environmental Sciences (research-oriented; divided into two programs – Oil Spill Modeling and Environmental Studies, the latter conducting science and socioeconomic research focused in areas of existing/proposed mining/drilling activities).

Special Interest Areas: Gas Hydrates (methane-containing, ice-like minerals – both a potential safety hazard to current drilling operations and a potential future energy source); Biotechnology (using marine species for developing new pharmaceuticals and biomaterials).

Key Issues: Reorganizing the Minerals Revenue Management program to match current general business practices; exploring a "royalty-in-kind" approach for collecting oil and gas royalties (as opposed to collection in cash).

Key Report: Outer Continental Shelf Petroleum Assessment (periodic assessment of recoverable oil and gas resources within the OCS; issued every 5 years).

Check Out on the Web: "MMS Facts, Figures and Information" (providing an introduction to the MMS; available under "Online Publications").

Established: 1982 **Employees:** 1800 **Budget** (FY02 Request): $1.25 billion

Budget Breakdown (FY02 Request; $ in millions): Leasing and Associated Payments ($983; for 3 permanent appropriations to states); OCS Lands Management ($126); Royalty Management ($83); General Administration ($43); Oil Spill Research ($6); National Forests Funds ($5; for payments to states); Land Leases for Allied Purposes ($2).

Budget Info Online: See Profile #219 for the DOI as a whole.

GPRA Reports Online (all located under "Strategic Planning"): Annual Performance Plan (FY02); Annual Performance Report (FY00); Strategic Plan (FY00-05).

Contact Info: 1849 C St. NW, Washington, DC 20240; (703) 787-1000.

Agency/Entity Head: R.M. Burton (Director)

225.   Dept. of Interior – National Park Service (NPS) (www.nps.gov)

Description/Mission: Federal agency (under the DOI) responsible for managing the National Park System (NPS, consisting of nearly 400 sites encompassing 84 million acres) which includes both National Parks and designated National Monuments (which includes not just actual monuments but also: preserves, historical sites/parks, memorials, battlefields, cemeteries, recreation areas, seashores, lakeshores, rivers, and parkways and trails). The NPS also coordinates both the Wild and Scenic Rivers System and the National Trails System. The NPS hosts nearly 300 million visitors each year.

A Closer Look: The NPS is a relatively decentralized agency, providing broad discretion to individual park managers with priorities and budgets set at the park-unit level. In addition, 80+% of NPS employees are based in the parks themselves.

Key Issue: NPS maintenance backlog (estimated at $4.9 billion: $2.7 for roads and bridges, $2.2 for non-road-related projects).

Key Report: Natural Resource Year in Review – 1999 (focused on the NPS; online).

Check Out on the Web: "Visit the Parks" (links to all National Parks web pages); "Park Planning" (online access to 100+ park planning documents).

Established: 1916 **Employees:** 20,400 **Budget** (FY02 Request): $2.77 billion

Budget Breakdown – Overall (FY02 Request; $ in millions): NPS Operations ($1470; see detailed breakdown below); Land and Water Conservation Fund State Grant Program ($450; for grants to states for recreation and conservation projects); Construction and Major Maintenance ($340; for 57 identified projects); Recreation Fee Usage ($162; visitor fee receipts used to support various projects; a mandatory appropriation); NPS Land Acquisition ($107; for acquiring land at 41 national parks in 25 states); Other Permanent Appropriations ($73); U.S. Park Police ($65); National Recreation and Preservation ($48; for local community programs to preserve natural and cultural resources); Historic Preservation Fund ($37; for matching grants to states and Indian tribes to preserve historically and culturally significant sites).

Budget Breakdown – NPS Operations (FY02 Request; $ in millions): Facility Operations and Maintenance ($477); Resource Stewardship ($312); Visitor Services ($289); Park Support ($266); External Administrative Costs ($127).

Budget Info Online: FY02 Budget Justification (see "NPS Greenbook"; located on the "Info Zone" webpage).

GPRA Reports Online: Annual Performance Plan (FY02) / Annual Performance Report (FY00) (located under "Budget" within the "Info Zone" webpage); Strategic Plan (FY01-05; located under "Park Planning" within the "Info Zone" webpage).

Major Management Challenges/Program Risks (per the GAO): Improved Management Needed (Recommendations: 1) prioritize the scientific assessment of the condition of NPS resources for planning/budgeting purposes; 2) gather more accurate data on the maintenance backlog to better set project/budget priorities; 3) improve Park Managers' accountability for achieving results; 4) address identified management problems in the concessions program, namely: inadequate staff qualifications/training, use of out-of-date practices, and general lack of accountability; 5) better manage the structural fire safety program for NPS's 30,000 building structures by fully specifying minimum expected standards and placing a higher priority on structural fire safety in general).

Contact Info: 1849 C St. NW, Washington, DC 20240; (202) 208-6843 (Public Affairs).

Agency/Entity Head: Fran P. Mainella (Director)

226.   Dept. of Interior – Office of Surface Mining, Reclamation and Enforcement (OSM or OSMRE) (www.osmre.gov)

Description/Mission: Federal agency (under the DOI) responsible for: 1) regulating active coal mining (which currently covers 4.4 million acres in 26 states as well as on Indian lands) and 2) reclaiming abandoned mines in accordance with the Surface Mining Control and Reclamation Act of 1977. A field-oriented agency. OSM also oversees the Abandoned Mine Reclamation Fund which is used to pay abandoned mine reclamation costs (funded via fees imposed on active coal production; the Fund's balance as of 3/01 is $1.3 billion, with $275 million collected annually).

Facts and Figures: Since 1977, some 140,000 acres of abandoned mine land have been reclaimed, with 12,000 acres reclaimed in FY00. However, a total of 560,000 acres have been identified as needing reclamation.

Key Activities: Regulation of Active Coal Mines (overseeing 24 existing state regulatory programs and providing matching grant funding to those state programs, while directly overseeing mining activities in other "non-primacy" states); Reclaiming Abandoned Mines (provides full funding for reclaiming mine lands abandoned prior to 1977).

Key Multi-Agency Program: Clean Water Initiative / Clean Water Action Plan (see Profile #248).

Key Issues: Acid Mine Drainage (particularly from abandoned mines; the Appalachian Clean Streams Initiative was set up to help address, funding 97 local projects from 1997-2000, with 35 projects planned in 2001, 40 in 2002).

Unique: OSM provides all their annual reports (1978-2000) on a CD-ROM – for free!

Check Out on the Web: Abandoned Mine Land Inventory System (identifying 560,000 acres as needing reclamation); "Statistics" page (provides data on both abandoned and active mines, including U.S. coal production figures since 1978).

Established: 1977 **Employees:** 640 **Budget** (FY02 Request): $361 million

Budget Breakdown (FY02 Request; $ in millions): Regulation and Technology ($102; $56 of this provided to the 24 states with approved state regulatory programs); Abandoned Mine Reclamation Fund ($258; for cleanup of mine lands abandoned prior to 1977).

Budget Info Online: FY02 Budget Justification (located under "Jobs, Budget and Administration").

GPRA Reports Online: Annual Performance Plan (FY02) / Annual Performance Report (FY00) (located under "Jobs, Budget and Administration"); Strategic Plan (FY00-05; available on the DOI website under "About DOI")

Contact Info: 1951 Constitution Ave. NW, Washington, DC 20240; (202) 208-2719; getinfo@osmre.gov

Agency/Entity Head: Jeffrey Jarrett (Director)

227.   Department of Justice (DOJ) (www.usdoj.gov)

Description/Mission: Federal-Cabinet level department responsible for the civil and criminal enforcement of U.S. laws and defense of U.S. interests according to those laws, while also providing federal leadership in preventing and controlling crime. Headed by the Attorney General of the U.S.

Operating/Organizational Structure: Comprised of 38 separate component organizations, including the Environment and Natural Resources Division (see Profile #228), one of 6 litigation divisions within DOJ.

Employees: 120,000 **Budget** (FY02 Request): $24.7 billion

Budget Info Online: FY02 Budget Justification (located on the DOJ home page).

GPRA Reports Online (both located on the DOJ home page): Annual Performance Plan (FY02) / Annual Performance Report (FY00); Strategic Plan (FY00-05).

OIG Reports Online: Audit and inspection reports; semiannual reports to Congress; special reports.

Contact Info: 950 Pennsylvania Ave. NW, Washington, DC 20530; (202) 353-1555; AskDOJ@usdoj.gov

Agency/Entity Head: John Ashcroft (Attorney General of the U.S.)

228.   Dept. of Justice – Environment and Natural Resources Division (ENRD) (www.usdoj.gov/enrd)

Description/Mission: Division (within the DOJ) responsible for: 1) the civil and criminal enforcement of federal environmental and natural resource laws, 2) the defense of the federal government's administration of federal environmental and natural resource laws, and 3) litigation relating to the use and protection of federally-owned public lands and natural resources. The ENRD also: represents the U.S. in its trust capacity for Indian tribes; acquires land by purchase or condemnation for use by the federal government; and defends the federal government against Fifth Amendment-related "takings" claims. Overall, the ENRD works with U.S. Attorneys and the FBI in investigation and handling of cases.

Organizational Structure – Key ENRD Sections (and activities/focus areas): Environmental Crimes (prosecuting individuals and businesses/corporations with a focus on pollution-related cases); Environmental Enforcement (civil enforcement, focused on pollution-related cases); Environmental Defense (represents the U.S. – principally the USEPA – in suits challenging the federal government's administration of federal environmental laws); Wildlife and Marine Resources (litigates both civil and criminal cases under federal wildlife laws and laws protecting marine fish and mammals; prosecutions focus on smugglers and black market dealers in protected wildlife); General Litigation (ensuring compliance with 70+ federal statutes dealing with land management of federally-owned properties and natural resources; includes litigation under the National Environmental Policy Act); Indian Resources (acting for individual Indians or Indian tribes); Land Acquisition (either by direct purchase or through condemnation proceedings).

Main Website Divisions: Mission Statement; FAQs; Division Sections; Current Topics; Legal Topics; FOIA; Employment.

Check Out on the Web: Either "Summary of Litigation Accomplishments" or "Press Releases" for a summary of accomplishments (both are listed under "Current Topics").

Founded: 1909 **Employees:** 635 (400 attorneys) **Budget** (FY02): $67 million (Note: budget request for all 6 DOJ litigation divisions – including ENRD – combined: $862 million)

Budget Info Online: See Profile #227 for the DOJ as a whole.

GPRA Reports Online: See Profile #227 for the DOJ as a whole.

Contact Info: 10th St. and Constitution Ave. NW, Washington, DC 20530; (202) 514-2000.

Agency/Entity Head: John C. Cruden (Acting Assistant Attorney General)

229.   Dept. of State (www.state.gov)

Description/Mission: Federal Cabinet-level department acting as the lead U.S. foreign affairs agency, formulating, representing, and implementing the President's foreign policy. The Secretary of State is the President's principal adviser on foreign policy and the person chiefly responsible for U.S. representation abroad. Principally through the State Department, the U.S. currently maintains diplomatic relations with some 180 of 191 countries overall, along with a multitude of international organizations.

Organizational Structure – Key Environmental Org: Bureau of Oceans and International Environmental and Scientific Affairs (OES; see Profile #230).

Contact Info: 2201 C St. NW, Washington, DC 20520; (202) 647-4000.

Agency/Entity Head: Colin Powell (Secretary)

230.   Dept. of State – Bureau of Oceans and International Environmental and Scientific Affairs (OES)
(www.state.gov/g/oes)

Description/Mission: Bureau (within the Dept. of State) that coordinates U.S. international policy regarding oceans and environmental issues, including representing the U.S. internationally on global warming/climate change and sustainable development.

A Closer Look: OES is located within the Office of Under-Secretary for Global Affairs, which coordinates U.S. foreign relations on a variety of global issues.

Key Issue Areas: Oceans; Global Climate Change; Sustainable Development; Invasive Species.

Contact Info: 2201 C St. NW, Washington, DC 20520; (202) 647-4000.

Agency/Entity Head: Paula Dobriansky (Under Secretary for Global Affairs); John F. Turner (Assistant Secretary – OES: the former President/CEO of The Conservation Fund – see Profile #34)

231.   Department of Transportation (DOT) (www.dot.gov)

Description/Mission: Federal Cabinet-level department overseeing the nation's transportation systems (including highway, rail, airline, ship, mass transit and oil/natural gas pipelines).

Facts and Figures: The U.S. transportation system is comprised of: 4 million miles of public roads; 120,000 miles of major railroads; 25,000 miles of commercially navigable waterways; 300 ports; 5,000 public use airports; 500 urban public transit operators; 2 million miles of oil and natural gas pipelines.

Operating/Organizational Structure: Organized into 11 operating administrations and bureaus, each with its own management and operating structure.

Key DOT Organizations (see Profiles #232-239, respectively): Coast Guard; Federal Aviation Administration (focus on: Office of Environment and Energy); Federal Highway Administration; Federal Transit Administration; Research and Special Programs Administration (includes: Office of Hazardous Materials Safety; Office of Pipeline Safety).

Key General Initiative: One DOT (encouraging collaboration and integration amongst the different operating Administrations comprising the DOT).

Key Environmental Issues (and focus areas): Public Transit (service; ridership); Transportation Pollution (mobile source emissions; greenhouse gas emissions; aircraft noise exposure; maritime oil spills; pipeline hazardous materials spills); Wetlands Protection and Recovery; Fisheries Protection (through the Coast Guard);

DOT Facility Cleanup.

Key Report: National Transportation Statistics (annual report; Chapter 4 provides energy consumption and pollution generated statistics; issued by the DOT's Bureau of Transportation Statistics; online at the BTS home page)

Main Website Divisions: DOT News; Doing Business with DOT; Safety; Dockets; Jobs and Education; About DOT; FOIA.

Check Out on the Web: National Transportation Library (a repository of materials from public and private organizations; organized into 16 categories, including "Energy and Environment").

Established: 1967 **Employees:** 100,000 **Budget** (FY02 Request): $60 billion (with $6.6 billion allocated to "Environment")

Budget Breakdown for "Environment" (FY02 Request: $ in billions): Federal Highway Administration ($2.67); Federal Transit Administration ($2.28); Coast Guard ($1.13); Federal Aviation Administration ($0.52); Research and Special Programs Administration ($0.02).

Budget Info Online: FY02 Budget (located on the Office of the Chief Financial Officer webpage).

GPRA Reports Online: Performance Plan (FY02) and Performance Report (FY00) (located under "About DOT"); Strategic Plan (FY00-05) (located under "About DOT").

OIG Reports Online: Audit and inspection reports; semiannual reports to Congress; "Top 10" Management Challenges (annual report).

Major Environmentally-Related Management Challenges/Program Risks (per the GAO): Transit Grants (see Profile #236 for the Federal Transit Administration for details); Pipeline Safety (see Profile #239 for the Office of Pipeline Safety for details); Surplus Maritime Administration Ships (112 surplus ships as of FY99, posing environmental threats both in storage and when scrapped/disposed of).

Contact Info: 400 7th St. SW, Washington DC 20590; (202) 366-4000; dot.comments@ost.dot.gov

Agency/Entity Head: Norman Mineta (Secretary)

232.   Dept. of Transportation – The Coast Guard (USCG) (www.uscg.mil)

Description/Mission: A multi-mission maritime service, positioned under the DOT during peacetime, the Secretary of the Navy during war or when the President directs. A unique federal entity serving both a national defense role as well as a broad scope of regulatory, law-enforcement, humanitarian, and emergency-response duties, all focused along the nation's coastlines. Amongst its duties, the USCG: 1) serves as the primary federal law enforcement agency for the 200-mile U.S. Exclusive Economic Zone, which covers 3.4 million square miles of ocean and 95,000 miles of coastline; 2) enforces National Marine Fisheries Service regulations, as well as regulations specified in regional fisheries management plans; and 3) responds to oil (or other hazardous material) spills along and around U.S. coastlines (maintaining National Strike Teams – located on the East, Gulf, and West coasts – for such responses; responds to 11,000+ pollution incidents annually).

Strategic Goals (and related activities): Maritime Safety (search and rescue; marine safety); Maritime Mobility (aids to navigation; ice operations); Maritime Security (enforce laws and treaties); National Defense (defense readiness); Protection of Natural Resources (domestic fisheries and marine sanctuaries enforcement activities; marine environmental protection).

Key Environmental Programs/Issues: Aquatic Nuisance Species (ANS) / Ballast Water Management (ANS are potentially introduced into U.S. waters through ship ballast water operations and/or hull fouling); Fisheries Protection/Enforcement (focused on preventing overfishing and foreign poaching); Oil Spill and Response; Marine Protected Species (protecting such species); Marine Partners Campaign (an environmental education and outreach program focused on pollution from boats).

Main Website Divisions: News and Events; Services We Provide; Units and Locations; Recruiting; Facts, Images, History and More.

Key Web Site Division: Marine Safety and Environmental Protection.

Established: 1915 **Personnel:** 36,000 (Active Duty) **Budget** (FY02 Request): $5.2 billion (with $1.13 billion allocated for "Environment")

Budget Breakdown For "Environment" (FY02 Request; $ in millions): Domestic Fisheries and Marine

Sanctuaries Enforcement Activities ($638; for: operating expenses –$523; acquisition, construction and improvements –$115); Marine Environmental Protection ($421; for: operating expenses –$375; acquisition, construction and improvements –$46); Oil Spill Recovery ($61); Environmental Compliance and Restoration ($17; for maintaining USCG compliance with environmental laws).

Budget Info Online: FY02 Budget in Brief (located under "News and Events").

GPRA Reports Online (both located under "News and Events"): FY02 Budget in Brief / Annual Performance Report (FY00); Strategic Plan (a 10-year plan; issued in 1999).

Contact Info: 2100 2nd St. SW, Washington, DC 20593; (202) 267-2229.

Agency/Entity Head: Admiral James M. Loy (Commandant)

233.   Dept. of Transportation – Federal Aviation Administration (FAA) (www.faa.gov)

Description/Mission: Federal regulatory agency (under the DOT) responsible for national civil aviation issues, focusing on safety, security and system efficiency. Operates a national network of airport towers, air route traffic control centers, and flight service stations.

Operating/Organizational Structure: FAA Headquarters is organized into 15 offices, including the Office of Policy, Planning and International Aviation, which, in turn, includes the Office of Environmental and Energy (see Profile #234).

Established: 1958 **Employees:** 50,000 **Budget** (FY02 Request): $13.3 billion (with $522 million allocated for "Environment")

Budget Breakdown for "Environment" (FY02 Request; $ in millions): Grants-in-Aid for Airports ($394; administered through the Airport Improvement Program for building soundproofing, purchasing of buffer zones, planning, etc.); Facilities and Equipment ($78); Operations ($42); Research, Engineering, and Development ($8).

Budget Info Online: FY02 Budget in Brief (on the Assistant Administrator for Financial Services [ABA] webpage).

GPRA Reports Online (on the Assistant Administrator for Financial Services [ABA] web page): FY00 Performance Plan.

Contact Info: 800 Independence Ave. SW, Washington, DC 20591; (202) 366-4000.

Agency/Entity Head: Jane F. Garvey (Administrator)

234.   Dept. of Transportation – Federal Aviation Administration – Office of Environment and Energy (FAA-AEE) (www.aee.faa.gov)

Description/Mission: Federal agency (under the DOT, within the FAA's Office of Policy, Planning and International Aviation) responsible for national civil aviation policy relating to environmental and energy matters, with particular emphasis on aircraft noise and exhaust emissions.

Organizational Structure – AEE Divisions: Noise; Emissions; Environment, Energy, and Employee Safety.

Key Issue: Noise Abatement (including through local land use planning).

Main Website Divisions (and key contents): Noise Ombudsman (provides annual summary reports); Aircraft Noise (airports; aircraft; ombudsman); Emissions (modeling and analysis; global air emissions; aircraft emissions); Mission Statement; What's New; Additional Information.

Check Out on the Web: Planning Toolkit (resource materials for compatible land use planning around airports).

Contact Info: 800 Independence Ave. SW, Washington, DC 20591; (202) 267-3033.

Agency/Entity Head: Carl Burleson (Director)

235.   Dept. of Transportation – Federal Highway Administration (FHWA) (www.fhwa.dot.gov)

Description/Mission: Federal agency (under the DOT) responsible for managing the federal highway system and its intermodal connections.

Operating/Organizational Structure: Divided into 5 core business units, including "Planning and Environment."

Main Programs: Federal-Aid Highway Program (providing federal financial assistance to the States to construct and improve the National Highway System, urban and rural roads, and bridges); Federal Lands Highway Program (providing access to and within National Forests, National Parks, Indian reservations and other public lands).

Key Environmental Programs: See below under "Budget Breakdown for Environment."

Main Website Divisions: What's New; FHWA Programs; Legislation and Regulations; Electronic Reading Room/FOIA; Press Room; FHWA Web Sites; About FHWA; Employee Phone Directories; Doing Business with FHWA; Search.

Check Out on the Web: "Planning, Environment, and Real Estate Services" program webpage for environmental information (www.fhwa.dot.gov/environment).

Employees: 2800 **Budget** (FY02 Request): $32.5 billion (with $2.7 billion allocated for "Environment")

Budget Breakdown for "Environment" (FY02 request; $ in millions): Congestion Mitigation and Air Quality Improvement Program ($1800; for funding transportation projects to reduce air emissions in non-attainment and maintenance areas; co-administered with the Federal Transit Administration); Transportation Enhancement Activities ($732; for 12 categories of projects including bicycle and pedestrian facilities, rail-trails, historic preservation and preservation of historic transportation facilities, landscape and beautification); Recreational Trails Program ($50); National Scenic Byways Program ($26); Transportation and Community and System Preservation Pilot Program ($25; for research and discretionary grants).

Budget Info Online: See Performance Plan (FY02) for budget information (located under "FHWA Programs").

GPRA Reports Online (both located under "FHWA Programs"): Performance Plan (FY02) and Performance Report (FY00); Strategic Plan (a 10-year plan; issued in 1998).

Contact Info: 400 7th St. SW, Washington, DC 20590; (202) 366-0537.

Agency/Entity Head: Mary Peters (Administrator)

236.   Dept. of Transportation – Federal Transit Administration (FTA) (www.fta.dot.gov)

Description/Mission: Federal agency (under the DOT) providing financial, technical, and planning assistance to local public mass transit systems (buses, rail, etc.) nationwide.

A Closer Look: While a key priority for the FTA obviously is to increase the availability of mass transit systems, it also seeks to reduce mass transit-related emissions as well (see below).

Key Environmental Programs: Congestion Mitigation and Air Quality Improvement Program (funding transportation projects to reduce air emissions in non-attainment and maintenance areas; co-administered with the Federal Highway Administration); Clean Fuels Program (financing: 1) purchase/lease of clean-fuel buses and associated facilities and 2) modification of existing facilities to accommodate clean-fuel buses).

Main Website Divisions: Bookshop; Links; Search; Grantees; Site Map; What's New; Contact.

Employees: 500 **Regional Offices:** 10 **Metro Offices:** 5 **Budget** (FY02 Request): $6.7 billion (with $2.3 billion allocated for "Environment")

Budget Breakdown for "Environment" (FY02 Request; $ in millions): Formula Grants ($1159; for: bus and railcar purchases, maintenance facility construction and improvement, and capital and operating needs associated with Clean Air Act requirements); Capital Investment Grants ($1009); Transit Planning and Research ($90); Administrative Expenses ($23).

Budget Info Online: See Profile #231 for the DOT as a whole.

GPRA Reports Online (both listed on the FTA home page): Online Performance Plan (FY02) and Performance Report (FY00); Strategic Plan (FY1998-02).

Major Management Challenges/Program Risks (per the GAO): Transit Grants (recommendations: increased funding to FTA for project oversight; additional prioritization of eligible projects to ensure that the most promising are funded).

Contact Info: 400 7th St. SW, Washington, DC 20590; (202) 366-4043.

Agency/Entity Head: Jennifer Dorn (Administrator)

237.   **Dept. of Transportation – Research and Special Programs Administration (RSPA)**
(www.rspa.dot.gov)

Description/Mission: Federal agency (under the DOT) responsible for administration of smaller DOT programs that do not fit the defined missions of the other 10 existing DOT administrations.

Organizational Structure – Key Offices (see Profiles #238 and 239): Office of Hazardous Materials Safety; Office of Pipeline Safety.

Established: 1977 **Budget** (FY02): $110 million (with $22.5 allocated for "Environment")

Budget Breakdown (Overall FY02 Request; $ in millions): Pipeline Safety ($54); Other Research and Special Programs ($42); Emergency Preparedness Grants ($14; to states/local communities for transportation emergency preparedness).

Budget Info Online: See Profile #231 for the DOT as a whole.

GPRA Reports Online: Strategic Plan (issued in 1998); also see Profile #231 for the DOT as a whole.

Contact Info: 400 7th St. SW, Washington, DC 20590.

Agency/Entity Head: Ellen Engleman (Administrator)

238.   **Dept. of Transportation – RSPA – Office of Hazardous Materials Safety (OHM)** (hazmat.dot.gov)

Description/Mission: Federal agency (under the DOT, within the RSPA) responsible for regulating commercial transportation of hazardous materials (except for bulk transportation via ships/tankers and transport via pipelines). Also known for its "Emergency Response Guidebook," an annual publication for first responders (firefighters, police, etc.) to a transportation incident involving a hazardous material.

Facts and Figures: Roughly 300 million hazardous material shipments (totaling over 3 billion tons) occur annually, with about 15,000 "incidents" taking place, about 400 of which are classified as "serious." Such "haz mat" incidents result in roughly 10 deaths, 400 injuries, and $35 million in property damage annually.

Basic Activities: Regulatory development; enforcement; training and information dissemination; domestic and international standards development; inter-agency cooperative activities.

Main Website Divisions: None per say – Click on the "Table of Contents" to get a detailed list of website content.

Check Out on the Web: Penalty Actions Reports (listing penalties issued for HazMat violations; annual report; online); Hazardous Materials Incident Data (annual report; online).

Budget Info Online: See Profile #231 for the DOT as a whole.

GPRA Reports Online: See Profile #231 for the DOT as a whole; also see the "HMPE Report" (an internal evaluation of DOT-wide hazardous materials transportation programs; located on OHM's home page).

Contact Info: 400 7th St. SW, Washington, DC 20590; (202) 366-0656; hmis@rspa.dot.gov

239.   **Dept. of Transportation – RSPA – Office of Pipeline Safety (OPS)** (ops.dot.gov)

Description/Mission: Federal agency (under the DOT, within the RSPA) responsible for regulating the transportation of natural gas, petroleum, and other hazardous materials by pipeline (there are 2 million miles of natural gas pipelines and 155,000 miles of hazardous liquid – crude/refined oil – pipelines in the U.S.). Most states have been certified by OPS to conduct inspections on intrastate pipelines, while OPS focuses on inspecting interstate pipelines.

A Closer Look: The program is funded by a user fee assessed on a per-mile basis on each pipeline OPS regulates.

Key Initiatives: National Pipeline Mapping System (a GIS database of natural gas transmission lines, hazardous liquid trunklines, and liquefied natural gas facilities); Oil Pollution Act Initiative (oil pipeline owners/operators are required by law to submit facility oil spill response plans to OPS for review and approval); Unusually Sensitive Areas (a risk management program for areas identified by OPS as unusually sensitive to environmental damage in the event of a hazardous liquid pipeline release).

Key Issue: Risk-Based Regulation (focusing on identified "high risk" areas).

Main Website Divisions: Table of Contents; What's New; Regulations; Pipeline Statistics; Online Library; Training and Publications; Contact Information; Special Concerns.

Check Out on the Web: Pipeline Statistics (annual accident/incident summaries; online).

Employees: 70 **Regional Offices**: 5 **Budget** (FY02 Request): $54 million

Budget Info Online: See Profile #231 for the DOT as a whole.

GPRA Reports Online: See Profile #231 for the DOT as a whole.

Major Management Challenges/Program Risks (per the GAO): Pipeline Safety (concerns over: 1) implementing a risk-based management approach before fully evaluating the results of a demonstration program; 2) relying less on states to inspect interstate pipelines; 3) pursuing an approach of working constructively with pipeline companies and reducing OPS's reliance on fines in enforcing regulations without evaluating the effect of such actions on regulatory compliance rates).

Contact Info: 400 7th St. SW, Washington, DC 20590; (202) 366-4595.

Agency/Entity Head: Stacey Gerard (Assistant Administrator)

2.2.2 Independent Agencies/Entities

240.   **Chemical Safety and Hazard Investigation Board (CSB)** (www.chemsafety.gov)

Description/Mission: Independent Federal entity responsible for investigating the causes of major chemical accidents at fixed facilities and issuing recommendations to prevent their re-occurrence. CSB is modeled after the National Transportation Safety Board (NTSB), which investigates transportation-related accidents. Like NTSB, CSB is a scientific investigation body; it is not an enforcement or regulatory agency.

Basic Activities: Accident Investigation; Research; Outreach.

Operating/Organizational Structure: Governed by a five-member board appointed by the President and confirmed by the Senate.

Main Website Divisions: About the CSB; CSB 5-Year Strategic Plan; Chemical Incidents Report Center; Investigations; ChemLinks (a searchable database); E-Mail Updates (a news service); Career Opportunities; Conferences and Meetings; Reporting Chemical Incidents; Library.

Check Out on the Web: Chemical Incident Reports Center (CIRC; a searchable online database of chemical incidents).

Established: 1997 **Board Members:** 5 **Staff:** 33 **Budget** (FY01 actual): $7.5 million

Budget Info Online: FY01 Budget Justification (on the CSB's home page)

GPRA Reports Online (both on the CSB's home page): Annual Report (FY98-00); Strategic Plan (FY01-05).

Contact Info: 2175 K St. NW, Suite 400, Washington, DC 20037-1809; (202) 261-7600; info@csb.gov

Board Members: Gerald V. Poje; Isadore Rosenthal; Andrea Taylor (2 seats are vacant)

241.   **Environmental Protection Agency (EPA)** (www.epa.gov)

Description/Mission: Independent Federal agency charged with "protecting human health and safeguarding the natural environment." Mostly known for regulating business and industrial activities to reduce pollution. EPA's specific programs are mainly driven by 12 major pieces of federal legislation. Day-to-day implementation of most major EPA regulatory programs has been delegated to the states with EPA retaining oversight authority.

Organizational Structure – Key Offices (see Profiles #242-245, respectively): Air and Radiation; Prevention, Pesticides, and Toxic Substances; Solid Waste and Emergency Response; Water.

Key Program Areas: Air; Pesticides; Pollution Prevention; Toxics and Chemicals; Water (covering drinking-, storm-, and waste-water); Wastes and Recycling (including both hazardous and solid waste).

Key Multi-Agency Programs (see Profiles #248 and 249, respectively): Clean Water Initiative / Clean Water Action Plan; Energy Star® Program.

Main Website Divisions: Information access is provided via 3 key ways: Browse EPA Topics (a directory-type listing of individual topics classified under 17 main headings); Where You Live (provides access to regional/local information); Programs (the choices offered are: by media and topic; general interest; research; geographic-focus; state, local and tribal; industry partnerships; agency offices and regions).

Check Out on the Web: "Where You Live" section (particularly "Search Your Community," providing access to zip code-level information from 4 key databases – EnviroFacts; EnviroMapper; Surf Your Watershed; UV Index); Sector Notebooks (a series of profiles containing key environmental information on 30+ major industrial sectors; located under "Compliance Assistance" on the Office of Enforcement and Compliance Assistance's webpage); Internet Newsbrief (a weekly sampling of new and/or useful Internet resources; listed categories include: EPA; environmental; government; international; business/corporate).

Established: 1970 **Employees:** 17,500 **Regional Offices:** 10 **Budget** (FY02): $7.3 billion

Budget Breakdown By Program Area (FY02; $ in millions): Water Programs ($3213); Waste Management Programs ($1511); Air Programs ($565); Management Programs ($432); Regulatory Compliance and Enforcement Programs ($411); Science Programs ($307); Pollution Prevention Programs ($298); Global and Cross Border Environmental Risk Programs ($283); Environmental Information Programs ($189); Food Programs ($108; focuses on pesticide residues on foods).

Budget Breakdown By Major Activity (FY02; $ in millions): State and Tribal Assistance Grants ($3289);

Environmental Program and Management ($1973); Superfund Program ($1268); Science and Technology ($641); Leaking Underground Storage Tank Program ($72); Inspector General ($34); Building and Facilities ($25); Oil Spill Response ($15).

Budget Breakdown By Funding Mechanism (FY02; $ in billions): Operating Program ($3.75; includes $1.06 for 21 "categorical" program grants to state/tribal governments); Water Infrastructure Financing ($2.23; for: wastewater infrastructure grants to states and localities –$1.30; drinking water infrastructure loans to states and localities –$0.82; Mexican border and Alaskan native villages projects –$0.11); Trust Funds ($1.34; for: Superfund –$1.27 [includes $0.10 for the "brownfields" program]; leaking underground storage tank program – $0.07).

Budget Info Online: FY02 Budget (under "About EPA").

GPRA Reports Online (all under "About EPA"): Annual Report (FY00); Annual Performance Plan (FY02); Strategic Plan (FY00-05).

OIG Reports Online: Audit and inspection reports; semiannual reports to Congress; Selected Accomplishments (quarterly newsletter); Management Challenges (annual report); Annual Superfund Report.

Major Management Challenges/Program Risks (per the GAO): Environmental and Performance Information Management (recommendations: 1) fill critical information gaps on environmental conditions and corresponding effects on human health; 2) achieve compatibility among federal/state databases to permit data aggregation; 3) establish more results-oriented – as opposed to output-oriented – performance measures; 4) strengthen security over computer information systems; 5) develop a comprehensive information management strategy addressing the aforementioned concerns); EPA's Human Capital (needing to formally assess human capital needs and align those needs with strategic goals); EPA-State Working Relationships (needing to address long-standing problems/disagreements – particularly in the area of regulatory enforcement – and develop a more effective partnership system; EPA is attempting to address this through its National Environmental Performance Partnership System); Superfund Program (while much-improved, EPA has not agreed with the GAO's recommendation to use a performance measure to track cleanup cost recovery outcomes).

Contact Info: 401 M St. SW, Washington, DC 20460; (202) 260-2090; public-access@epa.gov

Agency/Entity Head: Christie Todd Whitman (Administrator)

242. EPA – Office of Air and Radiation (OAR) (www.epa.gov/oar)

Description/Mission: Office within the EPA responsible for developing national programs, technical policies, and regulations for controlling air pollution and radiation exposure. Also provides air pollution, clean air, and air quality information.

Organizational Structure – Program Offices: Air Quality Planning and Standards; Atmospheric Programs; Transportation and Air Quality; Radiation and Indoor Air.

Key Report: National Air Quality and Emissions Trends Report (annual report on air pollution trends; online).

Key Web Site Topic Areas: Indoor Air Quality; Transportation/Fuels; Off-Road Equipment (farm and construction equipment; lawn and garden equipment; RVs; boats/ships; trains; airplanes); Acid Rain; Ozone Depletion; Climate Change; Visibility; Toxic Air Pollutants; Radiation.

Check Out on the Web: "Air Quality Where You Live" (can check local air quality by city or state).

Budget Info Online: See Profile #241 for the EPA as a whole.

GPRA Reports Online: See Profile #241 for the EPA as a whole.

Contact Info: 1200 Pennsylvania Ave. NW, Washington, DC 20460; (202) 564-7400.

Agency/Entity Head: Jeffrey R. Holmstead (Assistant Administrator)

243. EPA – Office of Prevention, Pesticides, and Toxic Substances (OPPTS) (www.epa.gov/opptsfrs)

Description/Mission: Office within the EPA responsible for developing national programs, technical policies, and regulations with respect to pollution prevention, pesticides, and toxic substances. Also provides information, education and technical assistance in these areas.

Organizational Structure – Program Offices: Pollution Prevention and Toxic Substances; Pesticides Programs; Science Coordination and Policy.

Programs (and focus areas): Pollution Prevention (persistent, bioaccumulative, and toxic – PBT – substances strategy; green products; business practices; design for environment – DfE – and green chemistry; state/local pollution prevention grant program); Toxic Substances (chemical right-to-know; chemical testing and information gathering; exposure assessment tools and models; persistent bioaccumulative toxic pollutants; risk-screening environmental indicators); Pesticides (antimicrobial pesticides; biopesticides; pesticide registration; pesticide re-registration and special reviews; pesticide use; labels and labeling; safety programs; integrated pest management; endangered species); Science Policy (biotechnology; endocrine disruptors).

Key Initiative: Chemical Right-to-Know (a 3-prong initiative to gather/disseminate information on toxic chemicals; a key effort is basic hazard testing of 2000+ "high production volume" chemicals).

Budget Info Online: See Profile #241 for the EPA as a whole.

GPRA Reports Online: See Profile #241 for the EPA as a whole.

Contact Info: 1200 Pennsylvania Ave. NW, Washington, DC 20460; (202) 260-2090.

Agency/Entity Head: Stephen L. Johnson (Assistant Administrator)

244.   **EPA – Office of Solid Waste and Emergency Response (OSWER)** (www.epa.gov/swerrims)

Description/Mission: Office within the EPA responsible for developing national programs, technical policies, and regulations for: 1) safely managing waste (including municipal, industrial, and hazardous waste), 2) preparing for and preventing chemical and oil spills, and 3) cleaning up contaminated property. Most well known for running the Superfund cleanup program (addressing 1500+ abandoned hazardous waste sites).

Organizational Structure – Program Offices (and focus areas): Solid Waste (regulation of: hazardous waste; municipal solid waste; industrial and special waste); Emergency and Remedial Response (Superfund site cleanup; oil spill program); Underground Storage Tanks (spill/leak prevention; corrective action/cleanup); Chemical Emergency Preparedness and Prevention Office (prevention and risk management planning; preparedness – emergency planning and community right-to-know; emergency response; counter-terrorism; international programs); Federal Facilities Restoration and Reuse (aids in cleanup of federal facilities – principally DoD, DOE, and DOI sites); Outreach and Special Projects Staff ("brownfields" program); Technology Innovation (innovative technologies for hazardous waste site cleanup).

Key Initiative: "Brownfields" program (cleanup and redevelopment of abandoned/under-utilized commercial/industrial sites).

Key Reports: National Biennial RCRA Hazardous Waste Report (biennial report on hazardous waste generated in the U.S.; online); Municipal Sold Waste Generation, Recycling and Disposal in the U.S. (1998 Fact Sheet; online).

Budget Info Online: See Profile #241 for the EPA as a whole.

GPRA Reports Online: See Profile #241 for the EPA as a whole.

Contact Info: 1200 Pennsylvania Ave. NW, Washington, DC 20460; (202) 260-2090.

Agency/Entity Head: Marianne L. Horinko (Assistant Administrator)

245.   **EPA – Office of Water (OW)** (www.epa.gov/ow)

Description/Mission: Office within the EPA primarily responsible for implementing the Clean Water Act and Safe Drinking Water Act, along with portions of several other statutes. Also administers the National Estuary Program (to identify, restore and protect nationally significant estuaries with 28 estuaries in the program).

Key Programs/Activities: State Revolving Fund [SRF] Program (providing revolving loans to states/localities for low-cost financing of a range of water quality infrastructure projects – wastewater and drinking water projects); National Pollution Discharge Elimination System [NPDES] Permitting (for wastewater/stormwater discharges); Drinking Water Standards (develops and issues "Maximum Contaminant Levels" – MCLs); Total Maximum Daily Load [TMDL] Program (states identify "impaired waterbodies" that do not meet water quality standards and develop reduction goals – TDMLs – designed to meet such standards).

Organizational Structure – Key Program Offices (and divisions within): Ground Water and Drinking Water (drinking water protection; standards and risk management); Wastewater Management (municipal support; water [NPDES] permits); Wetlands, Oceans and Watersheds (assessment and watershed protection; oceans and coastal protection; wetlands); Science and Technology (engineering and analysis; health and ecological criteria; standards and applied science).

Key Issues: Total Maximum Daily Load [TMDL] Program (a controversial program, yet to be implemented; EPA is currently reviewing and revising the program); Drinking Water Infrastructure Needs (a 2001 survey estimates that $151 billion in funding is needed over next 20 years).

Key Reports: National Public Water Systems Compliance Report (annual report on public drinking water system violations; online); National Water Quality Inventory: Report to Congress ("305(b) report"; biennial report on the quality of the nation's waters – rivers, streams, lakes, reservoirs, wetlands, estuaries, coastal waters, and groundwater; online); National Health Protection Survey of Beaches (annual voluntary survey of local beach health conditions and activities; online).

Check Out on the Web: Water Where You Live (state-level water information source); Atlas of America's Polluted Waters (provides state-level maps showing surface waters that do not meet state water quality standards); Wastewater Primer (intro to wastewater issues and corresponding EPA programs).

Budget Info Online: See Profile #241 for the EPA as a whole.

GPRA Reports Online: See Profile #241 for the EPA as a whole.

Contact Info: 1200 Pennsylvania Ave. NW, Washington, DC 20460; OW-General@epamail.epa.gov; (202) 260-2090.

Agency/Entity Head: Tracy Mehan (Assistant Administrator)

246.   General Accounting Office (GAO) (www.gao.gov)

Description/Mission: Independent federal agency serving as the investigative arm of Congress – critically evaluating federal programs, auditing federal expenditures, and issuing legal opinions. GAO's primary products are reports ("blue books") and testimony before Congress. Also issues correspondence (letters) – narrower in scope, of more limited interest, and issued without recommendations. Most reports are done at the request of members of Congress (often committee chairpersons and ranking minority members); other program reviews are required by law or are self-initiated under GAO's own authority. In 1999 alone, GAO published 1,163 reports and testified 229 times before dozens of congressional committees.

Basic Activities: Financial audits; program reviews; investigations; legal support; policy/program analyses.

Check Out on the Web: GAO Reports (provides convenient access to GAO's primary products – reports and testimony to Congress; to browse the collection, click on either "This Month in Review" or "Annual Index"; also check out the "Special Collections About Other Agencies" section); GAO's Performance and Accountability and High Risk Series (separate reports on the major management challenges and program risks facing major federal government departments and agencies).

Established: 1921 **Employees:** 3300 **Budget** (FY00): $378 million

Contact Info: 441 G St. NW, Washington, DC 20548; (202) 512-4800.

Agency/Entity Head: David Walker (Comptroller General)

247.   Nuclear Regulatory Commission (NRC) (www.nrc.gov)

Description/Mission: Independent Federal committee responsible for regulating all commercial (civilian) uses of nuclear energy – for generating electricity, medical uses, various research uses, etc. Issues licenses to (and regulates all) 103 operating commercial nuclear power plants and 10 facilities that produce fuel for the plants. Also regulates – along with 32 states having agreements with the NRC – almost 21,000 civilian entities that use nuclear materials (known as "nuclear material licensees"). Also regulates commercial radioactive waste storage, transportation, and disposal and commercial nuclear facilities decommissioning.

A Closer Look: Users fees recover 90% of the NRC's operating budget.

Operating/Organizational Structure: The NRC is headed by five Commissioners appointed by the President and confirmed by the Senate for 5-year terms.

Programs (and focus areas): Nuclear Reactor Safety (regulatory oversight of 104 licensed reactors, 103 of which are currently in operation); Nuclear Materials Safety (regulatory oversight of 24 fuel facilities, 2 gaseous diffusion plants and 20,000 nuclear material licensees); Nuclear Waste Safety (regulation of high-level radioactive waste disposal – i.e., regulatory oversight of the proposed Yucca Mountain project; regulatory oversight of the storage and transport of spent nuclear fuel; licensing of low-level nuclear waste disposal facilities; decommissioning of nuclear facilities); International Nuclear Safety (import/export licensing; working with related international organizations such as the International Atomic Energy Agency and the Nuclear Energy Agency).

Key Issue: Revised Reactor Oversight Process (moving to a "risk-informed and performance-based" process, focusing on "significant-risk" activities).

Key Publication: Nuclear Regulatory Commission Information Digest (online; covers: the NRC as a regulatory agency; U.S. and worldwide energy; operating nuclear reactors; nuclear material safety; radioactive waste).

Website Notes: Post-Sept. 11, the entire NRC website was taken "off-line" for a major redesign with partial access to "select content" restored in 12/01. At the time of publication of this Guide, it was unclear how much information would ultimately be restored for public access through the site.

Check Out on the Web (but may not be available – see "Website Notes" above): "Nuclear Reactors" page (extensive information provided, including detailed "Plant Information Books"); "News and Information" page (extensive resources provided; in particular, check out both "Nuclear Plant Performance" and "Nuclear Plant Information Assistant").

Established: 1974 **Employees:** 2800 **Budget** (FY02): $513 million

Budget Breakdown (FY02; $ in millions): Nuclear Reactor Safety ($231); Management and Support ($152); Nuclear Waste Safety ($63); Nuclear Materials Safety ($55); Inspector General ($6); International Nuclear Safety Support ($5).

Budget Info Online: FY02 Budget Estimate (under "Planning and Financial Management").

GPRA Reports Online (all under "Planning and Financial Management"): Annual Performance Report (FY00); Annual Performance Plan (FY02); Strategic Plan (FY00-05).

OIG Reports Online (all located under "Reference Library"): Audit and inspection reports; semiannual reports to Congress; Selected Accomplishments (quarterly newsletter); Management Challenges (annual report).

Major Management Challenges/Program Risks (per the GAO): Nuclear Power Plants (overcome obstacles to implementing a risk-informed regulatory approach; recommendations: 1) develop a comprehensive implementation strategy; 2) obtain staff "buy-in" and ensure that the general public is confident about the new approach; 3) reconsider making compliance with the new approach voluntary, effectively resulting in a dual regulatory system); Nuclear Material Licensees (overcome difficulties in implementing a risk-informed regulatory approach, mainly due to the sheer number of licensees involved – over 20,000 – and the diversity of activities they conduct; also adjusting as more states assume responsibility for regulating nuclear material users); Management Issues (develop a succession plan to address gaps due to retiring personnel, particularly in terms of maintaining technical competency; improve the NRC's new information system – ADAMS – which was developed to provide timely document access to both NRC staff and the general public, but is experiencing significant start-up problems).

Contact Info: 1 White Flint North, 1555 Rockville Pike, Rockville, MD 20852; (301) 415-7000.

Commissioners: Richard Meserve (Chairman); Greta Dicus; Niles Diaz; Edward McGaffigan; Jeffrey Merrifield.

2.2.3 Multi-Agency Programs

248. Clean Water Initiative / Clean Water Action Plan (www.cleanwater.gov)

Description: Cooperative, long-term, multi-agency effort to prepare and implement a Clean Water Action Plan designed to strengthen efforts to restore and protect water resources nationwide. Initiated in 10/97 on the 25th anniversary of passage of the Clean Water Act. The Action Plan – issued in 2/98 – lists 111 key action items and stresses a watershed-based approach in implementation.

Departments/Agencies Involved: Dept. of Agriculture (Natural Resources Conservation Service; Forest Service); Environmental Protection Agency; Dept. of Interior (Bureau of Land Management; Geological Survey; Fish and Wildlife Service; Office of Surface Mining); Army Corps of Engineers; National Oceanic and Atmospheric Administration [NOAA].

Key Associated Website: Watershed Information Network (gateway to information and resources/services for protecting water resources; www.epa.gov/win).

Check Out on the Web: "Accomplishments" section (based on key action items identified in the Clean Water Action Plan).

Budget (FY01 Request): $2.8 billion

Budget Breakdown by Department/Agency (FY01 Budget Request; $ in millions): Dept. of Agriculture ($1043; for: Natural Resources Conservation Service –$411; Forest Service –$627); Environmental Protection Agency ($762; for: state and tribal grants –$495; water quality program management –$267); Dept. of Interior ($395; for: Bureau of Land Management –$167; Geological Survey –$138; Fish and Wildlife Service –$58; Office of Surface Mining –$32); Army Corps of Engineers ($145; for: wetlands programs –$125; floodplain restoration initiative –$20); National Oceanic and Atmospheric Administration [NOAA] ($22: for polluted runoff, algal blooms and toxic contaminants); Interagency Projects ($394; for: Florida Everglades –$334; California Bay-Delta –$60).

249. Energy Star ® Program (www.energystar.gov)

Description: Voluntary labeling program (using the "Energy Star" label) designed to identify and promote energy-efficient products. Co-administered by the DOE and the EPA with each taking responsibility for particular product categories. The program covers new homes, most of the buildings sector, residential heating and cooling equipment, major appliances, office equipment, lighting, and consumer electronics. Initiated by the EPA in 1992 as a means to reduce carbon dioxide emissions.

Departments/Agencies Involved: Dept. of Energy; Environmental Protection Agency.

Website Notes: The website assists users in finding labeled products, homes and buildings, as well as letting users compare their home's / building's energy performance versus similar homes/buildings.

Contact Info: (888) STAR-YES

250. United States Global Change Research Program (USGCRP) (www.usgcrp.gov)

Description: Science-based research initiative (begun in 1989) to study "global change" (defined as "changes in the global environment that may alter the capacity of the Earth to sustain life"). Primary issues covered include climate fluctuations (on time scales varying from seasonal through centuries), stratospheric ozone depletion, UV radiation, atmospheric chemistry, changes in land cover and in terrestrial and marine ecosystems.

A Closer Look: Exactly one-half the total program budget ($820 million) goes to NASA for "observation hardware" – research and weather satellites and associated data and information systems.

General Focus Areas (and specific research areas): Atmospheric Composition (stratospheric ozone and UV radiation; photochemical oxidants; atmospheric modeling; atmospheric aerosols and radiation; toxics and nutrients; clouds); Changes in Ecosystems (changing land use and land cover; multiple stresses in ecosystems; changes in the global nitrogen cycle); Climate Variability and Change (natural climate patterns; global monsoon; land-atmosphere and ocean-atmosphere exchanges; impacts on weather; downscaling; anthropogenic perturbations); Global Carbon Cycle (examining the fate of carbon dioxide in the environment); Global Water Cycle (land surface interactions; atmospheric processes); Human Dimensions of Climate Change (studying potential human responses to global change).

Departments/Agencies Involved: Dept. of Agriculture (Agricultural Research Service; Economic Research Service; Forest Service [global change research program]; Natural Resources Conservation Service); Dept. of Commerce (National Oceanic and Atmospheric Administration [office of global programs]); Dept. of Energy (Office of Biological and Environmental Research); Dept. of Health and Human Services (National Institutes of Health, including the National Institute of Environmental Health Sciences); Dept. of the Interior (U.S. Geological Service [global change research program]); Environmental Protection Agency (Global Change Research Program); National Aeronautics and Space Administration (Earth Science Enterprise Program); National Science Foundation (Global Change Research Program); Smithsonian Institution.

Key Publication: U.S. National Assessment: The Potential Consequences of Climate Variability and Change (online; scientific assessments on the potential consequences of climate variability and change for the nation and potential mechanisms for adaptation; includes: 20 regional assessments; sectoral assessments [initial focus: agriculture; water; human health; forests; coastal areas and marine resources]; national synthesis [integrating key findings from the regional and sectoral assessments]).

Annual Report: "Our Changing Planet – FY02" (online under "About USGCRP").

Affiliated Org: U.S. Global Change Research Information Office (provides data/information on global change research, adaptation/mitigation strategies and technologies and related educational resources; www.gcrio.org).

Associated Website: Global Change Data and Information Service (GCDIS) (www.globalchange.gov; see Profile #455, located within Subsection 7.2 – "Information and Data Resource Websites and Gateways").

Established: 1989 **Budget** (FY02 Request): $1.64 billion

Budget Breakdown by General Focus Area (FY02 Request; $ in millions): Atmospheric Composition ($310); Changes in Ecosystems ($199); Climate Variability and Change ($486); Global Carbon Cycle ($221); Global Water Cycle ($309); Human Dimensions of Climate Change ($107).

Budget Breakdown by Dept./Agency (FY02 Request; $ in millions): Dept. of Agriculture ($56); National Oceanic and Atmospheric Administration ($93; for: science program –$69; observation program –$24); Dept. of Energy ($121); National Institutes of Health ($57); Dept. of the Interior – U.S. Geological Service ($22); Environmental Protection Agency ($22); National Aeronautics and Space Administration ($1072; for: science program –$253; observation program –$819); National Science Foundation ($187); Smithsonian Institution ($7).

Budget Info Online: FY02 Budget Request (found within USGCRP's annual report "Our Changing Planet"; located under "About USGCRP").

Contact Info: 400 Virginia Ave SW, Suite 750, Washington, DC 20024; (202) 488-8630; information@usgcrp.gov

Agency/Entity Head: Richard Moss (Director)

251.   Wildfire Management Initiative / National Fire Plan (www.fireplan.gov)

Description: Cooperative, long-term, multi-agency effort to manage the impacts of wildfires on communities and the environment. Initiated in 8/00 in response to the 90,000+ wildfires that consumed 7+ million acres in 2000.

Departments/Agencies Involved: Dept. of Agriculture (Forest Service); Dept. of the Interior (Bureau of Land Management; National Park Service; Fish and Wildlife Service; Bureau of Indian Affairs); National Association of State Foresters (a governmental association of the directors of state forestry agencies).

Key Activities (and focus areas): Firefighting Capacity (ensure adequate preparedness for future fire seasons); Rehabilitation and Restoration (restore landscapes and rebuild communities damaged by wildfire); Hazardous Fuel Reduction (to reduce fire risk); Community Assistance (work to ensure adequate protection).

Check Out on the Web: 10-Year Comprehensive Strategy (details overall program direction and goals); State Summary Reports (state-specific information).

Base Program Funding (FY01): $2.9 billion ($1.9 to the Forest Service; $1.0 to the DOI).

Program Budget (FY02 Request): $2.0 billion ($1.3 to the Forest Service; $0.66 to the DOI).

Subsection 2.3: Governmental Associations and Councils

Introduction/User's Guide:

Within this subsection, 34 governmental associations and councils (and related entities) are profiled, divided into the following two subsections:

2.3.1 – General Governmental Associations and Councils	(9 entries)
2.3.2 – Environmentally-Focused Governmental Associations and Councils	(25 entries)

In terms of individual entry contents, the following is a descriptive outline of standardized profile information provided for each organization listed within this subsection (please note that the exact contents provided varies by organization, being dependant upon applicability and/or availability):

[Profile #] Organization Name (Website Address)

A Top Federal Lobbying Group Per Fortune Magazine's Annual Survey: Noted as applicable with the organization's ranking for 2001 specified.

Description: Short summary of the organization, focusing on its membership, basic mission/focus and structure.

Basic Activities: Potential entries include: information exchange/services; training/technical assistance; meetings/conferences; policy research/analysis; advocacy.

Lobbying/Political Activities: Included if the organization is registered as a federal lobbyist under the Lobbying Disclosure Act (LDA) and/or maintains a Political Action Committee (PAC) with the name of the PAC specified.

Key Internal Groups: Noting relevant committees, working groups, advisory groups, task forces, etc.

Programs/Issues (and activities/focus areas): Providing specifics on the organization's activities/concerns.

Key Initiatives/Policy Priorities: Highlighting the organization's "high priority" activities/issues.

Key Reports/Publications: Listing specific reports and other publications judged to represent "essential reading" for interested parties, and noting if they are available online at the organization's website. (A summary listing of all such reports/publications is also provided in Appendix B.)

Website Notes: Significant notes concerning the organization's website – navigating hints, content notes, etc.

Check Out on the Web: Listing website-related content/features that particularly stand out ("worth a look").

Founded: Beginning year specified **HQ:** Noting city and state **Staff:** Overall staffing level **NP Status:** Formal IRS non-profit status (typically 501(c)(3) – exempt) **Revenue/Expenses:** Overall figures as obtained from IRS submittals (IRS Form 990) **Budget:** As obtained from non-IRS sources

Affiliated Orgs: Noted as applicable; based on IRS submittals and other information sources.

Contact Info: Providing: Street/mailing address; general telephone number; general email address (if established/available).

Key Personnel: Providing the name(s) and title(s) of key executives (President, Executive Director, etc.).

Organizational profiles for this subsection are divided into two smaller subsections (namely general associations and councils, presented in Subsection 2.3.1, followed by environmentally-focused associations and councils, presented in Subsection 2.3.2). Within each subsection, organizations are grouped according to the geographic focus of its members (national, state, or local), with profiles arranged alphabetically within each such grouping.

A Closer Look – Federal Lobbying Efforts:

It should be noted that one profiled association – the National Governors Association – is listed in Fortune magazine's annual survey as a "top federal lobbying group" for 2001 (ranked #21 of 87 listed groups), indicating NGA to be a "key player" in influencing general policy-making at the federal level.

A Closer Look – Affiliate Programs:

Most of the profiled general governmental associations – specifically the Council of State Governments, the National Conference of State Legislatures, the National Governors' Association, the International City/County Management Association, and the National Association of Counties – offer some type of membership-based affiliate program aimed at providing corporations/business trade groups with special access to government officials/decision-makers, directly and/or through designated advisory groups.

2.3.1 General Governmental Associations and Councils

2.3.1.1 State-Level General Governmental Associations and Councils

American Legislative Exchange Council (ALEC) (www.alec.org)
See Profile #412, located within Section 6 – "Opposing View Groups."

252.   **Council of State Governments (CSG)** (www.statenews.org)

Description: Research and service organization serving state governments (all 3 branches – executive, legislative, and judicial) and various associations of state officials. Maintains 4 Policy Groups, including an Environmental Policy Group (EPG) and an Agricultural Policy Group (APG). All Policy Groups are located within the CSG's Center for Leadership, Innovation and Policy.

A Closer Look: Offers an "Associates Program" aimed at corporations, offering "access to key decision-makers in the states" and "participation in discussions on policy development." Some 90 corporations and trade groups are listed under "Environment" for this program (see below for key business-related associate members).

Key Business-Related Associate Members (see separate profiles for each within Subsection 5.1 – "Business Trade Associations"): American Automobile Manufacturers Association; American Chemistry Council; American Crop Protection Association; American Forest and Paper Association; American Petroleum Institute; American Trucking Associations; Center for Energy and Economic Development; Chlorine Chemistry Council; Edison Electric Institute; Grocery Manufacturers of America; National Association of Realtors; National Rural Electric Cooperative Association; Nuclear Energy Institute; Steel Recycling Institute.

Basic Activities: Information exchange/services; training/technical assistance; policy research/analysis; leadership development.

Keys EPG Programs (and focus areas): Environmental Task Force (addressing current issues); State Environmental Initiative (matching grants program partnering state agencies and businesses with Asian governments and businesses); Toxics in Packaging Clearinghouse (information on reducing heavy metals – mercury, lead, cadmium, and hexavalent chromium – in packaging); Working at the Watershed Level (training in watershed planning and management).

Key Periodicals: ecos (Environmental Communiqué of the States; discusses policy, budget and legislative initiatives in all 50 states; $40/yr.).

Key Publication: Suggested State Legislation (annual volume of state legislation selected as exemplary by a dedicated CSG committee; covers a variety of topics, including "conservation and the environment").

Website Notes: The website address cited above is for "State News," run by the CSG and billed as "your one link to the states." The site essentially serves two purposes: it provides state-focused news and it serves as a gateway to the CSG as an organization (including its' EPG).

Founded: 1933 **Staff:** 190 **NP Status:** 501(c)(3) **Revenue/Expenses (for CSG as a whole; FY00):** $17.6/$16.8 million

Contact Info: PO Box 11910, 2760 Research Park Drive, Lexington, KY 40578; (859) 244-8000.

Key Personnel: Daniel Sprague (Executive Director); Karen Marshall (Sr. Policy Analyst for EPG)

253.   **National Conference of State Legislatures (NCSL)** (www.ncsl.org)

Description: Research and service organization for state/territorial lawmakers and staffs. Maintains 2 internal Assemblies: the Assembly on Federal Issues (directing NCSL's federal lobbying efforts) and the Assembly on State Issues (an information exchange forum for lawmakers and their staff). Overall, NCSL covers 23 issue areas, including both Environmental Protection and Natural Resources (see below for details). Affiliated with both the Council of State Governments and the National Governors Association (see Profiles #252 and 254, respectively). Has an affiliated tax-exempt non-profit organization – NCSL Foundation – that engages in research, technical assistance and educational activity.

A Closer Look: The NCSL Foundation "offers opportunities for businesses, national associations and unions seeking to improve the state legislative process" via a sponsorship program offering interaction with NCSL leadership and legislative leaders as well as participation in public policy studies with NCSL. Minimum sponsorship is $5000 annually; for $10,000 or more, sponsors can participate on a NCSL standing committee. See below for key business- and labor-related groups serving as sponsors.

Key Business-Related Foundation Sponsors (see separate profiles for each within Subsection 5.1 – "Business Trade Associations"): Alliance of Automobile Manufacturers; American Forest and Paper Association; American Plastics Council; Center for Energy and Economic Development; Edison Electric Institute; Grocery Manufacturers of America; National Association of Realtors; National Federation of Independent Business; Nuclear Energy Institute.

Key Labor Union Foundation Sponsors (see separate profiles for each within Subsection 5.2 – "Labor Unions"): AFL-CIO; International Association of Machinists and Aerospace Workers; International Brotherhood of Teamsters.

Basic Activities: Policy research/analysis; advocacy; information exchange/services; meetings/seminars; training/technical assistance; consulting services.

Environmental Protection Policy Issues (and focus areas): Air Quality; Environmental Audits; Environmental Remediation (hazardous waste; management of federal facilities; brownfields/urban renewal; solid waste management); Environmental Health (asbestos; children's health; indoor air quality; lead hazards; radon; toxics); Environmental Justice; Water Resources (beaches; drinking water; watersheds; Western water; wetlands).

Natural Resources Policy Issues (and focus areas): Emergency Management and Natural Disasters (bio-terrorism; eco-terrorism; hurricanes; state programs); Fishing, Hunting, and Wildlife ("canned" hunting; recreational hunting and fishing; trapping and poison bans); Forestry; Growth Management; Property Rights/Takings; Water Resources.

Key Publications: Environment Update (monthly; online); LegisBriefs (2-page concise analysis of a single issue; weekly; $79/yr subscription; can also purchase individual papers); State Legislative Reports (5-7 page comprehensive analysis of a single issue; $15 per paper).

Website Notes – Key Website Divisions (and contents of): Policy Issues (24 issues listed including: agriculture; energy and electric utilities; environmental protection; natural resources; transportation); State Legislatures (provides website links – both to the legislatures and to individual legislators); State-Federal Relations (12 specific issues addressed, including: agriculture and internal trade; energy and transportation; environment).

Check Out on the Web: 2000-2001 Policies (specific goals for state-federal action; located under "State-Federal Relations").

Founded: 1975 **Membership:** 32,000 **Staff:** 150 **Revenue/Expenses (NCSL Foundation; FY00):** $1.00/$1.04 million **Budget (NCSL as a whole):** $13 million

Revenue (NCSL Foundation; FY00): Contributions (56%); Government Grants (0%); Program Service Revenues (44%; from grants and contracts); Other (<1%).

Expenses (NCSL Foundation; FY00): Program Services (63%); Management and General (13%); Fundraising (24%).

Contact Info (HQ): 1560 Broadway, Suite 700, Denver, CO 80202; (303) 830-2200.

Contact Info (DC): 444 N Capitol St. NW, Suite 515, Washington, DC 20001; (202) 624-5400.

Key Personnel: William T. Pound (Executive Director)

254. National Governors' Association (NGA) (www.nga.org)

A Top Federal Lobbying Group Per Fortune Magazine's Annual Survey: Ranking for 2001: #21

Description: Research and service organization for state/territorial governors and their staffs. Formal membership consists of all the nation's governors. A key entity within NGA is its Center for Best Practices (CBP), which focuses on policy studies and is organized into 5 divisions, including Natural Resources Policy Studies.

A Closer Look: Offers a Corporate Fellows program to promote information exchange between the private sector and the Governors. Limits participation to 100 corporations, which must each contribute $12,000 annually to participate. Corporate feedback is mainly accomplished though NGA's CBP, with Corporate Advisory Groups established for each of the CBP's 5 policy studies areas, including natural resources, which has a 25-member Corporate Advisory Group.

Basic Activities: Policy research/analysis; information exchange/services; advocacy.

Key Environmental Issues (and focus areas) (Website Note: Details on the following are found on the "Center for Best Practices" webpage, under "Environment and Emergency Management"): Brownfield Redevelopment; Cleanup of the Nuclear Weapons Complex; Emergency Management (chemical emergency management; domestic terrorism; oil spill prevention); Energy (utility deregulation); Environmental Regulatory Innovations and Issues ("pay for performance" for environmental remediation projects; environmental electronic reporting; environmental justice); Growth and Quality of Life (suburban growth; urban revitalization; land and open space preservation; environmental and public health; climate change); Natural Resources and Land Preservation (private working lands conservation; invasive species; air quality; water quality).

Check Out on the Web: Governors' State-of-the-State Addresses (see "Governor's Speeches" on the "Governors" page); "NGA Policy Positions," "Legislative Issues," and "State Policy Issues" (all on the NGA home page); Legislative Priorities (located under "Legislative Update").

Founded: 1908 **Members:** 55 governors **Staff:** 87 **NP Status** (NGA-CBP): 501(c)(3) **Revenue/Expenses** (NGA-CBP; FY00): $7.0/$6.5 million **Budget** (for NGA overall): $10 to 25 million

Revenue (NGA-CBP; FY00): Contributions (57%); Government Grants (44%); Program Service Revenues (4%); Other (-4%; loss due to return of previous contributions from a particular funder).

Expenses (NGA-CBP; FY00): Program Services (72%; for: human resource policy studies –52%; natural resource policy studies –15%; economic development and commerce policy studies –5%); Management and General (21%); Fundraising (7%).

Contact Info (NGA-CBP): 444 N Capitol St. NW, Suite 267, Washington, DC 20001; (202) 624-5300.

Key Personnel: Raymond Scheppach (Executive Director)

2.3.1.2 Local-Level Governmental Associations and Councils

255.   International City/County Management Association (ICMA) (www.icma.org)

Description: Association of appointed managers/administrators in local governments throughout the world. ICMA developed and manages the Local Government Environmental Assistance Network (LGEAN; see Profile #459 located within Subsection 7.2 – "Information and Data Resource Websites and Gateways") in partnership with ECOS, NACO, EPA, and others. ICMA also serves as the organizational home for the Smart Growth Network (SGN; see Profile #116, located within Section 1.2 – "Public Interest Groups and Coalitions").

A Closer Look: Offers a Corporate Partnership program providing access to local government decision-makers. A minimum annual contribution of $5,000 annually is required to participate. Pledges of $10,000 or more gain membership on the ICMA Executive Director's Corporate Advisory Board.

Basic Activities: Information exchange/services; technical assistance.

Key Environmental Programs: Brownfields/Superfund; Energy Efficiency; Indoor Air; Intelligent Transportation Systems; Local Government Environmental Assistance Network; Natural Resources; Smart Growth Network; Wetlands and Watershed Management.

Website Note: Not much publicly accessible on ICMA's website, except through LGEAN or the SGN (see Profiles #459 and #116, respectively).

Founded: 1914 **Membership:** 8300 **Staff:** 120 **NP Status:** 501(c)(3) **Revenue/Expenses (FY00):** $19.6/$19.4 million

Contact Info: 777 N Capitol St. NE, Suite 500, Washington, DC 20002; (202) 289-4262.

Key Personnel: William Hansell (Executive Director)

256.   National Association of Counties (NACo) (www.naco.org)

Description: Association of counties – NACo's current membership of 1780 counties represents 60% of all counties nationwide. Develops, organizes and manages 30+ projects and programs divided into 6 categories, including "Environmental." Maintains a separate Research Foundation with a common Board of Directors.

Maintains affiliations with 26 different associations of professionally-related county officials.

A Closer Look: Offers a Corporate Membership program that provides access to local government leaders/decision-makers. Current program membership includes 130+ corporations and trade groups (see below for key business-related corporate members).

Key Business-Related Corporate Members (see separate profiles for each within Subsection 5.1 – "Business Trade Associations"): American Chemistry Council; American Petroleum Institute; American Trucking Associations; National Association of Home Builders; National Association of Realtors; National Rural Electric Cooperative Association; Nuclear Energy Institute.

Basic Activities: Technical assistance; info exchange/services; policy research/analysis; advocacy.

Environmental Programs/Projects (and focus areas): Energy Efficiency; Environmentally Preferable Purchasing; Local Government Environmental Assistance Network (LGEAN – see Profile #459, located within Subsection 7.2 – "Information and Data Resource Websites and Gateways"); Indoor Air Programs (radon; asthma; tobacco smoke; carbon monoxide); Smart Growth; Solid Waste; Water Programs (non-point source water pollution; source water protection; watershed management; wetlands protection; restoration challenge grant program; wastewater management); Joint Center for Sustainable Development; Western Community Stewardship Forum (focused on community-driven solutions to land-use issues in the rural West).

Check Out on the Web: Legislative Priorities (priority issues for counties; located under "Legislative Affairs").

Founded: 1935 **Members** 1780 counties (60% of all counties) **Staff:** 79 **NP Status:** 501(c)(4) (NACo); 501(c)(3) (NACo Research Foundation) **Revenue/Expenses** (NACo Research Foundation; 1999): $2.5/$4.2 million **Budget** (for NACo overall): $15 million

Contact Information: 440 1st St. NW, Suite 800, Washington, DC 20001; (202) 393-6226.

Key Personnel: Larry Naake (Executive Director)

257.   National Association of Towns and Townships (NATaT) (www.natat.org/natat)

Description: Association of local towns and townships.

Facts and Figures: Of the 39,000 general-purpose local governments in the U.S., 85% are under 10,000 in population and nearly one-half have less than 1000 residents.

Basic Activities: Policy research/analysis; advocacy; info exchange/services.

Priority Environmental Issues (and focus areas): Brownfields (funding for rural areas); Takings (maintaining local government control of growth); Water Infrastructure (federal funding issues).

Founded: 1976 **Members:** 11,000 local governments **Staff:** 5 **Budget**: $0.5 to 1 million

Contact Information: 444 N Capitol St. NW, Suite 208, Washington, DC 20001; (202) 624-3550; natat@sso.org

Key Personnel: Tom Halicki (Executive Director)

258.   National Center for Small Communities (NCSC) (www.smallcommunities.org/ncsc)

Description: Center providing information and training/technical assistance to small town decision-makers on a range of pertinent issues, including environmental planning and compliance. Formerly part of the National Association of Towns and Townships (see Profile #257); shares offices with NATaT and has the same Executive Director.

Basic Activities: Info exchange/services; training/technical assistance.

Environmental Issues: Drinking Water; Wastewater Treatment; Hazardous Material Emergency Response; Underground Storage Tanks.

Key Environmental Initiative: Small Town Wellhead and Source Water Protection Initiative (a cooperative project with the USEPA).

NP Status: 501(c)(3) **Revenue/Expenses (2000):** $0.47/$0.45 million

Contact Information: 444 N Capitol St. NW, Suite 208, Washington, DC 20001; (202) 624-3550; ncsc@sso.org

Key Personnel: Tom Halicki (Executive Director)

259.   National League of Cities (NLC) (www.nlc.org)

Description: Association of municipalities (cities, towns, villages, etc.) and state municipal leagues (state-level associations of municipalities). Maintains the NLC Institute as the education and training arm. NLC's environmental focus is with respect to general infrastructure issues (see below).

A Closer Look: Offers Associate membership to other interested parties (both private/public and non-profit/for-profit orgs).

Basic Activities: Policy research/analysis; advocacy; info exchange/services; training/technical assistance.

Key Environmental Issues (and activities/focus areas): Drinking, Storm, and Waste Water Infrastructure (co-founded the Water Infrastructure Network which is seeking $57 billion in federal support over 5 years for water infrastructure projects); Mass Transit (high-speed rail lines; TEA-21 funding).

Founded: 1924 **Members:** 1800 municipalities; 49 municipal leagues (which, in turn, represent another 18,000 municipalities) **Staff:** 95 **NP Status:** 501(c)(4) (NLC); 501(c)(3) (NLC Institute) **Revenue/Expenses** (NLC Institute; FY00): $1.93/$1.38 million **Budget** (for NLC overall): $11 million

Contact Info: 1301 Pennsylvania Ave. NW, Suite 550, Washington, DC 20004; (202) 626-3000; inet@nlc.org

Key Personnel: Donald Borut (Executive Director)

260.   Unites States Conference of Mayors (USCM) (www.usmayors.org)

Description: Association of cities with populations of 30,000 or more (non-voting associate membership is available to those cities under 30,000 in population). Undertakes/offers 14 Projects and Services, including "Environment" and "Sustainable Communities."

A Closer Look: Offers an Allied Membership program for non-profit organizations; currently has 21 such members.

Facts and Figures: There are 1050 cities in the U.S. with populations exceeding 30,000.

Basic Activities: Policy research/analysis; advocacy; information exchange/services; technical assistance.

Key Environmental Programs: Brownfields; Joint Center For Sustainable Communities; Municipal Waste Management Association (see Profile #281, located within Subsection 2.3.2 – "Environmentally-Focused Governmental Associations and Councils"); Recycling at Work; Urban Water Council.

Unique: "Clean Your Files Day" – promoting workplace recycling programs by urging employees to purge old files; targeted for the week of Earth Day (April 22).

Check Out on the Web: "Meet the Mayors" (particularly: "Mayors at a Glance" [search engine providing photo and contact information, including a link to the city's website]; "Cities Online" [summary listing of links to city websites]).

Founded: 1932 **Members:** 1100 cities **Staff:** 45 **NP Status**: 501(c)(3) **Revenue/Expenses (1998)**: $1.93/$1.38 million **Budget** (for USCM overall, including affiliated orgs): $7.6 million

Affiliated Orgs: Conference of Mayors Research and Education Fund; U.S. Mayor Enterprises, Inc.

Contact Info: 1620 1st St. NW, 4th Floor, Washington DC 20006; (202) 395-5750.

Key Personnel: J. Thomas Cochran (Executive Director)

2.3.2 Environmentally-Focused Governmental Associations and Councils

2.3.2.1 National-Level Environmentally-Focused Governmental Associations and Councils

261.   White House Council on Environmental Quality (CEQ) (www.whitehouse.gov/ceq)

Description: "Coordinates federal environmental efforts and works closely with agencies and other White House offices in the development of environmental policies and initiatives." The Council's Chair (appointed by the President and confirmed by the Senate) serves as the principal environmental policy adviser to the President and Vice President.

A Closer Look: Under the Executive Office of the President, the CEQ was established with passage of the National Environmental Policy Act of 1969 (NEPA).

Check Out on the Web: "NEPAnet" page (provides CEQ reports online, including: past Annual Reports and Environmental Quality Statistics [a series of environmental data tables covering 11 topic areas]).

Contact Info: 722 Jackson Pl. NW, Washington DC 20503; (202) 456-6224.

Key Personnel: James Connaughton (Chairman)

2.3.2.2 State-Level Environmentally-Focused Governmental Associations and Councils

262.   Association of American Pesticide Control Officials (AAPCO) (aapco.ceris.purdue.edu)

Description: Association of government officials responsible for regulatory control of pesticides. Principal AAPCO members are state/territorial pesticide regulatory officials responsible for implementing the Federal Insecticide, Fungicide and Rodenticide Act (FIFRA); each state/territorial pesticide regulatory agency designates one member as its voting representative for AAPCO. Membership is also open to federal regulatory officials and Canadian government officials. AAPCO meets twice a year, with its three-day spring meeting in Washington DC involving extensive discussions with relevant federal agencies (particularly the USEPA) as well as meeting with pesticide industry representatives.

A Closer Look: A primary goal of AAPCO is to encourage uniformity among the states/territories in their pesticide regulatory programs; to that extent, AAPCO has developed/adopted uniform policies and model legislation.

Basic Activities: Information exchange/services; policy/legislation development.

Key Group: State FIFRA Issues Research and Evaluation Group (consisting of 10 state pesticide officials – one from each EPA region – that meet periodically with EPA pesticide officials to discuss relevant issues).

Founded: 1947 **Members:** 55 state/territorial agency representatives **Staff:** 1 **Budget:** $0.01 to 0.025 million

Contact Info: (802) 472-6956; aapco@plainfield.bypass.com

Key Personnel: Donnie Dippel (President)

263.   Association of State and Interstate Water Pollution Control Administrators (ASIWPCA)
          (www.asiwpca.org)

Description: Association of executive officers (program administrators) of state/territorial and interstate water pollution control agencies/programs. Organized around 6 task forces (see below for key task forces).

Basic Activities: Information exchange/services; conferences/seminars; training/technical assistance; advocacy.

Key Task Forces: Groundwater Protection; State Revolving Loan Fund; Watershed Protection.

Programs: TMDL Program/Watershed Management; Non-Point Source Program; Confined Animal Feeding Operations; Wastewater Control; Water Quality Standards and Monitoring.

Founded: 1962 **Members:** 56 executive officers **HQ:** Washington, DC **Staff:** 6 **NP Status:** 501(c)(3)
Revenue/Expenses (FY00): $0.76/$0.72 million

Contact Info: (202) 898-0905; admin1@asiwpca.org
Key Personnel: Robbi Savage (Executive Director)

264.   Association of State and Territorial Health Officials (ASTHO) (www.astho.org)

Description: Association of executive officers of state/territorial public health agencies/programs. Also maintains a non-voting "alumni" membership category. Has 5 Policy Committees, including an Environmental Health Committee.

Basic Activities: Information exchange/services; policy research/analysis; advocacy.

Lobbying/Political Activities: Registered lobbyist under the LDA.

Environmental Health Committee Projects: Toxic Substance/Waste Sites (maintains a cooperative agreement with the federal government [through ATSDR] to enhance communications and information exchange).

Key Periodical: Environmental Health News (monthly electronic newsletter; online).

Founded: 1942 **Members:** 57 executive officers **HQ:** Washington, DC **Staff:** 23 **NP Status:** 501(c)(3)
Revenue/Expenses (FY00): $3.4/$3.3 million

Contact Info: (202) 371-9090

Key Personnel: Cheryl Beversdorf, RN (Executive VP)

265.   Association of State and Territorial Solid Waste Management Officials (ASTSWMO) (www.astswmo.org)

Description Association of executive officers of state/territorial solid waste management agencies/programs. Organized around 7 Waste Program Committees (see below).

Basic Activities: Information exchange/services; conferences/workshops; policy research/analysis; advocacy.

Waste Program Committees: Federal Facilities; Hazardous Waste; Industrial and Municipal Solid Waste; Pollution Prevention; Superfund/State Cleanup; Training and Information Exchange; Underground Storage Tanks.

Founded: 1974 **Members:** 56 executive officers **HQ:** Washington, DC **Staff:** 9 **Budget:** $1 to 2 million

Contact Info: (202) 624-5828

Key Personnel: Thomas Kennedy (Executive Director)

266.   Association of State Drinking Water Administrators (ASDWA) (www.asdwa.org)

Description: Association of executive officers (program administrators) of state/territorial drinking water agencies/programs. Other state and local drinking water regulatory personnel may participate as associate members. Maintains a number of standing and ad hoc committees. Particularly focused on working with the USEPA on Safe Drinking Water Act-related regulatory issues.

Basic Activities: Information exchange/services; training/technical assistance; policy research/analysis; advocacy.

Founded: 1984 **Members:** 56 executive officers **HQ:** Washington, DC **Staff:** 5 **NP Status:** 501(c)(3)
Revenue/Expenses (1999): $0.91/$0.75 million

Contact Info: (202) 293-7655; asdwa@erols.com

Key Personnel: Vanessa Leiby (Executive Director)

267.   Association of State Floodplain Managers (ASFPM) (www.floods.org)

Description: Association of professionals involved in floodplain management, including flood hazard mitigation, the National Flood Insurance Program, and flood preparedness, warning and recovery. Members are mainly various government officials, but also includes individuals from the private sector (principally from engineering/technical consulting firms and flood control product suppliers). Has 14 State Chapters. Maintains 12 committees (see below for key committees). Has an affiliated non-profit organization – the ASFPM Foundation – which focuses on training, education/public awareness and research activities.

Basic Activities: Training/technical assistance; information exchange/services; professional certification; policy research/analysis; advocacy.

Key Committees: Arid Regions; Coastal Issues; Flood Mitigation; Floodproofing/Retrofitting; Multi-Objective Management; Floodplain Regulations; Urban Stormwater.

Key Publication: National Flood Programs in Review 2000 (addresses key issues and identifies recommended actions).

Founded: 1977 **Membership:** 4500 **Staff:** 3 **HQ:** Madison, WI **Budget:** $0.1 to 0.25 million

Contact Info: (608) 274-0123

Key Personnel: Larry Larson (Executive Director)

268.   Association of State Wetland Managers (ASWM) (www.aswm.org)

Description: Professional membership association of individuals and organizations/agencies involved in protection and restoration of wetlands. Members are mainly various government officials, but also includes individuals from the private sector and academia.

Basic Activities: Training/technical assistance; information exchange/services.

Key Publication: Status and Trends Report (summary of wetland and wetland-related regulatory programs in all 50 states).

Founded: 1984 **Membership:** 950 **Staff:** 4 **HQ:** Berne, NY **NP Status:** 501(c)(3) **Revenue/Expenses (1999):** $0.27/$0.26 million

Contact Info: (518) 872-1804; aswm@aswm.org

Key Personnel: Jon Kusler (Executive Director)

269.   Council of State and Territorial Epidemiologists (CSTE) (www.cste.org)

Description: Association of government epidemiologists working in state/territorial or local public health agencies. Epidemiologists working in federal health agencies or academia can also join as associate members. Members are from every U.S. state/territory, along with Canada and Britain. Provides technical advice/assistance to the Association of State and Territorial Health Officials (see Profile #264) and federal public health agencies, particularly the Centers for Disease Control and Prevention (CDC). Also conducts advocacy on selected issues.

Basic Activities: Information exchange/services; training/technical assistance; standards development; policy research/analysis; advocacy.

General Priority Areas: Infectious diseases; chronic diseases and conditions; environmental health concerns.

Key Project: Environmental Epidemiology Capacity-Building (seek to facilitate development of environmental epidemiology capacity and competency at the state level).

Founded: 1951 **Members:** 400 **HQ:** Atlanta, GA **Staff:** 20 **Budget:** $2 to 5 million

Contact Info: (770) 458-3811

Key Personnel: Donna Knutson (Executive Director)

270.   Environmental Council of the States (ECOS) (www.sso.org/ecos)

Description: Association of state/territorial environmental commissioners. ECOS staff also carry out projects for the Environmental Research Institute of the States, an affiliated research- and education-focused non-profit. ECOS maintains close relations with the National Governors Association (see Profile #254).

Basic Activities: Policy research/analysis; information exchange/services.

Committees: Air; Water/Ecosystems; Waste; Compliance; Cross-Media; Planning.

Key Programs/Projects (and focus areas): Children's Environmental Health (document innovative state programs); National Childhood Asthma Prevention Campaign; Mercury (policy resolutions; outreach efforts); Core Performance Measures (state/EPA cooperative agreement); Enforcement (evaluate sources of data inconsistencies between the states and the EPA); Environmental Information Management (information exchange between the states and the EPA); Environmental Justice; Transportation (TEA-21); State Innovations; Management of Decentralized Wastewater Systems.

Key Periodicals: ECOStates (quarterly newsletter; online).

Key Reports: Mercury in the Environment (a compendium of state mercury activities; online); State

Environmental Agency Contributions to Enforcement and Compliance (a report to Congress; online); States Put Their Money Where Their Environment Is (summary of state environmental spending for FY00; online).

Check Out on the Web: "State Innovations" (innovative ideas from state environmental agencies).

Contact Info: 444 N Capitol St. NW, Suite 445, Washington, DC 20001; (202) 624-3660; ecos@sso.org

Key Personnel: Robert E. Roberts (Executive Director)

271.   International Association of Fish and Wildlife Agencies (IAFWA) (www.iafwa.org)

Description: Association of North American fish and wildlife resource agencies (state-level agencies in the U.S.). Also offers 3 non-voting memberships (affiliate/associate/contributing) to conservation-related governmental and non-governmental orgs and individuals. Maintains 36 committees composed of 700 professionals that monitor and advise on a wide range of pertinent issues.

Basic Activities: Information exchange/services; technical assistance; policy research/analysis; advocacy; litigation.

Lobbying/Political Activities: Registered lobbyist under the LDA.

Key Periodicals: Inside IAFWA (monthly electronic newsletter; online).

Founded: 1902 **Membership:** 300 **Staff:** 12 **Budget:** $0.5 to 1 million

Contact Info: 444 N Capitol St. NW, Suite 544, Washington, DC 20001; (202) 624-7890; iafwa@sso.org

Key Personnel: Robert L. McDowell (President)

272.   Interstate Council on Water Policy (ICWP) (www.icwp.org)

Description: Association of state and regional water resource management agencies. Also offers affiliate membership to interested private and public entities. Focuses on water quality and water quantity issues, particularly with respect to state-federal interaction.

A Closer Look: Shares offices and staff with the National Association of Flood and Stormwater Management Agencies (see Profile #284).

Basic Activities: Information exchange/services; policy research/analysis.

Interest Areas: Watershed Management; Dam Safety; Floodplain Management; Groundwater; Non-Point Source Pollution; Water Quality Standards; Water Conservation; Drought and Emergency Management; Wetlands Protection; State Water Rights; Climate Change; Hydropower Licensing; Endangered Species and Habitat; Water Supply; Water Resource Research and Data.

Founded: 1959 **Membership:** 28 agencies **Staff:** 4 **NP Status:** 501(c)(3) **Revenue/Expenses (FY00):** $0.137/$0.138 million

Contact Info: 1299 Pennsylvania Ave. NW, Suite 800, Washington, DC 20004; (202) 218-4196.

Key Personnel: Susan Gilson (Executive Director)

273.   National Association of State Conservation Agencies (NASCA) (www.nascanet.org)

Description: Association of state/territorial executive agencies responsible for the administration of soil, water and related natural resource programs. Works closely with the National Association of Conservation Districts (see Profile #282) and the USDA Natural Resources Conservation Service (see Profile #193, located within Subsection 2.2 – "Federal Governmental Agencies/Entities").

A Closer Look: While many NASCA member agencies are involved with state-level regulatory programs for water quality, none are designated as the primary water quality agency for their respective state/territory.

Basic Activities: Information exchange/services.

Website Notes: Unfortunately, the website currently provides relatively little information and what is provided appears to be a couple of years old.

Membership: 55 agencies **NP Status:** 501(c)(3) **Revenue/Expenses (2000):** $0.23/$0.15 million

Key Personnel: Harry Nikides (President); Jim Cox (Executive Director)

274.   **National Association of State Departments of Agriculture (NASDA)** (www.nasda-hq.org)

Description: Association of executive officers (commissioners, secretaries and directors) of state/territorial Departments of Agriculture. Organized based on 4 geographic regions; maintains 6 general policy committees and 2 special task forces. Focuses on policy advocacy efforts. Maintains an affiliated non-profit organization – the NASDA Research Foundation – to conduct agriculturally-oriented research, education, and training.

Basic Activities: Information exchange/services; policy research/analysis; advocacy.

Key Committees (and focus areas): Natural Resources and Environment (non-point source pollution and general water quality issues; watershed and coastal area management; public lands management; farmland management; general conservation issues; threatened and endangered species; property rights); Pesticide Regulation.

Check Out on the Web: "Legislative and Regulatory Affairs" section (provides NASDA's: policy statements; position statements; legislative issue papers; legislative backgrounders).

Founded: 1915 **Membership:** 54 executive officers **Staff:** 9 **Budget:** $0.5 to 1 million

Contact Info: 1156 15th St. NW, Suite 1020, Washington, DC 20005; (202) 296-9680; nasda@patriot.net

Key Personnel: Richard Kirchhoff (Executive VP/CEO)

275.   **National Association of State Energy Officials (NASEO)** (www.naseo.org)

Description: Association of officials from state/territorial energy offices (offices formed in response to the energy crisis of the early 1970s) and affiliates from the private and public sectors. Affiliated with the National Governors' Association (see Profile #254). Organized around 7 Committees (see below) and 2 Task Forces.

Basic Activities: Information exchange/services; training/technical assistance; policy research/analysis; advocacy.

Committees (and key issue areas): Buildings; Economic Development and Environmental Quality (energy efficiency; renewable energy); Electric and Gas Utilities (utility restructuring); Energy Data and Energy Security (petroleum-related issues); International; Issues Agenda (top advocacy priorities); Transportation.

Check Out on the Web: Issues 2000: NASEO's National Energy Issues Agenda (online).

HQ: Alexandria, VA **Staff:** 4 **NP Status:** 501(c)(3) **Revenue/Expenses (FY00):** $0.89/$0.83 million

Contact Info: (703) 299-8800; info@naseo.org

Key Personnel: Frank Bishop (Executive Director)

276.   **National Association of State Foresters (NASF)** (www.stateforesters.org)

Description: Association of directors of state/territorial forestry agencies. Seeks to promote sound forest management on both public and private lands. Has an affiliated non-profit organization – the NASF Foundation, which provides a grant to support NASF activities. Organized around a set of nearly 30 standing, select, and liaison committees (see below for key committees).

Basic Activities: Information exchange/services; training/technical assistance; policy research/analysis; advocacy.

Key Committees (and activities/focus areas): Forest Fire Protection; Forest Resource Management (assist private landowners); Urban and Community Forestry (community-based tree planting and care); Forest Health (pest suppression, control, and eradication); Water Resources (water quality protection); Conservation and Natural Resource Education; Federal Lands; Working Land Conservation (lands privately owned and actively managed for forest products); Sustainable Forestry Implementation.

Key Periodical: NASF Washington Update (monthly newsletter; online).

Check Out on the Web: State Forestry Statistics (bi-annual survey of state forestry programs; online); State Forestry Homepages (links to state forestry agency websites).

Founded: 1920 **HQ:** Washington, DC **Staff:** 5 **NP Status:** 501(c)(3) **Revenue/Expenses** (NASF Foundation; FY99): $0.079/$0.048 million

Contact Info: (202) 624-5415; nasf@sso.org

Key Personnel: William Imbergamo (DC Representative)

277.   National Association of State Park Directors (NASPD) (www.naspd.org)

Description: Association of chief administrative officers of state park agencies. Organized based on 6 geographic regions.

Basic Activities: Information exchange/services; policy research/analysis.

Check Out on the Web: "State Park Statistics" and "State Park Research" (providing relevant data and research); Official State Park Pages (an Internet gateway).

Founded: 1962 **Membership:** 50 executive officers **Budget:** $0.05 to 0.1 million

Contact Info: (520) 298-4924; naspdglen@home.com

Key Personnel: Glen Alexander (Executive Director)

278.   State and Territorial Air Pollution Program Administrators (STAPPA) (www.cleanairworld.org)

Description: Association of executive officers (program administrators) of state/territorial air pollution control agencies/programs. Organized around a set of 15 standing committees that focus on specific areas of air pollution control (see below for key committees). Formally affiliated with the Association of Local Air Pollution Control Officials (ALAPCO; see Profile #279), sharing offices and staff; essentially one organization (referred to as STAPPA/ALAPCO).

Basic Activities: Information exchange/services; policy research/analysis.

Key Committees: Agriculture; Air Toxics; Criteria Pollutants; Emissions and Modeling; Energy; Enforcement; Mobile Sources and Fuels; Monitoring; Permitting; Pollution Prevention and Sustainability; Stratospheric Ozone Protection and Global Warming.

Founded: 1968 **Membership:** 54 executive officers **HQ:** Washington, DC **Staff:** 6 **NP Status:** 501(c)(3) **Revenue/Expenses** (combined STAPPA/ALAPCO; FY00): $1.13/$1.11 million

Contact Info: (202) 624-7864

Key Personnel: William Becker (Executive Director)

2.3.2.3 Local-Level Environmentally-Focused Governmental Associations and Councils

279.   Association of Local Air Pollution Control Officials (ALAPCO) (www.cleanairworld.org)

Description: Association of government officials representing their local air pollution control agencies/programs. Members represent 165+ major metropolitan areas. Organized around a set of 15 standing committees that focus on specific areas of air pollution control (see below for key committees). Formally affiliated with the State and Territorial Air Pollution Program Administrators (STAPPA; see Profile #278), sharing offices and staff; essentially one organization (referred to as STAPPA/ALAPCO).

Basic Activities: Information exchange/services; policy research/analysis.

Key Committees: Agriculture; Air Toxics; Criteria Pollutants; Emissions and Modeling; Energy; Enforcement; Mobile Sources and Fuels; Monitoring; Permitting; Pollution Prevention and Sustainability; Stratospheric Ozone Protection and Global Warming.

Founded: 1971 **Membership:** Represents 220 local agencies/programs **HQ:** Washington, DC **Staff:** 6 **NP Status:** 501(c)(3) **Revenue/Expenses** (combined STAPPA/ALAPCO; FY00): $1.13/$1.11 million

Contact Info: (202) 624-7864

Key Personnel: William Becker (Executive Director)

280.   Association of Metropolitan Sewerage Agencies (AMSA) (www.amsa-cleanwater.org)

Description: Association of metropolitan sewerage (wastewater treatment) agencies. Affiliate members include interested private-sector companies.

A Closer Look: Wastewater treatment is typically handled through either municipal utilities or public works departments of local governments; service areas are often referred to as "sanitation/sanitary districts."

Basic Activities: Information exchange/services; meetings/conferences; policy research/analysis; advocacy.

Lobbying/Political Activities: Registered lobbyist under the LDA.

Legislative Priorities: Funding Initiatives (for: wet-weather grants; water infrastructure; biosolids reuse).

Priority Regulatory Issues: Infrastructure Funding; Total Maximum Daily Loads [TDML] Program; Proposed Sanitary Sewer Overflow Rule; Other Issues (namely: bio-solids management; mercury use and disposal; national pretreatment program; water quality standards; wet-weather programs).

Key Publication: Evaluation of Domestic Sources of Mercury (in household wastewater).

Founded: 1981 **Membership:** 260 agencies **Staff:** 4 **Budget:** $0.25 to 0.5 million

Contact Info: 1816 Jefferson Place NW, Washington DC 20036; (202) 833-AMSA; information@amsa-cleanwater.org

Key Personnel: Ken Kirk (Executive Director)

281. **Municipal Waste Management Association (MWMA)** (www.usmayors.org/uscm/mwma)

Description: Association of local municipal waste management agencies/programs. Active members are government officials representing their agencies/programs; private sector representatives can also join as Associate Members. Conducts legislative advocacy on key issues (see below). Maintains 5 committees (see below). Affiliated with the U.S. Conference of Mayors (see Profile #260).

A Closer Look: Municipal waste management is typically handled through either municipal utilities or public works departments of local government; private firms typically perform actual collection and disposal activities.

Basic Activities: Information exchange/services; policy research/analysis; advocacy.

Committees: Environment; Recycling; Operations; Waste-to-Energy.

Key Issues: Superfund; Brownfields Redevelopment; Clean Air Regulations; Clean Water Regulations; Waste-to-Energy.

Founded: 1982 **Members:** 43 cities/counties **HQ:** Washington, DC **Staff:** 3 **Budget:** $0.05 to 0.1 million

Contact Info: (202) 861-6760

Key Personnel: Geri Powell (Managing Director; from the U.S. Conference of Mayors)

282. **National Association of Conservation Districts (NACD)** (www.nacdnet.org)

Description: Association of local soil and water conservation districts and state/territorial associations. Founded on the philosophy that conservation decisions should be made at the local level; supports voluntary, incentive-driven conservation programs. Has 8 natural resource policy committees (see below). Works closely with the National Association of State Conservation Agencies (see Profile #273) and the USDA Natural Resources Conservation Service (see Profile #193, located within Subsection 2.2 – "Federal Governmental Agencies/Entities"). Primarily financed through contributions from member districts and state associations. Offers Associate Memberships to the general public.

A Closer Look: Conservation districts are local units of government – 3000 nationwide – established under state law to help private landowners manage and protect land and water resources on their lands.

Basic Activities: Policy research/analysis; information exchange/services; technical assistance; meetings/conferences.

Natural Resource Policy Committees: Agricultural Lands Resources; District Operations; Education; Environment and Resource Policy; Forest Resources; Grazing Lands and Public Lands Resources; Urban, Community, and Coastal Resources; Water Resources.

Check Out on the Web: "Districts on the Web" (links to local conservation districts' web pages).

Founded: 1946 **Members:** 3000 local districts; 54 state/territorial associations **Staff:** 45 **NP Status:** 501(c)(3)

Revenue/Expenses (2000): $5.7/$5.9 million

Contact Info (HQ): Box 855, League City, TX 77574; nacdinfo@nacdnet.org

Contact Info (DC): 509 Capitol Court NE, Washington, DC 20002; (202) 547-6223; washington@nacdnet.org

Key Personnel: Ernie Shea (CEO)

283.   National Association of County and City Health Officials (NACCHO) (IP Address: 129.41.41.25)

Description: Association of local public health officials representing their local public health departments (affiliate membership is also made available to the general public – both individuals and groups). NACCHO is an affiliate of the National Association of Counties (see Profile #256).

A Closer Look: There are nearly 3000 local public health agencies/departments nationwide – in cities, counties, townships, and districts.

Basic Activities: Information exchange/services; training/technical assistance; policy research/analysis; advocacy.

Key Programs (and focus areas): Community Environmental Health Assessment (producing an assessment tool for use by local communities); Superfund (relevant training and assistance to local communities); Environmental Health Practice (identifying environmental public health priorities, current needs, and future challenges); Indoor Air Quality ("Tools for Schools" training to address potential problems in K-12 schools).

Annual Report: 2001 report online.

Founded: 1966 **Members:** 3000 individuals; 700 jurisdictions **HQ**: Washington, DC **Staff:** 35 **NP Status:** 501(c)(3) **Revenue/Expenses (FY00):** $5.7/$5.8 million

Revenue Sources (2000): Federal Grants/Contracts (53%); Foundation Grants/Contracts (38%); Other (9%).

Contact Info: (202) 783-5550

Key Personnel: Thomas Milne (Executive Director)

284.   National Association of Flood and Stormwater Management Agencies (NAFSMA)
         (www.nafsma.org)

Description: Association of public agencies involved in flood and stormwater management. The vast majority of members are city or county agencies, while a few are state-level agencies. Private engineering firms can also join as "subscribers." Maintains 4 committees (see below).

Basic Activities: Information exchange/services; advocacy.

A Closer Look: Shares offices and staff with the Interstate Council on Water Policy (see Profile #272).

Committees: Stormwater; Flood Control; Watershed Management; Floodplain Management.

Founded: 1978 **Membership:** 110 agencies (mostly city/county-level agencies) **Staff:** 4 **NP Status:** 501(c)(3) **Budget:** $0.1 to 0.25 million

Contact Info: 1299 Pennsylvania Ave. NW, Suite 800, Washington, DC 20004; (202) 218-4122.

Key Personnel: Susan Gilson (Executive Director)

285.   National Association of Local Government Environmental Professionals (NALGEP)
         (www.nalgep.org)

Description: Association of local environmental officials, principally city and county managers responsible for environmental compliance and/or local environmental policy, representing their localities. Organizations with no direct relationship to a specific local government can also join as associate members.

Basic Activities: Information exchange/services; training/technical assistance; policy research/analysis.

Programs (and focus areas): Brownfields (a host of specific programs/projects initiated to promote cleanup and redevelopment of brownfields); Air Quality ("Clean Air Partnership" program with the USEPA and the states to identify tools and incentives for meeting national air quality objectives); Smart Growth (two separate projects: Smart Growth for Clean Water; Smart Growth Business Partnership).

Key Publication: Profiles of Business Leadership on Smart Growth ("presents the perspectives of business leaders in combating sprawl and promoting smart growth").

Founded: 1993 **Membership:** represents 140+ local government entities **HQ:** Washington, DC **Staff:** 3 **NP Status:** 501(c)(3) **Revenue/Expenses (1999):** $0.33/$0.33 million

Contact Info: (202) 638-6254; nalgep@spiegelmcd.com

SECTION 3: MULTILATERALS (MULTINATIONAL ORGANIZATIONS)

INTRODUCTION/USER'S GUIDE:

In this section, 26 environmentally-significant "multilaterals" – international organizations and associated entities consisting of, or otherwise actively involving, multiple nations or other significant parties (for instance, multinational corporations) – are profiled, divided into the following two subsections:

        3.1 – The United Nations System   (20 entries)
        3.2 – Other Multilaterals and Associated Entities   (6 entries)

For purposes of this Guide, the main focus is on the United Nations and its extended "family" of formally-affiliated organizations (including the World Trade Organization [WTO], the International Monetary Fund [IMF] and the World Bank) that are collectively known as "The UN System." In addition, several other key multilaterals were identified (e.g., the International Chamber of Commerce), which are profiled separately within the "Other Multilaterals and Associated Entities" subsection (Subsection 3.2).

In terms of individual entry contents, the following is a descriptive outline of standardized profile information provided for each organization listed within this section (please note that the exact contents provided varies by organization, being dependant upon applicability and/or availability):

[Profile #] Multilateral Name (Website Address)

Description/Mission: Providing a background summary of the multilateral's mission and activities.

A Closer Look: Providing further information on the multilateral, principally in terms of additional relevant facts and/or a discussion of key issues surrounding the multilateral itself (e.g., reform efforts, concerns raised by critics/observers, etc.).

Operating/Organizational Structure: Focusing on the governing structure utilized and key sub-entities.

Key Internal Groups: Noting relevant committees, working groups, advisory groups, task forces, etc.

Programs/Key Programs (and activities/focus areas): Indicating specific activities/areas of concern and/or current priorities.

Key Activities/Initiatives/Issues: Highlighting the multilateral's "high priority" activities/issues.

Key Reports/Publications: Listing specific reports and other publications judged to represent "essential reading" for interested parties, and noting if they are available online at the multilateral's website. (A summary listing of all such reports/publications is also provided in Appendix B.)

Annual Report: Only included if the report is available online at the multilateral's website; if so, the latest year available is specified. (Represents a key additional source of information on the multilateral's activities and accomplishments.)

Check Out on the Web: Listing website-related content/features that particularly stand out ("worth a look").

Founded: Beginning year specified **HQ:** Noting city and country **Staff:** Overall staffing level **Regional Offices:** Noting as applicable **Budget:** Noted if made available

Contact Info: Providing: City and country; general telephone number; general email address (if established/available).

Key Personnel: Typically citing the head of the multilateral's Secretariat (administrating body), with name and title provided, along with country affiliation.

A CLOSER LOOK – BACKGROUND INFORMATION ON MULTILATERALS

Multilaterals themselves are voluntary-based associations of nations or other significant parties (for instance, multinational corporations) that exist primarily to: 1) form a common agenda and 2) resolve disputes between participating parties through a formal international forum. Nation-based multilaterals are not governments themselves and do not create laws, but can (and do) facilitate adoption and enforcement of international conventions and other treaties.

Multilaterals generally have the same unique three-level operating/governing structure: 1) a supreme governing body (typically termed an "Assembly," "Conference," or "Board of Governors") that meets periodically (typically semi-annually, annually or once every two years) and is comprised of representatives from all member entities (nations or other significant parties); 2) an elected Council or Executive Board that acts as the governing body in-between meetings of the supreme governing body and is comprised of representatives from a subset of all member entities; and 3) a Secretariat (administering body) that manages day-to-day affairs (with the exact duties and scope of activities performed varying by organization), headed by a Secretary or Director-General.

In addition to the three commonly-found internal bodies listed above, multilaterals may (and frequently do) maintain various committees, commissions or other internal groups that carry out substantive portions of their overall agenda (particularly with respect to technical- and scientific-related activities).

Subsection 3.1: The United Nations System

Introduction/User's Guide:

Within this subsection, 20 environmentally-relevant entities of the United Nations and its extended "family" of formally-affiliated organizations (including the World Trade Organization [WTO], the International Monetary Fund [IMF], and the World Bank) are profiled.

Organizational profiles for this subsection are listed beginning on the next page and presented in alphabetical order, divided into the following sub-listings and arranged alphabetically within each such sub-listing:

> 3.1.1 – UN Commissions and Associated Entities
>
> 3.1.2 – UN Programmes and Associated Entities
>
> 3.1.3 – UN Specialized Agencies and Organizations (autonomous entities working with the UN through the UN's Economic and Social Council)
>
> 3.1.4 – UN Related Agencies and Organizations (autonomous entities working with the UN through the UN's General Assembly)
>
> 3.1.5 – UN-Associated Partnership Programs

In terms of individual entry contents, the reader is referred back to the beginning of Section 3 where a descriptive outline of standardized profile information provided is presented.

Subsection 3.1: The United Nations System

286.   United Nations (UN) (www.un.org)

Description/Mission: Originally established at the end of World War II to preserve peace through international cooperation and collective security. Now a centralized body for global efforts to solve a wide range of international problems. Most well known for peacekeeping and humanitarian efforts. Not a world government, nor does it make laws, but rather seeks to help resolve international conflict and formulate policy on international issues. Nearly every nation belongs to the UN, with current membership standing at 189 nations (out of 191 recognized nations worldwide).

Operating/Organizational Structure: The UN has 6 main organs (see below), along with a host of affiliated orgs/entities that, along with the UN itself, are collectively known as "the UN System." UN-affiliated orgs/entities fall into one of the following general classifications: Programmes and Funds; Commissions (both functional and regional); Specialized Agencies; Research and Training Institutes; Other UN Entities; Related Organizations.

Main UN Organs: The General Assembly (a kind of "parliament of nations"); the Security Council (responsible for maintaining international peace and security); the Economic and Social Council (coordinates economic and social work – see Profile #287); the Trusteeship Council (prepares trust territories for self-governance or independence); the International Court of Justice (the World Court, deciding disputes between nations); and the Secretariat (carries out the substantive and administrative work of the UN; its head is the Secretary-General).

Key UN Commissions/Programmes (all report to the UN's Economic and Social Council; see Profiles #288 and 290-291, respectively): UN Commission on Sustainable Development; UN Development Programme; UN Environment Programme.

Key UN Specialized Agencies (autonomous orgs working with the UN through the UN's Economic and Social Council; see Profiles #295-301, respectively): Food and Agricultural Organization of the UN; International Maritime Organization; International Monetary Fund; UN Industrial Development Organization; World Bank Group; World Health Organization; World Meteorological Organization).

Key UN Related Organizations (autonomous orgs working with the UN through the UN's General Assembly; see Profiles #302-303, respectively): International Atomic Energy Agency; World Trade Organization.

Key UN-Associated Partnerships (see Profiles #304-305, respectively): Critical Ecosystem Partnership Fund; Global Environment Facility.

Key Publication: Basic Facts About the UN (an abbreviated version available online under "About the UN").

Website Notes: To navigate through the "UN System," as well as to better understand its components, go to the interactive "Organizational Chart" given under "About the UN."

Founded: 1945 **Member Nations:** 189 **HQ:** New York, NY

Contact Info: 3 UN Plaza, New York, NY 10017; (212) 326-7000; inquiries@un.org

Key Personnel: Kofi Annan (of Ghana) (Secretary-General)

287.   United Nations Economic and Social Council (UN-ECOSOC) (www.un.org/esa/coordination/ecosoc)

Description/Mission: Coordinates the economic and social work of the UN/UN family, acting as a central forum for discussing international economic and social issues and for formulating policy recommendations. Under the overall authority of the UN General Assembly.

Operating/Organizational Structure: The Council is comprised of 54 member nations, elected by the General Assembly for 3-year terms. The Council meets throughout the year and holds a major session in July, during which a special meeting of Ministers discusses major economic and social issues.

A Closer Look: Most of the subsidiary/affiliated organizations of the UN System report at least in part to the Council, including all UN Programmes, Funds, Commissions, and Specialized Agencies (see Profile #286 for the UN as a whole for a listing of key specific organizations reporting to the Council).

Contact Info (Dept. of Economic and Social Affairs): 1 UN Plaza, Room DC1-1428; New York, NY 10017; (212) 326-7000; esa@un.org

Key Personnel: Martin Belinga-Eboutou (of Cameroon) (President)

3.1.1 UN Commissions and Associated Entities

288.   **United Nations Commission on Sustainable Development (UN-CSD)** (www.un.org/esa/sustdev)

Description/Mission: A UN Functional Commission created to ensure effective follow-up to the 1992 UN Conference on Environment and Development (UNCED; a.k.a. the "Earth Summit" held in Rio de Janeiro, Brazil), including monitoring and reporting on implementation of the agreements made at the local, national, regional and international levels. A primary focus of UN-CSD is Agenda 21, a 300-page "action plan" for achieving sustainable development in the 21st century, originally adopted at the 1992 Earth Summit. UN-CSD is tasked with concentrating on certain issues contained within Agenda 21 according to a set 5-year plan (see below), including organizing the 2002 World Summit on Sustainable Development to be held in Johannesburg, South Africa (see Profile #289). In addition, UN-CSD works on international sustainable forestry issues, following up on the "Forest Principles" statement adopted at the Rio Summit.

Operating/Organizational Structure: The UN-CSD is a Functional Commission of the UN Economic and Social Council (see Profile #287) and is comprised of 53 member nations.

2001 Agenda 21 Issues: Atmosphere; Energy; Information; International Cooperation; Transport.

2002 Agenda 21 Issues: "Rio plus 10 years" (a comprehensive review of all issues considered since the Rio summit in 1992).

Key Publication: Agenda 21 (online).

Check Out on the Web: "Issues" (for each Agenda 21 issue, provides: short summary; list of relevant documents; list of related websites); "National Info" (provides nation-specific sustainable development-related information – including indicators – covering 4 general areas: social; economic; natural resources; institutional).

Established: 1992

Contact Info (Division for Sustainable Development): 2 UN Plaza, Room DC2-2220, New York, New York 10017; (212) 963-0902; dsd@un.org

Key Personnel: Bedrich Moldan (of the Czech Republic) (Chairman)

289.   **United Nations World Summit on Sustainable Development** (www.johannesburgsummit.org)

Description/Mission: A follow-up meeting to the 1992 "Earth Summit" held in Rio de Janeiro, Brazil; this meeting is to be held in Johannesburg, South Africa in September 2002 (as such, the meeting is also being referred to as the "Johannesburg Summit" or "Rio +10," the latter in reference to the fact that it is the 10-year follow-up meeting to Rio). The focus of this meeting is on "adopting concrete steps and identifying quantifiable targets for better implementing Agenda 21" (Agenda 21 being the "action plan" for sustainable development adopted at Rio in 1992). The meeting is being organized by the UN Commission on Sustainable Development (see Profile #288), whose primary mission is to ensure effective follow-up to the original Earth Summit.

Website Notes: The website provides information and news concerning the upcoming summit, as well as offering background materials on past summits and providing other relevant information/news.

Contact Info (Division for Sustainable Development): 2 UN Plaza, Room DC2-2220, New York, New York 10017; (212) 963 0902; dsd@un.org

3.1.2 UN Programmes and Associated Entities

290. <u>United Nations Development Programme (UNDP)</u> (www.undp.org)

Description/Mission: A UN Programme created to provide development advice, advocacy and grant support; focuses on providing developing countries with consulting services and coalition building. Currently charged with carrying out a pledge made by world leaders at the UN Millennium Summit in 9/00 to cut poverty in half by 2015. Focuses on 6 priority practice areas, including "Energy and Environment."

A Closer Look: UNDP is completing a major reform effort begun in 1999, with a new focus (the aforementioned 6 priority practice areas, along with an emphasis on field activities), new leadership, and significant downsizing in headquarters staff.

Key Programs (and activities/focus areas): Global Environment Facility (GEF; a grant-making fund; see Profile #305); Small Grants Program (supports community-based NGO projects in developing countries that are related to the GEF's global agenda); Capacity 21 Program (works with developing/transitional countries to meet the goals of "Agenda 21" – guidelines for sustainable development adopted at the 1992 UN Earth Summit); Energy and Atmosphere Program (promotes sustainable energy through a variety of projects); Public-Private Partnerships for the Urban Environment (supports partnerships at the local level to assist small- and medium-sized cities in providing basic urban services – water, sanitation, and energy); Multilateral Fund of the Montreal Protocol (fund to assist developing countries implement the control measures specified in the Montreal Protocol to protect the ozone layer; operated in conjunction with UNEP, UNIDO and the World Bank); Office to Combat Desertification and Drought (spearheads UNDP's work to control desertification and prevent drought in affected program countries).

Key Reports: Human Development Report (annual report evaluating human development worldwide using 4 composite indices; each report also focuses on a different topical theme; online); World Energy Assessment: Energy and the Challenge of Sustainability (evaluates social, economic, environmental and security issues linked to energy, and the compatibility of different energy options with specified objectives in those areas; online).

Annual Report: 2001 report online.

Established: 1966

Contact Info: 1 UN Plaza, Floor 3, New York, NY 10017; (212) 906-5558; aboutundp@undp.org

Key Personnel: Mark Malloch Brown (of Britain) (Administrator)

291. <u>United Nations Environment Programme (UNEP)</u> (www.unep.org)

Description/Mission: Established by the UN General Assembly to be "the environmental conscience of the UN System." Works to "encourage sustainable development through sound environmental practices." Home to various environmentally-related Convention Secretaries (which provide administrative support for developing/implementing international agreements such as the Montreal Protocol, Basel Convention, Convention on Biological Diversity, etc.).

Functional Programs (and activities/focus areas): Environmental Information, Assessment, and Early Warning (provides environmental data and information); Environmental Policy Development and Law; Environmental Policy Implementation; Technology, Industry, and Economics (comprised of: the International Environmental Technology Centre – promotes/transfers "environmentally-sound technologies" for management of cities and freshwater resources; Production and Consumption Unit – promotes cleaner/safer production/consumption patterns; Chemicals Unit; Energy and Ozone Action Unit – supports phase-out of ozone-depleting substances; Economics and Trade Unit); Regional Cooperation and Representation (6 regional offices).

Current Priorities: Environmental Information, Assessment, and Research (including emergency response capacity and strengthening of early warning and assessment functions); Coordination of Environmental Conventions and Development of Policy Instruments; Fresh Water; Technology Transfer and Industry; Support to Africa.

Key UNEP-Associated Orgs (see Profiles #293-294, respectively): UNEP World Conservation Monitoring Center; UNEP/WMO Intergovernmental Panel on Climate Change.

Key Periodicals: Our Planet (magazine; online).

Key Publications (all online): Global Environmental Outlook 2000 (GEO-2000; outlines progress, identifies threats, and makes recommendations); Pachamama: Our Earth – Our Future (GEO-2000 written for youth); Cultural and Spiritual Values of Biodiversity.

Annual Report: 2000 report online.

Key UNEP-Associated Websites (see Profiles # 471, 292, and 467, respectively): EarthPrint (official online bookshop of UNEP; also offers environment-related publications from other UN family members plus others); UNEP Earthwatch (provides "a window on system-wide UN work to observe and assess the global environment"); UNEP Network (a multi-party partnership to make environmentally-relevant scientific information available over the Internet at a centralized website).

Check Out on the Web: Division of Technology, Industry, and Economics (DTIE; addresses a wide range of environmental issues with its activities being divided into 18 separate areas).

Established: 1972

Contact Info: Nairobi, Kenya; (254-2) 621234; eisinfo@unep.org

Key Personnel: Klaus Töpfer (of Germany) (Executive-Director)

EarthPrint (www.earthprint.com)
See Profile #471, located within Subsection 7.3 – "Media-Related Entities."

292. UNEP Earthwatch (earthwatch.unep.net)

Description/Mission: A UN Environment Programme website seeking to provide "a window on system-wide UN work to observe and assess the global environment." An interagency "Earthwatch Working Party" provides guidance to Earthwatch.

Key Website Divisions (and focus areas): Environment (emerging environmental issues; near real-time data; major environmental assessments); Special Topics (various topics).

Check Out on the Web: Emerging Environmental Issues.

UNEP Network (UNEP.net) (www.unep.net)
See Profile #467, located within Subsection 7.2 – "Information and Data Resource Websites and Gateways."

293. UNEP World Conservation Monitoring Center (www.unep-wcmc.org)

Description/Mission: A UN Environment Programme Center offering world biodiversity information and assessment. Closely linked to UNEP's Environmental Information, Assessment, and Early Warning program.

Operating/Organizational Structure: Organized into 3 Divisions: Information Services; Assessment and Early Warning; Conventions and Policy Support.

Programs (and focus areas): Habitats (forests; marine waters; freshwaters; mountains and mountain forests; polar regions); Species (wildlife trade; biodiversity assessment; species conservation databases – animals and plants); Regions (Africa, Latin America, Eurasia); Climate Change and Biodiversity; Protected Areas; Conventions and Agreements (information services regarding 20+ international agreements); iMaps (interactive map-based conservation data on the Internet).

Key Publication: World Atlas of Coral Reefs (assesses the distribution and status of the world's coral reefs).

Contact Info: Cambridge, UK; +44 (0) 1223 277722; info@unep-wcmc.org

Key Personnel: Mark Collins (Director)

294. UNEP/WMO Intergovernmental Panel on Climate Change (IPCC) (www.ipcc.ch)

Description/Mission: An international panel of experts established by the UN Environment Programme (see Profile #291) and the World Meteorological Organization (see Profile #301) to assess the scientific, technical and socio-economic aspects of human-induced climate change (i.e., global warming). IPCC's key product is a comprehensive Assessment Report, issued every 5 years.

A Closer Look: The IPCC does not carry out new research nor does it monitor climate related data; instead it bases its assessments mainly on published and peer-reviewed scientific/technical literature.

Operating/Organizational Structure: The IPCC has 3 Working Groups (WGs) and one Task Force: WG I assesses the science of climate change; WG II addresses the potential impacts of climate change and the options/capacity for adapting to it; WG III assesses options for limiting greenhouse gas emissions and otherwise mitigating climate change; the task force is known as the National Greenhouse Gas Inventories Task Force and is focused on developing and refining an internationally-agreed methodology for calculating and reporting national greenhouse gas emissions and removals.

Publications: Third Assessment Report – Climate Change 2001 (consists of separate reports from each of the three Working Groups, along with a Synthesis Report; corresponding "Summaries for Policymakers" and "Technical Summaries" are available online); Various Special Reports (includes: Regional Impacts of Climate Change; Aviation and the Global Atmosphere; Emissions Scenarios; Land Use, Land Use Change, and Forestry; Methodological and Technological Issues in Technology Transfer; all are available online as full text; corresponding "Summaries for Policymakers" are also available online).

Key Report: Third Assessment Report – Climate Change 2001 (see the Synthesis Report – Summary for Policymakers; online).

Established: 1988

Contact Info (Secretariat): Geneva, Switzerland; +41-22-730-8208; ipcc_sec@gateway.wmo.ch

Key Personnel: Rajendra Pachauri (of India) (Panel Chairman); Narasimhan Sundararaman (Secretary)

3.1.3 UN Specialized Agencies and Organizations

295.   Food and Agriculture Organization of the UN (FAO) (www.fao.org)

Description/Mission: A "Specialized Agency" of the UN (i.e., an autonomous organization working with the UN through the UN's Economic and Social Council) that works to "improve agricultural productivity and food security, and to better the living standards of rural populations." Acts as the lead UN agency for agriculture, forestry, fisheries and rural development. FAO's main functions are offering development assistance and information and support services, along with providing a forum for international cooperation.

Operating/Organizational Structure: Current membership stands at 183 nations (out of 191 recognized nations worldwide), along with the European Union. Governed by a Conference of member nations, which meets once every two years; an elected Council of 49 member nations acts as an interim governing body between meetings of the Conference, while an elected Director-General oversees the agency's day-to-day operations as head of a 3700-person Secretariat.

Key Departments (and divisions/focus areas): Agriculture (biotechnology; conservation agriculture; natural resources and environment; organic agriculture; pesticide management and pollution); Fisheries (marine fisheries; inland fisheries; aquaculture); Forestry (policy and planning; forestry products; forest resources); Sustainable Development (rural development; research, extension, and training; women and population).

Key Interdisciplinary Priority Areas: Biological Diversity; Biotechnology in Food and Agriculture; Ethics in Food and Agriculture; Organic Agriculture.

Key Reports: State of Food and Agriculture (annual report on developments affecting world agriculture; online); State of World Fisheries and Aquaculture (biennial report on developments affecting world fisheries and aquaculture; online); State of World Forests (biennial report on developments affecting world forests; online); World Fisheries and Aquaculture Atlas (a CD-ROM-based containing: 300+ original articles; graphs; maps; fact sheets; 5000 links to other documents and websites).

Check Out on the Web: "Statistical Databases" (online databases providing international statistics on various items, including: agricultural production; fertilizer and pesticide consumption; land use and irrigation; fisheries and forest data/products).

Established: 1945 **Member Nations:** 183 **HQ:** Rome, Italy **Staff:** 3700 **Budget (biennial – 2000-01):** $650 million

Contact Info: Rome, Italy; +39 06 5705 1; FAO-HQ@fao.org

Key Personnel: Jacques Diouf (of Senegal) (Director-General)

296.   International Maritime Organization (IMO) (www.imo.org)

Description/Mission: A "Specialized Agency" of the UN (i.e., an autonomous organization working with the UN through the UN's Economic and Social Council) responsible for improving maritime safety and preventing pollution from ships. Also involved in legal matters, including liability and compensation issues, and the facilitation of international maritime traffic. The current emphasis for IMO is on ensuring that adopted international conventions and other treaties are properly implemented by the countries that have accepted them.

Operating/Organizational Structure: Current membership stands at 160 nations (out of 191 recognized nations worldwide). Governed by an Assembly (comprised of all member nations), which meets biennially. A 32-member Council acts as an interim governing body between Assembly sessions. Technical work is carried out by 5 committees (including the Marine Environment Protection Committee) and various sub-committees, supported by a 300-person Secretariat headed by a Secretary-General.

Key Environmental Conventions Overseen By IMO: International Convention for the Prevention of Pollution from Ships (a.k.a. MARPOL; covers accidental and operational pollution by oil, chemicals, harmful substances in packaged form, sewage and garbage); International Convention on Oil Pollution Preparedness, Response, and Co-operation (OPRC; establishes a framework for combating major incidents or threats of marine pollution); Convention on the Prevention of Marine Pollution by Dumping of Wastes and Other Matter (a.k.a. "the London Convention"; regulates waste disposal at sea).

Key Marine Environment Protection Programs/Initiatives: Global Ballast Water Management Program (a 3-

year, $10 million initiative to assist developing countries address the problem of transfer of harmful aquatic organisms into ships' ballast water); London Convention Update (seeking to have a 1996 update to the original 1972 Convention addressing regulation of waste disposal at sea put into force); Group of Experts on the Scientific Aspects of Marine Environmental Protection (GESAMP; providing relevant scientific input to UN Agencies); Oil and Litter Information Network; Marine Electronic Highway (addressing management of highly congested and confined waters).

Established: 1948 **Member Nations:** 160 **HQ:** London, UK **Staff:** 300 **Budget (biennial – 1998-99):** $56 million

Contact Info: London, UK; +44 (0) 20 7735 7611

Key Personnel: William A. O'Neil (of Canada) (Secretary-General)

297.   International Monetary Fund (IMF) (www.imf.org)

Description/Mission: A "Specialized Agency" of the UN (i.e., an autonomous organization working with the UN through the UN's Economic and Social Council) established to "facilitate international monetary cooperation and financial stability while providing a permanent forum for consultation, advice and assistance on financial issues." Also seeks to "facilitate the expansion and balanced growth of international trade." Most well known for providing financial assistance (credits and loans) to countries with significant financial problems (as of 7/1/01, $65 billion in such credits/loans had been extended to 90 countries worldwide).

A Closer Look: Two separate notes: 1) the IMF is listed here due to its involvement in promoting international trade/globalization, as well as for its influence in countries receiving IMF aid, factors that can significantly affect environmental policy and/or environmental outcomes worldwide; and 2) the IMF is currently undergoing reform efforts, including placing increased emphasis on the "social dimensions" of its work as well as adding more transparency to its policymaking operations.

Operating/Organizational Structure: Current membership stands at 183 nations (out of 191 recognized nations worldwide). Governed by a Board of Governors (comprised of all member nations), which meets annually. A 24-member Executive Board supervises implementation of policies set by the Board of Governors and serves as an interim governing body between meetings of the full Board. The appointed Chairman of the Executive Board also serves as the Managing Director for the 2500-person IMF staff.

Key Activities: Surveillance (appraising members' exchange rate policies); Financial Assistance (including credits and loans extended to member countries with "balance of payments" problems); Technical Assistance (focused on fiscal and monetary policy).

Annual Report: 2001 report online.

Established: 1946 **Member Nations:** 183 **HQ:** Washington, DC **Staff:** 2500

Contact Info: 700 19th St. NW, Washington, DC 20431; (202) 623-7000; publicaffairs@imf.org

Key Personnel: Horst Köhler (of Germany) (Managing Director)

298.   United Nations Industrial Development Organization (UNIDO) (www.unido.org)

Description/Mission: A "Specialized Agency" of the UN (i.e., an autonomous organization working with the UN through the UN's Economic and Social Council) responsible for promoting industrialization throughout the developing world, in cooperation with all its member nations. Acts as a technical/management consultant, offering a host of services to developing countries.

A Closer Look: UNIDO appears to have embraced "sustainability" in promoting development – its stated mission is to "help countries pursue sustainable industrial development," while one of its two headquarters divisions focuses on environmental sustainability.

Operating/Organizational Structure: Current membership stands at 169 nations (out of 191 recognized nations worldwide). Governed via a General Conference of all member nations which meets once every two years. A 53-member Industrial Development Board acts as an interim governing body, meeting once or twice each year. An appointed Director-General runs day-to-day operations of UNIDO as head of a 650-person Secretariat.

UNIDO Divisions: Investment Promotion and Institutional Capacity-Building; Sector Support and Environmental Sustainability (consisting of 4 Branches: cleaner production and environmental; agro-industries and sectoral support; industrial energy and climate change; the Montreal Protocol); Field Operations and Administration (includes 5 Regional Bureaus).

Annual Report: 2000 report online.

Established: 1966 **Member Nations:** 169 **HQ:** Vienna, Austria **Staff:** 650 **Budget (biennial – 2000-01):** $133 million

Contact Info (HQ): Vienna, Austria; (+43 1) 26026; unido@unido.org

Contact Info (U.S.): 1 UN Plaza, Room DC1-1118, New York, NY 10017; (212) 963-6890; office.newyork@unido.org

Key Personnel: Carlos Magariños (of Argentina) (Director-General); Angelo D'Ambrosio (of Italy) (Managing Director of Sector Support and Environmental Sustainability)

299.   World Bank / World Bank Group (www.worldbank.org)

Description/Mission: A "Specialized Agency" of the UN (i.e., an autonomous organization working with the UN through the UN's Economic and Social Council) that provides loans and technical assistance to developing countries in an effort to reduce poverty and advance economic growth. Represents the largest source of development assistance to developing countries. Provided $17 billion in loans to its client countries during FY01, while working in 100+ developing economies. Finances private sector projects and encourages direct foreign investment by providing private investors with guarantees against political risk. Also offers investment marketing services and advice to developing countries.

A Closer Look: From an environmental perspective, the significant influence that the World Bank has on environmental policy and outcomes in the developing world is clear – witness that, at end of FY01, the Bank cites as having in its portfolio 95 active, stand-alone environmental projects worth $5 billion, along with another $11 billion of projects with clear environmental objectives. The Bank itself has been subject to criticism in the past (as well as present) for its selection of projects with environmental implications. In response, starting in the mid-1970's, the Bank developed a series of "Safeguard Policies" (10 policies, including: Environmental Assessment; Natural Habitats; Forestry; Pest Management) aimed at mitigating potential adverse effects on people or the environment. More recently – in the 1990's – the Bank began a targeted environmental assessment program, resulting in development of the aforementioned portfolio of projects with clear environmental objectives. As part of this latest effort, the Bank has sought more partnerships with the public and private sectors (see below for key partnership projects).

Operating/Organizational Structure: Current membership stands at 183 nations (out of 191 recognized nations worldwide). Composed of 5 separate institutions (see below) that specialize in different aspects of development. Governed overall by a Board of Governors (which includes all member nations) and a smaller Board of Executive Directors. A President manages the day-to-day affairs, assisted by a team of Managing Directors. Work is organized through Vice Presidential Units (VPUs) that focus on a particular region or sector – one such VPU is "Environmentally and Socially Sustainable Development." In addition, the Bank operates the World Bank Institute – its training and outreach arm – which includes a Sustainable Development program focused on environmental and natural resource management. Overall, the World Bank Group maintains a large staff (10,000 persons) with 100+ field offices located in 75+ countries.

World Bank Group Orgs (Note: the terms "World Bank" and "the Bank" technically refer only to the IBRD and the IDA): International Bank for Reconstruction and Development (IBRD); International Development Association (IDA); International Finance Corporation (IFC); Multilateral Investment Guarantee Agency (MIGA); International Center for the Settlement of Investment Disputes (ICSID).

Key "Development" Issues: Energy; Environment (see below for details); Infrastructure; Mining; Rural Development and Agriculture; Transport; Urban Development; Water Resources Management; Water Supply and Management.

Key "Environment" Issues (and focus areas): Natural Resources Management (biodiversity conservation; coastal and marine resources management; drylands management and combating desertification; forests and forestry; water resources management); Pollution (pollution management; news ideas in pollution regulation – focused on industrial pollution control in developing countries; clean air initiative – focused on improving urban air quality); Policy and Economics (environmental economics and indicators; environmental assessment); Energy and Environment; Global Commitments (Global Environment Facility operations [see below]; climate change; Montreal Protocol; Prototype Carbon Fund [see below]; 2002 Johannesburg Summit on Sustainable Development).

Key Partnership Projects: Global Environment Facility (see Profile #305; the Bank supports projects in: biodiversity conservation; global climate change; phase-out of ozone depleting substances; protection of international waters); Critical Ecosystem Partnership Fund (project funding aimed at safeguarding developing countries' biodiversity hotspots; see Profile #304 for details); World Bank/World Wildlife Fund Alliance for Forest Conservation and Sustainable Use (seeks to protect 125 million acres of highly threatened forest areas by 2005); Montreal Protocol's Multilateral Fund (supports programs in 20 countries to help enterprises convert to ozone-friendly technologies; have committed $445 million since 1991 for 550+ such projects); Prototype Carbon Fund (a $145 million fund to develop real-world experience/expertise on how carbon markets and trading could operate in developing/transitional nations to achieve reductions in greenhouse gas emissions; see separate website at www.PrototypeCarbonFund.org for details).

Key Reports: Making Sustainable Commitments (outlines a new environmental strategy for the World Bank; focuses on: biodiversity; climate change; forests; water resources); World Development Indicators (annual compilation of development-related data; organized into 6 sections, including "Environment"; also available: shorter summary versions and a CD-ROM containing a set of 550 time-series indicators).

Annual Report: 2001 report online.

Website Notes: Relevant information is best accessed off the "Development Topics" webpage – see above for "Key Development Issues" – while the World Bank Institute is accessed via the "Learning" webpage.

Established: 1944 **Member Nations:** 183 **HQ:** Washington, DC **Staff:** 10,000 **Field Offices:** 100+ in 75+countries

Contact Info (HQ): 1818 H St. NW, Washington, DC 20433; (202) 477-1234.

Contact Info (Environment Program): (202) 522-3773; eadvisor@worldbank.org

Key Personnel: James Wolfensohn (of Australia) (President); Ian Johnson (of the UK) (VP and Network Head for Environmentally and Socially Sustainable Development)

300.   World Health Organization (WHO) (www.who.org)

Description/Mission: A "Specialized Agency" of the UN (i.e., an autonomous organization working with the UN through the UN's Economic and Social Council) focused on improving human health worldwide. Specifically, WHO: 1) seeks to assist governments in strengthening human health services, providing technical assistance and aid; 2) works to prevent, control, and eradicate/eliminate diseases; 3) works to improve nutrition, housing, sanitation, recreation, economic or working conditions, and other aspects of environmental hygiene; 4) establishes international standards/guidelines for water, air quality, foods and biological, pharmaceutical, and similar products.

Operating/Organizational Structure: Current membership stands at 189 nations (out of 191 recognized nations worldwide). Governed by an Assembly (representing all member nations) which meets once a year. An elected 32-member Executive Board meets twice a year to facilitate the work of WHO. An appointed Director-General runs day-to-day operations as head of a 3500-person Secretariat.

Environmental Programs (and focus areas): Air Quality Management; Chemical Safety (international program on chemical safety); Children's Environmental Health; Climate and Health (climate change; El Nino); Environmental Burden of Disease (assess disease burden caused by environmental hazards); Food Safety (biotechnology; chemical contaminants; microbiological risk assessment); Noise; Occupational Health; Radiation Safety (ionizing radiation; UV radiation; electromagnetic fields); Solid Wastes (health care waste); Water and Sanitation (drinking water; water resources; sanitation).

Key Publications: Global Water Supply and Sanitation Assessment 2000 Report (online); Water, Sanitation and Health Electronic Library (a compendium of WHO information on water, sanitation and health; on CD-ROM); Guidelines for Drinking Water Quality (2nd edition; multiple volume set; partially online); Air Quality Guidelines (online).

Established: 1948 **Member Nations:** 189 **HQ:** Geneva, Switzerland **Staff:** 3500 **Regional Offices:** 6

Contact Info: Geneva, Switzerland; (+00 41 22) 791 21 11; info@who.ch

Key Personnel: Dr Gro Harlem Brundtland (of Norway) (Director-General) (she previously served as the chairperson of the World Commission of Environment and Development – a.k.a. the Brundtland Commission – which championed the concept of sustainable development).

301.   World Meteorological Organization (WMO) (www.wmo.ch**)**

Description/Mission: A "Specialized Agency" of the UN (i.e., an autonomous organization working with the UN through the UN's Economic and Social Council) that coordinates global scientific research on the Earth's atmosphere and climate and facilitates the global exchange of meteorological data. Along with the UNEP, established the UN's Intergovernmental Panel on Climate Change (see Profile #294).

Operating/Organizational Structure: Current membership stands at 185 nations (out of 191 recognized nations worldwide). Governed by a Congress (representing all member nations) which meets once every 4 years. A 36-member Executive Council meets each year to facilitate the work of the WMO. A Secretary-General runs day-to-day operations as head of a Secretariat.

Key Technical Programs (and focus areas): World Weather Watch (provides meteorological data/services worldwide; the "backbone" of the WMO's activities); World Climate (data and monitoring; applications and services; impact assessment and response strategies; research); Atmospheric Research and Environment (structure/composition of the atmosphere; physics/chemistry of clouds; weather modification; tropical meteorology; weather forecasting); Applications of Meteorology (agricultural; aeronautical; marine/oceanographic; public weather services); Hydrology and Water Resources (evaluating water resources; developing hydrological data networks and services).

Established: 1947 **Member Nations:** 185 **HQ:** Geneva, Switzerland

Contact Info: Geneva, Switzerland; +41 22 730 8111; ipa@www.wmo.ch

Key Personnel: Prof. G.O.P. Obasi (of Nigeria) (Secretary-General)

3.1.4 UN Related Agencies and Organizations

302.   International Atomic Energy Agency (IAEA) (www.iaea.int)

Description/Mission: An autonomous intergovernmental organization under the aegis of the UN as a "related organization," the IAEA serves as the primary intergovernmental forum for scientific and technical cooperation in the peaceful use of nuclear technology. The IAEA develops nuclear safety standards and operates an inspection system to ensure that nations comply with their commitments under the Non-Proliferation Treaty (and other non-proliferation agreements) to only use nuclear material and facilities for peaceful purposes.

Operating/Organizational Structure: Current membership stands at 132 nations (out of 191 recognized nations worldwide). Governed by a General Conference (consisting of all member nations) which meets once each year. A 35-member Board of Governors meets 5 times each year to facilitate the work of the IAEA. An appointed Director-General runs day-to-day operations as head of a 2200-person Secretariat.

Key Departments (and associated programs): Nuclear Energy (nuclear power; nuclear fuel cycle and waste technology; comparative assessment of energy sources; International Nuclear Information System – providing scientific and technical information); Nuclear Safety (nuclear installation safety; nuclear safety coordination; radiation protection and waste safety); Nuclear Sciences and Applications (food and agriculture; human health; physical and chemical sciences; water resources; marine environmental lab; other agency labs); Safeguards (non-proliferation-related activities).

Annual Report: 2000 report online.

Established: 1957 **Member Nations:** 132 **HQ:** Vienna, Austria **Staff:** 2200 **Budget (2001):** $230 million

Contact Info: Vienna, Austria; (+431) 2600-0; Official.Mail@iaea.org

Key Personnel: Dr. Mohamed El-Baradei (of Egypt) (Director-General)

303.   World Trade Organization (WTO) (www.wto.org)

Description/Mission: An autonomous intergovernmental organization recognized by the UN as a "related organization," the WTO is the only international organization dealing with the global rules of trade between nations. The WTO seeks to lower trade barriers to "ensure that trade flows as smoothly, predictably and freely as possible." At the heart of the WTO system – known as the multilateral trading system – are WTO agreements, negotiated and signed by the bulk of the world's trading nations. These agreements represent the legal ground-rules for international commerce. The complete set of rules consists of some 60 agreements and separate commitments ("schedules"), running some 30,000 pages in total. Trade disputes are channeled into a formal dispute settlement process. The WTO is the successor to the General Agreement on Tariffs and Trade (GATT), which was established following WW II. The WTO currently has 142 member nations, which collectively account for 90+% of all world trade.

Operating/Organizational Structure: Current membership stands at 142 nations (out of 191 recognized nations worldwide). Governed by a Ministerial Conference (consisting of all member nations) which meets at least once every two years. A General Council (normally ambassadors and heads of delegations based in Geneva) meets several times a year at the WTO's Geneva headquarters, including as the Trade Policy Review Board and the Dispute Settlement Body, to facilitate the work of the WTO. An appointed Director-General runs day-to-day operations as head of a 500-person Secretariat. However, as all decisions are made by the WTO member nations themselves, the WTO Secretariat does not perform the same decision-making duties normally granted to international bureaucracies. Instead, the WTO Secretariat's main duties are to provide technical and legal support/assistance.

A Closer Look: Overall concerns about the WTO abound, perhaps best summarized in (ironically) a WTO document entitled "10 Common Misunderstandings About the WTO," namely allegations that it: 1) dictates policy, 2) is for free trade at any cost, 3) allows commercial interests to take priority over development... 4) ...and over environmental concerns 5) ...and over health and safety concerns, 6) destroys jobs and worsens poverty, 7) renders small countries powerless, 8) is a tool of powerful lobbies, 9) forces weaker countries to join it, 10) is undemocratic. (One additional concern missing from this list: the WTO's seemingly remote and mysterious, "closed door" nature, at least partially attributable to the fact that the WTO's Director-General lacks decision-making powers – thus, no one person appears to be ultimately "in charge"/held accountable.) Such concerns were no doubt behind the protests that occurred at the WTO's Ministerial Conference held in Seattle in 1999.

From an environmental standpoint, the WTO currently has no specific agreement dealing with the environment. It does maintain a Committee on Trade and Environment (see below for its stated agenda); however, the committee's stated fundamental principles – 1) it is only competent to deal with trade, thus it limits its tasks to studying environmental issues/policies when they have a significant impact on trade and 2) when problems are identified, the solutions must uphold basic WTO principles (which are intended to lower trade barriers) – don't lend themselves to making the committee seem particularly "environmentally-friendly." Thus, significant concerns exist about the potential effects the WTO might/will have on the environment.

Agenda of the Committee on Trade and Environment (and focus areas): Trading System Rules, Multilateral Environmental Agreements, and Dispute Settlement Mechanisms; Environmental Protection and the Trading System (trade-related environmental policies; environmental review of trade agreements); Taxes and Other Environmental Requirements (environmental charges and taxes; standards and technical regulations; eco-labeling; packaging and recycling requirements); Transparency of Environmental Trade Actions; Environment and Trade Liberalization (effects of environmental measures on market access; environmental benefits of removing trade restrictions and distortions); Domestically Prohibited Goods (in particular, hazardous waste); Intellectual Property (relevant provisions of the Agreement on Trade-Related Aspects of Intellectual Property Rights); Services (as envisioned in the Decision on Trade in Services and the Environment); The WTO and Other Organizations (relations with intergovernmental and non-governmental organizations).

Key Report: Special Studies 4: Trade and the Environment (an in-depth look at key issues; online).

Annual Report: 2001 report online.

Check Out on the Web: Agenda of the Committee on Trade and Environment (listing the main conclusions reached and the current state of debate; online under "Environment" on the "Trade Topics" webpage).

Established: 1995 **Member Nations:** 142 **HQ:** Geneva, Switzerland **Staff:** 500 **Budget (2000):** $77 million

Contact Info: Geneva, Switzerland; (41-22) 739 51 11; enquiries@wto.org

Key Personnel: Mike Moore (Director-General)

3.1.5 UN-Associated Partnership Programs

304.   Critical Ecosystem Partnership Fund (CEPF) (www.cepf.net)

Description/Mission: A joint initiative seeking to better safeguard developing countries' biodiversity "hotspots" (highly threatened regions) by providing project funding primarily to non-governmental, community and grassroots organizations. Aims to invest at least $150 million over 5 years to advance biodiversity conservation projects in critical ecosystems, seeking to invest in a minimum of 5 hotspots per year. Founded by (see Profiles #35, 305 and 299, respectively): Conservational International (oversees day-to-day Fund management); the Global Environment Facility (provides strategic guidance); the World Bank (provides strategic guidance).

Initial "Hotspot" Focus Areas: Madagascar; West Africa (Ghana; Cote d' Ivoire; Liberia; Guinea; Togo; Sierra Leone); the Vilcabamba-Amboró Corridor (located in Peru and Bolivia).

Contact Info: 1919 M St. NW, Suite 600, Washington, DC 20036; (202) 912-1808; cepf@conservation.org

305.   Global Environment Facility (GEF) (www.gefweb.org)

Description/Mission: A grant-making trust fund established to "forge international cooperation and finance actions to address 4 critical threats to the global environment: biodiversity loss, climate change, degradation of international waters, and ozone depletion" (related work addressing land degradation is also eligible for GEF funding). GEF's $3+ billion project portfolio has served 140+ countries, covering the developing world, Eastern Europe, and the Russian Federation.

Operating/Organizational Structure: Current membership stands at 167 nations (out of 191 recognized nations worldwide). Governed by a Assembly (consisting of all member nations) which meets once every 3 years. A 32-member GEF Council functions as an independent board of directors, while a 40-person Secretariat assists in day-to-day operations. GEF itself is implemented by 3 UN System agencies, namely (see Profiles #290, 291 and 299, respectively): UNDP (responsible for technical assistance, capacity building, and the Small Grants Program for local NGOs); UNEP (responsible for scientific and technical input); the World Bank (acts as the repository for the trust funds; also responsible for investment projects and mobilizing private sector resources).

Programs (and focus areas) (see below for corresponding funding levels): Biodiversity Conservation (GEF serves as the financial mechanism for the Convention on Biological Diversity; projects focus on critical ecosystem types and the human communities found there); Climate Change (GEF serves as the financial mechanism for the UN Framework Convention on Climate Change; project categories include: energy efficiency; renewable energy; low greenhouse gas-emitting energy technologies; sustainable transport); International Waters Protection (project categories: water bodies; integrated land and water projects; contaminants); Ozone Depletion (focuses on phasing-out use of ozone destroying chemicals in the Russian Federation, Eastern Europe, and Central Asia); Land Degradation (focuses on desertification and deforestation projects, in accordance with the UN Convention to Combat Desertification).

Program Funding Levels (1991-1999 totals): Biodiversity Conservation ($991 million directly plus $1.5 billion in co-financing from others); Climate Change ($884 million directly plus $4.7 billion in co-financing); International Waters Protection ($360 million); Ozone Degradation ($155 million); Land Degradation ($350 million, includes co-financing).

Key Publication: Operational Report on GEF Programs (a detailed summary of all work undertaken since the fund's inception in 1991; online under "Map").

Check Out on the Web: "Outreach/Publications" and "Results" (provides a multitude of information on the GEF, including a self-evaluation of its results and identification of "lessons learned").

Established: 1991 **Member Nations:** 167 **HQ:** Washington, DC **Staff:** 40

Contact Info (Secretariat): 1818 H St. NW, Washington, DC 20433; (202) 473-0508; secretariatofgef@worldbank.org

Key Personnel: Mohamed T. El-Ashry (of Egypt) (Chairman and CEO)

Subsection 3.2: Other Multilaterals and Associated Entities

Introduction/User's Guide:

Within this subsection, four selected "other" (i.e., non-UN system) multilaterals of environmental relevance are profiled. In addition, two U.S.-focused groups that serve as the official U.S. affiliate to the multilaterals profiled here are themselves also profiled (namely, the U.S. Council for International Business, which serves as the U.S. affiliate to the International Chamber of Commerce, and the U.S. Energy Association, which serves as the U.S. affiliate to the World Energy Council).

Organizational profiles for this subsection are listed beginning on the next page, presented in alphabetical order.

In terms of individual entry contents, the reader is referred back to the beginning of Section 3 where a descriptive outline of standardized profile information provided is presented.

Subsection 3.2: Other Multilaterals and Associated Entities

306.   International Chamber of Commerce (ICC) (www.iccwbo.org)

Description/Mission: An international business association promoting "an open international trade and investment system and the market economy." Member companies and associations (from 130+ countries) are engaged in international business. Has formal "consultation" status with the United Nations and associated UN family members. Establishes voluntary international business rules and offers arbitration services via its International Court of Arbitration. [NOTE: The U.S. affiliate to the ICC is NOT the U.S. Chamber of Commerce, as one might expect, but rather the U.S. Council for International Business – see Profile #309].

Operating/Organizational Structure: The World Council is the supreme governing body for the ICC and meets semi-annually. World Council members are business executives either named as delegates by their respective national committees (which represent the ICC in their respective countries) or are directly invited if no national committee exists. A 15- to 30-member elected Executive Board (headed by an elected President) is responsible for implementing ICC policy. Various Commissions carry out the bulk of the substantive work, formulating policy and establishing voluntary international business rules. A Secretariat (headed by an appointed Secretary-General) works with the various Commissions to carry out the ICC's overall work program.

Environmental Issues Covered: Energy; Sustainable Development; Climate Change; Water; "BioSociety" (biotechnology); Trade and Environment; Waste Management.

Key Commissions (and activities/focus areas): Commission on Environment (prepare position statements; participate in meetings of the UN Commission on Sustainable Development; enhance its ICC website); Commission on Energy (prepare position statements; study future energy challenges); Commission on International Trade and Investment Policy (provide input into WTO negotiations; track WTO agreements; promote customs modernization and simplification of trade procedures).

Key Working Parties (and focus areas): Working Party on Sustainable Development (Business Action for Sustainable Development – see "key corporate initiatives" below for details); Joint Working Party on Climate Change (international negotiations on the UN Framework Convention for Climate Change); Joint Working Party on BioSociety (develop/manage the Global Roadmap for Modern Biotechnology – a 5-topic roadmap for establishing a "constructive dialogue critical to advancing the biotechnology industry"); Joint Working Party on Trade and Environment; Joint Working Party on Waste Management.

Key Corporate Initiatives: ICC/UNEP Awards (awards to businesses for environmental achievement and sustainable development partnerships); Business Action for Sustainable Development (initiative to create a business network for the 2002 UN Earth Summit); Company Showcase (present the environmental and sustainable development activities of 18 member companies through the ICC website); Global Compact (UN-business compact to uphold a set of core values in the areas of human rights, labor standards and environmental practice).

Founded: 1919 **HQ:** Paris, France

Contact Info (HQ): Paris, France; +33 1 49 53 28 28; webmaster@iccwbo.org

Contact Info (U.S.): See Profile #309 for the U.S. Council for International Business.

Key Personnel: Richard McCormick (President); Maria Livanos Cattaui (Secretary-General)

307.   International Union for Conservation of Nature and Natural Resources (IUCN) – The World Conservation Union (www.iucn.org)

Description/Mission: An international scientific/technical association that promotes and helps prepare/implement conservation and biodiversity strategies worldwide via a partnership bringing together 78 countries/states, 112 governmental agencies, 735 NGOs and some 10,000 scientists and experts from 181 countries. The work of the 10,000 scientists and experts (all of which volunteer their time) is coordinated through 6 separate Commissions (see below).

Operating/Organizational Structure: Technical/scientific work is accomplished through 6 separate Commissions (see below). The 1000-person Global Secretariat facilitates this work as well as implements IUCN policies and Global Programs (see below).

Commissions (and number of members): Protected Areas (1300 members); Species Survival (6800 members); Environmental, Economic and Social Policy (350 members); Ecosystem Management (250 members); Education and Communication (600 members); Environmental Law (550 members).

Global Programs (all focused on conservation/biodiversity): Biodiversity Policy; Climate Change; Economics; Education and Communication; Environmental Law; Forests; Monitoring and Evaluation; Protected Areas; Social Policy; Species Survival; Sustainable Use; Wetlands and Water Resources.

Key Periodicals: World Conservation (magazine; 2-4 times/yr; online).

Key Report: Red List of Threatened Species 2000 (online).

Annual Report: "Progress and Assessment Report for 2000" (online).

Founded: 1948 **HQ:** Gland, Switzerland **Staff:** 1000 **Offices:** In 42 countries **Budget** (2000; approximate U.S. $): $47 million

Funding Sources (2000): Government (80%); Multilaterals (10%); Non-Governmental Organizations (6%); Other (4%).

Contact Info (HQ): Gland, Switzerland; ++41-22-999-0001.

Contact Info (U.S. Multilateral Office): 1630 Connecticut Ave., 3rd Floor, Washington, DC 20009; (202) 518-2047; postmaster@iucnus.org

Key Personnel: Yolanda Kakabadse Navarro (President); Achim Steiner (Director-General); Scott Hajost (Executive Director – U.S. Office)

308. Organization for Economic Cooperation and Development (OECD) (www.oecd.org)

Description/Mission: An international, intergovernmental organization seeking to "help governments tackle the economic, social and governance challenges of a globalized economy." Composed of 30 member countries (representing the leading democratic and developed countries) while also maintaining relationships with some 70 other countries. Addresses a wide range of economic and social issues, grouped into 33 themes (see below for details). Best known for its publications ("documentation," including individual country surveys and reviews) and its statistical data.

Operating/Organizational Structure: Currently comprised of 30 member nations. Governed by a Council (consisting of all member nations) which provides guidance on the work of OECD's committees (which includes an Environmental Policy Committee). An appointed Director-General runs day-to-day operations as head of a Secretariat.

Key Themes Addressed: Agriculture, Food, and Fisheries; Biotechnology; Energy; Environment; Sustainable Development; Transport.

Environmental Focus Areas: Biosafety (focused on biotechnology); Chemical Safety; Climate Change, Energy, and Transport; Economic Policy and the Environment in Developing Countries; Environment and Sustainable Development; Environment in Emerging and Transition Countries; Environmental Impacts of Production and Consumption; Environmental Performance, Indicators, and Outlooks; Environmental Policies and Instruments; Environmental-Social Interface; Natural Resource Management; Sustainable Development, Environment and Development Cooperation; Trade Investment and Environment; Waste.

Key Publications (can fully browse each online, but can't print out): OECD Environmental Outlook (provides economy-based projections of environmental pressures and changes in the state of the environment through 2020); OECD Environmental Performance Reviews – Achievements in OECD Countries: No. 2 (peer reviews of environmental progress in each OECD country); Sustainable Development: Critical Issues; Environmentally-Related Taxes in OECD Countries: Issues and Strategies.

Annual Report: 2001 report online.

Check Out on the Web: Environmentally-Related Taxes Database (details environmentally-related taxes, fees, and charges levied in OECD member nations); Biotech Product Database (database of products derived using modern biotechnology and approved for commercial use in OECD member nations); BioTrack (database of field trials of genetically modified organisms).

Established: 1961 **Member Nations:** 30 **HQ:** Paris, France

Contact Info (HQ): Paris, France; +33 1.45.24.82.00; news.contact@oecd.org

Contact Info (U.S.): 2001 L St. NW, Suite 650, Washington, DC 20036; (202) 785-6323; washington.contact@oecd.org

Key Personnel: Donald J. Johnston (of Canada) (Secretary-General)

309. United States Council for International Business (USCIB) (www.uscib.org)

Description/Mission: A U.S.-based business council serving as the official U.S. affiliate of the International Chamber of Commerce (see Profile #306). Founded in 1945 to promote an open world trading system. Facilitates international trade through harmonization of commercial practices. Has an active membership base of 300+ multinational corporations, business associations, and law firms.

A Closer Look: Bills itself as "among the premiere pro-trade, pro-market liberalization organizations."

Operating/Organizational Structure: Maintains 50+ specialized policy committees and working groups, including an Environment Committee.

Environment Committee Activities: Promotes environmental trade and investment initiatives through the WTO, OECD, NAFTA and other regional initiatives; monitors the activities of the OECD; participates in the UN Commission on Sustainable Development (see Profile #288; maintains an Environmental Labeling Working Group.

Founded: 1945 **Members:** 300 companies and orgs **Staff:** 45 **Budget:** $7 million

Contact Info (HQ): 1212 Avenue of the Americas, New York, NY 10036; (212) 354-4480; info@uscib.org

Contact Info (DC): 1030 15th St. NW, Suite 800, Washington, DC 20005; (202) 371-1316.

Key Personnel: Thomas M.T. Niles (President); Norine Kennedy (V.P. for Environmental Affairs)

310. United States Energy Association (USEA) (www.usea.org)

Description/Mission: A mixed membership association that serves as the official U.S. Member Committee of the World Energy Council (see Profile #311). The USEA's work is focused on energy resource development and use both domestically and especially abroad. USEA members include: energy companies, manufacturers and trade associations; professional societies; governmental entities (including the U.S. Dept. of Energy); universities and research institutions.

A Closer Look: The USEA is nearly completed funded by government grants (see its revenue breakdown below). Budget-wise, its primary activity is organizing and conducting seminars and international exchange visits.

Major Initiatives (and activities/focus areas): Energy Partnerships (75 "cooperative partnerships" between U.S. orgs and counterparts in developing/transitional countries; seeks to convey U.S. experiences and business / regulatory practices abroad; focus areas: petroleum exploration, production, and transportation; natural gas distribution; electric power production, transmission, distribution, and utilization); National Energy Policy (issues an annual statement on national energy policy); Energy Efficiency (cosponsors an annual policy forum); Global Climate Change (focuses on emissions reductions in developing countries); Regulation/Restructuring (manages cooperative partnerships between U.S. regulatory commissions and similar agencies in other countries); Energy Trade (promotes exports of energy sector goods and services); Industry Recognition (awards program); Training (for various countries); Conference Organization (for various conferences).

Key Committees: Energy Efficiency; Global Climate Change; Energy Trade.

Annual Report: 2000 report online.

Founded: 1930 **Members:** 160 companies and orgs **Staff:** 30 **NP Status:** 501(c)(3) **Revenue/Expenses (2000):** $8.8/$8.7 million

Revenue (2000): Contributions (1%); Government Grants (93%); Program Service Revenues (3%); Other (3%).

Expenses (2000): Program Services (90%; for: organize/conduct seminars and exchange visits with federal agencies –84%; meetings and reports –4%; World Energy Council activities –2%); Management and General (10%); Fundraising (0%).

Contact Info: 1300 Pennsylvania Ave., Suite 550, Washington, DC 20004; (202) 312-1230.

Key Personnel: Barry Worthington (Executive Director)

<u>**The World Conservation Union**</u> (www.iucn.org)
See Profile # 307 for the "International Union for Conservation of Nature and Natural Resources (IUCN)".

311.   <u>World Energy Council (WEC)</u> (www.worldenergy.org)

Description/Mission: A non-governmental, international council focused on energy resource development and use worldwide. WEC membership consists of autonomous country Member Committees, whose members reflect a range of local and national energy companies and organizations. The U.S. Member Committee is the U.S. Energy Association (see Profile #310).

Operating/Organizational Structure: Currently comprised of 95 autonomous country Member Committees. Governed by a Council (consisting of all Member Committees) which meets annually in an Executive Assembly to provide guidance on the WEC's Work Programme. The Work Programme is carried out through two Standing Committees – a Programme Committee (consisting of both Technical and Regional Programmes; the latter focused on: Africa, Asia, Europe, and Latin America/the Caribbean) and a Studies Committee (focused on policy studies). A Secretary-General runs day-to-day operations as head of a 12-person Secretariat, while 4 Regional Coordinators carry out the work of the Regional Programmes.

A Closer Look: The WEC was incorporated as a public charity in the UK in 2001.

Associated Orgs: WEC Services Limited (a private company serving as a trading subsidiary of the WEC); WEC Foundation (a charitable fund used to help finance WEC's Studies, Technical, and Regional Programmes).

Technical Programme Sub-Groups (and activities/focus areas): Performance of Generating Plants Committee (collection and analysis of power plant performance data); Cleaner Fossil Fuels Systems Committee (promotes such fuels/systems); Survey of Energy Resources (conducts periodic worldwide surveys); Survey of Energy Efficiency Policies (focuses on indicator trend analysis and identification of "best practices"); Greenhouse Gas Reduction Projects (an industry initiative to establish a world-wide inventory of projects reducing greenhouse gas emissions); Committee on Renewables (promotes use of biomass-, wind-, solar-, geothermal-, and hydro-based energy as well as utilization of industrial waste heat as an energy source).

Key Publication: WEC Survey of Energy Resources (periodic report based on a worldwide survey).

Annual Report: 2000 report online.

Check Out on the Web: Energy Data Center (a nation-based database of descriptive and statistical energy data collected by the WEC; provides information on energy reserves, production capacity, consumption, and emissions; energy efficiency indicators are also available for 29 countries).

Established: 1924 **HQ:** London, UK **Staff:** 12 **Budget** (Work Programme only; approx. U.S. $): $0.65 million

Contact Info (HQ): London, UK; (+44 20) 7734 5996; info@worldenergy.org

Contact Info (U.S.): See Profile #310 for the U.S. Energy Association.

Key Personnel: Antonio del Rosario (Chairman); Gerald Doucet (of Canada) (Secretary-General)

SECTION 4: POLITICAL ORGANIZATIONS

INTRODUCTION/USER'S GUIDE:

In this section, 6 key political organizations of environmental relevance are profiled, divided into the following two subsections:

      4.1 – Political Parties   (4 entries)

      4.2 – Other Political Groups   (2 entries)

In terms of individual entry contents, a descriptive outline of standardized profile information provided for each organization listed is given at the beginning of each subsection.

Subsection 4.1: Political Parties

Introduction/User's Guide:

Within this subsection, profiles are provided of the two major political parties (Democratic and Republican), along with two key "third parties" that actively "weigh in" (on relatively opposite ends of the spectrum) on environmental issues (namely, the Green and Libertarian Parties).

The profiles provided focus on each Party's official 2000 Party Platform (as presented on their respective websites), examining in particular their stated positions on environmental issues.

In terms of individual entry contents, the following is a detailed outline of standardized information provided for each political party listed within this section (please note that the exact contents provided varies by organization, being dependant upon applicability and/or availability):

[Profile #] Party Name (Website Address)
Slogan: As adopted/used by the Party.
Description: A short summary of the Party, focusing on its governing structure.
Elected Positions Held/Registered Voters: Provided for the two listed "third parties" (Green and Libertarian) to give perspective on their relative standing compared to the two major parties (Democratic and Republican).
A Closer Look: Providing further information on the Party, principally in terms of additional relevant facts and/or a closer examination of the Party and its viewpoints/general outlook.
Key Party Principles/Values: As obtained from the Party's website.
2000 Party Platform: Summarizing key portions of the Party's official platform as adopted at their 2000 national convention, focusing on the Platform's stated environmental principles/positions.
Check Out on the Web: Listing website related content that particularly stand out ("worth a look").
Founded: Beginning year specified
Contact Info: Providing: Street/mailing address; general telephone number; general email address (if established/available).
Key Personnel: Noting the name of the Party's current Chairman.

Organizational profiles for this subsection are listed beginning on the next page.

A Closer Look:

Given the current Republican administration, the Republican Party entry is likely of most interest, as its 2000 Party Platform was obviously influenced/molded by now-President Bush and thus would be expected to largely reflect his overall views and intended political agenda.

In addition, the Libertarian Party entry is also of potential interest, given that general libertarian ideology is behind a significant portion of the organizations/entities profiled under the "Opposing Views" section of this Guide (Section 6).

Subsection 4.1: Political Parties

312.   **Democratic Party (Democratic National Committee)** (www.democrats.org)

Description: National political party founded by Thomas Jefferson. The Democratic National Committee – consisting of about 450 Party members, including 13 elected officers – serves as the governing structure for the Party.

2000 Party Platform – Key Environmental Issues/Positions: Everglades restoration; protecting the Florida and California coasts and the Artic National Wildlife Refuge from oil and gas drilling; preserving untouched forests from logging and development; ending ocean disposal of contaminated dredge spoils; improving auto fuel efficiency and energy efficiency; cleaning up aging power plants; rebuilding and improving transportation infrastructure and diversifying transportation sources; instituting cleaner auto fuels and cleaner trucks and buses; nuclear waste disposal; ratifying the Kyoto greenhouse gas emissions Protocols.

Check Out on the Web: 2000 Democratic National Platform (the official agenda for the national party).

Founded: 1792

Contact Info: 430 S. Capitol St. SE, Washington, DC 20003; (202) 863-8000.

Key Personnel: Terry McAuliffe (Party Chairman)

313.   **Republican Party (Republican National Committee)** (www.rnc.org)

Description: National political party founded in the mid-1850's by anti-slavery activists. The Republican National Committee serves as the governing structure for the Party.

Key Party Principles: Individuals, not government, can make the best decisions; decisions are best made close to home; all people are entitled to equal rights.

2000 Party Platform – Key Environmental Principles: Economic prosperity and environmental protection must advance together, with prosperity giving the wherewithal to advance environmental protection; government's main role is to provide market-based incentives to meet/exceed environmental standards; environmental regulations should be based on the best science, peer-reviewed and made publicly available; environmental policy should focus on achieving results, not crafting bureaucratic processes; government should undertake consistent enforcement of environmental standards; government should work cooperatively to ensure that environmental policy meets the particular needs of geographic regions and localities; states and localities should be provided with flexibility, authority and finality to deal with environmental concerns.

2000 Party Platform – Key Environmental Issues (and associated positions): Brownfields/Superfund (seek voluntary-based cleanups); Endangered Species Act (seek to add market incentives to the program); Global Warming (scrap the Kyoto Protocol, which is viewed as ineffective, unfair and not based on the best science; conduct more research on causes/impacts of global warming); Property Rights (protect such rights based on the view that "environmental stewardship has best advanced where property is privately held"; seek to enforce the "takings clause" of the 5th Amendment); Public Lands (provide greater state and local roles in both decision-making and land management; make national parks accessible to all; preserve access to public lands for multiple uses; promote sustainable forest management in place of no growth policies "because so many people in rural America rely on public forest for their livelihood"); Agriculture (fight the European Union's import restrictions of U.S. crops and livestock; pledge to exempt food exports from any new trade sanctions; support biotech and biomass research; support the ethanol tax credit; protect farmers access to safe "crop protection products" [i.e., pesticides]; adopt water quality standards based on best science to address hypoxia and runoff issues); Energy (increase domestic supplies of fossil fuels; provide tax incentives for energy production; seek oil and natural gas on federal lands, including the Artic National Wildlife Refuge; advance clean coal technology; maintain the ethanol tax credit; expand renewable energy resource tax credits; provide tax incentives for residential solar power); Transportation (support intercity passenger rail systems and development of a national high-speed rail system; give states and localities flexibility to set their own transportation priorities).

2000 Party Platform – Key Regulatory Reform Principles: Make sound science – with peer-reviewed risk assessments and full disclosure – the basic for regulation; target the most serious risks; require periodic review of existing regulations; require agency disclosure of costs to consumers and small businesses of proposed regulations; require a "regulatory budget" that explains the likely costs for meeting regulatory requirements; use cost/benefit analysis for evaluating regulations; retrain civil servants to work with people affected by regulation; withdraw certain Executive Orders issued by the Clinton Administration.

Check Out on the Web: Republican Platform 2000 (the official agenda for the national party); The Republican Oath (core general beliefs of Party members).

Founded: 1854

Contact Info: 310 1st St., SE, Washington, DC 20003, (202) 863-8500; info@rnc.org

Key Personnel: Jim Gilmore (Party Chairman)

314.   Green Party of the U.S. (Association of State Green Parties) (www.gpus.org)

Slogan: "Building a more democratic society."

Description: National political party most well-known for nominating Ralph Nader for President in 2000.

Elected Positions Held: Green Party members currently hold 120+ elected local-level positions in 20+ states.

A Closer Look: Although commonly thought of (based on its name) as the "environmental" party, the Green Party's platform actually covers a wide range of social issues, while "environmentalism" is but one of 10 stated key values (see below).

Key Party Values: Respect for Diversity; Social Justice; Grassroots Democracy; Feminism; Community-Based Economics (encouraging employee ownership and workplace democracy); Decentralization; Environmentalism ("ecological wisdom"); Nonviolence; Personal and Global Responsibility; Future Focus (long-term thinking).

2000 Party Platform – Issues Addressed: Democracy; Social Justice and Equal Opportunity; Environmental Sustainability (focus areas: energy policy; nuclear issues; waste management; fossil fuels; renewable energy; transportation policy; clean air/ greenhouse effect/ ozone depletion; land use; water; agriculture; biological diversity); Economic Sustainability.

Check Out on the Web: Green Party Platform – 2000 (the official agenda for the national party).

Founded: 1996

Contact Info: PO Box 18452, Washington, DC 20036; (202) 232-0335; capeconn@attbi.com

315.   Libertarian Party (www.lp.org)

Slogan: "The party of principle."

Description: National political party that bills itself as "America's largest and most successful third party." Party beliefs are deeply rooted in both individual rights (especially property rights) and free market capitalism. An 18-member elected National Committee serves as the governing structure for the Party.

Elected Positions Held: Libertarian Party members currently hold about 500+ elected local-level positions in 44 states and 1 elected state-level position (a New York State Supreme Court judge).

Registered Voters: About 225,000 voters are registered as Libertarian (less than 0.2% of all 156 million registered voters overall).

A Closer Look: The basic philosophy of the Libertarian Party/libertarians in general might be most accurately characterized as "freedom and free enterprise taken to the extreme" – the rights of the individual are held paramount (the Party holds that "all individuals have the right to live in whatever manner they chose, so long as they do not forcibly interfere with the equal right of others to live in whatever manner they chose"), while the "free market" is held in similar high esteem (the Party calling for the elimination of all government regulation and all government taxes and subsidies, while also calling for privatization of all public/social services). As a result, government in general is not held in very high esteem (being referred to as "the cult of the omnipresent state" in the 2000 Party Platform) and the Party seeks to largely abolish it (see the "2000 Party Platform" entry below), leaving essentially only the police and court system for law enforcement (which would be specifically focused on just criminal and contractual law) and a sharply reduced military maintained strictly for national defense purposes only. "Governance" would instead be provided though the free market and the legal system based on private property rights and full/strict liability laws.

Key Party Principles: Government must not violate the three basic rights of individuals, namely the: 1) right to life, 2) right to liberty of speech and action, and 3) right to property; Oppose all government inference in the areas of voluntary and contractual relations among individuals – individuals should be free to deal with one another as free traders in a free market.

2000 Party Platform – Key Environmental Positions: Completely abolish relevant federal governmental agencies – including the EPA, BLM, USFS, BOR, Ag Dept., DOE, NRC, DOT; end all government subsidies and taxes; sell off/transfer all public lands to private ownership (including National Parks and wilderness and recreation areas); privatize public utilities (energy, water, sewage, etc.); replace the existing bureaucratic system with a "super-free" market system based on private property rights and full/strict liability laws (whereby pollution of another's property would be dealt with as a violation of individual rights, subject to legal action, with property rights defined for water and air).

2000 Party Platform – Other Notable Positions: Repeal all laws dealing with "victimless crimes" (drugs, prostitution, gambling, etc.) and gun control; repeal all taxes; eliminate all government subsidies; lift all trade barriers; repeal all consumer protection and OSHA worker safety and health legislation/regulation; eliminate zoning laws and building codes; end government-provided health insurance and care; privatize currently-public schools and colleges; withdraw from the UN, the World Bank and the IMF; privatize NASA.

Check Out on the Web: National Platform – 2000 (the official agenda for the national party).

Founded: 1971

Contact Info: 2600 Virginia Ave. NW, Suite 100, Washington, DC 20037; (202) 333-0008; hq@lp.org

Key Personnel: James W. Lark (Party Chairman)

Subsection 4.2: Other Political Groups

Introduction/User's Guide:

Within this subsection, profiles are provided for two key political groups – the "New Democrats" / Democratic Leadership Council and Republicans for Environmental Protection. These groups were included in this Guide as they each present views/visions that differ from their respective mainstream counterparts. (The League of Conservation Voters is also cross-listed under this section, but, as a "watchdog" group, its full entry is included within Subsection 1.2 – "Public Interest Groups and Coalitions.")

Organizational profiles for this subsection are listed beginning on the next page, arranged in alphabetical order. In terms of individual entry contents, the standardized format adopted for Section 1 ("Environmental Non-Governmental Organizations") was utilized (for further details on that format, the reader is referred back to the beginning of Section 1).

Subsection 4.2: Other Political Groups

316.   New Democrats / Democratic Leadership Council (DLC) (www.ndol.org)

Description/Mission: "New Democrats" is the term applied to a subset of Democrats seeking to reform ("modernize") Democratic Party policies and programs. The Democratic Leadership Council is the founding organization for the movement and seeks to advance the New Democrat agenda through a national network of elected officials and community leaders as well as though its affiliated think tank – the Progressive Policy Institute. Past DLC chairs include former President Bill Clinton, House Minority Leader Richard Gephardt and Senator Joseph Lieberman.

A Closer Look: New Democrat policies seek to define a "Third Way" for governing by "adopting enduring progressive values to the new challenges of the information age." Examples put forth of New Democrat ideas include national service, work-based welfare reform, charter schools, community policing, an expanded earned-income tax credit, and market incentives for environmental protection.

Lobbying/Political Activities: Registered lobbyist under the LDA.

New Democrat Orgs: Democratic Leadership Council (the founding organization); Progressive Policy Institute (the DLC's affiliated think tank); House New Democrat Coalition (a group of 74 moderate, pro-growth House members); Senate New Democrat Coalition (a group of 19 moderate, pro-growth Senate members); New Democrat Network (a PAC for New Democrats; not formally affiliated with the DLC).

Environmental Issues: Second Generation Policy (a proposed new policy approach – seeking to modernize regulation using performance-based, market-oriented and civic-minded strategies to drive continuous and efficient improvement); Climate Change; Natural Resources; Sprawl; Energy; Trade; Civic Solutions ("civic environmentalism").

Periodicals: The New Democrat (bimonthly magazine); Blueprint: Ideas for a New Century (policy journal).

Check Out on the Web: The Hyde Park Declaration (a statement of New Democrat principles and a broad national policy agenda for the next decade).

Founded: 1985

Contact Info: 600 Pennsylvania Ave. SE, Suite 400, Washington, DC 20003; (202) 546-0007.

Key Personnel: Senator Evan Bayh [D-IN] (Chairman)

317.   REP America / Republicans for Environmental Protection (www.repamerica.org)

Slogan: "The environmental conscious of the GOP."

Description/Mission: An independent, grassroots organization promoting more centrist views/approaches regarding environmental issues within the Republican Party. Republicans for Environmental Protection is REP America's separate political action network.

Basic Activities: Public education; advocacy; research.

Environmental Issues: National Forests; Oceans; Wetlands; Global Climate Change; Energy; "Takings"; Federal Public Lands.

Periodicals: The Green Elephant (quarterly newsletter; partially online).

Unique: Biennial "Heroes and Zeros" Awards (honoring/deriding specific Republican members of Congress).

Check Out on the Web: "Policy Papers" section (all online); the book "The Making of a Conservative Environmentalist" by REP America member Gordon K. Durnil.

Founded: 1995 **Staff:** 5 **State Chapters:** 34 **NP Status:** 501(c)(3) (REP America); 501(c)(4) (Republicans for Environmental Protection)

Contact Info: PO Box 7073, Deerfield IL 60015; (847) 940-0320; marREP@aol.com

Key Personnel: Jim Scarantino (Executive Director)

League of Conservation Voters (LCV) (www.lcv.org)

See Profile #73 within Subsection 1.2 – "Public Interest Groups and Coalitions."

SECTION 5: OTHER INTERESTED PARTIES

INTRODUCTION/USER'S GUIDE:

In this section, two sets of "other interested parties" – namely business- and labor-related groups – that can (and do) "weigh in" on environmental issues are profiled, divided into the following two subsections:

      5.1 – Business Trade Associations, Coalitions/Councils and Related Entities   (81 entries)

      5.2 – Labor Unions   (8 entries)

In terms of individual entry contents, a descriptive outline of standardized profile information provided for each type of organization listed is given at the beginning of each subsection.

Subsection 5.1: Business Trade Associations, Coalitions/Councils and Related Entities

Introduction/User's Guide:

Within this subsection, 81 profiles are provided covering a range of business trade associations, coalitions, councils, and related entities that can (and do) "weigh in" on environmental issues. (For purposes of this Guide, "business/business groups" includes traditional manufacturing/industrial operations, commercial businesses, and other related operations/entities such as utilities, farming/agriculture, and construction/land development.) (Note: Business groups and coalitions that work in a relatively progressive fashion on environmental issues are separately profiled in Section 1.3 – "Progressive Business Groups and Coalitions.")

The bulk of the entries included within this subsection consist of organizations/entities comprised solely of business interests, with the following notable exceptions:

- Four energy-focused coalition groups listed include some non-business members (both the American Coal Foundation and the Coalition for Affordable and Reliable Energy include labor union members, while both the National Hydrogen Association and the Nuclear Energy Institute include universities and other research centers as members).

- The Chemical Industry Institute of Toxicology is technically an independent research institute, but is openly funded by business interests; hence it is included within this subsection.

- The American Forest Foundation (and its affiliated Institutes for Journalism and Natural Resources program), while nominally presenting itself as an independent organization and being the recipient of some limited funding from federal governmental agencies, is primarily backed by business – specifically paper and timber/wood products interests – including maintaining a "historic and continuing relationship" with the American Forest and Paper Association (a business trade group) that involves using AFPA employees and facilities. Hence the AFF is included within this subsection.

- The Greening Earth Society, while nominally presenting itself as an independent organization, was founded by the Western Fuels Association (which retains a leadership position within the Society) and formally partners with the National Mining Association. Furthermore, the Society is reportedly financed by coal-based utilities. Hence the GES is included within this subsection.

In terms of individual entry contents, the following is a descriptive outline of standardized profile information provided for each organization listed within this subsection (please note that the exact contents provided varies by organization, being dependant upon applicability and/or availability):

[Profile #] Organization Name (Website Address)
A Top Federal Lobbying Group Per Fortune Magazine's Annual Survey: Noted as applicable with the organization's ranking for 2001 specified.
Description: A short summary of the organization, particularly in regards to its membership makeup and extent (for example, "Represents 500 companies with a combined 80% market share").
A Closer Look: Providing further information on the organization, principally in terms of additional relevant facts and/or – in select cases – a critical examination of the organization itself.
Lobbying/Political Activities: Included if the organization is registered as a federal lobbyist under the Lobbying Disclosure Act (LDA) and/or maintains a Political Action Committee (PAC) with the name of the PAC specified.
Key Members: Listing both individual companies (those with well-known names are typically noted) as well as any business group profiled within this subsection.
Key Issues/Initiatives (and the org's activities/positions/viewpoints): Generally based on information obtained from the organization's website.
Key Reports/Publications: Listing specific reports and other publications judged to represent "essential reading" for interested parties, and noting if they are available online at the organization's website. (A summary listing of all such reports/publications is also provided in Appendix B.)

Associated Websites: Listing distinct websites separate from the organization's main website, along with a short description and corresponding web address (URL).

Website Notes: Significant notes concerning the organization's website – navigating hints, content notes, etc.

Check Out on the Web: Listing website related content/features that particularly stand out ("worth a look").

Founded: Beginning year specified **Membership:** Noted if figures made available **Staff:** Overall staffing level

Budget: As obtained from non-IRS sources of information (website, other reference material, etc.)

The following is also included if the organization is a (501(c)(3))-exempt non-profit:

NP Status: Formal IRS non-profit status **Revenue/Expenses:** Overall figures as obtained from IRS submittals

Revenue: Providing a percentage breakdown based on IRS submittals (IRS Form 990). Categories considered: Contributions (non-governmental public support from individuals, foundations, businesses, etc.); Government Grants; Program Service Revenues; Other (a variety of miscellaneous sources including: membership dues; investment income; special events; inventory sales [typically publications]).

Expenses: Providing a percentage breakdown based on IRS submittals (IRS Form 990). Categories considered: Program Services (broken down by specific program/service when available); Management and General (administration and overhead expenses); Fundraising.

Affiliated Orgs: Noted as applicable; based on IRS submittals and other sources (website, etc.).

Key Personnel: Typically citing the name and title of the chief paid executive (President, Executive Director, etc.), along with the total financial compensation they receive per IRS submittals (IRS Form 990).

Organizational profiles for this subsection are listed in alphabetical order following this introductory material..

A Closer Look – Federal Lobbying Efforts:

21 of the business groups profiled within this subsection are listed in Fortune magazine's annual survey as top federal lobbying groups for 2001, indicating their relatively strong ability to influence general policymaking at the federal level (for comparative purposes, only one environmental public interest group – the Sierra Club at #52 – was included in the Fortune list for 2001). The specific business groups and their corresponding Fortune survey ranking positions are as follows (for reference, a total of 87 organizations were listed by Fortune for 2001):

Alliance of Automobile Manufacturers (AAM): #58   Business Roundtable: #26

American Chemistry Council (ACC): #85   Edison Electric Institute (EEI): #51

American Electronics Association (AeA): #60   National Association of Home Builders (NAHB): #11

American Farm Bureau Federation (AFB): #15   National Association of Manufacturers (NAM): #10

American Forest and Paper Association (AFPA): #63   National Association of Realtors (NAR): #9

American Hospital Association (AHA): #13   National Automobile Dealers Association (NADA): #39

American Petroleum Institute (API): #35   National Federation of Independent Businesses (NFIB): #3

American Trucking Associations (ATA): #30   National Rural Electric Cooperative Association (NREC): #54

Associated Builders and Contractors (ABC): #40   Nuclear Energy Institute (NEI): #80

Associated General Contractors of America (AGC): #47   U.S. Chamber of Commerce: #7

Biotechnology Industry Organization (BIO): #76

Unfortunately, many of the above groups take a decidedly adversarial and "hard-nosed," aggressive approach in dealing with environmental public interest groups in particular and relevant environmental issues in general (especially regarding gov't regulations), based primarily on "bottom-line" economic considerations (see below).

A Closer Look – General Positions Taken By Business Trade Groups

In examining the specific positions taken on environmental issues by the business trade groups profiled in this subsection, two fundamental stances clearly emerge, namely that such groups generally:

- Oppose government regulations affecting its members (particularly proposed new regulations).

- Support programs offering business opportunities for its members (for example, government funding programs for building municipal water and wastewater treatment facilities are generally strongly supported by construction industry trade groups).

These basic stances can be readily explained by considering that the overall motivation of business trade groups is to adopt positions in the best "business interest" for their member firms, where "business interest" is defined in financial ("bottom line") terms. Under such an outlook, environmental regulations are generally viewed as simply a "cost" to business, a cost that business seeks to minimize (as it does with other cost items).

In place of government regulations (or similar mandates), business trade groups frequently put forth two general alternatives:

- Market-based programs that provide financial incentives to achieve intended goals.

- Cooperative public-private partnerships that involve voluntary participation by businesses.

In areas where regulatory control is already well-established, business trade groups generally seek:

- "National uniformity" whereby regulations are set at the national level and uniformly applied throughout the country. Such national uniformity is often sought by businesses to avoid the problems associated with differing sets of regulations applying in differing states and/or localities. (On the other hand, when national regulations are proposed covering areas previously unregulated, business trade groups frequently oppose such regulation, based on the argument that it should be left up to individual states and localities – rather than the federal government – to establish such regulations).

- A cooperative approach to enforcement, de-emphasizing the use of fines and other penalties.

A Closer Look – Key Concerns Cited By Business Trade Groups

Business trade groups tend to focus on three areas of concern related to the general policy-/decision-making process employed by government, namely:

- The cost of regulatory compliance to businesses (often also framed in terms of the potential ultimate cost(s) to consumers). This concern is typically accompanied by a call for mandatory full cost-benefit analysis prior to any new rulemaking.

- The need to consider risk in policy-/decision-making (particularly in terms of calling for use of comparative risk assessment studies to establish priorities in addressing various potential concerns).

- The need for the use of "sound science" in policy-/decision-making.

While appearing quite reasonable and relatively straightforward on the surface, the above three areas actually represent highly contentious issues in practice. Economic and risk analyses (particularly cost-benefit analysis and comparative risk assessments) are controversial as they are each subject to relatively large uncertainties and variability in calculation, while "sound" science can involve a relatively subjective evaluation that does not always take into account the general nature of science as a whole and scientists in particular (that is, the relatively cautious, critical and non-absolute nature of scientists, whom typically provide only qualified answers to questions – particularly to non-scientists – thus tending to leave the impression that many issues remain open to vigorous debate within the scientific community when such is not necessarily the case).

As such, critics/observers note that these three areas of concern potentially can represent a convenient means for business (as well as non-business) groups to consistently question and/or downplay raised environmental concerns (as well as potential solutions to address such concerns), rather than actually serving as part of a legitimate priority-setting framework. Such potentially disingenuous usage is of particular concern with respect to the non-business "opposing view" groups identified in Section 6 of this Guide (see that section for further details).

Subsection 5.1: Business Trade Associations, Coalitions/Councils and Related Entities

318.   Alliance of Automobile Manufacturers (AAM) (www.autoalliance.org)

A Top Federal Lobbying Group Per Fortune Magazine's Annual Survey: Ranking for 2001: #58

Description: Trade alliance representing 13 new car and light truck manufacturers which, in turn, collectively account for 90+% of U.S. vehicle sales (one major manufacturer notably absent from AAM is Honda). AAM essentially replaced the American Automobile Manufacturers Association, which ceased operations in 2000.

A Closer Look: Despite the obvious impacts of the auto industry on the environment, relatively very little information is provided on the AAM website regarding environmental issues. Overall, however, AAM's general viewpoint is perhaps best expressed by one of their five stated fundamental goals: "To promote market-based, cost-effective solutions in preference to mandates on public policy issues."

Lobbying/Political Activities: Registered lobbyist under the LDA.

Key Issues (and AAM's positions): Auto Fuel Efficiency Standards (staunchly opposes increasing CAFE standards; favors consumer tax incentives instead).

Check Out on the Web: "Advanced Technology" section (provides information on alternative fuel, hybrid, electric and fuel cell vehicles).

319.   Alliance for Energy and Economic Growth (www.yourenergyfuture.org)

Description: A recently-formed (5/01) coalition of 500+ energy users and providers (the latter being mostly small groups) promoting an increased supply of traditional energy sources (i.e., fossil fuels and nuclear power).

A Closer Look: The Alliance clearly appears to have been formed to promote the Bush Administration's proposed National Energy Policy released in 5/01 – the same time that the Alliance was formed. The Alliance claims that "nothing less than our quality of life is at stake" if such energy policy reform is not implemented. While nominally acknowledging the benefits of increased efficiency and conservation, no representatives from renewable energy / energy efficiency groups are part of the Alliance.

Key Business Trade Group Members (see separate profiles for each within this subsection): Alliance of Automobile Manufacturers; Aluminum Association; American Chemistry Council; American Farm Bureau Federation; American Forest and Paper Association; American Gas Association; American Iron and Steel Institute; American Petroleum Institute; American Plastics Council; Associated Builders and Contractors; Associated General Contractors; Association of Home Appliance Manufacturers; Business Roundtable; Coalition for Affordable and Reliable Energy; Edison Electric Institute; Electronics Industry Alliance; National Association of Manufacturers; National Electrical Manufacturers Association; National Mining Association; National Petrochemical and Refiners Association; Nuclear Energy Institute; Rubber Manufacturers Association; U.S. Chamber of Commerce.

Key Labor Union Members (see separate profile within Subsection 5.2 – "Labor Unions"): United Mine Workers of America.

320.   Alliance for Understandable, Sensible and Accountable Government Rules (www.allianceusa.org)

Description: An alliance of 1000+ businesses and trade associations established to "promote an open, sensible and accountable federal regulatory process." The Alliance supports legislative reforms "which would inject common sense into the federal rulemaking process," including requiring cost-benefit analyses and risk assessments for major rules.

A Closer Look: The Alliance's website is officially sponsored by the Business Roundtable (see Profile #342) and provides web-links to prominent conservative/libertarian "opposing view" think tanks, namely: Cato Institute, Competitive Enterprise Institute, Heartland Institute, Heritage Foundation, and Reason Public Policy Institute (see separate profiles for each within Section 6 – "Opposing View Groups").

Key Business Trade Group Members (see separate profiles for each within this subsection): Aluminum Association; American Chemistry Council; American Farm Bureau Federation; American Forest and Paper Association; American Iron and Steel Institute; American Petroleum Institute; American Plastics Council; American Trucking Associations; Associated Builders and Contractors; Business Roundtable; Edison Electric

Institute; Electronics Industry Alliance; Grocery Manufacturers of America; National Association of Manufacturers; National Electrical Manufacturers Association; National Federation of Independent Businesses; National Petrochemical and Refiners Association; U.S. Chamber of Commerce.

321.   Aluminum Association (AA) (www.aluminum.org)

Description: Trade association representing producers of primary and secondary aluminum ("secondary" meaning recycled) and semi-fabricated aluminum products. Member companies operate 200 plants in 27 states.

Facts and Figures: The top markets for the aluminum industry are transportation, beverage cans and other packaging, and infrastructure. The industry is a major user of electricity, with an annual energy bill of $2 billion. Recycling, however, saves almost 95% of the energy needed to produce virgin aluminum. In 1998, 1/3 of the total U.S. aluminum supply was from recycled aluminum while 64 of the 102 billion aluminum cans produced were recycled.

Lobbying/Political Activities: Registered lobbyist under the LDA.

Key Issues (and AA's positions): Energy Usage; Perfluorocarbon (PFC) Emissions from Aluminum Smelting (PFCs being potent greenhouse gases); Recycling Programs (supports market-based incentives while opposing government mandates).

Founded: 1933 **Members:** 62 companies **Staff:** 30 **Budget:** $5 to 10 million

American Automobile Manufacturers Association

See Profile #318 for the "Alliance of Automobile Manufacturers."

322.   American Bioenergy Association (ABA) (www.biomass.org)

Description: Trade association representing the U.S. biomass industry (which includes production of power, transportation fuels and chemicals from biomass).

Key Issues (and ABA's activities/positions): Federal Research Program (monitors DOE's R&D budget for biomass power and biofuels); Production Tax Credit (promoting extension and expansion of existing tax credits for biomass); Biomass Ethanol Oxygenate (seeks inclusion of biomass in a renewable fuels standard).

323.   American Chemistry Council (ACC) (www.americanchemistry.com)

A Top Federal Lobbying Group Per Fortune Magazine's Annual Survey: Ranking for 2001: #85

Description: The primary trade association for the chemical industry; formerly known as the Chemical Manufacturers Association (CMA). Has 190 members which collectively produce 90% of the world's supply of basic industrial chemicals.

A Closer Look: ACC is particularly known for founding and coordinating the "Responsible Care"® program – a voluntary environmental, health and safety initiative which critics have characterized as just a public relations campaign originally launched in response to release of industrial toxic emissions data under the USEPA's Toxics Release Inventory (TRI) program.

Lobbying/Political Activities: Registered lobbyist under the LDA.

Key Corporate Members: Many " household names" including: 3M; BASF; Calgon; DuPont; Dow; Eastman Kodak; General Electric Plastics; Exxon; Procter and Gamble.

Key Issues/Initiatives (and activities/focus areas): Long-Term Research Initiative (a $100 million, 5-year health and environmental research effort related to chemical use; much of the research is to be conducted by the Chemical Industry Institute of Toxicology – see below); High Production Volume Chemical Challenge (a USEPA-coordinated effort to conduct environmental and health screening tests on 2800 high-production chemicals by 2004); Endocrine Disruption Research.

Key Report (online under "Responsible Care"): Responsible Care Progress Report.

Key Affiliated Orgs/Websites (and activities/focus areas): Chorine Chemistry Council (c3.org; promotes chlorine use; members include Dow, DuPont, Occidental, and Olin Chemical; also operates the Water Quality and Health Council, which promotes chlorine use for water and wastewater treatment); ChemicalGuide.com (www.chemicalguide.com; provides "Responsible Care" program-related information – namely: what they do;

performance; public safety; community service – for 1700 individual chemical facilities throughout the U.S.); Chemical Industry Institute of Toxicology [CIIT] (www.ciit.org; conducts research on the health effects of chemicals, pharmaceuticals, and consumer products; supported by the ACC and 30+ major chemical and related corporations); CEFIC (www.cefic.be; the European Chemical Industry Council, representing 40,000 European chemical companies accounting for more than 30% of the world's total chemical production); International Council of Chemical Association [ICCA] (www.icca-chem.org; council of leading trade associations representing chemical manufacturers worldwide).

Founded: 1872 **Members:** 190 companies **Staff:** 285 **Budget:** $28 million

324.   American Coal Foundation (ACF) (www.acf-coal.org)

Description: A business- and labor-backed organization formed to develop, produce and disseminate coal-related educational programs and materials designed for teachers and students.

A Closer Look: Support for ACF comes from coal producers, electric utilities, railroads, manufacturers of mining equipment and supplies, and organized labor.

NP Status: 501(c)(3) **Revenue/Expenses (2000):** $0.31/$0.30 million

Revenue (2000): Contributions (95%); Government Grants (0%); Program Service Revenues (3%); Other (2%).

Expenses (2000): Program Services (84%; for public education and promotion); Management and General (10%); Fundraising (6%).

Key Personnel: Mary Butterworth (Executive Director; 2000 compensation: $55,500)

325.   American Crop Protection Association (ACPA) (www.acpa.org)

Description: Trade association representing manufactures, formulators and distributors of crop protection, pest control and biotechnology products (that is, pesticides and related products). Has nearly 50 active members including various chemical pesticide manufacturers (see below).

Affiliated Org: A companion group of APCA is Responsible Industry for a Sound Environment (RISE – see Profile #387, located within this subsection), a lobbying and public relations-focused coalition group that operates the Pest Facts Information Center (see Profile #385, located within this subsection).

Key Corporate Members: BASF; Dow; DuPont; Monsanto.

Lobbying/Political Activities: Registered lobbyist under the LDA; maintains a PAC (Crop Protection Political Action Committee).

Key Issues (and activities/focus areas): Agricultural Health Study (a long-term research study on the health of farmers, farm families and agricultural chemical applicators; conducted jointly by 3 federal agencies – NCI, NIEHS, USEPA); Biotechnology; Endocrine Disruption; Food Quality Protection Act (assessment standards for pesticides; maximum permissible pesticide residue levels on food); Water Quality (pesticide contamination).

Founded: 1933 **Members:** 86 companies **Staff:** 28 **Budget:** $7 million

326.   American Electronics Association (AeA) (www.aeanet.org)

A Top Federal Lobbying Group Per Fortune Magazine's Annual Survey: Ranking for 2001: #60

Description: Trade association representing 3500 member companies that span the high tech-spectrum, including computers, software, semiconductors, Internet technology and telecommunications.

A Closer Look: Environmental issues are not currently a public policy priority issue for AeA (instead, education, privacy, taxation, international trade, and broadband deployment are).

Lobbying/Political Activities: Registered lobbyist under the LDA.

Key Issues (based on a list cited by a sister organization, the Electronics Industries Alliance – see Profile #354): Toxic Chemicals (focused on lead and mercury use in electronics); CRT/Electronic Products Recycling/End-of-Life Management; Energy Efficiency (focused on the USEPA Energy Star ® Program); Design for the Environment.

Founded: 1943 **Members:** 3500 companies **Staff:** 110 **Budget:** $15 million

327.   American Farm Bureau Federation (AFB) (www.afb.org)

A Top Federal Lobbying Group Per Fortune Magazine's Annual Survey: Ranking for 2001: #15

Description: The nation's largest farm trade association, representing 2,800+ county-level Farm Bureaus in the U.S. and Puerto Rico (officially, AFB members are 50 state-level Farm Bureaus plus the Puerto Rico Farm Bureau which, in turn, represent the 2800+ county-level Farm Bureaus). Overall, AFB represents 48 million individuals and 4 million families.

A Closer Look: AFB has a reputation as an aggressive, hard-nosed group that is unafraid of taking on the federal government, particularly the USEPA, on environmental issues, much less environmental groups. AFB itself seeks to promote an image of its members as being mostly small family farmers struggling to survive, while downplaying the role of corporate agro-businesses in the farming industry. For further information on AFB, see *Amber Waves of Gain*, an exposé of AFB put forth by Defenders of Wildlife (see Profile #39 within Subsection 1.2 – "Public Interest Groups and Coalitions").

Lobbying/Political Activities: Registered lobbyist under the LDA.

Key Issues (and AFB's positions/viewpoints): Food Quality Protection Act (concerned over USEPA's mandated re-evaluation of allowable pesticide residue limits on foods); Non-Point Source Pollution (wants the USEPA's TDML program scrapped in favor of a voluntary, incentive-based program; argues that TDML allows USEPA to effectively "take over" all state water quality programs); Concentrated Animal Feeding Operations (opposes a proposed USEPA rule to expand its regulatory authority over such operations); Alternative Energy (promotes the use of ethanol – made from corn and other farm grains – as an alternative vehicle fuel); Biotechnology (wants a comprehensive strategy assuring domestic and international acceptance of products "enhanced" by biotechnology); Regulatory Reform (wants an immediate moratorium on federal regulations and seeks a risk assessment and cost-benefit analysis requirement for all proposed regulations).

Founded: 1919 **Members:** 50 state Farm Bureaus and the Puerto Rico Farm Bureau **Staff:** 160 **Budget:** $16 million

328.   American Forest and Paper Association (AFPA) (www.AFPA.org)

A Top Federal Lobbying Group Per Fortune Magazine's Annual Survey: Ranking for 2001: #63

Description: Trade association representing the paper, wood and forest products industry. Membership consists of 200+ companies and related trade associations and includes manufacturers of 80+% of the paper, wood and forest products collectively produced in the U.S.

A Closer Look: AFPA is involved in two particularly controversial endeavors labeled "greenwash" by critics, namely: 1) the American Forest Foundation and its associated Institutes for Journalism and Natural Resources (organizations linked to paper and timber/wood products interests, including being formally affiliated with the AFPA) and 2) AFPA's own Sustainable Forest Initiative ^{SM} (launched in response to the sustainable forest certification program offered by the independent Forest Stewardship Council – see Profile #54 within Subsection 1.2 – "Public Interest Groups and Coalitions").

Lobbying/Political Activities: Registered lobbyist under the LDA; maintains a PAC (American Forest and Paper Association Political Action Committee).

Key Initiatives (and activities/focus areas): Sustainable Forest Initiative ^{SM} (SFI; established in 1994, now the world's largest sustainable forest certification program, covering 94 million acres in North America); Agenda 2020 (a collaborate research effort with the Dept. of Energy, begun in 1994; covers six areas: sustainable forest management; environmental performance; energy performance; recycling; improved capital effectiveness; sensors and control).

Key Issues (and AFPA's focus areas/viewpoints): Sustainable Forestry (AFPA offers the Sustainable Forest Initiative program – see above); State Recycling/Recycling Content Laws (newspaper content; general recycling programs; government procurement mandates), Forest Service's "Roadless Area Conservation" policy (AFPA opposes); Climate Change/Greenhouse Gas Emissions Control (AFPA: opposes the Kyoto Protocol; wants forests to count as carbon sequestration; wants emissions reduction credits included for biomass fuels).

Key Publications (all online under "Industry Information and Programs"): Comparative Analysis of the Forest Stewardship Council (FSC) and the Sustainable Forest Initiative (SFI) Certification Programs; Sustainable Forest Initiative Program Annual Progress Report; Environmental, Health and Safety Progress Report.

Affiliated Orgs (see Profiles #329 and #367, respectively): American Forest Foundation; Institutes for Journalism and Natural Resources.

Founded: 1993 (merger of 3 orgs) **Members:** 200 companies/orgs **Staff:** 156 **Budget (1995):** $36 million

329.   American Forest Foundation (AFF) (www.affoundation.org)

Description: A forest-oriented organization that runs 3 separate programs (see below for details). Closely linked to industry (see below); hence its listing here.

A Closer Look: AFF funding is dominated by paper and timber/wood products companies; it also has a "historic and continuing relationship" with the American Forest and Paper Association (see Profile #328), including using AFPA employees and facilities to conduct its work. AFF also receives a limited amount of financial support from government agencies (specifically the Forest Service, the Bureau of Land Management, and the Environmental Protection Agency) – a total of $221,000 in 2000 (representing 5% of the total revenue generated by AFF that year).

Major Corporate Funders (FY00): American Petroleum Institute; Georgia-Pacific; International Paper; Weyerhaeuser Foundation.

Programs: American Tree Farm System (a certification program for private landowners managing their land as "tree farms"); Institutes for Journalism and Natural Resources (see Profile #367); Project Learning Tree ® (a pre-K thru 12 environmental education program focused on forests).

Affiliated Orgs (see Profiles #328 and 367, respectively): American Forest and Paper Association; Institutes for Journalism and Natural Resources.

NP Status: 501(c)(3) **Revenue/Expenses (2000):** $4.4/$3.6 million

Revenue (2000): Contributions (47%); Government Grants (5%); Program Service Revenues (14%; from: sales of educational materials –8%; meeting revenue –5%; advertising –1%); Other (34%; from investment income).

Expenses (2000): Program Services (83%; for: American Tree Farm System; Institutes for Journalism and Natural Resources; Project Learning Tree ®); Management and General (12%); Fundraising (5%).

Key Personnel: Laurence Wiseman (President; 2000 compensation: $215,365)

330.   American Gas Association (AGA) (www.aga.org)

Description: Trade association representing 189 local natural gas utilities. Other members include natural gas pipeline companies, marketers, gatherers, and international gas companies.

Lobbying/Political Activities: Registered lobbyist under the LDA; maintains a PAC (Gas Employees Political Action Committee).

Key Issues: Global Climate Change; Nitrogen Oxide (NOx) Emission Limits.

Key Initiative: Natural Gas STAR Program (a voluntary partnership with the USEPA to reduce methane emissions).

Key Report: Fueling the Future: A Policy Blueprint (details 8 policy goals and implementation steps designed to ensure that natural gas "fuels the future"; online).

Founded: 1918 **Members:** 275 companies **Staff:** 180 **Budget:** $56 million

331.   American Hospital Association (AHA) (www.aha.org)

A Top Federal Lobbying Group Per Fortune Magazine's Annual Survey: Ranking for 2001: #13

Description: Trade association representing hospitals, heath care systems and networks and other health care providers.

A Closer Look: AHA is concerned with a multitude of health care issues, so environmental issues – mainly in the form of medical waste management/disposal – don't currently register on AHA's radar screen.

Lobbying/Political Activities: Registered lobbyist under the LDA; maintains a PAC (American Hospital Association Political Action Committee).

Key Issues: Medical Waste Management/Disposal (particularly with respect to medical waste incineration issues); Mercury Use (phasing out use of mercury thermometers and other mercury-containing medical products/devices).

Founded: 1898 **Members:** 6000 institutions; 50,000 individuals **Staff:** 800 **Budget:** $81 million

332.   American Hotel and Lodging Association (AHLA) (www.ahma.com)

Description: Federation of state lodging associations throughout the U.S. with some 13,000 property members worldwide, collectively representing 1.7+ million guest rooms. Has several committees, including an Engineering and Environment Committee. Formerly known as the American Hotel and Motel Association (AHMA).

Lobbying/Political Activities: Registered lobbyist under the LDA; maintains a PAC (American Hotel and Motel Political Action Committee).

Key Issues: Energy Management and Conservation; Water Use and Conservation.

Founded: 1910 **Members:** 13,000 properties **Staff:** 60 **Budget:** $18 million

American Hotel and Motel Association (AHMA) (www.ahma.com)

See Profile #332 for the "American Hotel and Lodging Association."

333.   American Iron and Steel Institute (AISI) (www.steel.org)

Description: Trade association representing North American steel producers. AISI membership consists of 39 primary steel producers, including integrated and electric furnace steelmakers, and 154 associated or affiliated members, which are suppliers to, or customers of, the industry (affiliate members make downstream steel products such as cold rolled strip, pipe and tube, and coated sheet). Member companies account for more than two-thirds of the raw steel produced in North America.

Facts and Figures: The steel industry is energy-intensive with its aggregated average energy consumption representing over 10% of that used by industry overall and 2-3% of the total energy consumed in the U.S. Energy purchases represent about 15-20% of the total manufacturing cost of steel. About 60% of the energy required to produce steel is derived from coal, and most of that is needed to produce coke, an essential material for the conversion of iron ore to iron. Recycled steel accounts for about two-thirds of the steel produced in the U.S.

Lobbying/Political Activities: Registered lobbyist under the LDA; maintains a PAC (American Iron and Steel Institute Political Action Committee).

Key Issues (and AISI's positions/viewpoints): Clean Air Act/Air Pollution Control (focuses on the costs to the steel industry); Clean Water Act/Water Pollution Control (focuses on water recycling by steelmakers and emphasizes other water pollution sources, particularly non-point sources); Global Climate Change (AISI has assumed a leadership role in the Global Climate Coalition – see Profile #363); Regulatory Procedure Reform (emphasizes risk-benefit versus cost analysis; calls for relative risk ranking); Hazardous Waste (concerned about the potential costs of the RCRA Corrective Action program); Superfund (concerned in relation to the RCRA Corrective Action program); Recycling (focuses on recycling/reclamation being treated as a regular industrial process, not as waste treatment or disposal); Auto Fuel Efficiency Standards (opposes raising the CAFE standards).

Founded: 1855 **Members:** 200 companies/associate members **Staff:** 50 **Budget:** $5 to 10 million

Affiliated Org: Steel Recycling Institute (see Profile #391).

334.   American Petroleum Institute (API) (www.api.org)

A Top Federal Lobbying Group Per Fortune Magazine's Annual Survey: Ranking for 2001: #35

Description: Trade association representing the entire oil and natural gas industry, including: exploration and production, transportation, refining, and marketing. Membership includes 400+ corporations. API provides its members with representation on state issues in 33 states east of the Rocky Mountains as well as on all federal issues.

A Closer Look: API has toned down the rhetoric that used to be on their website, while adding an extensive section on "Environmental Commitment" which focuses on seven separate areas. Nonetheless, API maintains a reputation with environmental groups as being an aggressive, hard-nosed adversary.

Lobbying/Political Activities: Registered lobbyist under the LDA.

Key Issues (and API's positions/viewpoints): New Source Review (contends that USEPA's interpretation of NSR regulations seriously restricts the abilities of oil refineries to expand, upgrade, or perform routine maintenance on equipment); Superfund (wants program funding to come from general revenues, rather than industry taxes); National Energy Strategy (wants: environmental regulations "modernized" and institution of an "Energy Impact Analysis" requirement on government decisions/actions; also questions the economic sanctions currently imposed on three major oil producers – Iran, Iraq and Libya); Oil and Natural Gas Exploration (seeks expanded access for drilling on public lands and offshore); Global Climate Change (focuses on the "debate/uncertainty" over likely causes and the severity of climate change, while claiming that the Kyoto Protocol would result in "millions of lost jobs" and "unnecessarily disrupt the lives of American families" while being an approach that "at best would make only slight progress towards solving climate change"; contends that only voluntary efforts are needed for now); Clean Air [Reformulated] Gasolines (seeks to reduce the number of such formulations).

Key Report: Overview of the Oil and Natural Gas Industry's Environmental, Health and Safety Performance (online).

Founded: 1919 **Members:** 400+ companies **Staff:** 455 **Budget:** $82 million

335.   American Plastics Council (APC) (www.americanplasticscouncil.org)

Description: Trade association representing the U.S. plastics industry with a stated mission of "ensuring that plastics are the preferred material in a more environmentally-conscious world." APC is comprised of 23 of the leading plastic resin manufacturers, plus one affiliated trade association (the Vinyl Institute, representing the vinyl industry; see Profile #396). APC's membership collectively represents 80+% of monomer and polymer production and distribution capacity in the U.S. Maintains several associated websites (see below).

A Closer Look: The APC website focuses on promoting the benefits of plastics, stressing potential resource conservation in using plastics versus other materials.

Lobbying/Political Activities: Registered lobbyist under the LDA.

Key Issues (and APC's focus areas/viewpoints): Plastics Recycling/Recyclability (focuses on community, commercial and electronics recycling); Disposal of Plastics (APC promotes increased use/acceptance of non-recycled plastics as a fuel source – "plastics-derived fuel"); Potential Human Health Effects (areas of concern: plastic baby bottles; plastic toys and teethers; plastic food wrap and containers; plastics in the microwave; plastic medical devices; APC seeks to dispel the concerns raised).

Associated Websites: Plastics.org (www.plastics.org; "Gateway to plastics on the Internet"); Plastics Resource (www.plasticsresource.com; information on plastics and the environment); Plasticsinfo.org (www.plasticsinfo.org; information on plastics and human health); Automotive Learning Center (www.plastics-car.com; promotes use of plastics in automobiles); Teachingplastics.org (www.teachingplastics.org; a "virtual plastics classroom").

Website Notes: A multitude of information is made available on the APC's various websites.

Founded: 1991 **Members:** 23 companies; 1 trade association **Staff:** 60 **Budget:** $25 to 50 million

336.   American Trucking Associations (ATA) (www.truckline.com)

A Top Federal Lobbying Group Per Fortune Magazine's Annual Survey: Ranking for 2001: #30

Description: Trade association representing the U.S. trucking industry, with membership including 2500+ trucking companies (per the U.S. Dept. of Transportation, there are 500,000+ trucking companies in the U.S.; however, the vast majority – 95% – are small, having 20 or less trucks, with almost 50% having only a single truck).

Lobbying/Political Activities: Registered lobbyist under the LDA; maintains a PAC (Truck Political Action Committee).

Key Issues (and ATA's focus areas/viewpoints): Clean Air Issues (focuses on diesel fuel and associated emissions; ATA concerned over low-sulfur fuel mandates and emissions standards for nitrogen oxides, hydrocarbons, and particulate matter; opposes establishment of "boutique" diesel fuels); Fuel Use (the trucking industry uses 43 billion gallons of fuel – diesel and gas – annually; hence its concern).

Associated Website: GreenTruck (provides information on environmental compliance at trucking and vehicle maintenance facilities).

Founded: 1933 **Members:** 4200 companies/associate members **Staff:** 290 **Budget** (2000; as cited on ATA'a website): $44 million

Revenue Sources (2000; as cited on ATA'a website): Business Activities, Contract Research, and Litigation (66%); Membership Dues and Sponsorship Contributions (34%).

337.   American Wind Energy Association (AWEA) (www.awea.org)

Description: Trade association representing the wind power industry. Has 200 member companies, including power plant developers, wind turbine manufacturers, and utilities.

Lobbying/Political Activities: Registered lobbyist under the LDA; maintains a PAC (American Wind Energy Association Political Action Committee – a.k.a. WindPAC).

Key Issues (and AWEA's focus areas/viewpoints): Production Tax Credit Extension (seeks extension of the existing 1.5 cent per kilowatt-hour tax credit); Renewables Portfolio Standard (seeks establishment of such standards); Federal Research Program (advocates for increases in the Dept. of Energy's R&D budget for wind energy); Electricity Transmission Grid Access (seeks grid access that accommodates the naturally intermittent/variable nature of wind energy production); Bird Deaths (AWEA cites figures indicating an extremely low rate compared to deaths caused by vehicles, tall structures, and plate glass; nonetheless, a research effort is underway to address the problem).

Check Out on the Web: "Energy Policy" section (provides a variety of resources on wind power for regulators and policymakers); Wind Energy Fact Sheets (on a variety of topics; online under "Publications").

Founded: 1974 **Members:** 200 companies; 650 individuals **Staff:** 14 **Budget:** $2 to 5 million

338.   Associated Builders and Contractors (ABC) (www.abc.org)

A Top Federal Lobbying Group Per Fortune Magazine's Annual Survey: Ranking for 2001: #40

Description: Trade association of the construction industry, specifically representing 23,000 contractors, subcontractors, material suppliers and related firms. The majority of ABC's members are small businesses.

Lobbying/Political Activities: Registered lobbyist under the LDA; maintains a PAC (Associated Builders and Contractors Political Action Committee).

Key Issues (and ABC's positions/viewpoints): Clean Water Act (advocates for full reauthorization of the State Revolving Fund which provides funding to states for water-related infrastructure projects; seeks wetlands permitting reform, including variable requirements based on perceived wetland "value" and providing compensation to landowners for wetlands designation); Endangered Species Act (seeks major reforms, including: 1) strengthening scientific requirements for listing and designation, 2) offering incentives in place of federal mandates for conservation, 3) compensating landowners for property "takings" as a result of the ESA); Superfund (seeks major reform of cleanup contractor liability and lender provisions; contends that current provisions discourage firms from doing the work as well as resulting in excessive cleanup times and costs); Regulatory Reform (seeks across-the-board requirements for agencies to weigh risks and perform cost/benefit analyses on regulations; also advocates for targeted regulatory relief proposals).

Founded: 1950 **Members:** 23,000 companies/firms **Staff:** 80 **Budget:** $7 million

339.   Associated General Contractors of America (AGC) (www.agc.org)

A Top Federal Lobbying Group Per Fortune Magazine's Annual Survey: Ranking for 2001: #47

Description: Trade association of the construction industry, specifically representing 36,000+ firms, including 8000 general contractors and 14,000 specialty-contracting firms.

A Closer Look: AGC is known for aggressively "plays both sides of the fence" on environmental issues, on one hand touting/promoting their work as "green" (from their website: "Construction is … one of the most effective means of enhancing the environment," while cited environmental enhancements include "building safe schools, constructing water and wastewater treatment plants, developing protection for streams and rivers, and remediating hazardous waste sites"), while at the same time opposing environmental laws/regulations directly affecting their industry (for instance, AGC's "Recommendations to the USEPA" paper – issued 1/01 – calls for significant changes in existing/proposed air, water, wetland, endangered species, environmental enforcement, and relevant contractor liability laws/regulations). Overall, though, AGC appears clearly driven by financial considerations and not any true underlying desire to be "environmentally-friendly," perhaps best exemplified by its newly formed "Environmental Action Foundation" (EAF). The EAF's stated focus is on conducting a public relations campaign (termed "enhancing the construction industry's environmental image" on its website), while its rather dubious "proactive environmental activities…range from promoting the return of hard science in schools to ensuring sensible application of environmental laws." Even more revealing are the rather misleading applications actually involved in specific EAF projects: under "Promoting Environmental Awareness Campaigns" is an EAF-funded campaign formed in response to a Sierra Club lawsuit attempting to halt certain road construction projects in California, while under "Assisting in Environmental Litigation" is EAF involvement in a lawsuit opposing implementation of stormwater pollution regulations in Georgia.

Lobbying/Political Activities: Registered lobbyist under the LDA; maintains a PAC (Associated General Contractors Political Action Committee).

Key Issues (and AGC's viewpoints/activities): Growth (promotes "quality growth" over conventional "smart growth" with "quality growth" stressing road-building to relieve traffic congestion, while considering "backyards and local playgrounds" to be "open space"; encourages members to become planning/land use commissioners); Infrastructure (promotes infrastructure-related construction projects of all sorts, but particularly road/highway construction); Recycling/Reclamation (focuses on construction and demolition waste).

Key Publication: Building Better Communities: A Toolkit for "Quality Growth" (designed for AGC members to respond "at a moment's notice" to smart growth initiatives with "facts, statistics, and examples"; online).

Founded: 1918 **Members:** 36,000 companies/firms **Staff:** 90 **Budget:** $10 million

Revenue (Non-Dues Income Only; 2001; as cited on AGC's website): $6.3 million.

340.   Association of Home Appliance Manufacturers (AHAM) (www.aham.org)

Description: Trade association representing home appliance manufacturers with membership divided into three categories: major appliances, portable appliances, and industry suppliers.

A Closer Look: One of AHAM's key duties is developing technical standards for the industry.

Lobbying/Political Activities: Registered lobbyist under the LDA; maintains a PAC (Association of Home Appliance Manufacturers Political Action Committee).

Key Issues (and AHAM's viewpoints): Federal Energy Efficiency Standards Program (supports existing federal [DOE] standards – AHAM backed their initial enactment to replace disparate state standards with a uniform federal standard – but opposes any new/upgraded standards; claims that calculated energy savings from the standards are exaggerated, while alleging that the DOE has maladministered the program, causing "great financial harm" to manufacturers; supports voluntary initiatives – such as accelerated replacement or early retirement, aimed at consumers – instead of regulation of industry); Global Climate Change (supports market-based programs and goals; opposes "any mandatory, coordinated and harmonized means and measures approach such as the heavily bureaucratic and regulatory European approach"; opposes international harmonization of energy standards as being impractical); Recycling/Disposal (supports recycling – operates the Appliance Recycling Information Center [see below for information] – but opposes mandated minimum content, design specifications or disposal fees as "unnecessary regulatory burdens and taxes").

Check Out on the Web: Energy Efficiency and Consumption Trends (statistics provided covering 1972-1996 for dishwashers, clothes washers, freezers, refrigerators and room air conditioners; online under "Statistics"); Appliance Recycling Information Center (particularly the "Information Bulletins" provided online; located under "Recycling").

Founded: 1967 **Members:** 173 companies **Staff:** 14 **Budget:** $2 to 5 million

341.   Biotechnology Industry Organization (BIO) (www.bio.org)

A Top Federal Lobbying Group Per Fortune Magazine's Annual Survey: Ranking for 2001: #76

Description: Trade organization representing the biotech industry, focused on promoting biotechnology (including production of genetically engineered foods). Has 700+ members, including corporate heavyweights Dow and DuPont.

Lobbying/Political Activities: Registered lobbyist under the LDA.

Key Issues (and BIO's viewpoints): Labeling of Biotech Foods (BIO opposes mandatory labeling; also concerned about labeling of non-biotech foods to differentiate them from biotech foods).

Founded: 1993 (merger of 2 orgs) **Members:** 720 companies **Staff:** 34 **Budget:** $5 to 10 million

342.   Business Roundtable (www.brtable.org)

A Top Federal Lobbying Group Per Fortune Magazine's Annual Survey: Ranking for 2001: #26

Description: A business association whose formal membership consists of the chief executive officers (CEOs) of leading U.S. corporations that, in turn, maintain a combined workforce of more than 10 million employees in the U.S. The Roundtable focuses on 9 issue areas, including "Environment, Technology and the Economy."

A Closer Look: The Roundtable has a single objective: "to promote policies that will lead to sustainable, non-inflationary, long-term growth in the U.S. economy."

Lobbying/Political Activities: Registered lobbyist under the LDA.

Key Issues (and the Roundtable's viewpoints): Climate Change (promotes new technology as the answer, while citing 38 regulatory, tax and trade barriers that they contend hinder relevant technological innovations from reaching the marketplace); Performance-Based Environmental Management (promotes "managing for performance" legislation – stressing results over process – over traditional "command and control" regulations).

Key Report: Blueprint 2001: Drafting Environmental Policy for the Future (focuses on: "high-quality" science and technology; "managing for performance"; market-driven approaches) (online).

343.   Can Manufacturers Institute (CMI) (www.cancentral.com)

Description: Trade association representing the metal (aluminum and steel) can manufacturing industry and its suppliers (including aluminum and steel manufacturers). CMI has 100+ member companies which collectively produce more than 98% of cans annually in the U.S. (130 billion cans in total).

Lobbying/Political Activities: Registered lobbyist under the LDA.

Key Issues (and CMI's positions/viewpoints): Deposit Laws / "Bottle Bills" (opposes creation of any such new laws; where already implemented – in 9 states – wants such recycling to "pay for itself"); "Restrictive Packaging Measures" (defined by CMI as "any measure that would restrict the use of any package based on any specified set of criteria"; opposes any efforts to "restrict consumer choice of packaging material based upon criteria other than public health," including advance disposal fee programs or the creation of refillable packaging mandates).

Founded: 1938 **Members:** 120 companies **Staff:** 9 **Budget:** $11 million

344.   Center for Energy and Economic Development (CEED) (www.ceednet.org)

Description: A business-based coalition of 200 member companies – primarily coal producers, utilities, and railroads – seeking to "maintain and enhance the option of coal-based electricity generation in the U.S."

Key Issues (and CEED's positions/viewpoints): Global Climate Change (opposes the Kyoto Treaty); Ozone Transport (focuses on emissions from Midwest power plants causing ozone problems in Northeast cities, which CEED dismisses as "a myth"); Mercury Emissions From Coal Plants (disputes the potential effects on human health); Electric Utility Restructuring (concerned over state environmental laws potentially restricting use of coal-generated electricity).

Members: 200 companies **Budget** (as cited on CEED's website): $5 million

Chamber of Commerce of the U.S.A. (www.uschamber.com)

See Profile #394 for the "U.S. Chamber of Commerce."

345.   ChemicalGuide.com (www.chemicalguide.com)

Description: An American Chemistry Council website (see Profile #323) providing "Responsible Care®" program-related information (specifically: what they do; performance; public safety; community service) for 1700 individual chemical manufacturing facilities throughout the U.S.

346.   Chemical Industry Institute of Toxicology (CIIT) (www.ciit.org)

Description: A chemical industry-supported toxicology research institute for assessing the human health effects of chemicals, pharmaceuticals, and consumer products.

A Closer Look: CIIT is supported by 34 major companies (including: Dow; DuPont; ExxonMobile; Occidental Chemical; Solutia) and the American Chemistry Council (see Profile #323).

Research Programs: Chemical Carcinogenesis; Endocrine, Reproductive, and Developmental Toxicology; Neurotoxicology; Respiratory Toxicology.

Founded: 1974 **Staff:** 160 **Budget:** $17 million

Chemical Manufacturers Association (www.americanchemistry.com)

See Profile #323 for the "American Chemistry Council."

347.   Chorine Chemistry Council (CCC) (c3.org)

Description: A business council of the American Chemistry Council (see profile #323) designed to promote chlorine use. The CCC also operates the Water Quality and Health Council (see Profile #398), a business council which promotes the use of chlorine for water and wastewater treatment.

Key Corporate Members: Dow; DuPont; Occidental; Olin Chemical.

Lobbying/Political Activities: Registered lobbyist under the LDA.

Key Issue: Dioxins and Endocrine Disrupters (both potentially produced from various applications of chlorine).

Founded: 1992 **Budget:** $5 to 10 million

348.   Coalition for Affordable and Reliable Energy (CARE) (www.careenergy.com)

Description: A mixed-member coalition of nearly 50 entities (mostly business trade organizations; hence its listing here) promoting a "sound energy policy" that stresses increased use of coal (from their website: "coal must be an essential part of the solution to our energy problems").

Key "Opposing View" Group Members (see separate profiles for each within Section 6 – "Opposing View Groups"): Americans for Tax Reform; Frontiers of Freedom Institute.

Key Business Trade Group Members (see separate profiles for each within this subsection): Aluminum Association; American Iron and Steel Institute; American Trucking Associations; Center for Energy and Economic Development; Edison Electric Institute; Fertilizer Institute; National Association of Manufacturers; National Mining Association; National Rural Electric Cooperative Association; U.S. Chamber of Commerce.

Key Labor Union Members (see separate profile located within Subsection 5.2 – "Labor Unions"): United Mine Workers of America.

Key Issues: Global Climate Change; Toxics Release Inventory Reporting; Visibility and Regional Haze; New Source Review; Ozone Transport; Mountaintop Mining; Mercury Emissions.

349.   Coalition for Vehicle Choice (CVC) (www.vehiclechoice.org)

Description: A mixed-member coalition (led by the "Big 3" U.S. automakers – Daimler-Chrysler, Ford and General Motors) created to "preserve the freedom of Americans to choose motor vehicles that meet their needs and their freedom to travel."

A Closer Look: The CVC is generally recognized as a thinly-veiled effort by the "Big 3" U.S. automakers focused on opposing/eliminating CAFE (federal fuel efficiency) standards. The CVC takes an aggressive stance, complete with dubious/inflammatory claims such as asserting that CAFE represents a "war on farmers" who use pickup trucks and characterizing those asking for an increase in the standards as being "anti-vehicle." One interesting facet of the CVC is that no other automakers (other than the "Big 3") are listed as members.

Key "Opposing View" Group Members (see separate profiles for each within Section 6 – "Opposing View Groups"): American Legislative Exchange Council; Citizens for A Sound Economy; Competitive Enterprise Institute.

Key Business Trade Group Members (see separate profiles for each within this subsection): American Farm Bureau Federation; American Hospital Association; American Iron and Steel Institute; Associated Builders and Contractors; Associated General Contractors; National Association of Home Builders; National Association of Manufacturers; National Automobile Dealers Association; National Mining Association; Rubber Manufacturers Association; U.S. Chamber of Commerce.

Key Issues (and CVC's positions/viewpoints): Federal Fuel Efficiency Standards (staunchly opposes raising the CAFE standards); Auto Emissions (seeks flexibility in new tailpipe emission standards).

350.   Council for Biotechnology Information (CBI) (www.whybiotech.com)

Description: A business-backed organization founded by leading biotechnology companies to create a comprehensive communications (i.e., public relations) campaign promoting biotechnology. Known for its print and TV ads touting biotechnology. Promotes biotech crops as potentially helping to conserve soil, water, and land while also reducing the amount chemical pesticides needed.

A Closer Look: The CBI website is "upbeat," emphasizing the possibilities of biotechnology and contains a multitude of references to governmental and scientific documents, yielding an authoritative air to the information presented.

Founding Members: Major biotech firms (namely: Aventis; BASF; Bayer; Dow; Dupont; Monsanto; Syngenta) and key business trade associations (namely the American Crop Protection Association and the Biotechnology Industry Organization – see Profiles #325 and 341, respectively).

Ecotourism Society (www.ecotourism.org)

See Profile #369 for "(The) International Ecotourism Society" (TIES).

351.   Edison Electric Institute (EEI) (www.eei.org)

A Top Federal Lobbying Group Per Fortune Magazine's Annual Survey: Ranking for 2001: #51

Description: Trade association comprised of 200 shareholder-owned electric companies, 45+ international affiliates and 140+ industry-related associates worldwide. U.S. members collectively generate 75% of all U.S. electricity and serve 70% of all ultimate customers in the nation.

Lobbying/Political Activities: Registered lobbyist under the LDA; maintains a PAC (Power PAC of the Edison Electric Institute).

Key Issues (and EEI's activities/viewpoints): New Source Review (contends that the current program is too complicated and needs reform); Global Climate Change (in partnership with the Dept. of Energy, EEI has established the Climate Challenge – a voluntary initiative to reduce greenhouse gas emissions by electric utilities); Multi-Emissions (promotes an alternative market-based approach to reducing air emissions); Mercury Emissions (questions the threat to the public from such emissions); Toxics Release Inventory [TRI] Reporting (provides a "communications kit" for its member companies); Solid Waste (coordinates the U.S. Solid Waste Activities Group, an informal consortium of 80 utilities and several industry trade groups that addresses solid and hazardous waste issues); Electric/Alternative Fuel Vehicles (supports incentives for purchases of such vehicles).

Check Out on the Web: Our Energy Future (discusses key issues – fuel diversity; using electricity wisely; expanding the system; systems reliability; competition); E Seal Program (an energy efficiency certification system for new homes, typically yielding a 10-30% reduction in space heating, cooling and water heating energy consumption; 165,000 homes certified thus far; information located under "Energy Services Group").

Website Notes: A generally informative website.

Founded: 1933 **Members:** 200 electric companies **Staff:** 280 **Budget:** $64 million

352.   Electric Power Research Institute (EPRI) (www.epri.com)

Description: A research and development consortia created by U.S. electric utilities to "develop innovative solutions to energy problems." Serves 1000+ energy organizations worldwide. Involved in a host of environmentally-related technical projects on air, water, and solid/hazardous waste issues, as well as maintaining an extensive program in nuclear power (including nuclear waste management). Also runs EPRIsolutions, Inc., a wholly-owned subsidiary that works with companies worldwide to implement EPRI-developed technologies for improving electric power generation, distribution, and use.

A Closer Look: EPRI strongly promotes both coal and nuclear energy, while performing relatively little research regarding energy efficiency and associated technologies. One key "environmentally-friendly" initiative being pursued is development of electric grid-connected hybrid vehicles.

Lobbying/Political Activities: Registered lobbyist under the LDA.

Key Research Areas (and key specific topics) for 2002: Environment (air quality/global climate change; EMFs/ occupational health and safety; land and groundwater; water ecosystems); Power Generation (fossil steam plants and combustion turbines; renewable and hydroelectric power; nuclear power); Power Delivery (includes research on energy utilization, which, in turn, includes some limited research on energy efficiency).

Key Report: Electricity Technology Roadmap (a 6-volume research and development roadmap focusing on the next 25 years; "Summary and Synthesis" report online).

Annual Report: 2000 report online.

Founded: 1972 **Members:** 660 utilities **Staff:** 750 **NP Status:** 501(c)(3) **Revenue/Expenses (1998):** $355/$398 million

Revenue (1998): Contributions (0%); Government Grants (0%); Program Service Revenues (28%; from specific project funding); Other (73%; from: membership dues –67%; misc. 6%).

Expenses (1998): Program Services (52%); Management and General (48%); Fundraising (0%).

Key Personnel: Kurt Yeager (President and CEO; 1998 compensation: $585,031)

353.   Electric Power Supply Association (EPSA) (www.epsa.org)

Description: Trade association representing competitive electric power suppliers, including independent power producers, merchant generators and power marketers. These suppliers collectively account for more than a third of the nation's installed electrical generating capacity. EPSA seeks to "open up" (deregulate) the electric power industry. EPSA itself was formed in 1997 by a merger of two separate trade groups – the National Independent Energy Producers and the Electric Generation Association.

Lobbying/Political Activities: Registered lobbyist under the LDA; maintains a PAC (Electric Power Supply Association Political Action Committee).

Key Issues (and EPSA's positions/viewpoints): Renewable Portfolio Standards (conditionally supports "moderate" standards); Global Climate Change (favors flexible, market-driven emissions reduction programs within an overall global agreement that includes developing countries); Environmental Disclosure (seeks voluntary disclosure only, based on consumer demands; want fuel use information to be considered "confidential information"); Air Quality in Electric Industry Restructuring (seeks regulatory reform to reduce "barriers to market entry" such as the New Source Performance Standards and the New Source Review program; seeks to maintain fuel source diversity, including both renewable and non-renewable sources).

Founded: 1997 (by a merger of 2 orgs) **Members:** 85 companies **Staff:** 12 **Budget:** $2 to 5 million

354.   Electronic Industries Alliance (EIA) (www.eia.org)

Description: Trade alliance representing 80% of the U.S. high tech industry, with 2300 members. EIA itself is an alliance of six autonomous trade business associations: Telecommunications Industry Association; Consumer Electronics Association; Electronic Components, Assemblies, and Materials Association; Government Electronics and Information Technology Association; JEDEC-Solid State Technology Association; Electronics Industries Foundation. EIA is also known as the Electronic Industries Association.

A Closer Look: Environmental issues are addressed through EIA's Environmental Issues Council (EIC), which, in turn, is organized around specific issue-area Working Groups.

Lobbying/Political Activities: Registered lobbyist under the LDA.

Key Issues (and EIA's activities/viewpoints): Toxic Chemicals (focuses on lead and mercury; EIA opposes regulating or banning their use in electronics); CRT/Electronic Products Recycling/End-of-Life Management; Energy Star ® Program (EIA is a formal partner in this government-led energy efficiency program – see Profile # 249 for details); Design for the Environment.

Key Initiatives: Consumer Education Initiative (encourages consumers to reuse/recycle used electronics such as TVs, VCRs, personal computers, and cell phones; includes a separate website [www.eiae.org] that directs interested parties to local charities, needy schools, neighborhood and community de-manufacturers, and other local and national recycling programs that collect used electronics): EIA Electronics Recycling Project (a one-year grant program funding regional/state recycling initiatives for home electronic products).
Founded: 1924 **Members:** 2300 companies **Staff:** 200 **Budget:** $42 million

355.   Environmental Bankers Association (EBA) (www.envirobank.org)

Description: Trade association representing the financial services industry, including banking and non-banking financial institutions, insurers, and asset management firms. Members include lending institutions, property/casualty/life insurers, the environmental consulting and appraisal community, and attorneys. The stated mission of the EBA is to "protect and preserve bank net income and assets from environmental exposure and liability resulting from lending and trust activities through the employment of environmental risk management."
Founded: 1994 **Members:** 60 institutions **Staff:** 3 **Budget:** $0.05 to 0.1 million

356.   Environmental Industry Associations (EIA) (www.envasns.org)

Description: Trade association that was formerly the National Solid Wastes Management Association (NSWMA) and now is an umbrella organization that includes both NSWMA and the Waste Equipment Technology Association (see Profiles #383 and 397, respectively).
Lobbying/Political Activities: Registered lobbyist under the LDA.
Founded: 1982 **Members:** 2000 companies **Staff:** 85 **Budget:** $10 to 25 million

357.   Environmental Technology Council (ETC) (www.etc.org)

Description: Trade council representing commercial environmental management firms that recycle, treat and/or dispose of industrial and hazardous wastes as well as firms involved in cleanup of contaminated sites/properties. Formerly known as the Hazardous Waste Treatment Council.
Lobbying/Political Activities: Registered lobbyist under the LDA.
Key Issues (and ETC's positions/viewpoints): Federal Regulation of Hazardous Waste (identifies two perceived "key gaps" in such regulation and correspondingly calls for the USEPA to: 1) designate more wastes as "hazardous," and thus subject to regulation under the federal RCRA hazardous waste program and 2) designate more chemicals as subject to reporting under the federal EPCRA "Community Right-to-Know"/Toxic Release Inventory program).
Founded: 1982 **Members:** 15 companies **Staff:** 3 **Budget:** $1 to 2 million

358.   (The) Fertilizer Institute (TFI) (www.tfi.org)

Description: Trade association representing 300+ companies that collectively represent 90+% of the U.S. fertilizer industry.
Lobbying/Political Activities: Registered lobbyist under the LDA; maintains a PAC (Fertilizer Institute Political Action Committee – a.k.a. FERT PAC).
Key Issues (and TFI's activities/viewpoints): Fertilizer Use (focus areas: nutrient management plans; certified crop advisors; precision agriculture – using GPS technology; conservation buffers); Gulf of Mexico Hypoxia (working with the USEPA and the USDA on an action plan to reduce oxygen depletion in the northern Gulf of Mexico); EPA's Total Maximum Daily Load Program (opposes implementation of the federal program; supports state and local efforts that are voluntary and incentive-based); Metals in Fertilizers (TFI has established safe screening levels for 12 metals in fertilizer products).
Founded: 1970 **Members:** 325 companies; 200 individuals **Staff:** 30 **Budget:** $2 to 5 million

359.   FossilFuels.org (www.fossilfuels.org)

Description: An industry-associated website promoting the use of fossil fuels ("one of the Creator's greatest gifts to mankind"), while also seeking to discount global warming concerns over such use.

A Closer Look: The website is put forth by the Greening Earth Society (see Profile #364), which, in turn, was founded by the Western Fuels Association and partners with the National Mining Association (see Profile #380).

360.   Foundation for Clean Air Progress (www.cleanairprogress.org**)**

Description: A business-backed organization set up to "provide public education and information about air quality progress" with an expressed aim of "present(ing) the situation…from the perspective of the glass being half-full, rather than half empty." The website itself focuses on ground-level ozone levels.

A Closer Look: Foundation members represent a coalition of business/industry groups, many of which are transportation related. In 1999, the group's three principal officers were affiliated with the American Highway Users, American Trucking Associations, and the American Petroleum Institute. Virtually all (99%) of the group's expenses for 1999 went to the well-known public relations firm Burson-Marsteller to conduct a PR campaign on behalf of the group.

Key Business Trade Group Members (see separate profiles for each within this subsection)**:** American Chemistry Council; American Farm Bureau Federation; Center for Energy and Economic Development; Electric Edison Institute; National Association of Manufacturers; National Association of Realtors; U.S. Chamber of Commerce.

NP Status: 501(c)(3) **Revenue/Expenses (1999):** $0.35/$0.35 million

Revenue (1999): Contributions (99%); Government Grants (0%); Program Service Revenues (0%); Other (<1%).

Expenses (1998): Program Services (99%; for public education campaign [run by an outside consultant, specifically the PR firm Burson-Marsteller]); Management and General (1%); Fundraising (0%).

Key Personnel: William Fay (President; affiliated with American Highway Users); Allen Schaeffer (Secretary; affiliated with the American Trucking Associations); Arthur Wiese (Treasurer; affiliated with the American Petroleum Institute).

361.   Geothermal Energy Association (GEA) (www.geotherm.org**)**

Description: Trade association promoting the expanded use of geothermal energy for electrical power generation and direct-heat uses. Represents 50 member companies, including many which develop geothermal resources worldwide.

Founded: 1987 **Members:** 50 companies **Staff:** 7 **Budget:** $0.25 to 0.5 million

362.   Glass Packaging Institute (GPI) (www.gpi.org**)**

Description: Trade organization representing the North American glass container industry. Maintains 3 classes of membership: glass container manufacturers, "closure" (lid/cap) manufacturers and "associates" (industry-supporting companies).

A Closer Look: GPI activities include: a public relations program promoting the sales and recyclability of glass containers; lobbying efforts to "oppose legislative and regulatory threats to packaging on the federal, state, and local levels."

Lobbying/Political Activities: Registered lobbyist under the LDA.

Key Issues (and GPI's positions/viewpoints): Deposit Systems / "Bottle Bills" (strongly opposes); Recovery / Recycled Content Mandates (conditionally supports); Volume-Based Solid Waste Fees (supports to encourage recycling); National Recycling Legislation (would potentially support, but believes best left to local/state/regional authorities).

Founded: 1945 **Members:** 7 companies; 26 associate members **Staff:** 6 **Budget:** $5 million

363.   Global Climate Coalition (GCC) (www.globalclimate.org**)**

Description: A coalition of business trade organizations focused on global climate change.

A Closer Look: Originally comprised of individual corporate members, but after the defections of key members – including DaimlerChrysler, Ford, General Motors, Shell, Texaco, and Dow – GCC became a trade association-only organization in 3/00. The GCC has clear ties to conservative/libertarian-based "opposing view" groups (see

"Climate Web-Links Cited" below). A four-prong strategy is employed by GCC, namely: 1) question the science behind the "theory" of global warming and its possible impacts, 2) strongly oppose ratification of the Kyoto Treaty, stressing the potential economic consequences ("harming the U.S. economy"; "enormous costs to U.S. citizens/taxpayers") and lack of specific reduction commitments from developing nations, 3) promote alternative voluntary, market-based solutions using advanced technology applications and, most recently, 4) stress voluntary efforts businesses have made in reducing their greenhouse gas emissions.

Lobbying/Political Activities: Registered lobbyist under the LDA.

Climate Web-Links Cited on Website (see separate profiles for each within Section 6 – "Opposing View Groups"): Center for the Study of Carbon Dioxide and Global Change; Competitive Enterprise Institute; George C. Marshall Institute; Greening Earth Society; The Heartland Institute; Reason Public Policy Institute; The Science and Environmental Policy Project.

364.   Greening Earth Society (GES) (www.greeningearthsociety.org)

Description: A business-backed and conservative-associated organization promoting the "benefits" of carbon dioxide emissions ("our message is that CO2 is required for life on earth and that the earth is actually getting greener thanks to increasing CO2 levels"). GES operates the FossilFuels.org website (see Profile #359), where fossil fuels are said to be "one of the Creator's greatest gifts to mankind." Closely linked to industry (see below); hence its listing here.

A Closer Look: The GES was founded by the Western Fuels Association, which also maintains a leadership position within the Society; it also partners with the National Mining Association (see Profile #380) and is reportedly funded by coal-based utilities.

Key Affiliations: Townhall.com (conservative group network).

365.   Grocery Manufacturers of America (GMA) (www.gmabrands.com)

Description: Trade organization representing manufacturers of "groceries" (food, beverages, and consumer products). Has 140+ members, including many well-known names (see below). Grocery store chains are not members of GMA, however.

Key Corporate Members: Anheuser-Busch; Bristol-Myers Squibb; Clorox; CocaCola; Colgate-Palmolive; Del Monte; General Mills; Georgia-Pacific; Kodak; Nabisco; Philip-Morris; Proctor and Gamble.

A Closer Look: The GMA formally weighs in on many environmental issues; in many cases, it calls for national standards to replace state and local measures.

Lobbying/Political Activities: Registered lobbyist under the LDA; maintains a PAC (Grocery Manufacturers of American Political Action Committee).

Key Issues (and GMA's positions/viewpoints): Advanced Disposal Fees (opposes such "front-end" fees as "discriminatory taxes"; supports "waste-end" – point of disposal – fees instead); Beverage Container Deposits / "Bottle Bills" (opposes as "expensive and inefficient"; supports municipal curbside recycling programs instead); Biotechnology (promotes "foods derived from biotechnology" – i.e., genetically modified; promotes "agricultural biotechnology" as making farmlands more productive, thereby reducing the need for agricultural lands); Biotechnology Labeling Legislation (opposes mandatory labeling of biotech foods; feels that consumers should "pay a price" for assurances that food is non-biotech, as with the organic food market); Environmental Labeling (such as "recyclable" or "ozone-friendly"; opposes state-specific laws, seeking national uniformity instead); Environmental Procurement (opposes state initiatives to use Green Seal guidelines in making state government purchases; has established their own ad-hoc coalition to "provide state procurement officers with a proper framework to assess environmental attributes"); Mandatory Product Disclosure (opposes mandatory disclosure of information – such as the recycled content of packages and chemical ingredients in products – as being "arbitrary" and offering "questionable benefit"); Precautionary Principle (considers it to be "a serious, imminent threat to U.S. domestic food policy and international trade"; opposes adoption by the European Union, Codex, or the WTO); rBST Regulation (opposes state-specific labeling of milk containing the growth hormone rBST); Superfund Reform (focuses on repealing retroactive liability; considers GMA member companies to be "classic examples of unintended victims of this failed government program"); Voluntary Environmental Self-Assessments and Self-Disclosure (seeks disclosure protection and penalty immunity for all federal environmental laws and for similar state/local laws); Warnings on Product Labels (opposes California's Prop 65 warning program and similar efforts).

Founded: 1908 **Members:** 145 companies **Staff:** 43 **Budget:** $8 million

366.   Institute of Scrap Recycling Industries (ISRI) (www.isri.org)

Description: Trade association representing the scrap processing and recycling industry with 1500 member companies that process, broker, and industrially consume scrap commodities (including metals, paper, plastics, glass, rubber, and textiles) and associated equipment/service providers.

Facts and Figures: In 1999, U.S. scrap recyclers handled 120 million tons of recyclables (mostly iron/steel and paper/paperboard – 60 and 47 million tons, respectively).

A Closer Look: A primary objective of ISRI is promoting "Design for Recycling" (designing and manufacturing goods that, at the end of their useful lives, can be recycled safely and efficiently).

Lobbying/Political Activities: Registered lobbyist under the LDA; maintains a PAC (Institute of Scrap Recycling Industries Political Action Committee).

Key Issues (and ISRI's activities/viewpoints): Design for Recycling (promotes as noted above); Mercury In Vehicles (calls for a nationwide recovery and collection system to remove mercury-containing switches from end-of-life vehicles, with help from automakers); Brownfields Redevelopment (seeks program reform in existing liability provisions); Superfund Recycling Equity Act (seeks to help in implementing the Act which provides liability relief to scrap recycling businesses); Basel Convention (seeks to help in implementing the Convention which governs international movement of hazardous waste).

Founded: 1987 (merger of 2 orgs) **Members:** 1500 companies **Staff:** 38 **Budget:** $5 to 10 million

367.   Institutes for Journalism and Natural Resources (IJNR) (www.affoundation.org)

Description: A program of the American Forest Foundation (see Profile #329) which involves taking journalists on expedition-style journeys, complemented by seminar-style discussions, in an effort to "improve the quality of the public conversation and debate on natural resource and environmental issues." 200+ mid-level and senior journalists have participated since IJNR was established in 1995. Closely linked to industry (see below); hence its listing here.

A Closer Look: Despite its independent, academic-sounding name, IJNR is actually closely linked to industry – it is a program of the American Forest Foundation (see Profile #329), an organization funded primarily by paper and timber/wood products companies and one that has a "historic and continuing relationship" with the American Forest and Paper Association (see Profile #328), including using AFPA employees and facilities to conduct its work. In addition, IJNR's co-founder and current Executive Director – Frank Allen – comes from the *Wall Street Journal*, well-known for its "business-first" thinking on environmental issues.

Programs/Projects/Activities: Various "Institutes" (expedition-style programs); Campus Outreach and Recruiting; Internships and Residencies; Other Career-Development Support; Wallace Stegner Initiative (long-term assessment of the "quality and persistence of news coverage throughout the North American West").

Founded: 1995 **HQ:** Missoula, MT **NP Status:** 501(c)(3) **Revenue/Expenses (2000):** $1.03/$0.80 million
Revenue (2000): Contributions (99%); Government Grants (0%); Program Service Revenues (0%); Other (1%).
Expenses (2000): Program Services (80%; for: Stegner Initiative –31%; Arcadian Institute –13%; Golden Gate Institute –13%; Pacific Northwest Institute –11%; various other programs/activities –12%); Management and General (14%); Fundraising (7%).
Key Personnel: Larry Wiseman (Chairman; also serves as the President of the American Forest Foundation); Frank Allen (Executive Director).

368.   Integrated Waste Services Association (IWSA) (www.wte.org)

Description: Trade association representing the national waste-to-energy (WTE) industry. Members include owners/operators of WTE facilities representing 67 plants that process 84,000 tons of trash each day (overall, there are 102 operating WTE plants in the U.S. burning about 14% of the trash generated nationwide – 97,000 tons each day – producing 2,800+ megawatts of electricity).

Lobbying/Political Activities: Registered lobbyist under the LDA; maintains a PAC (REPAC Integrated Waste Services Association).

Key Publication: Directory of Waste-to-Energy Plants 2000 (information on the 102 operating WTE plants in the U.S.; online).

Founded: 1991 **Members:** 50 companies **Staff:** 3 **Budget:** $1 to 2 million

369.   (The) International Ecotourism Society (TIES) (www.ecotourism.org)

Description: Business membership group (and associated website) promoting tourism as a viable tool for conservation and sustainable development. TIES membership totals 1700 (in 70+ countries) and includes tour operators, eco-lodges, and eco-businesses.

Website Notes: The website is essentially divided in two – one part for the general public, one part for professionals (see below). For easier navigating, go to the "Index" page to access the site's contents.

Website Contents: Travel Choice (information for the general public on eco-travel, with links provided to member businesses); Eco-Professional (separate resources for: 1) researchers – market data; selected research papers; information on ecotourism libraries and university programs; 2) conservationists – projects; success stories; selected papers; 3) businesspeople – TIES member business reports; ecotourism operating guidelines).

Check Out on the Web: Ecotourism Statistical Fact Sheets (for both the U.S. and the world; online under "Ecotourism Market Data" on the "Researcher" webpage); Bookstore (offers ecotourism planning, conservation, and management documents); TIES Annual Initiatives (identifies key issues in ecotourism).

NP Status: 501(c)(3) **Revenue/Expenses (FY01):** $0.47/$0.47 million

Revenue (FY01): Contributions (58%); Government Grants (0%); Program Service Revenues (13%; from training and education); Other (29%; from: membership dues –25%; misc. –4%).

Expenses (FY01): Program Services (72%; for: research –30%; membership resource center –27%; education and training –12%; international program –3%; honorarium –<1%); Management and General (28%); Fundraising (0%).

Key Personnel: Megan Epler Wood (President)

370.   National Association of Home Builders (NAHB) (www.nahb.com)

A Top Federal Lobbying Group Per Fortune Magazine's Annual Survey: Ranking for 2001: #11

Description: A business federation of 850 state and local builder trade associations. About one-third of NAHB's 200,000 members are homebuilders and/or remodelers, with the remainder working in associated fields (mortgage finance, building products and services, etc.). NAHB members construct 80% of new housing units annually in the U.S.

Facts and Figures: Residential construction typically accounts for about 5% of all spending annually in the U.S., making home building one of the largest (and thus most influential) industries.

A Closer Look: The NAHB takes an aggressive, hard line against government regulation and growth controls (from NAHB's 1999 President Bruce Smith: "The housing marketplace … is increasingly threatened by a vast array of government regulations and growth controls"; also see "Key Issues" below). In taking this stance, the NAHB consistently cites: 1) the "Great American Dream" of owning a single-family detached house in the suburbs and/or 2) the specter of "pushing homeownership beyond the reach of millions of prospective home buyers" as rationale for opposing proposals that might potentially slow growth and/or increase housing costs. More evidence of the NAHB's general viewpoint is given within the "Environmental Education" section of their website, where information on environmental regulatory programs is provided and targeted students (college students in construction management programs) are encouraged to debate – pro and con – those regulations, within the context of a housing affordability versus environmental protection trade-off.

On the other hand, the NAHB's Research Center does maintain some "green" programs – namely in construction waste management, energy, and "green" building (see below for details) – although policy-wise, the NAHB strictly opposes government intervention except in the limited case of non-regulatory, voluntary, market-driven programs. Overall, much like other construction-related associations (such as the Associated General Contractors – see Profile #339), it is readily apparent that the NAHB embraces being "green" only when there is significant financial incentive to do so.

Lobbying/Political Activities: Registered lobbyist under the LDA; maintains a PAC (Build Political Action Committee).

Key Issues (and NAHB's activities/viewpoints): Smart Growth (their version focuses on 1) cleanup and redevelopment of contaminated brownfields and 2) "infill" of urban/inner suburban areas; on the other hand, addressing suburban sprawl – the typical focus of smart growth programs – is not on their agenda; the NAHB also opposes open space purchases that "block development" and they also seek to have government spread infrastructure improvement costs to existing residents as well as to developers/new home-buyers); Clean Air Act (primarily concerned that highway projects may be stopped or delayed due to air quality concerns, resulting in reduced growth); Wetlands (in a provocative report, "Even the Government Must Obey the Law," the NAHB accuses the federal government of "repeatedly and willfully breaking the law" in the case of Tulloch wetlands rule; also alleges that the U.S. Army Corp of Engineers "cut a back room deal" with environmental groups to establish the Tulloch rule; calls for comprehensive reform of the entire federal wetlands program); Endangered Species Act (calls the new "4(d)" rule – which makes local government outline what activities are/are not allowed for salmon protection – a possible "death knell for local land use authority"; attempts to reduce the issue down to "people versus fish" – from the NAHB's 2000 President Robert Mitchell: "People should not discriminate against their children, minorities and senior citizens…for the sake of fish and other animals").

Key NAHB Research Center Programs: Construction Waste Management (emphasizing material recycling and reuse); Energy (focusing on various efficiency measures); Green Building (sponsoring an annual National Green Building Conference).

Key Report: Housing Facts, Figures, and Trends 2001 (a statistical summary; also includes a section on green building; online).

Key Technical Publication: Environmentally Green/Economically Green: Tools for a Green Land Development Program (issued in partnership with the USEPA; online); A Guide to Developing Green Building Programs (describes program development and green building techniques).

Founded: 1942 **Members:** 850 state/local builder associations; 194,000 individuals **Staff:** 285 **Budget:** $25 to 50 million

371.   National Association of Manufacturers (NAM) (www.nam.org)

A Top Federal Lobbying Group Per Fortune Magazine's Annual Survey: Ranking for 2001: #10

Description: Trade association representing manufacturers; billed as the nation's largest industrial trade association. Has 14,000 members (including 10,000 small- and mid-sized companies and 350 member associations) with member companies collectively producing over 80% of all manufactured goods in the U.S. Also affiliated with 130 state/local business associations through its National Industrial Council and 200 manufacturing trade associations through its Association Council. NAM maintains 5 policy committees, including one on "Resources, Environment and Regulation Policy," which also covers energy issues.

A Closer Look: NAM's overall "Pro-Growth Policy Agenda for 2001" includes a call for "modernization" of hazardous waste, clean water, and clean air regulations, while also calling for increased domestic development of fossil fuel energy sources. NAM often frames positions from the viewpoint of small businesses and overall takes a dim view of government regulation (from a recent [6/01] letter to the USEPA concerning a proposed regulation: "Any new law, regulatory policy, guidance, directive, interpretation or other agency decision – in whatever form – is expensive and time-consuming. The people who make things in America must divert their attention from their productivity and quality goals to deal with bureaucracies, inspectors, complainants, lawyers and courts").

Lobbying/Political Activities: Registered lobbyist under the LDA.

Key Issue Areas (and NAM's key positions/viewpoints) – Energy and Natural Resource Issues: Energy Supply/Efficiency (opposes mandated efficiency standards such as CAFE, while favoring drilling for Alaskan oil; promotes coal and nuclear energy over natural gas; advocates for adoption of an "Energy Impact Statement" requirement for federal decision-making); Electricity (opposes market set-asides, preferences, or mandates for renewable energy sources; supports cogeneration, distributed generation, and combined heat and power systems); Global Climate (opposes the Kyoto Protocol as "irreparably flawed"; favors voluntary efforts over mandated cutbacks in greenhouse gas emissions); Nuclear Power/Waste Disposal (supports siting Yucca Mountain for nuclear waste disposal, calling it "high time to move forward"); Mining Law Reform (opposes federal royalties on hardrock mining, including those designed to fund cleanup of abandoned mines; works with the National Mining Association on mining issues); Endangered Species Act Reform (one of NAM's top legislative priorities; alleges that the law is "used more to stop development rather than saving endangered species" and that is has "cost Americans tens of thousands of jobs and millions of dollars"; NAM wants species listing to be based on weighing the economic effect along with the biological risk to the species).

Key Issue Areas (and NAM's key positions/viewpoints) – Environmental Issues: Environmental Justice (while supporting the general concept, implies that an associated delay in permitting threatens efforts to revitalize abandoned industrial sites); Hazardous Waste Cleanup (seeks comprehensive reform of Superfund, calling for "phase-out of this broken program"; also seeks specific reforms in the RCRA Corrective Action program to speed up cleanup operations; supports federal legislation promoting "brownfields" revitalization); Water Quality (seeks more flexibility in the EPA's TMDL program; opposes a proposed new rule governing wastewater discharges from metal products and machinery operations); Environmental Information Use (opposes collection of material accounting data under the EPA's Toxic Release Inventory program); Compliance and Enforcement (wants federal legal barriers removed to promote voluntary environmental self-audits and disclosure by industry); Biotechnology (opposes mandatory labeling of biotech foods).

Key Issue Areas (and NAM's key positions/viewpoints) – Air Quality Issues: Regional Haze (concerned over the EPA's proposed emissions rules addressing visibility-impairing air pollutants); New Source Review Program (calls the program "onerous…(with) complicated and uncertain applicability rules"; seeks substantial reforms focused on increasing flexibility and reducing time requirements for associated permitting); National Ambient Air Quality Standards (opposes the EPA's new ozone and particulate matter standards as being "based on incomplete science and no cost-benefit test"); Multi-Emissions Legislation (while supporting the general concept, opposes including carbon dioxide in any such proposal).

Key Report: Preliminary Report on Environmental Trends (summary information, mostly extracted from federal government sources; online).

Founded: 1895 **Members:** 14,000 companies **Staff:** 180 **Budget:** $16 million

372. National Association of REALTORS ® (NAR) (nar.realtor.com)

A Top Federal Lobbying Group Per Fortune Magazine's Annual Survey: Ranking for 2001: #9

Description: Trade association representing the real estate industry. NAR's 750,000 members (composed of individuals involved in all aspects of residential and commercial real estate – brokers, salespersons, property managers, appraisers, etc.) belong to one or more of some 1,700 local associations/boards and 54 state/territory associations.

A Closer Look: Overall, NAR emphasizes: 1) "the American dream of homeownership," 2) the rights of property owners, 3) local decision-making (rather than at the state or federal level), and 4) use of financial incentives rather than regulations. NAR launched a "Smart Growth Initiative" in 3/00, aimed at making NAR "the leading land-use voice" on this issue (see below for specific initiative components) and urges its members to become active in local land-use planning. NAR also maintains a Congressional PAC that explicitly considers a candidate's stand on "smart growth" when making campaign contributions. From an environmental protection perspective, NAR's smart growth blueprint (see below) emphasizes private property rights, local control over land use decisions, and redevelopment of brownfields, while expressing concerns over open space preservation practices, wetlands policies, the Endangered Species Act, clean air standards, and federal mandates in general. NAR also seeks limits on impact fees imposed for infrastructure-related costs directly attributable to new development.

Lobbying/Political Activities: Registered lobbyist under the LDA; maintains a PAC (National Association of Realtors Political Action Committee).

Key Smart Growth Initiative Components (and NAR's activities): Research (conducts: a biannual national survey of public opinion; customized state/local surveys); Training (urges members to become active in local land-use planning); Technical Assistance on Legislation and Regulation (provides customized state smart growth legislation); Advocacy Publications; Federal Lobbying and Communications Program.

Key 2001 Priority Issues (and NAR's positions/viewpoints): Brownfields Legislation (advocates for program funding and elimination of owner liability); Land and Water Conservation Fund (against the fund, claiming it infringes on the rights of property owners); Planning Grants to States (advocates for federal funds to states to assist localities in planning).

Key Publication: Meeting the Challenge of Growth: A Blueprint for Realtor Action (the blueprint for NAR's "Smart Growth Initiative"; online).

Founded: 1908 **Members:** 750,000 individuals **Staff:** 450 **Budget:** $54 million

373.   National Automobile Dealers Association (NADA) (www.nada.org)

A Top Federal Lobbying Group Per Fortune Magazine's Annual Survey: Ranking for 2001: #39

Description: Trade association representing franchised new car and light truck dealers (both domestic and import), with nearly 20,000 members owning/operating nearly 40,000 separate franchises.

Lobbying/Political Activities: Registered lobbyist under the LDA; maintains a PAC (Dealers Election Action Committee of the NADA).

Key Issues (and NADA's positions/viewpoints): Auto Fuel Economy (opposes "large and rapid increases" in federal CAFE standards; supports consumer tax incentives to purchase fuel-efficient vehicles).

374.   National Electrical Manufacturers Association (NEMA) (www.nema.org)

Description: Trade association representing manufacturers of electrical equipment, with 600+ member companies. Principally known for development of technical standards for the industry, publishing 500+ standards. Maintains an Environmental, Health and Safety Council and an Energy Policy Center.

Lobbying/Political Activities: Registered lobbyist under the LDA; maintains a PAC (National Electrical Manufacturers Association Political Action Committee).

Key Issues (and focus areas): Dry Batteries (recycling/disposal); Electromagnetic Fields (potential human health effects); Energy (climate change; energy efficiency; energy transmission and distribution); International Trade (foreign market barriers; European Union regulations/directives); Mercury-Containing Lamps (labeling; recycling/disposal).

Key Project: Thermostat Recycling Corporation (a non-profit corporation owned by 3 NEMA member companies; aids in the collection of used, wall-mounted, mercury-switch thermostats for subsequent mercury recovery and re-use).

Founded: 1926 **Members:** 630 companies **Staff:** 95 **Budget:** $8 million

375.   National Endangered Species Act Reform Coalition (NESARC) (www.nesarc.org)

Description: A coalition of various parties seeking to reform the Endangered Species Act ("restoring balance to the ESA" is their motto). Former U.S. Senator James A. McClure serves as Chairman of the Coalition, while specific members include farming groups, energy firms/utilities, water users, natural resource extraction firms, land owners, and land development groups.

A Closer Look: A strong "property rights" tone is used to justify reform; the Coalition emphasizes providing incentives and/or compensation to property owners in addressing endangered species issues.

Key Business Trade Group Members (see separate profiles for each within this subsection): American Farm Bureau Federation, Electric Edison Institute, National Association of Homebuilders.

Lobbying/Political Activities: Registered lobbyist under the LDA; maintains a PAC.

376.   National Federation of Independent Businesses (NFIB) (www.nfibonline.com)

A Top Federal Lobbying Group Per Fortune Magazine's Annual Survey: Ranking for 2001: #3

Description: Trade association representing small and independent businesses, with 600,000 members. Nearly three-quarters of NFIB member businesses have less than 10 employees; about one-half of its members are in service or retail, with another one-fourth in construction or manufacturing. NFIB maintains offices in both Washington, DC and all 50 state capitals.

Lobbying/Political Activities: Registered lobbyist under the LDA; maintains a PAC (National Federation of Independent Businesses Safe Trust).

Key Issues (and NIFB's positions/viewpoints): Superfund (seeks a small business exemption from current

Superfund liability); Regulation (in general, seeks to make government regulations less costly and complicated for small businesses; focuses in particular on OSHA health and safety regulations).
Founded: 1943 **Members:** 600,000 individuals **Staff:** 1000 **Budget:** $70 million

377.   National Golf Course Owners Association (NGCOA) (www.ngcoa.org)

Description: Business membership association representing golf course owners in both the U.S. and Canada.

A Closer Look: NGCOA's stated mission – "to consider the problems of operation, management, and promotion of golf by profit-oriented, tax-paying owners and operators of golf courses" – suggests that the group is not very receptive to raised concerns in general and not likely to be very eco-friendly in particular. Its membership in Responsible Industry for a Sound Environment (see Profile #387) – which seeks to justify chemical pesticide use in general and particularly on golf courses (a key environmental issue for golf courses) – appears to confirm such observations.

Key Issue (and focus areas): Pesticide Use (health concerns; water contamination).

Website Notes: The publicly-accessible portion of NGCOA's website provides relatively little information.

Founded: 1976 **Members:** 3000 **Staff:** 4 **Budget:** $1 to 2 million

378.   National Hydrogen Association (NHA) (www.hydrogenUS.com)

Description: Mixed industry/small business and university/research center member association seeking to foster the development of hydrogen energy technologies and their utilization in industrial and commercial applications. Overall, NHA seeks to act as a national focal point for hydrogen interest and information transfer.

A Closer Look: NHA members include: auto manufacturers; fuel cell developers; gas producers; and chemical companies.

Key Project: Hydrogen Commercialization Plan (developing and implementing a strategic plan for achieving a hydrogen-based economy; carried out in conjunction with the U.S. Dept. of Energy).

Key Publication: Hydrogen Commercialization Plan (a "living document"; current version online).

Founded: 1989 **Members:** 70 companies and universities/research centers **Budget:** $0.25 to 0.5 million

379.   National Hydropower Association (NHA) (www.hydro.org)

Description: Trade association representing the U.S. hydropower industry. Has 150 members, including utilities and power producers, equipment manufacturers, consultants and law firms. NHA members collectively own or operate 60% of non-federal hydroelectric generating capacity in the U.S.

Lobbying/Political Activities: Registered lobbyist under the LDA.

Key Issues (and NHA's positions/viewpoints): Hydropower Licensing Reform (seeks reforms to streamline the re-licensing process, including establishing FERC as the final arbitrator); Electricity Restructuring (seeks inclusion of hydropower as part of any renewable portfolio standard; advocates for government tax incentives for hydropower generation/use); R&D Appropriations (advocates for increased federal funding to the Dept. of Energy for hydropower research and development); Decommissioning and Dam Removal (views dam removal strictly as a means of last resort to address environmental concerns).

Founded: 1983 **Members:** 150 companies/firms **Staff:** 5 **Budget:** $0.5 to 1 million

380.   National Mining Association (NMA) (www.nma.org)

Description: Trade association representing the U.S. mining industry. Created in 1995 when the National Coal Association merged with the American Mining Congress. NMA membership consists of coal, metal and hardrock mining operations, mineral processors, and other related businesses.

A Closer Look: Partners with the Greening Earth Society, a business-backed organization promoting the "benefits" of carbon dioxide emissions (see Profile #364).

Lobbying/Political Activities: Registered lobbyist under the LDA; maintains two PACs (CoalPAC and MinePAC).

Key Issues (and focus areas): Environment (abandoned mine land cleanup; air quality; community right-to-know/Toxics Release Inventory reporting; land subsidence; mine land reclamation; mine waste; water quality; wetlands, bird and animal habitat); Land Use (Endangered Species Act reform; revision of hardrock surface management regulations; mountaintop mining; millsites; the General Mining Law and related amendments; the National Monuments/Antiquities Act; private property rights); Energy (climate change policy).

Check Out on the Web: Mining Statistics (summary facts and statistics).

Founded: 1995 (by a merger of 2 orgs) **Members:** 400 companies **Staff:** 80 **Budget:** $12 million

381. National Petrochemical and Refiners Association (NPRA) (www.npradc.org)

Description: Trade association representing the petroleum refining and petrochemical manufacturing industries, with almost 500 member companies, including virtually all U.S. refiners and petrochemical manufacturers. Formerly known as the National Petroleum Refiners Association.

Lobbying/Political Activities: Registered lobbyist under the LDA.

Key Issues (and NPRA's positions/focus areas): Climate Change (opposes the Kyoto Protocol, but supports market-based programs to address greenhouse gas emissions); Diesel Sulfur (opposes the new 15 ppm sulfur cap for 2006/7; wants a 50 ppm cap for 2010 instead); Gasoline Sulfur (focused on the USEPA's "Tier 2 rule"); New Source Review (seeking a more flexible permitting process; also concerned over targeted enforcement efforts for alleged non-compliance); Superfund Taxes; Urban Air Toxics (focused on the USEPA's "anti-backsliding" toxics standard for gasoline).

Founded: 1902 **Members:** 490 companies **Staff:** 28 **Budget:** $1 to 2 million

382. National Rural Electric Cooperative Association (NRECA) (www.nreca.org)

A Top Federal Lobbying Group Per Fortune Magazine's Annual Survey: Ranking for 2001: #54

Description: Trade association representing 900 cooperative electric utilities (both consumer-owned and public power districts) serving 32 million people in 46 states.

A Closer Look: Advocates on general rural community and economic development issues, as well as on energy issues.

Lobbying/Political Activities: Registered lobbyist under the LDA; maintains a PAC (Action Committee for Rural Electrification).

Key Priority Issues (and NREC's viewpoints): Climate Change (carbon dioxide should not be regulated as an air pollutant; greenhouse gas reduction actions should focus on voluntary programs that are cost-effective); New Source Review (seeking to reform with respect to allowing maintenance and repair of coal-fired electric power plants); Clean Coal Technologies (supports increases federal funding for research, development, and deployment of such technologies).

Key Publication: Annual Meeting Resolutions (contains NRECA member-ratified new and continuing public policy resolutions; over 150 resolutions for 2001, focused on a wide variety of energy and rural area issues; online).

Founded: 1942 **Members:** 900 electric utilities **Staff:** 500 **Budget:** $140 million

383. National Solid Wastes Management Association (NSWMA) (www.nswma.org)

Description: Trade association representing solid and medical waste management industry, including firms providing collection, recycling, and disposal services and companies offering legal and consulting services to the industry. NSWMA itself is part of the Environmental Industry Associations (see Profile #356).

A Closer Look: NSWMA maintains two policy-focused groups: the Medical Waste Institute and the Landfill Institute.

Key Issues (and focus areas): Interstate Waste/Waste Flow Control (centering around the Supreme Court ruling that the U.S. Constitution's "commerce clause" prohibits states or local governments from banning or placing special burdens on out-of-state waste and/or directing where waste should be processed or disposed of); Superfund (potential liability for solid waste companies); Medical Waste Management/Disposal (incineration; alternative treatment/disposal technologies; mercury-contaminated waste; conflicting regulation and lack of coordination/communication between government agencies); Landfills (financial assurance requirements under

RCRA).

Key Publications (both online): Garbage By the Numbers (a summary data report); Size of the U.S. Solid Waste Industry (a summary report).

Financial Info: See Profile #356 for "Environmental Industry Associations."

384.   Nuclear Energy Institute (NEI) (www.nei.org)

A Top Federal Lobbying Group Per Fortune Magazine's Annual Survey: Ranking for 2001: #80

Description: Trade organization representing the nuclear energy and nuclear technologies industry. NEI has 260+ corporate members in 15 countries. Overall membership includes: companies that operate nuclear power plants and associated fuel suppliers; companies involved in non-power nuclear applications (including: nuclear medicine; food processing and agricultural applications; industrial applications); and universities/research institutes.

Lobbying/Political Activities: Registered lobbyist under the LDA; maintains a PAC (Nuclear Energy Institute Federal Political Action Committee).

Key Issues (and NEI's viewpoints/focus areas): Clean Air (promotes nuclear energy as an essential component of measures to limit emissions of greenhouse gases and other key air pollutants); Energy Security (contends that a diverse mix of energy sources is desirable and that nuclear energy is essential in ensuring such a mix); Electricity Deregulation (asserts that nuclear energy is competitive in the new electricity marketplace); Regulation (seeks major reforms in the regulatory process, one that NEI perceives as "burdensome, costly and not safety-focused"); License Renewal (about one-third of all nuclear power plants will need to apply for renewal by 2003); Used Fuel Management (favors transport to a central interim storage facility until a permanent national disposal facility is made ready); Low-Level Waste Management (seeks to maintain access to the one remaining facility – in Barnwell, SC – while also calling on states to open up new facilities over the next 10-15 years to accommodate wastes from shutdown nuclear plants); International Trade (focused on helping China build standardized nuclear power plants based on U.S. advanced plant designs).

Website Notes: An extensive website, with a multitude of information provided (although some has been removed following September 11 – particularly information regarding specific nuclear power plants that was formerly made available online).

Founded: 1981 **Members:** 370 **Staff:** 140 **Budget:** $27 million

385.   Pest Facts Information Center (www.pestfacts.org)

Description: An "information resource" website regarding pests and pesticides put forth by Responsible Industry for a Sound Environment (RISE; see Profile #387), a lobbying and public relations organization representing manufacturers, formulators, distributors and other members of the "specialty pesticides" industry.

A Closer Look: See Profile #387 for RISE.

Website Notes: Not that much information is currently provided on the website.

Associated Website: SchoolPestFacts.com (focuses on the "threats to kids" from pests – insects, weeds and diseases – and emphasizes use of chemical pesticides to address those "threats"; the website is operated by both RISE and the American Crop Protection Association – see Profiles # 387 and 325, respectively).

386.   Renewable Fuels Association (RFA) (www.ethanolRFA.org)

Description: Trade association for the U.S. ethanol fuel industry, "working to secure a strong marketplace for ethanol." RFA members include ethanol producers (public/private companies and farmer-owned cooperatives), fuel retailers and blenders, and agricultural organizations. RFA producer members collectively account for 90% of U.S. fuel ethanol production. RFA works to promote ethanol use in both regular gas and diesel fuel, as well as use as a fuel source in fuel cells for both transportation and stationary power applications.

Lobbying/Political Activities: Registered lobbyist under the LDA.

Check Out on the Web: Industry Outlook (an in-depth look at the U.S. ethanol industry as of 2/01).

Founded: 1981 **Members:** 75 companies **Staff:** 5 **Budget:** $1 to 2 million

387.   Responsible Industry for a Sound Environment (RISE) (www.pestfacts.org)

Description: A lobbying- and public relations-focused organization representing manufacturers, formulators, distributors and other members of the "specialty pesticides" industry (includes pesticides used in homes and schools, landscape uses, and urban pest and vegetation control). Many key members of RISE are large chemical companies (see "key members" list below). RISE operates the Pest Facts Information Center, an "information resource" website regarding pests and pesticides (see Profile #385).

A Closer Look: RISE is affiliated with the American Crop Protection Association (see Profile #325), sharing ACPA's Washington, DC offices. A telling sign of RISE's general viewpoint is conveyed by the list of "Health and Safety" web-links posted on its Pest Facts Information Center website, which includes "opposing view" organizations/websites such as the American Council on Science and Health, JunkScence.com, and the Mountain States Legal Foundation (see separate profiles for each within Section 6.2 – "Opposing View Groups"). A key concern of RISE appears to be dealing with questions raised over chemical pesticide use on golf courses, as they provide a dedicated section addressing that particular issue on the "Pest Facts" website (in that regard, it should also be noted that the National Golf Course Owners Association – see Profile #377 – is a member of RISE).

Key Corporate Members: BASF; Clorox; Dow; Dupont; FMC; Monsanto; Rohm and Haas; Scotts.

388.   Rubber Manufacturers Association (RMA) (www.rma.org)

Description: Trade association representing the U.S. finished rubber products industry. Comprised of two divisions: the Tire Group (which includes the 7 major U.S. tire manufacturers) and the General Products Group (which has 100+ members).

Facts and Figures: 60% of rubber production is used for tire manufacturing.

Lobbying/Political Activities: Registered lobbyist under the LDA.

Key Issue: Scrap Tire Disposition (some 300 million scrap tires are currently stockpiled, with nearly 275 million scrap tires generated in 2000 alone; amongst disposition options, some 125 million scrap tires were used as a fuel source in 2000).

Founded: 1900 **Members:** 135 companies **Staff:** 22 **Budget:** $2 to 5 million

389.   Solar Electric Power Association (SEPA) (www.solarelectricpower.org)

Description: A coalition of 80+ electric utilities and energy service providers and 30 photovoltaic (PV) industry organizations (manufacturers, installers, etc.) promoting the commercial use of solar electric power. SEPA members collectively account for nearly 50% of total U.S. electricity sales, serving 40+ million customers.

Basic Activities: Helps establish standards for PV systems and their interconnection to the utility grid; hosts cross-industry workshops; manages educational and outreach campaigns.

Key Project: TEAM-UP (Technology Experience to Accelerate Markets in Utility Photovoltaics; a partnership with the U.S. Dept. of Energy providing cost-sharing for selected PV business ventures).

390.   Solar Energy Industries Association (SEIA) (www.seia.org)

Description: Trade association representing U.S. solar energy manufacturers, dealers, distributors, contractors and installers. Has 500+ member companies.

Lobbying/Political Activities: Registered lobbyist under the LDA.

Key Issues (and SEIA's viewpoints/activities): Federal Research Program (advocates for increases in the Dept. of Energy's research and development budget for solar energy); Residential Solar Tax Credit (advocates for a tax credit for purchases of residential solar electric or water heating equipment); Production Tax Credit (advocates for a tax credit similar to that currently in place for wind energy); Federal Net Metering/ Interconnection Standards (seeks to standardize the way individuals/businesses can feed excess solar energy into the electric grid and receive credit for that generated energy).

Founded: 1974 **Members:** 500+ companies **Staff:** 5 **Budget:** $0.5 to 1 million

391.   Steel Recycling Institute (SRI) (www.recycle-steel.org)

Description:. A unit of the American Iron and Steel Institute (see Profile #333) that promotes recycling of all steel products. Formerly known as the Steel Can Recycling Institute.

Lobbying/Political Activities: Registered lobbyist under the LDA.

Focus Areas: Cans; Cars; Appliances; Construction Materials.

Founded: 1988 **Members:** 19 steel companies **Staff:** 30 **Regional Offices:** 5 **Budget:** $2 to 5 million

392.   Sustainable Buildings Industry Council (SBIC) (www.sbicouncil.org)

Description:. Business council promoting "integrated, energy efficient, 'whole buildings'" both within and outside the building industry. Council members include builders, manufacturers, architect and engineering firms, utilities, and consultants. SBIC particularly focuses on promoting use of passive solar strategies and "whole building design" (a collaborative design approach).

Basic Activities: Education/training programs; publications/informational services.

Key Technical Publication: Designing Low-Energy Buildings (a set of guidelines for using passive solar design and energy efficiency strategies in all types of buildings; also includes the "ENERGY-10" software design tool).

Founded: 1980 **Members:** 70 companies/firms **Staff:** 8 **Budget:** $0.1 to 0.25 million

393.   Synthetic Organic Chemical Manufacturers Association (SOCMA) (www.socma.com)

Description:. Trade association representing manufacturers/processors of synthetic organic chemicals worldwide. Has 300+ member companies. Maintains a multitude of specialized affiliated groups (councils, working groups, task forces, committees, etc.).

A Closer Look: An interesting membership requirement for SOCMA is "commitment and implementation" of the American Chemistry Council's "Responsible Care"® program (see Profile #323 for further program details).

Lobbying/Political Activities: Registered lobbyist under the LDA.

Key Issues: Federal Environmental Laws/Regulations; EPA Activities; International Trade.

Founded: 1921 **Members:** 300+ companies **Staff:** 45 **Budget:** $12 million

394.   United States Chamber of Commerce (www.uschamber.com)

A Top Federal Lobbying Group Per Fortune Magazine's Annual Survey: Ranking for 2001: #7

Description: Business trade organization representing 3+ million businesses, 3000 state and local Chambers of Commerce and 800+ business associations; 96% of members are small businesses (100 or less employees). Also known as the Chamber of Commerce of the U.S.A.

A Closer Look: Under the leadership of Thomas Donohue since 1997, the Chamber clearly has adopted a "business versus the environment" stance. Amongst the major themes of Donohue's stated agenda is "fighting extreme environmentalists," and it appears those two words – extreme and environmentalist – always go together in his view. Further insight into Donohue's general viewpoint can be gained from the fact that he serves on the Board of Directors of the libertarian-based think tank the Hudson Institute (see Profile #429, located within Section 6.2 – "Opposing View Groups"). His Vice-President for Environmental and Regulatory Affairs – Bill Kovacs – has an equally alarming mindset that again clearly seeks to place business before the environment – according to the Chamber's website, Kovacs is "passionate in his belief that our nation can have a healthy and clean environment only by having a healthy business community that generates the wealth to maintain it." Further indication of the current general Chamber thinking is found under the "What We Do" section of their website – the first item listed is "lobby government to keep regulators off your back." But perhaps of most concern overall is the Chambers continued publication of "The Environmentalists' Little Green Book," a collection of alleged quotes from environmentalists typically presented in an out-of-context manner.

Lobbying/Political Activities: Registered lobbyist under the LDA; maintains a PAC (National Chamber Alliance for Politics).

Key Affiliated Programs/Organizations: Grassroots Action Information Network (GAIN; a network of business activists and a team of lobbyists); National Chamber Foundation (the Chamber's public policy think tank); Institute for Legal Reform (litigation arm of the Chamber).

Key Issues (and the Chamber's key positions/viewpoints) – Environment and Energy: Air Quality Requirements (considers new USEPA requirements – including those for soot and smog – to "not have been shown to carry any real health or environmental benefits"); Brownfields (wants site cleanups to be administered at the state and local level, with cleanup standards established independent of existing federal [CERCLA and RCRA] standards); Clean Water (opposes USEPA efforts to implement new intake, TMDL, and mixing-zone rules "until the costs and benefits are proven and backed by sound science"); Data Access (seeks FOIA access to non-governmental data [developed by third-party universities or non-profits] that is used to support federal regulations); Electricity Restructuring (promotes a state-by-state approach to electricity restructuring, along with federal legislation to remove interstate regulatory barriers to competition; supports repeal of PUHCA); Energy Strategy (supports the Bush Administration's energy plan; has joined the Alliance for Energy and Economic Growth – see Profile #319, located within this subsection); Environmental Justice (seeks to prevent implementation of USEPA's environmental justice guidance document; claims environmental justice is used by USEPA to prevent industrial development; also claims USEPA has no statutory authority to implement the program); Forest Roads (opposes efforts to eliminate road construction in sections of national forests based on alleged economic impacts to local communities, particularly in terms of reduced funding for local schools); Kyoto Global Climate Treaty (opposes the Kyoto Protocol in favor of incentives for developing high-efficiency technologies and transferring efficient technologies to developing nations); Local Development Restrictions (claims that several proposed USEPA regulations – concerning air quality, water permitting and environmental justice, among others – will "restrict new developments, freeze economic expansion, and force businesses to close"); Nuclear Waste (focused on establishing an interim storage facility at Yucca Mountain while work continues on finding/building a permanent repository); Property Rights/ Endangered Species (supports legislation to make it easier for property owners to have so-called "takings" claims heard in federal court); Total Maximum Daily Loads (wants USEPA to withdraw or modify its proposed TMDL rules, considered by the Chamber to be "needlessly expensive, unworkable and cumbersome… (while) unlikely to provide additional environmental benefit).

Key Issues (and the Chamber's key positions/viewpoints) – Food and Agriculture: Biotechnology (seeks to promote use of biotechnology in food, medicine, agriculture, textiles and other products; vows to "work diligently to counter the propaganda of anti-technology activists"); Food Safety (a telling statement: "Under the guise of improving food safety, radical environmental groups are capitalizing on consumers' fears about food safety to expand their fundraising efforts. Baseless allegations, actual fabrication of evidence, "eco" terrorism, and other parts of the anti-capitalism, anti-globalization protest movement are serious problems facing the food industry"); Genetically Modified Organisms and the European Union (claims that the European Union has implemented a *de facto* moratorium on biotech crop approvals; supports international trade rules that reduce trade barriers against biotech commodities).

Key Issues (and the Chamber's key positions/viewpoints) – Transportation: CAFE Standards (opposes raising the standards, alleging it would "result in increased fatalities and injuries…restrict consume choice and cost American jobs"); Quality Growth (promotes "quality growth" as opposed to conventional "smart growth"; seek policies that "accommodate, rather than stifle, growth"); TEA-21 (focuses on ensuring that collected highway user fees are only used to repair/expand the nation's surface transportation infrastructure).
Staff: 1100 **Budget:** $66 million

---

395.   United States Council for Automotive Research (USCAR) (www.uscar.org)
Description: An umbrella management organization for various technical research partnerships formed by the "Big 3" U.S. automakers (Daimler-Chrysler, Ford, and General Motors). A key program of USCAR is the Partnership for a New Generation of Vehicles (PNGV), a federal government-USCAR partnership program formed in 1993 to develop and produce affordable, fuel-efficient, low-emissions vehicles that meet current performance standards.
USCAR Consortia/Partnerships (in addition to PNGV): Advanced Battery Research; Automotive Composites; Automotive Materials; Electrical Wiring Components; Environmental Research; Low Emissions Technologies; Low Emission Paint; Natural Gas Vehicle Technology; Occupant Safety Research; Supercomputer Automotive Applications; Vehicle Recycling.
Key Issue: PNGV Program (in 1/02, the Bush Administration proposed eliminating the PNVG program in favor of its own proposed "Automotive Fuel Cell Initiative").
Check Out on the Web: "2000 Concept Cars" (presents the results of the current PNGV program – prototype

cars achieving 72-80 mpg fuel efficiency; located under "About PNGV").

United States Council for International Business (USCIB) (www.uscib.org)
See Profile #309, located within Subsection 3.2 – "Other Multilaterals."

United States Energy Association (USEA) (www.usea.org)
See Profile #310, located within Subsection 3.2 – "Other Multilaterals."

396. Vinyl Institute (VI) (www.vinylinfo.org)

Description: Trade association representing manufacturers of vinyl, including vinyl-packaging materials. An affiliate of the American Plastics Council (see Profile #335).

A Closer Look: The Institute's website seeks to convey a positive message, emphasizing the potential beneficial aspects of plastics use, while also promoting plastics recycling and seeking to allay raised concerns over the general safety of vinyl products (see "Key Issues" below). In addition, the website is used to promote the vinyl industry's formal commitment to the American Chemistry Council's "Responsible Care®" program (see Profile #323 for a details on that particular program), as well as its own "Partnership for Humanity," a joint project with the Chlorine Chemistry Council (see Profile #347) supporting Habitat for Humanity.

Key Corporate Members: Chemical giants BASF, Dow, Occidental, and Rohm and Haas.

Key Issues: General Calls For Banning Vinyl (due to a host of raised concerns, including: problems with recycling; concerns that incineration of vinyl wastes can result in dioxin and acid gas emissions, along with heavy metals being left behind in the ash; potential decomposition of vinyl in landfills, giving off toxic vinyl chloride monomer; potential health concerns over use of vinyl chloride monomer – a cancer-causing agent – to make vinyl products; potential release of hydrogen chloride gas during fires; concerns over potential health hazards in both food-contact and medical applications).

Associated Website: vinyl.org ("the vinyl industry's portal page").

Founded: 1982 **Members:** 32 companies **Staff:** 4 **Budget:** $2 to 5 million

397. Waste Equipment Technology Association (WASTEC) (www.wastec.org)

Description: Trade association representing firms affiliated with the solid/hazardous waste equipment industry (including recycling systems). Part of the Environmental Industry Associations (see Profile #356). WASTEC focuses on technical activities (including equipment standards development and technical project working groups) through its Technical Programs Division while performing advocacy work through its Executive Programs Division.

Founded: 1972 **Financial Info:** See Profile #356 for "Environmental Industry Associations."

398. Water Quality and Health Council (WQHC) (no website)

Description: A business council of the American Chemistry Council (see Profile #323) which promotes the use of chlorine for both water and wastewater treatment). Operated through ACC's Chlorine Chemistry Council (see Profile #347).

Subsection 5.2: Labor Unions

Introduction/User's Guide:

Within this subsection, 8 key labor unions are profiled, including the national "umbrella" union, the American Federation of Labor – Congress of Industrial Organizations (AFL-CIO), which collectively represents 80% of all unionized workers.

In terms of individual entry contents, the following is a descriptive outline of standardized profile information provided for each labor union listed within this subsection (please note that the exact contents provided varies by organization, being dependant upon applicability and/or availability):

[Profile #] Union Name (Website Address)

A Top Federal Lobbying Group Per Fortune Magazine's Annual Survey: Noted as applicable with ranking for 2001 provided.

Description: A short summary of the union, particularly in regards to its membership and whether it is a member of the AFL-CIO.

A Closer Look: Providing further information on the union, principally in terms of additional relevant facts.

Lobbying/Political Activities: Included if the union is registered as a federal lobbyist under the Lobbying Disclosure Act (LDA) and/or maintains a Political Action Committee (PAC), with the name of the PAC specified.

Key Issues (and the union's viewpoints): Based on information obtained from the union's website.

Organizational profiles for this subsection are listed beginning on the next page, presented in alphabetical order.

A Closer Look – Union Involvement in Environmental Issues:

While often remaining relatively neutral on environmental issues overall – typically becoming involved only if the particular issue can/will significantly affect relevant union jobs (positively or negatively) and/or potentially impact worker health or safety – labor unions can (and do) play a major role when engaged because of their relatively large political influence. (In that regard, it should be noted that all eight unions profiled in this subsection are listed in Fortune magazine's annual survey as top federal lobbying groups for 2001, indicating their relatively strong ability to influence general policymaking at the federal level.)

Subsection 5.2: Labor Unions

399.   American Federation of Labor – Congress of Industrial Organizations (AFL-CIO) (www.aflcio.org)

A Top Federal Lobbying Group Per Fortune Magazine's Annual Survey: Ranking for 2001: #6

Description: Voluntary federation of 64 national and international labor unions, representing 13+ million workers combined (about 80% of all unionized workers).

A Closer Look: Opposed Gale Norton's nomination as Interior Secretary for the Bush Administration, calling it "a massive affront to environmentalists and to all who are concerned about…the earth."

Lobbying/Political Activities: Registered lobbyist under the LDA; maintains a PAC (AFL-CIO Committee on Political Education/Political Contribution Committee [COPE]).

Key Issues (and the AFL-CIO's positions): Energy Policy (opposes the Kyoto Protocol; opposes electricity restructuring; supports fuel diversity, including fossil fuels, nuclear, hydro and renewables).

400.   International Association of Machinists and Aerospace Workers (IAMAW) (Machinists Union) (www.iamaw.org)

A Top Federal Lobbying Group Per Fortune Magazine's Annual Survey: Ranking for 2001: #74

Description: Union representing 730,000 active and retired employees in shipbuilding, manufacturing, aerospace, railroads and airlines. A member of the AFL-CIO.

Lobbying/Political Activities: Registered lobbyist under the LDA; maintains a PAC (Machinists Non-Partisan Political League).

Key Issues (and IAM's positions): Forests (supports the American Forest and Paper Association's Sustainable Forest Initiative [SM]; supports the federal timber supply program; supports full funding for the federal forest roads program).

401.   International Brotherhood of Teamsters (IBT) (The Teamsters) (www.teamster.org)

A Top Federal Lobbying Group Per Fortune Magazine's Annual Survey: Ranking for 2001: #25

Description: Union with 1.4 million members representing "everyone from A to Z." Structured to promote strong local unions (there are 521 local Teamster unions located nationwide). Has 16 trade divisions that serve as an information clearinghouse for the local IBT unions. A member of the AFL-CIO.

A Closer Look: In a highly publicized event, the Teamsters broke ranks with the AFL-CIO in opening supporting the Bush Administration's proposal to open up the Artic National Wildlife Refuge to oil and gas drilling.

Lobbying/Political Activities: Registered lobbyist under the LDA; maintains a PAC (Democratic-Republican-Independent Voter Education [DRIVE]).

Key Issues (and the Teamster's positions): Artic Oil Drilling (supports drilling in ANWR).

402.   International Union, United Automobile, Aerospace and Agricultural Implement Workers of America (United Auto Workers Union – UAW) (www.uaw.org)

A Top Federal Lobbying Group Per Fortune Magazine's Annual Survey: Ranking for 2001: #33

Description: Union representing 750,000 active members and 500,000 retired members in the U.S., Canada and Puerto Rico. Represents employees in the automotive, heavy truck, farm/heavy equipment, and aerospace/defense industries, but principally known for representing workers for the "Big 3" U.S. automakers (Daimler-Chrysler, Ford, and General Motors). A member of the AFL-CIO.

Lobbying/Political Activities: Registered lobbyist under the LDA; maintains a PAC (United Auto Workers Political Action Committee).

Key Issues (and the UAW's positions): Auto Fuel Efficiency Standards (opposes raising CAFE standards).

403.   Sheet Metal Workers International Association (SMWIA) (www.smwia.org)

A Top Federal Lobbying Group Per Fortune Magazine's Annual Survey: Ranking for 2001: #77

Description: Union representing 150,000 craftspersons employed in the U.S. and Canadian sheet metal industry. A member of the AFL-CIO.

Lobbying/Political Activities: Registered lobbyist under the LDA; maintains a PAC (Sheet Metal Workers International Association Political Action Committee).

404.   United Association of Plumbers and Pipefitters (UA) (www.ua.org)

A Top Federal Lobbying Group Per Fortune Magazine's Annual Survey: Ranking for 2001: #83

Description: Building trades union representing 290,000 craftspersons across North America employed in the fabrication, installation and servicing of piping systems. Members belong to one of 418 local UA unions. A member of the AFL-CIO.

Lobbying/Political Activities: Registered lobbyist under the LDA; maintains a PAC (United Association Political Education Committee).

Key Issues (and the UA's positions): Artic Oil Drilling (supports drilling in ANWR); Clean Air Standards (opposed to the EPA's new ozone and particulate standards).

United Auto Workers Union (UAW) (www.uaw.org)

See Profile #402 for "International Union, United Automobile, Aerospace and Agricultural Implement Workers of America."

405.   United Brotherhood of Carpenters and Joiners of America (UBC) (Carpenters Union) (www.necarpenters.org/UBC.htm)

A Top Federal Lobbying Group Per Fortune Magazine's Annual Survey: Ranking for 2001: #72

Description: Union representing 400,000+ members through affiliated local unions throughout North America. Members include carpenters, framers, millwrights, pile drivers, cabinet workers, floor coverers and asbestos abatement workers. Recently disaffiliated itself from the AFL-CIO.

Lobbying/Political Activities: Registered lobbyist under the LDA; maintains a PAC (Carpenters' Legislative Improvement Committee).

Website Note: Doesn't yet have a website of its own – shares part of the website of its New England regional chapter.

406.   United Mine Workers of America (UMWA) (www.umwa.org)

A Top Federal Lobbying Group Per Fortune Magazine's Annual Survey: Ranking for 2001: #69

Description: Union representing about 40% of all employed miners, with an overall membership of 240,000 in 1998. A member of the AFL-CIO.

Lobbying/Political Activities: Registered lobbyist under the LDA; maintains a PAC (Coal Miners Political Action Committee).

Key Issues (and UMWA's positions): Global Climate Change (opposes the Kyoto Protocol; opposes carbon taxes and market-based "cap and trade" systems; favors implementing more energy-efficient technologies); Clean Air Standards (opposes the EPA's new ozone and particulate standards); Ozone Transport (opposes federal intervention in the ozone non-attainment problem in the northeast; wants decision-making left up to the states).

SECTION 6: "OPPOSING VIEW GROUPS"

INTRODUCTION/USER'S GUIDE:

In this section, profiles are provided of 35 non-business groups (and associated entities) that are typically labeled by critics/observers as "anti-environmental" based on their views and/or activities (although none understandably classify themselves as such; in fact, at least some refer to themselves as "the real environmentalists"). The section is divided into the following two subsections:

> 6.1 – Key Policy Research Institutions ("Think Tanks") (4 entries)
> 6.2 – Other Organizations and Entities   (31 entries)

In terms of individual entry contents, the following is a descriptive outline of standardized profile information provided for each organization/entity listed within this section (please note that the exact contents provided varies by organization, being dependant upon applicability and/or availability):

[Profile #] Organization/Entity Name (Website Address)

A Top Federal Lobbying Group Per Fortune Magazine's Annual Survey: Noted as applicable with the organization's ranking for 2001 specified.

Description: A short summary of the organization, particularly in regards to its basic focus and activities.

A Closer Look: Providing further information on the organization, principally in terms of presenting a critical examination in light of its labeling by critics/observers as being "anti-environmental."

Lobbying/Political Activities: Included if the organization is registered as a federal lobbyist under the Lobbying Disclosure Act (LDA) and/or maintains a Political Action Committee (PAC), with the name of the PAC specified.

Key Issues (and activities/focus areas/viewpoints of the org): Generally listed based on information obtained from the organization's website.

Key Initiatives/Projects: Highlighting the organization's "high priority" issues/activities.

Key Reports/Publications: Listing specific reports and other publications judged to represent "essential reading" for interested parties, and noting if they are available online at the organization's website. (A summary listing of all such reports/publications is also provided in Appendix B.)

Annual Report: Only included if the report is available online at the organization's website; if so, the latest year available is specified. (Represents a key additional source of information on the organization's activities.)

Associated Websites: Listing distinct websites separate from the org's main website, along with a short description.

Website Notes: Significant notes concerning the main website – navigating hints, content notes, etc.

Check Out on the Web: Listing website-related content/features that particularly stand out ("worth a look").

Founded: Beginning year specified **HQ:** Noting city and state **Staff:** Overall staffing level **NP Status:** Formal IRS non-profit status (typically 501(c)(3) – exempt) **Revenue/Expenses:** Overall figures as obtained from IRS submittals (IRS Form 990) **Budget:** As obtained from non-IRS sources (annual report, website, etc.)

Revenue: Providing a percentage breakdown based on IRS submittals (IRS Form 990). Categories considered: Contributions (non-governmental public support from individuals, foundations, businesses, etc.); Government Grants; Program Service Revenues; Other (a variety of miscellaneous sources including: membership dues; investment income; special events; inventory sales [typically publications]).

Expenses: Providing a percentage breakdown based on IRS submittals (IRS Form 990). Categories considered: Program Services (broken down by specific program/service when available); Management and General (administration and overhead expenses); Fundraising.

Affiliated Orgs: Noted as applicable, based on IRS submittals and other sources (annual report, website, etc.).

Key Personnel: Typically citing the name and title of the chief paid executive (President, Executive Director, etc.), along with the total financial compensation they receive per IRS submittals (IRS Form 990).

Key Affiliations: Noting if the organization is a listed member of **Townhall.com** (a Heritage Foundation-based network of conservative groups) and/or the **Freedom Network** (a libertarian-based network of groups).

A CLOSER LOOK – The Prevailing Ideology Behind The Profiled Groups:

The "opposing view" organizations/entities listed within this section typically can be classified based on general political ideology as either being conservative or libertarian in nature (note: for a general background on libertarian ideology, see Profile #315 for the Libertarian Party, located within Subsection 4.1 – "Political Parties"). Overall, these groups' views on the environment are driven by and large by a shared general ideological belief in limiting government intervention – especially at the federal level – in the "free market" (that is, the capitalist economic system in place in the U.S.; by extension, these groups also typically strongly advocate for "free trade" worldwide).

However, a split in ideological belief occurs when looking at the exact extent of government intervention these groups wish to limit – while both sets of groups seek to limit both government regulation and taxes, libertarian-based groups also seek to limit all forms of government subsidies, while conservative-based groups typically view government subsidies as appropriate "market tools." In addition, while libertarians seek to privatize all public lands, conservatives generally seek only to make such lands available for resource extraction (obtaining minerals, timber, oil, etc.) or other use by private interests without necessarily seeking to sell off the lands themselves to private interests.

A CLOSER LOOK – "Free-Market Environmentalism":

Based on the above fundamental beliefs, both sets of "opposing view" groups (conservative- and libertarian-based) generally have put forth and/or embraced various versions of a so-called "new environmentalism" that is promoted as an alternative to current mainstream environmentalism. At its core, this "new environmentalism" is based on a reliance on the free market system – instead of existing environmental laws and regulations – to protect the environment (hence, it is typically referred to as "free-market environmentalism," although it also has been referred to as "civic," "community-based," or "common sense" environmentalism by different groups). Intertwined with this core belief in the free market are several other common tenants, including in particular:

- Strong private property rights (based on a relatively broad interpretation of the so-called "Takings Clause" of the Fifth Amendment to the U.S. Constitution).
- Decentralized decision-making (having decisions preferably made at the state/local level rather than through federal rulemaking).
- Evaluating and/or prioritizing issues based on risk (using formal risk-assessment methodology, including comparative-risk analysis) and economics (using formal cost/benefit analysis).
- Use of "sound science" (as opposed to so-called "junk science") in policy-/decision-making.

While appearing relatively reasonable (and potentially desirable) on the surface – particularly when viewed on a piecemeal basis – it is the proposed application of these principles – particularly when considering their overall combined effect – that typically earns these groups (and "free-market environmentalism" in general) an "anti-environmental" label by critics/observers. Specific areas of concern cited by critics/observers are as follows:

- Efforts by such groups are typically focused on removing the existing law/regulation-based control structure, with relatively little put forth regarding exactly how the free market system will step in to provide natural resource conservation and/or environmental protection (while in general market-based tools are acknowledged as being potentially effective in certain cases, critics/observers charge that these groups would consistently put the market ahead of the environment in carrying out such applications).
- The strong property rights stance taken by such groups is viewed by critics/observers as akin to a "right-

to-pollute"/"right-to-harm-or-deplete-natural resources" stance and/or effectively an attempt to extract financial compensation for not polluting or harming/depleting natural resources (i.e., seeking payment for acting responsibly/"doing the right thing").

- The promotion of decentralized decision-making down to the state/local level by such groups is seen by critics/observers as a strategy to more readily influence the decision-making process towards removing the various regulatory-based protections currently in place, potentially resulting in a so-called "race to the bottom," whereby states and localities feel obligated to sacrifice environmental protection/resource conservation in favor of maintaining/increasing economic activity (under the logic that businesses will seek to locate environmentally-impacting activities where conditions are most favorable – i.e., where environmental protection/resource conservation requirements are weakest).

- The emphasis put forth by such groups on use of formal risk and economic analyses (both areas of which are controversial as they are each subject to large uncertainties and variability in calculation), along with the "sound vs. junk" science debate frequently brought up by these groups are both viewed by critics/observers as representing convenient means for these groups to consistently question and/or downplay raised environmental concerns (as well as potential solutions to address such concerns) rather than actually serving as a legitimate priority-setting framework.

Taken in total, critics charge, "free-market environmentalism" represents nothing more than a veiled attempt to remove the regulatory control structure currently in place without substituting any effective alternative means to ensure that environmental protection and appropriate resource conservation will continue to take place. It has also been characterized as the latest reincarnation of the so-called "Wise Use" movement of the early 1990s – a movement that focused on private property rights and decentralized decision-making in seeking to remove existing federal regulatory controls and other government mandates with respect to use of natural resources (for which it was labeled as "anti-environmental" in nature).

A CLOSER LOOK – Key Government Officials' Ties to Opposing View Groups:

It should be noted that three current high-ranking government officials within the Bush Administration have close ties with opposing view groups profiled in this section, namely:

- Gale Norton (Secretary of the Interior): Norton spent four years (1979-83) as a staff attorney at the Mountain States Legal Foundation [see Profile #431], which was founded by the controversial James Watt, who served as Secretary of the Interior under the Regan Administration until he was forced to resign, due in part to his views on the need for natural resource conservation (Norton herself served as Assistant Solicitor for conservation and wildlife within the DOI from 1985-87). Norton also has served as an Advisory Board member for Defenders of Property Rights [see Profile #420], as well as reportedly has had close ties with the Pacific Research Institute [see Profile #436]. (It should also be noted that as head of the DOI, Norton is promoting a "new environmentalism" within the DOI that closely resembles the so-called "free-market environmentalism" previously discussed above.)

- Lynn Scarlett (Assistant Secretary for Policy, Management and Budget under DOI Secretary Gale Norton): Prior to her appointment at the DOI, Scarlett served as the President of the libertarian Reason Foundation [see Profile #410].

- John Graham (Administrator of the Federal Office of Information and Regulatory Affairs – a.k.a. "Regulatory Czar" – within the Office of Management and Budget): Prior to his appointment, Graham served as the Founding Director of the Harvard Center for Risk Analysis [see Profile # 427].

Subsection 6.1: Key Policy Research Institutions ("Think Tanks")

Introduction/User's Guide:

Within this subsection, four leading "opposing view" policy research institutions – two libertarian-based think tanks (the Cato Institute and the Reason Public Policy Institute) and two strongly conservative thinks tanks (the Competitive Enterprise Institute and the Heritage Foundation) – are profiled. All four cover a range of policy issues, but each substantially focuses in on environmental issues.

Organizational profiles for this subsection are listed beginning on the next page, presented in alphabetical order (for a descriptive outline of the standardized profile information provided, see the beginning of this section).

A Closer Look:

A "think tank" is a somewhat loosely defined term typically applied to independent organizations whose main activity consists of research/analysis of public policy issues and whose main output typically is in the form of written reports/briefs primarily aimed at policy-/decision-makers. At traditional think tanks – such as the Brookings Institution – an academic environment is maintained, with research staff being formally referred to as "scholars."

While at least superficially maintaining a traditional type of academic atmosphere, each of the think tanks listed within this subsection go substantially beyond the relatively passive nature of traditional think tanks to aggressively "market" their ideas to policy- and decision-makers, likely because of their non-centrist views.

Subsection 6.1: Key Policy Research Institutions ("Think Tanks")

407.   Cato Institute (www.cato.org)

Description: Libertarian-based think tank advocating for free markets/free trade, limited government (including minimal government regulation), and individual rights. Conducts policy research in 14 areas, including Natural Resources and Environmental Studies, where it advocates for so-called "free-market environmentalism" (relying solely on the free market and private property rights – instead of environmental laws and regulations – to protect the environment and natural resources).

A Closer Look: Cato's list of "fellows" includes the humor writer P.J. O'Rourke and the magicians Penn and Teller.

Key Policy Research Areas (and activities/focus areas): Natural Resources and Environmental Studies (covers a wide range of topics; also promotes "free-market environmentalism"); Regulatory Studies (seeks far-reaching "regulatory rollback"); Risk and Science Studies (focuses on so-called "junk science").

Founded: 1977 **HQ:** Washington, DC **Fellows/scholars:** 15 fellows; 60 adjunct scholars **NP Status:** 501(c)(3) **Revenue/Expenses (2000):** $12.4/$12.2 million

Revenue (2000): Contributions (89%); Government Grants (0%); Program Service Revenues (6%; from conference registration fees); Other (5%).

Expenses (2000): Program Services (63%; for: publications –48%; forums/seminars –15%); Management and General (21%); Fundraising (16%).

Key Personnel: Edward Crane (President; 2000 compensation: $315,164)

Key Affiliations: Townhall.com (conservative group network); Freedom Network (libertarian group network).

408.   Competitive Enterprise Institute (CEI) (www.cei.org)

Description: Conservative think tank advocating for free markets/free trade and limited government (including minimal government regulation). Focuses on 3 issue areas affecting business/industry: Environment; Health and Safety; Technology. Promotes so-called "free-market environmentalism" (relying solely on the free market and private property rights – instead of environmental laws and regulations – to protect the environment and natural resources). Also publishes the *Cooler Heads Newsletter* for the Cooler Heads Coalition (see Profile #419).

A Closer Look: In general accordance with its name, CEI believes that for business enterprises to be "competitive," they should be "unfettered" by environmental, health and safety regulations – CEI appears to never have met a regulation they like, with their "Free Market Legal" program specifically designed to "develop new tools for challenging government regulations." In this effort, they "take no prisoners" (see the "Check Out on the Web" entry below), having been cited as "one of Washington's feistiest think tanks" by the *Boston Globe*. For their efforts on behalf of business/industry, the *Wall Street Journal* named CEI as "the best environmental think tank." In general, CEI focuses on getting their word out via press releases and op-ed pieces.

Key Departments: Competition and Regulation Policy (seeks regulatory reform); Environmental Policy; Free Market Legal Program (a.k.a. "Death by Regulation Program").

Key Center: Center for Environmental Education Research (contends that current K-12 environmental education is biased and based on "environmentalist propaganda").

Key Issues: Air Pollution; Biotech and Food Regulation; Chemical and Environmental Risk; Energy and Electricity; Environmental Education; Federal Lands; Global Warming; Property Rights; Private Conservation; Regulatory Reform and Deregulation; Solid and Hazardous Waste; Trade and International Environment; Transportation; Water and Wetlands; Wildlife and Marine Resources.

Key Publication: Earth Report 2000 (CEI's own assessment of the state of the planet).

Check Out on the Web: "Sell Out of the Month" (past "sell outs" includes the U.S. Chamber of Commerce, Ford Motor Co., Sen. Trent Lott, Rep. Don Young, and Steve Forbes – a strong indication of CEI's reputation for "feistiness").

Founded: 1984 **HQ:** Washington, DC **Staff:** 35 **NP Status:** 501(c)(3) **Revenue/Expenses (FY00):** $2.7/$3.2 million

Revenue (FY00): Contributions (97%); Government Grants (0%); Program Service Revenues (<1%); Other

(2%).

Expenses (FY00): Program Services (77%; for: environmental studies program –47%; publications –8%; regulatory reform program –7%; free market legal program –6%; economic studies program –6%; media outreach –3%); Management and General (12%); Fundraising (11%).

Key Personnel: Fred L. Smith, Jr. (President; FY00 compensation: $150,000)

Key Affiliations: Townhall.com (conservative group network); Freedom Network (libertarian group network).

409. Heritage Foundation (www.heritage.org)

Description: Conservative think tank advocating public policy based on "free enterprise, limited government, individual freedom, traditional American values, and a strong national defense." Covers 28 issue areas, including Energy and the Environment. Operates Town Hall – a "one-stop mall of ideas" from the conservative movement (see Profile #440, located within Subsection 6.2 – "Other 'Opposing View' Organizations and Entities").

Key Issues (and focus areas): Energy and the Environment (energy; environmental reform; air; water; Superfund; global warming; global environmentalism; natural resources); Regulation; Smart Growth; Urban Issues.

Key Publication: Issues 2000: The Candidate's Briefing Book (see Chapter 5: Environment, which provides insight as to conservatives' viewpoints on environmental issues).

Annual Report: 2000 report online.

Check Out on the Web: PolicyExperts.org (a searchable online database of 2250 conservative, free-market policy experts and 500 public policy organizations; offers a means to investigate the backgrounds of individuals and organizations; also available in paper format).

Founded: 1973 **HQ:** Washington, DC **Fellows:** 30 **Staff/Management:** 170 **NP Status:** 501(c)(3)
Revenue/Expenses (2000): $38/$33 million

Revenue (2000): Contributions (72%; includes: cash –61%; non-cash –11%); Government Grants (0%); Program Service Revenues (1%); Other (27%; from: investment income –25%; misc. –2%).

Expenses (2000): Program Services (79%; for: research programs –47%; media and government programs –18%; education programs –14%); Management and General (3%); Fundraising (18%).

Key Personnel: Edwin Feulner (President; 2000 compensation: $527,723)

Key Affiliations: Townhall.com (conservative group network); Freedom Network (libertarian group network).

410. Reason Public Policy Institute (RPPI) / Reason Foundation (www.rppi.org)

Description: Libertarian-based think tank advocating for free markets/free trade, limited government (including minimal government regulation), and individual rights. Advocates for so-called "free-market environmentalism" (relying solely on the free market and private property rights – instead of environmental laws and regulations – to protect the environment and natural resources). RPPI is part of the Reason Foundation, which is best known for its magazine *Reason* (which covers culture, politics, science and technology, and business, with a reported 60,000-copy circulation rate).

A Closer Look: RPPI/Reason focuses on getting its word out, promoting the exact number of its media appearances, speaking engagements, and print citations in its annual report. A telling statement from their website: the controversial reporter John Stossel of ABC News "proudly credits Reason with changing his outlook from one trusting government to protect people to one trusting markets." The former President of the Reason Foundation – Lynn Scarlett – currently serves as the Assistant Secretary for Policy, Management and Budget within the U.S. Dept. Of Interior under DOI Secretary Gale Norton.

General Issues Addressed: Environment; Education and Child Welfare; Privatization and Government Reform; Transportation; Urban Land Use and Economic Development.

Environmental Focus Areas: Air Quality; Climate Change; Environmental Information; Environmental Risk; New Environmentalism; Waste and Recycling.

Annual Report: 2000 report online.

Associated Websites: NewEnvironmentalism (emphasizes: financial incentives over penalties/fines; flexibility over regulation; private stewardship, gained by providing incentives; local over federal decision-making);

Privatization.org (promotes transferring government services – such as health care services, social services, public safety, and infrastructure – to the private sector; publishes an annual "Privatization Report" that tracks the latest trends in privatization); UrbanFutures.org (promotes voluntary, private-sector, and market-oriented solutions to urban problems; focuses on economic development policy and land-use planning).

Founded: 1997 **HQ:** Los Angeles, CA **Staff:** 17 **NP Status:** 501(c)(3) **Revenue/Expenses** (Reason Foundation; FY00): $5.3/$5.2 million

Revenue (Reason Foundation; FY00): Contributions (76%); Government Grants (0%); Program Service Revenues (22%; from: subscription sales –15%; mailing list sales –3%; ad income –2%; research income –2%); Other (2%).

Expenses (Reason Foundation; FY00): Program Services (81%; for: *Reason* magazine; Reason Public Policy Institute; annual conference; various privatization studies); Management and General (3%); Fundraising (16%).

Key Personnel – Reason Public Policy Institute: Adrian Moore (Executive Director); Kenneth Green (Director of Environmental Programs).

Key Personnel – Reason Foundation: David Nott (President)

Key Affiliations: Freedom Network (libertarian group network).

Subsection 6.2: Other Organizations and Entities

Introduction/User's Guide:

Within this subsection, profiles are provided of 31 other "opposing view" organizations and entities that are typically labeled by critics/observers as "anti-environmental" based on their views and/or activities (this list excludes business groups as a whole, which are separately covered within Subsection 5.1 – "Business Trade Associations, Coalitions/Councils and Related Entities").

The resulting list is diverse in nature, ranging from the taxpayer group Americans for Tax Reform to Harvard University's Center for Risk Analysis. It includes two notable law firms (the Mountain States Legal Foundation and the Washington Legal Foundation) as well as several self-styled "think tanks" of lesser note than the four profiled in the preceding subsection (Subsection 6.1). A common thread between many of these organizations is membership in either Townhall (the Heritage Foundation's network of conservative groups) or the Freedom Network (a libertarian-based network of groups) – in fact, a fair amount of the organizations listed are members of both networks (such membership is noted within the individual profiles provided).

Organizational profiles for this subsection are listed beginning on the next page, presented in alphabetical order (for a descriptive outline of the standardized profile information provided, see the beginning of this section).

A Closer Look:

It should be noted that one profiled group – Americans for Tax Reform – is listed in Fortune magazine's annual survey as a "top federal lobbying group" for 2001 (ranked #64 of 87 listed groups), indicating ATR to be a "key player" in influencing general policy-making at the federal level.

Subsection 6.2: Other Organizations and Entities

411. American Council on Science and Health (ACSH) (www.acsh.org)

Description: An organization billing itself as a "consumer education consortium concerned with issues related to food, nutrition, chemicals, pharmaceuticals, lifestyle, the environment, and health."

A Closer Look: ACSH is a libertarian-associated group that critics cite as being a business-backed organization focused on attempting to downplay health risks, particularly environmentally-related health risks. A pro-business/anti-environmental slant is evident when considering its stated mission (which includes "to defend the achievements and benefits of responsible technology within America's free-enterprise system"), combined with an article that recently appeared in its *Priorities for Health* magazine entitled, "Environmentalism, Animal Rights Activism, and Eco-Nazism." ACSH cites funding from over 300 sources, but doesn't "name any names"; according to the Environmental Working Group (see Profile #51), ACSH has been funded over the years by chemical manufacturers such as Dow Chemical, DuPont, Exxon, Monsanto, and Uniroyal Chemical. ACSH's Board of Advisors include several controversial individuals well-known for their contrarian views that key environmentally-related risks are overestimated, namely: Stephen Safe (who focuses on the risks posed by endocrine disrupting chemicals); Dennis T. Avery (who focuses on the risks posed by chemical pesticide use, as well as those posed by biotechnology / genetically modified foods – see Profile #429 [located within this subsection] for his employer, the Hudson Institute); and S. Fred Singer (who argues that global warming is not real – see Profile #439 [located within this subsection] for his Science and Environmental Policy Project).

Founded: 1978 **Staff:** 11 **HQ:** Washington, DC **NP Status:** 501(c)(3) **Revenue/Expenses (FY00):** $1.86/$1.72 million

Revenue (FY00): Contributions (96%); Government Grants (0%); Program Service Revenues (0%); Other (4%).

Expenses (FY00): Program Services (75%; for: scientific and educational programs –47%; Dr. Koop.com fund – 6%; elderly diet fund –6%; tobacco issue fund –5%; children as hostages fund –3%; other misc. programs/services –7%); Management and General (14%); Fundraising (11%).

Key Personnel: Dr. Elizabeth Whelan (President; FY00 compensation: $253,785)

Key Affiliations: Freedom Network (libertarian group network).

412. American Legislative Exchange Council (ALEC) (www.alec.org)

Description: A membership association for conservative state lawmakers who "share a common belief in limited government, free markets, federalism, and individual liberty." ALEC maintains 10 different national policy task forces which provide forums for ALEC member legislators and the private sector to discuss issues, develop policies and write model legislation on a variety of topics. One such task force is Energy, Environment, Natural Resources, and Agriculture (EENRA), which promotes "free market environmentalism" (relying solely on the free market and private property rights – instead of environmental laws and regulations – to protect the environment and natural resources).

Key Issues (EENRA Task Force): Agriculture; Biotechnology; Energy Infrastructure; Environmental Education; Environmental Health; National Monument Designation; Property Rights; Urban Growth; Water Quality.

Key Projects: Model Legislation (generating proposed state-level legislation on a variety of topics); "Putting Expert Testimony on Environmental Health Issues Under the Microscope" (developing tools to assist legislators in evaluating scientific testimony to detect so-called "junk science").

Annual Report: 2000 report online.

Website Notes: The publicly-accessible portion of the ALEC website offers little specific information to visitors.

Founded: 1973 **Members:** 2400 **Staff:** 30 **HQ:** Washington, DC **NP Status:** 501(c)(3) **Revenue/Expenses (2000):** $5.7/$5.5 million

Revenue (2000): Contributions (81%); Government Grants (0%); Program Service Revenues (17%; from conferences and seminars); Other (2%).

Expenses (2000): Program Services (74%; for: national conferences –40%; policy task forces –23%; public affairs –6%; membership services –5%); Management and General (14%); Fundraising (12%).

Key Personnel: Duane Parde (Executive Director; 2000 compensation: $141,953)

Key Affiliations: Townhall.com (conservative group network); Freedom Network (libertarian group network).

413. <u>**Americans for Tax Reform (ATR)**</u> (www.atr.org)

A Top Federal Lobbying Group Per Fortune Magazine's Annual Survey: Ranking for 2001: #64

Description: A libertarian-associated coalition of 80,000+ taxpayers and taxpayer advocacy groups with a simple mission: "oppose all tax increases at the state and federal levels as a matter of principle." An associated mission is to reduce the size of government, particularly the federal government. Focuses on the cost of federal regulations.

A Closer Look: Listed policy links on ATR's website include several major conservative-/libertarian-associated think tanks/groups, namely: American Legislative Exchange Council; Cato Institute; Competitive Enterprise Institute; Heritage Foundation; Reason Foundation (see separate profiles for each within this overall section – Subsections 6.1 and 6.2).

Lobbying/Political Activities: Registered lobbyist under the LDA.

Key Issues (and ATR's viewpoints/activities): Global Warming (strongly opposes the Kyoto Protocol, believing that it would cause an economic depression in the U.S.; a "proud member" of the Cooler Heads Coalition – see Profile #419, located within this subsection).

HQ: Washington, DC **NP Status:** ATR – 501(c)(4); ATR Foundation – 501(c)(3) **Revenue/Expenses** (ATR Foundation; 2000): $0.96/$1.85 million

Key Personnel: Grover Norquist (President)

Key Affiliations: Freedom Network (libertarian group network).

414. <u>**Blue Ribbon Coalition**</u> (sharetrails.org)

Description: A special interest group pushing for access to public lands for four-wheel drive vehicles, motorcycles/dirt bikes, ATVs, snowmobiles and watercraft, along with access for horses and mountain bikes.

A Closer Look: Neither a true coalition in the normal sense of the word, nor "blue ribbon" in its makeup – both the group's officers and its listed supporters are heavily drawn from/associated with industries/businesses that directly benefit from increased public access to government lands. The group's outlook is perhaps best exemplified by the following two quotes prominently appearing on their website: "United to defend access for motorized recreation nationwide" and "Preserving our natural resources FOR the public instead of FROM the public." Refers to opponents as "anti-recreation."

Key Campaign: Maintaining snowmobile access in Yellowstone and Grand Teton National Parks.

Founded: 1987 **HQ:** Pocatello, ID **NP Status:** 501(c)(3) **Revenue/Expenses (2000):** $0.88/$0.83 million

Revenue (2000): Contributions (28%); Government Grants (0%); Program Service Revenues (20%; from: member contributions to a legal fund); Other (52%; from: membership dues –34%; magazine/advertising –13%; misc. –5%).

Expenses (2000): Program Services (96%; for public education); Management and General (4%); Fundraising (0%).

Key Personnel: Clark Collins (Executive Director)

415. <u>**Capital Research Center (CRC)**</u> (www.capitalresearch.org)

Description: A conservative-based "philanthropy watchdog" group that focuses in particular on "tax-exempt political advocacy groups that seek to expand the power of government." Maintains "Green Watch" (see Profile #426, located within this subsection), an online database and research service dedicated to "monitoring the leadership, activities and funding of the liberal environmentalist movement."

HQ: Washington, DC **NP Status:** 501(c)(3) **Revenue/Expenses (2000):** $2.8/$1.4 million

Revenue (2000): Contributions (87%); Government Grants (0%); Program Service Revenues (<1%); Other (12%; from investment income).

Expenses (2000): Program Services (68%); Management and General (20%); Fundraising (12%).

Key Personnel: Terrence Scanlon (President; 2000 compensation: $206,000)

Key Affiliations: Townhall.com (conservative group network).

416.   <u>**Center for the Defense of Free Enterprise**</u> (www.cdfe.org)

Description: A special interest group focused on private property rights, particularly with respect to alleged government "takings" of land. Seeks to prevent such "takings" from occurring, while "restoring" government land to private individuals. As part of this effort, the group seeks to have the Endangered Species Act repealed in its entirety.

A Closer Look: The organization itself is actually a very small group run by the founders of the so-called "Wise Use Movement" of the early 1990s – Alan Gottlieb and Ron Arnold.

Founded: 1976 **HQ:** Bellevue, WA **NP Status:** 501(c)(3) **Revenue/Expenses (2000):** $0.064/$0.042 million

Revenue (2000): Contributions (57%); Government Grants (0%); Program Service Revenues (41%); Other (1%).

Expenses (2000): Program Services (91%; for: public education –72%; legal action –19%); Other (9%).

Key Personnel: Alan Gottlieb (President); Ron Arnold (Vice-President)

417.   <u>**Center for the Study of Carbon Dioxide and Global Change**</u> (www.co2science.org)

Description: A conservative-associated group focused on offering "editorials and mini-reviews" of recently published scientific journal articles on "atmospheric carbon dioxide enrichment" (that is, rising carbon dioxide levels in the atmosphere) and associated global warming, principally through publication of an online review magazine – CO2 Science Magazine.

A Closer Look – The Center's Focus: The Center's focus is clearly is on attempting to dispute the scientific evidence supporting global warming's occurrence, while also arguing that rising carbon dioxide levels are actually good for the planet (hence, their use of the term "carbon dioxide enrichment"). Thus, the Center calls for no action on reducing carbon dioxide emissions (the Center's stated policy prescription: "leave well enough alone and let nature and humanity take their inextricably intertwined course. All indications are that both will be well served by the ongoing rise in atmospheric carbon dioxide").

A Closer Look – Behind the Center: While its' name implies it to be a non-partisan scientific research institute, the Center falls well short of such a billing. The Center's showcase magazine – appearing at first glance to be a serious scientific publication – actually is just an opinion piece (offering "editorials and mini-reviews"), not subject to the normal peer-review process characteristic of scholarly scientific journals and scientific work in general. Furthermore, use of statements such as "climate alarmists periodically terrorize the public" belie the supposed non-partisan nature of the organization. Perhaps more telling – and of more concern overall – however, is that the group itself appears to be little more than a small "family affair" – Sherwood Idso is president, Keith Idso vice-president, Ann Idso secretary, and Julene Idso operations manager (in fact, the only non-Idso staff members consist of an "operations consultant" and two college student interns). In addition, Craig Idso was formerly the Center's president and now serves as a "scientific advisor" to the group.

Staff: 4 **HQ:** Tempe, AZ **NP Status:** 501(c)(3) **Revenue/Expenses (2000):** $0.32/$0.27 million

Revenue (2000): Contributions (99%); Government Grants (0%); Program Service Revenues (0%); Other (1%).

Expenses (2000): Program Services (89%; for: report dissemination and commentary); Management and General (11%); Fundraising (<1%).

Key Personnel: Sherwood Idso (President); Craig Idso (former President; 2000 compensation: $112,697); Keith Idso (Vice-President; 2000 compensation: $59,065).

Key Affiliations: Townhall.com (conservative group network).

418.   <u>**Citizens for a Sound Economy (CSE)**</u> (www.cse.org)

Description: A conservative- and libertarian-associated organization that seeks to "recruit, educate, train and mobilize volunteer activists to fight for less government, lower taxes, and more freedom." CSE covers several issues, including "Environment," where it promotes so-called "free-market environmentalism" (relying solely on the free market and private property rights – instead of environmental laws and regulations – to protect the environment and natural resources). CSE has an affiliated non-profit organization – the CSE Educational Foundation – that shares facilities/staff and has common board members.

Lobbying/Political Activities: Registered lobbyist under the LDA.

Key Issues (and CSE's positions): Global Warming (disputes the scientific evidence supporting its occurrence; calls for no regulation of carbon dioxide emissions, stressing associated costs); Energy (calls for: opening public lands for fossil fuel exploration; less spending on renewable energy; no increase in auto fuel efficiency standards).

Founded: 1985 **Staff:** 60 **HQ:** Washington, DC **NP Status:** CSE – 501(c)(4); CSE Ed Foundation – 501(c)(3)

Revenue/Expenses (CSE Ed Fund; 2000): $6.7/$6.4 million **Revenue** (CSE; 2000): $8.5 million

Revenue (CSE Ed Fund; 2000): Contributions (97%); Government Grants (0%); Program Service Revenues (0%); Other (3%).

Expenses (CSE Ed Fund; 2000): Program Services (80%; for: state chapter activities –39%; regulatory policy program –29%; tax and budget policy program –9%; membership services –3%); Management and General (11%); Fundraising (9%).

Affiliated Orgs: Citizens for the Environment (a 501(c)(4) non-profit organization)

Key Personnel: Paul Beckner (President, CSE and CSE Ed Fund; combined 2000 compensation from CSE/CSE Ed Fund: $250,000)

Key Affiliations: Townhall.com (conservative group network); Freedom Network (libertarian group network).

Coalition for Vehicle Choice (CVC) (www.vehiclechoice.org)

See Profile #349 within Subsection 5.1 – "Business/Industry Trade Associations, Coalitions/Councils and Related Entities."

419. Cooler Heads Coalition / Global Warming Information Page (www.globalwarming.org)

Description: A conservative- and libertarian-associated coalition of groups focused on the issue of global warming, offering the Global Warming Information Page in that regard.

A Closer Look – The Coalition's Focus: The focus of the Coalition and its associated website clearly is on attempting to discount/downplay global warming as a problem (hence the "cooler heads" moniker). The group's general outlook is perhaps best stated by the following taken from their "Global Warming Information Page" website: "The risks of global warming are speculative; the risks of global warming policies are all too real." The Coalition's website focuses on the potential costs to consumers for addressing global warming, while also attempting to raise doubts about the prevailing science regarding global warming. The group also questions the use of alternative and renewable energy sources as a whole.

A Closer Look – Behind the Coalition: The Cooler Heads Coalition itself is a sub-group of the 24-member, so-called "National Consumer Coalition," with members being various "opposing view" groups, including (see separate profiles for each within this overall section): Competitive Enterprise Institute; National Center for Policy Analysis; National Center for Public Policy Research; Political Economy Research Center; and several TownHall.com-associated groups (including: Defenders of Property Rights; Frontiers of Freedom; Heartland Institute; and Pacific Research Institute). The Global Warming Information Page website is paid for and maintained by "Consumer Alert," one of the Coalition's listed members and a member of the libertarian-based Freedom Network.

Founded: 1997

420. Defender of Property Rights (DPR) (www.defendersproprights.org)

Description: A conservative-based group founded to "counterbalance the governmental threat to private property as a result of a broad range of regulations." DPR's environmental focus is on the Endangered Species Act and perceived government "land grabs."

A Closer Look: An active litigant – involved in 100+ court cases since it was formed in 1991. DPR's Board of Advisors includes several well-known conservatives, including former Reagan advisor Ed Meese, former Supreme Court Justice nominee Robert Bork, Senator Orrin Hatch, and current Solicitor General Ted Olson.

Website Notes: The publicly-accessible portion of the DPR website offers little specific information to visitors.

Founded: 1991 **HQ:** Washington, DC **NP Status:** 501(c)(3) **Revenue/Expenses (2000):** $0.33/$0.35 million

Revenue (2000): Contributions (99%); Government Grants (0%); Program Service Revenues (0%); Other (1%).

Expenses (2000): Program Services (82%; for: litigation –42%; public education –22%; legislative analysis and regulatory analysis –14%; intern program –2%; lobbying –2%); Management and General (10%); Fundraising (8%).

Key Personnel: Nancie Marzulla (President/Director; 2000 compensation: $50,004); Roger Marzulla (Chairman; 2000 compensation: $50,004).

Key Affiliations: Townhall.com (conservative group network).

421.   Federalist Society for Law and Public Policy Studies (www.fed-soc.org)

Description: A conservative- and libertarian-associated legal society seeking to "reorder priorities within the legal system to place a premium on individual liberty, traditional values, and the rule of law." Founded on the principles that "the state exists to preserve freedom, the separation of governmental powers is central to our Constitution, and it is emphatically the province and duty of the judiciary to say what the law is, not what it should be." The Society is a membership-based organization with 3 main membership divisions, namely: Student; Faculty; Lawyer. It maintains 15 practice groups, including one on "Environmental Law and Property Rights."

A Closer Look: The Society's Board of Visitors includes several well-known conservatives, including former Reagan advisor Ed Meese, former Supreme Court Justice nominee Robert Bork, and Senator Orrin Hatch.

Founded: 1982 **Staff:** 15 **HQ:** Washington, DC **NP Status:** 501(c)(3) **Revenue/Expenses (FY00):** $3.0/$2.6 million

Revenue (FY00): Contributions (88%); Government Grants (0%); Program Service Revenues (8%); Other (4%).

Expenses (FY00): Program Services (90%; for: speakers bureau –22%; chapter and membership services –16%; fellows program –12%; symposium and conference –11%; other conferences –10%; practice activities –10%; general programs –8%); Management and General (4%); Fundraising (6%).

Key Personnel: Eugene Meyer (Executive Director; FY00 compensation: $107,000)

Key Affiliations: Townhall.com (conservative group network); Freedom Network (libertarian group network).

422.   Foundation for Research on Economics and the Environment (FREE) (www.free-eco.org)

Description: A conservative- and libertarian-associated organization promoting "free market environmentalism" (relying solely on the free market and private property rights – instead of environmental laws and regulations – to protect the environment and natural resources) by offering 3 seminar programs (see below).

A Closer Look: FREE is well known for its controversial practice of offering junket-like seminars to Federal judges. The criticism has obviously hit a nerve – FREE has a carefully crafted response to such criticism prominently displayed on the home page of their website.

Programs: Seminars for Federal Judges (past lecturers have included Bruce Ames of UC-Berkeley and George Gray of Harvard's Center for Risk Analysis – see Profile #427); Seminars for Law Professors; Environmental Entrepreneurship Seminars.

Staff: 5 **HQ:** Bozeman, MT **NP Status:** 501(c)(3) **Revenue/Expenses (2000):** $1.02/$0.62 million

Revenue (2000): Contributions (96%); Government Grants (0%); Program Service Revenues (0%); Other (4%).

Expenses (2000): Program Services (66%; for: federal judges conferences and seminars –44%; law professor seminars 11%; media and environmental issues seminars –11%); Management and General (15%); Fundraising (19%).

Notable Funding Sources – Conservative Foundations: Olin Foundation; Scaife Foundation.

Key Personnel: John Baden (Chairman; 2000 compensation: $137,587)

423.   The Freedom Network / Free-Market.Net (www.free-market.net)

Description: The Freedom Network is a libertarian-associated, membership-based organization for both individuals and organizations (with 120+ organizations being listed as official "partners") while Free-Market.Net serves as an associated libertarian Internet portal for news, information and other resources.

A Closer Look: Both The Freedom Network and Free-Market.Net are funded by the Henry Hazlitt Foundation, a foundation specifically set up to support libertarian ideas.

HQ: Chicago, IL **NP Status:** 501(c)(3) **Revenue/Expenses** (2000; Henry Hazlitt Foundation): $0.22/$0.21

million

Revenue (2000; Henry Hazlitt Foundation): Contributions (86%); Government Grants (0%); Program Service Revenues (2%); Other (12%; from membership dues).

Expenses (2000; Henry Hazlitt Foundation): Program Services (72%; all for Free-Market.net / The Freedom Network); Management and General (17%); Fundraising (11%).

Key Personnel: Chris Whitten (President; 2000 compensation: $40,000)

424. Frontiers of Freedom (FoF) (www.ff.org)

Description: A conservative organization "committed to the preservation of personal freedoms, the right to private property and the sanctity of the first amendment." Focuses on 10 issue areas, including the Endangered Species Act and Global Warming (see below for details). Has an affiliated non-profit organization – the Frontiers of Freedom Institute – that shares facilities/staff and has common board members.

A Closer Look: FoF views environmental groups as "anti-capitalist extremists." The group's Founder and current Chairman of the Board is ex-Senator Malcolm Wallop of Wyoming (well-known for his pro-businesss/anti-environmental views while in Congress), while S. Fred Singer (founder of the Science and Environmental Policy Project – see Profile #439 within this subsection) is an Adjunct Fellow.

Key Issues (and FoF's positions/viewpoints): Endangered Species Act (calls for its complete repeal, viewing it as an "assault on personal freedoms"); Global Warming (attempts to "debunk" the science; emphasizes the potential costs of actions to address).

HQ: Arlington, VA **NP Status:** FoF – 501(c)(4); FoF Institute – 501(c)(3) **Revenue/Expenses** (FoF Institute; 1999): $0.102/$0.070 million

Revenue (FoF Institute; 1999): Contributions (100%); Government Grants (0%); Program Service Revenues (0%).

Expenses (FoF Institute; 1999): Program Services (86%; for public policy research); Management and General (14%); Fundraising (<1%).

Key Affiliations: Townhall.com (conservative group network).

Key Personnel: Malcolm Wallop (Chairman of the Board; ex-Senator of Wyoming).

425. George C. Marshall Institute (www.marshall.com)

Description: A think tank billing itself as being "dedicated to providing rigorous, unbiased technical analyses of scientific issues which impact public policy." Focuses on environmental issues and national defense.

A Closer Look: Bruce Ames of UC-Berkeley (known for his contrarian views on the risks of chemical pesticide use) is on the Institute's Board.

Key Issues (and the Institute's viewpoints): Global Warming (disputes the prevailing science, while promoting its own "sun-climate linkage" theory).

HQ: Washington, DC **NP Status:** 501(c)(3) **Revenue/Expenses (1999):** $0.50/$0.46 million

Revenue (1999): Contributions (99%); Government Grants (0%); Program Service Revenues (<1%); Other (1%).

Expenses (1999): Program Services (73%); Management and General (16%); Fundraising (11%).

Key Personnel: Jeffrey Salmon (Executive Director; 1999 compensation: $102,796)

Global Warming Information Page (www.globalwarming.org)

See Profile #419 for the "Cooler Heads Coalition" within this subsection.

426. Green Watch (www.green-watch.com)

Description: An online database and research service dedicated to "monitoring the leadership, activities and funding of the liberal environmentalist movement."

A Closer Look: Green Watch is a project of the Capital Research Center (see Profile #415), a conservative "philanthropy watchdog" that focuses in particular on "tax-exempt political advocacy groups that seek to expand the power of government."

Website Notes: The database appears out-of-date; apparently, it is no longer maintained.

Key Affiliations: Townhall.com (conservative group network).

Greening Earth Society (GES) (www.greeningearthsociety.org)

See Profile #364 within Subsection 5.1 – "Business/Industry Trade Associations, Coalitions/Councils and Related Entities."

427.   Harvard Center for Risk Analysis (HCRA) (www.hcra.harvard.edu)

Description: A research center within Harvard University's School of Public Health with the stated mission of "promoting reasoned public responses to health, safety and environmental hazards" via use of risk analysis.

A Closer Look: Why would a university research center (out of Harvard University, no less) be listed here as an "opposing view group"? Because, despite the detailed conflict of interest policy put forth by the Center, critics charge that it is little more than a scientific mouthpiece for business/industry, more akin to the American Council on Science and Health (see Profile #411, located within this subsection) than a typical academic research group (even the *Washington Post* has referred to the Center as "industry-backed"). Indeed, Center funding sources are dominated by business/industry (see below), along with notable ultra-conservative foundations, casting doubt on the impartiality of the results it produces, which do appear to consistently favor industry's interests (take for example, the Center's report "Toxic Pollution from Power Plants: Large Emissions, Little Risk"). In fact, Dr. David Ozonoff, chairman of the Environmental Health Department at Boston University, contends that much of the research conducted by the Center has amounted to "having the client shoot an arrow, and then the analyst paints a target around it." Further, by stated design, HCRA goes far beyond the traditional academic role of scientific/technical research by aggressively seeking to shape federal and state policy via a vigorous outreach effort to policymakers, journalists, and opinion-makers. The Center aggressively promotes comparative risk assessment – a controversial approach that critics charge is inherently subject to bias – as a rigorous scientific method to shape public health policy. As part of this effort, founding director John Graham – now the Bush Administration's controversial "regulatory czar" within the Office of Management and Budget – has sought to "deliver his message directly to the American people" by appearing on popular TV shows such as *Good Morning America* and the *Today* show, along with prime time specials (including with ABC's controversial John Stoussel).

Programs (and key activities/focus areas): Environmental Science ("refining" the precautionary principle; risk-based reform of the regulatory process; kids risk project; benefit-cost assessment for non-carcinogenic chemicals; global climate change and stratospheric-ozone depletion; contingent valuation of environmental health risk); Food Safety and Agriculture (advisory committee on agricultural health risks; study of "risk/risk tradeoffs" – focusing on the ban on organophosphate and carbamate pesticides; risk of conventional and organic produce); Motor Vehicles and Public Health (fuel economy, safety, and environmental protection); Economic Evaluation of Medical Technology.

Notable Funding Sources – Conservative Foundations: Bradley Foundation; Koch Foundation; Olin Foundation.

Notable Funding Sources – Business Trade Groups and Related Orgs (see separate profiles for each within Subsection 5.1 – "Business/Industry Trade Associations, Coalitions/Councils and Related Entities"): American Automobile Manufacturers Association; American Chemistry Council; American Crop Protection Association; American Petroleum Institute; Center for Energy and Economic Development; Chlorine Chemistry Council; Edison Electric Institute; Electric Power Research Institute; Grocery Manufacturers of America; National Association of Home Builders.

Notable Funding Sources – Corporations: Auto (Ford; General Motors); Oil/Petroleum (Amoco; Arco; Atlantic Richfield; British-Petroleum; Chevron; Citgo; Exxon; Mobil; Shell; Texaco; Unocal); Chemical (Air Products; BASF; Ciba Geigy; Dow; DuPont; FMC; ICI; Monsanto; Rohm and Haas; Union Carbide); Paper (Boise Cascade; Fort James; Georgia Pacific; International Paper; James River; Mead).

Budget: $3 million

428.   Heartland Institute (www.heartland.org)

Description: A conservative- and libertarian-associated think tank that while boldly proclaiming "solutions to every public policy problem," actually focuses on three issues: education, health care and the environment. Promotes "free market environmentalism" (relying solely on the free market and private property rights – instead of environmental laws and regulations – to protect the environment and natural resources) which the Institute calls "common-sense environmentalism."

Founded: 1984 **Staff:** 11 **HQ:** Chicago, IL **NP Status:** 501(c)(3) **Revenue/Expenses (2000):** $1.34/$1.37 million

Revenue (2000): Contributions (58%); Government Grants (0%); Program Service Revenues (25%; from publications); Other (17%; from gifts received prior to 2000 that were earmarked for activities in 2000).

Expenses (2000): Program Services (82%; for: publications –61%; "policy fax" and Internet information services –12%; members services –9%); Management and General (11%); Fundraising (7%).

Public Support Sources: Foundations (1/3); Corporations (1/3); Individuals (1/3).

Key Personnel: Joseph Bast (President/CEO; 2000 compensation: $64,167)

Key Affiliations: Townhall.com (conservative group network); Freedom Network (libertarian group network).

429. Hudson Institute (www.hudson.org)

Description: A libertarian-associated think tank billing itself as a futurist organization that is "skeptical of conventional wisdom, optimistic in the ability of technology to solve problems, and believing in individuality and free institutions." Maintains 6 policy centers, including the Center for Global Food Issues which addresses agricultural and related environmental policy.

A Closer Look: The Center for Global Food Issues is run by Dennis T. Avery whose well-known contrarian viewpoints are perhaps best expressed by the title of his book, "Saving the Planet with Pesticides and Plastics."

Key Issues (and the Institute's positions/viewpoints): Food Biotechnology / Genetically Modified Foods (promotes the use and consumption of); Trade (promotes free trade in agricultural products); Pesticides (disputes raised concerns over use of chemical pesticides); Organic Foods (alleges various problems with organic farming).

Founded: 1961 **HQ:** Indianapolis, IN **Staff:** 50 **NP Status:** 501(c)(3) **Revenue/Expenses (FY00):** $8.8/$7.6 million

Revenue (FY00): Contributions (39%); Government Grants (0%); Program Service Revenues (54%; from: independent research –52%; government fees/contracts –2%); Other (7%).

Expenses (FY00): Program Services (78%); Management and General (18%); Fundraising (4%).

Key Personnel: Herbert London (President; FY00 compensation: $147,917)

Key Affiliations: Freedom Network (libertarian group network).

Institutes for Journalism and Natural Resources (IJNR) (www.affoundation.org)

See Profile #367 within Subsection 5.1 – "Business/Industry Trade Associations, Coalitions/Councils and Related Entities."

430. JunkScience.com (www.junkscience.com)

Description: A libertarian-associated website providing various news stories and commentaries on a host of science-related issues, many environmentally-related, posted in an attempt to expose alleged "junk" (bad) science (their slogan is "all the junk that's fit to debunk").

A Closer Look: Most posted stories emanate from either FoxNews.com or the Washington Times, neither generally considered an objective/non-partisan news source. The website itself is run by Steven J. Milloy, a columnist for FoxNews.com and an adjunct scholar at the libertarian-based Cato Institute think tank (see Profile #407, located within Subsection 6.1 – "Key Policy Research Institutions").

Website Notes: The website itself is rather haphazardly put together with little rhyme or reason (its home page typically runs 15-20 printed pages in length).

431. Mountain States Legal Foundation (MSLF) (www.mountainstateslegal.com)

Description: A conservative non-profit law firm dedicated to "individual liberty, the right to own and use property, limited government, and the free enterprise system."

A Closer Look: MSLF was started by James Watt (the controversial Dept. of Interior Secretary under the Reagan Administration, ultimately forced to resign in large part due to his views on resource conservation which were widely assailed as being "anti-environmental"), while the current Interior Secretary – Gale Norton – spent 4 years there as a staff attorney.

Environmental Focus Areas: The Endangered Species Act; Wetlands Regulation; Public Lands.

Founded: 1976 **HQ:** Denver, CO **NP Status:** 501(c)(3) **Revenue/Expenses (2000):** $3.4/$2.6 million

Revenue (2000): Contributions (99%); Government Grants (0%); Program Service Revenues (0%); Other (1%).

Expenses (2000): Program Services (65%; for legal activities); Management and General (15%); Fundraising (20%).

Key Personnel: William Perry Pendley (President; 2000 compensation: $170,000)

Key Affiliations: Townhall.com (conservative group network).

432.   National Anxiety Center (www.anxietycenter.com)

Description: A website that, in an attempted humorous fashion, seeks to "debunk junk science, junk politics, junk education, greens and global anything." Goes by the slogan "the good news is… the bad news is wrong."

An (Attempted Humorous) Closer Look: The website represents a one-man operation run by Alan Caruba, a public relations consultant (available for hire) and ex-reporter (for two local weekly newspapers, circulation rate not noted). His PR "organization" (consisting of himself) publishes the booklet "Getting Famous," billed as a guide to writing successful press releases (no kidding – enough said!).

433.   National Center for Policy Analysis (NCPA) (www.ncpa.org)

Description: A conservative- and libertarian-associated think tank with a stated goal of "developing and promoting private alternatives to government regulation and control, solving problems by relying on the strengths of the competitive, entrepreneurial private sector." Focuses on 7 program areas, including "Environment."

A Closer Look: Two notes: 1) NPCA's Environment program is relatively small (receiving only 3% of NCPA's 2000 budget, with only one dedicated staff member), and the program's webpage mostly provides just web-links to other sites and 2) NCPA's Policy Chairman is Pete duPont (a member of the DuPont Chemical family – his father ran both DuPont and General Motors during his career).

Founded: 1983 **HQ:** Dallas, TX **Staff:** 26 **NP Status:** 501(c)(3) **Revenue/Expenses (2000):** $6.7/$5.5 million

Revenue (2000): Contributions (96%); Government Grants (0%); Program Service Revenues (2%); Other (2%).

Expenses (2000): Program Services (81%; for: marketing –35%; research and publications –27%; conferences – 12%; internet –7%); Management and General (8%); Fundraising (11%).

Funding Sources (2000): Foundations (71%); Corporations (18%); Individuals (11%)

Key Personnel: John Goodman (President; 2000 compensation: $292,500)

Key Affiliations: Townhall.com (conservative group network); Freedom Network (libertarian group network).

434.   National Center for Public Policy Research (NCPPR) (www.nationalcenter.org)

Description: A conservative- and libertarian-associated think tank that House Rep. Tom DeLay calls "THE Center for conservative communications." NCPPR covers a range of public policy issues, but is very focused on the environment. The Center's Environmental Policy Task Force advocates for "free market environmentalism" (relying solely on the free market and private property rights – instead of environmental laws and regulations – to protect the environment and natural resources).

A Closer Look: Overall, the Center measures its success in terms of the number of media interviews and citations it achieves. In that regard, the website itself is basically a series of posted short documents – papers, press releases, editorials, etc. The postings reveal NCPPR to be an aggressive, no-holds-barred outfit – posted papers include "Speaker Gingrich and the Environmental Movement: Two Peas in a Pod" and "Environmentalists Rob Elderly Widows of Retirement Money" (the latter reflecting NCPPR's general strategy of using eye-catching alleged "horror stories" as a means to "combat government regulations"). Personnel-wise, NCPPR's

Environmental Program Director – Tom Randall – possesses less-than-impressive credentials, being a former advertising executive with a degree in advertising, while his wife – a former business executive – serves as the Director of the Center's Energy Program.

Founded: 1982 **NP Status:** 501(c)(3) **Revenue/Expenses (2000):** $5.2/$5.2 million

Revenue (2000): Contributions (100%); Government Grants (0%); Program Service Revenues (0%).

Expenses (2000): Program Services (72%; for: general public education –64%; environmental/regulatory reform program –5%; minority issues program –2%; Center for Environmental Justice –1%); Management & General (1%); Fundraising (27%).

Funding Sources (2000): Individuals (93%); Corporations (4%); Foundations (3%).

Key Personnel: Amy Ridenour (President; 2000 compensation: $126, 975); David Ridenour (Vice-President; 2000 compensation: $92,775); Tom Randall (Environmental Program Director); Gretchen Randall (Energy Program Director).

Key Affiliations: Townhall.com (conservative group network); Freedom Network (libertarian group network).

435.   **National Wilderness Institute (NWI) (**www.nwi.org**)**

Description: A conservative organization billing itself as the "voice of reason on the environment." Promotes "free market environmentalism" (relying solely on the free market and private property rights – instead of environmental laws and regulations – to protect the environment and natural resources).

Focus Areas: Endangered Species; "Land Use Rights"; Environmental Regulations.

Founded: 1989 **HQ:** Alexandria, VA **NP Status:** 501(c)(3) **Revenue/Expenses** (1999): $0.27/$0.25 million

Revenue (1999): Contributions (99%); Government Grants (0%); Program Service Revenues (0%); Other (1%).

Expenses (1999): Program Services (68%; for: public education and member outreach –35%; programs and seminars –33%); Management and General (22%); Fundraising (10%).

Key Personnel: Robert Gordon (Executive Director; 1999 compensation: $50,039)

Key Affiliations: Freedom Network (libertarian group network).

436.   **Pacific Research Institute for Public Policy (PRI) (**www.pacificresearch.org**)**

Description: A conservative- and libertarian-associated think tank promoting public policies that emphasize "a free economy, private initiative, and limited government." Operates 4 centers, including the Center for Environmental and Regulatory Reform, which promotes "free market environmentalism" (relying solely on the free market and private property rights – instead of environmental laws and regulations – to protect the environment and natural resources) which they refer to as "new resource economics."

A Closer Look: PRI hosts a gala annual dinner, which in the past has featured well-known conservative speakers such as Steve Forbes, George Will, and William Bennett.

Key Publication: Index of Environmental Indicators (an annual report giving PRI's own assessment of environmental trends in the U.S.).

Founded: 1979 **HQ:** San Francisco, CA **Staff:** 17 **NP Status:** 501(c)(3) **Revenue/Expenses (2000):** $4.3/$3.5 million

Revenue (2000): Contributions (94%); Government Grants (0%); Program Service Revenues (2%); Other (4%).

Expenses (2000): Program Services (86%; for: research; publications; policy briefings; conferences and forums); Management and General (6%); Fundraising (8%).

Key Personnel: Sally Pipes (President; 2000 compensation: $195,000)

Key Affiliations: Townhall.com (conservative group network); Freedom Network (libertarian group network).

437.   **PolicyExperts.org (The Heritage Foundation Resource Bank) (**www.policyexperts.org**)**

Description: A website providing a "searchable online database of the conservative movement," indexing over 2200 conservative, free-market policy experts and 500 public policy organizations by area of expertise, including "Natural Resources, Environment and Science." Based on a book published by the conservative think tank, The Heritage Foundation (see Profile #409, located within Subsection 6.1 – "Key Policy Research Institutions").

A Closer Look: The website represents a convenient means to investigate the backgrounds of individuals and organizations.

438.   Political Economy Research Center (PERC) (www.perc.org)

Description: A libertarian-associated group self-described as a pioneer in the concept of "free market environmentalism" (relying solely on the free market and private property rights – instead of environmental laws and regulations – to protect the environment and natural resources).

A Closer Look: PERC is headed by Terry L. Anderson, a libertarian-based economist who is also a senior fellow with the Hoover Institution, a conservative think tank. PERC's specific proposals – calling both for repeal of key environmental laws (including the Endangered Species Act and the Superfund toxic waste cleanup law) and for the federal government to sell off the National Parks and other public lands – follow strict libertarian views (see Profile #315 for a discussion of the Libertarian Party and libertarian views in general). A key component of PERC's overall effort is in attempting to influence environmental education (from K-12 through college) by offering workshops, teacher's guides, curriculum, etc. that focus on so-called "free-market environmentalism."

Key Publication: Free Market Environmentalism (updated 2001).

Founded: 1980 **HQ:** Bozeman, MT **Staff:** 24 **NP Status:** 501(c)(3) **Revenue/Expenses (2000):** $1.81/$1.54 million

Revenue (2000): Contributions (96%); Government Grants (0%); Program Service Revenues (0%); Other (4%).

Expenses (2000): Program Services (81%; for: research projects, publications, and environmental education programs –73%; conferences and seminars –8%); Management and General (12%); Fundraising (6%).

Funding Sources: Foundations (92%); Individuals/Misc. (7%); Corporations (1%).

Key Personnel: Terry Anderson (Executive Director; 2000 compensation: $93,100)

Key Affiliations: Freedom Network (libertarian group network).

439.   Science and Environmental Policy Project (SEPP) (www.sepp.org)

Description: Self-billed as an "educational group" with a mission to "clarify the diverse problems facing the planet."

A Closer Look: SEPP was started by S. Fred Singer (an electrical engineer by background), perhaps the single most outspoken skeptic of global warming's occurrence. As such, SEPP focuses on attempting to discount global warming as a significant problem. (A revealing side-note: amongst SEPP's other concerns – viewed as more valid than global warming – is "the protection of Earth and its inhabitants from the effects of asteroid impact.")

Website Notes: The site content is rather stale, with relatively little updated information provided.

Founded: 1990 **HQ:** Arlington, VA **NP Status:** 501(c)(3) **Revenue/Expenses (2000):** $0.212/$0.123 million

Revenue (2000): Contributions (90%); Government Grants (0%); Program Service Revenues (<1%); Other (10%; from investment income).

Expenses (2000): Program Services (88%; for: communications –37%; contract research –24%; workshops – 14%; student stipends –13%); Management and General (10%); Fundraising (2%).

Key Personnel: S. Fred Singer (President/Director)

440.   Townhall.com (www.townhall.com)

Description: An Internet portal for "conservative news and information," providing web-links to 80+ member organizations. A project of the conservative think tank The Heritage Foundation (see Profile #409, within Subsection 6.1 – "Key Policy Research Institutions").

A Closer Look: The website represents a convenient means to investigate the backgrounds of organizations.

Key Affiliations: Freedom Network (libertarian group network).

441.   Washington Legal Foundation (WLF) (www.wlf.org)

Description: A litigation and advocacy group with one goal: "to defend and promote the principles of free enterprise and individual rights." Advocates for free-enterprise principles, limited government, private property rights, and reform of the civil and criminal justice system. WLF covers multiple practice areas, including "environmental and property rights law," wherein WLF seeks to "help create a body of law that will serve as a precedent for those seeking to protect their property rights." Generates "In All Fairness," a monthly op-ed page "advertorial" appearing in the NY Times (one example ad: "When Radicals Regulate," which targets the USEPA).

A Closer Look: WLF has a reputation as an aggressive, hard-nosed group whose general outlook is perhaps best summed up from this statement taken from their website: "Environmental extremist groups, activist courts, government bureaucrats that are not held accountable and the media all foster the false notion that the environment is always threatened by economic activities."

Key Programs/Divisions (and activities/focus areas): Litigation Program (court cases; administrative and regulatory proceedings; judicial misconduct investigations; attorney and judicial reform actions and petitions); Legal Studies Divisions (legal studies publications, "micro-marketed" to selected individuals/groups); Communications Outreach Program (print and electronic media; public education campaigns; seminars and briefings; opinion editorials); Economic Freedom Law Clinic (a pro-business law clinic housed within George Mason University).

Founded: 1977 **HQ:** Washington, DC **NP Status:** 501(c)(3) **Revenue/Expenses (2000):** $4.2/$2.5 million
Revenue (2000): Contributions (88%); Government Grants (0%); Program Service Revenues (0%); Other (12%; from investment income).

Expenses (2000): Program Services (64%; for: legal programs and documents –51%; surveys and educational materials –13%); Management and General (30%); Fundraising (6%).

Key Personnel: Daniel Popeo (Chairman/Director; 2000 compensation: $271,593)

SECTION 7: OTHER ENTITIES AND WEBSITES OF NOTE

In this section, 52 environmentally-relevant entities and websites not covered elsewhere in this Guide are profiled, divided into the following four subsections:

7.1 – Internet Directories	(6 entries)
7.2 – Information and Data Resource Websites and Gateways	(21 entries)
7.3 – Media-Related Entities (News/Magazines/Books/Videos)	(22 entries)
7.4 – Job- and Career-Oriented Organizations and Websites	(3 entries)

In terms of individual entry contents, a descriptive outline of standardized profile information provided for each entity listed is given at the beginning of each subsection

Subsection 7.1: Internet Directories

Introduction/User's Guide:

Within this subsection, six "Internet Directories" – websites that primarily provide a directory-based set of web-links to a variety of other websites – are profiled.

Profiles of the selected Internet directories are presented beginning on the next page, arranged in alphabetical order. The profiles themselves are intended to provide a brief description of the website (including key site contents) as well as of the organization behind the website.

A Closer Look:

Unfortunately, as reflected in the fortunes of industry leader Yahoo, the ability of Internet directory websites to maintain financial viability has been called into serious question. This has resulted in a considerable reduction in the number of available directories, with concerns over how well maintained the remaining sites are in terms of adding new links and/or deleting/updating old links. Such concerns are particularly applicable with respect to environmentally-focused directory websites, which have a relatively limited potential audience compared to all-encompassing sites like Yahoo.

Subsection 7.1: Internet Directories

442.   About.com – Environmental Issues (environment.about.com)

Slogan: "The Human Internet." ™

Description: A unique Internet directory search tool consisting of several hundred "Guide Sites" (organized into 23 basic categories), each run by a professional Guide screened and trained by About. The Guide's background (education, professional experience, philosophy), photo, and contact information is included on their individual site. The "Environmental Issues" Guide Site – located under the "News and Issues" category, is divided into 29 sub-categories (termed "Subjects").

Key Site Contents: Articles (providing a background summary and relevant web-links for particular issues); Forums; Chat; Newsletter (can sign-up for "Environmental Issues," an electronic newsletter).

A Closer Look: The site was recently consolidated down from 36 to 23 basic categories, with the number of Guide Sites reduced from 700+ to "several hundred." In addition, the Guide position for the "Environmental Issues" site was vacant as of 4/02.

443.   Amazing Environmental Organization Web Directory (www.webdirectory.com)

Description: An Internet directory search tool billed as "the largest exclusively environmental organization directory on the Web." Includes sites from over 100 countries, organized into 30 basic sub-directories. The site also includes a Bulletin Board.

444.   EnviroLink Network (envirolink.netforchange.com)

Slogan: "The online environmental community" ®

Description: An Internet directory/environmental information clearinghouse; also offers free Internet services to non-profits through an associated organization – Network for Change. Started at Carnegie Mellon University in 1991.

A Closer Look: The recent financial picture for the organization (raising only $4000 while expending $26,000 in 2000) does not bode well for the future of the organization/website. Further, the "membership system" for Network for Change has been "suspended indefinitely."

Key Site Contents: Organizations; Educational Resources; Government Resources; Progressive Career Resources; Actions You Can Take; Related Topics; News Headlines; Products and Services; In Depth; In Your Community; Events; Community Dialogue (online discussions).

Founded: 1991 **NP Status:** 501(c)(3) **Revenue/Expenses (2000):** $0.004/$0.026 million

445.   Environmental Yellow Pages ® (enviroyellowpages.com)

Slogan: "The environmental industry's telephone directory."

Description: An online business-to-business yellow page directory; also provides some educational resources (see below). Listings include Canada, Mexico, the United Kingdom, Italy, Australia and India along with the U.S.

Key Site Contents – Educational Resource Categories: Associations; Ecology; Education; Global Warming; Government; Health; Jobs, K-12; Materials Exchange; News, Organizations; Pollution Prevention; References; Societies; Sustainability; Weather.

446.   EnviroOne (www.enviroone.com)

Description: An environmental Internet portal – essentially a Yahoo! focused on the environment. Billed as "your one stop center for all your environmental needs."

Key Site Contents: News Headlines; Categories (offering 36 basic subdirectories); Local (providing access to localized environmental information); Hot Programs/Issues (focus areas: ambient air quality; Superfund; brownfields; children; business assistance; urban sprawl; global warming), Forums (separate forums for: researchers; environmental professionals; concerned citizens; students and teachers; book/software reviews).

Check Out on the Web: Free member/affiliate sign-up, providing: web page customization; free e-mail; post and review resumes; post and review available jobs; receive job and resume alerts; promote your site and/or business; and submit environmental news, press releases, and event announcements.

447. **Yahoo Environment and Nature Directory**
   (dir.yahoo.com/Society_and_Culture/Environment_and_Nature)

Description: Yahoo remains the #1-used Internet search tool; thus, its listing here. The "Environment and Nature" directory is somewhat oddly placed under "Society and Culture," but it is the correct place to look for most relevant environmental links. 54 sub-categories are provided, including one for "Web Directories" in case you need to search for even more environmental links.

Subsection 7.2: Information and Data Resource Websites and Gateways

Introduction/User's Guide:

Within this subsection, profiles are provided of 21 "Information and Data Resource Websites and Gateways" – websites that primarily provide access to specialized sources of information and/or data either directly (e.g., the National Library for the Environment website) or via a collection of web-links (i.e., a "gateway" website such as the Global Change Data and Information Service website). Many of the websites listed focus on providing government-generated or government-related information/data. All of the listed websites can be expected to yield relatively non-partisan, objective information, with the possible exception of the Map Cruzin website, which was listed for its technical mapping/GIS resources and not for its associated environmental advocacy work.

Profiles of the selected websites are presented beginning on the next page, arranged in alphabetical order. The profiles themselves are intended to provide a brief description of the website, focusing on the exact information resources made available on or through it, along with a discussion of the organization behind the website.

In terms of individual entry contents, the following is a descriptive outline of standardized profile information provided (please note that the exact contents provided varies, being dependant upon applicability and/or availability):

[Profile #] Website Name (Website Address)

Description: A brief description of the website, focusing on the information/data resources made available on or through it.

Behind the Website: Identifying the organization responsible for the website.

A Closer Look: Providing further information on the website/organization, principally in terms of additional relevant facts.

Resources Provided/Topic Areas Addressed: Providing more detail on the exact information/data resources made available on or through the website.

Key Reports/Publications: Listing specific reports and other publications judged to represent "essential reading" for interested parties, and noting if they are available online at the website. (A summary listing of all such reports/publications is also provided in Appendix B.)

Associated Websites: Listing distinct websites separate from the profiled website, along with a short description and corresponding web address (URL).

Website Notes: Significant notes concerning the main website – navigating hints, content notes, etc.

Check Out on the Web: Listing website-related content/features that particularly stand out ("worth a look").

Contact Info: Provided in selected cases as deemed appropriate/relevant.

Subsection 7.2: Information and Data Resource Websites and Gateways

448.   Capitol Reports / Environmental News Link (www.caprep.com)

Description: A website offering environmental policy news and related research tools.

Behind the Website: The website is put forth by Capital Reports, a firm specializing in environmental policy reporting.

News Services Offered: Environmental "News Link" (online news from Capital Hill, presented in two formats: News Briefs [latest news, uncategorized] and News Digest [recent news grouped by category – air, biotechnology, etc.]); Environmental Issues Report (an environmental policy newsletter; issued twice per month; $95/yr online; $195 in print).

Research Tools Offered: Gateway webpages offering relevant web-links to: Federal Register/Code of Federal Regulations; Federal Agencies; State Agencies; Congress; State Legislatures; Federal Courts; State Courts; Federal Legislation; State Legislation.

Website Notes: Click on "Site Tour" to get started using the site.

Center for Renewable Energy and Sustainable Technology (CREST) (www.crest.org)

See Profile #22, located within Subsection 1.2 – "Public Interest Groups and Coalitions."

449.   CorporateRegister.com (www.corporateregister.com)

Description: A website offering an online database of published corporate environmental and social reports. The database currently has 2800+ reports, including 300+ from the U.S.

Behind the Website: The website is put forth by Next Step Consulting, a London-based consulting firm specializing in developing and evaluating corporate environmental and social reports.

450.   Eco-Labels.org (www.eco-labels.org)

Description: A "one-stop" online resource for eco-labels found on food and wood products (eco-labels being a seal or logo indicating that a product has met a set of established environmental or social standards). One can search by label, product, or certifier as well as find out more about the standards themselves. The website currently covers 82 labels generated under 40 separate certifying programs as offered by 37 different certifying organizations (see below for a further breakdown).

Behind the Website: The website is put forth by Consumers Union (the publisher of Consumer Reports), an independent, non-profit testing and information organization aimed at aiding/informing consumers.

Eco-Label Categories (and the number of such labels included on the website): Organic (22); Pest Management (6); Social Responsibility (4); Sustainable Agriculture (7); Sustainable Fishing (1); Animal Welfare (1); Sustainable Wood (3); General Claims (43; one example – "dolphin safe").

Check Out on the Web: What Makes A Good Eco-Label (a description of the criteria used to evaluate eco-labels).

Energy Efficiency and Renewable Energy Network (EREN) (U.S. Dept. of Energy – (www.eren.doe.gov)

See Profile #202, located within Subsection 2.2 – "Federal Governmental Agencies/Entities."

451.   Environmental Education Link (EE-Link) (www.eelink.net)

Description: A website providing links to environmental education (EE) resources on the Internet. The stated goal of EE-Link is to provide the best EE materials; thus, any suggested link must pass an established set of criteria before being added to the site.

Behind the Website: The website is a USEPA-funded project of the North American Association for Environmental Education (see Profile #143, located within Subsection 1.4 – "Student- and Education-Oriented Groups").

EE Resources Provided Online For: Professionals; Teachers/Classroom Use (K-12); Students (K-12 and higher education); Grants; Jobs; Organizations and Projects; General Environmental Information and Data.

452.   Environmental Media Services (EMS) (www.ems.org)

Description: An online environmental and public health information clearinghouse/resource center aimed at journalists, but a valuable information source for all interested parties. For each topic area covered on the website, a fact sheet or backgrounder typically is provided, along with a list of additional resources (contacts, reports, press releases, etc.). The resources provided are designed to meet information needs ranging from a few quick facts through a detailed backgrounder. Selected websites addressing all sides of an issue are also given. The homepage features significant current news items with links to additional resources.

A Closer Look: EMS partners with many well-respected environmental organizations. Its founder – journalist Arlie Schardt – was head of the Environmental Defense Fund (now Environmental Defense) in the 1970s.

Topic Areas Addressed: Chemicals and Health; Climate and Air; Education and Media; International Trade and Development; Land and Transportation; Oceans and Water; Plants and Animals.

Key Publication: Guide to Nonprofit Environmental Communications Organizations 2001 (online).

Website Notes: Go to the "Topics" webpage for a summary listing of all specific topics covered on the site.

Check Out on the Web: "E-Mail Update Service" (news updates; 2-3 times/month).

453.   FedStats (www.fedstats.gov)

Description: A Federal government Internet gateway for accessing statistics from 100+ Federal agencies. One is able to search for desired statistics via a multitude of ways, including by topic, by geography area, and by agency.

Website Notes: The site is compact, direct, and to-the-point, making a wealth of government data available with just a few keystrokes. Even provides a listing of "Kids' Pages" made available on agency websites.

454.   FirstGov ^{TM} (www.first.gov)

Slogan: "Your first click to the U.S. government."

Description: A Federal government Internet gateway to 30 million pages of government info, services, and online transactions. The search engine provided reportedly can search every word of every U.S. government document on the Internet in a quarter of a second or less. One can also search by topic – 18 topics are listed, including "Environment and Energy." The site also has an extensive set of links to various governmental organizations (namely: Federal Executive; Federal Legislative; Federal Judicial; State and Local; International) as well as links one can use to contact the government online or otherwise (listed by topic, by agency, and to state governors).

Behind the Website: The website is administered by the federal governement's General Service Administration.

Fuel Cells 2000 (www.fuelcells.org)

See Profile #18 for the "Breakthrough Technologies Institute," located within Subsection 1.2 – "Public Interest Groups and Coalitions."

455.   Global Change Data and Information Service (GCDIS) (www.globalchange.gov)

Description: A Federal government Internet gateway for accessing global change data. The site is principally focused on global climate change, but also considers other related global change issues (including: ozone depletion; El Nino; tropical deforestation).

Behind the Website: The website is put forth by the U.S. Global Change Research Program (USGCRP; a multi-federal agency national research program – see Profile #250, located within Subsection 2.2.3 – "Multi-Agency Programs"), along with the U.S. Global Change Research Information Office (part of the USGCRP, implemented through the Center for International Earth Science Information Network at Columbia University).

Provides Web-Links To: Data Sources (divided into 12 disciplines); News; Specific Agency Programs; Agency Research; Publications; USGCRP Links.

Key Initiative: Carbon Cycle Science Program (to identify/quantify sources and sinks for carbon dioxide and other greenhouse gases and understand how these sources/sinks will function in the future).

Key Report: Climate Change Impacts on the U.S.: The Potential Consequences of Climate Variability and Change (online).

Check Out on the Web: Ask Dr. Global Change (answers your questions).

456.   Global Cities Project Online (www.globalcities.org)

Description: An online information clearinghouse aimed at providing local governments and businesses with relevant information and resources on sustainable development and environmental policies and programs within 11 topic areas (see below). An online database houses 5700 environmental policies and programs implemented by local governments across the U.S. (access to the database requires paid membership, however).

Behind the Website: The website is a project of the Environmental Policy Center, a non-profit organization focused on environmental policy at the local level.

Topic Areas Addressed: Air Quality; Energy Efficiency; Environmental Management; Land Use; Open Space; Solid Waste; Toxics/Hazardous Waste; Transportation; Urban Forestry; Water Efficiency; Water Quality.

Contact Info: c/o Environmental Policy Center, 2962 Fillmore St., San Francisco, CA 94123; (415) 775-0791; epc@globalcities.org

457.   GreenBiz.com (www.greenbiz.com)

Slogan: "The resource center on business, the environment, and the bottom line."

Description: An online information clearinghouse/resource center on environmental/sustainability issues created for businesses, particularly small- and mid-sized companies and others that typically lack the time, expertise, or financial resources to obtain such information. 2000+ resources are listed on the site.

Behind the Website: The website is a project of the National Environmental Education and Training Foundation (see Profile #142, located within Subsection 1.4 – "Student- and Education-Oriented Groups") and was created by the Green Business Network (a separate non-profit organization), which continues to maintain the site. A major project sponsor is the USEPA.

Resources (and focus areas/specific contents) Provided Online: Business Toolbox (research reports; "tools" – checklists, assessments, software, etc.; "essentials" – issue briefs; "how-to's" – hands on help); Reference Desk (government gateway; organization directory; web guide – handpicked sites; corporate websites; bookstore; mentor center; awards directory); News Center (news; features; columns); Job Link (jobs; resumes; career tools); Bookstore (100 selected titles listed, each reviewed by GreenBiz).

Key Publication: Greening Your Business: A Primer for Smaller Companies (offers tips and cites resources culled from GreenBiz.com's other resources; useful for companies of all sizes, not just smaller ones; online under "Essentials").

Website Notes: The website lives up to its billing: "a wealth of news, information and resources, all free." Provides pertinent material, logically organized and smartly presented. The key is that its creators take a carefully selective approach (rather than an all-inclusive, "everything goes" approach) to gathering/posting resources.

Check Out on the Web: Most everything, but particularly "Corporate Websites" (providing direct links to the environmental pages/environmental reports of 250+ corporations) and GreenBiz Essentials ("two-minute briefings on key business issues").

Contact Info: c/o Green Business Network, 6 Hillwood Place, Oakland, CA 94610; (510) 451-1300.

458.   Idealist.Org (www.idealist.org)

Description: An online resource center providing non-profit and volunteering related information and resources. Provides worldwide listings (from 150+ countries) of: 25,000 nonprofit/community organizations; 12,000 services/programs; and 5000 resources (books, videos, etc.). Also lists: volunteer opportunities; internships; jobs; career fairs; events; campaigns. All listings are searchable by focus area, one of which is "Environment." Also provides an extensive Nonprofit Career Center and "Tools for Orgs" (offering web-based guides for starting, running and funding a nonprofit).

Behind the Website: A project of Action Without Borders, a non-profit dedicated to promoting and facilitating volunteerism and community action.

Periodicals: Ideas in Action (newsletter; 6-12 times/yr.)
Founded: 1995 **Staff:** 10 **NP Status:** 501(c)(3) **Budget** (Action Without Borders): $0.3 million
Contact Info: New York, NY; (212) 843-3973; info@idealist.org

459.   Local Government Environmental Assistance Network (LGEAN) (www.lgean.org)

Description: An online information clearinghouse/resource center providing environmental management, planning, and regulatory information for local government officials and their staffs.

Behind the Website: The website was developed and is maintained by the International City/County Management Association (see Profile #255, located within Subsection 2.3.1 – "General Government Associations and Councils") in partnership with the Environmental Council of the States, the National Association of Counties, the USEPA, and others.

Resources Provided Online: "Hot Topics" (information on 17 topics, providing for each: issue summary; what's new; legislative/regulatory updates and activities; publications; other websites); "Toolbox" (providing interactive software or documents that require user input; covers 12 topic areas).

Check Out on the Web: "Plain English Briefs of Environmental Laws" and "Plain English Regulatory Guides" (both on the "Regulatory Information" webpage).

Contact Info: (877) 865-4326; lgean@icma.org

460.   MapCruzin.com (www.mapcruzin.com)

Description: An environmental and socio-demographic resource website focusing on mapping/use of Geographic Information Systems (GIS). Provides access to free GIS software, maps and data, as well as offers off-line consulting services in that specialized arena. The website also provides a set of "Resource" pages covering a scattershot of issues.

Behind the Website: The website is run by the Clary Meuser Research Network, a small private firm offering consulting services focused on environmental and socio-demographic research, GIS analysis, and WebMap project services.

Check Out on the Web: E-Risk Maps (a collection of environmental risk maps available on the web).

461.   National Library for the Environment (NLE) (cnie.org)

Description: An online library/Internet gateway focused on the environment and environmental issues. Through the website, one can access both National Library for the Environment (NLE) resources (see below) as well as a host of resources offered by NLE's parent organization, the National Council for Science and the Environment (NCSE) (see below).

Behind the Website: The website is a program of the National Council for Science and the Environment (NCSE), a neutral, science-based organization supported by nearly 500 academic, scientific, environmental, and business organizations

NLE Online Resources (consisting of categorized and annotated links to nearly 2000 resources overall): Reference Resources (databases, dictionaries, laws, etc.); Toxicology Resources; Professional Resources (awards; careers; conferences and meetings; journals); Yellow Pages.

NSCE Resources Provided Online at NLE: Congressional Research Service [CRS] Reports (1100+ policy-oriented reports and issue briefs on environmental and related topic areas prepared for Congress; divided into 26 categories); Environmental Education Programs and Resources; Internet Reference Desk; Native Americans and The Environment; PopEnvironment (abstracts and links to 14,000+ resources dealing with population-environment linkages); PopPlanet (provides in-depth Country Briefing Books exploring population, health and environment connections for 15 countries in Africa, Central America and Southeast Asia); Daily Planet (links to 13 daily sources of environmental news plus 300+ online magazines, newspapers and TV stations in 57 countries); USenvironment (provides State Briefing Books – state-specific information on environmental issues).

Check Out on the Web: CRS Reports (provides access to the same policy-oriented reports and issue briefs Congress is receiving/reviewing); State of the Environment Reports (a "Featured Link" providing links to 140+ state, local, regional, national and international "state of the environment" reports); Environmental Journals

Online (listed under "Professional Resources," it provides links to 170+ environmental journals grouped by the amount of free online content).

462.   <u>**National Safety Council's Environmental Health Center**</u> (www.nsc.org/ehc.htm)

Description: A resource website providing technical information on a wide range of environmental health issues. Provided resources are categorized by both topic (see the specific list below) and by intended audience (namely: Journalists; Educators; General Public; Children; Professionals).

Behind the Website: The website is operated by the National Safety Council, a well-respected non-political, non-governmental, non-profit, (501(c)(3))-exempt organization that serves as a primary source of safety and health information in the U.S.

Topics (and focus areas) Addressed: Air Quality (mobile source emissions; indoor air quality; radon); Children's Environmental Health (lead poisoning; pesticides; overexposure to the sun; poor air quality); Climate Change; Disaster Recovery (fire; earthquakes; floods); Hazardous Chemicals (the USEPA's Risk Management Program); Radiation/Radioactive Waste; Solid Waste (electronic product recovery and recycling); Water/Coasts (drinking water sources; coastal and marine issues).

Check Out on the Web: "For Journalists" section (especially: Environmental Writer [published 10 times/yr; online]; TipSheet [published biweekly; online]; Climate Change Update [published bi-monthly; online]; Chemical Backgrounders [provides short summaries for 80+ specific hazardous chemicals]); Directory (FAQs on a wide range of issues); Environmental Links (a selective listing of "best sites").

Associated Website: Crossroads (a safety, health and environment search engine and news network; located at www.crossroads.nsc.org).

463.   <u>**National Technical Information Service (NTIS)**</u> (www.ntis.gov)

Description: A governmental agency billed as "providing the largest, central resource for obtaining (at some cost) government-funded scientific, technical, engineering, and business related information." Overall, NTIS provides access to 2+ million government publications covering 350+ subject areas. The NTIS website's electronic catalog includes 400,000+ publications plus CD-ROMs, data-files, and audiovisuals. The website groups publications and other products into 4 categories, including "Environment," which contains 80,000+ publications/products – items produced by government agencies since 1990 – with the focus being on pollution-related information (see the listing below), mostly generated by the USEPA.

A Closer Look: The NTIS is part of the Technology Administration of the U.S. Dept. of Commerce.

Environment Collection Topic Areas: Air Pollution and Control; Environmental, Health and Safety; Noise Pollution and Control; Pesticides Pollution and Control; Radiation Pollution and Control; Solid Waste Pollution and Control; Water Pollution and Control.

Contact Info: (703) 605-6000; info@ntis.gov

464.   <u>**Right-to-Know Network (RTK Net)**</u> (www.rtk.net)

Description: An online information clearinghouse providing free public access to key government databases regarding the environment as well as concerning housing/bank loans.

Behind the Website: The website is operated by two non-profit public interest groups – OMB Watch (see Profile #88, located within Subsection 1.2 – "Public Interest Groups and Coalitions") and the Center for Public Data Access.

Online Environmental Databases (and focus areas/specific contents): Toxic Release Inventory (toxic chemicals released/transferred from industrial facilities); Biennial Reporting System (hazardous waste generation/tracking data); Comprehensive Environmental Response, Compensation, and Liability Information System (Superfund site information); Docket (civil court cases filed on behalf of the USEPA); Emergency Response Notification System (data on toxic spills/releases); Resource Conservation and Recovery Act Information System (hazardous waste handler permits); Toxic Substances Control Act Test Submissions (studies on the effects of specific chemicals); Accidental Release Information Program (data on chemical accidents); Facility Indexing System (names, addresses and ID numbers of facilities regulated by the USEPA); Permit Compliance System (surface water permits issued under the Clean Water Act).

Other Key Online Resources: Risk Management Plans (provides Executive Summaries of submitted reports).
Contact Info: 1742 Connecticut Ave. NW, Washington DC 20009; (202) 234-8494.

465.   Scorecard (www.scorecard.org)

Description: An online information clearinghouse providing free public access to key environmental data. Draws from 400+ scientific and governmental databases to generate user-customized profiles of environmental quality. Known for an easy-to-use interface, with an emphasis on providing localized information. Focused on the U.S., but also has a companion site for Canada ("Pollution Watch") that focuses on toxic chemical releases.

Behind the Website: The website is operated by Environmental Defense (see Profile #48, located within Subsection 1.2 – "Public Interest Groups and Coalitions").

Online Databases (and focus areas/specific contents): Air (criteria air pollutants; hazardous air pollutants); Water (Clean Water Act status; watershed indicators); Land (lead hazards; potential sources of land contamination/Superfund sites); Waste (toxic chemical releases from industrial facilities; animal waste from factory farms); Environmental Policy (setting environmental priorities/comparative risk project results); Chemical Information (profiles of 6800 chemicals).

Check Out on the Web: "Pollution Rankings" (powerful feature to identify where "hot spots" might be).

Contact Info (c/o Environmental Defense): (212) 505-2100; Contact@environmentaldefense.org

466.   Thomas (thomas.loc.gov)

Slogan: "Legislative information of the Internet."

Description: A federal government-developed Internet gateway to federal legislative information (see below). Overall, provides a convenient way to stay up to-date on official happenings on Capital Hill.

Behind the Website: The website is a project of the Library of Congress.

Key Online Resources (and focus areas/specific contents): Legislation (bill summary and status; bill text; public laws by law number); Congressional Record (including roll call votes); House and Senate Committee Information (reports; home pages; schedules; hearings).

Check Out on the Web: FAQs; The Legislative Process (an excellent primer); Library of Congress Web Links.

467.   United Nations Environment Programme Network (UNEP.net) (www.unep.net)

Description/Mission: A United Nations-led partnership to make relevant scientific information available over the Internet at a centralized website. Initiated by UNEP in 9/00.

Topics Addressed/Resources Provided: Artic; Climate Change; GEO-3 (access to core datasets associated with UNEP's Global Environmental Outlook program); Country Profiles (for each country, provides: national environmental outlook; domestic environmental profile; international environmental profile; environmental indicators – air and climate; freshwater; forests; threatened animals; protected areas).

Contact Info: Arendel, Norway; eisinfo@unep.org

468.   United States State and Local Gateway (www.statelocal.gov)

Description: A federal government-developed Internet gateway designed to give state and local government officials and employees convenient access to federal information.

Key Resources (and focus area/specific contents) Provided Online: Info By Topic (listing 11 topic areas, including "Environment/Energy"); Info By Type (funding; best practices; tools; training; laws/regulations; contacts; FAQs); Current Issues (4 issues, including: brownfields; sustainable communities); News (by subject; by agency; from the White House); Reference Page (divided into 16 areas, including "environment/energy"); State/Local Links; Federal "One-Stop" Pages; Federal Agency Links.

Subsection 7.3: Media-Related Entities (News/Magazines/Books/Videos)

Introduction/User's Guide:

Within this subsection, profiles are presented of 22 media-related entities – those providing environmentally-related news, magazines, books, or videos. The resulting list covers a wide range of potential interests.

Profiles of the selected media-related entities are presented beginning on the next page, arranged in alphabetical order. The profiles themselves are intended to provide a brief description of the entity, focusing on the information/viewpoints offered.

In terms of individual entry contents, the following is a descriptive outline of standardized profile information provided (please note that the exact contents provided varies, being dependant upon applicability and/or availability):

[Profile #] Entity Name (Website Address)

Description: A brief description of the entity, focusing on the information/viewpoints offered.

A Closer Look: Providing further information on the entity, principally in terms of additional relevant facts.

Contents/Topics Covered/Other Features: Providing more detail on the exact media-related information/resources made available on or through the entity's website.

Website Notes: Significant notes concerning the entity's website – navigating hints, content notes, etc.

Check Out on the Web: Listin website-related content/features that particularly stand out ("worth a look").

Contact Info: Provided in selected cases as deemed appropriate/relevant.

Subsection 7.3: Media-Related Entities (News/Magazines/Books/Videos)

469.   **Adbusters** (www.adbusters.org)

Description: A non-profit, reader-supported, 85,000-copy circulation magazine "concerned about the erosion of our physical and cultural environments by commercial forces." Offers philosophical articles as well as activist commentary from around the world addressing issues ranging from genetically modified foods to media concentration. In addition, conducts several "social marketing" campaigns (see below). Published by the Adbusters Media Foundation, which also runs PowerShift, an advocacy advertising agency.

A Closer Look: While Adbusters doesn't usually address environmental issues directly, it does extensively examine closely related consumerism and corporate globalization issues – hence its listing here.

Campaigns (and activities/focus areas): Corporate Crackdown (seeks to bring corporations back under civil control); First Things First (a manifesto challenging ad designers, stating that "too much design energy is being spent to promote pointless consumerism, and too little to helping people understand an increasingly complex and fragile world"); Media Carta (a "battle for media democracy – the right of meaningful access to the power to communicate"; touches on issues ranging from media concentration to "infodiversity," from who owns the airwaves to free speech versus commercial speech); Buy Nothing Day (promotes rejecting consumerism by "buying nothing" on the day after Thanksgiving, the busiest shopping day of the year); TV Turnoff Week (the last week of April); The Big Question ("Is economic progress killing the planet?"); Fools Fest (April 1; "tweaking the nose of those in power and authority," as well as highlighting unquestioning conformity by the general public); Reclaiming Urban Space (focused on reducing car use in cities; sponsors "Car Free Day"); Commercial-Free Schools ("debranding" schools from commercial interests).

Periodical: Adbusters (magazine; 5 times/yr; partially online; subscription cost: $30/yr.)

Check Out on the Web: Spoof Ads (parodies of famous product ads); Uncommercials (promoting current campaigns).

Contact Info: Vancouver, BC; (800) 663-1243; info@adbusters.org

470.   **E-Magazine.com** (www.emagazine.com)

Description: The online version of E/The Environment Magazine, a bi-monthly magazine aimed at the general public.

Magazine Divisions: Features; Green Living; E Word (from the Editor); Currents; In Brief; Updates; Feedback (Ask E [Questions and Answers]; Advice and Dissent [Letters to the Editor]).

Online Access: Can fully access current and archived issues online.

Hard Copy Subscription: $20/yr.

Contact Info: Marion, OH; (815) 734-1242.

471.   **EarthPrint** (www.earthprint.com)

Description: The official online bookshop of the United Nations Environment Programme (UNEP). Also offers environment-related publications from other UN family members plus selected other international organizations. Publications are categorized into 50+ topic areas.

Contact Info: Hertfordshire, England; +44 1438 748 111; customerservices@earthprint.com

472.   **(The) Ecologist** (www.theecologist.org)

Slogan: "Rethinking basic assumptions."

Description: Billed as "the world's longest running environmental magazine," founded in 1970. Re-launched in 2000 to cover a range of environmental, social and economic issues. A nonprofit monthly magazine, UK-based and read in over 150 countries. Seeks to provide: 1) hard-hitting, investigative reports, 2) provocative articles challenging the conventional wisdom, and 3) people-oriented stories on issues such as the environment, labor, the media, health care, consumer protection, and cultural trends.

Online Access: Archives provided based on established categories.

Hard Copy Subscription: About $40/yr.

Contact Info: London, England; +44 (0)1795 414963; theecologist@thegalleon.co.uk

473.   Environment and Energy Daily (www.eenews.net)

Description: A daily newsletter tracking environmental and energy legislation in Congress, covering hearings, markups, bill introductions, floor actions, positions of key legislators, stakeholders and more. Consists of a 20-40 page (paper and electronic) edition on Mondays and email/website-based editions Tuesday through Thursday. **Subscription service only** ($900/yr) – can sign up for a 30-day free trial subscription. Published by E&E Publishing.

Contact Info (E&E Publishing): Washington, DC; (202) 628-6500; pubs@eenews.net

474.   Environment News Service (ENS) (ens.lycos.com)

Description: A service providing environmentally-related news online. Part of the Lycos Network (an Internet portal/search engine company).

Key Online Content Provided: Headlines (latest environmental news); Environmental News Index (groups prior environmental news articles first by month, then by specific day); E-Wire (press releases).

Environmental Media Association (EMA) (www.ema-online.org)

See Profile #50, located within Subsection 1.2 – "Public Interest Groups and Coalitions."

Environmental Media Services (EMS) (www.ems.org)

See Profile #452, located within Subsection 7.2 – "Information and Data Resource Websites and Gateways."

475.   Environmental News Link (Capitol Reports) (www.caprep.com)

Description: A website offering environmental policy news (both free and paid services). Offered by Capital Reports, a firm specializing in environmental policy reporting.

Free News Services Offered Online: Environmental "News Link" (offering news from Capital Hill, presented in two formats: News Briefs [latest news, uncategorized] and News Digest [recent news grouped by category – air, biotechnology, etc.])

Key Periodical: Environmental Issues Report (environmental policy newsletter; 2 times/month; $95/yr online; $195 in print).

Website Notes: Click on "Site Tour" to get started using the site.

Contact Info (c/o Capitol Reports): Cameron Park, CA; (530) 676-9334.

476.   Environmental News Network (ENN®) (www.enn.com)

Description: A website providing environmentally-related news online, offering both traditional news reports as well as in-depth features and other related resources (see below). Members are granted full site access and can receive ENN's Daily News directly through e-mail (note: ENN membership is free of charge).

A Closer Look: ENN was started in 1993 originally as a monthly print publication (*Environmental News Briefing*) which subsequently was discontinued in favor of the current website presentation format.

Key Online Content Provided: News (current news; archived news [note: limited archives provided]; press releases; daily newscast; environment show; earthnews radio); In-Depth (topics; features; slideshows; special reports); Interact (forum; chats; congressional contacts; media contacts).

Topics Covered In-Depth: Alternative Energy; Alternative Transportation; Animals; Coral Reefs; Earth Day; The Bush Presidency; Global Warming; Genetically Modified Foods; Population; Recycling; Social Responsible Investing; Wildfires; Special Reports.

477.   Greenwire (www.eenews.net)

Description: Designed as a "must read" electronic-only daily newsletter for people with a professional interest in environmental politics and policy, covering federal, state and international environmental issues. The daily news briefing summarizes the most important environmental coverage from hundreds of print, broadcast and online sources, along with original reporting. **Subscription service only** ($1800/yr) – can sign up for a 30-day free trial subscription. Published by E&E Publishing.

Contact Info (E&E Publishing): Washington, DC; (202) 628-6500; pubs@eenews.net

478.   Grist Magazine (www.gristmagazine.com)

Slogan: "Gloom and doom with a sense of humor." "A beacon in the smog."

Description: A "must-read" online environmental magazine true to its credo: "Pull no punches, take no prisoners, and accept no advertising." A project of the Earth Day Network (see Profile #41, located within Subsection 1.2 – "Public Interest Groups and Coalitions").

Magazine Contents: Best of the Rest (summaries of articles in other periodicals); Books Unbound (views; reviews; interviews); Counter Culture (fun facts and figures); Daily Grist (top environmental news from across the globe); Do Good (online actions you can take); Global Citizen (sustainable living); Ha (a cartoon); Heat Beat (climate change information); In My Humble Opinion (op-ed page); Letters to the Editor; The Main Dish (various writings); Muckraker (gossip column on the environmental scene); My Week and Welcome to It (daily diary entries); Out on a Limb (profiles of "oddballs, kooks, and other inspiring environmentalists"); Zed (another cartoon).

Other Website Features: Archives (old magazine issues); Grist by Email (sign up for free Daily Grist or Weekly Grist).

479.   High Country News (www.hcn.org)

Slogan: "A paper for people who care about the West."

Description: A bi-weekly newspaper (founded in 1970) reporting on the natural resources, public lands, and changing communities of the 11 Western states. Offers environmental news, analysis and commentary, particularly with respect to water, logging, wildlife, grazing, wilderness, and growth issues (see also "key topic areas covered" below). 20,000 subscribers nationwide. The HCN-associated website offers online access to archived copies of the newspaper (including by topic area), as well as other pertinent features (see below).

Key Topic Areas Covered: Communities; Consensus; Endangered Species; Mining; Native Americans; Parks and Monuments; Politics; Politics of the West; Water; Wilderness; Wildlife.

Online Access: Online archives from 1993.

Hard Copy Subscription: $32/yr.

Website Features: Online HCN Archives (from 1993); eNewsletter (bi-weekly; via email; also online); Writers on the Range (HCN's syndicated column service; online); Radio HCN (half-hour weekly program; online via RealAudio).

Contact Info: Paonia, CO; (800) 905-1155 / (970) 527-4898.

480.   Island Press (www.islandpress.org)

Description: An environmentally-oriented, non-profit book publisher. Publishes 35-40 books annually, with over 186,000 publications sold in 2000. Seeks to translate technical information into a book format that is accessible and informative to citizen-activists, educators, students, and professionals. Sells its own books, along with those from the ICUN and The Nature Conservancy.

A Closer Look: While Island Press is the business name for the organization, its formal legal name is the Center for Resource Economics.

Contact Info: Covelo, CA; (800) 828-1302; service@islandpress.org

481.   Living on Earth (www.loe.org)

Description: A weekly environmental news and information radio program (providing features, interviews and commentary) distributed by National Public Radio (NPR). 230+ NPR stations broadcast the program. All past shows are archived online – both in text, as well as audio (using RealPlayer). Can also purchase cassette tapes of the programs (see the website for details).

482.   Our Stolen Future (www.ourstolenfuture.org)

Description: A website focused on the 1996 book "Our Stolen Future" by Theo Colborn (along with Dianne Dumanoski and John Peterson Myers), which explores the science of endocrine disruption (how synthetic chemicals affect the endocrine systems of humans and wildlife). The website itself reviews the book and provides new/emerging science in the endocrine disrupter field.

A Closer Look: The website was created (and is maintained) by John Peterson Myers, a co-author of the book.

Check Out on the Web: "Myths vs. Reality" (responding to critics' specific charges regarding the book and the associated science behind it).

483.   Rachel's Environment and Health Weekly (www.rachel.org)

Description: A newsletter (named in honor of Rachel Carson, author of the famous book *Silent Spring*) that addresses technical environmental and health issues (focusing on toxic substances and other environmental hazards) in an easily-understandable way and often put into a political context. Much of the information covered is found only in scientific and medical journals. First published in 1986 and now issued about 3 times/month, each newsletter addresses a single topic.

A Closer Look: Published by the Environmental Research Foundation, a 501(c)(3)-exempt non-profit public interest group specializing in providing information on hazardous substances and hazardous technologies to grassroots citizens groups, libraries and individuals.

Online Access: Complete archives (from Issue #1) online.

Subscription Service: Via email/paper subscription.

Contact Info (c/o Environmental Research Foundation): Annapolis, MD; (410) 263-1584 / (888) 272-2435; erf@rachel.org

484.   Reuters Daily World Environment News (www.planetark.org/dailynewshome.cfm)

Description: A website providing worldwide environmental news stories from the Reuters news network. One can search the online archives based on specific issue (with 100 possibilities listed) or by keyword. The website also serves as the online home of Reuters' Environmental News Pictures, which provides environmentally-related photos from around the world. The website itself is located on "Planet Ark," an Australian-focused environmental website.

Society of Environmental Journalists (SEJ) (www.sej.org)

See Profile #177, located within Subsection 1.5 – "Professional Societies." (Cross-listed here as the SEJ website provides significant news/journalism content open to non-members.)

485.   Stateline.org (www.stateline.org)

Slogan: "Your source for state news."

Description: A website offering state-specific news and background information on a variety of issues, including Land Use (which covers three areas: Growth Management; Transportation; and Environment). One can view the news (obtained from national/state newspapers) in two ways: by issue or by state. Only that day's news is listed, but an archive (from 1999 on) is maintained that is searchable by keyword. One can also sign up to receive emailed news alerts on specific issues.

A Closer Look: Funded by the Pew Charitable Trust, a well-known and respected charitable foundation.

Website Notes: The website essentially serves two purposes: 1) provides state-focused news and 2) serves as the website presence for the Council of State Governments (see Profile #252, located within Subsection 2.3.1 – "General Governmental Associations and Councils").

486.   TomPaine.com (www.tompaine.com)

Description: An online "journal of opinion" that "seeks to enrich the national debate on controversial public issues by featuring the ideas, opinions, and analyses too often overlooked by the mainstream media." Covers 4 major areas: Environment; Money and Politics; Media Criticism; History. Known for their weekly ad appearing on the op-ed page of the *New York Times*.

A Closer Look: A project of the Florence Fund, a 501(c)(3)-exempt non-profit (the journal's publisher – John Moyers – is also the Executive Director of the Florence Fund).

487.   Video Project (www.videoproject.org)

Slogan: "Media for a safe and sustainable world."

Description: A distributor of environmental and other social issue videos and CD-ROMs for teachers and the general public. Some 250+ titles are currently made available.

A Closer Look: Co-founded by Adam Werbach, former President of the Sierra Club.

Contact Info: (800) 4PLANET; video@videoproject.net

488.   World Environment (www.worldenvironment.com)

Description: A website providing environmental news stories obtained from a wide variety of sources worldwide. Part of the World News Network (see Profile #489).

Environmental News Categories Addressed: Global Warming; Polar News; Animals; Forests; Nature; Oceans; Pollution.

489.   World News Network (www.wnnetwork.com)

Description: A news organization that obtains news stories from a wide variety of sources worldwide and presents them on a series of individual webpages based on specific topic areas.

General News Categories Addressed: Business and Industries; Countries; Entertainment; Environment; Health; Politics; Science and Education; Society; Sport; World News (by region/country).

Key Environmentally-Related News Pages: Ecology; Energy Review (a portal to various energy-related WNN news sites); Farming; Global Warming; Genetically Modified Foods; Hydroelectric Power; Hydrogen Guide; Nature; Nuclear Waste; Pollution; Population; Polar News; Whaling.

Website Notes: The network is somewhat confusing, with a multitude of different sites listed, overlapping coverage areas, and differing lists of topics provided at different locations.

490.   Yahoo!® News – Full Coverage of Science (dailynews.yahoo.com/fc/Science)

Description: Yahoo daily news webpage providing access to full coverage of science-related news stories and other information/resources (see below) obtained from a wide variety of sources. On the above-cited webpage, links are provided to both "Top Stories" as well as to full coverage (see below) of about 30 separate Science subcategories, including "Environment and Nature" as well as other more specific environmentally-related topic areas such as "Global Warming and Climate Change." One can also search for new stories/resources based on keyword.

A Closer Look: Our personal first choice for keeping up on the daily news regarding the environment and environmental issues.

Information/Resources Provided ("Full Coverage"): News Stories; Opinion and Editorials; Magazine Articles; Audio; Video; Related Websites: Online News Sources; Related Yahoo Full Coverage Categories; Yahoo Categories (a directory-based Internet search tool).

Subsection 7.4: Job- and Career-Oriented Organizations and Websites

Introduction/User's Guide:

Within this subsection, profiles are provided of three job- and career-oriented organizations and associated websites that specialize in the environmental arena (large, all-encompassing job/career websites like "HotJobs" or "Monster.com" are not considered here). Likely because of their specialized nature, just a few such organizations/websites were identified overall.

Entries for the selected organizations/websites are presented beginning on the next page, arranged in alphabetical order. The profiles themselves are intended to provide a brief description of the organization/website, focusing on the information/services offered, along with other relevant information.

Subsection 7.4: Job- and Career-Oriented Organizations and Websites

491.   Environmental Career Center / EnvironmentalCareer.com (www.environmental-jobs.com)

Description: An environmental career organization that provides both job listings and career resources.

Job Categories Listed: Biological and Ecological; Forestry, GIS, and Natural Resources; Environmental Science and Engineering; Environmental Education and Communications; Policy, Advocacy, and Environmental Activism; Career Changers and Environmental Support; Federal; State.

Key Periodical: National Environmental Employment Report (monthly newspaper providing complete job listings and career news; typically lists 500+ jobs; by subscription only – from $19 [3 months] to $89 [24 months] for individuals).

Founded: 1980

Contact Info: Hampton, VA; (757) 727-7895; eccinfo@environmentalcareer.com

492.   Environmental Career Opportunities (ECO) (ecojobs.com)

Description: A subscription-only environmental job listing service (cost: from $29 for 2 months to $129 for one year). Listings are accessible either online or via bi-weekly newsletters. Typically contains 500+ listings; a few are made available for free online, shown as example listings. Published by the Brubach Corporation.

Job Categories Listed: Conservation and Natural Resources; Environmental Policy, Legislation, and Regulation; Environmental Advocacy, Outreach, and Communications; Environmental Engineering and Scientific; Outdoor and Environmental Education; Higher Education; International; Internships; Environmental Degree Programs.

Founded: 1990

Contact Info: Stanardsville, VA; (800) 315-9777.

493.   Environmental Careers Organization (ECO) (www.eco.org)

Description: A non-profit organization promoting environmental careers through a paid internship program, an annual two-day National Environmental Career Conference, and career-oriented publications. ECO's key activity is arranging paid student internships: 600+ internships (lasting from 3 months to 2 years) are offered every year with a variety of organizations (non-profits; corporations; government agencies; foundations). Interns are officially "ECO Associates." The program is highly competitive, with 30,000+ applicants for the 600+ slots. ECO also maintains an intern alumni network of 7000 individuals.

Key Programs (and activities/focus areas): Diversity Initiative (seeks to increase multicultural diversity in the environmental field); Sustainable Communities Leadership Program (a fellowship program for college students; fellows work 3-6 months on sustainability projects in California); EPA Program (a formal internship program with the USEPA); Corporate, State, and Local Programs (programs sponsored by corporations and state/local government agencies).

Periodicals: Connections (newsletter; online).

Key Publications: The Complete Guide to Environmental Careers in the 21st Century; Environmental Studies 2000 (a national study examining interdisciplinary undergraduate environmental studies programs and the career experiences of their alumni); Increasing Diversity in the Environmental Field (a report from the National Roundtable on Diversity in the Environment).

Annual Report: 2000 report online.

Founded: 1972 **Regional Offices:** 4 **NP Status:** 501(c)(3) **Budget:** $15 million

Revenue (2000): Contributions (10%); Government Grants (0%); Program Service Revenues (90%; from: internship contract fees –86%; environmental program fees –4%).

Expenses (2000): Program Services (84%; for: intern placement program –82%; acquire/use grant funds –2%); Management and General (15%); Fundraising (1%).

Contact Info: Boston, MA; (617) 426-4375.

Key Personnel: John Cook, Jr. (President)

Green Corps (www.greencorps.org**)**
See Profile #58, located within Subsection 1.2 – "Public Interest Groups and Coalitions."

Idealist.Org (www.idealist.org**)**
See Profile #458, located within Subsection 7.2 – "Information and Data Resource Websites and Gateways."

APPENDIX A: Summary Listing of Organizations and Other Entities Profiled

Appendix A provides a summary listing of the 493 organizations and other entities profiled in this Guide. The listing is organized based on the presentation order and general format used in the Guide. Individual entries include the Profile reference number, organization name and corresponding website address. In addition, organization focus areas (as listed in the Guide) are provided for most of the Environmental NGOs (see the beginning of Section 1 of the Guide for further details).

1. ENVIRONMENTAL NON-GOVERNMENTAL ORGANIZATIONS (NGOs)

1.1 POLICY RESEARCH INSTITUTIONS ("THINK TANKS")

1. Center for Clean Air Policy (CCAP) (www.ccap.org) [Pollution/Public Health]
2. Environmental and Energy Study Institute (EESI) (www.eesi.org) [Multiple Focus Areas]
3. H. John Heinz Center for Science, Economics and the Environment (www.heinzctr.org) [Conservation/Pollution]
4. Inform, Inc. (www.informinc.org) [Pollution/Business Practices/Transportation]
5. Resources For the Future (RFF) (www.rff.org) [Multiple Focus Areas]
6. Tellus Institute (www.tellus.org) [Energy/Business Practices/Sustainable Development]
7. Worldwatch Institute (www.worldwatch.org) [Multiple Focus Areas]

1.2 PUBLIC INTEREST GROUPS AND COALITIONS

8. 20/20 Vision (www.2020vision.org) [Action Alert Center]
9. African Wildlife Foundation (AWF) (www.awf.org) [Conservation]
10. Alliance to Save Energy (ASE) (www.ase.org) [Energy]
11. American Council for an Energy-Efficient Economy (ACEEE) (www.aceee.org) [Energy]
12. American Farmland Trust (AFT) (www.farmland.org) [Conservation]
13. American Forests (www.americanforests.org) [Conservation]
14. American Oceans Campaign (AOC) (www.americanoceans.org) [Conservation/Pollution]
15. American Rivers (www.amrivers.org) [Conservation]
16. Appliance Standards Awareness Project (ASAP) (www.standardsasap.org) [Energy]
17. Beyond Pesticides/ National Coalition Against the Misuse of Pesticides (www.beyondpesticides.org) [Pollution/Public Health]
18. Breakthrough Technologies Institute (Fuel Cells 2000) (www.fuelcells.org) [Energy]
19. Campaign for Safe and Affordable Drinking Water (CSADW) (www.safe-drinking-water.org) [Public Health]
20. Center for Health, Environment and Justice (CHEJ) (www.chej.org) [Pollution/Public Health]
21. Center for a New American Dream (CNAD) (www.newdream.org) [Consumerism]
22. Center for Renewable Energy and Sustainable Technology (CREST) (www.crest.org) [Energy]
23. Children's Environmental Health Network (CEHN) (www.cehn.org) [Public Health]
24. Clean Air Trust (CAT) (www.cleanairtrust.org) [Pollution]
25. Clean Car Campaign (www.cleancarcampaign.org) [Pollution]
26. Clean Water Action (CWA) (www.cleanwateraction.org) [Pollution/Public Health]
27. Clean Water Fund (CWF) (www.cleanwaterfund.org) [Pollution/Public Health]

28.   Clean Water Network (CWN) (www.cwn.org) [Pollution/Public Health]

29.   Clear the Air Campaign (www.cleartheair.org) [Pollution/Public Health]

30.   Climate Action Network (CAN) (www.climatenetwork.org) [Global Warming]

31.   Coalition for Environmentally Responsible Economies (CERES) (www.ceres.org) [Business Practices]

32.   Coastal Conservation Association (CCA) (www.joincca.org) [Conservation]

33.   Concern, Inc. (no web address) [Sustainable Development]

34.   (The) Conservation Fund (www.conservationfund.org) [Conservation]

35.   Conservation International (CI) (www.conservation.org) [Conservation/Business Practices]

36.   Consortium for Energy Efficiency (CEE) (www.cee1.org) [Energy]

37.   Corporate Watch / CorpWatch.org (www.corpwatch.org) [Corporations/Globalization]

38.   Cousteau Society (www.cousteausociety.org) [Conservation]

39.   Defenders of Wildlife (www.defenders.org) [Conservation]

40.   Ducks Unlimited (DU) (www.ducks.org) [Conservation]

41.   Earth Day Network (www.earthday.net) [Energy/Earth Day]

42.   Earth Island Institute (EII) (www.earthisland.org) [Activism Support/Training]

43.   Earthjustice Legal Defense Fund (www.earthjustice.org) [Conservation/Pollution/Public Health]

44.   Earth Share (www.earthshare.org) [Workplace Giving]

45.   Earthwatch Institute (www.earthwatch.org) [Scientific Research]

46.   Endangered Species Coalition (ESC) (www.stopextinction.org) [Conservation]

47.   Environmental Alliance for Senior Involvement (EASI) (www.easi.org) [Senior Citizen Involvement]

48.   Environmental Defense (ED) (www.environmentaldefense.org) [Multiple Focus Areas]

49.   Environmental Law Institute (ELI) (www.eli.org) [Multiple Focus Areas]

50.   Environmental Media Association (EMA) (www.ema-online.org) [Media]

51.   Environmental Working Group (EWG) (www.ewg.org) [Pollution/Public Health]

52.   Essential Information (www.essential.org) [Activism Support/Training]

53.   Forest Service Employees for Environmental Ethics (FSEEE) (www.afseee.org) [Conservation]

54.   Forest Stewardship Council U.S. (FSC-US) / U.S. Working Group (www.fscus.org) [Conservation]

55.   Friends of the Earth (USA) (FoE) (www.foe.org) [Multiple Focus Areas]

56.   Friends of the Earth International (FoEI) (www.foei.org) [Multiple Focus Areas]

57.   Grassroots Recycling Network (GRRN) (www.grrn.org) [Pollution]

58.   Green Corps (www.greencorps.org) [Activism Support/Training]

59.   Greenpeace (International) (www.greenpeace.org) [Multiple Focus Areas]

60.   Greenpeace (USA) (www.greenpeaceusa.org) [Multiple Focus Areas]

61.   Green Seal (www.greenseal.org) [Product Standards]

62.   Health Care Without Harm (HCWH) (www.noharm.org) [Pollution/Public Health]

63.   Health Track (www.health-track.org) [Pollution/Public Health]

64.   Institute for Agriculture and Trade Policy (IATP) (www.iatp.org) [Agriculture]

65.   Institute for Global Communications (IGC) (www.igc.org) [Internet Hosting]

66.   Institute for Local Self-Reliance (ILSR) (www.ilsr.org) [Sustainable Development]

67.   Interfaith Center on Corporate Responsibility (ICCR) (www.iccr.org) [Business Practices]

68.   International Right to Know Campaign (IRTK) (www.irtk.org) [Information Disclosure/Right-to-Know]

69.   Izaak Walton League of America (IWLA) (www.iwla.org) [Conservation]

70.   Jane Goodall Institute (JGI) (www.janegoodall.org) [Conservation]

71.   Keep America Beautiful (KAB) (www.kab.org) [Pollution/Public Health]

72.   Land Trust Alliance (LTA) (www.lta.org) [Conservation]

73.   League of Conservation Voters (LCV) (www.lcv.org) [Politics]

74. League of Conservation Voters Education Fund / Vote Environment (www.voteenvironment.org) [Politics]
75. Mineral Policy Center (MPC) (www.mineralpolicy.org) [Pollution/Public Health]
76. National Arbor Day Foundation (www.arborday.org) [Arbor Day/Tree Planting]
77. National Audubon Society (NAS) (www.audubon.org) [Conservation]
78. National Environmental Trust (NET) (environet.policy.net) [Multiple Focus Areas]
79. National Fish and Wildlife Foundation (NFWF) (www.nfwf.org) [Conservation]
80. National Geographic Society (www.nationalgeographic.com) [Conservation/Scientific Research]
81. National Parks Conservation Association (NPCA) (www.npca.org) [Conservation]
82. National Recycling Coalition (NRC) (www.nrc-recycle.org) [Pollution]
83. National Religious Partnership for the Environment (NRPE) (www.nrpe.org) [Religious-Based]
84. National Wildlife Federation (NWF) (www.nwf.org) [Conservation]
85. Natural Resources Defense Council (NRDC) (www.nrdc.org) [Multiple Focus Areas]
86. (The) Nature Conservancy (TNC) (www.nature.org) [Conservation]
87. Ocean Conservancy (www.oceanconservancy.org) [Conservation]
88. Office of Management and Budget (OMB) Watch / Focus Project (www.ombwatch.org) [Gov't Watchdog]
89. Peregrine Fund (www.peregrinefund.org) [Conservation]
90. Pesticide Action Network (International) (PAN) (www.pan-international.org) [Pollution/Public Health]
91. Pesticide Action Network North America (PANNA) (www.panna.org) [Pollution/Public Health]
92. Pew Center on Global Warming (www.pewclimate.org) [Global Warming]
93. Pew Oceans Commission (www.pewoceans.org) [Conservation]
94. Physicians for Social Responsibility (PSR) (www.psr.org) [Pollution/Public Health]
95. Pinchot Institute (www.pinchot.org) [Conservation]
96. Population Action International (PAI) (www.populationaction.org) [Population]
97. Population Reference Bureau (PRB) (www.prb.org) [Population]
98. PR Watch / Center for Media and Democracy (CMD) (www.prwatch.org) [PR Industry]
99. Public Citizen (www.citizen.org) [Pollution/Public Health]
100. Public Employees for Environmental Responsibility (PEER) (www.peer.org) [Whistleblower Support]
101. Public Interest Research Interest Group (PIRG) (www.uspirg.org) [Multiple Focus Areas]
102. Rails-to-Trails Conservancy (RTC) (www.railtrails.org) [Trail-Building]
103. Rainforest Action Network (RAN) (www.ran.org) [Conservation]
104. Rainforest Alliance (www.rainforest-alliance.org) [Conservation]
105. Redefining Progress (www.rprogress.org) [Economics]
106. Resource Renewal Institute (RRI) (www.rri.org) [Sustainable Development]
107. River Network (www.rivernetwork.org) [Conservation]
108. Rocky Mountain Elk Foundation (RMEF) (www.rmef.org) [Conservation]
109. Rocky Mountain Institute (RMI) (www.rmi.org) [Multiple Focus Areas]
110. Safe Energy Communication Council (SECC) (www.safeenergy.org) [Energy]
111. Save Our Environment Action Center (www.saveourenvironment.org) [Action Alert Center]
112. Save The Redwoods League (www.savetheredwoods.org) [Conservation]
113. Scenic America (www.scenic.org) [Scenic Conservation]
114. SeaWeb (www.seaweb.org) [Conservation]
115. Sierra Club (www.sierraclub.org) [Multiple Focus Areas]
116. Smart Growth Network (SGN) (www.smartgrowth.org) [Sprawl/Smart Growth]
117. Sprawl Watch Clearinghouse (www.sprawlwatch.org) [Sprawl/Smart Growth]

118. Strategies for the Global Environment (no web site) [Global Issues]
119. Surface Transportation Policy Project (STPP) (www.transact.org) [Transportation]
120. Surfrider Foundation (www.surfrider.org) [Conservation/Pollution]
121. Sustainable Communities Network (SCN) (www.sustainable.org) [Sustainable Development]
122. Teaming With Wildlife (TWW) (www.teaming.com) [Conservation]
123. Tides Center (www.tides.org) [Activism Support/Training]
124. Trout Unlimited (TU) (www.tu.org) [Conservation]
125. Trust for Public Land (TPL) (www.tpl.org) [Conservation]
126. Turning Point Project (www.turnpoint.org) [Global Issues]
127. Union of Concerned Scientists (UCS) (www.ucsusa.org) [Multiple Focus Areas]
128. United States Green Building Council (USGBC) (www.usgbc.org) [Green Building Construction]
129. Water Keeper Alliance (www.keeper.org) [Pollution]
130. (The) Wilderness Society (TWS) (www.wilderness.org) [Conservation]
131. Wildlife Conservation Society (WCS) (www.wcs.org) [Conservation]
132. Working for Change / Working Assets (www.workingforchange.com) [Action Alert Center / Activist Support/Training]
133. World Resources Institute (WRI) (www.wri.org) [Multiple Focus Areas]
134. World Wildlife Fund (WWF) (www.worldwildlife.org) [Conservation]

1.3 PROGRESSIVE BUSINESS GROUPS AND COALITIONS

135. Business for Social Responsibility (BSR) (www.bsr.org) [Business Practices]
136. Global Environmental Management Initiative (GEMI) (www.gemi.org) [Business Practices]
137. World Business Council for Sustainable Development (WBCSD) (www.wbcsd.ch) [Business Practices]

1.4 STUDENT- AND EDUCATION-ORIENTED GROUPS

138. Campus Ecology Program (National Wildlife Federation) (www.nwf.org/campusecology) [Conservation]
139. Center for Environmental Citizenship (CEC) (www.envirocitizen.org) [Activism Support/Training]
140. Envirothon (www.envirothon.org) [Academic Competition]
141. National Association of University Fisheries and Wildlife Programs (NAUFWP) (www.ag.iastate.edu/departments/aecl/naufwp) [Environmental Education]
142. National Environmental Education and Training Foundation (NEETF) (www.neetf.org) [Environmental Education]
143. North American Association for Environmental Education (NAAEE) (www.naaee.org) [Environmental Education]
144. Second Nature (www.secondnature.org) [Sustainable Development]
145. Sierra Student Coalition (SSC) (www.ssc.org) [Multiple Focus Areas]
146. Student Conservation Association (SCA) (www.sca-inc.org) [Conservation]
147. Student Pugwash USA (www.spusa.org) [Implications of Science and Technology]
148. University Leaders for a Sustainable Future (ULSF) (www.ulsf.org) [Sustainable Development]
149. YMCA Earth Services Corps (YESC) (www.yesc.org) [Community Service]

1.5 PROFESSIONAL SOCIETIES

150. Air and Waste Management Association (AWMA) (www.awma.org)
151. American Chemical Society (ACS) (www.acs.org)

152.   American Fisheries Society (AFS) (www.fisheries.org)
153.   American Institute of Hydrology (AIH) (www.aihydro.org)
154.   American Planning Association (APA) (www.planning.org)
155.   American Public Health Association (APHA) (www.apha.org)
156.   American Public Works Association (APWA) (www.pubworks.org)
157.   American Society of Landscape Architects (ASLA) (www.asla.org)
158.   American Water Resources Association (AWRA) (www.awra.org)
159.   American Water Works Association (AWWA) (www.awwa.org)
160.   Association for Environmental Health and Sciences (AEHS) (www.aehs.com)
161.   Association of Energy Engineers (AEE) (www.aeecenter.org)
162.   Association of Environmental and Resource Economists (AERE) (www.aere.org)
163.   Association of Environmental Engineering and Science Professors (AEESP) (www.aeesp.org)
164.   Ecological Society of America (ESA) (esa.sdsc.edu)
165.   Forest History Society (FHS) (www.lib.duke.edu/forest)
166.   Golf Course Superintendents Association of America (GCSAA) (www.gcsaa.org)
167.   National Association for Environmental Management (NAEM) (www.naem.org)
168.   National Association of Environmental Professionals (NAEP) (www.naep.org)
169.   National Environmental Health Association (NEHA) (www.neha.org)
170.   National Environmental Training Association (NETA) (www.ehs-training.org)
171.   National Ground Water Association (NGWA) (www.ngwa.org)
172.   National Wildlife Rehabilitators Association (NWRA) (www.nwrawildlife.org)
173.   Outdoor Writers Association of America (OWAA) (www.owaa.org)
174.   Renewable Natural Resources Foundation (RNRF) (www.rnrf.org)
175.   Society for Ecological Restoration (SER) (www.ser.org)
176.   Society of American Foresters (SAF) (www.safnet.org)
177.   Society of Environmental Journalists (SEJ) (www.sej.org)
178.   Society of Environmental Toxicology and Chemistry (SETAC) (www.setac.org)
179.   Soil and Water Conservation Society (SWCS) (www.swcs.org)
180.   Solid Waste Association of North America (SWANA) (www.swana.org)
181.   Water Environment Federation (WEF) (www.wef.org)
182.   (The) Wildlife Society (TWS) (www.wildlife.org)

2.   GOVERNMENTAL ORGANIZATIONS

2.1   CONGRESSIONAL COMMITTEES

2.1.1   House Committees

183.   House Committee on Agriculture (agriculture.house.gov)
184.   House Committee on Energy and Commerce (energycommerce.house.gov)
185.   House Committee on Resources (resourcescommittee.house.gov)
186.   House Committee on Transportation and Infrastructure (www.house.gov/transportation)

2.1.2   Senate Committees

187.   Senate Committee on Agriculture, Nutrition, and Forestry (www.senate.gov/~agriculture)

188. Senate Committee on Commerce, Science, and Transportation (www.senate.gov/~commerce)
189. Senate Committee on Energy and Natural Resources (energy.senate.gov)
190. Senate Committee on Environment and Public Works (www.senate.gov/~epw)

2.2 FEDERAL GOVERNMENTAL AGENCIES/ENTITIES

2.2.1 Cabinet Department-Associated Agencies/Entities (arranged by Department)

191. Dept. of Agriculture (USDA) (www.usda.gov)
192. Dept. of Agriculture – Forest Service (FS) (www.fs.fed.us)
193. Dept. of Agriculture – Natural Resources Conservation Service (NRCS) (www.nrcs.usda.gov)
194. Dept. of Commerce (DOC) (home.doc.gov)
195. Dept. of Commerce – National Oceanic and Atmospheric Administration (NOAA) (www.noaa.gov)
196. Dept. of Commerce – NOAA – National Marine Fisheries Service (NMFS) (www.nmfs.noaa.gov)
197. Dept. of Commerce – NOAA – National Ocean Service (NOS) (www.nos.noaa.gov)
198. Dept. of Commerce – NOAA – Office of Oceanic and Atmospheric Research (OAR) (www.oar.noaa.gov)
199. Dept. of Defense (DoD) (www.defenselink.mil)
200. Dept. of Defense – Army Corps of Engineers (ACE) (www.usace.army.mil)
201. Dept. of Energy (DOE) (www.energy.gov)
202. Dept. of Energy – Energy Efficiency and Renewable Energy Network (EREN) (www.eren.doe.gov)
203. Dept. of Energy – Energy Information Administration (EIA) (www.eia.doe.gov)
204. Dept. of Energy – National Energy Technology Laboratory (NETL) (www.netl.doe.gov)
205. Dept. of Energy – National Renewable Energy Laboratory (NREL) (www.nrel.gov)
206. Dept. of Energy – Office of Civilian Radioactive Waste Management (OCRWM) (www.rw.doe.gov)
207. Dept. of Energy – Office of Energy Efficiency and Renewable Energy (EERE) (www.eren.doe.gov/ee.html)
208. Dept. of Energy – Office of Environmental Management (EM) (www.em.doe.gov)
209. Dept. of Energy – Office of Fossil Energy (FE) (www.fe.doe.gov)
210. Dept. of Energy – Office of Nuclear Energy, Science and Technology (NE) (www.ne.doe.gov)
211. Dept. of Health and Human Services (HHS) (www.hhs.gov)
212. Dept. of Health and Human Services – Centers for Disease Control (CDC) (www.cdc.gov)
213. Dept. of Health and Human Services – CDC – Agency for Toxic Substances and Disease Registry (ATSDR) (www.atsdr.cdc.gov)
214. Dept. of Health and Human Services – CDC – National Center for Environmental Health (NCEH) (www.cdc.gov/nceh)
215. Dept. of Health and Human Services – Food and Drug Administration (FDA) (www.fda.gov)
216. Dept. of Health and Human Services – FDA – Center for Food Safety and Applied Nutrition (CFSAN) (www.cfsan.fda.gov)
217. Dept. of Health and Human Services – National Institutes of Health (NIH) (www.nih.gov)
218. Dept. of Health and Human Services – NIH – National Institute of Environmental Health Sciences (NIEHS) (www.niehs.nih.gov)
219. Department of the Interior (DOI) (www.doi.gov)
220. Dept. of Interior – Bureau of Land Management (BLM) (www.blm.gov)
221. Dept. of Interior – Bureau of Reclamation (USBR/BoR) (www.usbr.gov)
222. Dept. of Interior – Fish and Wildlife Service (FWS) (www.fws.gov)
223. Dept. of Interior – Geological Service (USGS) (www.usgs.gov)
224. Dept. of Interior – Minerals Management Service (MMS) (www.mms.gov)

225.   Dept. of Interior – National Park Service (NPS) (www.nps.gov)
226.   Dept. of Interior – Office of Surface Mining Reclamation and Enforcement (OSMRE) (www.osmre.gov)
227.   Department of Justice (DOJ) (www.usdoj.gov)
228.   Dept. of Justice – Environment and Natural Resources Division (ENRD) (www.usdoj.gov/enrd)
229.   Dept. of State (www.state.gov)
230.   Dept. of State – Bureau of Oceans and International Environmental and Scientific Affairs (OES) (www.state.gov/g/oes)
231.   Department of Transportation (DOT) (www.dot.gov)
232.   Dept. of Transportation – Coast Guard (USCG) (www.uscg.mil)
233.   Dept. of Transportation – Federal Aviation Administration (FAA) (www.faa.gov)
234.   Dept. of Transportation – Federal Aviation Administration – Office of Environment and Energy (FAA-AEE) (www.aee.faa.gov)
235.   Dept. of Transportation – Federal Highway Administration (FHWA) (www.fhwa.dot.gov)
236.   Dept. of Transportation – Federal Transit Administration (FTA) (www.fta.dot.gov)
237.   Dept. of Transportation – Research and Special Programs Administration (RSPA) (www.rspa.dot.gov)
238.   Dept. of Transportation – RSPA – Office of Hazardous Materials Safety (OHM) (hazmat.dot.gov)
239.   Dept. of Transportation – RSPA – Office of Pipeline Safety (OPS) (ops.dot.gov)

2.2.2   Independent Agencies/Entities

240.   Chemical Safety and Hazard Investigation Board (CSB) (www.chemsafety.gov)
241.   Environmental Protection Agency (EPA) (www.epa.gov)
242.   EPA – Office of Air and Radiation (OAR) (www.epa.gov/oar)
243.   EPA – Office of Prevention, Pesticides, and Toxic Substances (OPPTS) (www.epa.gov/opptsfrs)
244.   EPA – Office of Solid Waste and Emergency Response (OSWER) (www.epa.gov/swerrims)
245.   EPA – Office of Water (OW) (www.epa.gov/ow)
246.   General Accounting Office (GAO) (www.gao.gov)
247.   Nuclear Regulatory Commission (NRC) (www.nrc.gov)

2.2.3   Multi-Agency Programs

248.   Clean Water Initiative / Clean Water Action Plan (www.cleanwater.gov)
249.   Energy Star Program (www.energystar.gov)
250.   United States Global Change Research Program (USGCRP) (www.usgcrp.gov)
251.   Wildfire Management Initiative / National Fire Plan (www.fireplan.gov)

2.3   GOVERNMENTAL ASSOCIATIONS AND COUNCILS

2.3.1   General Governmental Associations and Councils

2.3.1.1 State-Level General Governmental Associations and Councils

252.   Council of State Governments (CSG) (www.statenews.org)
253.   National Conference of State Legislatures (NCSL) (www.ncsl.org)
254.   National Governors' Association (NGA) (www.nga.org)

2.3.1.2 Local-Level General Governmental Associations and Councils

255. International City/County Management Association (ICMA) (www.icma.org)
256. National Association of Counties (NACo) (www.naco.org)
257. National Association of Towns and Townships (NATaT) (www.natat.org/natat)
258. National Center for Small Communities (NCSC) (www.smallcommunities.org/ncsc)
259. National League of Cities (NLC) (www.nlc.org)
260. United States Conference of Mayors (USCM) (www.usmayors.org)

2.3.2 Environmentally-Focused Governmental Associations and Councils

2.3.2.1 National-Level Environmentally-Focused Governmental Associations and Councils

261. White House Council on Environmental Quality (CEQ) (www.whitehouse.gov/ceq)

2.3.2.2 State-Level Environmentally-Focused Governmental Associations and Councils

262. Association of American Pesticide Control Officials (AAPCO) (aapco.ceris.purdue.edu)
263. Association of State and Interstate Water Pollution Control Administrators (ASIWPCA) (www.asiwpca.org)
264. Association of State and Territorial Health Officials (ASTHO) (www.astho.org)
265. Association of State and Territorial Solid Waste Management Officials (ASTSWMO) (www.astswmo.org)
266. Association of State Drinking Water Administrators (ASDWA) (www.asdwa.org)
267. Association of State Floodplain Managers (ASFM) (www.floods.org)
268. Association of State Wetland Managers (ASWM) (www.aswm.org)
269. Council of State and Territorial Epidemiologists (CSTE) (www.cste.org)
270. Environmental Council of the States (ECOS) (www.sso.org/ecos)
271. International Association of Fish and Wildlife Agencies (IAFWA) (www.iafwa.org)
272. Interstate Council on Water Policy (ICWP) (www.icwp.org)
273. National Association of State Conservation Agencies (NASCA) (www.nascanet.org)
274. National Association of State Departments of Agriculture (NASDA) (www.nasda-hq.org)
275. National Association of State Energy Officials (NASEO) (www.naseo.org)
276. National Association of State Foresters (NASF) (www.stateforesters.org)
277. National Association of State Park Directors (NASPD) (www.naspd.org)
278. Association of State and Territorial Air Pollution Program Administrators (STAPPA) (www.cleanairworld.org)

2.3.2.3 Local-Level Environmentally-Focused Governmental Associations and Councils

279. Association of Local Air Pollution Control Officials (ALAPCO) (www.cleanairworld.org)
280. Association of Metropolitan Sewerage Agencies (AMSA) (www.amsa-cleanwater.org)
281. Municipal Waste Management Association (MWMA) (www.usmayors.org/uscm/mwma)
282. National Association of Conservation Districts (NACD) (www.nacdnet.org)
283. National Association of County and City Health Officials (NACCHO) (IP Address: 129.41.41.25)
284. National Association of Flood and Stormwater Management Agencies (NAFSMA) (www.nafsma.org)
285. National Association of Local Government Environmental Professionals (NALGEP) (www.nalgep.org)

3.   MULTILATERALS (MULTINATIONAL ORGANIZATIONS)

3.1   THE UNITED NATIONS SYSTEM

286.   United Nations (UN) (www.un.org)
287.   United Nations Economic and Social Council (UN-ECOSOC) (www.un.org/esa/coordination/ecosoc)

3.1.1   UN Commissions and Associated Entities

288.   United Nations Commission on Sustainable Development (UN-CSD) (www.un.org/esa/sustdev)
289.   United Nations World Summit on Sustainable Development (www.johannesburgsummit.org)

3.1.2   UN Programmes and Associated Entities

290.   United Nations Development Programme (UNDP) (www.undp.org)
291.   United Nations Environment Programme (UNEP) (www.unep.org)
292.   UNEP Earthwatch (earthwatch.unep.net)
293.   UNEP World Conservation Monitoring Center (www.unep-wcmc.org)
294.   UNEP/WMO Intergovernmental Panel on Global Warming (IPCC) (www.ipcc.ch)

3.1.3   UN Specialized Agencies and Organizations

295.   Food and Agriculture Organization of the UN (FAO) (www.fao.org)
296.   International Maritime Organization (IMO) (www.imo.org)
297.   International Monetary Fund (IMF) (www.imf.org)
298.   United Nations Industrial Development Organization (UNIDO) (www.unido.org)
299.   World Bank / World Bank Group (www.worldbank.org)
300.   World Health Organization (WHO) (www.who.org)
301.   World Meteorological Organization (WMO) (www.wmo.ch)

3.1.4   UN Related Agencies and Organizations

302.   International Atomic Energy Agency (IAEA) (www.iaea.int)
303.   World Trade Organization (WTO) (www.wto.org)

3.1.5   UN-Associated Partnership Programs

304.   Critical Ecosystem Partnership Fund (CEPF) (www.cepf.net)
305.   Global Environment Facility (GEF) (www.gefweb.org)

3.2   OTHER MULTILATERALS AND ASSOCIATED ENTITIES

306.   International Chamber of Commerce (ICC) (www.iccwbo.org)
307.   International Union for Conservation of Nature and Natural Resources (IUCN) – The World Conservation Union (www.iucn.org)

308.   Organization for Economic Cooperation and Development (OECD) (www.oecd.org)
309.   United States Council for International Business (USCIB) (www.uscib.org)
310.   United States Energy Association (USEA) (www.usea.org)
311.   World Energy Council (WEC) (www.worldenergy.org)

4.   POLITICAL ORGANIZATIONS

4.1   POLITICAL PARTIES

312.   Democratic Party (Democratic National Committee) (www.democrats.org)
313.   Republican Party (Republican National Committee) (www.rnc.org)
314.   Green Party of the U.S. (Association of State Green Parties) (www.gpus.org)
315.   Libertarian Party (www.lp.org)

4.2   OTHER POLITICAL GROUPS

316.   New Democrats / Democratic Leadership Council (DLC) (www.ndol.org)
317.   REP America / Republicans for Environmental Protection (www.repamerica.org)

5.   OTHER INTERESTED PARTIES

5.1   BUSINESS TRADE ASSOCIATIONS, COALITIONS/COUNCILS AND RELATED ENTITIES

318.   Alliance of Automobile Manufacturers (AAM) (www.autoalliance.org)
319.   Alliance for Energy and Economic Growth (www.yourenergyfuture.org)
320.   Alliance for Understandable, Sensible and Accountable Government Rules (www.allianceusa.org)
321.   Aluminum Association (AA) (www.aluminum.org)
322.   American Bioenergy Association (ABA) (www.biomass.org)
323.   American Chemistry Council (ACC) (www.americanchemistry.com)
324.   American Coal Foundation (ACF) (www.acf-coal.org)
325.   American Crop Protection Association (ACPA) (www.acpa.org)
326.   American Electronics Association (AeA) (www.aeanet.org)
327.   American Farm Bureau Federation (AFB) (www.afb.org)
328.   American Forest and Paper Association (AFPA) (www.afandpa.org)
329.   American Forest Foundation (AFF) (www.affoundation.org)
330.   American Gas Association (AGA) (www.aga.org)
331.   American Hospital Association (AHA) (www.aha.org)
332.   American Hotel and Lodging Association (AHLA) (www.ahma.com)
333.   American Iron and Steel Institute (AISI) (www.steel.org)
334.   American Petroleum Institute (API) (www.api.org)
335.   American Plastics Council (APC) (www.americanplasticscouncil.org)
336.   American Trucking Associations (ATA) (www.truckline.com)
337.   American Wind Energy Association (AWEA) (www.awea.org)
338.   Associated Builders and Contractors (ABC) (www.abc.org)
339.   Associated General Contractors of America (AGC) (www.agc.org)
340.   Association of Home Appliance Manufacturers (AHAM) (www.aham.org)

341. Biotechnology Industry Organization (BIO) (www.bio.org)
342. Business Roundtable (www.brtable.org)
343. Can Manufacturers Institute (CMI) (www.cancentral.com)
344. Center for Energy and Economic Development (CEED) (www.ceednet.org)
345. ChemicalGuide.com (www.chemicalguide.com)
346. Chemical Industry Institute of Toxicology (CIIT) (www.ciit.org)
347. Chorine Chemistry Council (CCC) (c3.org)
348. Coalition for Affordable and Reliable Energy (CARE) (www.careenergy.com)
349. Coalition for Vehicle Choice (CVC) (www.vehiclechoice.org)
350. Council for Biotechnology Information (CBI) (www.whybiotech.com)
351. Edison Electric Institute (EEI) (www.eei.org)
352. Electric Power Research Institute (EPRI) (www.epri.com)
353. Electric Power Supply Association (EPSA) (www.epsa.org)
354. Electronic Industries Alliance (EIA) (www.eia.org)
355. Environmental Bankers Association (EBA) (www.envirobank.org)
356. Environmental Industry Associations (EIA) (www.envasns.org)
357. Environmental Technology Council (ETC) (www.etc.org)
358. (The) Fertilizer Institute (TFI) (www.tfi.org)
359. FossilFuels.org (www.fossilfuels.org)
360. Foundation for Clean Air Progress (www.cleanairprogress.org)
361. Geothermal Energy Association (GEA) (www.geotherm.org)
362. Glass Packaging Institute (GPI) (www.gpi.org)
363. Global Climate Coalition (GCC) (www.globalclimate.org)
364. Greening Earth Society (GES) (www.greeningearthsociety.org)
365. Grocery Manufacturers of America (GMA) (www.gmabrands.com)
366. Institute of Scrap Recycling Industries (ISRI) (www.isri.org)
367. Institutes for Journalism and Natural Resources (IJNR) (www.affoundation.org)
368. Integrated Waste Services Association (IWSA) (www.wte.org)
369. (The) International Ecotourism Society (TIES) (www.ecotourism.org)
370. National Association of Home Builders (NAHB) (www.nahb.com)
371. National Association of Manufacturers (NAM) (www.nam.org)
372. National Association of Realtors (NAR) (nar.realtor.com)
373. National Automobile Dealers Association (NADA) (www.nada.org)
374. National Electrical Manufacturers Association (NEMA) (www.nema.org)
375. National Endangered Species Act Reform Coalition (NESARC) (www.nesarc.org)
376. National Federation of Independent Businesses (NFIB) (www.nfibonline.com)
377. National Golf Course Owners Association (NGCOA) (www.ngcoa.org)
378. National Hydrogen Association (NHA) (www.hydrogenUS.com)
379. National Hydropower Association (NHA) (www.hydro.org)
380. National Mining Association (NMA) (www.nma.org)
381. National Petrochemical and Refiners Association (NPRA) (www.npradc.org)
382. National Rural Electric Cooperative Association (NRECA) (www.nreca.org)
383. National Solid Wastes Management Association (NSWMA) (www.nswma.org)
384. Nuclear Energy Institute (NEI) (www.nei.org)
385. Pest Facts Information Center (www.pestfacts.org)
386. Renewable Fuels Association (RFA) (www.ethanolRFA.org)

387. Responsible Industry for a Sound Environment (RISE) (www.pestfacts.org)
388. Rubber Manufacturers Association (RMA) (www.rma.org)
389. Solar Electric Power Association (SEPA) (www.solarelectricpower.org)
390. Solar Energy Industries Association (SEIA) (www.seia.org)
391. Steel Recycling Institute (SRI) (www.recycle-steel.org)
392. Sustainable Buildings Industry Council (SBIC) (www.sbicouncil.org)
393. Synthetic Organic Chemical Manufacturers Association (SOCMA) (www.socma.com)
394. United States Chamber of Commerce (www.uschamber.com)
395. United States Council for Automotive Research (USCAR) (www.uscar.org)
396. Vinyl Institute (VI) (www.vinylinfo.org)
397. Waste Equipment Technology Association (WASTEC) (www.wastec.org)
398. Water Quality and Health Council (WQHC) (no website)

5.2   LABOR UNIONS

399. American Federation of Labor – Congress of Industrial Organizations (AFL-CIO) (www.aflcio.org)
400. International Association of Machinists and Aerospace Workers (IAMAW) (Machinists Union) (www.iamaw.org)
401. International Brotherhood of Teamsters (IBT) (The Teamsters) (www.teamster.org)
402. International Union, United Automobile, Aerospace and Agricultural Implement Workers of America (United Auto Workers Union – UAW) (www.uaw.org)
403. Sheet Metal Workers International Association (SMWIA) (www.smwia.org)
404. United Association of Plumbers and Pipefitters (UA) (www.ua.org)
405. United Brotherhood of Carpenters and Joiners of America (UBC) (Carpenters Union) (www.necarpenters.org/UBC.htm)
406. United Mine Workers of America (UMWA) (www.umwa.org)

6.   "OPPOSING VIEW" GROUPS

6.1   KEY POLICY RESEARCH INSTITUTIONS ("THINK TANKS")

407. Cato Institute (www.cato.org)
408. Competitive Enterprise Institute (CEI) (www.cei.org)
409. Heritage Foundation (www.heritage.org)
410. Reason Public Policy Institute (RPPI) / Reason Foundation (www.rppi.org)

6.2   OTHER ORGANIZATIONS AND ENTITIES

411. American Council on Science and Health (ACSH) (www.acsh.org)
412. American Legislative Exchange Council (ALEC) (www.alec.org)
413. Americans for Tax Reform (ATR) (www.atr.org)
414. Blue Ribbon Coalition (sharetrails.org)
415. Capital Research Center (CRC) (www.capitalresearch.org)
416. Center for the Defense of Free Enterprise (www.cdfe.org)
417. Center for the Study of Carbon Dioxide and Global Change (www.co2science.org)
418. Citizens for a Sound Economy (CSE) (www.cse.org)

419. Cooler Heads Coalition / Global Warming Information Page (www.globalwarming.org)
420. Defender of Property Rights (DPR) (www.defendersproprights.org)
421. Federalist Society for Law and Public Policy Studies (www.fed-soc.org)
422. Foundation for Research on Economics and the Environment (FREE) (www.free-eco.org)
423. (The) Freedom Network / Free-Market.Net (www.free-market.net)
424. Frontiers of Freedom (FoF) (www.ff.org)
425. George C. Marshall Institute (www.marshall.com)
426. Green Watch (www.green-watch.com)
427. Harvard Center for Risk Analysis (HCRA) (www.hcra.harvard.edu)
428. Heartland Institute (www.heartland.org)
429. Hudson Institute (www.hudson.org)
430. JunkScience.com (www.junkscience.com)
431. Mountain States Legal Foundation (MSLF) (www.mountainstateslegal.com)
432. National Anxiety Center (www.anxietycenter.com)
433. National Center for Policy Analysis (NCPA) (www.ncpa.org)
434. National Center for Public Policy Research (NCPPR) (www.nationalcenter.org)
435. National Wilderness Institute (NWI) (www.nwi.org)
436. Pacific Research Institute for Public Policy (PRI) (www.pacificresearch.org)
437. PolicyExperts.org (The Heritage Foundation Resource Bank) (www.policyexperts.org)
438. Political Economy Research Center (PERC) (www.perc.org)
439. Science and Environmental Policy Project (SEPP) (www.sepp.org)
440. Townhall.com (www.townhall.com)
441. Washington Legal Foundation (WLF) (www.wlf.org)

7.   OTHER ENTITIES AND WEBSITES OF NOTE

7.1   INTERNET DIRECTORIES

442. About.com – Environmental Issues (environment.about.com)
443. Amazing Environmental Organization Web Directory (www.webdirectory.com)
444. EnviroLink Network (envirolink.netforchange.com)
445. Environmental Yellow Pages (enviroyellowpages.com)
446. EnviroOne (www.enviroone.com)
447. Yahoo Environment and Nature Directory
      (dir.yahoo.com/Society_and_Culture/Environment_and_Nature)

7.2   INFORMATION AND DATA RESOURCE WEBSITES AND GATEWAYS

448. Capitol Reports / Environmental News Link (www.caprep.com)
449. CorporateRegister.com (www.corporateregister.com)
450. Eco-Labels.org (www.eco-labels.org)
451. Environmental Education Link (EE-Link) (www.eelink.net)
452. Environmental Media Services (EMS) (www.ems.org)
453. FedStats (www.fedstats.gov)
454. FirstGov (www.first.gov)
455. Global Change Data and Information Service (GCDIS) (www.globalchange.gov)

456.   Global Cities Project Online (www.globalcities.org)
457.   GreenBiz.com (www.greenbiz.com)
458.   Idealist.Org (www.idealist.org)
459.   Local Government Environmental Assistance Network (LGEAN) (www.lgean.org)
460.   MapCruzin.com (www.mapcruzin.com)
461.   National Library for the Environment (NLE) (cnie.org)
462.   National Safety Council's Environmental Health Center (www.nsc.org/ehc.htm)
463.   National Technical Information Service (www.ntis.gov)
464.   Right-to-Know Network (RTK Net) (www.rtk.net)
465.   Scorecard (www.scorecard.org)
466.   Thomas (thomas.loc.gov)
467.   United Nations Environment Programme Network (UNEP.net) (www.unep.net)
468.   United States State and Local Gateway (www.statelocal.gov)

7.3   MEDIA-RELATED ENTITIES (NEWS/MAGAZINES/BOOKS/VIDEOS)

469.   Adbusters (www.adbusters.org)
470.   E-Magazine.com (www.emagazine.com)
471.   EarthPrint (www.earthprint.com)
472.   (The) Ecologist (www.theecologist.org)
473.   Environment and Energy Daily (www.eenews.net)
474.   Environment News Service (ENS) (ens.lycos.com)
475.   Environmental News Link (Capitol Reports) (www.caprep.com)
476.   Environmental News Network (ENN) (www.enn.com)
477.   Greenwire (www.eenews.net)
478.   Grist Magazine (www.gristmagazine.com)
479.   High Country News (www.hcn.org)
480.   Island Press (www.islandpress.org)
481.   Living on Earth (www.loe.org)
482.   Our Stolen Future (www.ourstolenfuture.org)
483.   Rachel's Environment and Health Weekly (www.rachel.org)
484.   Reuters Daily World Environment News (www.planetark.org/dailynewshome.cfm)
485.   Stateline.org (www.stateline.org)
486.   TomPaine.com (www.tompaine.com)
487.   Video Project (www.videoproject.org)
488.   World Environment (www.worldenvironment.com)
489.   World News Network (www.wnnetwork.com)
490.   Yahoo News – Full Coverage of Science (dailynews.yahoo.com/fc/Science)

7.4   JOB- AND CAREER-ORIENTED ORGANIZATIONS AND WEBSITES

491.   Environmental Career Center / EnvironmentalCareer.com (www.environmental-jobs.com)
492.   Environmental Career Opportunities (ECO) (ecojobs.com)
493.   Environmental Careers Organization (ECO) (www.eco.org)

APPENDIX B: Summary Listing of Key Lists/Reports/Publications

Appendix B provides a summary listing of the approximately 200 specific lists, reports and other publications identified in the organizational profiles contained in this Guide that are judged to represent "essential reading" for interested parties. Many of the items listed are available for free at the source organization's website.

Items are listed within this appendix according to the following table of contents, with each item entry containing a cross-reference to the organizational profile in this Guide from which it was obtained (i.e., the corresponding Profile reference number):

TABLE OF CONTENTS – APPENDIX B:

B2.7   Global/Regional Evaluation Reports/Publications
- By Multilaterals
- By Non-Governmental Organizations

B2.8   Market-Based Policy/Taxes/Government Spending/General Economics Reports/Publications

B2.9   Politically-Related Reports/Publications

B2.10 Population-Environment Linkages Reports/Publications

B2.11 Public Health Reports/Publications
- Drinking Water
- Toxic Chemicals

B2.12 Sprawl/Smart Growth/Land Use Planning Reports/Publications

B2.13 State Activities/Contributions Reports/Publications

B2.14 Directories of Organizations and Groups

B2.15 Other Miscellaneous Reports/Publications

APPENDIX B1: KEY LISTS

B1.1   Conservation Lists

Top 20 Most Threatened Major Land Resource Areas (based on agricultural production, development pressure and land quality; contained in the report "Farming on the Edge"). *American Farmland Trust.* 1997. (see Profile #12).

Most Endangered Rivers in the U.S. (annual report). *American Rivers.* (see Profile #15).

Top 10 Coral Reef Hotspots (worldwide). *Conservation International.* 2/02. (see Profile #35).

2000 IUCN Red List of Threatened Species (identifies plant and animal species at risk for extinction worldwide). *International Union for Conservation of Nature and Natural Resources (IUCN).* 9/00. (see Profile #307).

10 Refuges in Crisis (key National Wildlife Refuges so identified; contained in the report "Refuges in Crisis"). *National Audubon Society.* 2000. (see Profile #77).

WatchList (identifies at-risk North American bird species before they become endangered; updated annually). *National Audubon Society and Partners in Flight.* (see Profile #77).

Parks in Jeopardy (annual list identifying the 10 most endangered National Parks). *National Parks Conservation Association.* (see Profile #81).

25 Most Wasteful and Damaging Corps of Engineers Water Projects in the U.S. (contained in the report "Troubled Waters"). *National Wildlife Federation and Taxpayers for Common Sense.* 3/00. (see Profile #84).

Last Chance Landscapes (annual list identifying key national landscapes with both a pending threat and a potential solution). *Scenic America.* (see Profile #113).

15 Most Endangered Wild Lands (annual report). *The Wilderness Society.* (see Profile #130).

Scorecard of Ecosystem Conditions and Changing Capacities (global evaluation contained in the book "World Resources 2000-2001"). *World Resources Institute.* 4/00. (see Profile #133).

B1.2   Pollution Lists

Top 20 Hazardous Substances (ASTDR/EPA Priority List, an annual government evaluation). *Agency for Toxic Substances and Disease Registry (ASTDR), U.S. Dept. of Health and Human Services.* (see Profile #213).

The Greenest Vehicles and the Meanest Vehicles for the Environment (annual lists based on emissions and fuel efficiency values). *American Council for an Energy-Efficient Economy.* (see Profile #11).

Automaker Pollution Rankings for Average New Vehicles (contained in the report "Pollution Lineup: An Environmental Ranking of Automakers"). *Union of Concerned Scientists.* 4/00. (see Profile #127).

B1.3   Politically-Related Lists

Top "Dirty Money Taker" Lists (identifies politicians accepting the most money from identified "anti-environmental interest groups"). *Environmental Working Group.* (see Profile #51).

National Environmental Scorecard (biennial report on the environmental voting records of all congressional members). *League of Conservation Voters.* (see Profile #73).

Heroes and Zeros (annual list of congressional members so identified based on their public interest voting records). *Public Interest Research Group.* (see Profile #101).

Heroes and Zeros (biennial list of Republican congressional members so identified based on their environmental records). *REP America / Republicans for Environmental Protection.* (see Profile #317).

B1.4   Other Lists

State Gold and Green Rankings (ranking of states based on 20 "gold" economic and 20 "green" environmental indicators – available for 1994 and 2000). *Institute for Southern* Studies (available from the *Green Business Network* at *GreenBiz.com).* 2001. (see Profile #457).

30 Most Sprawl-Threatened Cities (covering large, medium and small cities; obtained from the report "The Dark Side of the America Dream"). *Sierra Club.* 1998. (see Profile #115).

Signals of the OECD Environmental Outlook (key environmental issues assigned green, yellow, or red lights; contained in the book "OECD Environmental Outlook"). *Organization for Economic Cooperation and Development.* 4/01. (see Profile #308).

National Environmental Report Card on Environmental Knowledge (annual evaluation with grades assigned based on a survey of American adults). *National Environmental Education and Training Foundation.* (see Profile #142).

APPENDIX B2: KEY REPORTS/PUBLICATIONS

B2.1   Conservation Reports/Publications

Biodiversity/Wildlife:

Our Living Resources: A Report to the Nation on the Distribution, Abundance, and Health of U.S. Plants, Animals and Ecosystems. *Geological Survey (National Biological Service), U.S. Dept. of Interior.* 1995. (see Profile #223).

Status and Trends of the Nation's Biological Resources. *Geological Survey, U.S. Dept. of Interior.* 1999. (see Profile #223).

State Wildlife Diversity Program Funding: A 1998 Survey (details state-level wildlife funding sources, levels, trends and needs). *International Association of Fish and Wildlife Agencies.* 1999. (see Profile #271).

Refuges in Crisis (focuses on 10 key National Wildlife Refuges so identified). *National Audubon Society.* 2000. (see Profile #77).

Precious Heritage: The Status of Biodiversity in the U.S. (edited book). *Nature Conservancy and the Association for Biodiversity Information.* 3/00. (see Profile #86).

Cultural and Spiritual Values of Biodiversity. *United Nations Environment Programme.* 2000. (see Profile #291).

The Global 200: A Representative Approach to Conserving the Earth's Distinctive Ecoregions (a guiding strategy for conserving global biodiversity). *World Wildlife Fund.* 3/98 (draft manuscript). (see Profile #134).

Forests:

Resources Planning Act (RPA) Assessment of Forest and Range Lands (annual report focused on criteria and indicators of sustainable forest and range management). *Forest Service, U.S. Dept. of Agriculture.* (see Profile #192).

A Vision for the U.S. Forest Service – Goals for the Next Century (edited book). *Resources For the Future.* 9/00. (see Profile #5).

Seeing the Forests for Their Green (assessment of the economic benefits of forest protection, recreation and restoration). *Sierra Club.* 8/00. (see Profile #115).

Forest of Discord: Options for Governing Our National Forests and Federal Public Lands (task force report analyzing critical policy issues). *Society of American Foresters.* 1999. (see Profile #176).

Forest Management Certification Programs (task force report comparing 6 specific programs). *Society of American Foresters.* 1999. (see Profile #176).

The Economic Value of Forest Ecosystem Services (review of economic estimates). *The Wilderness Society.* 3/01. (see Profile #130).

Freshwater and Wetlands:

Most Endangered Rivers in the U.S. (annual report). *American Rivers.* (see Profile #15).

Resource Stewardship Report 2000 (examines water resources stewardship issues facing the Bureau of Reclamation). *Bureau of Reclamation, U.S. Dept. of Interior.* 2000. (see Profile #221).

Status and Trends of Wetlands in the Conterminous U.S. 1986 to 1997 (report to Congress). *Fish and Wildlife Service, U.S. Dept. of the Interior.* 1997. (see Profile #222).

Troubled Waters: Congress, the Corps of Engineers, and Wasteful Water Projects (identifies 25 Corps of Engineers water projects viewed as the most wasteful and environmentally damaging). *National Wildlife Federation and Taxpayers for Common Sense.* 3/00. (see Profile #84).

Oceans/Marine Life:

Our Living Oceans: Report on the Status of U.S. Living Marine Resources. *National Marine Fisheries Service, U.S. Dept. of Interior.* 1999. (see Profile #197).

Status of Fisheries of the U.S. (annual report to Congress). *National Marines Fisheries Service, U.S. Dept. of Commerce.* (see Profile #197).

Turning to the Sea: American's Ocean Future (ocean policy recommendations to protect, restore, and explore U.S. ocean resources). *National Oceanic and Atmospheric Administration (NOAA), U.S. Dept. of Commerce.* 1999. (see Profile #195).

Ocean Briefing Book (overview and synthesis of specific issues; online – periodically updated). *SeaWeb.* (see Profile #114).

Public Lands:

Public Lands Statistics (data-intensive annual report on Bureau of Land Management-managed public lands). *Bureau of Land Management, U.S. Dept. of Interior.* (see Profile #220).

Public Rewards from Public Lands (quantifies the worth of the Bureau of Land Management-managed public lands in economic, social and environmental terms). *Bureau of Land Management, U.S. Dept. of Interior.* 2000. (see Profile #220).

15 Most Endangered Wild Lands (annual report). *The Wilderness Society.* (see Profile #130).

Other Miscellaneous:

Farming on the Edge (identifying the nation's most threatened farming/agricultural regions). *American Farmland Trust and Northern Illinois University.* 3/97. (see Profile #12).

Land and Water Conservation Fund: An Assessment of Its Past, Present and Future. *The Conservation Fund.* 2000. (see Profile #34).

Ecological Fact Sheets (short summaries of key issues, along with a list of contacts for further information). *Ecological Society of America.* (see Profile #164).

Issues in Ecology. (a continuing series presenting major ecological issues in an easy-to-read format understandable by non-scientists; 9 reports thus far). *Ecological Society of America.* (see Profile #164).

Natural Resource Year in Review (annual report focused on the National Park System). *National Park Service, U.S. Dept. of Interior.* (see Profile #225).

National Resources Inventory. (statistical survey to assess soil, water and related resources on non-Federal U.S. lands; issued every 5 years). *Natural Resources Conservation Service, U.S. Dept. of Agriculture.* (see Profile #193).

B2.2   Pollution Reports/Publications

Air Pollution:

Power to Kill (quantifies potential death and disease from 51 power plants charged with violating the CAA's New Source Review regulations). *Clean Air Task Force (for the Clear the Air Campaign).* 7/01. (see Profile #29).

Death, Disease and Dirty Power (quantifies potential health impacts of fine-particle air pollution – soot – from power plants, as well as expected health benefits from reduction of such emissions). *Clean Air Task Force (for the Clear the Air Campaign)*. 10/00. (see Profile #29).

National Air Quality and Emissions Trends Report (annual report on air pollution trends). *Environmental Protection Agency (Office of Air and Radiation)*. (see Profile #242).

Above the Law: How the Government Lets Major Air Polluters Off the Hook (analysis of Clean Air Act violations by industry and associated government enforcement activities). *Environmental Working Group*. 5/99. (see Profile #51).

Lethal Legacy: The Dirty Truth About the Nation's Most Polluting Power Plants (examining older, coal-burning power plants). *Public Interest Research Group*. 4/00. (see Profile #101).

Clearing the Air with Transit Spending (evaluates public transit spending and smog in the 50 largest U.S. cities, with grades assigned). *Sierra Club*. Fall, 2001. (see Profile #115).

Automaker Pollution Rankings for Average New Vehicles (contained in the report "Pollution Lineup: An Environmental Ranking of Automakers"). *Union of Concerned Scientists*. 4/00. (see Profile #127).

Rolling Smokestacks: Cleaning Up America's Trucks and Buses (proposed blueprint for reducing air emissions and increasing the fuel efficiency of trucks and buses). *Union of Concerned Scientists*. 10/00. (see Profile #127).

Greener SUVs: A Blueprint for Cleaner, More Efficient Light Trucks (proposed blueprint for reducing air emissions and increasing the fuel efficiency of SUVs and light trucks). *Union of Concerned Scientists*. 7/99. (see Profile #127).

Hazardous Waste/Toxics:

Toxics in Vehicles: Mercury (examines implications for recycling and disposal). *Ecology Center, Great Lakes United and the University of Tennessee Center for Clean Products and Clean Technologies* (available at the *Clear Car Campaign* website). 2/01. (see Profile #25).

Mercury in the Environment (a compendium of state mercury activities). *Environmental Council of the States and the Clean Air Network*. 1/01. (see Profile #270).

National Biennial RCRA Hazardous Waste Report (biennial report on hazardous waste generated in the U.S.). *Environmental Protection Agency (Office of Solid Waste and Emergency Response)*. (see Profile #244).

Polluting Our Future (documents toxic chemical releases of concern for child development, learning and behavior). *National Environmental Trust, Physicians for Social Responsibility, and Learning Disabilities Association of America*. 9/00. (see Profile #78).

Cleaning Up the Nuclear Weapons Complex: Does Anyone Care? *Resources For the Future*. 1/00. (see Profile #5).

Defense Environmental Restoration Program (DERP) Annual Report to Congress (outlines status of DoD's cleanup activities addressing 27,000+ sites at 8,500+ military installations and properties). *U.S. Dept. of Defense*. (see Profile #199).

Solid Waste/Recycling:

Wasting and Recycling in the U.S. (examines the state of both "wasting" and recycling, along with a proposed "agenda for action"). *Grassroots Recycling Network and the Institute for Local Self-Reliance*. 3/00. (see Profile #57).

Welfare for Waste (examines how federal taxpayer subsides can discourage recycling). *Grassroots Recycling Network, Friends of the Earth, Materials Efficiency Project and Taxpayers for Common Sense*. 4/99. (see Profile #57).

Municipal Sold Waste Generation, Recycling and Disposal in the U.S.: Facts and Figures for 1998. *Environmental Protection Agency (Office of Solid Waste and Emergency Response).* 4/00. (see Profile #244).

Leveling the Playing Field for Recycling: A Policy Report on Virgin Material Subsidies. *National Recycling Coalition.* 9/99. (see Profile #82).

U.S. Recycling Economic Information Study (study of the U.S. recycling and reuse industry). *National Recycling Coalition (prepared by R.W. Beck, Inc).* 7/01. (see Profile #82).

Electronic Product Recovery and Recycling Baseline Report: Recycling of Selected Electronic Products in the U.S. *National Safety Council.* 5/99. (see Profile #462).

Garbage By the Numbers (summary data report). *National Solid Wastes Management Association.* 9/01. (see Profile #383).

Water Pollution:

Evaluation of Domestic Sources of Mercury (mercury in household wastewater). *Association of Metropolitan Sewerage Agencies.* 8/00. (see Profile #280).

National Health Protection Survey of Beaches (annual report based on a voluntary survey of local beach health conditions and activities nationwide). *Environmental Protection Agency (Office of Water).* (see Profile #245).

National Water Quality Inventory: Report to Congress ("305(b) report") (biennial report on the quality of the nation's waters). *Environmental Protection Agency (Office of Water).* (see Profile #245).

Clean Water Report Card: How the Regulators are Keeping Up with Keeping Our Water Clean (grading states on their Clean Water Act NPDES permit program). *Friends of the Earth and the Environmental Working Group.* 3/00. (see Profile #55).

Pollution Paralysis II: Code Red for Watersheds (examining non-point source water pollution control efforts). *National Wildlife Federation.* 4/00. (see Profile #84).

Polluters' Playground: How the Government Permits Pollution (examines facilities in "significant non-compliance" with their Clean Water Act permits). *Public Research Interest Group.* 5/01. (see Profile #101).

State of the Beach (annual report summarizing the health of U.S. beaches). *Surfrider Foundation.* (see Profile #120).

Fertile Ground – Nutrient Trading's Potential to Cost Efficiently Improve Water Quality (focus on U.S. watersheds). *World Resources Institute.* 2000. (see Profile #133).

Pollution Prevention / Materials Policy:

Going Green (an online resource kit for pollution prevention in health care). *Health Care Without Harm.* (see Profile #62).

Expanding the Public's Right-to-Know: Materials Accounting Data as a Tool for Promoting Environmental Justice and Pollution Prevention. *Inform, Inc.* 2000. (see Profile #4).

Extended Producer Responsibility: A Materials Policy for the 21st Century. *Inform, Inc. and the Materials Efficiency Project.* 2000. (see Profile #4).

Waste at Work: Prevention Strategies for the Bottom Line. *Inform, Inc.* 1999. (see Profile #4).

Other Miscellaneous:

Prime Suspects: The Law Breaking Polluters America Fails to Inspect. (analysis of state environmental enforcement programs). *Environmental Working Group.* 7/00. (see Profile #51).

National Transportation Statistics. (annual report, Chapter 4 of which is "Transportation, Energy and Environment"). *Bureau of Transportation Statistics, U.S. Dept. of Transportation*. (see Profile #231).

B2.3   Business Practices and/or Sustainable Development Reports/Publications

Greening Your Business: A Primer for Smaller Companies (web-based primer potentially useful for companies of all sizes). *The Green Business Network / GreenBiz.com*. (see Profile #457).

KPMG International Survey of Environmental Reporting. (surveys corporate environmental reporting worldwide). *KPMG International* (report available on *GreenBiz.com*). 9/99. (see Profile #457).

Sustainable Development: Critical Issues. *Organization for Economic Cooperation and Development*. 6/01. (see Profile #308).

Regulating for the Inside: Can Environmental Management Systems Achieve Policy Goals? (edited book). *Resources For the Future*. 4/01. (see Profile #5).

Green Plans: Working Strategies for a Sustainable Future (a primer on "green plans"– long-term environmental management strategies seeking to achieve sustainability). *Resource Renewal Institute*. 2000. (see Profile #106).

The Economic Renewal Guide (toolkit for helping communities achieve sustainable economic development) *Rocky Mountain Institute*. 1997 (3rd ed.). (see Profile #109).

Natural Capitalism (book promoting an environmentally friendly business model). *Rocky Mountain Institute*. 1999. (see Profile #109).

Agenda 21 (action plan for achieving sustainable development in the 21st century, originally adopted at the 1992 Earth Summit). *United Nations Commission on Sustainable Development*. (see Profile #288).

Sustainable Building Technical Manual (green building practices for design, construction, and operations). *U.S. Green Building Council*. Unknown pub date. (see Profile #128).

Eco-Efficiency – Creating More Value With Less Impact (reference source for eco-efficiency). *World Business Council for Sustainable Development*. 10/00. (see Profile #137).

Sustainability Through the Market – Seven Keys to Success (examining how sustainability could be achieved using market forces). *World Business Council for Sustainable Development*. 4/01. (see Profile #137).

B2.4   Climate Change/Global Warming Reports/Publications

Emissions of Greenhouse Gases in the U.S. (annual report). *Energy Information Administration, U.S. Dept. of Energy*. (see Profile #203).

Voluntary Reporting of Greenhouse Gases (annual report on voluntarily-reported reductions in greenhouse gas emissions and carbon sequestration). *Energy Information Administration, U.S. Dept. of Energy*. (see Profile #203).

An Introduction to the Economics of Climate Change Policy (explores differences in forecasts made). *Pew Center on Global Climate Change*. 7/00. (see Profile #92).

Climate Change: Science, Strategies and Solutions (an edited book). *Pew Center on Global Climate Change*. 8/01. (see Profile #92).

Climate Change Economics and Policy: An RFF Anthology (a collection of relevant Issues Briefs). *Resources For the Future*. 2/01. (see Profile #5).

Climate: Making Sense and Making Money (makes the case that global climate change can be addressed not at a cost but at a profit). *Rocky Mountain Institute*. 11/97. (see Profile #109).

The American Way to the Kyoto Protocol: An Economic Analysis to Reduce Carbon Pollution. *Tellus Institute (prepared for the World Wildlife Find)*. 7/01. (see Profile #6).

Greenhouse Gangsters vs. Climate Justice (examines oil companies records and tactics and calls for "climate justice"). *Transnational Resource and Action Center* (now *Corporate Watch*). 11/99. (see Profile #37).

Third Assessment Report – Climate Change 2001 (consists of separate reports from each of three Working Groups, along with a Synthesis Report). *UNEP/WHO Intergovernmental Panel on Climate Change (IPCC)*. 2001. (see Profile #294).

Climate Change Impacts on the U.S.: The Potential Consequences of Climate Variability and Change. *U.S. Global Change Research Program*. 2000. (see Profile #250).

A Climate and Environmental Strategy for U.S. Agriculture (examines potential strategy for U.S. agriculture operating under the Kyoto Protocol). *World Resources Institute*. 11/00. (see Profile #133).

B2.5   Education Related Reports/Publications

Ecodemia (environmental management innovations at college campuses). *Campus Ecology Program of the National Wildlife Federation*. (see Profile #138).

State of the Campus Environment (national report card on environmental performance and sustainability in higher education). *Campus Ecology Program of the National Wildlife Federation*. 2001. (see Profile #138).

Environmental Studies 2000 (national study examining interdisciplinary undergraduate environmental studies programs and the career experiences of their alumni). *Environmental Careers Organization*. 2001. (see Profile #493).

Environmental Educational Materials: Guidelines for Excellence Workbook. *North American Association for Environmental Education*. 2000. (see Profile #141).

Public Policies for Environmental Protection (edited book aimed at college students). *Resources For the Future*. 8/00 (2nd. Edition). (see Profile #5).

The RFF Reader in Environmental and Resource Management (a primer on environmental and natural resources policy; recommended for college coursework). *Resources For the Future*. 1/99. (see Profile #5).

Sustainability Assessment Questionnaire (offers a qualitative assessment of the extent to which a college or university is "sustainable"). *University Leaders for a Sustainable Future*. (continually updated). (see Profile #148).

Talloires Declaration (a 10-point action plan committing signing colleges and universities to sustainability and environmental literacy in teaching and practice). *University Leaders for a Sustainable Future*. 1990. (see Profile #148).

B2.6   Energy Reports/Publications

Energy Resources/Use:

Annual Energy Review (annual report providing historical energy statistics – U.S. and international – from 1949 on). *Energy Information Administration, U.S. Dept. of Energy*. (see Profile #203).

Annual Energy Outlook (annual report providing midterm – 20 year – forecasts of energy supply, demand and prices for the U.S.). *Energy Information Administration, U.S. Dept. of Energy*. (see Profile #203).

International Energy Outlook 2001 (international energy projections through 2020). *Energy Information Administration, U.S. Dept. of Energy*. 3/01. (see Profile #203).

Outer Continental Shelf Petroleum Assessment (assessment of recoverable oil and gas resources within the Outer Continental Shelf; issued every 5 years). *Minerals Management Service (Resource Evaluation Division), Dept of Interior.* (see Profile #224).

Transportation Energy Data Book (annual publication). *Oak Ridge National Lab (U.S. Dept. of Energy).* (see Profile #201).

World Energy Council Survey of Energy Resources (periodic report based on a worldwide survey). *World Energy Council.* (see Profile #311).

Proposed National Energy Policies:

A Responsible Energy Policy for the 21ˢᵗ Century. *Natural Resources Defense Council.* 3/01. (see Profile #85).

A New Energy Future: Options for a Smarter, Cleaner Energy Future. *Public Research Interest Group.* 5/01. (see Profile #101).

Clean Energy Blueprint (proposed national energy policy plan). *Union of Concerned Scientists.* 2001. (see Profile #127).

Energy Innovations: A Prosperous Path to a Clean Environment (outlines an alternative national energy strategy – the "innovative path"). *Union of Concerned Scientists; Alliance to Save Energy; American Council for an Energy-Efficient Economy; Natural Resources Defense Council; Tellus Institute.* 1997. (see Profile #127).

Energy Efficiency:

Consumer Guide to Home Energy Savings (periodically revised). *American Council for an Energy-Efficient Economy.* (Profile #11).

Green Book: The Environmental Guide to Cars and Trucks (annual report evaluating new cars and light trucks based on both fuel efficiency and air emissions values). *American Council for an Energy-Efficient Economy.* (Profile #11).

Most Energy Efficient Appliances (annual report). *American Council for an Energy-Efficient Economy* (Profile #11).

Opportunity Knocks: Capturing Pollution Reductions and Consumer Savings from Updated Appliance Efficiency Standards. *Appliance Standards Awareness Project and the American Council for an Energy-Efficient Economy.* 3/00. (see Profile #16).

Fossil Fuels:

Cleaner Power: The Benefits and Costs of Moving from Coal Generation to Modern Power Technologies. *Environmental Law Institute.* 5/01. (see Profile #49).

Drilling To The Ends Of The Earth: The Case Against New Fossil Fuel Exploration. *Rainforest Action Network.* Unknown Publication Date. (see Profile #103).

Coal: America's Past, America's Future? (a critical look at coal as an energy source). *Tellus Institute (prepared for the World Wildlife Fund).* 5/01. (see Profile #6).

Nuclear Energy:

Nuclear Regulatory Commission Information Digest (periodic report covering: NRC as a regulatory agency; U.S. and worldwide energy; operating nuclear reactors; nuclear material safety; radioactive waste). *Nuclear Regulatory Commission.* (see Profile #247).

Renewable Energy Sources:

The Role of Renewable Resources in U.S. Electricity Generation – Experience and Prospects. *Resources For the Future.* 9/00. (see Profile #5).

Clean Power Surge: Ranking the States (ranks state commitments to increasing renewable electricity use). *Union of Concerned Scientists.* 4/00. (see Profile #127).

Hydrogen:

Hydrogen Commercialization Plan (strategic plan for achieving a hydrogen-based economy). *National Hydrogen Association (in conjunction with the U.S. Dept. of Energy).* 10/00. (see Profile #378).

A Strategy for Hydrogen Transition (using fuel cells for energy generation). *Rocky Mountain Institute.* 4/99. (see Profile #109).

Other Miscellaneous:

Brittle Power: Energy Strategy for National Security (examines vulnerability of U.S. energy systems to attack/disaster). *Rocky Mountain Institute.* 1981 (re-released 10/01). (see Profile #).

B2.7   Global/Regional Evaluation Reports/Publications

By Multilaterals:

The State of Food and Agriculture (annual report on developments affecting world agriculture). *Food and Agriculture Organization of the United Nations.* (see Profile #295).

The State of World Fisheries and Aquaculture (biennial report on developments affecting world fisheries and aquaculture). *Food and Agriculture Organization of the United Nations.* (see Profile #295).

The State of World Forests (biennial report on developments affecting world forests). *Food and Agriculture Organization of the United Nations.* (see Profile #295).

World Fisheries and Aquaculture Atlas (CD-ROM containing: 300+ original articles; graphs; maps; fact sheets; 5000 links to other documents and websites). *Food and Agriculture Organization of the United Nations.* 2001. (see Profile #295).

OECD Environmental Outlook (provides economy-based projections of environmental pressures and changes in the state of the environment to 2020). *Organization for Economic Cooperation and Development.* 4/01. (see Profile #308).

OECD Environmental Performance Reviews – Achievements in OECD Countries: No. 2 (peer reviews of environmental progress in each OECD country). *Organization for Economic Cooperation and Development.* 5/01. (see Profile #308).

Human Development Report (annual report evaluating human development worldwide using 4 composite indices; each report also focuses on a different topical theme). *United Nations Development Programme.* (see Profile #290).

The State of the World Population 2001 (focuses on population-environmental change interactions). *United Nations Population Fund.* 2001. (see Profile #286).

World Energy Assessment: Energy and the Challenge of Sustainability (evaluates social, economic, environmental and security issues linked to energy, and the compatibility of different energy options with objectives in those areas). *United Nations Development Programme, United Nations Dept. of Economic and Social Affairs, and the World Energy Council.* 9/00. (see Profile #290).

Global Environmental Outlook 2000 (outlines progress, identifies threats, and makes recommendations). *United Nations Environment Programme.* 1999. (see Profile #291).

Pachamama: Our Earth – Our Future (youth-oriented introduction to worldwide environmental challenges; based on the UNEP report "Global Environmental Outlook 2000"). *United Nations Environment Programme.* 1999. (see Profile #291).

World Atlas of Coral Reefs (map-based assessment of status and distribution of the world's coral reefs). *United Nations Environment Programme World Conservation Monitoring Centre.* 2001. (see Profile #293).

World Development Indicators (annual compilation of development-related data; organized into 6 sections, including "Environment"; also available: shorter summary versions and a CD-ROM containing 550 time-series indicators). *World Bank.* (see Profile #299).

Global Water Supply and Sanitation Assessment 2000 Report. *World Health Organization and the United Nations Children's Fund.* 2000. (see Profile #300).

Water, Sanitation and Health Electronic Library (a CD-ROM-based compendium of World Health Organization [WHO] information on water, sanitation and health). *World Health Organization.* 2001. (see Profile #300).

By Non-Governmental Organizations:

Critical Consumption Trends and Implications (evaluates global food, fiber, and fishery sectors, arguing that production and consumption patterns are integrally linked). *World Resources Institute.* 8/99. (see Profile #133).

Pilot Analysis of Global Ecosystems Reports ("big picture" view of the world's ecosystems; five separate reports, covering: agro-ecosystems; forests; grasslands; coastal and marine ecosystems; freshwater ecosystems). *World Resources Institute.* 2000-2001. (see Profile #133).

Reefs at Risk (map-based assessment of threats to the world's coral reefs). *World Resources Institute.* 1998. (see Profile #133).

Watersheds of the World (assessment of the ecological value and vulnerability of the world's watersheds). *World Resources Institute.* 1998. (see Profile #133).

The Weight of Nations (examining material outflows from industrial economies). *World Resources Institute.* 2000. (see Profile #133).

World Resources Report (biennial report of global environmental trends). *World Resources Institute.* (see Profile #133).

State of the World (annual report on current global environmental issues). *Worldwatch Institute.* (see Profile #7).

Vital Signs (annual report on global trends in environmental and related areas). *Worldwatch Institute.* (see Profile #7).

B2.8   Market-Based Policy/Taxes/Government Spending/General Economics Reports/Publications

Green Scissors Report (annual report identifying federal programs and subsidies viewed as "environmentally harmful spending"). *Friends of the Earth, Public Interest Research Group, and Taxpayers for Common Sense.* 2001. (see Profile #55).

Paying for Pollution (a "Green Scissors" report identifying taxpayer subsidies of polluting energy programs). *Friends of the Earth, Public Interest Research Group, and Taxpayers for Common Sense.* 2000. (see Profile #55).

Environmentally-Related Taxes in OECD Countries: Issues and Strategies. *Organization for Economic Cooperation and Development.* 10/01. (see Profile #308).

Tax Waste, Not Work (proposes a revenue-neutral tax shift to resource taxes or emission permits). *Redefining Progress.* 4/97. (see Profile #105).

Genuine Progress Report (annual report based on a calculated "General Progress Indicator," intended as an alternative to Gross Domestic Product). *Redefining Progress.* (see Profile #105).

Experience with Market-Based Environmental Policy Instruments (summary of policies implemented worldwide). *Resources For the Future.* 1/00. (see Profile #5).

B2.9   Politically-Related Reports/Publications

National Environmental Scorecard (annual report on congressional voting records). *League of Conservation Voters.* (see Profile #73).

Congressional Scorecard (annual report on congressional members' public interest voting records). *Public Research Interest Group.* (see Profile #101).

B2.10   Population-Environment Linkages Reports/Publications

Forest Futures – Population, Consumption and Wood Resources (explores the link between population and forests). *Population Action International.* 1999. (see Profile #96).

Nature's Place – Human Population and the Future of Biodiversity (explores the link between population and biodiversity). *Population Action International.* 2000. (see Profile #96).

People in the Balance – Population and Natural Resources at the Turn of the Millennium (concise summary exploring population linkages with: water; land; forests; fisheries; carbon dioxide emissions; and biodiversity). *Population Action International.* 2000. (see Profile #96).

B2.11   Public Health Reports/Publications

Drinking Water:

Measuring Up: Grading the First Round of Right To Know Reports (grades 400+ SDWA "consumer confidence reports" in 20 states). *Campaign for Safe and Affordable Drinking Water.* 3/00. (see Profile #19).

National Public Water Systems Compliance Report (annual report on public drinking water system violations). *Environmental Protection Agency (Office of Water).* (see Profile #245).

Toxic Chemicals:

National Report on Human Exposure to Environmental Chemicals (assessment of the U.S. population's potential exposure to 27 environmental chemicals using bio-monitoring). *Centers for Disease Control and Prevention (National Center for Environmental Health), U.S. Dept. of Human Health Services.* 3/01. (see Profile #214).

The Poisonwood Rivals (examining the potential dangers of touching arsenic-treated wood). *Environmental Working Group and The Healthy Building Network (part of the Institute for Local Self-Reliance).* 11/01. (see Profile #51).

Our Stolen Future (examines endocrine-disrupting chemicals). *Our Stolen Future.* 3/97. (see Profile #482).

Nowhere to Hide: Persistent Toxic Chemicals in the U.S. Food Supply. *Pesticide Action Network North America and Commonwealth.* 3/01. (see Profile #91).

In Harm's Way (identifying potential threats to child development from toxic chemicals). *Physicians for Social Responsibility (Greater Boston Chapter).* 5/00. (see Profile #94).

B2.12   Sprawl/Smart Growth/Land Use Planning Reports/Publications

Growing Smart Legislative Handbook (models statutes for planning and change management). *American Planning Association*. 9/98 (Phase I and II Interim Edition). (see Profile #154).

Planning Communities for the 21ˢᵗ Century (examines the status of state planning enabling statutes and statutory reform efforts in the U.S.). *American Planning Association*. 12/99. (see Profile #154).

The Home Town Advantage ("how to defend your Main Street against chain stores…and why it matters"). *Institute for Local Self-Reliance*. 2000. (see Profile #66).

Profiles of Business Leadership on Smart Growth ("presents the perspectives of business leaders in combating sprawl and promoting smart growth"). *National Association of Local Government Environmental Professionals*. Unknown publication date. (see Profile #285).

Sprawl Reports (continuing series of reports – 5 thus far – on sprawl impacts and proposed solutions). *Sierra Club*. 1998-2001. (see Profile #115).

B2.13   State Activities/Contributions Reports/Publications

State Environmental Agency Contributions to Enforcement and Compliance (a report to Congress). *Environmental Council of the States*.2001. (see Profile #270).

States Put Their Money Where Their Environment Is (summary of state environmental spending for FY 2000). *Environmental Council of the States*. 2001. (see Profile #270).

Gold and Green 2000 (ranks states on 20 "gold" economic and 20 "green" environmental indicators). *Institute for Southern Studies (available from the Green Business Network at "GreenBiz.com")*. 2001. (see Profile #457).

B2.14   Directories of Organizations and Groups

Guide to Nonprofit Environmental Communications Organizations 2001. *Environmental Media Services*. 2001. (see Profile #50).

Conservation Directory (annual guide to environmental organizations worldwide). *National Wildlife Federation*. (see Profile #84).

River and Watershed Conservation Directory (annual listing of grassroots river and watershed conservation groups, local agencies, and governments). *River Network*. (see Profile #107).

Fuel Cell Directory (listing of fuel cell related businesses, research institutes and various orgs; updated semi-annually). *Breakthrough Technologies Institute*. (see Profile #18).

B2.15   Other Miscellaneous Reports/Publications

Amber Waves of Gain (an expose of the business trade group the American Farm Bureau Federation). *Defenders of Wildlife*. 4/00. (see Profile #39).

The Complete Guide to Environmental Careers in the 21ˢᵗ Century. *Environmental Careers Organization*. (see Profile #493).

Major Management Challenges and Program Risks. (annual reports on the performance and accountability of major federal government agencies and programs). *General Accounting Office*. (see Profile #246).

National Report Card on Environmental Attitudes, Knowledge and Behaviors (annual evaluation based on a survey of American adults). *National Environmental Education and Training Foundation*. (see Profile #142).

Congressional Research Service Reports (various policy-oriented reports and issue briefs prepared for Congress). Available online at the *National Library for the Environment*. (see Profile #461).

A Guide to Environmental Statutes and Regulations That Promote Public Access Activities (Appendix C of "A Citizen's Platform for Our Environmental Right-to-Know"; provides summaries of major statutes and associated key Internet and other resources). *OMB Watch*. 3/01. (see Profile #88).

National Environmental Policy During the Clinton Years. *Resources For the Future*. 9/01. (see Profile #5).

The Consumer's Guide to Effective Environmental Choices. *Union of Concerned Scientists*. 1999. (see Profile #127).

Agriculture Fact Book 2000 (provides information and data on U.S. agriculture and describes all USDA programs). *U.S. Dept. of Agriculture (Office of Communications)*. 11/00. (see Profile #191).

Making Sustainable Commitments (details a new environmental strategy for the World Bank; focuses on: biodiversity; climate change; forests; water resources). *World Bank*. 9/01. (see Profile #299).

Special Studies 4: Trade and the Environment (an in-depth look at key issues). *World Trade Organization*. 10/99. (see Profile #303).

SUPPORTER DONATION FORM

DIRECTIONS: Please complete this form and mail it along with your check or money order (sorry, no credit cards) to:

> **Environmental Frontlines**
> **P.O. Box 43**
> **Menlo Park, CA 94026**

Contact Information For Questions Or Comments:

> E-Mail: info@envirofront.org   Phone (8-5 PST M-F): (650) 323-8452

Supporter Information:*

> Name:_____

> Organization:_____

> Address:_____

> _____

> Phone:_____

> E-Mail:_____

> * All information is kept strictly confidential and is not sold or otherwise disclosed to third parties.

Support Level:
$20___ $35*___ $50___ $65**___ $100___   Other____

All supporters will receive our annual newsletter, *News from the Frontlines*.

* Donations of $35 or more qualify for a free gift (coffee or travel mug bearing the EF logo).

> Indicate your preference: Coffee Mug__   Travel Mug__   Neither_____

** Donations of $65 or more qualify for a complimentary copy of *The Environmental Guidebook* (in addition to a coffee or travel mug bearing the EF logo).

> Indicate your preference: Coffee Mug__   Travel Mug__   Neither_____

> I do___ do not_____ wish to receive a complimentary copy of the Guidebook.

How did you hear about Environmental Frontlines?_____

THANK YOU FOR SUPPORTING ENVIRONMENTAL FRONTLINES!